INDUSTRIAL
AUTOMATION

INDUSTRIAL AUTOMATION
Circuit Design and Components

DAVID W. PESSEN
Department of Mechanical Engineering
Technion, Israel Institute of Technology
Haifa, Israel

WILEY

A Wiley-Interscience Publication

JOHN WILEY & SONS

New York ● Chichester ● Brisbane ● Toronto ● Singapore

Library of Congress Cataloging in Publication Data:

Pessen, David W.
  Industrial automation.

  "A Wiley–Interscience publication."
  Bibliography: p.
  1. Electronic control.   2. Automation.   3. Switching
circuits.   I. Title.
TK7881.2.P47   1989   670.42'7   88-28002

ISBN 0-471-60071-7

Printed in the United States of America

10 9 8 7 6 5 4 3 2

PREFACE

The word *Automation* means different things to different people. This book deals mainly with the automation of mechanical industrial production systems. Furthermore, it concentrates on the control circuits and devices (be they electronic, electromechanical, or pneumatic) needed to actuate the overall system, and the stress is on *on–off* (i.e., binary) control as opposed to continuous feedback control (i.e., analog or proportional control used in process control or servo systems).

As implied by the subtitle, our concern is with micro- rather than macroautomation. This means the automation of small- or medium-size systems—so-called automation islands—rather than of a large production plant as a whole. (Macroautomation deals with computer supervision and coordination of many such individual automation islands within a plant, but this is beyond the scope of this book.)

This book is the first to combine all the various topics relevant to low-cost automation under one cover. While there are many books dealing with some of the topics, no single book combines all of them as is done here.

It is impossible to discuss control methods without taking into account the hardware at our disposal. Hence, Chapters 1, 2, and 4 deal mainly with hardware considerations. Since motion is the dominant variable in mechanical systems, the first chapter deals with different types of motion actuators. Chapter 2 discusses sensors for sensing position and other variables. Chapter 3 presents an introduction to switching theory, since this topic is necessary for Chapter 4, which discusses the different kinds of available switching elements, and for later chapters.

Chapter 5 deals with the design of electric-ladder diagrams. These are used not only for hard-wired relay circuits, but, even more important, form the basis for programming programmable controllers. Because of the importance of this subject, three different methods (one of them new) for designing ladder diagrams are described. Chapter 6 is an extension of Chapter 5, and deals with random-input systems.

Chapter 7 covers pneumatic control circuits. A number of good books on industrial pneumatics have been published, and this chapter does not pretend to compete with these. Rather, its purpose is to provide an introduction to this wide-reaching subject, which should be useful where time limitations preclude studying a whole book. Four methods for pneumatic-circuit design are presented, three of which are little known.

Chapters 9, 10, and 11 deal with the all-important field of flexible automation, including the use of microcomputers. Chapter 10, which covers the vital topic of programmable controllers, is especially detailed, and can almost be considered a small textbook on the subject.(Because of the dearth of books devoted to programmable controllers, this chapter should be especially useful both to students and to industrial practitioners.

Chapter 8 covers a number of auxiliary topics, and the book concludes with a discussion of assembly automation (Chapter 12) and robotics (Chapter 13).

While much of this book is based on material published elsewhere and well known, a number of original techniques and circuit-design methods are also presented. Most of these have been published by me in various journals, but this is the first time they have been integrated into a single book. Even where well-known methods are covered, they have been modified in order to make them easier to use. The emphasis is on practical methods, immediately applicable to industrial problems, rather than purely theoretical considerations. The aim is to enable the reader to select the most appropriate control method for a given application (see the flow chart presented for this purpose in Appendix B), and, having done so, to be able to design the necessary circuit without the help of outside consultants.

The material serves as the basis for a one-semester course on industrial automation that I have taught for a number of years to fourth-year mechanical engineering students at Technion, and also at Cornell University. At the same time, the book has also been written with the practicing engineer and technologist in mind. It is self-contained, requires little previous background, and, with its detailed and clear explanations, is definitely suitable for self-study. A large number of practice problems are presented, since much of the material cannot really be mastered thoroughly without problem-solving. Although the chapters are arranged in a certain logical order and should preferably be read in that order, this is not absolutely necessary. To help readers who may wish to skip certain chapters, a great number of cross-references between the various sections of the book are given, so that topics that may have been missed can easily be located.

At least four of the topics discussed (fluid-power systems, switching theory, microcomputers, and robotics) are taught as completely independent courses in many engineering schools. Since this book must cover them together with many other topics, the discussion is by necessity very brief, and does not pretend to be more than an introduction to each of these subjects. However, a great number of references are given, and these are not only of academic interest, but provide practical, immediately applicable information. Thus, the reader interested in an in-depth treatment of any topic has a source for additional material.

DAVID W. PESSEN

Haifa, Israel

CONTENTS

INDUSTRIAL
AUTOMATION

CHAPTER 1

MOTION ACTUATORS

The term *industrial automation* is very broad and involves many kinds of variables. The most dominant of these is undoubtedly motion. This chapter, therefore, begins with a brief discussion of the various types of motion and of mechanisms for converting one type of motion to another. The remainder of the chapter surveys different kinds of available motion actuators, both electric and pneumatic/hydraulic.

1.1 TYPES OF MOTION AND MOTION CONVERSION

1.1.1 Linear and Angular Motion

Motion can be classified as being either linear or angular. Angular motion, in turn, can consist of oscillating motion through a limited angle, or it can be continuous rotary motion, such as that produced by an electric motor. One type of rotary motion important in automatic machinery is an intermittent kind, such as produced by indexing devices, which are discussed later in this section.

The linear motion induced in a rigid object is governed by Newton's second law of motion

$$F = ma \qquad (1-1)$$

where

F = resultant of all forces acting on an object,
m = mass of the object,
a = resulting linear acceleration.

1

A common problem is to calculate the time required to move a given object of mass m through a certain distance s, for example, by means of a pneumatic or hydraulic cylinder. While the force produced by a cylinder (which is discussed in Section 1.4) is not really completely constant, it is assumed to be so for the purpose of this discussion. It follows from Equation (1-1) that a constant force F produces a constant acceleration a, so that the well-known equation for constant acceleration applies:

$$s = 0.5at^2 \qquad (1\text{-}2)$$

where

$s =$ displacement,
$t =$ time

and the initial velocity and displacement at $t = 0$ are assumed zero. Substituting a from Equation (1-1) into Equation (1-2) and solving for t gives

$$t = (2ms/F)^{1/2} \qquad (1\text{-}3)$$

which gives the time required to move mass m through distance s by means of a constant force F.

Similarly, Newton's law applied to angular motion reads

$$T = J\alpha \qquad (1\text{-}4)$$

where

$T =$ resultant of all torques acting on a mass rotating about a fixed axis,
$J =$ moment of inertia of the mass about its axis of rotation,
$\alpha =$ angular acceleration

and the angular displacement equation analogous to Equation (1-2) is

$$\theta = 0.5\alpha t^2 \qquad (1\text{-}5)$$

where $\theta =$ angular displacement.

As before, substituting α from Equation (1-4) into (1-5) and solving for t gives

$$t = (2J\theta/T)^{1/2} \qquad (1\text{-}6)$$

The situation becomes more complicated when the driving motor is connected to inertia load J through a gear drive, usually a gear reduction, as shown in Fig. 1.1. The moment of inertia J must now be replaced by an equivalent

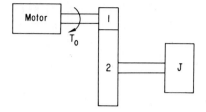

Fig. 1.1. Rotating mass driven through a gear reduction.

moment of inertia $J_{eq.}$ "felt" by the motor shaft, as expressed by

$$T_0 = J_{eq.}\alpha_1 \qquad (1\text{-}7)$$

The speed ratio n is expressed by

$$n = \omega_2/\omega_1 = \alpha_2/\alpha_1 = R_1/R_2 \qquad (1\text{-}8)$$

where

ω_1 and ω_2 = angular gear velocities,
α_1 and α_2 = angular gear accelerations,
R_1 and R_2 = gear pitch radii.

Neglecting friction losses, the force F transmitted at the gear teeth equals

$$F = T_1/R_1 = T_2/R_2 \qquad (1\text{-}9)$$

where T_1 and T_2 are the respective net torques acting on the two gears. Substituting Equation (1-8) into (1-9) gives

$$T_1 = R_1 T_2/R_2 = nT_2 \qquad (1\text{-}10)$$

Taking gear 1 as a free body gives

$$T_0 - T_1 = \alpha_1 J_1$$

or

$$T_0 = \alpha_1 J_1 + T_1 = \alpha_1 J_1 + nT_2 \qquad (1\text{-}11)$$

Taking gear 2 as a free body gives

$$T_2 = \alpha_2 J_2 \qquad (1\text{-}12)$$

(assuming no exterior loads acting on mass J). Substituting Equations (1-8), (1-11), and (1-12) into Equation (1-7) gives the equivalent moment of inertia as

$$J_{eq.} = T_0/\alpha_1 = (\alpha_1 J_1 + nT_2)/\alpha_1 = J_1 + nT_2/\alpha_1$$
$$= J_1 + n^2 T_2/\alpha_1 = J_1 + n^2 J_2 \qquad (1\text{-}13)$$

Thus, the load inertia J_2 is "reflected" back to the motor shaft by multiplying it by the square of the speed ratio n. For a sufficiently large speed reduction ($n \ll 1$), the reflected moment of inertia may become negligible. On the other hand, if $n > 1$, then $J_{eq.}$ is increased considerably.

For an analysis of drives with several gear reduction stages, and for a method of gear-train inertia minimization, see Ref. (1.1). The subject of inertia minimization is also discussed in Ref. (1.2).

1.1.2 Intermittent Rotary Motion

In many types of automatic machinery (such as machine tools, automatic assembly work stations, etc.), intermittent rotary motion, or *indexing*, is required. Various cam devices and ratchet mechanisms are available for this purpose, but one of the best-known intermittent-motion devices is the Geneva wheel, which is illustrated in Fig. 1.2. As the driver rotates continuously, the driving pin attached to it enters one of the four slots on the driven wheel. The

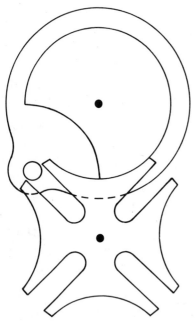

Fig. 1.2. Geneva wheel.

wheel then rotates through 90 degrees before the pin leaves the slot, whereupon the wheel remains stationary until the pin engages the next slot. If the device is properly designed, the pin enters and leaves the slot in a direction tangential to the slot surface, so that impact forces are minimized. The raised round surface extending over 270 degrees of the driver serves to produce self-locking, that is, preventing the driven wheel from moving during the stationary period.

A typical application of the Geneva wheel is driving a rotary table that is part of a production line, where there are four work stations 90 degrees apart. As the wheel rotates, the workpiece is brought to the next station, where some operation is performed on it while the table remains stationary. Geneva wheels with anywhere from 3 to 12 slots have been constructed, so that more than four work stations can be accommodated.

An analysis of Geneva wheels can be found in most textbooks on mechanism kinematics; see, for example, Ref. (1.3). For a detailed survey of various intermittent rotary-motion devices, see Ref. (1.4). A very useful discussion, including dynamic effects in Geneva wheels, is found in Ref. (1.5). Special types of Geneva mechanisms, together with other kinds of indexing mechanisms, are described in Ref. (1.6), pp. 13–14; Ref. (1.7), pp. 114–122, and Ref. (1.8), pp. 26–36. Various commercially available indexing drives for synchronizing motions are shown in Ref. (1.9).

1.1.3 Conversion of Rotary to Linear Motion

A common problem in automatic machinery is to convert rotary to linear motion or vice-versa. The three most common ways of accomplishing this are

1. rack-and-pinion drives,
2. power (lead) screws,
3. linkages.

In rack-and-pinion drives, see Fig. 1.3, a spur-gear wheel (the pinion) meshes with a geared rack. If the wheel drives the rack, the device converts rotary to linear motion. Conversely, if the rack is the driver (for instance, if a cylinder piston rod is connected to the rack), then the device converts linear to rotary motion. Regardless of the number of teeth on the pinion, the relation between the velocities is given by

$$V = \omega R \qquad (1\text{-}14)$$

where

V = linear rack velocity [mm/sec],

ω = angular pinion velocity [rad/sec],

R = pinion pitch radius [mm].

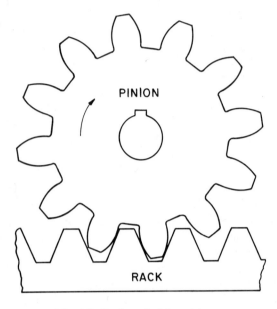

Fig. 1.3. Rack-and-pinion drive.

If the load attached to the rack has mass m, then, as shown by an analysis similar to that carried out before for a gear drive, the equivalent moment of inertia of this mass as reflected back to the pinion shaft is given by mR^2, so that the total equivalent moment of inertia equals

$$J_{eq.} = J_1 + mR^2 = J_1 + m(V/\omega)^2 \qquad (1\text{-}15)$$

where J_1 = moment of inertia of the pinion plus pinion shaft.

Conversely, if the rack is the driver, then the moment of inertia J_1 attached to the pinion shaft must be reflected back to the rack, and the equivalent linear inertia as felt by the piston driving the rack is

$$m_{eq.} = m + J_1/R^2 \qquad (1\text{-}16)$$

For light or intermediate loads, the rack-and-pinion drive can be replaced by various types of belt or chain drives. Here the rack is replaced by a toothed belt or chain, and a sprocket wheel replaces the pinion. Equations (1.14)–(1.16) still apply. For a detailed description of such systems, see Section 7 of Ref. (1.1).

A second method of converting rotary to linear motion is using a power screw (also called lead screw) to drive a nut. For each turn of the screw, the nut advances a distance equal to the lead of the screw thread. The various parameters involved in power-screw design are

Lead = distance the thread or nut advances during one turn,

Pitch = distance between corresponding points on adjacent threads,

N = number of continuous threads or *starts* on the screw (usually 1, 2, or 3).

Hence, we can write

$$\text{Lead} = N \cdot \text{Pitch} \tag{1-17}$$

Lead angle λ (lambda) is the angle of the line tangent to the pitch helix, measured with respect to the plane normal to the screw axis, and D_m is the mean thread diameter. Hence,

$$\lambda = \arctan(\text{Lead}/\pi D_m) \tag{1-18}$$

The relationship between screw and nut velocities is given by a relation analogous to Equation (1-14) for rack-and-pinion drives:

$$V = n \cdot \text{Lead} = \omega \cdot \text{Lead}/2\pi = (\omega D_m \cdot \tan \lambda)/2 \tag{1.19}$$

where

V = nut velocity [mm/sec],

n = rotational screw velocity [rev/sec],

ω = angular screw velocity [rad/sec].

The dynamic coefficient of friction f in power screws is usually assumed to be 0.12–0.15 (depending on surface finish and lubrication). The static-friction coefficient can be expected to be about twice as much. The friction angle β is defined as

$$\beta = \arctan f \tag{1-20}$$

so that β can be expected to be 7–9 degrees (or twice as much for the static-friction angle). If this friction angle becomes greater than the lead angle, that is, if $\beta > \lambda$, the screw becomes self-locking, which means that the screw can drive the nut in either direction, but the nut cannot drive the screw in any direction. Whereas this property may be very desirable in many applications, it means that most power screws *cannot* be used to convert linear to rotary motion, unlike rack-and-pinion drives. If such conversion is required, the power screw should have a lead angle λ greater than 20 degrees to assure smooth operation under static-friction conditions.

Power screws usually have either square threads or Acme (i.e., tapered) threads. The efficiency of square threads can be shown to be

$$\text{Efficiency} = \frac{\tan \lambda}{\tan (\lambda + \beta)} \tag{1-21}$$

See Ref. (1.10) or any other book on machine elements for the derivation of this relation. Since self-locking requires $\beta > \lambda$, it is obvious that any self-locking power screw has an efficiency less than 50%, with much lower values being common, depending on λ. The theoretical efficiency of Acme-thread power screws is lower still, but this is compensated for by the higher manufacturing accuracy attainable with Acme threads.

To get around the low efficiencies of power screws, ball (or roller) screws are often used. A ball screw, see Fig. 1.4, is essentially a power screw having a set of balls rolling between the screw and nut, as in a ball bearing. A recirculating track is built into the nut, so that the same balls are reused as the nut rides along the screw. Since the balls replace the sliding friction in conventional power screws by rolling friction, the efficiency of ball screws is high, typically 70–90%.

Because of this low friction, ball screws are not self-locking, so that a thrust applied to the nut causes the screw to turn, that is, linear motion is converted to rotary motion. The main drawback of ball screws is their higher cost, obviously due to their greater complexity and number of parts. For engineering data on ball screws, see Ref. (1.11). For a comparison between power, ball, and roller screws, see Refs. (1.12) and (1.13).

Ball screws are the basis for many specialty devices useful in automatic machinery. For example, an automatic reversing mechanism described in Ref. (1.14) consists of a ball screw with a double set of threads, one right- and the other left-handed. As the nut reaches the screw end, it automatically picks up the other thread and moves back in the opposite direction. Automatic reversing is thus obtained at each stroke end without the need for reversing motors, cams, clutches, or limit switches.

The third method of converting rotary to linear motion, or vice versa, uses mechanical linkages. The most common of these is the slider–crank mechanism used in internal-combustion engines, piston compressors, and pumps, etc., as shown in Fig. 1.5. Continuous crank rotation produces reciprocating linear motion of the slider or piston, and vice versa. However, the slider motion is *not* proportional to the crank rotation, but follows an approximately sinusoidal relationship.

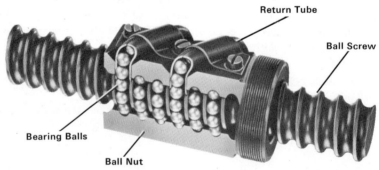

Fig. 1.4. Ball screw. (Courtesy of Thomson Saginaw Ball Screw Co., Inc.)

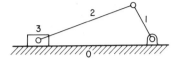

Fig. 1.5. Slider–crank mechanism (0 is the base, 1 is the crank, 2 is the connecting rod, and 3 is the slider).

There exist numerous "straight-line mechanisms," most based on the common four-bar linkage. They avoid the need for sliders (which require expensive guiding surfaces and have more friction losses), but the motion generated only approximates a straight line, and even that only for a limited range of crank angles. The most "ancient" of these mechanisms is the Watt linkage, which was invented by James Watt of steam-engine fame for guiding the cross-head of his steam engine along an approximately straight path. More sophisticated straight-line linkages are described in Refs. (1.15) and (1.16), and also in pages 72–77 of Ref. (1.8).

A microcomputer program written in BASIC for animating the motion of four-bar mechanisms is given in Ref. (1.17). The resulting screen display for one of the mechanisms from Ref. (1.15) is reproduced in Fig. 1.6, and it shows the quality of the straight line produced by one of the coupler points.

For converting linear to rotary motion, we can use the slider–crank mechanism of Fig. 1.5 or the so-called cross-link mechanism, which again makes use of the four-bar linkage. Reference (1.18) describes how to determine the optimum configuration. A typical cross-link mechanism from that reference is reproduced in Fig. 1.7. As the input arm is driven horizontally, the hinged output arm at the top rotates, and, for a limited angular range, this rotation is almost proportional to the linear horizontal motion. Also the vertical displacement of the input arm is very small.

For collections of various practical mechanisms useful for automatic machinery, the reader is referred to Refs. (1.7) and (1.8).

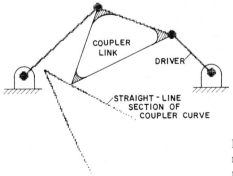

Fig. 1.6. Screen display for the animation of a four-bar straight-line mechanism.

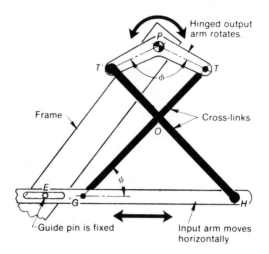

Fig. 1.7. Cross-link mechanism for converting linear to rotary motion. (Reprinted from *Machine Design*, July 20, 1978. Copyright 1978 by Penton Publishing, Inc. Cleveland, Ohio.)

1.2 ELECTRIC LINEAR ACTUATORS

Three different methods of generating linear motion by electric means are discussed in this section: (1) solenoids, (2) linear induction motors, and (3) rotating motors driving a power screw or a pinion and rack.

1.2.1 Solenoids

Solenoids are electromechanical devices consisting of an electromagnetic coil and a plunger (also called an armature), as shown in Fig. 1.8. When current is sent through the coil, the resulting magnetic field draws the plunger into a sleeve within the coil, thus converting electrical energy into linear motion.

Typical force–stroke curves of a solenoid are shown in Fig. 1.9. There are a number of important factors to consider when selecting a solenoid for a given application, and these are briefly outlined in what follows.

An important point in interpreting force–stroke curves such as shown in Fig. 1.9 is the duty-cycle factor, labeled f on the curves. This is defined as

$$f = \frac{on \text{ time}}{on \text{ time} + off \text{ time}} \tag{1-22}$$

Since the allowable solenoid load is determined by the temperature reached by the coil, the duty-cycle factor is of primary determining importance. As can be seen from the figure, the allowable load at $f = 0.1$ is about 5 to 10 times as high as at $f = 1$ (i.e., continuous operation).

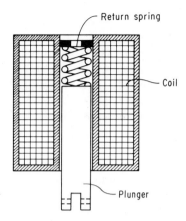

Fig. 1.8. Solenoid.

Another important fact to be noted from the figure is that the force developed drops drastically with increasing stroke (i.e., as the plunger moves farther out of the coil), due to the increasing air gap. This means that the stroke that can actually be utilized may be severely limited, especially since the break-away force needed to start moving the load is often much greater than the force required to hold it.

A basic decision to be made is whether to use an alternating- or direct-current solenoid. The ac solenoid bypasses the need for a special dc power supply, but it is noisier, and much more likely to burn out if excessively loaded. This is so because, when the plunger is outside the coil, coil impedance is very low, producing a very high inrush current that continues to flow until the plunger enters the coil and is seated against its stop. As opposed to ac solenoids, a dc solenoid has the same coil resistance whether the plunger is inside or outside the coil. On the other hand, ac solenoids develop more force at the beginning than dc solenoids of the same size, precisely because of this high inrush current.

In dc solenoids, coil inductance produces high reverse-voltage transients when the solenoid is shut off and the stator magnetic field collapses. (This effect

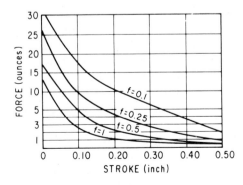

Fig. 1.9. Typical force–stroke curves for a 0.5″-diameter solenoid.

is similar to the high voltages applied to spark plugs by automobile ignition coils.) To prevent serious degradation of switch contacts caused by arcing, suppression devices should be used, especially in applications where the solenoid is switched *on/off* at high rates. The simplest suppression means is a diode connected across the coil winding, which limits reverse voltage to the supply-voltage level. However, the solenoid terminals must then be polarized to prevent damage to the diode. More sophisticated arc-suppression methods consist of circuits with various combinations of capacitors, resistors, and/or diodes; see page 230 of Ref. (1.19).

For ac solenoid applications in which the load is liable to vary and exceed the available solenoid force, coil-burnout protection methods should be used. These could consist of a thermal cutout device or of a preloaded tension spring inserted between the plunger and load. The preload spring force must be greater than the normal load. If the load should become excessive, the spring opens up and enables the plunger to continue moving until seated against its stop (i.e., the spring acts as a kind of mechanical fuse).

For applications where current consumption must be minimized (e.g., battery-operated devices), dc solenoids with magnetic latching can be used. Permanent magnets hold the plunger in place at each stroke end, eliminating the holding current normally required. Only a short current pulse is needed to latch the plunger in position. A current pulse of opposite polarity shifts the plunger to the opposite position.

Many other factors should be considered when selecting a solenoid. The reader is referred to information found in most manufacturers' catalogs, and also to Ref. (1.20), an excellent summary of the subject, and Refs. (1.21) and (1.22).

Apart from linear solenoids, there are also rotary solenoids, and these are mentioned in Section 1.3.3. A fairly recent development is the proportional solenoid, in which the final plunger position is proportional to the input current. Thus, these are analog rather than *on/off* devices, and as such are outside the scope of this book.

1.2.2   Linear Induction Motors

Linear induction motors (LIMs) change electric energy into a constant-force straight-line motion in either direction, without resorting to gears, power screws, or mechanical linkages. Basically, the LIM is a squirrel-cage induction motor that has been split along its axis of rotation and unrolled onto a flat plane. The result is a flat motor, with the primary containing the windings, and the secondary consists of a flat conductor (armature), as shown in Fig. 1.10. LIMs require some means, such as bearings or wheels, for maintaining the air gap between the primary and secondary as small as possible.

If the flat secondary is rolled up into a long rod, we get a round-rod LIM, as shown in Fig. 1.11. Here, the rod is supported by a bearing at each end of the primary. From an electrical standpoint, the length of the rod, and hence the

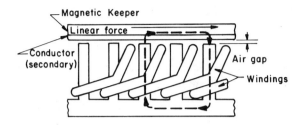

Fig. 1.10. Flat linear induction motor.

available stroke length, is unlimited. However, for very long rods, adequate bearing support must be provided along the rod length.

Normally, three-phase ac current is required to actuate LIMs, although single-phase current can be used under certain conditions, albeit with reduced available power. When ac current is applied to the primary, a field is induced in the secondary, so that the primary and secondary repel each other. Whichever element is free to move then provides the linear motion. Thus, where round-rod LIMs are used for long-stroke applications, almost half of the space can be saved by keeping the rod stationary and having the primary with its coils traverse the rod. (Of course, a coiled cord or other means is then needed to supply power to the primary as it travels along the rod.)

LIMs have several advantages as compared to solenoids: most important, the attainable stroke is virtually unlimited, and the available force remains constant along the whole stroke. Unlike solenoids, the motion of the LIM can be cushioned at the end of the stroke using bumpers, springs, or dashpots. In fact, the LIM can in itself be used an an electric shock absorber by applying a decelerating force to some other body; see Ref. (1.23).

The synchronous speed (i.e., no-load speed) of LIMs is usually very high. Methods for controlling the speed are discussed in Refs. (1.23) and (1.24), where the reader will also find general information about the characteristics and selection of LIMs. Reference (1.25) describes a LIM-driven linear actuator. Information on LIMs is also available in manufacturers' catalogs; see Ref. (1.26) for their names.

For a discussion of the high positioning accuracy attainable with linear motors, see Ref. (1.27).

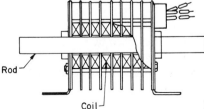

Fig. 1.11. Round-rod linear induction motor.

1.2.3   Rotating Motors Driving Rotary-to-Linear Motion Converter

Electric motors are discussed in the next section. However, here is the logical place to mention linear-motion generation by means of a rotating electric motor connected either to a rack-and-pinion combination or to a power or ball screw.

Such combinations can be purchased as a single unit called an "electromechanical linear actuator." Such an actuator, for example, might consist of a motor with thermal overload protection driving a spur-gear speed reducer, an overload clutch, and, finally, a ball screw that provides the linear motion.

The user can, of course, purchase these various components separately and assemble them. One problem to be solved is what to do when the nut reaches either end of the screw. Use of an overload clutch is one solution. Another consists of a pair of limit switches cutting off motor power at each stroke end.

1.3   ELECTRIC ROTARY ACTUATORS

1.3.1   Electric Motors

Over and beyond the simple division into ac and dc motors, electric motors come in an almost endless variety. To cover the subject even superficially would require more space than justified by the scope of this chapter. Since the various motor types, and information on motor rating and selection, are thoroughly discussed in many sources—unlike the situation with some of the other elements covered in this chapter—we confine ourselves to referring the reader to several of these useful sources.

An excellent discussion of various motor types, including available methods of speed control, is found in Ref. (1.1), pages 329–344. Another useful source is Ref. (1.19), or any one of the yearly Electrical Reference Issues published by that same publication. Even more detailed is the "Electric Motors Reference Issue" listed as Ref. (1.23). Another comprehensive survey of different motor types is found in Ref. (1.28). The reader can, of course, always fall back on commonly available electrical engineering handbooks, such as Refs. (1.29) and (1.30). A "buyer's guide" for commercially available motors and motor controls is included in Ref. (1.26).

A discussion of smaller ac motors in particular can be found in Ref. (1.31). A good discussion on how to estimate motor acceleration, based on the motor's speed–torque curve, is given in Ref. (1.32).

For a thorough discussion of small dc motors and their speed control, see Ref. (1.33), and for more of the same, see Ref. (1.34).

It is well known that dc motor speed is easily controlled by regulating either field or armature voltage. However, thanks to solid-state technology, variable-speed drives for ac motors are very common. The subject is covered in many of the references cited before, and also in Refs. (1.35)–(1.39). This last reference also includes a listing of commercially available motor-control systems.

1.3.2 Step Motors and Their Control

Step motors (also called stepping or stepper motors) convert pulse inputs to incremental shaft rotation: each pulse produces a certain incremental shaft displacement, or step, typically 1.8 to as high as 90 degrees, depending on motor design. Since the step-motor input signal is digital in nature, it is an ideal rotary-motion actuator for use with microcomputer or hard-wired switching circuits. The most common step-motor application is probably in analog quartz watches, where tiny step motors drive the hands.

Step motors present a number of pronounced advantages, as compared to conventional electric motors:

1. Since the step-motor shaft angle bears an exact relation to the number of input pulses, the motor provides an accurate open-loop positioning system, without the need for closing the loop with a position encoder, comparator, and servo amplifier, as is done in conventional closed-loop servo systems.

2. If the step motor receives a continuous train of pulses at constant frequency, it rotates at a constant speed, provided neither load torque nor pulse frequency are excessive for the given motor. The step motor can thus take the place of a velocity servo, again, without the need for a closed-loop system. By changing pulse frequency, the motor speed can be controlled. Even low velocities can be maintained accurately, which is difficult to do with conventional dc motors.

3. By receiving a short burst of pulses, the step motor can generate intermittent rotary motion. It can, therefore, act as an indexing device (similar to the Geneva wheels discussed in Section 1.1.2).

4. By connecting the step-motor shaft to a power screw or a rack-and-pinion drive, precisely controlled linear positioning is obtained. Ready-made units of this type, i.e., step motors connected to a built-in helix screw, are commercially available and find wide application in floppy-disk drives, printers, and other computer peripherals.

5. By feeding an identical pulse train to several step motors, precise synchronization can be achieved.

6. Step motors are inherently low-speed devices. Thus, the need for reduction gearing is usually avoided. (If high velocities are required, this, of course, becomes a drawback.)

7. If the motor stator is kept energized during standstill, the motor produces an appreciable holding torque. Thus, the load position can be locked, without the need for clutch-brake arrangements. The motor can be stalled in this manner indefinitely without adverse effects.

There are, of course, also drawbacks: many step motors have low efficiencies, as low as 30%. If the load is excessive, or if the pulse rate is too high, the step motor is liable to "lose" pulses, so that positioning accuracy is lost completely.

With high load inertias, overshoot and oscillation can occur unless proper damping is applied, and, under certain conditions, the step motor may become downright unstable. And, finally, step motors are only available in low- or medium-hp ratings, up to a couple of hp. (In theory, larger step motors could be built, but the large power transistors needed to drive them are too expensive.)

How do step motors actually operate? They can be classified according to five or six general types, which are described and compared in the previously cited Refs. (1.1), (1.19), and (1.23). We confine ourselves here to the two most common types: permanent-magnet and variable-reluctance step motors. (A third type, the hybrid step motor, is a combination of these two.)

A permanent-magnet step motor in its simplest form is shown in Fig. 1.12. The motor has a permanent-magnet rotor that, in this example, has two poles, though often many more poles are used. The stator is made of soft iron with a number of pole pieces and associated windings. Only four windings (grouped into two sets of two windings each) are used in this example. These windings must be excited sequentially in a certain order. Whereas this is commonly done by solid-state switching circuits, mechanical switches are shown in the figure, since their operation is easier to visualize.

Assume the switches to be in the positions shown. Windings 1 and 3 are energized, and, as a result, the pole pieces have the polarities shown. The rotor is thus forced into the position shown, with its S pole centered between the two N pole pieces, and its N pole between the two lower S pole pieces.

If we now imagine the position of switch *A* changed, then winding 2 is energized instead of winding 1. As a result, the right upper pole piece becomes S instead of N, and the left lower one N, so that the rotor is forced to rotate 90 degrees counterclockwise. Changing switch *B* produces the next 90-degree step, etc. The rotor is thus forced to realign itself continuously, according to the prevalent magnetic fields. If it is desired to reverse the direction of rotation, the order of changing the switch positions need only be reversed.

As already mentioned, the switching is usually done electronically. Each pulse received by the switching circuit produces one shift in stator polarity, and hence one motor step. Many motors have more than four stator pole pieces— and possibly also more rotor poles—resulting in smaller step angles. As

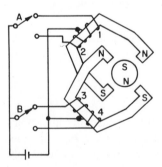

Fig. 1.12. Permanent-magnet step motor (90-degree steps, four-phase).

mentioned before, typical step angles for permanent-magnet step motors range from 90 to as low as 1.8 degrees. When there are more pole pieces, the switching sequences becomes more complicated. The pole windings are connected in so-called *phases*, with all windings belonging to the same phase energized at the same time. Typically, the number of phases can range from as low as two to as high as eight. The more phases the motor has, the smoother is its output torque.

The accuracy of a given step depends to a great extent on the motor construction and on the shaft load, and ranges typically from 1 to 5% of step angle. However, it is important to realize that the overall accuracy of a series of steps equals the absolute accuracy of the final step. In other words, the position error does not accumulate. For example, the no-load accuracy of a typical step motor may be 3% of the step angle. Assuming an 1.8-degree step angle, the final shaft position is accurate to within 0.054 degrees, no matter whether a single step or 10,000 steps were executed.

One characteristic feature of permanent-magnet step motors is that they have a so-called residual or detent torque when power to the stator windings is cut off. This is due to the magnetic field produced by the permanent-magnet rotor, which tends to keep the rotor in its last position. This detent torque is naturally much lower than the holding torque produced when the stator is energized, but it does help in keeping the shaft from moving due to outside forces. In some applications, this feature can, of course, be a disadvantage, since it prevents motor "freewheeling."

The second step-motor type discussed here is the variable-reluctance motor, shown in Fig. 1.13. The rotor is made of magnetic material, but it is not a permanent magnet, and it has a series of teeth (eight in this case) machined into it. As with the permanent-magnet step motor, the stator consists of a number of pole pieces with windings, in this case, numbering 12 arranged in three phases (labeled 1, 2, and 3, respectively) and connected to four windings per phase. The rotor attempts to align itself so as to minimize the magnetic reluctance between rotor and stator. In the figure, phase 1 is assumed energized. If we now

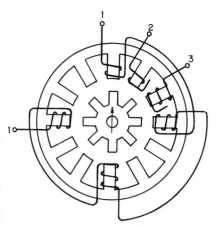

Fig. 1.13. Variable-reluctance step motor (15-degree steps, three-phase).

deenergize phase 1 and energize phase 2, the rotor rotates counterclockwise so that the four rotor teeth nearest to the four pole pieces belonging to phase 2 align themselves with these. The step angle of the motor equals the difference in angular pitch between adjacent rotor teeth and adjacent pole pieces; in this case, $45 - 30 = 15$ degrees.

Because of this difference relationship, variable-reluctance step motors can be designed to operate with considerably smaller step angles than permanent-magnet step motors. However, they do not provide any detent torque when not energized (although this becomes an advantage when freewheeling is desired). Other advantages of variable-reluctance step motors include faster dynamic response (due to smaller rotor inertia), and the ability to accept higher pulse rates.

Among the drawbacks: their output torque is lower than that of a permanent-magnet step motor of similar size, and they tend to become unstable when the pulse frequency approaches the natural frequency of motor plus load (a kind of "resonance"). When in resonance, motor operation becomes noisy, and, much worse, the motor can actually lose steps, or even halt completely and oscillate back and forth helplessly.

For general information on step motors, the reader is referred to Refs. (1.40)–(1.43). For guidelines on selecting proper step-motor size for a given application, see Ref. (1.44). Many step-motor manufacturers (see Ref. 1.26 for listing) provide useful literature on the subject. In order to evaluate the specifications and data presented in catalogs, it is necessary to understand several terms, in addition to those already mentioned. These terms relate to Fig. 1.14, which shows a typical torque–speed curve.

Figure 1.14 shows two separate curves: the *pull-in torque* curve, which relates to bidirectional or start–stop operation, and the *pull-out torque* curve, which relates to continuous-speed operation. Assume a constant frictional load torque T_F on the motor shaft. As shown by the dashed lines in the figure, this determines a certain *pull-in rate*, which is defined as the maximum pulse rate (i.e., rotational velocity) at which the motor is able to start or stop the given friction load T_F

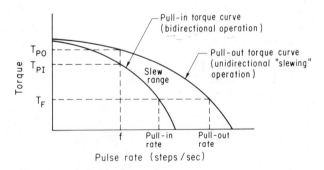

Fig. 1.14. Step-motor torque–speed curve.

without losing or overshooting a step. The same dashed T_F line also determines the *pull-out rate*, defined as the maximum constant pulse rate at which the motor is able to drive the friction load T_F after the motor has been *slewed* up to the maximum speed.

The area between these two curves is called the *slew range*. For many motors, especially of the variable-reluctance type, the slew range contains an unstable or resonance region that should be avoided. The motor should be accelerated from the pull-in rate as fast as possible in order to pass through this resonance region and reach the pull-out rate in minimum time.

If the motor is operated with a given pulse rate f, the vertical dashed line in Fig. 1.14 indicates the *pull-out torque* T_{PO} and the *pull-in torque* T_{PI}. These are defined as the maximum allowable friction loads at the given pulse rate f for undirectional and bidirectional operation, respectively.

The difference between the pull-in and pull-out rates, as seen from the figure, is caused by the inertia of the rotor and any inertia load connected to it. If it were not for inertia, pull-in and pull-out rates would be identical.

Actually, plots of step-motor characteristics, such as Fig. 1.14, are misleading, because the curves depend not only on the motor itself, but just as much on the motor controller used to drive it. The motor controller, which has a decisive effect on motor performance, basically has three different functions, as shown in Fig. 1.15.

The sequence-logic section of the controller accepts the pulse-train input, and also receives a binary direction signal indicating in which direction the motor is to step. It then produces the appropriate switching sequence, so that each motor phase is energized at the proper time. Reference (1.45) presents a good discussion of various sequencing-logic schemes.

The power-driver section consists of power transistors supplying necessary voltage and current to drive the motor. For a description of different power-driver circuits, see Ref. (1.40).

The third section of the controller suppresses the large reverse-voltage transients produced by the inductance of the motor windings when each phase is deenergized, which might otherwise damage the controller. (The identical problem is discussed in Section 1.2.1 on solenoids.)

High-quality step-motor controllers are expensive (in the $50–100 range), often costing more than the step motor itself. The question arises whether the do-it-yourselfer could not put together a controller for a fraction of the above price. The answer is a qualified yes.

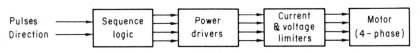

Fig. 1.15. Step-motor controller (four phase).

The simplest and undoubtedly the most inexpensive way of driving a step motor is to use the 50- or 60-Hz ac power line to drive a two-phase step motor. The motor acts like a synchronous ac motor, and indexes two steps for each cycle of line frequency. No electronics are needed, since all power is supplied directly by the power line. The motor is turned *on* or *off* using a simple switch or relay. Of course, we lose the ability to control motor speed, since the stepping rate is fixed by the power-line frequency. Reference (1.46) describes different ways of implementing this approach.

Another approach is to put together a sequence-logic circuit using inexpensive electronic integrated circuits (ICs). Various ways of doing this are described in a number of articles; see, for example, Refs. (1.47) and (1.48). The pulses feeding such a circuit could be supplied by an electronic timing circuit (also available in IC form), or they could come from an appropriately programmed microprocessor or microcomputer.

Step-motor drivers in the form of single-chip integrated circuits are available at reasonable prices; see, for example, Ref. (1.49). Since such circuits usually output only small currents and voltages (typically 1.5 A at 20 V dc), they are mainly useful for driving small permanent-magnet step motors. However, by using the circuit outputs to drive power transistors, larger motors can also be driven. As previously stated, the pulse train feeding such a single-chip controller has to be externally supplied.

At this stage, the reader will probably ask the following logical question: Why pay up to $100 for a commercial step-motor controller, when we can use one of the methods previously mentioned at one-tenth the cost? The answer lies in the fact, already stated, that the controller has a decisive effect on step-motor performance. A good controller performs a number of important functions, over and beyond producing the correct switching sequence for the motor phases:

1. As explained in connection with Fig. 1.14, the permissible pulse rate for starting an inertia load (i.e., the pull-in rate) is much lower than the permissible pulse rate once the motor has reached speed (pull-out rate). A good controller brings the motor up to its maximum speed gradually, a process called "ramping," in such a manner that no pulses are lost. Similarly, a good controller produces controlled deceleration when the motor is to be stopped. Since step-motor torque varies with speed, the optimum ramping profile is closer to an exponential curve than a straight line, and a good controller takes this into account. The controller should also be able to accept a pulse train at a fixed frequency higher than the pull-in rate, release these pulses at the correct rate for controlled acceleration, and then make up for lost time so that no pulses are lost in the process. For a software solution to the ramping problem, see Ref. (1.50).

2. To obtain high stepping rates, such as above 1000 pulses/sec, sophisticated controllers are required. The problem is how to get large currents into and out of the motor windings at a sufficiently high rate, in spite of winding inductance. Primitive controllers can only provide small currents at low stepping rates,

resulting in very low motor power (for which the derogatory term "flea power" has been used).

3. A third function is that of preventing overshooting and oscillation when the motor is to be stopped. This requires damping of some sort. Mechanical damping devices can be used, but these reduce the available motor torque, and also mostly require a motor with a double-ended shaft. Therefore, electronic damping methods are usually preferred. Special damping circuits are available for this purpose; see Refs. (1.1) and (1.23). Another technique, called *back-phase damping*, consists of switching the motor into the reverse direction to provide deceleration during the final portion of the last step. When the final position has been reached, the normal phase is again switched on, at which point the rotor should have come to a halt. Another method, called *delayed last-step damping*, consists of delaying the switching of the very last step until the rotor has coasted into the final position. Good controllers use these techniques in one way or another. For a discussion of step-motor damping methods, see Ref. (1.51).

4. The more sophisticated controllers are able to provide so-called *microstepping*. This technique permits the motor shaft to be positioned at places other than the natural stable points of the rotor. It is accomplished by proportioning the current in two adjacent motor windings. Instead of operating the windings in the *on–off* mode, the current in one winding is decreased slightly, but increased in the adjacent winding. In other words, the controller is called upon to generate analog rather than digital outputs.

Typical microstep sizes commonly used are 1/10, 1/16, 1/32, or 1/64 of a full step. Microstepping has several beneficial effects: the motor resolution (i.e., the attainable positioning accuracy) is greatly improved; operation is smoother, especially at low speeds; instability or resonance effects can usually be avoided; and finally, the problem of damping can easily be eliminated. The price that must be paid for all this is a much more complicated and expensive controller. For example, the controller needs digital-to-analog converters to modulate the winding voltages. For further information on microstepping, see Refs. (1.52)–(1.55).

References (1.56) and (1.57) describe techniques for microstepping a linear induction motor, providing a linear actuator for which a phenomenal accuracy (of better than 0.0001″) is claimed.

For more information on modern step-motor controllers, the reader is referred to Ref. (1.58). For a sophisticated programmable single-chip step-motor controller designed to be driven by a microcomputer, see Ref. (1.59).

1.3.3 Rotary Solenoids

Rotary solenoids, unlike motors, can generate only limited angular rotation. Furthermore, they are basically *on–off* devices, just like linear solenoids, so that intermediate angular positions cannot be obtained.

Most rotary solenoids are of the helical type: they are basically linear dc solenoids whose linear motion is converted to rotary motion by means of steel balls that ride in matching inclined cam grooves between armature and stator. Both left- and right-handed strokes from 5 to 200 degrees are obtainable with different models. When the solenoid is deenergized, the output shaft is returned to its neutral position by means of a scroll spring mounted between shaft and stator case.

As explained in Section 1.2.1, solenoids inherently have high end forces but very low starting forces. In helical rotary solenoids, this problem can be alleviated by changing the profile of the cam grooves. At the start, the groove incline is high, while it tapers off toward the stroke end. In this way, the output torque can be kept fairly constant throughout the stroke.

Rotary solenoids are comparatively low-cost devices, are rugged and compact, and are claimed to have long life. For more information, see Ref. (1.60).

1.4 FLUID-POWER LINEAR ACTUATORS

1.4.1 Fluid Power: Pneumatics vs. Hydraulics

Fluid power denotes the use of a pressurized fluid to drive linear or rotary actuators. The subject can be broadly divided into two fields: pneumatics and hydraulics. In the first, the working fluid is compressed air, and in the second, it usually is oil (sometimes water–oil emulsions).

The two fields have a great deal in common, but there are also some basic differences:

(a) *Pressure Levels.* Typical pressures in industrial pneumatic circuits range from 5 to 10 bar (75 to 150 psi), whereas hydraulic circuits commonly operate at pressures up to 200 bar (3000 psi), or even much higher. The reason for this difference can be pinpointed on the compressibility of air. If pneumatic systems were operated at 200 bar, the compressed air would be storing a tremendous amount of potential energy, presenting a serious safety hazard. Oil, on the other hand, is almost incompressible. Therefore, if an oil line in a hydraulic system should burst, the oil pressure drops almost immediately, and there is no danger of explosion. The fact that pneumatic systems operate at so much lower pressures has important implications with respect to several of the other differences that follow.

(b) *Actuating Forces.* Because of the relatively low air pressures used, pneumatic actuators can produce only low- or medium-size forces, whereas hydraulic actuators are suitable for very high loads. Or, to put it another way, a pneumatic cylinder needs a much larger diameter than a hydraulic cylinder driving the same load,

(c) *Element Cost.* Hydraulic cylinders and valves can cost from 5 to 10 times more than similar-size pneumatic elements. This can be explained by the much better workmanship and surface finish required in hydraulic elements. If a pneumatic element should have a small leak, some compressed air is wasted, but the system continues to function. In hydraulic systems, on the other hand, leaks cannot be tolerated. First of all, hydraulic oil is expensive, so that a leak represents a financial loss. But worse, oil leaks cause safety hazards, since most oils are inflammable and create slippery conditions on floors. In many industries (e.g., food, textile, etc.), leaking oil can ruin the manufactured product. Since hydraulic elements are built to function at so much higher pressures, their working surfaces must be manufactured to very close tolerances and have a fine surface finish so as to avoid leaks *without* the need for sliding seals; all this accounts for their high cost. Pneumatic elements, by comparison, use sliding O rings or other flexible seals to prevent leakage, so that manufacturing requirements are much less severe.

(d) *Transmission Lines.* Here, too, there is a big cost difference: hydraulic transmission lines are usually made of metal tubing with expensive fittings, needed to withstand the high working pressures and to avoid leaks. In pneumatics, inexpensive flexible plastic tubing is used, and the fittings can usually be connected by hand, without using wrenches. Also, in hydraulic systems, return lines are needed to return the oil from each cylinder back to the reservoir. In pneumatic systems, by comparison, only a single line is needed, since the air is simply exhausted back to the atmosphere after it has done its job. All this accounts for the higher installation costs of hydraulic systems.

(e) *Speed Control.* Because of the compressibility of air, it is difficult to control the speed of pneumatic cylinders or motors accurately. Therefore, whenever constant actuator speeds are required—despite sudden load changes—a hydraulic system (or a combined hydraulic–pneumatic system) should be chosen.

(f) *The Power Source.* In hydraulic systems, constant-displacement pumps are used, to that the oil flow rate is constant, regardless of load pressure. The pump *does not produce pressure*, but rather a constant flow. The pressure developed in the system depends on the opposing load. The situation is exactly the opposite in pneumatic systems: a pressure regulator connected at the compressor–receiver outlet keeps air pressure essentially constant, whereas the air flow rate into any given cylinder is determined by the load. This basic difference makes itself felt in the design of hydraulic vs. pneumatic circuits.

(g) *Actuation Speeds.* Since compressed air expands very quickly, the piston velocities in pneumatic cylinders are usually very high, provided the actuating valves and air-supply tubing are properly sized. In hydraulic cylinders, piston velocity is usually lower, being determined by the flow rate of the pump.

To summarize: pneumatic systems, because of their lower cost, are usually preferred in industrial automation, unless the loads are very high, or accurate speed control is required. Hydraulic systems, on the other hand, are preferred in high-load applications (e.g., in lifting machinery, earth-moving equipment, agricultural machinery, etc.), or where accurate speed control or positioning is required, such as in numerically controlled machine tools, robotics, etc.

Since the subject of hydraulics is immense, it cannot be covered properly within the limits of this book. We therefore confine outselves to referring the reader to a few of the many excellent textbooks on the subject; see Refs. (1.61)–(1.69). For current updates, and for information on equipment suppliers, see Refs. (1.70)–(1.72).

Turning now to the field of pneumatics: pneumatic cylinders, rotary actuators and motors are discussed in the remainder of this chapter. Chapter 4 covers, among other topics, pneumatic valves and other pneumatic logic elements. The design of pneumatic circuits is discussed in Chapter 7.

1.4.2 Pneumatic Cylinders

The moment *pneumatics* are mentioned, the most-commonly asked question is: Why bother with pneumatics, when we are living in the electronic age? The answer is simple: while nothing can compete with electronics when it comes to information-processing, electrical devices are left far behind wherever medium or large forces must be applied over appreciable distances.

Example. As seen from Fig. 1.9, a typical 0.5″-diameter solenoid has a 0.5″ stroke, and can develop a maximum sustained force (curve for f = 1) of about 13 ounces = 0.8 lb, (and this drops off to 0.03 lb at the extension end of the stroke). By comparison, a 0.5″-diameter cylinder operated at 80 psi (typical air pressure used in pneumatic circuitry) produces a force equal to $F = pA = (80)(\pi/4)(0.5)^2 = 16$ lb. Thus:

1. A pneumatic cylinder can produce a force typically 20 times as large as the *maximum* force of a solenoid with identical diameter.
2. The solenoid force drops off sharply, whereas the cylinder force remains almost constant throughout its stroke.
3. Solenoid strokes are very limited, typically equal approximately to the solenoid diameter. By comparison, cylinders can have strokes up to 15 times the piston diameter.
4. If a solenoid is overloaded, the coil is liable to overheat and burn out. An overloaded cylinder, by comparison, simply stalls; there is nothing to burn out.
5. The piston speed can easily be regulated, if desired, by placing adjustable restrictions (needle valves) in the exhaust lines. This cannot be done with solenoids.

For limited angular motion, various types of pneumatic *rotary actuators* are available. For continuous rotary motion, *pneumatic motors* can be used (e.g., in pneumatic power tools, such as those used in garages to tighten nuts), and these have a much higher power-to-weight ratio than equivalent electric motors.

Having (we hope) answered the previously posed question to the reader's satisfaction, we now discuss pneumatic cylinders and other cylinder-like devices. Without going into details about exact constructional features, we can classify cylinders into several types according to basic functions, as shown in Fig. 1.16.

Figure 1.16(a) is a single-acting cylinder, having a single air-inlet line. When this line is pressurized, the piston extends. If the inlet line is exhausted to atmosphere, the piston retracts due to the return spring mounted on the rod side of the piston. If the load, by itself, is able to push the piston back (e.g., due to gravity, such as in lifting devices), then the spring can be dispensed with. Single-acting cylinders with a return spring are limited in length (i.e., stroke), because the spring force that must be overcome while extending increases with the stroke. For long strokes, this force becomes excessive, and leaves less working force at the piston rod. The advantage of single-acting cylinders lies in their reduced air consumption: no air need be wasted for retracting the piston as with double-acting cylinders, Fig. 1.16(b), which have a second air inlet at the piston-rod end for retraction.

The double-acting cylinder, Fig. 1.16(b), produces less force during retraction, because the piston-rod cross-sectional area is subtracted from the active piston

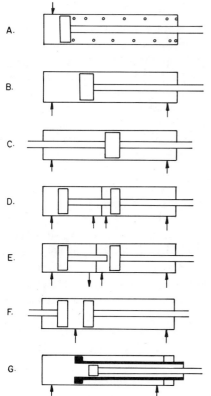

Fig. 1.16. Basic cylinder types: (a) single-acting cylinder, (b) double-acting cylinder, (c) double rod-end cylinder, (d) tandem cylinder, (e) three-position cylinder, (f) adjustable-stroke cylinder, and (g) telescoping cylinder.

area under pressure. If equal forces in both directions are required, a cylinder with double rod ends must be used; see Fig. 1.16(c). The two rod ends work in the push–pull mode.

Figure 1.16(d) is a tandem cylinder, which consist of two pistons operating in separate sections along the same axis and with a common piston rod. Since the available force is doubled, this design is useful if larger forces are required, but a single cylinder with a larger diameter cannot be accommodated. The same design can also be used as a pneumatic–hydraulic drive. For this purpose, both sides of one cylinder are filled with oil and are connected by a line containing a needle valve. When air pressure is applied to the second cylinder, the oil is forced through the needle valve. Thus, the oil-filled cylinder acts as a dashpot and permits accurate and smooth control of cylinder speed, in spite of the air compressibility.

Figure 1.16(e) is a three-position cylinder. It is quite similar to the tandem cylinder, except that the left piston rod is not connected to the right piston, and the left cylinder is shorter than the right one. With the left piston extended, the retraction of the right piston is limited to an intermediate position determined by the stroke of the left piston. With the left piston retracted, the right piston is able to retract fully.

In Fig. 1.16(f), the cylinder stroke can be adjusted by screwing the left-hand piston in or out. By using the shortest possible stroke needed for a given job, more rapid cycling is achieved, and air consumption is reduced.

Figure 1.16(g) is a telescoping cylinder. When pressure is applied to the left side, the inner cylinder acts as a piston and extends. Once it has reached the end of its stroke, the innermost piston begins to extend. The available stroke is thus almost doubled, compared to a normal cylinder having the same retracted length. For a discussion of telescoping cylinders, see Ref. (1.73).

An in-depth technical report on cylinders is found in Ref. (1.74). Figure 1.17, which is taken from this reference, shows some of the many ways in which cylinders can be utilized. This leads to a topic frequently neglected: proper cylinder mounting. Cylinders are basically reliable devices, but can be ruined quickly by improper mounting. Cylinders are designed for push–pull (i.e., in-line) loads, but they are not meant to act as load guides. Side loads or bending moments should be absorbed by separate guide surfaces and *not* by the cylinder; otherwise, they quickly ruin the bearing surfaces and seals of piston and of rod. Various common cylinder mounts are discussed in Refs. (1.63), (1.66), (1.67), (1.69), (1.70), (1.72), and (1.74)–(1.76). Most manufacturers offer a variety of different mounts for their cylinders. Manufacturers' catalogs or other technical literature usually provide guidelines as to the proper mount selection, depending on the type of loading.

Certain manufacturers offer so-called linear-thrust devices, consisting of a cylinder mounted between a set of guide shafts. These shafts absorb all side loads or bending moments, so that the piston rod sees a pure in-line load.

Another important factor is proper choice of piston and rod diameters. The piston diameter must be large enough to overcome the load (both static and

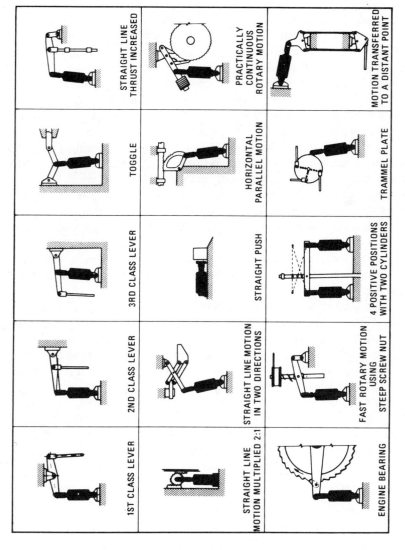

Fig. 1.17. Fifteen ways of using cylinders. (Reprinted from *Hydraulics & Pneumatics*, March 1976. Copyright 1976, by Penton Publishing, Inc., Cleveland, Ohio.)

inertia loads), taking friction losses within the cylinder and pressure drops in the air supply lines into account. The piston-rod diameter is especially important for long cylinders with compressive loads, where there might be danger of rod failure due to buckling. Many of the references cited previously present tables and nomographs helpful in proper cylinder sizing.

Another factor contributing to long cylinder life is proper piston braking at the end of the stroke. The piston should not slam into the cylinder cap at full speed. The problem is especially serious with long cylinders, where the piston often reaches maximum speed (determined by pressure difference and load conditions). For short cylinders, this maximum speed is usually never reached. Estimation of piston velocity is treated in Refs. (1.77) and (1.78). Also, some of the previously cited references present tables for estimating maximum piston velocities, e.g., Refs. (1.67), (1.69), (1.74), and (1.77).

One way to brake pistons at the end of their stroke is by using cushioned cylinders, as shown in Fig. 1.18. As the piston nears the end of stroke, the so-called cushion spear enters a mating cavity in the cylinder body, which forces the trapped air to exhaust through a needle valve. The resulting back pressure decelerates the piston. A built-in check valve bypasses the needle valve and permits fast start-up when the piston velocity is reversed. Proper needle-valve adjustment is important for good cushioning. If the needle valve is closed too much, the piston may bounce back rather than come to a smooth halt. Even worse, pressure buildup may be so high as to damage the cylinder. The problem is discussed in detail in Ref. (1.74).

For long cylinders whose pistons reach maximum velocity, and especially with high-inertia loads, the kinetic energy may simply be too high to be absorbed safely by the air cushion, because its braking action only begins toward the end of the stroke. In that case, exterior means for braking the piston must be used. The simplest method is placing a needle valve (with check-valve bypass) in the cylinder exhaust line. Long before the end of the stroke is reached, back pressure begins to build up and starts decelerating the load, The case of high-inertia loads is analyzed in Ref. (1.79), where guidelines for sizing the needle valve are given. See also Ref. (1.78), pages 399–404 of Ref. (1.67), and pages 237–238 of Ref. (1.68) for cylinder-braking methods.

1.4.3 Short-Stroke Pneumatic Actuators

As described in Ref. (1.80), new types of cylinders are evolving to meet changing needs. For example, a number of special actuators are available for applications where only very short strokes are required. Some of these devices bear a close resemblance to conventional cylinders, others, less so.

Several manufacturers offer very compact flat cylinders with short strokes. Some of these have a diameter-to-height ratio similar to that of an aspirin tablet, with strokes as small as $\frac{1}{8}''$. Certain of these cylinders can be purchased with attached fingers or similar gripping devices, so that they can be used as pneumatically driven robotic grippers for "pick-and-place" applications.

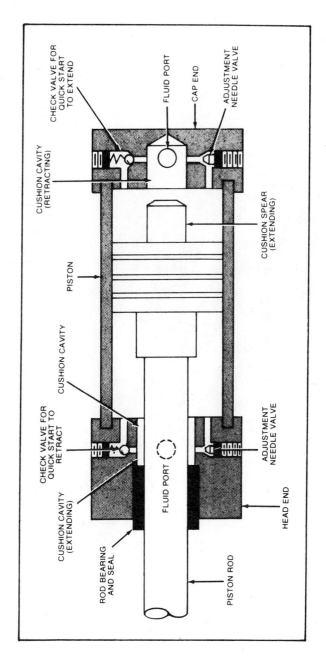

Fig. 1.18. Cylinders with cushions. (Reprinted from *Hydraulics & Pneumatics*, March 1976. Copyright 1976, by Penton Publishing, Inc., Cleveland, Ohio.)

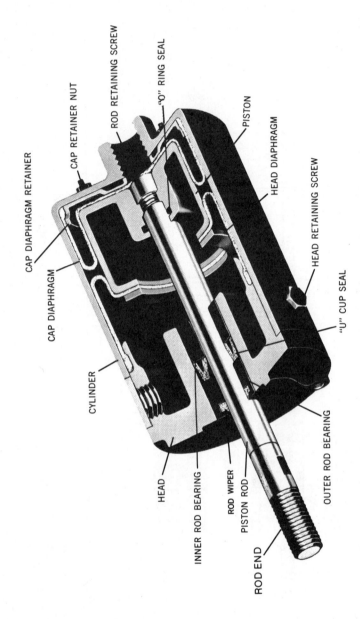

CAP DIAPHRAGM RETAINER

CAP RETAINER NUT

ROD RETAINING SCREW

"O" RING SEAL

PISTON

CAP DIAPHRAGM

HEAD DIAPHRAGM

CYLINDER

HEAD RETAINING SCREW

"U" CUP SEAL

HEAD

INNER ROD BEARING

ROD WIPER

PISTON ROD

OUTER ROD BEARING

ROD END

Fig. 1.19. Rolling-diaphragm cylinder. (By permission of Bellofram Corp.)

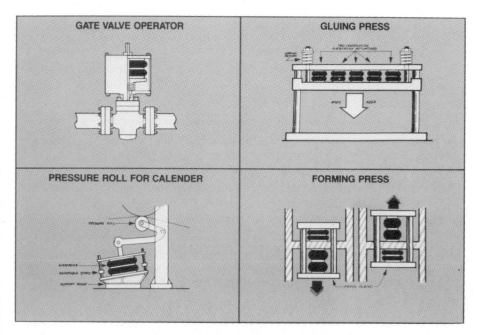

Fig. 1.20. Four typical "Airstroke" actuator applications. (By permission of Firestone Industrial Products Co., Division of The Firestone Tire & Rubber Co.)

Another type of short-stroke actuator is the rolling-diaphragm cylinder, as shown in Fig. 1.19. The piston consists of a metal cup connected to two convoluted elastomer diaphragms, which roll along the cylinder bore as the piston moves. These diaphragms replace the piston seal in conventional cylinders. Their advantage lies in complete absence of leakage past the piston, and in practically zero breakout friction. Thus, these cylinders are extremely sensitive and respond to very low air pressures. (With properly selected springs, rolling-diaphragm cylinders can even be used for proportional positioning applications, with piston movement proportional to air pressure.) Since no lubrication is required, the cylinder exhaust does not carry any contaminating oil mist, so that these cylinders find application in the food and drug industries. Their two main limitations are that working pressure is limited to about 125 psi and the maximum stroke-to diameter ratio is 1. See also Ref. (1.81).

A third type of short-stroke actuator is the so-called "Airstroke" actuator; see Ref. (1.82). It consists of one or more hollow rubber bodies, reminiscent of automobile-tire inner tubes. When pressurized, the body expands and can apply a considerable force due to its large diameter, albeit over a very short stroke. Several typical applications of this actuator are illustrated in Fig. 1.20. It can claim several advantages compared to conventional cylinders:

1. Lower cost than cylinders having the same force capacity.
2. Available in very large diameters (up to 37″), with correspondingly large forces.
3. No maintenance or lubrication required.
4. Practically frictionless (just as rolling-diaphragm cylinders).
5. No mounting problems, since the device can absorb side loads, and can even turn through an arc of up to 30 degrees.

For further examples of pneumatic clamping actuators consisting of various types of elastomer fingers or grippers, see Ref. (1.83).

1.5 FLUID-POWER ROTATING ACTUATORS

1.5.1 Rotary Actuators for Limited Rotary Motion

Unlike pneumatic or hydraulic motors (discussed in the next section) that can rotate continuously, rotary actuators oscillate through a limited angle. One way to achieve this is to take a conventional cylinder and connect its piston rod to any of the linear-to-rotary motion devices covered in Section 1.1.3 (i.e., rack-and-pinion drives, power screws, or linkages), and, indeed, some of these combinations are shown in Fig. 1.17. However, there are many commercial devices especially designed for this purpose, see Ref. (1.84), and these are generally more compact and efficient than a "do-it-yourself" combination.

Several types of rotary actuators are shown in Fig. 1.21. Figures 1.21(a) to (e) use pistons within cylinders, whose linear motion is then converted to rotary motion by various means. Figures 1.21(f) to (h) inherently produce rotary motion. All these actuators produce high instantaneous torques, but at relatively low speeds. Since no parts extend or retract, they are less sensitive to contamination than cylinders, and thus very reliable.

In Fig. 1.21(a), the piston has an internal thread with a high helix angle and drives a rotating shaft with a meshing helical groove. As the piston reciprocates, the shaft oscillates through an angular range than can exceed 360 degrees. Because of the high helix angle, the device is self-locking, that is, external loads acting on the shaft produce no movement.

Figs. 1.21(b), uses a slider–crank mechanism. The device is simple, but there is no self-locking, and the crank angle is limited to about 110 degrees.

The Scotch-yoke actuator, Fig. 1.21(c), uses two pistons connected by a rigid rod, which drives the shaft through a pin riding within a slot. The shaft angle is limited to 90 degrees. The torque developed at the two stroke ends is double the intermediate torque. This is useful in applications where high torques are needed at the beginning of the stroke to overcome static friction and inertia loads.

Figure 1.21(d) uses a rack-and-pinion drive. The generated torque remains

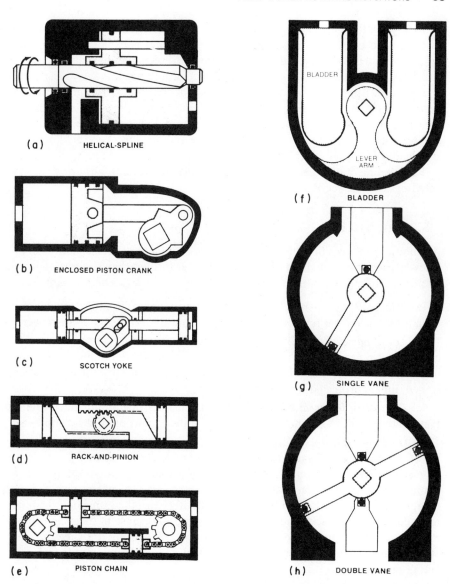

(a)   HELICAL-SPLINE

(b)   ENCLOSED PISTON CRANK

(c)   SCOTCH YOKE

(d)   RACK-AND-PINION

(e)   PISTON CHAIN

(f)   BLADDER

(g)   SINGLE VANE

(h)   DOUBLE VANE

Fig. 1.21. Different types of rotary actuators. (Reprinted from *Hydraulics & Pneumatics*, December 1976. Copyright 1976, by Penton Publishing, Inc., Cleveland, Ohio.)

constant, and the shaft can produce several complete rotations, depending on rack length. The use of two racks driving the same pinion from opposite sides, as shown in the figure, doubles the available torque and balances the forces acting on the pinion. These actuators are able to produce very large torques with high efficiencies. In the actuator of Fig. 1.21(e), a chain driving two sprocket wheels takes the place of the rack and pinion.

In Fig. 1.21(f), two expanding rubber bladders drive a lever arm back and forth, as one bladder is pressurized while the second is exhausted. The shaft angle is limited to about 110 degrees, but the design has the advantages of relatively low price, and the complete absence of internal leakage.

Figure 1.21(g) is a single-vane actuator, which can rotate through about 270 degrees. Differential pressure applied to the vane rotates the shaft. The double-vane actuator, Fig. 1.21(h), works in similar fashion, but is completely balanced, and produces twice the torque for the same size and pressure. Vane actuators are simple and relatively inexpensive.

For a listing of manufacturers, with technical details about the various rotary actuators offered, see Ref. (1.70) or (1.71).

1.5.2 Air Motors

Air motors produce continuous rotary motion, with many models bidirectional. They operate at higher speeds, but produce lower torques than rotary actuators. Compared to electric motors, air motors have several important advantages:

(a) *Higher Power-to-Weight Ratio.* Air motors are light and compact, and usually weigh several times less than electric motors having the same power.

(b) *Overloading Capability.* An overloaded air motor simply stalls, but continues to produce high torque. It can remain in the stalled condition indefinitely without risk of damage. Electric motors usually burn out when stalled, unless protected by a thermal cutout.

(c) *Operating Temperature Range.* Air motors can operate at much higher temperatures. They are self-cooling because of the expansion of the compressed air passing through the motor.

(d) *Speed and Direction Control.* The speed of air motors is easily controlled by means of a needle valve mounted in the exhaust line. By using a five-connection three-position actuating valve with a closed-center position (see Chapter 4), the air motor can be stopped instantly (with the trapped air helping to brake the motor) and reversed. (Electric motors, because of their high rotor inertia, take much longer to stop.) Furthermore, by shifting the valve into its closed-center position, the air motor can be locked in position, in spite of a load acting on the shaft.

(e) *Safety.* Air motors are inherently explosion proof.

As always, there are also drawbacks:

(a) *Price.* Air motors are usually more expensive than equivalent electric motors, especially in the smaller sizes (because of the low cost of small mass-produced electric motors).

(b) *Efficiency.* The efficiency of air motors is much lower than electric motors, often as low as 30%. As a result, air consumption is high, which increases operating cost considerably. If we multiply this already low efficiency with that of the compressor, we may reach an overall efficiency as low as 20%. (To be realistic, we should also take part of the cost of the air compressor into account. If a number of air motors are to be installed, it may be necessary to purchase a larger compressor.)

For a detailed comparison between air and electric motors, see Ref. (1.85). Discussion of the different types of available air motors is found in Refs. (1.86) and (1.87). For an in-depth analysis of air-motor dynamics, see pages 256–260 of Ref. (1.68).

There are several different air-motor types, the most common being vane motors, piston motors, and turbine motors. A typical vane motor is shown in Fig. 1.22. A rotor mounted eccentrically within a round housing has four (or more) radial slots, each with a sliding vane. When the rotor turns, the vanes are pressed against the inner housing surface by centrifugal force, so that the vane tip acts as seal. (To provide sealing before the rotor reaches speed, a small spring in each slot under the vane presses the vane outwards.) As pressurized air reaches one side of the rotor, the pressure difference across each vane produces a torque, making the rotor turn. The air expands, and, finally, is exhausted on the other side of the rotor. During each revolution, each vane slides in and out once.

Vane motors are compact and have high power-to-weight ratios since they operate at high speeds. However, they do not operate well at low speeds. For low-speed operation, a vane motor with built-in gear reducer should be used.

Piston motors contain several small pistons moving either radially or axially. They can supply higher low-speed torque than vane motors. They are usually larger and more expensive than vane motors of identical power. However, if the piston motor can be used without gear reduction, it may turn out cheaper than a vane rotor with gear reduction.

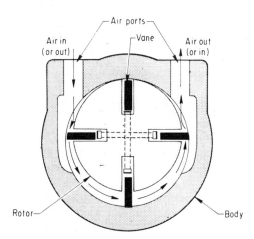

Fig. 1.22. Reversible vane-type air motor. (Reprinted from *Machine Design*, March 18, 1971. Copyright 1971, by Penton Publishing, Inc., Cleveland, Ohio.)

Turbine air motors, see Ref. (1.88), are more expensive than most other types, but provide several important advantages: their efficiency is much higher (about 70%), they are much more compact, and they have no sliding parts, and hence no lubrication and wear problems. However, they operate efficiently only at very high speeds (in the 10,000 to 50,000 rpm range). As a result, they are almost always used with a built-in planetary gear reducer. One well-known use of miniature-size turbine motors is in high-speed dental drills.

Another air-motor type is based on the gerotor element, a three-lobed rotor rotating within a housing having four internal matching lobes and bays. This motor, described in Ref. (1.89), falls on exactly the opposite side of the spectrum than turbine air motors: the gerotor air motor has high starting torque, and inherently runs at low speeds, eliminating the need for external gear reducers. Compared to vane motors, its efficiency is high, and, since the relative motion between rotor and housing is mainly rolling, wear is minimized. Although the gerotor air-motor cost is higher, this is partially offset by the fact that no external gear reduction is required.

REFERENCES

1.1. *Design and Application of Small Standardized Components*, Data Book 757, Stock Drive Products, New Hyde Park, NY, 1983.

1.2. T. Black, "Designing Low-Inertia Instrument Drives," *Product Engineering*, Dec. 1979, pp. 31–33.

1.3. J. Shigley, *Theory of Machines*, Mc-Graw-Hill, New York, 1961.

1.4. J. Bickford, "Design Guide: Mechanisms for Intermittent Rotary Motion," *Machine Design*, Dec. 23, 1965, pp. 119–131.

1.5. F. Yeaple, "Geneva Mechanisms for Indexing," *Product Engineering*, Aug. 1979, pp. 39–43.

1.6. P. Jensen, "Machinery Mechanisms," *Product Engineering*, Oct. 26, 1964, pp. 108–115.

1.7. N. Chironis, *Machine Devices and Instrumentation*, McGraw-Hill, New York, 1966.

1.8. N. Chironis, *Mechanisms, Linkages, and Mechanical Controls*, McGraw-Hill, New York, 1966.

1.9. S. Gibson, "Synchronizing Motions and Indexing Drives," *Machine Design*, July 25, 1985, pp. 89–94.

1.10. V. Faires, *Design of Machine Elements*, Macmillan, New York, 1965.

1.11. J. Rutkiewicz, "Ball Bearing Screw Design Basics," *Power Transmission Design*, June 1978, pp. 42–45.

1.12. S. Lochmoeller, "Power Screw or Ball Screw?" *Machine Design*, Mar. 11, 1976, pp. 76–79.

1.13. G. de Charette, "Comparing Ball and Roller Screws," Machine Design, Sept. 11, 1980, pp. 119–123.

1.14. Ball Reverser—Automatic Reciprocating Actuators, catalog, Norco Inc., PO Box 405, Georgetown, CT 06829.

1.15. D. Tesar and J. Vidosic, "Analysis of Approximate Four-bar Straight-line Mechanisms," *Journal of Engineering for Industry*, Aug. 1965, pp. 291–297.

1.16. N. Chironis, "Unique Linkage Produces Precise Straight-line Motion," *Product Engineering*, June 8, 1970, pp. 100–101.

1.17. D. Pessen, "Mechanism Animation on a Personal Computer," *Mechanical Engineering*, Oct. 1984, pp. 33–35.

1.18. R. Hadekel, "Converting Linear to Rotary Motion with Cross-link Mechanisms," *Machine Design*, July 20, 1978, pp. 64–67.

1.19. Electrical and Electronics Reference Issue, *Machine Design*, May 19, 1988.

1.20. R. Acker, "Solenoids," *Machine Design*, Apr. 1, 1971, pp. 148–151.

1.21. V. Coughlin, "Solenoid Selection and Protection,"*Design Engineering*, Oct. 1980, pp. 45–48.

1.22. L. Williamson, "What You Always Wanted to Know About Solenoids," *Hydraulics & Pneumatics*, Part 1: Sept. 1980, pp. 85–87; Part 2: Oct. 1980, pp. 182–183.

1.23. Electric Motors Reference Issue, *Machine Design*, April,11, 1974.

1.24. S. Cory, "The Nature of Linear Induction Motors," *Machine Design*, Aug. 23, 1984, pp. 111–113.

1.25. "LIM Drives Actuator for Unlimited Stroke," *Product Engineering*, June 1979, pp. 20, 22, 26.

1.26. "1987 Control Products Specifier,"*Control Engineering*, (Special Issue), Nov. 1986.

1.27. B. Triplett, "Linear Motors Combine Muscle with a Fine Touch," *Machine Design*, May 7, 1987, pp. 94–97.

1.28. S. Davis, "Wide World of Electric Motors/Subsystems," *Design Engineering*, May 1982, pp. 49–65.

1.29. E. Werninck (Ed.), *Electric Motor Handbook*, McGraw-Hill, New York, 1978.

1.30. D. Fink and J. Carrall (Eds.), *Standard Handbook for Electrical Engineers*, Section 18, McGraw-Hill, New York, 1968.

1.31. N. Sclater, "Fractional-hp ac Motors," *Design Engineering*, May 1980, pp. 35–37.

1.32. F. Yeaple, "AC Motor Acceleration Estimates," *Design Engineering*, Jan. 1981, pp. 43–44.

1.33. *DC Motors—Speed Controls—Servosystems: An Engineering Handbook*, Electro-Craft Corp., Hopkins, Mn 55343, 1980.

1.34. "Forum on DC Motors," *Product Engineering*, Oct. 1979, pp. 29–34.

1.35. Three articles on Motor Control, *I & CS*, April 1988, pp. 29–40.

1.36. S. Bailey, "Motor Drives 1985," *Control Engineering*, Mar. 1985, pp. 159–163.

1.37. S. Bailey, "New Motor Drives Can be Tailored to Loads,"*Control Engineering*, Aug. 1984, pp. 84–88.

1.38. H. Murphy and T. Gilmore, "Trends in ac-Drive Technology," *Control Engineering*, Sept. 1984, pp. 183–186.

1.39. P. Cleaveland, "Motor Controls: A Technology Update," *I & CS*, Mar. 1984, pp. 50–55.

1.40. G. Flynn, "Drive Versatility— Get it With a Stepper," *Product Engineering*, Aug. 1979, pp. 48–52.

1.41. D. Jones, "Step Motors Versus dc Motors," *Design Engineering*, Jan. 1980, pp. 43–46.

1.42. P. P. Acarnley, *Stepping Motors: A Guide to Modern Theory and Practice*, Peter Peregrinus, London, 1984.

1.43. B. Carlisle, "Stepping Motors: Edging into Servo Territory," *Machine Design*, Nov. 6, 1986, pp. 88–93.

1.44. C. de sa e Silva, "What Size Stepper?," *Machine Design*, Dec. 14, 1972, pp. 136–143.

1.45. G. Singh, "Step-motor Systems,"*Power Transmission Design*, Part 1: Feb. 1978, pp. 27–32; Part 2: May 1978, pp. 36–40; Part 3: June 1978, pp. 50–54.

1.46. M. Hoberman, "A Simplified Approach to Stepper Motor Control," *Control Engineering*, Sept., 1973, pp. 67–69.

1.47. O. Neumann, "C-MOS Circuit Controls Stepper Motor," *Electronics*, Sept. 8, 1982, pp. 165, 167.

1.48. T. Nguyen, "Logic and Driver Circuit Allow Microprocessor to Control 4-phase Stepper Motor," *Electronic Design*, Feb. 19, 1981, pp. 189–190.

1.49. Sprague Engineering Data Sheet 26184.10 on UCN4204/5 Stepper Motor Translator/Driver, Sprague Electric Co., Worcester, MA 01606, 1986.

1.50. B. Lafreniere, "Software for Stepping Motors," *Machine Design*, Apr. 26, 1979, pp. 213–217.

1.51. V. Coughlin, "Damping and the Step Motor," *Design Engineering*, Sept. 1980, pp. 55–57.

1.52. S. J. Bailey, "Lessening the Gap Between Incremental and Continuous Motion Control," *Control Engineering*, Feb. 1987, pp. 72–76.

1.53. E. Pritchard, "Curing Step Motor Resonance," *Machine Design*, Jan. 10, 1980, pp. 127–128.

1.54. E. Pritchard, "Step Motor Accuracy at Low Frequencies," *Machine Design*, July 24, 1980, pp. 111–112.

1.55. V. Coughlin, "Step Motors with Micro Control," *Design Engineering*, June 1981, pp. 49–51.

1.56. H. Morris, "Microstepping a Linear Motor," *Control Engineering*, Feb. 1985, pp. 83–84.

1.57. E. R. Pelta, "Precise Positioning Without Gear Trains," *Machine Design*, Apr. 23, 1987, pp. 79–83.

1.58. S. Bailey, "Step Motion Control 1985," *Control Engineering*, Aug. 1985, pp. 49–52.

1.59. E. Klingman and K. Moty, "A Third-generation Stepper Motor Controller," *Robotics Age*, Part 1: Dec. 1984, pp. 26–30; Part 2: Feb. 1985, pp. 31–34.

1.60. B. J. Yost, "Rotary Solenoids," *Machine Design*, Aug. 24, 1972, pp. 89–92.

1.61. R. Henke, *Introduction to Fluid Power Circuits and Systems*, Addison-Wesley, Reading, MA, 1970.

1.62. G. Keller, *Hydraulic System Analysis*, Published by Hydraulics & Pneumatics Magazine, Cleveland, OH 44113, 1974.

1.63. D. Pease, *Basic Fluid Power*, Prentice Hall, Englewood Cliffs, NJ, 1967.

1.64. J. Pippenger, *Industrial Hydraulics*, 3rd ed., McGraw-Hill, New York, 1979.

1.65. J. Pippenger, *Hydraulic Valves and Controls: Selection and Application*, Dekker, New York, 1984.

1.66. H. Stewart and J. Storer, *Fluid Power*, Howard W. Sams, Indianapolis, IN, 1973.

1.67. F. Yeaple, *Fluid Power Design Handbook*, Dekker, New York, 1984.

1.68. F. Yeaple, *Hydraulic and Pneumatic Power and Control*, McGraw-Hill, New York, 1966.

1.69. *Design Engineers Handbook*, Bull. 0224-B1, Parker-Hannifin Corp., Cleveland, OH, 1979.

1.70. *Fluid Power Handbook and Directory*, published biannually by Hydraulics & Pneumatics Magazine, Cleveland, OH 44113, 1988–1989.

1.71. Annual Designers Guide to Fluid Power Products, *Hydraulics & Pneumatics*, Jan. 1988.

1.72. Fluid Power Reference Issue, *Machine Design*, Sept. 15, 1988.

1.73. D. Combs, "Special Considerations for Designing with Telescoping Cylinders," *Hydraulics & Pneumatics*, Sept. 1987, pp. 53–56.

1.74. T. Goldoftas, "Cylinders for Profit-making Designs," *Hydraulics & Pneumatics*, Mar. 1976, pp. HP1–HP32.

1.75. L. Boulden, "Controlling Aerosols with Oil-less Cylinders," *Machine Design*, Jan. 9, 1975, pp. 95–99.

1.76. F. Yeaple, "Making Air Cylinders Behave," *Design Engineering*, Aug. 1981, pp. 37–42.

1.77. W. Baier, "Calculate Instantaneous Piston Velocity this Easy Way," *Hydraulics & Pneumatics*, June 1963, pp. 98–102.

1.78. C. Hedges, "How to Control Cylinder Speed," *Hydraulics & Pneumatics*, Feb. 1979, pp. 50–53.

1.79. M. Kerber and D. Pessen, "Controlled Exhaust Brakes Pneumatic Cylinders Smoothly," *Hydraulics & Pneumatics* (International Edition), Jan. 1971, pp. 31–36.

1.80. K. J. Korane, "Pneumatic Cylinders Adapt to Changing Needs," *Machine Design*, Feb. 26, 1987, pp. 74–77.

1.81. L. Matthys and P. Marchetti, "Precise Pneumatic Positioning with Diaphragm Air Cylinders," *Machine Design*, Apr. 24, 1980, pp. 80–83.

1.82. Airstroke Actuators, Catalog ASAM-185, Firestone Industrial Products Co., Noblesville, IN.

1.83. G. Neubauer, "Pneumatic Grippers," *Machine Design*, Nov. 25, 1982, pp. 69–71.

1.84. I. Chang, "How to Choose a Rotary Actuator," *Hydraulics & Pneumatics*, Dec. 1976, pp. 66–69.

1.85. E. Brooks, "Air Motors Challenge Electrics," *Machine Design*, Sept. 21, 1978, pp. 130–133.

1.86. E. Brooks, "Basic Facts You Should Know About Air Motors," *Hydraulics & Pneumatics*, Feb. 1973, pp. 54–56.

1.87. J. Webb, "Tips on Selecting Air Motors for Controlled Rotary Power," *Machine Design*, Mar. 18, 1971, pp. 104–107.

1.88. R. Graham, "Turbine Air Motors Shed their High-cost Image," *Machine Design*, Nov. 26, 1981, pp. 93–98.

1.89. J. Mahanay, "Gerotor Air Motor," *Machine Design*, Feb. 6, 1986, pp. 75–77.

CHAPTER 2

SENSORS

In Chapter 1, various motion actuators were described. To control these, it is necessary to detect the result of the motion, that is, a change in position. Therefore, the stress in this chapter is on binary position sensors, both electric and pneumatic. However, binary sensors for other variables, such as liquid level, pressure, temperature and flow, are also discussed.

2.1 BINARY (ON-OFF) VS. ANALOG (PROPORTIONAL) SENSORS

Sensors are either binary or analog devices. Binary sensors produce *on–off* signals; for example, a limit-switch contact might close whenever the switch is mechanically actuated. The contact is either open or closed; there is no intermediate position. Hence, limit switches are binary sensors that can be used to indicate whether or not a certain machine part—for instance, a cylinder piston—has reached a certain position. Analog sensors, by comparison, produce so-called proportional or analog signals. Thus, a linear potentiometer might be used to indicate piston motion, with the voltage measured at the potentiometer slide wire proportional to the motion.

As a second example, consider temperature measurement. A simple thermostat (such as used in refrigerators, electric irons, etc.) opens or closes a contact when a certain temperature is reached. Hence, thermostats represent binary sensors. On the other hand, thermocouples produce voltages proportional to the temperature measured, and therefore represent analog sensors.

As stated in the preface, this book deals mainly with binary, or *on–off*, control, as opposed to continuous feedback control. Hence, the discussion in this chapter is limited to binary sensors. The subject of analog sensors (transducers) is, of course, an important topic in itself, and it is covered in detail in many books, e.g., Ref. (2.1) or (2.2).

2.2 ELECTRIC POSITION SENSORS

2.2.1 Limit Switches

Limit switches consist of mechanically actuated electrical contacts. The contacts open or close when some machine component reaches a certain position (i.e., limit) and actuates the switch. Limit switches have been in use for many decades, and, because of their extreme simplicity and low cost, will most likely continue to be popular for decades to come, even though they must compete with various types of more sophisticated sensors, which are discussed in following sections.

For a detailed guide to limit switches, see Ref. (2.3) and also Refs. (2.4)–(2.10). Limit switches are manufactured by hundreds of companies and come in an almost unlimited number of configurations. In attempting to classify these, we must distinguish between the type of actuation (i.e., the mechanical aspect, or the "outside" of the switch), and the type of contacts (i.e., the electrical aspect, or the "inside").

Four of the most common actuating methods are shown in Fig. 2.1. The overtravel plunger, Fig.1(a), is used with in-line operating motion, where overtravel must be accommodated. Roller actuation, Fig. 2.1(b), permits overtravel, reduces actuating forces, and is frequently used to sense piston motion of pneumatic/hydraulic cylinders. The pin-plunger actuation, Fig. 2.1 (c), is used in applications with limited operating motion and little overtravel, but where maximum precision and repeatability is required (e.g., in thermostats or other instruments). Lever actuation, Fig. 2.1(d), is used where actuating forces must be kept minimum. The elasticity of the lever permits a certain amount of overtravel.

Some of the other actuation methods include the wobble stick (which permits the actuating force to be applied from any direction and with a great amount of overtravel), the fork lever (which causes the switch to remain in its tripped position as the actuator travels beyond the switch, and with the switch returned

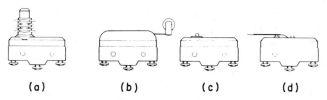

(a)	(b)	(c)	(d)

Fig. 2.1. Common actuation methods for limit switches: (a) overtravel plunger, (b) lever-roller, (c) pin plunger, and (d) lever. (Courtesy MICRO SWITCH, a Honeywell Division.)

to its normal position on the return stroke), and the one-way actuator (usually consisting of a roller mounted on a hinged link, so that the switch is actuated only briefly during the actuator's forward stroke).

Limit switches come in a wide range of sizes, from tiny light-duty switches used in instruments or small mechanical devices, to large heavy-duty switches used in heavy industrial machinery and equipped with elaborate protective enclosures providing various degrees of watertightness and explosion-proofing. This difference makes itself felt in the required actuating forces, the current capacity of the contacts, and, of course, the price, which can vary by a factor of 100 for different types of limit switches (from 50 cents up to about $50).

In many automation applications, the limit switches represent the weakest link of the control system: it has been estimated that about 90% of failures can be attributed to limit switches or other sensors. This can be explained by the fact that the sensors are almost always located "where the action is," that is, they are exposed to heat, moisture, corrosive atmosphere, vibration, high impact forces, etc. However, failure frequently is simply due to misuse or even gross abuse of the limit switches, which basically are reliable elements if properly selected and applied. A number of "do's and don'ts" can be found in Refs. (2.4) and (2.8)–(2.10). Among the common abuses are:

1. Using the limit switch as a mechanical stop. This is a sure way to obtain quick failure. The switch should be positioned so that the actuator does not ram the switch lever or plunger beyond its overtravel limit. If necessary, external blocks should be used to stop actuator motion.
2. Allowing high impact forces. To avoid these, the actuator should have a cam surface with a small slope, so that the switch roller is depressed gradually.
3. Applying side forces on the switch roller or lever can ruin switch bearings quickly. Actuator forces must be applied in the proper direction, depending on switch design.
4. Switching excessive currents (to be discussed later).

Turning now to the switch contacts, these can be classified as normally open (NO) or normally closed (NC), as illustrated in Fig. 2.2. These two types are also referred to as single-pole single-throw (SPST) contacts. The majority of limit switches contain both an NO and an NC contact, but with a common pole, producing a so called single-pole double-throw (SPDT) configuration, as shown in the figure. These are also referred to as "change over" or "transfer" contacts.

The contact symbols and the way they should be drawn often causes confusion. It might help the reader to imagine the spring that is part of the switch (but not shown on the symbol) tending to press the moving contact down. Therefore, in the "normal" position, the moving contact is down as far as it can go, whereas in the "actuated" position, the contact is pushed up against the spring. The "normal" condition of a contact is defined as the position in which

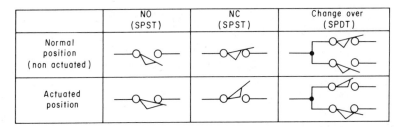

	NO (SPST)	NC (SPST)	Change over (SPDT)
Normal position (non actuated)			
Actuated position			

Fig. 2.2. Limit-switch symbols for different contact configurations.

the switch is *not* actuated (e.g., with the switch uninstalled and lying on a storeroom shelf), and this has nothing to do with whether the contacts are NO or NC.

In any circuit diagram, it is customary to draw each switch contact (no matter whether it is NO or NC) the way it appears at the beginning of a machine cycle, with the system at rest. For example, cylinders frequently have two limit switches mounted along the piston-rod path, in order to indicate piston position. One of these switches (say, switch *A*) is usually mounted to be actuated when the cylinder is retracted, whereas the second (switch *B*) is actuated when the cylinder is completely extended. Assume that the cylinder is retracted at the beginning of a cycle. We would therefore draw all contacts of switch *A* (no matter whether NO or NC) in their actuated position, whereas contacts of switch *B* would be drawn in their normal position. This convention is followed in the coming chapters (see, e.g., Fig. 5.9).

SPDT contacts can be further classified as providing either "break-before-make" (BBM) or "make-before-break" (MBB) switching. This is shown in Fig. 2.3. In the BBM arrangement, both contacts are open for a brief moment during switching, whereas the MBB arrangement produces a temporary overlap with both contacts closed, providing continuity in current flow. Standard SPDT contacts are generally of the BBM type. If MBB is required, it must be so specified.

There are also switches having more than one pole, for example, with double-pole double-throw (DPDT) contacts. These simply duplicate the SPDT arrangement and are useful where independent circuits must be operated simulta-

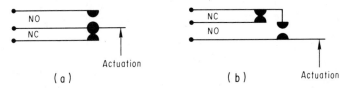

Fig. 2.3. SPDT switch with (a) break-before-make (BBM) contacts, and (b) make-before-break (MBB) contacts.

neously. However, if multiple poles are required, it is usually cheaper to use a simple standard switch, and connect its NO contact to operate the coil of a multicontact relay. Such a relay generally costs less than a special switch with complicated contact arrangement. (See the discussion of "cloning" in Section 5.2.)

As mentioned before, excessive currents are one of the main reasons for contact failure; see Ref. (2.7). The critical moment occurs during switching, when contact is broken. The problem is most serious with inductive loads (especially with direct current), where very high voltages are generated when contact is broken. The resulting arcing can quickly ruin switch contacts. A variety of arc-suppression circuits are available to protect the contacts. These use combinations of resistors, capacitors, and diodes connected as shown in Fig. 2.4. It also helps to use limit switches with snap action, which produces fast opening and closing of the contacts, thus tending to reduce arcing.

For more information on limit-switch selection, see the previous references and, of course, manufacturers' catalogs.

One manufacturer, see Ref. (2.11), makes so-called tape switches. These come in the form of long ribbons, which, when pressed at any point, close the contact. They are also available built into mats, which can be placed under carpets. These devices can be used as alarms, for automatically opening doors when stepped on, and in safety applications (e.g., giving the possibility of sending an emergency stop signal from any location to which the tape is led). While these tape switches are not strictly limit switches, they are mentioned here since they respond to physical contact.

2.2.2 Mercury Switches

Mercury switches are small hermetically sealed glass tubes containing two contact terminals and sufficient mercury to bridge these. The switch is opened or closed by tilting the tube, causing the mercury to run into or out of the terminal region. Mercury switches have several advantages:

1. The actuation force is low, since the switch is actuated by tilting.
2. Since the terminals are wetted by a fairly large amount of mercury, contact resistance is very small.
3. Current interruption does not harm the mercury. Thus, there are no contacts to burn out. The only limitation is overheating produced by arcing. With light loads, mercury switches provide extremely long life.

However, there are also several drawbacks:

1. Mounting is critical, since unwanted tilt can cause false actuation.
2. Vibration can cause false actuation.
3. They are not suitable for high cycling rates because of mercury inertia.

Preventing contact erosion

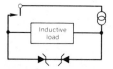

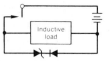

Diode zener: Adding a zener in series with the diode speeds up de-energization of the inductive load.

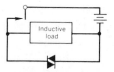

Varistor: The resistance of this device is very high at applied voltage but decreases to a small value at high transient peaks. If the varistor carries 10% load current, it will limit the transient to about twice the source voltage. This technique is also used in ac circuits.

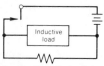

Resistor: Peak transient voltage developed upon opening the contact depends on the size of the resistor across the inductive load. However, the resistor wastes power while the load is energized.

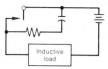

Resistor-capacitor: Initial values of resistance and capacitance for an R-C network may be calculated from: $R = E/10\,I(^{50/I})$, and $C = I^2/10$, where R = resistance, ohms; E = voltage before closing; C = capacitance, μF; and I = current before closing, mA. Peak rather than rms values of voltage and current must be used to calculate arc suppression of ac loads.

To ensure adequate suppression on ac or dc, the R-C network should be tested. If necessary, resistance and capacitance values can be adjusted to eliminate arcing at the contacts.

Zener-zener: Back-to-back zener diodes work similar to the resistor-only method.

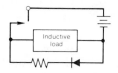

Diode-resistor: Works similar to the diode-zener combination.

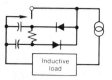

Diode: A diode connected across the load blocks the applied voltage at contact closure, but provides a path for the energy stored in the load when the contacts open.

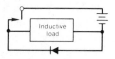

Resistor-capacitor-diode (ac): In ac circuits, this network can be connected either across the load or the contacts. For 115 Vac, PIV of the diodes should be 400 V, working voltage rating of the capacitors should be 200 Vac. and the resistor should be 100 kΩ , 1W.

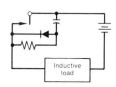

Resistor-capacitor-diode (dc): The capacitor charges through the diode but can discharge only through the resistor. Thus, the voltage drop across the contacts is zero as they open. This circuit is used for extremely inductive loads. The capacitor value is chosen so that the peak voltage to which it charges does not cause a breakdown of the diode, the contact gap, or the capacitor.

Fig. 2.4. Arc-suppression circuits. (Reprinted from *Machine Design*, May, 13, 1982. Copyright 1982, by Penton Publishing, Inc., Cleveland, Ohio.)

2.2.3 Reed Switches

A reed switch consists of two leaf springs (the reeds) sealed in a small glass tube, with their two free ends overlapping and almost touching, as shown in Fig. 2.5. When a magnet approaches the tube, the reeds assume opposite magnetic polarity, attracting each other sufficiently to make contact. Thus, unlike limit switches, reed switches are actuated without physical contact with the actuating element.

Since reed switches are filled with inert gas during sealing, their contacts are resistant to corrosion and contamination. The overlapping reed ends are usually plated to reduce contact resistance. Thus, reed switches are reliable long-life devices, with service life above 100 million operations, provided their current capacity is not exceeded.

Reed switches come in different sizes, from about 50 mm long, down to miniature switches typically 20 mm long and 2 mm in diameter. Current capacity might vary from 0.1 to 5 A, depending on switch size.

Figure 2.5 illustrates several ways of actuating reed switches. In Fig. 2.5(a), the magnet is oriented parallel to the reed switch, but moves perpendicular to it. As the magnet reaches a certain distance, the contacts close. As the magnet passes over the reed switch, the contacts remain closed up to a certain point and then open again. The approximate range of contact closure is indicated by the heavy line to the left of the figure. By mounting several reed switches parallel to each other, the magnet actuates each in turn as it passes over them. Thus, by attaching a magnet to a piston rod, a number of piston positions can be detected. Such a system could thus replace a number of limit switches mounted along the piston-rod path.

Figure 2.5(b) shows a parallel magnet moving parallel to the reed switch. This method provides three contact closures for maximum magnet travel or a single closure if travel is limited. In between, the contacts open, because both reed ends assume the same magnetic polarity, thus repelling each other.

In Fig. 2.5(c), the magnet is oriented and moves perpendicular to the reed switch. This provides two different contact closures, with contacts open when the magnet center is near the switch. Note that the magnet path must be offset from the switch center, otherwise both reed ends would be attracted to the magnet, so that the contacts would never close.

In Fig. 2.5(d), magnet orientation is perpendicular, but the magnet motion is parallel to the reed switch. Here, too, there are two contact closures. The contacts open when the magnet is centered with respect to the reed switch, for the same reason mentioned in connection with Fig. 2.5(c).

To obtain a normally closed contact, the scheme of Fig. 2.5(e) is used. A bias magnet permanently attached to the reed switch tends to keep the contacts closed. If a second magnet with opposite polarity is brought into proximity, the two magnets neutralize each other, causing the contacts to open.

In Fig. 2.5(f), a bias magnet is also used to keep the contacts normally closed. When a magnetic shield is inserted between the magnet and reed switch, the magnetic flux is shunted, causing the contacts to open.

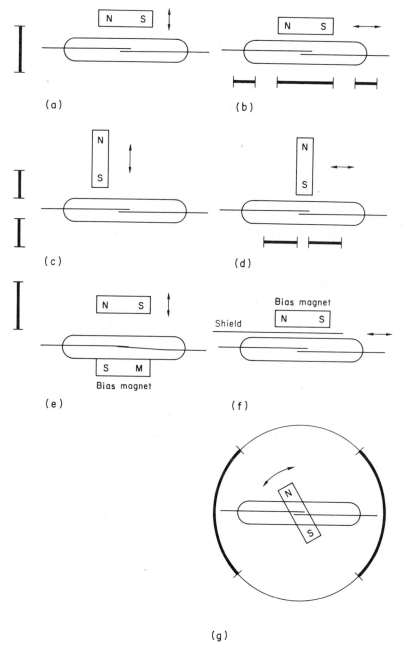

Fig. 2.5. Methods for actuating reed switches: (a) parallel magnet, perpendicular motion, (b) parallel magnet, parallel motion, (c) perpendicular magnet, perpendicular motion, (d) perpendicular magnet, parallel motion, (e) normally closed contact with bias magnet, (f) magnetic shield operation, and (g) rotary magnet motion.

Fig. 2.6. Cylinder with built-in reed switches. (© Bimba Manufacturing Company.)

Finally, Fig. 2.5(g) shows a magnet rotating with respect to the switch, producing two contact closures for each rotation.

A number of manufacturers supply pneumatic cylinders with built-in reed switches to indicate piston position, as shown in Fig. 2.6. Usually, one or more reed switches can be moved along a track on the cylinder to select the exact piston position at which the contacts close. The magnet is inside the cylinder attached to the piston (which means that the cylinder wall must be made of non-magnetic material). This method eliminates the need for mounting limit switches along the piston-rod path; see Refs. (1.80) and (2.12). For a method of improving reed-switch resolution and piston-positioning accuracy, see Ref. (2.13).

To protect reed contacts from arcing, any of the protection methods of Fig. 2.4 can be used. Reed switches can also be damaged by careless cutting, bending, or soldering of the reed leads, which can break the seal between the lead and glass tube. Precautions to be taken are described in Ref. (2.14).

For an in-depth discussion of reed switches, see Ref. (2.15). Although this reference is somewhat dated, it contains useful and relevant information.

2.2.4 Photoelectric Sensors

Photoelectric sensors consist basically of a source emitting a light beam and a light-sensing detector receiving the beam. The object to be sensed interrupts or reflects the beam, thereby making its presence known without physical contact between sensor and object.

The light-sensing detectors in photoelectric sensors are based either on photoconduction or photogeneration. One form of photoconductive detector consists of light-sensitive material whose resistance drops sharply when exposed to light. Another form is nonhomogeneous, and contains either a single junction (p-n photodiode) or two junctions (n-p-n phototransistor). Photogenerative (photovoltaic) detectors, on the other hand, generate a small voltage when exposed to light, typically 0.45 V per cell (but several cells can be connected in series). Since the voltages and currents produced by all detectors are small, they must be amplified electronically. For an in-depth discussion of photodetectors and typical application circuits, see Refs. (2.16)–(2.18). See also Chapters 12 and 13 of Ref. (2.2). For new developments in miniature photoelectric sensors, see Refs. (2.19) and (2.20).

Photoelectric sensors operate according to one of the following three modes of operation, see Fig. 2.7: (a) through beam, (b) reflection from target, and (c) retroreflection.

(a) In the through-beam mode of operation, the emitter and detector are mounted in separate housings which must be aligned carefully so as to face each other exactly. As the target to be detected approaches, it breaks the beam. This mode of operation has several advantages: the operating range can be as long as 100 m, provided the beam is concentrated, the air fairly clean, and the emitter and detector accurately aligned. Also, position sensing is more precise than with the other modes.

There are small very inexpensive ($1 to $2 each) "opto slotted coupler/interrupter modules" available; see Ref. (2.21). These contain both emitter (infrared LED) and detector (phototransistor) prealigned within a sealed unit. However, the opening between the two is only 3 mm, so that only very thin targets (e.g., sheets, webs, encoder discs, etc.) can be sensed.

An interesting variation of the through-beam principle is used in some smoke detectors (such as in domestic fire alarms). Here, a baffle installed between emitter and detector normally blocks the light beam. However, when smoke is present, the smoke particles refract and scatter sufficient light around the baffle to activate the detector; see Ref. (2.17).

(b) In the reflection mode, the emitter and detector are built into a single housing, which reduces wiring and mounting costs. The target, when it reaches the proper location, reflects the beam back into the detector. The electronic circuit connected to the detector must be adjusted for sensitivity, depending on

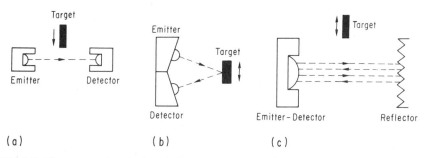

Fig. 2.7. Three operating modes of photoelectric sensors: (a) through-beam, (b) reflection from target, and (c) retroreflection.

reflectivity and distance of the target. Since only part of the emitted light returns to the detector, this mode is only suitable for fairly small distances, and the air must be reasonably clean of contaminants The method can also be used to detect liquid level, or to detect the difference in reflectivity between different objects.

(c.) In the retroflection mode, a special reflector (typically a formed plastic surface with small embedded spheres or pyramids) reflects the light beam back into the detector, regardless of the angle of incidence, unless it is interrupted by the target. Here, too, emitter and detector are mounted in the same housing. This method permits sensing at greater distances, up to 10 m in the absence of atmospheric contaminants. However, if the target itself is highly reflective (e.g., a metal can), a polarizing filter may be needed, so that the detector will respond only to reflection from the retroreflector. Also, the retroreflector size must be matched to the target size. For instance, a small target, such as the tip of a drill bit, cannot be detected if a large retroreflector is used.

No matter which of the operating modes is used, it is vital to keep the "windows" of the emitter and detector clean. Dust or oil mist can cover the windows so as to put the sensor quickly out of action.

Three developments have dramatically improved the performance of photo-electric sensors. These are the use of light-emitting diodes (LEDs), producing infrared rather than visible light; the use of pulsed light; and the invention of fiber optics. The use of infrared has a double advantage: LEDs produce infrared more efficiently than visible light, and silicon light detectors are more sensitive to infrared light. Also infrared-light beams are better able to penetrate air contaminants, and there is less of a problem with ambient light reaching the detector.

Using pulsed light, rather than a constant light beam, has two advantages, both of which considerably increase the maximum target range: First, short-duration high-intensity pulses can be used, which can penetrate longer distances. A constant light beam of the same intensity would cause overheating of the emitter. Second, by pulsing the LED at a given frequency, it becomes possible to distinguish between a light beam and ambient light. This is done by passing the detector signal through an electric filter designed to pass only the LED frequency. For a typical electronic circuit producing this light pulsing and filtering, see Ref. (2.22). It should be noted that LEDs, unlike incandescent lamps used in the past, lend themselves ideally for pulsing.

One of the drawbacks of photoelectric sensors is their inability to tolerate high temperatures (above 50 to 100°C) and other harsh environmental conditions. However, the use of fiber optics in conjunction with photoelectric sensors bypasses these problems; see Ref. (2.23). By using fiber-optic cable to transmit the light beam from the LED to the target, and a second cable to transmit the beam back to the detector, the sensor can be completely removed from the area where high temperatures prevail. Since optical fibers are immune to electrical noise, no shielding is necessary and installation is easy.

Furthermore, optical fibers are available in extremely small sizes (small enough to permit insertion into hypodermic needles in medical applications), which facilitates installation where space is at a premium. Finally, using fiber optics bypasses the problem of explosion-proofing in applications with explosive atmospheres.

There are, of course, drawbacks: apart from the increased cost when using fiber optics, the target range is limited to a few inches, and care must be taken not to break the optical cable by bending it too sharply.

2.2.5 Ultrasonic Sensors

These are similar to photoelectric sensors, except that ultrasonic sound waves are used instead of light beams. Ultrasonic sensors, which are used in autofocusing cameras, are also available for industrial applications. They can be used in the reflective mode (with emitter and detector built into the same unit), or in the through-beam mode (with emitter and detector in separate units), as shown in Fig. 2.8. They are suitable for a range of several meters, and, unlike photoelectric sensors, can be used to sense transparent objects. Their drawbacks include relatively high cost and sensitivity limited to about 2 mm. Also, they tend to be influenced by high ambient-noise levels, and by strong air motion. For further details, see Ref. (2.3).

2.2.6 Inductive Proximity Sensors

Strictly speaking, the reed switches and photoelectric and ultrasonic sensors discussed so far are all proximity sensors. However, the term "proximity sensor" generally refers to devices based on inductive, capacitive, or magnetic effects, which, with appropriate electronics, can sense the presence of an object.

Fig. 2.8. AGASTAT ultrasonic proximity sensors. (Courtesy of Amerace Corp.)

These proximity sensors are usually packaged in one of two ways, as shown in Fig. 2.9. Some come in standard limit-switch enclosures, which facilitate interchangeability and maintenance. Others, named the threaded-barrel type, are more compact.

Most inductive proximity sensors operate by generating a high-frequency electromagnetic field that induces eddy currents in the metal target. The sensor inductance is part of an oscillator circuit. When the target (which must be a conducting material) nears the sensor, the oscillations are damped. The resulting change in oscillator current actuates a solid-state switch.

For more information on inductive sensors, see Refs. (2.24) and (2.25). The former provides a table listing manufacturers of different sensors and proximity switches. The latter provides useful graphs and information to help determine maximum sensing distance (typically ranging from 2 to 30 mm), which depends on the target size, thickness, material, and on temperature; it also provides practical advice on sensor selection and application. As explained there, sensors must not be mounted too closely together (since they interfere with each other), or with their sensing face too close to metallic objects other than the target. The article also discusses connecting proximity switches. The switch is either "load powered" (i.e., connected in series with the load, but without a separate power connection, so that the switch simply closes a circuit), or "line powered" (i.e., applying a voltage to the load), and the article shows electric circuits for both cases.

Fig. 2.9. Proximity sensors. (Courtesy of Baumer Electric.)

2.2.7 Capacitive Proximity Sensors

These contain a damped RC oscillator. When a target, which need *not* be of conducting material, is brought within operating range of the sensor, the resulting change in capacitance causes the circuit to actuate a solid-state switch. Typical maximum sensing distances can range from 5 to 40 mm, depending on sensor design and target material.

The main advantage of capacitive proximity sensors is that they are not limited to metallic targets. Thus, they can be used to detect the level of a liquid or solid material inside a vessel. They can even detect the presence of objects inside sealed containers. However their switching accuracy is affected by humidity and temperature.

2.2.8 Magnetic Proximity Sensors

Reed switches, discussed previously, could also be included here, since they utilize magnetism. However, this section deals only with magnetic sensors without moving contacts.

2.2.8.1 *Magnetic Inductance or Reluctance Sensors.* Sensors based on these effects usually comprise a permanent magnet surrounded by a wire coil. When an object made of ferrous material approaches the sensor, the magnetic flux through the coil is changed, which generates a small voltage at the coil terminals. This, properly amplified, actuates a solid-state switch. Note that the sensor itself requires no exterior power source (though the associated amplifier, of course, does). Since the sensor contains no electronics, it can tolerate relatively high temperatures.

Magnetic sensors of this type have two major drawbacks. First, they are only suitable for targets of magnetic material. Second, their output voltage depends on target speed, so that they are not suitable for detecting stationary targets. One typical application is that of determining shaft speed; see Ref. (2.26). By mounting a gear on the shaft, the sensor, mounted near the gear circumference, produces voltage pulses as each tooth approaches and recedes, with pulse frequency proportional to shaft speed. For further discussion see Ref. (2.5) and (2.27).

2.2.8.2 *Hall-Effect Sensors.* Though the Hall effect was discovered over a hundred years ago, it has only lately become the basis for a large group of simple inexpensive sensors. Figure 2.10 illustrates the Hall effect. A current source sends a current i through a flat conductor. If this conductor has a magnetic field H applied to it (with the magnetic flux perpendicular to the conductor), a voltage difference is produced across the conductor perpendicular to current flow, as indicated in the figure, with the output or "Hall voltage" proportional to the vector cross product $i \times H$. This Hall voltage is very small (in the order of millivolts), and must therefore be amplified to be utilized.

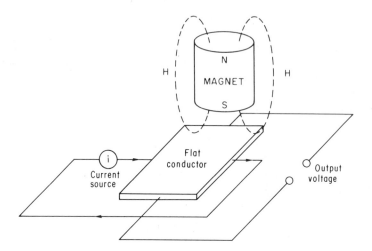

Fig. 2.10. Illustration of the Hall effect.

The Hall sensor is thus an analog device, since Hall voltage increases as the magnet approaches. However, by connecting the sensor to an electronic circuit (containing an amplifier, a hysteresis flip-flop, and a comparator), it becomes a binary sensor, whose output switches from low to high as the magnet reaches a certain distance from the sensor. Hysteresis is included to prevent output dither should the magnet stop near the switching point. All these electronic functions are carried out in an integrated circuit, which also includes the Hall sensor itself. The resulting chips are very compact and inexpensive (as little as $1).

Hall-effect sensors bear a strong resemblance to reed switches: In both, the switching is caused by a magnet. Indeed, most of the modes of actuating reed switches illustrated in Fig. 2.5 are also applicable to Hall-effect sensors. There is, of course, a basic difference: While reed switches are subject to contact bounce and arcing, Hall-effect sensors are solid-state devices with no moving parts, so that these problems are avoided. As with reed switches, at least one manufacturer supplies pneumatic cylinders with built-in Hall-effect sensors to indicate piston position; see Refs (1.80) and (2.12).

In order to exploit the just-stated advantage, one well-known manufacturer of mechanical limit switches offers a "Hall-effect limit switch." From the outside, this device looks exactly like a conventional limit switch, with roller and operating lever. However, this lever does not close mechanical contacts. Instead, the lever causes a tiny magnet to approach a Hall sensor built into the device together with associated electronics, and this does the actual switching.

The different actuation modes for Hall-effect sensors are illustrated in Refs. (2.28)–(2.30), which also describe various electronic circuits used to interface the sensor with other elements. The first two of these references also show a number of typical applications. Hall-effect sensors are also discussed in Refs. (2.5) and

(2.27). In the past, Hall-effect devices were subject to erratic performance due to aging and temperature effects (which change the magnet's properties), and also due to mechanical stress (which can produce false offset voltages). However, these problems are today minimized by proper design, as described in Ref. (2.31).

Other problems connected with Hall-effect sensors are the need to select a suitable magnet (which must be sized to actuate the switch at the required distance), and the fact that the resolution obtainable cannot match that of photoelectric or inductive proximity sensors. However, Hall-effect sensors offer small size (as small as 5 mm square for the complete IC chip) and low cost.

2.2.8.3 Wiegand-Effect Sensors.
Wiegand-effect sensors are not as well known as the other types discussed. Like Hall-effect sensors, they also operate in the presence of a magnetic field. But, unlike them, they produce voltage pulses without requiring external electric power.

A Wiegand-effect sensor consists of "Wiegand wires" and a sensing coil. The wires are short strands of specially fabricated ferromagnetic material (which can even be imbedded in plastic credit cards or similar objects). The sensing coil is either wound around the Wiegand wire (producing a "Wiegand module"), or placed near it. In addition, there must be one or two outside magnets. By moving the Wiegand wires with respect to the magnetic field, or alternatively, by having one or more permanent magnets move with respect to the Wiegand module, short voltage pulses, up to several volts, are produced.

Wiegand-effect sensors are now available in compact self-contained units, as pictured in Fig. 2.11. For more details, the reader is referred to Refs. (2.27) and (2.32).

Fig. 2.11. Wiegand-effect proximity sensors. (Courtesy of Sensor Engineering Co.)

2.3 PNEUMATIC POSITION SENSORS

The reader may wonder why we are concerned with pneumatic position sensors, considering the wide variety of available electric sensors. The reasons are threefold:

1. As is discussed in Chapter 4, we often prefer to construct a control circuit using pneumatic valves or other pneumatic logic elements, especially where the motion actuators used are pneumatic cylinders or motors, requiring a compressed-air supply anyway. Under these conditions, it is also advantageous to use pneumatic sensors, since electric sensors require additional voltage-to-pressure transducers (e.g., solenoid valves) to translate the electric to pneumatic signals. (Similarly, it would not make sense to use pneumatic sensors in conjunction with electric or electronic switching elements.) In general, it pays to stay with the same power medium all the way through, so as to avoid the need for additional interface equipment.

2. Some pneumatic sensors have desirable properties, such as small size, simplicity, low cost, and robustness, which are difficult to match with electric sensors.

3. In applications dealing with explosive or inflammable materials, pneumatic sensors provide absolute safety. Electric sensors, by comparison, require expensive explosion-proof casings, unless they are certified to be "intrinsically safe".

2.3.1 Pneumatic Limit Valves

Pneumatic limit valves are the pneumatic equivalent of mechanical limit switches. The various actuating methods that can be used are similar to the ones described in connection with limit switches (see Fig. 2.1), and the same precautions against mechanical abuse listed in Section 2.2.1 apply here also.

The difference between limit switches and valves is that, in the latter, the actuating arm or plunger shifts a so-called directional-control valve, rather than electric contacts, as illustrated in Fig. 2.12. Since directional-control valves and their symbols are discussed in detail in Chapter 4, we confine ourselves here to a brief explanation. Figure 2.12(a) shows a so-called 3/2 valve (meaning 3 connections/2 positions). The valve pictured is normally closed, so that the outlet line is exhausted to atmosphere when the valve is not actuated. When the valve is actuated, the roller is depressed against the return spring at the bottom, so that the valve opens and passes supply pressure to the outlet line.

Figure 2.12(b) shows a 5/2 valve (5 connections/2 positions), which has two independent outlet lines, one normally open and the second normally closed. Such a valve is analogous to a limit switch with changeover (SPDT) contacts.

Limit valves are undoubtedly the most common of all pneumatic position sensors. They are robust, reliable, and can provide high output pressures (equal

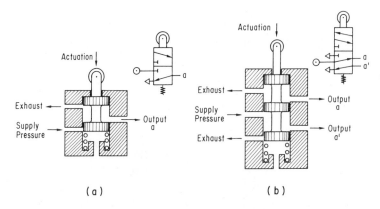

Fig. 2.12. Pneumatic limit valves and their fluid-power symbols: (a) a 3/2 valve, and (b) a 5/2 valve.

to the supply pressure used). Their only drawbacks are their relatively large size and their requirement for relatively high actuating forces. A typical small 3/2 limit valve is pictured in Fig. 2.13.

2.3.2 Back-Pressure Sensors

In its simplest form, the back-pressure sensor consists of a hole or small nozzle exhausting air to the atmosphere. When the hole is blocked, the pressure backs up, and this increased back pressure signals the presence of an object.

The action of a back-pressure sensor is illustrated in Fig. 2.14. Note that a restriction must be placed between the supply-pressure inlet and the nozzle. This restriction could be a short length of capillary tubing or a small hole drilled into a plug inserted in the tube. Its purpose is to produce sufficient pressure drop, so as to get a low output pressure P_O when the nozzle is open. If the sensed object blocks the nozzle outlet, the restriction has no effect, and output pressure P_O almost equals supply pressure P_S (assuming negligible leakage through the blocked nozzle, and also that the load fed by output pressure P_O does not draw air at steady state). On the other hand, when the nozzle is open, the restriction acts like an electrical voltage divider, and produces an output pressure P_O given by

$$\frac{P_O}{P_S} = \frac{\text{flow resistance of nozzle}}{\text{flow resistance of restriction + nozzle}}$$

Thus, to obtain a sufficiently low P_O with an open nozzle, the flow resistance of the restriction should be at least 10 times that of the nozzle. Typical diameter values are 0.5 mm for the restriction and 1 mm for the nozzle. Since laminar flow

Fig. 2.13. A 3/2 limit valve. (Courtesy of Telemecanique.)

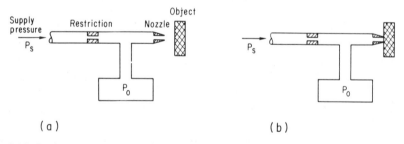

Fig. 2.14. Back-pressure sensor with (a) output pressure P_O low and (b) output pressure P_O high.

resistance is inversely proportional to the fourth power of the hole diameter, this produces a ratio of $P_O/P_S = 1/17$. If hole diameters are too large, air consumption is excessive and the emerging air stream is noisy. On the other hand, holes with too small diameters produce slow dynamic response, and become easily clogged. To prevent clogging, good air filters must be used, preferably of the coalescing type, which remove all oil from the compressed air.

It should be noted that a microscopic gap between nozzle and object (in the order of 0.02 mm) is already sufficient to make P_O go low. Therefore, the object

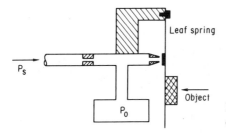

Fig. 2.15. Back-pressure sensor with overtravel protection.

can be sensed only if it practically touches the nozzle. On the other hand, the nozzle should not be expected to act as mechanical stop for the object (which typically might be the piston rod of a pneumatic cylinder). To prevent damage to the nozzle, provision for overtravel must be provided, as illustrated in Fig. 2.15. The nozzle is not blocked by the object to be sensed, but rather by a pad attached to a flexible leaf spring, which can tolerate sufficient elastic deflection to absorb the overtravel.

In applications where the presence of a nonmoving object must be detected, the nozzle could consist of a hole drilled into the base on which the object sits. See, for example, Problem 6.8 of Chapter 6, which deals with a die-protection system. As seen from the figure associated with that problem, the sensor is a hole drilled into the bottom die. No other type of sensor can compete with this as to simplicity and ruggedness.

It is interesting to note that air hoses placed on the ground at gas stations, and that ring a bell whenever a car drives over them, make use of the back-pressure principle. Another common application of the back-pressure sensor is that of the "bubble tube" to detect liquid level in vessels (or even level of solids), as shown in Fig. 2.16. Here, the sensor is simply a tube inserted into the vessel. As the level rises, the tube opening is covered, causing an increase in back pressure P_O. If an electric output is desired, P_O could be connected to a pressure switch (see Section 2.5.2).

For an in-depth discussion of back-pressure sensors and their applications, see Ref. (2.33).

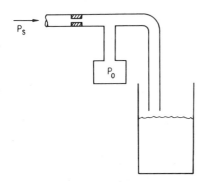

Fig. 2.16. Detecting liquid level with a bubble tube.

2.3.3   Coiled-Spring Sensors

Coiled-spring sensors consist of a piece of tubing with an air supply, at whose end a tightly wound helical spring is cemented. The other end of the spring is terminated by a plastic rod, as shown in Fig. 2.17. As long as no object touches the rod, the spring coils touch each other with negligible air leakage, and the output pressure P_O is high. If an object displaces the rod (by as little as 6 degrees), the spring is bent, producing gaps between the adjacent coils through which air flows. Because of the supply-line restriction, output pressure P_O becomes low.

Coiled-spring sensors are simple, inexpensive, and offer several other advantages. The rod need only be deflected by a few degrees to produce low output, and yet the device can tolerate considerable overtravel without damage to the spring. Furthermore, only small actuating forces are required, and these can be applied from any direction perpendicular to the rod. While coiled-spring sensors are commercially available, see Ref. (2.34), they can easily be built by the user choosing spring and rod dimensions appropriate for the application. For long life, the spring should be chosed so that the elastic limit of its material is not exceeded.

2.3.4   Annular Back-Pressure Sensors

The annular back-pressure sensor (also called the cone-jet or annular-jet sensor) is the pneumatic equivalent of an electric proximity sensor, that is, no mechanical contact between the sensor and object is required. Furthermore, the

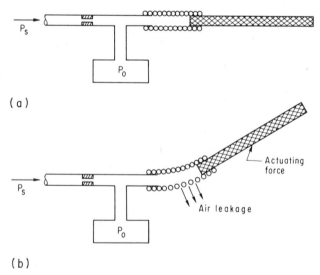

Fig. 2.17. Coiled-spring sensor with (a) output pressure P_O high, and (b) output pressure P_O low.

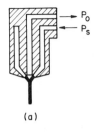

(a)

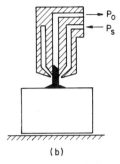

(b)

Fig. 2.18. Annular back-pressure sensor with (a) output pressure P_O low, and (b) output pressure P_O high.

object–sensor distance is not critical (unlike with conventional back-pressure sensors), and it can be as large as 20 mm.

As illustrated in Fig. 2.18, sensor supply pressure P_S is let into an annular space, so that a conical jet forms at the nozzle. This jet tends to suck air from the central output-signal bore of the device, so that output pressure P_O is partial vacuum. If an object nears the nozzle, the conical jet is prevented from forming so that P_O becomes high.

The drawbacks of this sensor are relatively high air consumption and relatively high cost as compared to conventional back-pressure sensors. Also, the output pressure P_O that can be obtained is very low, so that the signal must generally be amplified. This is done by means of special binary pneumatic amplifying relays or by using pneumatic valves with sensitive diaphragms in their pilot lines; see Chapter 4. For more information on annular back-pressure sensors, see Refs. (2.35) and (2.36).

2.3.5 Interruptable-Jet Sensors

The interruptable-jet sensor, in its simplest form, is shown in Fig. 2.19. It consists of a nozzle and receiver tube. The nozzle has air supply P_S, so that a jet emerges from it and enters the receiver, thus producing a small output pressure P_O (typically 20% of the supply pressure). If an object is placed between the nozzle and receiver, the jet is interrupted and P_O drops to zero. For a 0.5 mm nozzle diameter, the gap between nozzle and tube should be no greater than 20 or 30 mm; otherwise, output pressure is too low to be useful. This limits the width of the sensed objects. Increasing nozzle diameter permits use of a wider gap, but also increases air consumption considerably.

The main problem associated with this kind of sensor is its sensitivity to dust. The jet tends to pick up ambient dust and carry it into the receiver, clogging it after a short time. To overcome this problem, the sensor of Fig. 2.20 can be used. The receiver tube has its own nozzle fed by an air supply through a restriction. With no object in the gap, the jet coming from the left nozzle is stronger than the

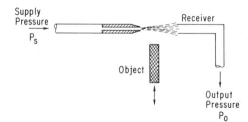

Fig. 2.19. Interruptable-jet sensor.

right jet (because of the restriction in the latter). As a result, the two jets collide near the right nozzle exit, and the resulting collision plane prevents most of the air from this nozzle from escaping, so that output pressure P_O is high. (In a way, this system represents a back-pressure sensor that senses the presence of a collision plane.) If an object is in the gap, there is no collision plane, so that air escapes freely from the nozzle and P_O is low. Since a clean supply of air is continuously purged from both nozzles, the danger of clogging is very small. A typical industrial application of such sensors is described in Ref. (2.37).

A third variation of interruptable-jet sensors is shown in Fig. 2.21. A third jet impinges on the other two, and thus prevents formation of the collision plane, so that the output pressure P_O is normally low. If an object blocks this third jet, the collision plane forms and P_O goes high. The advantage of this method is that objects as wide as 150 mm can be sensed, since the third nozzle can be placed relatively far away.

In a way, interruptable-jet sensors represent the pneumatic equivalent of photoelectric sensors operating in the through-beam mode. While simple and relatively inexpensive, they have the drawback that only relatively thin objects can be sensed, since air jets do not carry as far as light beams. As with annular back-pressure sensors, the output pressures obtainable are very low (typically a few inches of water), so that amplification is generally needed. For a comprehensive discussion of interruptable-jet sensors and various ways of applying them, see Refs. (2.33) and (2.36).

2.3.6 Threshold Sensors

A large percentage of position-sensing applications pertain to pneumatic cylinders, where a signal must be produced to indicate the end of the piston stroke. While limit valves are commonly used for this, sometimes there is

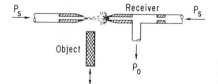

Fig. 2.20. Dirt-insensitive interruptable-jet sensor.

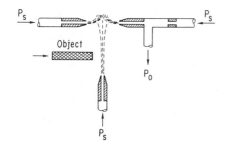

Fig. 2.21. Interruptable-jet sensor with remote actuation.

insufficient space for mounting them. The threshold sensor provides a solution to this problem. It consists of a pneumatic valve that is sensitive to the back pressure produced in the exhaust end of a cylinder (due to the flow resistance of the cylinder actuating valve or of a special needle valve inserted in the exhaust line for this purpose). When the piston comes to a halt, this back pressure drops to zero.

The threshold valve is designed to produce an output pressure when the exhaust back pressure reaches a low threshold, indicating the end of the piston stroke. Since the threshold valve can be connected by tubing to the cylinder exhaust, it can be mounted wherever convenient. An additional advantage is that the threshold valve produces a signal no matter where the piston stops, which makes it very useful for variable-stroke applications. However, this same feature can also be a drawback: The sensor produces an output signal even when the stroke has not been completed due to a malfunction (e.g., the machine jamming). However, this problem can be overcome by using an interlocking option; see Ref. (2.38).

It is interesting to note that two manufacturers supply theshold sensors built into the cylinder-connection fittings; see Refs (2.12) and (2.39). This eliminates extra tubing and makes for a neat compact assembly. The sensor has a sensitive diaphragm to respond to cylinder back pressure, and this opens a poppet valve when the back pressure has dropped to less than 10% of the supply pressure. Its response time is 3 msec.

2.4 COMPARISON BETWEEN DIFFERENT POSITION SENSORS

As discussed in the beginning of Section 2.3, pneumatic position sensors have their own defined field of application, so that they do not really compete with electric sensors. The real competition is between mechanically actuated limit switches and the various types of solid-state proximity sensors.

Many recent articles discuss the pros and cons of each method, see, e.g., Refs. (2.40)–(2.44). All experts agree that the use of solid-state proximity sensors is becoming more widespread. Most, however, also agree that mechanical limit switches will continue to be used widely because of their simplicity and low cost.

Table 2.1. Comparison between Different Position Sensors

Sensor	Possible Targets	Typical Maximum Sensing Distance	Typical Maximum Switching Rate (Hz)	Environmental Sensitivities	Advantages	Drawbacks
Limit switch	Any	0 (needs physical contact)	3	Temperature, moisture	Simple, inexpensive	Physical contact, contact arcing
Mercury switch	Any	0 (needs physical contact)		Vibration, mounting angle	Low contact resistance, sealed unit	Physical contact, only SPST contact
Reed switch	Magnet	20 mm	500	Vibration	Small size, inexpensive	Contact arcing, requires magnet actuator
Photoelectric	Opaque, semi-transparent	0.1 to 50 m (depending on target shape)	100–1000	Dust, dirt, ambient light	Good resolution	
Ultrasonic	Nonporous, large	From 30 mm to 10 m	50	Noise, air motion		Poor resolution, needs large target
Inductive	Conductive material	Ferrous: 50 mm Nonferrous: less	300–5000 Over 1000	Other nearby sensors	Good resolution; usually fails *on*	

Capacitive	Most solids, liquids	30 mm	500	Humidity, temperature		Complex circuitry, false triggering
Magnetic inductance	Ferromagnetic	50 mm (depending on target mass)	300	Other nearby sensors	Good resolution	Collects debris, no static sensing, complex circuitry
Hall effect	Magnet	20 mm	100,000	Temperature	Simple, inexpensive	Poor resolution, requires magnet actuator
Wiegand effect	Magnet		100,000			No static sensing, requires magnet actuator
Limit valve	Any	0 (needs physical contact)			High pressure output	Physical contact
Back-pressure	Any	0 (needs physical contact)	400	Dust	Very simple	Physical contact
Coiled-spring	Any	0 (needs physical contact)			Very simple	Physical contact
Annular back-pressure	Must have flat surface	20 mm	50–500			Low pressure output
Interruptable jet	Thin	20 to 150 mm	60			Low pressure output

They have become smaller and have been improved in other ways, so that, if properly applied, can provide a life expectancy of 10–50 million switching operations. Their cost is less than half that of the average proximity switch. Furthermore, limit switches are not temperature-sensitive as most proximity sensors, whose operating point is liable to shift with temperature. Another advantage of limit switches is that they can be mounted side-by-side, whereas most proximity sensors interfere with each other if mounted too closely.

By comparison, solid-state proximity switches do not suffer from contact bounce or from mechanical shock. Their life expectancy is basically unlimited, and their cycling rate can be as high as 1000 closures per second. Limit switches, however, should not exceed 2 or 3 closures per second, because of overheating. Thus, applications involving continuous high switching rates are best handled by solid-state proximity sensors.

The question of life expectancy can be vital in some applications and unimportant in others. Thus, a limit switch that is actuated once an hour reaches 10 million operations (assuming that to be its maximum life) only after 1141 years! Thus, it would be senseless to replace such a limit switch by an expensive solid-state sensor just for the sake of increased life expectancy. On the other hand, if the switch is actuated once a second, 10 million operations are reached after less than four months, and such low life expectancy is unacceptable in most cases.

The features of different sensors are compared in Table 2.1. (The data given there only indicate order of magnitude.) A listing of manufacturers of different types of limit and proximity switches can be found in Ref. (2.45)

To make an intelligent choice between the great number of available position sensors, the following factors and questions should be considered:

1. Output signal: High or low voltage? High or low current? High or low pressure?
2. Mechanical contact with the sensed object: Is it permissible?
3. Available space.
4. Environmental conditions.
5. Nature of target: size, shape, and material.
6. Sensor-to-target distance: both maximum and minimum.
7. Positional accuracy required for the application.
8. Speed of target.
9. Switching rate: both momentary and long-term.
10. Reliability and life expectancy: What is the cost of failure?

2.5 POINT SENSORS FOR VARIABLES OTHER THAN POSITION

As stated at the beginning of the chapter, we are concerned here solely with binary sensors. Thus, we do not discuss various types of measurement transducers that give voltages proportional to the variable measured, but confine ourselves to level, pressure, temperature, and flow switches, which switch whenever the variable reaches a certain point. Such switches are often called "point sensors".

Point sensors are frequently utilized as alarm devices that actuate visual or audible alarms or even shut down the process whenever a dangerous condition is detected. To fulfill this function, alarm switches should be special dedicated devices, completely separate from the normal analog measuring instruments used to send feedback signals to the continuous control system. Preferably, alarm switches should utilize a different technology than the normal measuring instrument, and they should be selected to be "failsafe" (i.e., fail in such a way as to automatically signal an alarm or a shutdown). In a way, alarm switches represent a last line of defense against malfunctions in a regular control system; see Ref. (2.46).

The symbols used for various types of point-sensor switches are shown in Fig. 2.22. All are shown with a nonactuated normally open contact. Naturally, these switches also come with other contact configurations, as illustrated in Fig. 2.2 in connection with limit switches.

For a listing of manufacturers of various types of level, pressure, temperature and flow switches, see Ref. (2.45).

2.5.1 Level Switches

Point-level sensors (i.e., level switches) are used to send a signal when the level in a tank or vessel reaches a certain height. The medium sensed can be a liquid, a slurry, or even a solid (in powder or granular form). Many of the methods of position detection discussed so far are directly applicable to level sensing, since we can regard the liquid or solid level as being just another object or target whose proximity is to be detected. We will, therefore, briefly review the list of position sensors discussed so far and see to what extent the same principles can be applied to level switches:

Limit Switches. By using a float (spherical or cylindrical) connected to a snap-action limit switch, we get a simple level switch of a type very popular in industry. Obviously, this switch is only applicable for liquids. The limit-switch housing has to be watertight and the wires somehow brought to the outside.

Mercury Switches. Their actuation is similar to limit switches. As the float rises, its lever arm tilts the sealed mercury switch, closing its contacts.

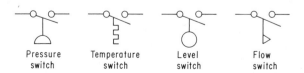

| Pressure switch | Temperature switch | Level switch | Flow switch |

Fig. 2.22. Symbols for various sensor switches (normally open contacts).

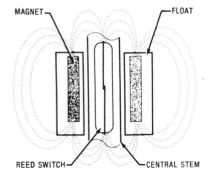

MAGNET FLOAT

REED SWITCH CENTRAL STEM

Fig. 2.23. Reed switch used as a level sensor. (Courtesy of Gems Sensors.)

Reed Switches. This is an ideal application for reed switches. As shown in Fig. 2.23, the float contains an annular magnet surrounding the reed switch. As the float reaches a certain level, the contacts close, Since the reed switch is hermetically sealed, it is automatically waterproof. Alternatively, the float, containing a magnet, moves along the inner wall of the vessel, with the reed switch mounted outside. This eliminates electrical connections inside the vessel, but the vessel must be of nonmagnetic material.

Photoelectric Sensors. These can be used in several ways to detect level. For example, as illustrated in Fig. 2.24, a glass prism can be mounted at a desired height within a vessel. Ordinarily, the light beam sent by an LED is reflected so as to hit a photodiode mounted facing the other side of the prism. However, when the prism is submerged in liquid, the light beam is deflected by refraction, so that the output beam does not reach the photodiode. By utilizing optical fibers to transmit the light, the LED and photodiode can be kept outside the tank. In a more compact version of the same idea, the LED and photodiode are enclosed in a single sealed probe having a prism-shaped tip, which is inserted in the vessel.

Capacitive Proximity Sensors. These are especially suitable for solid materials, where floats cannot be used. As the material rises, it displaces air between the capacitance probe and the vessel wall, which changes the dielectric between the probe and ground and thus the capacitance. Since

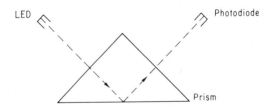

LED   Photodiode

Prism

Fig. 2.24. Liquid-level detection by light-beam refraction.

capacitive sensors are expensive, they are used mainly as analog rather than point sensors.

Hall-Effect Sensors. These can be utilized in the same manner as previously described for reed switches. The Hall sensor replaces the reed switch and is mounted either inside or outside the vessel.

Pneumatic Back-Pressure Sensors. These are especially useful for slurries or powders and use the bubble–tube principle described in Section 2.3.2 (see Fig. 2.16).

Apart from these methods, there are other ways to construct point-level sensors *not* based on regular position-sensing methods. A very simple method is to install two wire electrodes in the tank. As the level rises, the electrodes are shorted. Naturally, this method is only applicable for conducting liquids. Another simple method is to install a pressure switch at the vessel bottom. When the level reaches a certain height, the pressure produced by the liquid head actuates the pressure switch.

References (2.47) and (2.48) list various other methods of sensing level. While most of these refer to analog level sensors, it is obvious that any such sensor, if desired, can be converted into a point sensor by means of electronic circuits containing a hysteresis flip-flop (to prevent excessive dither), a comparator, and a solid-state switch. Reference (2.49) has a table listing over 150 manufacturers of level-sensing equipment.

In conclusion, it should also be mentioned that many level switches actually contain two operating points with separate contacts. This is useful for high–low operation, where one contact might actuate an alarm, whereas the second initiates some emergency control action.

2.5.2 Pressure Switches

Pressure switches generally consist of the following three elements: (a) a pressure-sensing element, such as a diaphragm, metal bellows, piston, etc.; (b) a calibrating spring opposing the deflection of the pressure-sensing element, thus translating pressure into motion; and (c) electrical contacts that are actuated when spring deflection reaches a certain point (frequently, standard limit switches are used for this purpose, with the plunger actuated by the spring motion).

Pressure switches come in a tremendous variety of designs. In selecting a pressure switch, each of the following points should be considered:

1. *Type of Pressure To Be Sensed.* Four types of pressures can be sensed. (a) Gage pressure (i.e., pressure above atmospheric pressure). Most pressure switches are of this type. (b) Vacuum (i.e., pressure below atmospheric pressure). (c) Absolute pressure. (d) Differential pressure (difference between two pressures). A typical application for a differential pressure switch is sensing the pressure drop across an oil filter to detect clogging.

Fig. 2.25. Several pressure switches with a fixed set point. (Courtesy of Hobbs Div., Stewart-Warner Corp.)

2. *Adjustments Required.* The simplest pressure switches are factory-set to switch at a fixed pressure; see Fig. 2.25. Because of their low cost, these are popular for OEM (original-equipment manufacturer) applications (e.g., to actuate oil-pressure warning lights in automobiles). They also have the advantage of being tamper-proof.

The majority of industrial pressure switches have adjustable set points, as shown in Fig. 2.26, which are field-adjusted. Some of these (especially if a Bourdon tube is used as the pressure-sensing element) have an accurate pressure scale, which greatly facilitates adjusting the set point. Others have only a rough scale, and others, no scale at all (i.e.,"blind adjustment"). To adjust these, an external pressure gage must be temporarily connected. The set-point adjusting screw can be placed outside the switch case (convenient if frequent readjustment is required), or inside the case (which helps to prevent tampering).

Pressure switches come with or without a dead band. In switches without a dead band, contact movement is linear with the movement of the sensing element, giving a single switching point, as shown in Fig. 2.27(a). Such switches can be very accurate, but are sensitive to pressure fluctuations about the set point, producing constant contact opening and closing (with arcing). They are also more sensitive to vibration. To avoid this, a dead band is built in, so that contacts open and close at different pressure levels, as shown in Fig. 2.27(b). This is usually achieved using a toggle mechanism or Belleville (disk) springs. The pressure range between the deactuation and actuation points represents the dead band, or pressure differential, within which no switching occurs. As with the set point, some pressure switches have a fixed built-in dead band, whereas in others, the dead band is field-adjustable, depending on the sensitivity desired.

3. *Usable Pressure Range.* This is defined as the minimum and maximum pressures at which the switching point can be set. It is generally recommended to select the pressure range so that the set point is near the middle of the range,

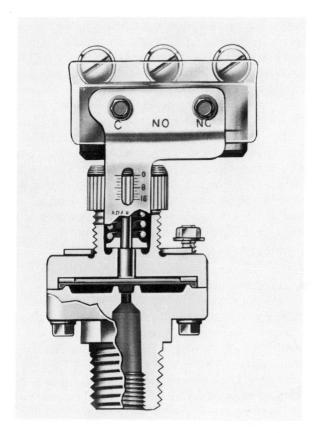

Fig. 2.26. Pressure switch with an adjustable set point. (Courtesy of IMO Delaval Inc., Barksdale Controls Division, Los Angeles, California 90058.)

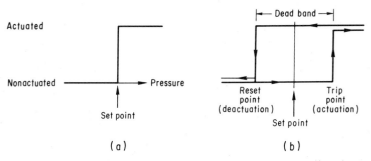

Fig. 2.27. Pressure-switch characteristics (a) without and (b) with a dead band.

since this represents a good compromise between accuracy and life expectancy. To illustrate: pressure switches typically have an accuracy of about 1% of full range. If we need a set point of, say, 50 psi, but select a pressure switch with a 0–1000 psi range, the accuracy is ±10 psi, which is very poor compared to the set point. By selecting a switch with a 0–100 psi range, the accuracy is improved by a factor of 10 to ±1 psi. On the other hand, if the set point is near the upper end of the range, the accuracy is even better, but the life expectancy is reduced, because the pressure-sensing element suffers larger deflections.

The top of the pressure range should not be confused with the so-called proof pressure or with burst pressure. The rated proof pressure is the maximum pressure the sensing element can tolerate without suffering permanent deformation, and it should be high enough to prevent damage due to pressure surges. The burst pressure is the pressure producing catastrophic switch failure, and it is usually several times the rated proof pressure.

4. *Types of Pressure-Sensing Elements.*

(a) DIAPHRAGMS. These provide high-force outputs and therefore good accuracy. They are usually used for low pressures, up to about 500 psi. Special designs are available for ultralow pressures (as low as 0.02 psi). Such ultralow pressure switches can be used in conjunction with interruptable-jet sensors or other types of pneumatic sensors (see Sections 2.3.2, 2.3.4, and 2.3.5) to sense objects pneumatically but to obtain electric output signals. Several such applications are described in Ref. (2.50).

(b) METAL BELLOWS. These also provide high-force outputs, but have larger deflections than diaphragms. They can be used for intermediate pressures, up to about 2500 psi. However, they are more failure-prone than other elements, due to fatigue effects at their bends or seams.

(c) BELLEVILLE (DISK) SPRINGS. A limp diaphragm seals the pressure source and transfers force to the Belleville spring, which is a saucer-shaped disk. As the force applied on the convex surface increases, the disk snaps into a concave shape, thus actuating the switch contacts. Because of this snap action, the switch automatically contains a fairly large dead band. This sensor can be used for very low pressure ranges, but is also available for pressures up to 6000 psi.

(d) BOURDON TUBES. These are tubes bent through a 270-degree angle, with an oval cross section. As pressure inside the tube increaes, the tube tends to straighten, so that the motion of the tube tip is proportional to the pressure change. Since the tube itself acts as spring, no additional spring is required. Bourdon-tube switches can be used for pressures up to about 25,000 psi, but are sensitive to vibration, and the set point tends to drift with temperature. Bourdon tubes are often used in pressure switches where pressure indication is also required. However, because of their low-force output, they are not very suitable where heavy switch contacts must be actuated.

(e) PISTONS. Piston sensors can withstand very high pressures (over 25,000 psi) and high overpressures without suffering damage. However, they require seals, whose friction restricts the obtainable accuracy and repeatability. Teflon seals are better than O rings in this respect.

5. *Enclosures.* Many types of pressure-switch enclosures are available, and choice depends on the answers to such questions as: Is the switch intended to be mounted in a cabinet or outdoors? Is a dustproof enclosure needed? Is explosion-proofing required? Must the enclosure be hermetically sealed to protect against atmospheric corrosion or moisture buildup? Is the switch subject to shock or vibration? What type of electric conduit is used? Will the sensed medium cause corrosion to the sensing element? (If so, a chemical seal may be required.)

6. *Types of Contacts.* As with level switches, some pressure switches have double contacts actuated at different set points, with one contact serving as the alarm and the other initiating corrective action.

Apart from conventional mechanical contacts, other contact types can be used. Sometimes mercury switches are used for reliability and long life, but these are only suitable if little vibration is present, and they only provide the equivalent of a SPST contact. The use of solid-state switches as part of the pressure switch is becoming more prevalent. In most of these, the pressure-sensing element moves a tiny magnet sufficiently to actuate a Hall-effect switch; see Ref. (2.51). In another design, pressure-sensing is performed by semiconductor strain gages and switching by solid-state triacs, which are capable of switching up to 3 A continuous load. However, even solid-state pressure switches cannot provide an unlimited service life, because of eventual fatigue failure of the pressure-sensing element.

For further information on pressure switches, see pages 106–112 of Ref. (2.4), Ref. (2.6), Parts 3 and 4 of Ref. (2.10), and Refs. (2.51)–(2.54).

2.5.3 Temperature Switches

Simple temperature switches come with a fixed set point. Temperature switches with an adjustable set point are often called thermostats. Thermostats are not meant for alarm functions, but are directly connected to the controlled process so as to regulate the temperature. Thus, thermostats provide a simple form of on–off control.

Temperature switches have many features in common with pressure switches. In both, a sensing element deflects and thus actuates the switch, which can have mechanical contacts or be a solid-state switch. Thus, most of the points mentioned in the previous section also apply to temperature switches. The main difference lies in the sensing elements used, the most common of which are:

(a) *Bimetal Strips.* These consist of two different metals cemented together, and formed into a U-shaped strip, see Fig. 2.28. One metal is typically brass, with a high coefficient of thermal expansion, whereas the other is a special alloy with a very low coefficient. From the figure, as temperature increases, the brass expands more than the alloy, so that the strip, in attempting to straighten, bends to the right until, at a certain temperature, the contacts open. With decreasing temperature, the brass contracts and the contacts close. In a way, bimetal strips can be considered the thermal equivalent of Bourdon tubes, and, indeed, they

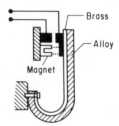

Fig. 2.28. Bimetal temperature switch.

have similar characteristics. Although bimetal strips are simple and inexpensive, their accuracy is limited by the low force produced. Also, they are sensitive to shock and vibration.

To obtain a dead band, a small magnet is mounted so as to attract a piece of iron attached to the moving contact, as shown in the figure. As the contacts near each other, the magnetic attraction increases until, at a certain point, the moving contact snaps into the closed position. Since this increases the magnetic force even more, the temperature must now increase considerably above the closure point for the contacts to open, thus creating a dead band. By screwing the magnet in or out, the dead band can be adjusted.

(b) *Bimetal Disks.* A bimetal sheet is formed into a convex disk, producing a Belleville, or disk, spring. Similarly to Belleville pressure sensors, the disk snaps into its concave shape at a certain temperature. Bimetal disk sensors usually are simple and inexpensive devices with fixed set points and fairly large dead bands.

(c) *Liquid- or Gas-filled Sensors.* These consist of a sensing bulb filled with liquid (typically mercury or xylene), or an inert gas, and connected to a pressure-sensing element, such as a bellows, diaphragm, or Bourdon tube. As temperature rises, the liquid or gas expands, which increases pressure on the pressure-sensing element, and, in turn, actuates the contacts. Sometimes, volatile liquids are used, whose vapor pressure increases with temperature. Since these sensors are based on pressure effects, they are called "pressure thermometers." A typical liquid-filled temperature switch is shown in Fig. 2.29.

As seen from the figure, the liquid-filled bulb is sometimes connected to the sensing element by a long run of capillary tubing (up to 50 m is quite common), so that the bulb and switch can be mounted in different locations. Such remote mounting protects the sensing element and contacts from high temperature or other detrimental effects. However, it increases cost, and also slows down the speed of response.

(d) *Mercury-in-Glass Thermometer.* This consists of a mercury-filled bulb connected to a glass capillary tube. Two platinum wires sealed into the glass wall act as normally open contacts. With rising temperature, the mercury expands, enters the glass tube, and shorts the wires. The method is useable up to about 100°C.

(e) *Reed Temperature Switch.* These are specially designed reed switches (see Section 2.2.3) surrounded by two toroid-shaped magnets separated by a

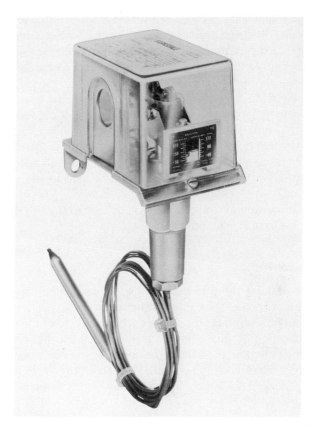

Fig. 2.29. Liquid-filled temperature switch. (Courtesy of IMO Delaval Inc., Barksdale Controls Division, Los Angeles, California 90058.

similarly shaped piece of ferrite. Since the ferrite normally conducts magnetic flux, the reed contacts are normally closed. At a certain temperature, the ferrite loses its ability to conduct magnetic flux (the so-called Curie effect), which causes the contacts to open. While the set-point temperature of such switches cannot be field-adjusted, almost any set point, up to about 300°C, can be obtained by proper formulation of the ferrite material. For a detailed discussion of such switches, see Ref. (2.55).

(f) *Thermistor Sensors.* Thermistors are solid-state devices whose resistance drops sharply with rising temperature. By using appropriate electronic circuitry, this effect can be utilized to actuate a solid-state switch.

(g) *Thermocouples and Resistance Thermometers.* These can be used for very high temperatures (up to 2000°C). They normally provide continuous analog outputs, but, by using appropriate electronic circuits, can be used to actuate solid-state switches.

One important difference between pressure and temperature sensors is their speed of response. Whereas pressure sensors respond almost immediately to pressure changes, temperature sensors have considerable time lags, because of the time required for heat to transfer from the medium to the sensor. This lag depends not only on sensor design, but even more so on the medium, and its velocity with respect to the sensor. (High velocities increase heat transfer, and thus decrease time lag.) Typical time constants of these lags can vary from as low as several seconds (attainable with flowing liquids) up to several minutes (for nonflowing air or gases). In applications where fast switch response is vital, this factor should be taken into account by selecting a sensor with fast response and mounting it at a location having maximum flow velocity rather than at a stagnation point.

For further discussion of temperature switches, see Refs. (2.4), (2.6), Part 5 of Ref. (2.10), Refs. (2.53), (2.54), and 2.56)

2.5.4   Flow Switches

Flow switches indicate the presence of flow, actuating the contacts when a certain flow rate is reached. Most flow switches are based on the use of a reed switch. The fluid flow displaces the magnet, which then closes the reed contacts. A typical application is sensing water flow in "demand hot-water heaters." When water begins to flow, the switch contacts close and actuate a control relay, which in turn, energizes the heater coil. On loss of flow, the switch opens, turning the heater off. See Ref. (2.45) for a listing of flow-switch manufacturers.

REFERENCES

2.1.   E. Doebelin, *Measurement Systems: Application and Design*, McGraw-Hill, New York, 1983.

2.2.   J. Alloca and A. Stuart, *Transducers—Theory and Applications*, Reston Publ. Co., Reston, VA, 1984.

2.3.   E. Rudisill and F. Yeaple, "Guide to Limit Switches," *Product Engineering*, Nov. 12, 1962, pp. 84–101.

2.4.   Electric Motors and Controls Reference Issue, *Machine Design*, April 24, 1975, pp. 92–116.

2.5.   Electrical and Industrial Electronics Reference Issue, *Machine Design*, May 14, 1987.

2.6.   R. Smeaton (Ed.), *Switchgear and Control Handbook*, McGraw-Hill, New York, 1987.

2.7.   J. Lockwood, "Applying Snap-acting Switches," *Machine Design*, Oct. 2, 1969, pp. 122–127.

2.8.   J. Lockwood, "Hostile Environments vs. Snap-acting Switches," *Machine Design*, Feb. 5, 1970, pp. 128–133.

2.9.   J. Copland, "Limit Switches: Don't Complicate the Uncomplicated," *Machine Design*, Nov. 28, 1974, pp. 79–82.

2.10. M. Szabo, "Electric Controls for Fluid Power Systems," *Hydraulics & Pneumatics*, Part 1: June, 1976, pp. 54–58; Part 2: August 1976, pp. 66–68; Part 3: Sept. 1976, pp. 110–113; Part 4, Oct. 1976, pp. 166–169; Part 5, Dec. 1976, pp. 62–63.

2.11. *Press-at-any-Point Sensing Switches*, Catalog C–14, Tapeswitch Corp. of America, Farmingdale, NY 11735.

2.12. E. Jacobs, "Making Fluid Power Cylinders Smart," *Hydraulics & Pneumatics*, May 1986, pp. 56–63.

2.13. A. Baz, "Positioning Accuracy of Magnetic Reed Switches," *Journal of Fluid Control*, Vol. 16, No. 4, 1986, pp. 41–54.

2.14. W. Bruenger, "Tips on Altering Reed Switches," *Machine Design*, Aug. 9, 1973, p. 113.

2.15. L. Dumbauld, "Dry Reed Switches and Switch Modules," *Control Engineering* (Special Report), July 1963, pp. 75–105.

2.16. S. M. Juds, *Photoelectric Sensors and Controls*, Dekker, New York, 1988.

2.17. T. Green and J. Tait, "The Fine Points of Sensing Light," *Machine Design*, Sept. 11, 1980, pp. 124–128.

2.18. W. Filichowski, "Photoelectric Systems: Industry's Electronic Eyes," *Machine Design*, Oct. 7, 1976, pp. 102–106.

2.19. D. Bahniuk, "Shrinking the Size of Light Sensors," *Machine Design*, Feb. 26, 1987, pp. 80–83.

2.20. C. Strack, "New Photoelectric and Proximity Sensors are Smaller, More Versatile," *I & CS*, Nov. 1986, pp. 71–74.

2.21. Opto Slotted Coupler H21A1 and H22A1 Data Sheets, *Optoelectronic Device Data*, p. 3–34, Motorola Inc., Phoenix, AZ, 1983.

2.22. N. Flueckiger, "Protecting Photoelectrics from False Signals," *Machine Design*, June 26, 1980, pp. 100–103.

2.23. R. Fayfield, "Fiber Optics and Photoelectric Sensing, a Good Combination," *Instruments and Control Systems*, Mar. 1982, pp. 45–49.

2.24. J. Hall, "Position Sensor and Proximity Switch Update," *I & CS*, July 1984, pp. 22–28.

2.25. P. Garlewsky and R. Dolson, "A Guide to Inductive Proximity Switches," *Instruments & Control Systems*, Oct. 1981, pp. 49–52.

2.26. G. Haynes, "Using Magnetic Speed Sensors," *I & CS*, Nov. 1985, pp. 51–57.

2.27. L. Teschler, "Transducers for Digital Systems," *Machine Design*, July 12, 1979, pp. 64–75.

2.28. *Hall Effect IC Application Guide*, Bulletin 27701, 1980, Sprague Electric Co., Concord, NH 03301.

2.29. "V. Coughlin, "Designing with Hall-effect Sensors," *Design Engineering*, Dec. 1983, pp. 47–49.

2.30. D. Brockman and R. Nelson, "Hall-effect Sensors,"*Machine Design*, Oct. 16, 1975, pp. 123–127.

2.31. J. Hines and T. Lantzsch, "New Life for Hall-effect Sensors," *Machine Design*, Oct. 10, 1985, pp. 83–87.

2.32. M. Sinko, "Simple Sensors that Need no Power," *Machine Design*, April 26, 1979, pp. 154–158.

2.33. L. Walle, "Understanding Air Jet Sensors," *Hydraulics & Pneumatics*, June 1974, pp. 66–70; July 1974, pp. 82–84; Nov. 1974, pp. 72–76; Dec. 1974, pp. 62–64.

2.34. *Spring Sensor Data Sheet*, Air Logic Div., Fred Knapp Engraving Co., Racine, WI, 1981.

2.35. *Fluid Sensor Catalog*, Festo, Esslingen, West Germany.

2.36. J. Kirschner and A. Schmidlin, "Fluidic Sensors—A Survey," *Fluidics Quarterly*, Vol. 8, No. 1, 1976, pp. 1–18.

2.37. F. Martin, "Inside Story of the Racquets with Pneumatics," *Hydraulics & Pneumatics*, Oct. 1980, pp. 167–169.

2.38. D. Payne, "Sensing the Position of Pneumatic Cylinders," *Machine Design*, July 12, 1984, pp. 97–99.

2.39. R. Beercheck, "On-board Controls for Pneumatic Cylinders," *Machine Design*, Dec. 6, 1984, pp. 142–144.

2.40. G. Flynn, "Mechanical vs Proximity Limit Switches," *Design Engineering*, Mar. 1980, pp. 43–46.

2.41. E. Wolff, "Solid State vs. Electromechanical," *Product Engineering*, July 1979, pp. 41–44.

2.42. F. Hardcastle, "How to Apply Position Sensors," *Instruments & Control Systems*, May 1982, pp. 52–57.

2.43. H. Morris, "Object Detection Techniques Range from Limit Switches to Lasers," *Control Engineering*, Nov. 1980, pp. 65–70.

2.44. S. Bailey, "Proximity Sensor: Key Link in Product Motion Controls," *Control Engineering*, Oct. 1981, pp. 92–96.

2.45. "Annual Designers Guide to Fluid Power Products," *Hydraulics & Pneumatics*, Jan. 1988, pp. 155–159.

2.46. W. Flynn, "Alarm Switches," *Control Engineering*, Mar. 1985, pp. 85–88.

2.47. S. Bailey, "Level Sensor '80: A Key Partner in Productivity," *Control Engineering*, Oct. 1980, pp. 75–79.

2.48. S. Bailey, "Analysis of Material-sensor Interaction Essential to Proper Level Meter Selection," *Control Engineering*, Dec. 1981, pp. 67–70.

2.49. P. Cleaveland, "Level Monitoring and Control," *I & CS*, Oct. 1985, pp. 37–44.

2.50. *Pressure Sensors and Switches*, Catalog, Fairchild Industrial Products, Dumont Instrumentation Inc., Commack, NY 11725.

2.51. P. Godfrey, "Choosing the Right Pressure Switch," *Instruments & Control Systems*, Apr. 1979, pp. 31–34.

2.52. J. Sandford, "Pressure Switches for Simple, Reliable Control," *Instruments & Control Systems*, Nov. 1976, pp. 27–32.

2.53. Electrical and Electronics Reference Issue, *Machine Design*, May 14, 1981, pp. 176–188.

2.54. S. Bailey, "Temperature and Pressure Switches: Guardians of Loops," *Control Engineering*, Aug. 1986, pp. 47–51.

2.55.   N. Miller, "Magnetic-reed Temperature Switches," *Instruments and Control Systems*, May 1973, pp. 55–57.

2.56.   "Guide to Selecting Temperature Switches," *Instruments & Control Systems*, May 1973, pp. 77–85.

CHAPTER 3

INTRODUCTION TO SWITCHING THEORY

In order to design logic circuits efficiently, it is necessary to have at least a rudimentary knowledge of switching theory. This is based on so-called switching or Boolean algebra (named after George Boole, who invented it in the last century).

It would be difficult to visualize modern technology without the use of switching circuits. Digital computers, even pocket calculators, are comprised of thousands of switching circuits that are microscopically contained within their integrated circuits or "IC chips." Another example of a switching circuit is an elevator control system. The system receives an input signal each time a passenger presses a button inside the elevator or an "UP" or "DOWN" button on any floor of the building. Also, as the elevator passes a given floor, a limit switch, or other position sensor, is actuated, informing the switching circuit of the elevator location. The circuit must then evaluate all these input signals and instruct the elevator whether to stop or to go; and, if the latter, in which direction. The most extensive switching system in existence is probably the telephone system, which permits us to reach telephones in far-away places simply by dialing a number. (The most sophisticated of all switching systems is, undoubtedly, the human brain, but biological systems are not the subject of this book.)

There are many good textbooks on switching theory; see, for example, Refs. (3.1)–(3.10). However, most of these were written by and for electrical engineers, and hence mainly stress techniques useful for designing computers or telecommunication systems. Most of these techniques are, unfortunately, not applicable for our purposes. We concentrate only on those methods useful for designing automation control circuits.

3.1 BINARY ELEMENTS

The sensors discussed in Chapter 2, and the switching elements to be covered in the next chapter, operate, for the most part, in the so-called "*on–off*" mode. This means that, at any given moment, they can only be in one of two positions. Such elements are called "binary elements," and they are the basic components of so-called "logic circuits," whose design is covered in succeeding chapters.

The classic example of a binary element is an electric switch or relay contact. A contact is either open or closed; there is no intermediate position. The limit valves discussed in Chapter 2 are also binary elements. In contrast to switch contacts, a valve can be partially open. However, valves intended to serve in logic circuits are designed to operate in the *on–off* mode. When such a valve passes from the open to the closed position, it, of course, passes through an intermediate state, but this state lasts only for a very brief period of time and is not utilized in logic circuits. (So-called proportional valves, as used in feedback control systems, usually operate in partially open positions, but such systems are not the subject of this book.)

A third example of a switching element is the transistor. Although transistors, as used in amplifiers, radios, televisions, and other "analog" circuits, do have intermediate states, transistors used in digital circuits operate in the on–off mode. They either conduct or do not conduct current.

3.2 BINARY VARIABLES

It is customary to label the two states of a binary element using the symbols 0 and 1. For example, if a certain element such as a switch contact, relay contact, or transistor is labeled A, then the statement $A = 0$ signifies that the element is open (i.e., does not conduct current), whereas $A = 1$ signifies that the element is closed (i.e., conducts). The letter A thus stands for a binary variable, which can have only one of two discrete values, 0 or 1, unlike variables in conventional algebra, which can have an infinite number of values, from minus to plus infinity.

We should not consider these symbols 0 and 1 as numerical values. They are nothing more than symbols standing for a certain state. We could just as well label these states 7 and 8 or "Green" and "Red."

In the previous example, the binary variable A represents the state of a conducting element such as a contact or transistor. However, binary variables can also represent many other activities. For instance, A could represent the actuation of a push-button or a limit switch, in which case $A = 0$ signifies that the switch is not being actuated, and $A = 1$ signifies actuation.

Frequently, a binary variable represents a voltage level or signal in a certain line. It is customary to label the state having the higher energy level as 1 or "high," and the lower energy level as 0 or "low." Thus, in typical TTL (transistor-transistor logic) circuits, the voltage level is switched from approximately 0.2 to 3.6 V. To be on the safe side and leave some room for small deviations from normal operation, it is customary to define any voltage below 0.4 V (the maximum expected low-level output) as "Logic 0," and any voltage above 2.4 V (the minimum expected high-level output) as "Logic 1."

In pneumatic systems, a binary variable such as p could represent pressure level in a certain line, in which case $p = 0$ signifies that the line is exhausted to atmosphere, and $p = 1$ signifies a pressurized line (with the pressure usually equal to system supply pressure, whatever that might be).

3.3 BASIC LOGIC GATES

Logic gates, the subject of this section, can be implemented in various ways, such as by switch or relay contacts, transistor or diode circuits, pneumatic valves, or other pneumatic elements. These various switching elements are the subject of Chapter 4. In this chapter, we use switch contacts exclusively to illustrate the operation of the various logic gates, since contacts are probably easier to visualize than other types of elements.

Figure 3.1 shows a push-button switch with a normally open contact. The switch symbol includes a small spring, which tends to push the contact bar upward against the push button, thus keeping the switch in its normally open position as long as the button is not being depressed. (These springs, however, are frequently not shown in schematic drawings.)

The left contact point of the switch in the figure is connected to a voltage, as indicated by the symbol "1." The push-button actuation is defined by binary variable A, and variable T represents the voltage level at the right contact point. We can then set down the following two statements:

If $A = 0$ (push button is not actuated), then $T = 0$ (voltage level is low).
If $A = 1$ (push button is actuated), then $T = 1$ (voltage level is high).

This results in the equation:

$$T = A$$

and the switch is said to represent a *YES* gate.

Consider next a push-button switch with a normally closed contact, as shown in Fig. 3.2. (Again, note the spring pressing the contact bar upward.) We can state:

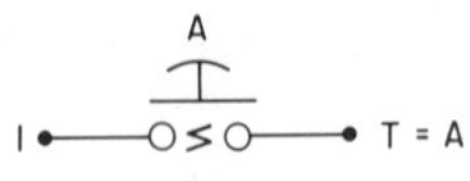

Fig. 3.1. YES gate. 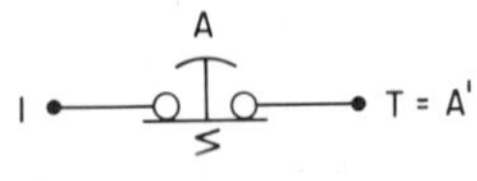   **Fig. 3.2.** NOT gate.

If $A = 0$ (push button is not actuated), then $T = 1$ (voltage level is high).
If $A = 1$ (push button is actuated), then $T = 0$ (voltage level is low).

In order to express these contact states algebraically, we must first define Boolean *negation*, or *inversion*, using the prime symbol, as follows:

$$0' = 1 \quad \text{and} \quad 1' = 0$$

These two relations represent axioms of Boolean algebra. (*Note:* In many textbooks, the overbar is used instead of the prime, in which case we could write $\bar{0} = 1$ and $\bar{1} = 0$.) In other words, if some variable $c = 0$, then $c' = 1$; and, conversely, if $c = 1$ then $c' = 0$. We can now express operation of the switch in Fig. 3.2 by the equation

$$T = A' \quad \text{(or, alternatively, } T = \bar{A})$$

and such a switch is said to represent a *NOT* gate.

Figure 3.3 shows two normally open switch contacts connected in series. Here $T = 1$ only if *both* push buttons A AND B are actuated. This represents an *AND* gate, and its equation is written as

$$T = A \cdot B$$

The dot between letters A and B stands for the operation defined as Boolean multiplication (sometimes called *conjunction*). Just as in ordinary algebra, the multiplication sign can be omitted, it always being implied whenever two letters are written next to each other, so that the previous equation is usually written

$$T = AB$$

Note that the term AND as used here has nothing in common with arithmetic addition or multiplication, and should really be read as "AND ALSO."

The operation of logic gates, such as the AND gate, can also be described by means of so-called *truth tables*. As shown in Fig. 3.3, a truth table must have a separate column for each input variable, and an additional column for the output variable. The number of rows equals the number of input combinations,

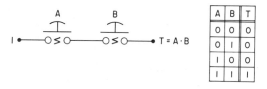

Fig. 3.3. Active AND gate and its truth table.

B
A •———O ≤ O———• T = A · B   **Fig. 3.4.** Passive AND gate.

which is equal to 2^n, where n is the number of input variables. The truth table simply lists all possible input combinations, and shows the resulting output for each.

It should be stressed that AND gates can have more than two input variables, since any number of switches could be connected in series. Thus, adding a third switch to Fig. 3.3 results in

$$T = ABC$$

and the resulting truth table would now have eight rows instead of four. For this case, $T = 1$ only if A AND B AND $C = 1$. The number of input channels available in a gate is termed the *fan-in* of the gate.

Figure 3.4 shows a single normally open switch, just as in Fig. 3.1, but here the left contact point is labeled A rather than 1. This means that this point is not connected to any defined voltage, but rather to a point, which may or may not be at a high voltage level, depending on the momentary state of variable A. We can state that $T = 1$ only if $A = 1$ AND $B = 1$, so that we again have an AND gate with the equation $T = AB$. This represents a *passive* gate, meaning that it is not connected to any energy source, but relies on the input variable A to supply the energy required to energize the output line (unlike the *active* gate of Fig. 3.3, which is connected to an energy source designated as 1). The difference between active and passive gates is discussed in Chapter 4.

Figure 3.5 shows two normally open switches connected in parallel. $T = 1$ if either A OR B is actuated. This is an OR gate, and its equation is written as

$$T = A + B$$

The plus sign stands for Boolean addition (sometimes called *disjunction*), but, again, this has nothing in common with arithmetic addition. This OR gate has a fan-in of 2, but, here too, we could increase the fan-in by connecting more switches in parallel, giving $T = A + B + C + \cdots$.

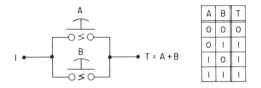

Fig. 3.5. OR gate and its truth table.

3.4 BASIC THEOREMS OF SWITCHING ALGEBRA

The symbols $+$, $\cdot$, $'$, 0, and 1 defined so far have a somewhat different meaning than in arithmetic. We must, therefore, use a completely new set of algebraic theorems, some of which may appear somewhat strange at first. The most important of these follow, with the physical interpretation written next to some of them:

$$0 \cdot 0 = 0 \qquad \text{(two open switches in series)} \qquad (1)$$

$$0 + 0 = 0 \qquad \text{(two open switches in parallel)} \qquad (2)$$

$$1 \cdot 1 = 1 \qquad \text{(two closed switches in series)} \qquad (3)$$

$$1 + 1 = 1 \qquad \text{(two closed switches in parallel)} \qquad (4)$$

While the first three equations agree with what we learned in elementary school, the last one does not. Obviously, $1 + 1$ cannot equal 2, because there is no "2" in Boolean algebra. The equation $1 + 1 = 1$ means that if both contacts connected in parallel are closed, then the system conducts.

Similarly, we can write

$$1 \cdot 0 = 0 \cdot 1 \ = 0 \qquad \text{(closed and open switches in series)} \qquad (5)$$

$$1 + 0 = 0 + 1 = 1 \qquad \text{(closed and open switches in parallel)} \qquad (6)$$

We now list theorems for a single variable:

$$X + 0 = X \qquad (7)$$

$$X \cdot 1 = X \qquad (8)$$

$$X + 1 = 1 \qquad (9)$$

$$X \cdot 0 = 0 \qquad (10)$$

Each equation can be visualized or interpreted physically by means of a switch circuit. For instance, in the circuit of Fig. 3.6, we see that the open switch 0 has no effect whatsoever on system output, which depends only on the position of switch X. This circuit therefore illustrates Equation (7), $X + 0 = X$.

The previous equations can be utilized to simplify more complicated Boolean

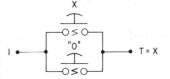

Fig. 3.6. Interpretation of the relation $X + 0 = X$.

expressions. For example, if in the equation $T = A + B + C + D + \cdots$, one of the terms equals 1, then, from Equation (9), we know that $T = 1$. Similarly, if in the equation $T = ABCD\ldots$, one of the variables equals 0, then, from Equation (10), $T = 0$.

Four additional theorems involving a single variable X follow:

$$X + X = X \tag{11}$$

$$X \cdot X = X \tag{12}$$

$$X + X' = 1 \tag{13}$$

$$X \cdot X' = 0 \tag{14}$$

It is suggested that the reader attempt to interpret each of the above relations using switch circuits. The Equations (11) and (12) signify that if in expressions like $T = A + B + C + C + D$ or $T = ABCCD$, any term, such as C, appears twice, then the second C is redundant and can be dropped.

Going on to functions of two variables X and Y, we have the following theorems:

$$X + Y = Y + X \tag{15}$$

$$X \cdot Y = Y \cdot X \tag{16}$$

$$\left. \begin{array}{l} X + XY = X \\[6pt] X(X + Y) = X \end{array} \right\} \text{absorption laws} \tag{17} \tag{18}$$

$$(X + Y')Y = XY \tag{19}$$

$$XY' + Y = X + Y \tag{20}$$

$$XY + Y' = X + Y' \tag{20A}$$

Theorems (17) and (18) are termed "*absorption laws*," because in both, variable Y is absorbed and disappears.

In Theorems (18) and (19), parentheses appear for the first time. Their purpose, just as in conventional algebra, is to determine the order in which operations are carried out. In the absence of parentheses, we first carry out the operation of negation (inversion), then that of Boolean multiplication, and, finally, that of Boolean addition. We show later that parentheses can be opened up just as in conventional algebra, and likewise we are allowed to place a common factor in front of parentheses. According to these principles, the prime symbol in Equation (20) applies only to the variable Y (i.e., not to the product XY), since otherwise we would have written $(XY)'$.

Theorem (20A) is not really different from (20), since we can always change the name of any variable. In order to get from Theorem (20) to (20A), we need only change the original variable Y to y' and Y' to y. After making that substitution, we return to capital letters, that is, change y back to Y.

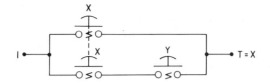

Fig. 3.7. Interpretation of absorption law $X + XY = X$.

As before, it is suggested that the reader attempt to interpret each of Theorems (15)–(20) by means of switch circuits. For example, absorption law (17) can be illustrated by the circuit of Fig. 3.7. It is clear from the figure that actuation of switch Y (i.e., $Y = 1$) does not assure an output voltage T. To obtain $T = 1$, we must actuate switch X (which has a double contact). Once this is done, the status of switch Y has no effect whatever on the result, since current flows through the upper contact of switch X in any case. Thus, switch Y is superfluous, and the output depends only on the status of switch X.

There are many theorems relating to three variables, but only the most important are listed:

$$X + Y + Z = (X + Y) + Z = X + (Y + Z) \tag{21}$$

$$XYZ = (XY)Z = X(YZ) \tag{22}$$

$$XY + XZ = X(Y + Z) \tag{23}$$

$$(X + Y)(X + Z) = X + YZ \tag{24}$$

$$(X + Y)(Y + Z)(Z + X') = (X + Y)(Z + X') \tag{25}$$

$$XY + YZ + ZX' = XY + ZX' \tag{26}$$

$$(X + Y)(X' + Z) = XZ + X'Y \tag{27}$$

If there are three or more variables, it becomes difficult to visualize the theorem by means of switch circuits. In order to prove any theorem of Boolean algebra, we can use one of two methods: mathematical induction or algebraic proof. Both of these are now illustrated.

In mathematical induction, we attempt to show that the theorem is valid for every possible combination of values of the variables. This method is difficult to apply in conventional algebra, since every variable could assume an infinite number of values. However, the method becomes practical in Boolean algebra, since each variable can only be 0 or 1, so that the number of possible combinations is strictly limited, being equal to 2^n, where n is the number of variables.

We now prove Theorem (23) by mathematical induction. Since this theorem involves three variables, we must test $2^3 = 8$ different combinations. If the theorem is shown to be correct for each one of these, it is proved to be true. The test is carried out in the following truth table:

X	Y	Z	XY	XZ	$XY + XZ$	$Y + Z$	$X(Y + Z)$
0	0	0	0	0	0	0	0
0	0	1	0	0	0	1	0
0	1	0	0	0	0	1	0
0	1	1	0	0	0	1	0
1	0	0	0	0	0	0	0
1	0	1	0	1	1	1	1
1	1	0	1	0	1	1	1
1	1	1	1	1	1	1	1

Since the results in the column labeled $XY + XZ$ are identical to those in column $X(Y + Z)$ for every possible combination, the theorem is proved true. It is thus demonstrated that parentheses can be opened up, as already mentioned.

While mathematical induction is based on "brute force" (and thus not considered "elegant" by some), it is very efficient, since it always succeeds in proving that a given equation is true or false, as the case may be. The only problem is that for equations involving a large number of variables, the required truth table becomes exceedingly long.

The second method, that of algebraic proof, is illustrated on Theorem (26). In this method, we are only permitted to use other theorems that have already been proved. Next to each operation, the number of the theorem on which that operation is based is noted:

$$XY + YZ + ZX' = XY + 1(YZ) + ZX' \qquad \text{according to (8)}$$
$$= XY + (X + X')(YZ) + ZX' \qquad \text{according to (13)}$$
$$= XY + XYZ + X'YZ + ZX' \qquad \text{according to (23)}$$
$$= XY(1 + Z) + X'Z(Y + 1) \qquad \text{according to (23)}$$
$$= XY(1) + X'Z(1) \qquad \text{according to (9)}$$
$$= XY + X'Z \qquad \text{according to (8)}$$

We complete the list of theorems with the so-called De Morgan theorems, which are very useful in manipulating Boolean expressions:

$$(X + Y + Z + \cdots)' = X'Y'Z' \cdots \tag{28}$$
$$(XYZ \cdots)' = X' + Y' + Z' + \cdots \tag{29}$$

or, in its most general form:

$$f(X_1, X_2, \ldots, X_n, +, \cdot)' = f(X_1', X_2', \ldots, X_n', \cdot, +) \qquad (30)$$

This last expression states, in symbolic form, that we obtain the negation (inversion) of any function f by replacing each variable X_i by X_i', each $+$ by $\cdot$, and each $\cdot$ by $+$.

For example, if $T = X + X'Y$, then

$$
\begin{aligned}
T' &= (X + X'Y)' \\
   &= X' \cdot (X'Y)' && \text{according to (30)} \\
   &= X' \cdot (X + Y') && \text{according to (30)} \\
   &= X'X + X'Y' && \text{according to (23)} \\
   &= 0 + X'Y' && \text{according to (14)} \\
   &= X'Y' && \text{according to (7)}
\end{aligned}
$$

The proof of De Morgan's theorem can be found in Ref. (3.1) and other textbooks on switching theory.

3.5 ALGEBRAIC SIMPLIFICATION OF BINARY FUNCTIONS

The main purpose of the various theorems just presented is to facilitate the simplification of binary functions. Where do these functions come from? They are usually the result of translating the practical requirements of a given control problem into the logic language of Boolean algebra. Toward the end of this chapter, we give two examples of such problems and their resulting binary functions.

To illustrate the process of simplification, suppose we have the function that follows. We first open the parentheses using Theorem (23), and then, relying on Theorem (14), cancel any expression having the general form XX'. The result is as follows:

$$
\begin{aligned}
&(x + y')(y + z')(z + x')(xyz + x'y'z') \\
&= (xy + xz' + y'y + y'z')(z + x')(xyz + x'y'z') \\
&= (xyz + xz'z + y'z'z + xyx' + xz'x' + y'z'x')(xyz + x'y'z') \\
&= (xyz + x'y'z')(xyz + x'y'z') \\
&= xyz + x'y'z' && \text{according to (12)}
\end{aligned}
$$

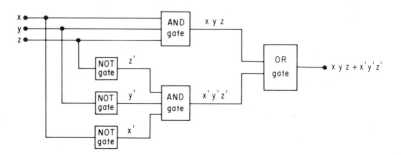

Fig. 3.8. Logic-gate implementation of a binary function.

This simplified function can now be implemented using a logic circuit, as shown in Fig. 3.8. This implementation requires three NOT gates, two AND gates, and one OR gate, or a total of six gates, whereas the implementation of the original function would have required a total of ten gates (three NOT, three AND, and four OR gates). So far we have not discussed the various types of gates, such as relay contacts, electronic gates, or different kinds of pneumatic elements, all of which are described in Chapter 4. However, it should be obvious that the use of the simplified function results in considerable savings of equipment and, therefore, of money, regardless of the type of gate used. Thus, the practical importance of being able to simplify binary functions is evident.

We conclude this section with a further example:

$$abcd + abc' + abd' = ab[(cd + c') + d'] \qquad \text{according to (21) and (23)}$$
$$= ab[(c' + d) + d'] \qquad \text{according to (20a)}$$
$$= ab(c' + 1) \qquad \text{according to (13)}$$
$$= ab(1) \qquad \text{according to (9)}$$
$$= ab \qquad \text{according to (8)}$$

In this case, the simplification achieved is even more striking. Instead of six gates required for implementing the original function, one single AND gate suffices for the simplified function.

3.6 KARNAUGH MAPS

While the algebraic method of simplifying binary functions is useful for simple cases, it is more and more time-consuming as the function becomes more complex. Also, in many cases, a "trick" of some sort is required, and it is frequently difficult to know for sure that the result cannot be simplified even further. We now describe a graphical method, based on the so-called Karnaugh

Fig. 3.9. Karnaugh map for two variables.

map, that does not suffer from these drawbacks. The method is applicable to complex functions; and it always produces the simplest possible result, without relying on tricks. Also, the method is generally much faster than the algebraic one.

We first show how the Karnaugh map is constructed, and, afterwards, how it is utilized for function simplification. The Karnaugh map includes 2^n squares arranged in matrix form, where n is the number of variables in the function to be simplified. For example, Fig. 3.9 shows the Karnaugh map for two variables, say a and b. Each of the $2^2 = 4$ squares in the map represents one of the four possible combinations of the two variables. The upper row represents $a = 0$ (or $a' = 1$), and the lower row $a = 1$. Similarly, the left column represents $b = 0$ (or $b' = 1$), and the right column $b = 1$. For the purpose of this explanation, the *address* has been written in each square of Fig. 3.9, though this is usually not done. For example, the address in the right top square is $a'b$. This means that this particular square represents the combination $a'b = 1$ (in other words, $a = 0$ and $b = 1$).

Similarly, Fig. 3.10 shows the Karnaugh map for the three variables a, b, and c, and again the correct address has been entered in each one of the $2^3 = 8$ squares. The assignment of the variables to the different rows and columns can be done in different ways, provided the following basic property of all Karnaugh maps is preserved: *the respective addresses of any two adjacent squares must differ in only one variable.* For example, the addresses of the two leftmost squares in the top row are identical except for the variable c, since the left square has c' whereas the right one has c.

For the purpose of this rule, adjacent squares are defined as having a common boundary. Thus, squares touching only at their corners are not considered adjacent. On the other hand, the left column is considered adjacent to the right column, as if the map were wound around and the two edges glued together. Thus, the left and right squares in the bottom row are considered adjacent, and, indeed, they differ only in the variable b.

Figure 3.11 shows a four-variable Karnaugh map, having $2^4 = 16$ squares.

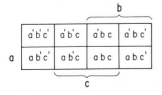

Fig. 3.10 Karnaugh map for three variables.

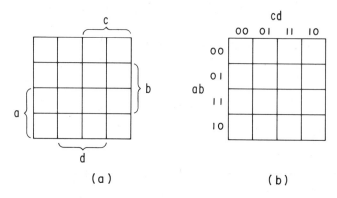

(a)   (b)

Fig. 3.11. Two ways of labeling a four-variable Karnaugh map.

The addresses of the squares are not listed; only the rows and columns have been labeled. This can be done in two different ways, as shown in Figs. 3.11(a) and (b), respectively. The two methods are equivalent and their use a matter of personal preference. Note that, in Fig. 3.11(a), only the regions a, b, c, and d but not a', b', c', and d' are labeled. It is implied that any region not included in, say, b belongs to $b' = 1$ (or $b = 0$). Thus, the square in the upper right-hand corner represents $a'b'cd' = 1$, which means that $a = 0$, $b = 0$, $c = 1$, and $d = 0$. Note that each row or column in these maps represents a Boolean product of two variables. Thus, the uppermost row represents $a'b' = 1$ ($a = 0$ and $b = 0$); the lowest row, $ab' = 1$; the second column from the left, $c'd = 1$; etc.

As in all Karnaugh maps, here, too, adjacent squares differ by only a single variable. As explained for Fig. 3.10, the right and left edges are considered adjacent. However, here the top and bottom edges are *also* considered adjacent. Thus, the address of the uppermost square in the leftmost column ($a'b'c'd'$) differs from the lowest square in the same column ($ab'c'd'$) only in the variable a.

We now illustrate now Karnaugh maps are used to simplify binary functions, for instance, the function T defined by the expression

$$T = a'b'cd' + a'bc'd' + bc'd + a'bcd' + abc'd' + abcd' + ab'c'd' + ab'cd'$$

It is very time-consuming to simplify this function algebraically, and the problem is better solved using a Karnaugh map. This function is expressed as a sum of eight products. This signifies that $T = 1$ provided any one of these eight terms, which are joined together by the $+$ sign (OR operation), equals 1. We, therefore, fill in the Karnaugh map by entering a 1 in every square corresponding to one of these eight terms, as shown in Fig. 3.12. Note that the term $bc'd$ covers two squares. Since the variable a is not specified in this term, it can be either 0 or 1, so that the term covers both $abc'd$ and $a'bc'd$ squares.

Any square not having a 1 is a 0, which signifies that $T = 0$ whenever the combination of the four variable states corresponds to that square's address. For

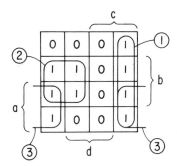

Fig. 3.12. Function simplification with a Karnaugh map.

example, if $a'b'c'd' = 1$, then $T = 0$, since combination $a'b'c'd'$ is not included in the present sum-of-products expression defining T. Therefore, a 0 is entered in the square at the left upper corner, which has the address $a'b'c'd'$. In other words, the Karnaugh map provides a "mapping" of the function T, showing for which of the 16 possible combinations of the four variables we get $T = 0$ and for which $T = 1$.

After the map has been filled in, the next step is to *loop* adjacent squares containing a 1 into *cells* having 2, 4, or even 8 squares. Each 2-square cell must contain two squares that are considered adjacent according to the definition previously given. For a four-variable Karnaugh map, a 2-square cell has an address consisting of a product of three variables. Several such 2-square cells are shown in the example of Fig. 3.13.

A 4-square cell consists of a combination of four squares, each containing a 1, in the form of a 4×1 matrix or a 1×4 matrix (see cell 1 in Fig. 3.12) or a 2×2 matrix (see cell 2). Since the two edges of the map are considered adjacent, cell 3 also represents a legitimate 4-square cell. For a four-variable Karnaugh map, a 4-square cell has an address consisting of a product of only two variables. For example, cell 2 in Fig. 3.12 has the address bc'. The four corner squares of the map also provide a 4-square cell with address $b'd'$ if each contains a 1, but in this example there is no such cell, since one of the four corners contains a 0.

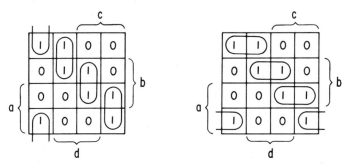

Fig. 3.13. Function having two similar solutions.

We can easily see that the larger the cell, the shorter the address. Thus, an 8-square cell, which covers half the map, has an address consisting of only a single variable. For example, if the first and the last rows of the map contain only 1s, we could loop these two rows into an 8-square cell having the address b'. Note that a cell must contain $2^n = 1, 2, 4, 8$, etc. squares, where n is any positive integer. Thus, 3-, 5-, and 6-square cells are not legitimate, since the address of such "cells" could not be expressed as a product of the variables.

The looping process must take place according to the following three rules:

1. Each square containing a 1 must be covered by at least one cell. (A square may be covered by more than one cell, if this should prove advantageous.)
2. The number of cells should be as small as possible.
3. Each cell should be as large as possible. (If a square containing a 1 has no adjacent squares with a 1, it remains by itself; i.e., a "1-square cell.")

While rule 1 must be observed, the other two rules are not absolute, but are intended to produce an optimum (i.e., simplest) solution.

Figure 3.12 shows how all the squares containing a 1 would be looped into 4-square cells, for this particular example. Since these cells cover all the combinations for which the function $T = 1$, the simplified function consists of the Boolean sum of all the cell addresses, in this case:

$$T = cd' + bc' + ad'$$

The reader will agree that this result is much simpler than the original function.

Frequently, there is more than one result. For example, compare the two Karnaugh maps of Fig. 3.13. Both represent the same function T, since all the 1s and 0s appear in the same squares. (*Note:* Here, and in many of the following examples, we shall not list the individual terms of the original unsimplified function. To save time, the function is mapped directly on the map.) In both maps, there are four 2-square cells, but the solutions are completely different, namely:

For the left map: $T = b'c'd' + a'c'd + bcd + acd'$
For the right map: $T = a'b'c' + a'bd + abc + ab'd'$

There is no obvious advantage for one solution over the other, both requiring the same number of logic gates for their implementation (four NOT gates, four AND gates, and one OR gate).

Sometimes, a problem has several solutions that are *not* similar, and the question arises how to find the optimum (i.e., the simplest) solution. Before showing a method for doing so, it is necessary to define two new terms.

A *prime cell* (also called a *prime implicant* in the literature) is defined as a cell not entirely included in a larger cell. For example, in the Karnaugh map of Fig. 3.12, we can combine squares $a'bc'd$ and $abc'd$ into a 2-square cell $bc'd$, but this is not a prime cell, since it is part of an even larger cell bc'. This 4-square cell bc' is a prime cell, since it is not included in any 8-square cell.

An *essential prime cell* (also called an *essential prime implicant*) is defined as a *prime cell* that includes at least one square containing a 1 that *cannot* be included in any other *prime cell*. For example, square $a'bc'd$ in Fig. 3.12 is part of prime cell bc' only. Therefore, the 4-square cell bc' is considered an essential prime cell, since there is no other prime cell that can cover this square. Actually, each one of the three cells looped in Fig. 3.12 is an essential prime cell (cell 1 because of the square $a'b'cd'$, and cell 3 because of square $ab'c'd'$). On the other hand, cell bd', which was not looped in Fig. 3.12 and is not utilized in the final solution, is a perfectly legitimate prime cell, but is *not* an essential prime cell. Each of its four squares can be covered by at least one other prime cell.

When attempting to loop the 1 squares in a Karnaugh map, we should begin by searching for all essential prime cells and loop these first. If these essential prime cells cover all the 1 squares (as is the case in Fig. 3.12), then the procedure is completed, and we have arrived at the optimum solution. On the other hand, if there are any 1 squares remaining without cover, then these have to be covered using nonessential prime cells, which means that there is more than one way of doing so. The solution selected in the end is chosen using common sense, again using the three rules listed previously.

In general, it can be said that we are not interested in cells that are not prime cells. A prime cell is nearly always preferable, even if it covers a 1 that has already been covered, because the address of a prime cell is always shorter than that of a smaller cell, and it is, therefore, easier to implement the function. (There are occasional exceptions to this principle, as illustrated in Section 3.10.)

The method described generally produces the optimum simplification of the original function. Consider the example of Fig. 3.14. This Karnaugh map contains three essential prime cells. (In each one, an asterisk has been drawn in the square that has no other possible coverage and thus makes the prime cell an essential one.) Since these three cells, between them, cover all the 1 squares, the optimum solution is $T = c'd' + ab + b'd$. If we approach the problem without first looking for essential prime cells, we might loop 4-square cells such as ac' or

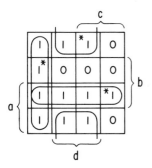

Fig. 3.14. Function simplification using essential prime cells.

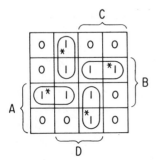

Fig. 3.15. Use of essential prime cells.

$b'c'$. However, both of these are useless, since they do not cover any squares that are not, in the end, covered by some essential prime cell.

An even more extreme example is shown in Fig. 3.15. Here, there are four 2-square cells, all of which are essential prime cells. We are tempted to loop the 4-square prime cell BD, but this cell is not essential and, in the end, is useless.

As a final example, consider the Karnaugh map of Fig. 3.16. Here, there are two essential prime cells bd and $b'c'd'$. However, they leave the $a'b'c'd$ square without coverage, and this square must then be looped either horizontally (giving $a'b'c'$) or vertically (giving $a'c'd$). Both of these cells are nonessential prime cells, and we end up with two alternative solutions:

$$T = bd + b'c'd' + a'b'c'$$

or

$$T = bd + b'c'd' + a'c'd$$

3.7   THE "DON'T CARE" CONDITION

It frequently happens that we "don't care" about the state of a given binary function for a specific combination of input variables. This is due to two possible reasons. (a) The specific combination of input variables is physically impossible. (b) The combination of input variables is possible, but it is completely

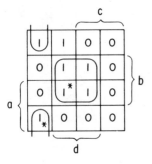

Fig. 3.16. Karnaugh map with two alternative solutions.

unimportant to us whether the function T is 1 or 0 for this particular combination. To illustrate these two cases, we present a practical example for each one.

Suppose we are designing a switching circuit to control an elevator, which determines at which floor the elevator is to stop. Assume that the binary function T, which plays a role in this circuit, is a function of several binary input variables a, b, c, d, etc., and $a = 1$ indicates that the elevator is presently going up, whereas $b = 1$ means that it is going down. Therefore, $ab' = 1$ means that the elevator is going up and not going down, and $a'b = 1$ that it is not going up but going down. The combination $a'b' = 1$ signifies that the elevator is standing (i.e., not going up and not going down). Finally, the combination $ab = 1$ is physically impossible, since the elevator obviously cannot go both up and down at the same time. Therefore, we don't care whether T is 0 or 1 for $ab = 1$, since this combination could never turn up anyway.

If that is the case, then it doesn't matter whether there is a 0 or a 1 in the Karnaugh map for T in any square whose address includes the combination ab. We are, therefore, free to enter either a 0 or a 1 in all such squares, depending on what is more convenient for us. This "don't care" condition is represented in the Karnaugh map by the Greek letter phi, ϕ (the superposition of 0 and 1), or simply by a dash, "—".

A good example for the second case, in which a given input combination is possible but the resulting state of the function unimportant, is provided by the set–reset flip-flop discussed in Section 3.9. If an S signal exists, the flip-flop is in the SET condition, in which output $y = 1$. If the S signal is now removed, the flip-flop remains SET, as long as signal $R = 0$. Assume now that the flip-flop is part of a switching circuit, and we wish to derive an expression for the so-called excitation function S, which defines under what conditions we must make $S = 1$. Assume that presently $y = 1$, and we wish y to remain 1. In this situation, we require $R = 0$, but don't care about S. Although an $S = 1$ signal is not needed at this time, it also does no harm. Therefore, we can enter a ϕ or "—" in the Karnaugh map for S into all squares that represent the above situation.

The presence of "—" entries in the Karnaugh map makes it easier for us to simplify the function. Each "—" entry can be interpreted as either 0 or 1, depending on which is more advantageous. (The matter is analogous to the joker in a pack of cards.) As an example, consider Fig. 3.17. If there were no "—" entries in the map, we would need two 2-square cells to cover the three 1 squares in the bottom row, and an additional 1-square cell for the isolated 1 square in the second row. However, the "—" entry in the bottom row enables us to loop the entire row as a 4-square cell (an essential prime cell). The remaining 1 in the second row can be looped together with any of the three adjacent "—" entries, giving three alternative solutions:

$$T = ab' + a'bc'$$

$$T = ab' + a'bd$$

$$T = ab' + bc'd$$

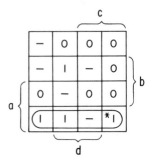

Fig. 3.17. Karnaugh map with "don't care" conditions.

Depending on which of these three solutions is chosen, the remaining unused "—" entries are interpreted as 0.

We can now summarize the advantages of the Karnaugh-map method:

1. It is faster and easier than algebraic simplification, and requires less effort to arrive at the optimal solution.
2. If there is more than one possible solution, the map immediately shows the different alternatives.
3. "Don't care" conditions are easily taken into account.

3.8 KARNAUGH MAPS FOR MORE THAN FOUR VARIABLES

Because of the advantages just enumerated, it is natural to attempt to use Karnaugh maps for functions of more than four variables. Many textbooks show how the Karnaugh map can be used with five or even six variables, but most go on to state that the method becomes impractical for more than six variables. This is simply not so, and it will be shown in this section that the method can easily be used for up to eight variables.

We begin with five variables and work our way up to eight. The five-variable Karnaugh map is really three-dimensional, and consists of 2 four-variable maps placed on top of each other, as shown in Fig. 3.18(a). It can be visualized as a two-floor building, each floor having an identical floor plan. Each cube, or "room," now has five adjacent cubes. Four of these are those corresponding to the four adjacent squares on the same floor, and the fifth is at the same location, but above or below it.

As seen from Fig. 3.18(a), the various cubes on each floor are defined by the four variables a, b, c, and d, and the two floors are differentiated by the fifth variable e. As an example, the five cubes adjacent to cube $ab'cde$ have been cross-hatched on the figure, and their respective addresses are $a'b'cde$, $abcde$, $ab'c'de$, $ab'cd'e$, and $ab'cde'$. Note that here, too, the basic property of the Karnaugh map is preserved: *the respective addresses of two adjacent cubes differ in only one variable.*

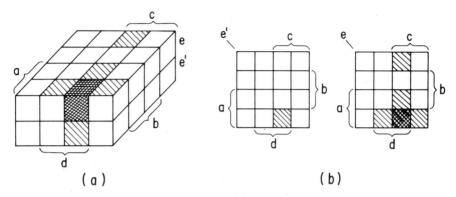

(a)   **(b)**

Fig. 3.18. (a) Three-dimensional five-variable Karnaugh map, and (b) its development.

Since three-dimensional maps are awkward to work with, we do what an architect would do: draw the plan of each floor separately, and place these two-dimensional plans side by side. This is done in Fig. 3.18(b), and we now have a five-variable Karnaugh map, which consists of 2 four-variable *submaps* placed next to each other, although they really belong on top of each other.

To show how such a map is used, consider the function

$$T = a'b'c'd' + a'bde' + a'b'cde' + ab'c'd' + a'bc'de + abcde + abcd'e$$

with conditions $a'b'cd' = 1$ and $acde' = 1$ both specified impossible. This function is mapped in Fig. 3.19. Note that all squares corresponding to an impossible condition get a "don't care" entry. (Entering a 0 in such squares is a common mistake. A 0 in the $abcde'$ square, for example, does *not* mean that $abcde' = 0$. Rather, it means that the function $T = 0$ when $abcde' = 1$.) Here, too, the proper way of looping squares is to first search for essential prime cells. There are three of these in this map, and they have been marked by asterisks in those squares that cannot be covered by any other prime cell. (Loops between

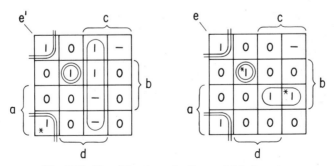

Fig. 3.19. Simplification of a five-variable function.

the two submaps are indicated by double lines.) There remain two squares ($a'b'cde'$ and $a'bcde'$) that cannot be covered by essential prime cells, and they are best covered by nonessential prime cell cde'. The resulting simplified function is

$$T = b'c'd' + a'bc'd + cde' + abce$$

The principle of the six-variable Karnaugh map is basically the same as for five variables, except that the two-story "building" of Fig. 3.18(a) now becomes a four-story one, as shown in Fig. 3.20(a). Each cube now has six adjacent cubes, rather than five. Again, four of these correspond to the four adjacent squares on the same floor, and the remaining two correspond to the same location, but on adjacent floors. As seen from the figure, the cube location on a given floor is defined by the four variables a, b, c, and d, whereas the four floors are differentiated by ef', ef, $e'f$, and $e'f'$. As an example, the six cubes adjacent to cube $ab'cde'f'$ have been cross-hatched on the figure, and the reader can check that each of their addresses differs from $ab'cde'f'$ in only one variable. Note also that the top and bottom floors are considered adjacent (just as the top and bottom rows of a four-variable Karnaugh map are adjacent).

As before, this Karnaugh map is drawn in the form of 4 two-dimensional four-variable submaps, as shown in Fig. 3.20(b). Here, too, the first and last submaps in the row are considered adjacent.

As an example of the use of such a map, consider the six-variable function

$$T = A'BC'F' + AB'C'DE'F + ABDF + ACDE$$

$$+ ACD'E + A'C'DE' + A'C'DEF'$$

with the conditions $A'B'C'D' = 1$ and $A'BCD'F = 1$ both specified as impossible.

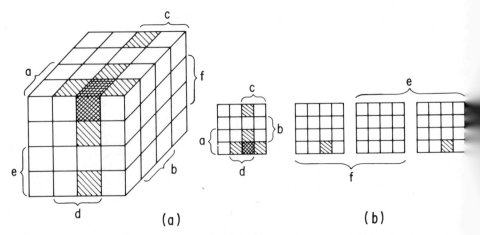

Fig. 3.20. (a) Three-dimensional six-variable Karnaugh map, and (b) its development.

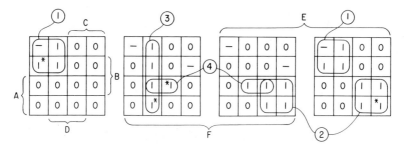

Fig. 3.21. Simplification of a six-variable function.

The Karnaugh map for this function is shown in Fig. 3.21. To help the reader follow the solution, the cells have been numbered, both on the map and on the resulting solution. There are four essential prime cells, and they cover all the 1 squares, so that there is only one possible solution:

$$T = A'C'F' + ACE + C'DE'F + ABDF$$
$$① \qquad ② \qquad ③ \qquad ④$$

As we go on to seven and eight variables, the maps become four-dimensional, and it is impossible to display them as a three-dimensional drawing. However, as before, we can place the individual submaps side by side, and if the reader has mastered the five- and six-variable Karnaugh maps, there should be no difficulty with seven or eight variables.

Let us first visualize a three-variable Karnaugh map covering the variables g, e, and f, as shown in Fig. 3.22. Each square has three adjacent squares, as indicated by the cross-hatching for square $ef'g'$, for example. If we now visualize each square turning into a four-variable submap covering variables a, b, c, and d, and if we draw these submaps in the same relative positions as in Fig. 3.22 but with some space between them, then we obtain the seven-variable Karnaugh map shown in Fig. 3.23. Since the row and column labels for a, b, c, and d are

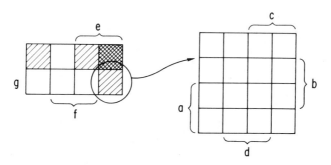

Fig. 3.22. Creation of a seven-variable Karnaugh map.

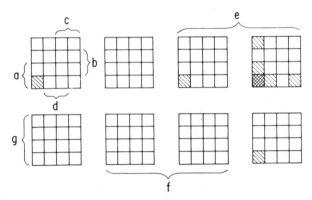

Fig. 3.23. A seven-variable Karnaugh map.

identical for all submaps, they are only shown once. Again, for the purpose of illustration, a particular square $ab'c'd'ef'g'$ has been marked, and its seven adjacent squares are indicated by cross-hatching.

Rather than illustrating the use of this seven-variable map, we proceed directly to the eight-variable Karnaugh map. This evolves from the four-variable map covering variables $e, f, g,$ and $h,$ as shown in Fig. 3.24. Each square has four adjacent squares, as indicated by the cross-hatching for the square $e'fg'h,$ for example. If we now visualize each square turning into a four-variable submap covering variables $a, b, c,$ and $d,$ and if we draw these submaps in the same relative position as in Fig. 3.24 but with some space between them, then we obtain an eight-variable Karnaugh map, similar to that of Fig. 3.25.

To illustrate the use of this eight-variable Karnaugh map, we take some shortcuts. Rather than list the original unsimplified function, which is very tedious, the various terms of this function are already entered in the map of Fig. 3.25. Also, only the "1" and "—" conditions are entered. To save time and effort, the squares in which the function $T = 0$ are left blank.

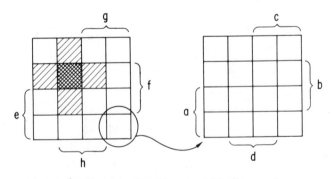

Fig. 3.24. Creation of an eight-variable Karnaugh map.

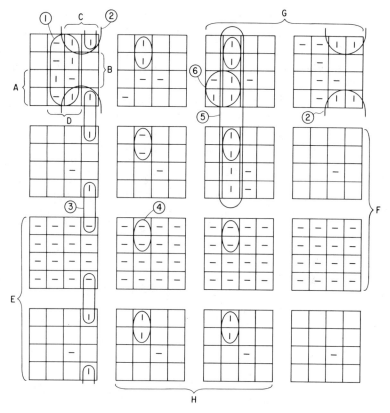

Fig. 3.25. Simplification of an eight-variable function.

The method of looping this map is basically the same as that used previously, but we formally summarize the procedure:

1. Go through all the squares in each submap in some systematic order, and check each 1 square. (Squares with "—" entries are not checked here.) If any such square can be covered by *only one* prime cell, then we have located an essential prime cell, and it should be looped and numbered. (For the purpose of this check, the square must be checked not only against adjacent squares within the same submap, but also against the identical square in all adjacent submaps.)

2. If a 1 square can be covered by *more than one* prime cell, disregard it for the time being, and continue on to the next 1 square.

3. Any 1 square that has already been included in a loop need not be checked anymore.

4. After all the unlooped 1 squares have been checked, there are two possibilities:

(a) If all 1 squares have been covered, the looping procedure is completed.
(b) If any 1 squares remain without cover, they must then be covered using nonessential prime cells, and, by definition, there is more than one way of doing so. The choice should be made so that the number of cells is minimum.

5. Write the simplified function as the Boolean sum of the addresses of the respective cells, labeling each term with the same number as used for the corresponding cell. (This is highly recommended, as it greatly helps avoid mistakes and facilitates checking the solution.)

Following this procedure, the solution for the eight-variable map of Fig. 3.25 follows. There are five essential prime cells, and the only 1 square remaining uncovered can be covered in two different ways, giving two alternative solutions:

$$T = DE'F'G'H' + B'CE'F'H' + B'CD'G'H'$$
$$\quad\quad ① \quad\quad\quad ② \quad\quad\quad ③$$
$$+ A'C'DEH + C'DE'GH + AC'E'F'GH$$
$$\quad\quad ④ \quad\quad\quad ⑤ \quad\quad\quad ⑥$$

$$(or\ AB'C'D'E'F'H)$$

For functions of more than eight variables, the Karnaugh-map method must be abandoned, although, under certain conditions, it can still be used for even up to 12 variables; see Fig. 5.48 and also Ref. (3.11). However, there exist several numerical methods for handling such problems, the best-known of which is the so-called Quine–McCluskey method, described in most textbooks on switching theory; see, for example, Refs. (3.1)–(3.7). Most of these numerical methods are very tedious when done by hand, but they become quite practical using a computer; see Ref. (3.5).

3.9 ADDITIONAL LOGIC GATES AND FLIP-FLOPS

In addition to the AND, OR, and NOT gates discussed so far, there are several other important gates. Before describing these, we briefly discuss commonly used gate symbols.

Unfortunately, there is no universally accepted set of symbols. The International Standards Organization (ISO) recommended a set of symbols over 10 years ago, and these are gaining international acceptance, except in the United States, where older symbols are still widely used. Even within the United States, there is no national consensus, and at least three different sets of symbols are used. We, therefore, use the ISO symbols in this book. Five different sets of symbols are shown in Fig. 3.26.

Note that the small circle—whether appearing in an input or output line—represents Boolean inversion or negation. Thus, a circle at the output of an OR

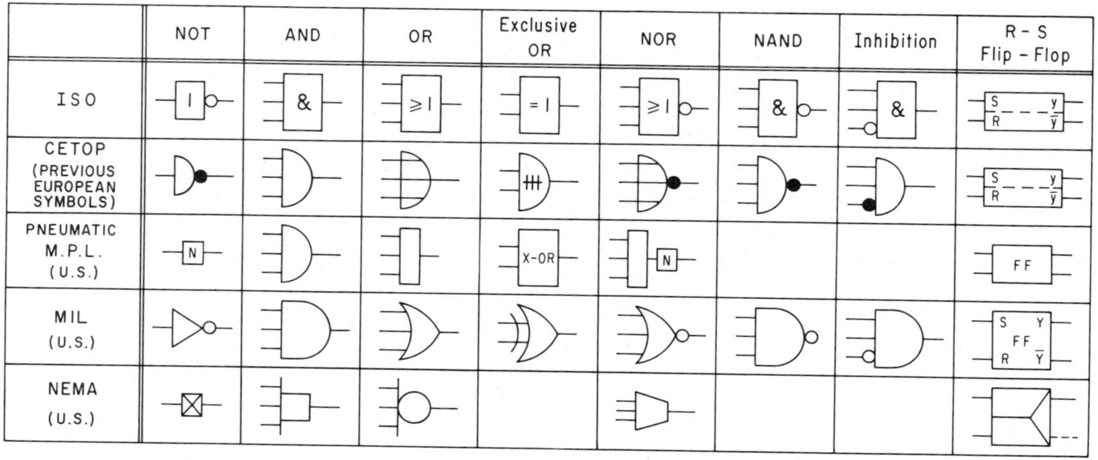

Fig. 3.26. Commonly used logic-gate symbols.

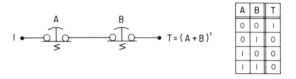

A	B	T
0	0	I
0	I	0
I	0	0
I	I	0

Fig. 3.27. NOR gate and its truth table.

gate converts the OR into a NOR gate (discussed in what follows). The $\geqslant 1$ designation inside the OR gate symbol means that gate output is "high," provided the number of "high" input signals is equal to or greater than 1.

Figure 3.27 shows two normally closed switches connected in series. This system only conducts provided neither the first NOR the second switch is actuated; hence, it provides a NOR gate, whose equation is

$$T = A \downarrow B = A'B' = (A + B)'$$

where the symbol $\downarrow$ represents the NOR operation. The second form $(A + B)'$ shown can be obtained from the first form $A'B'$ using De Morgan's theorem, or it can be obtained from physical considerations (i.e., $T = 0$ if either $A = 1$ OR $B = 1$). This second form also shows that the NOR gate is a combination of a NOT and an OR.

NOR gates are important for two reasons. First, they are easily obtained electronically or pneumatically, as is shown in Chapter 4. Second, the NOR gate is what is called a *universal gate*, which means that it is possible to obtain any Boolean function using NOR gates alone. For example, a NOT gate is a NOR gate with a single input. If the actual element should have more than one input line, these additional inputs are simply connected to 0 (i.e., to ground for electronic elements or to atmosphere for pneumatic ones), so that the NOR becomes a NOT gate, as shown in Fig. 3.28.

An OR gate can be obtained by connecting a NOR gate and a NOT gate in series, as shown in Fig. 3.29. If either A OR B equals 1, then $C = 0$, giving an output of $T = 1$.

An AND gate is obtained by using two NOT gates and one NOR gate connected as shown in Fig. 3.30. In other words, each AND gate "costs" three NOR gates.

If NOR gates were utilized simply as direct replacements for the other gates, as shown in Figs. 3.28–3.30, an excessive number of NOR gates would be required, and the resulting circuits would be very wasteful. Fortunately, there

A •——
0 •——$\geqslant 1$ —— • $T = A'$ **Fig. 3.28.** NOR gate acting as a NOT gate.

A •
B •　≥ 1　$C = (A+B)'$　≥ 1　• $T = C' = A + B$　　**Fig. 3.29.** Two NOR gates acting as an
　　　　　　0 •　　　　　　　　　　　　　OR gate.

are special, much more efficient, techniques for implementing circuits using NOR gates, and one of these is described in Section 3.10.

If we connect two normally closed switches in parallel, as shown in Fig. 3.31, we obtain a so-called NAND gate. The system does NOT conduct if both A AND B are actuated (i.e., it conducts if either switch is *not* actuated). The equation of the NAND gate is, therefore,

$$T = A \mid B = (AB)' = A' + B'$$

where the vertical line | represents the NAND operation. It can be seen that this gate is a combination of a NOT and AND, hence, the name NAND. NAND gates are very common in electronic circuits, and the NAND gate is also a universal gate. It is left as an exercise for the reader to demonstrate how NOT, OR, and AND gates can be produced using NAND gates only.

As with OR and AND gates, the fan-in of NOR and NAND gates can be increased above 2 simply by providing more input lines.

Figure 3.32 shows a circuit with two switches, each having double contacts (one normally open and the other normally closed). The output T is defined by

$$T = A \oplus B = AB' + A'B$$

where the $\oplus$ symbol represents the Exclusive-OR (also termed XOR) operation. In the XOR gate, output $T = 1$, provided $A = 1$ or $B = 1$, but not if both $A = 1$ and $B = 1$ (contrary to an ordinary OR gate). A circuit, such as shown in Fig. 3.32, is useful for controlling a room light from two different switch locations A and B. Also, Exclusive-OR gates are extremely important in computers, since binary addition is carried out using XOR operations. If we add two binary bits, there are four different possibilities:

$$
\begin{array}{cccc}
0 & 0 & 1 & 1 \\
+0 & +1 & +0 & +1 \\
\hline
=0 & =1 & =1 & =10
\end{array}
$$

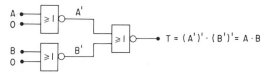

Fig. 3.30. Three NOR gates acting as an AND gate.

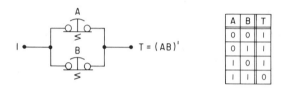

Fig. 3.31. NAND gate and its truth table.

A	B	T
0	0	I
0	I	I
I	0	I
I	I	0

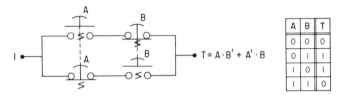

$T = A \cdot B' + A' \cdot B$

Fig. 3.32. Exclusive-OR gate and its truth table.

A	B	T
0	0	0
0	I	I
I	0	I
I	I	0

It is seen that the least significant bit of the sum always has the value shown in the truth table of Fig. 3.32.

Another type of gate included in the symbol table of Fig. 3.26 is the INHIBITION gate, which is really an AND gate, but with one of its input lines inverted. A 1 signal in this inverted input line "inhibits" the output signal from becoming 1, hence, the name. An INHIBITION gate with a fan-in = 2 is obtained by connecting a normally open and a normally closed switch in series, as in Fig. 3.33, and its equation is $T = AB'$.

The various operating characteristics (fan-in, fan-out, switching speed, 0 and 1 levels, etc.) of different logic gates (electronic, relay, pneumatic, etc.) are discussed in Chapter 4.

We conclude this section by discussing the most common types of flip-flops, or bistable elements, so called because they have two different stable output states.

The logic gates discussed so far represent *combinational systems,* that is, the gate output depends only on the present combination of input signals. By contrast, flip-flops are *memory* elements, since flip-flop output depends not only on the present state of the inputs, but also on the previous flip-flop state.

$T = A \cdot B'$

A	B	T
0	0	0
0	I	0
I	0	I
I	I	0

Fig. 3.33. *INHIBITION* gate and its truth table.

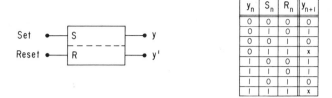

y_n	S_n	R_n	y_{n+1}
0	0	0	0
0	1	0	1
0	0	1	0
0	1	1	x
1	0	0	1
1	1	0	1
1	0	1	0
1	1	1	x

Fig. 3.34. RS flip-flop and its truth table.

The most basic type of flip-flop is the *RS flip-flop* (Reset–Set), which is shown schematically in Fig. 3.34. The two flip-flop inputs S and R can be either 0 or 1. However, they are not permitted to be 1 at the same time, as the flip-flop operation is not well defined for that case. The flip-flop has an output y (also called a *state variable*), and also its inverted value y'. If $S = 1$, the flip-flop becomes *set*, which means that $y = 1$ and $y' = 0$. If S now returns to 0, the flip-flop "remembers" that S had been 1, and maintains $y = 1$. Additional S signals have no effect. If R becomes 1 (assuming that $S = 0$), the flip-flop is *reset*, so that $y = 0$ and $y' = 1$. Again, R can then return to 0, and y remains 0 until a new S signal appears. Until that time, additional R signals have no effect.

Figure 3.34 also shows the truth table defining flip-flop operation. The subscript n in the table indicates the present state, and $n + 1$ the resulting succeeding state. The x in the output column indicates an undefined state. The equation of the RS flip-flop can be written as $y_{n+1} = R'(S + y_n)$.

Using the information in this truth table, we can construct a flip-flop actuation table, as shown in Fig. 3.35. It indicates the S and R signals required to obtain a certain result. Note the "don't care" states appearing in the first and last rows of the table, previously mentioned in Section 3.7.

In Chapters 4 and 5, it is shown how RS flip-flops can be obtained using a single switching element, such as a relay or pneumatic valve. However, RS flip-flops can also be constructed with two logic gates, as shown in Fig. 3.36. In Fig. 3.36(a), two NOR gates are used, with each gate output fed back to one of the inputs of the other gate. If $S = 1$ while $R = 0$, the upper-gate output labeled y' becomes 0. As a result, both inputs of the lower gate are 0, so that output y becomes 1. Since y is fed back as input to the upper gate, output y' remains 0

y_n (initial)	y_{n+1} (final)	Required S	Required R
0	0	0	—
0	1	1	0
1	0	0	1
1	1	—	0

Fig. 3.35. Actuation table for an RS flip-flop.

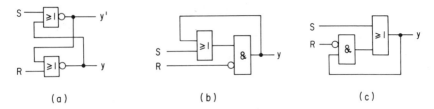

Fig. 3.36. Three flip-flop circuits using two logic gates.

when S returns to 0. The moment R becomes 1, the flip-flop switches to $y' = 1$ and $y = 0$. If both S and R are 1 concurrently, both gate outputs y' and y are 0 (which is a logic contradiction, but this condition is illegal anyway). Hence, this particular flip-flop is said to be "reset dominating." Most electronic RS flip-flops are constructed from two NOR gates using this circuit.

Figure 3.36(b) shows a flip-flop constructed from an OR and an INHIBITION gate, but this flip-flop only has a single output y. If y' is also required, an additional NOT gate has to be used. If both $S = R = 1$, the INHIBITION gate produces $y = 0$, so that this flip-flop is also reset-dominating.

Figure 3.36(c) shows a third flip-flop, also constructed from an OR and an INHIBITION gate, and with single output y. If both $S = R = 1$, the OR gate produces $y = 1$, so that this flip-flop is set-dominating.

Figure 3.37 shows a *JK flip-flop* and its truth table. This is very similar to the RS flip-flop, with J being the set signal and K the reset signal. The only difference is that here both J and K are permitted to be 1 concurrently, and this causes y to "flip" (i.e., change state). The JK flip-flop (usually implemented electronically) frequently comes with a clock-pulse input, labeled CP in the figure. The J and K inputs only take effect when CP goes from 0 to 1, that is, at the leading edge of the clock pulse. (Sometimes, the falling edge is used.) To complete the cycle and permit a new transition, the clock signal must first return to 0. Clocked systems, also called synchronous systems, are very common in computer circuits, where an internal clock produces pulses at a fixed frequency.

The *T flip-flop* (where T stands for "trigger") shown in Fig. 3.38 finds wide application in counting circuits (see Chapter 8), and as "frequency dividers" in

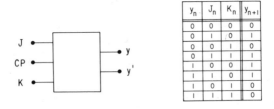

y_n	J_n	K_n	y_{n+1}
0	0	0	0
0	1	0	1
0	0	1	0
0	1	1	1
1	0	0	1
1	1	0	1
1	0	1	0
1	1	1	0

Fig. 3.37. JK flip-flop and its truth table.

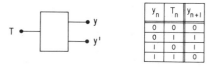

y_n	T_n	y_{n+1}
0	0	0
0	I	I
I	0	I
I	I	0

Fig. 3.38. T flip-flop and its truth table.

timing circuits (e.g., electronic quartz watches). This flip-flop has only one input, labeled T. Whenever an up-going pulse (leading edge) appears in the T line, the output y flips.

The final flip-flop to be mentioned here (though there are still others) is the D *flip-flop* (where D stands for "delay"), which is shown in Fig. 3.39. This has a D ("data") and a CP ("clock pulse") input. Whenever a clock pulse appears, output y accepts the D-input value that existed before the appearance of the clock pulse. In other words, the D input is delayed by one clock pulse, hence, the name "delay." As seen from the truth table, the new state y_{n+1} is always independent of the old state, which distinguishes the flip-flop from all previous ones.

Both T and D flip-flops frequently have an additional "CLEAR" input. A CLEAR pulse always produces $y = 0$, regardless of the flip-flop's previous state.

3.10 LOGIC-CIRCUIT DESIGN

In this section, we discuss ways of combining logic gates in the most efficient manner.

When simplifying a binary function using Karnaugh maps, the result appears as a sum-of-products expression. We could implement this expression directly, using either logic gates or switch contacts, but it is frequently advantageous to first factor out any common term present in the expression.

Assume, for example, that the simplified sum-of-product expression is $T = AB + AC$. We would require four switch contacts to implement this function (i.e., one for each letter, or *literal*, appearing in the expression). However, by factoring out A, we get $T = A(B + C)$, which requires only three contacts.

If electronic or pneumatic logic gates are used to implement the function, the number of logic operations must be counted, rather than the number of literals. In this case, the original expression requires three gates (two AND and one OR gate), whereas the factored expression requires only two gates (one AND and

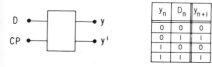

y_n	D_n	y_{n+1}
0	0	0
0	I	I
I	0	0
I	I	I

Fig. 3.39. D flip-flop and its truth table.

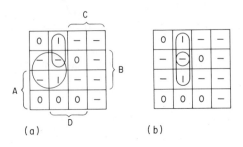

(a)

(b)

Fig. 3.40. Example of the nonselection of a prime cell.

one OR). Thus, no matter how the function is to be implemented, it often pays to first factor out common variables that may be present.

We now demonstrate that it is occasionally of advantage to select a cell that is *not* a prime cell, in complete contradiction to what was stated in Section 3.6. Assume that the Karnaugh map of a certain function T appears as in Fig. 3.40. If we went strictly by the rules laid down in Section 3.6, we would select the prime cell BC', as shown in Fig. 3.40(a). The resulting function would be $T = BC' + A'C'D$, and this would require five switch contacts, or, alternatively, five logic gates (two NOT, one OR, and two AND gates). If we were to factor out C', we would get $T = C'(B + A'D)$, which would require only four contacts, but still five logic gates.

In the Karnaugh map of Fig. 3.40(b), the 2-square cell $BC'D$ is selected rather than the 4-square prime cell BC'. The resulting function $T = BC'D + A'C'D$ appears more complicated at first sight. However, the term $C'D$ can be factored out, giving $T = C'D(B + A')$, and this requires four contacts as before, but only four gates (two NOT, one OR and one AND), a savings of one gate.

Another example is shown in Fig. 3.41, which represents a multiple-output system. There are two output variables T_1 and T_2, each of which actuates something else in the physical system, but both are functions of the same input variables A, B, C, and D. The Karnaugh maps for T_1 and T_2 are shown in the figure, and the resulting simplified functions are $T_1 = AC' + BD$ and $T_2 = A'B' + BCD$. To implement these, we require a total of three NOT gates, two OR gates, and four AND gates.

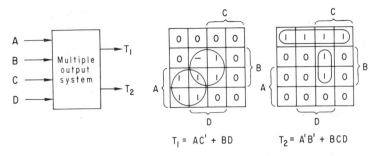

$T_1 = AC' + BD$ $T_2 = A'B' + BCD$

Fig. 3.41. Nonselection of a prime cell in a multiple-output system.

If we now replace the 4-square prime cell BD in the T_1 map by the 2-square cell BCD (which is permissible since the $A'BC'D$ square has a "don't care" entry and the $ABC'D$ square is already covered by the AC' cell), then only three AND gates are required. The explanation for this is that the T_2 function requires an AND gate to give the BCD product in any case, and the modified T_1 function can share this AND gate and thus eliminate the AND gate previously assigned to produce BD. (*NOTE:* This does not work with contact implementation.)

In this simple example, the desirable modification of the T_1 function can be discovered easily using common sense. For more complicated multiple-output systems, and especially those having more than two output functions, this becomes difficult, and a more systematic method is needed to discover possible function modifications. The subject is beyond the scope of this book, but the reader can find a good description of such a method in Refs. (3.5) and (3.7).

As stated in Section 3.9, both NOR and NAND gates are universal gates. Thus, any required function can be implemented using NOR or NAND gates alone, but special design methods are required to accomplish this economically. Such a method is now illustrated for NOR-gate implementation.

It is assumed that the required function has already been simplified and appears in standard sum-of-products form. The method consists of working backwards, that is, we assume that we already have the required function at the right end of the diagram, and, working toward the left, we add the necessary NOR gates and connections. The procedure is best illustrated by an example.

Assume we wish to design a NOR circuit giving the function

$$T = CD + A'B'C + ABC'$$

To facilitate the work, it is recommended to write down and keep before us the two standard forms of the NOR function, which were already noted in Section 3.9:

$$T = x_1 \downarrow x_2 \downarrow x_3 \cdots = x_1'x_2'x_3' \cdots = (x_1 + x_2 + x_3 + \cdots)'$$

We now compare the function to be implemented to these two standard forms and come to the conclusion that our sum-of-products form corresponds more closely to the second of the above two standard forms, except that the prime sign is missing. To get our function into this second form, we need an inverter or NOT gate, that is, a single-input NOR gate, and this is shown at the right end of Fig. 3.42.

The input to this NOR gate must be $T' = (CD + A'B'C + ABC')'$, which exactly matches the second standard form of the NOR function. Therefore, T' is obtained by a second NOR gate, which must have the various product terms of T as inputs. We continue working backwards and note that each product term corresponds to the first standard form of the NOR function. (A NOR gate acts like an AND gate provided the various inputs are first inverted.) Thus, each product term requires an additional NOR gate. Finally, we provide NOT gates,

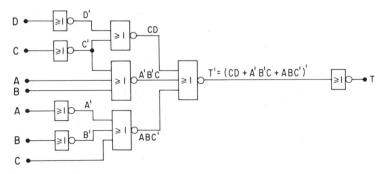

Fig. 3.42. "1-method" solution for $T = CD + A'B'C + ABC'$.

where necessary, to supply these inverted inputs to each of the NOR gates. The final solution for the above example requires nine NOR gates. (We assume here that the input variables are only available in uninverted form. If the inverted inputs are already available, the four NOT gates in the previous solution are not required.)

The reader may believe that we are done, but actually we have only completed one-half of the job. The second half of the procedure consists of applying the 'O method'. This means that we again map the original function on the Karnaugh map, but this time we loop all 0s appearing on the map into cells. The rules for looping the 0s are identical to those for looping 1s. (1) Each zero must be covered at least once. (2) We want a minimum number of cells. (3) Each cell should be as large as possible. The result of the looping for this example is shown in Fig. 3.43. Since we have looped the 0s, the resulting sum-of-products expression represents T' rather than T, and we have

$$T' = A'C' + B'C' + ACD' + BCD'$$

Inverting gives

$$T = (A'C' + B'C' + ACD' + BCD')'$$

and this automatically places the function into the second standard form of the

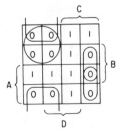

Fig. 3.43. "0-method" looping for $T = CD + A'B'C + ABC'$.

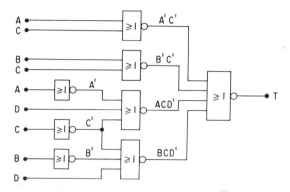

Fig. 3.44. "0-method" solution for $T = CD + A'B'C + ABC'$.

NOR function, so that we save the NOT gate needed at the right end of the "1-method" solution in Fig. 3.42.

Again, we begin the diagram at the right end and work backwards. The resulting solution, Fig. 3.44, requires only eight NOR gates instead of nine.

On the average, the 0-method solution requires one NOR gate less than the 1-method, since the final NOT gate is eliminated. However, the matter depends on the respective 1 and 0 locations on the Karnaugh map, and there are many cases where the 1-method gives better results. In general, both methods must be tried before making the final choice.

For an even more economical NOR-gate method, the reader is referred to Ref. (3.12). The method presented there is somewhat more difficult to master, but frequently results in a further reduction of the number of gates required.

In conclusion, it should be stressed that the method illustrated can also be used for NAND-gate circuits. In that case, the function to be implemented should be compared to the two standard forms of the NAND function

$$T = x_1 \,|\, x_2 \,|\, x_3 \cdots = (x_1 x_2 x_3 \cdots)' = x_1' + x_2' + x_3' + \cdots$$

and the more suitable form selected. Here, too, both the 1-method and 0-method solution must be tried before making the final choice. However, when using NAND gates, the 1-method solution, on the average, requires one gate less than the 0-method.

3.11   PRACTICAL EXAMPLES OF SWITCHING SYSTEMS

Two examples are presented in this section, which more or less summarize the material of this chapter.

Example 1. A generator in a certain plant is able to supply up to 100 kW power. This power is used to drive up to five difference machines, which have the following power requirements:

Machine A uses 51 kW
Machine B uses 40 kW
Machine C uses 20 kW
Machine D uses 20 kW
Machine E uses 10 kW

It is known for certain that machines B and C never run concurrently.

If too many machines are running concurrently, the generator overloads, and it becomes necessary to cut in an emergency generator by means of a signal T. Design a switching system using only NOR gates that will supply the required function for T.

SOLUTION. We begin by entering the data in a truth table. Since there are five input variables, the truth table should have 32 rows. However, studying the given data, we realize that, without machine A, the total load can never exceed 100 kW. In other words, if $A = 0$, then $T = 0$ regardless of the other four input variables. We can, therefore, eliminate variable A from the truth table and the resulting Karnaugh maps, which cuts their size down by one-half. The resulting truth table is shown in Fig. 3.45.

Figure 3.46 shows the data from the truth table entered into the Karnaugh map. Figure 3.46(a) shows the 1-method result as $T = ABD + ABE + ACDE$, and this function requires 10 NOR gates for its implementation. Figure 3.46(b) shows the 0-method result as $T' = A' + D'E' + B'C' + B'D' + B'E'$, and this requires only six NOR gates, as shown in Fig. 3.47. (*Note:* The various input variables A to E are supplied by switches that are actuated whenever the respective machine is turned *on*. If these switches should have double contacts (i.e., both NO and NC), they automatically supply the inverted input variable, so that the NOT gates assigned for this purpose are eliminated. In that case, both the 1-method and 0-method require only five NOR gates each.)

B (40)	C (20)	D (20)	E (10)	T
0	0	0	0	0
0	0	0	I	0
0	0	I	0	0
0	0	I	I	0
0	I	0	0	0
0	I	0	I	0
0	I	I	0	0
0	I	I	I	I
I	0	0	0	0
I	0	0	I	I
I	0	I	0	I
I	0	I	I	I
I	I	0	0	—
I	I	0	I	—
I	I	I	0	—
I	I	I	I	—

Imposible conditions

Fig. 3.45. Truth table for example 1 (assuming $A = 1$)

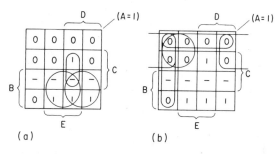

Fig. 3.46. Karnaugh maps for Example 1: (a) 1-method and (b) 0-method.

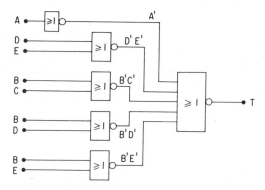

Fig. 3.47. NOR-gate implementation of the solution for Example 1 (0-method).

Example 2. A pump supplies water to a large reservoir, as shown in Fig. 3.48. The pump is actuated by switch S. The water level is sensed by two pressure switches A and B, set to 2 and 3 m, respectively (i.e., $A = 1$ if the level exceeds 2 m, and $B = 1$ if it exceeds 3 m). Two on–off valves C and D control the amount of water withdrawn from the tank, with C being the larger of the two. Each valve has a limit switch mounted on its stem, which transmits a signal when the valve is open.

To prevent the water level from dropping too low, the pump is to be actuated if any of the following should occur:

1. Water level has dropped below 2 m.
2. Water level is between 2 and 3 m, and valve C is open.
3. Water level is above 3 m, but both valves are open.

The function S for actuating the pump is to be derived.

SOLUTION. The three requirements specified can be translated directly into

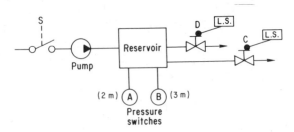

Fig. 3.48. Example 2.

the following Boolean expression, without the need for a truth table:

$$S = A' + AB'C + ABCD$$

This function is mapped in the Karnaugh map of Fig. 3.49, where all squares in the $A'B$ row receive "don't care" entries, because the water level obviously cannot be below 2 m and above 3 m at the same time. The resulting simplified function is function is

$$S = A' + B'C + CD$$

The logic implementation of this function is shown in Fig. 3.50. Implementing this function using only NOR gates (or NAND gates) is left as an exercise.

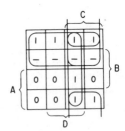

Fig. 3.49. Karnaugh map for Example 2.

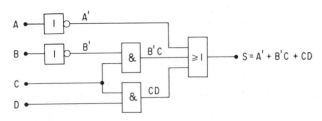

Fig. 3.50. Logic implementation of the solution for Example 2.

PROBLEMS

Simplify the following binary functions algebraically:

3.1. $(ab + (b' + c')' + a'c$

3.2. $w + w'xyz + w'xy'z' + w'xyz' + w'xy'z$

3.3. $xyz + xyz' + xy'z + xy'z' + x'z$

3.4. $(abcd + abc' + abd')'$

3.5. $(a + b + c)(a + b + c')$

Simplify the following binary functions using a Karnaugh map:

3.6. Repeat Problem 3.1. *Hint:* First open parentheses using De Morgan's theorem.

3.7. Repeat Problem 3.2.

3.8. Repeat Problem 3.3.

3.9. Repeat Problem 3.4. *Hint:* Invert equation and map the zeros.

3.10. $T = a'b'c'd' + a'b'cd + a'bc'd' + a'b'cd' + ab'cd + a'b'c'd$

3.11. $T = c'd' + ac' + a'b'c'd + abc + a'cd'$

3.12. $T = (a + bc)[c' + a'(b + c)]d'e' + (b + d)(b' + d') + b'c'de.$ *Hint:*   First open parentheses.

3.13. $T = A'B'C'E' + A'B'CD' + ABC'DE' + AB'C'E' + ABCD'E'$
$+ B'C'D'E + A'B'C'DE + CD'E$

3.14. $T = a'bc'd' + abc'd + ab'cd + ab'cd'$, with the following conditions being impossible: $a'b'c'd' = 1$, $a'b'cd' = 1$, $a'bc'd = 1$, and $abcd = 1$.

3.15. $T = A'B'C'D' + A'B'C'D + A'BCD' + ABC'D' + AB'C'$, with the following conditions being impossible: $A'BC' = 1$ and $ABC = 1$.

3.16. $T = A'B'C'D' + AB'CD' + ABCDE + ABC'D'F'$, with the following conditions being impossible: $AB'C'D' = 1$, $ABC'D = 1$, $A'BCD = 1$, and $A'B'CD' = 1$.

3.17. $T = AC'EFH' + ACEFG'H' + AC'DEF'H' + A'BDE'G'$
$+ A'B'CD'EFG'H' + ABCDE'FG'H$, with the following conditions being impossible: $B'CD'FGH' = 1$, $C'DGH = 1$, and $E'F'GH' = 1$.

3.18. Design a circuit producing the Exclusive-OR function using only NOR gates.

3.19. Design a circuit to implement the function of Problem 3.11 using only NOR gates.

3.20. Design a circuit to implement the following function using only NOR gates: $T = A'CDE' + A'B'DE + A'BCD + AB'CD'E$, with the following conditions being impossible: $AB = 1$, $BC'D = 1$, and $ACD'E' = 1$.

3.21. Repeat Problem 3.19, but using only NAND gates.

3.22. Show how NOT, AND, and OR gates can be obtained using only NAND gates.

REFERENCES

3.1. A. Marcovitz and J. Pugsley, *An Introduction to Switching System Design*, Wiley, New York, 1971.

3.2. A. Friedman, *Logical Design of Digital Systems*, Pitman, London, 1975.

3.3. D. Givone, *Introduction to Switching Theory*, McGraw-Hill, New York, 1970.

3.4. S. Caldwell, *Switching Theory and Logical Design*, Wiley, New York, 1958.

3.5. H. Nagle, B. Carroll, and J. Irwin, *An Introduction to Computer Logic*, Prentice-Hall, Englewood Cliffs, NJ, 1975.

3.6. T. Kohonen, *Digital Circuits and Devices*, Prentice-Hall, Englewood Cliffs, NJ, 1972.

3.7. F. Hill and G. Peterson, *Introduction to Switching Theory and Logical Design*, Wiley, New York, 1968.

3.8. F. Fitch and J. Surjaatmadja, *Introduction to Fluid Logic*, McGraw-Hill/ Hemisphere Publ. Co., New York, 1978.

3.9. D. Zissos, *Logic Design Algorithms*, Oxford University Press, London and New York, 1971.

3.10. N. Morris, *Logic Circuits*, McGraw-Hill, New York, 1969.

3.11. D. Pessen, "Use of Karnaugh Maps to Simplify Boolean Functions of up to 12 Variables," *Seventh Cranfield Fluidics Conference*, Stuttgart, West Germany, 1975, Paper X2.

3.12. D. Pessen, "Design Method for Near-Optimal NOR Logic Circuits," *Fluidics Quarterly*, Vol. 9, No. 2, Apr. 1977, pp. 1–22.

CHAPTER 4

INDUSTRIAL SWITCHING ELEMENTS

In Chapter 3, logic gates and flip-flops were defined. These can be implemented in different ways, electrically or pneumatically. In this chapter, the more common types of switching elements available for industrial use are described under the following headings:

1. Electronic logic gates
2. Relays
3. Pneumatic valves
4. Pneumatic moving-part logic (MPL)
5. Fluidic elements

The chapter concludes with a comparison between these elements from the standpoint of cost, reliability, and convenience.

4.1 ELECTRONIC LOGIC GATES

Logic gates can be implemented with diodes, as shown in Fig. 4.1, where diodes provide AND and OR gates. However, such gates attenuate the voltage, and the resulting deterioration makes it undesirable to cascade several gates in series. Therefore, electronic logic gates commonly use transistors to amplify the signal back to a standard level. This is illustrated in Fig. 4.2, which shows one type of three-input NOR gate implemented with a simple n-p-n bipolar junction transistor.

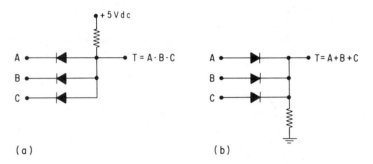

Fig. 4.1. Diode logic gates: (a) an AND gate and (b) an OR gate.

As long as all three inputs x, y and z are "LO" (i.e., low, or logic O), the transistor base (labeled B) is below zero voltage and the transistor does not conduct. As a result, output T connected to collector C is "HI" (logic 1), which is somewhat less than supply voltage V_{CC}. If any input goes HI, the transistor conducts, and the current flow from collector C to emitter E produces a voltage drop across the resistor sufficient to make output T go LO.

Single-transistor gates provide either the NOR or NAND function (and also the NOT function, which is really a single-input NOR). As shown in Chapter 3, all other basic functions (AND, OR, Exclusive-OR, flip-flops, etc.) can be constructed from NOR gates alone. Hence, gates providing these functions require more than one transistor.

4.1.1 Common Electronic Gate Families

There are a number of electronic gate families, and these are identified by often unfamiliar acronyms. Since this does not purport to be an electronics textbook, we limit ourselves here to listing and briefly describing these and some other acronyms. For a more detailed treatment, see Refs. (4.1)–(4.3).

The transistor circuits can be coupled in different ways, leading to the

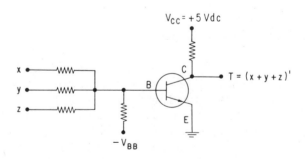

Fig. 4.2. NOR-gate circuit.

following families or systems:

RTL *(resistor-transistor logic)*
DTL *(diode-transistor logic)*
TTL *(transistor-transistor logic)*

Of these, TTL is today the most commonly used system.

Integrated circuits (ICs) contain a number of gates on a single chip, as compared to circuits built of discrete transistors and other components. When discussing ICs, we refer to

SSI *(small-scale integration,* with up to 12 gates per IC),

MSI *(medium-scale integration,* with up to 100 gates per IC)

LSI *(large-scale integration,* (with up to 2000 gates per IC)

Presently, we have reached VLSI *(very-large-scale integration),* XLSI *(extra-large-scale integration),* and the sky's the limit.

Conventional TTL integrated circuits have been largely replaced by LS-TTL *(low-power Schottky TTL)* elements. These employ so-called Schottky diodes to increase switching speed, and use considerably less power than the older TTL type.

ICs are frequently packaged in so-called DIP format, which stands for *"dual in-line package."* These are typically 8 by 20 mm large, with either 14 or 16 "pins" or leads, half on each side. Larger ICs with 48 pins or more also exist.

For building experimental circuits, so-called prototype boards are very useful. These have hundreds of holes arranged in matrix formation, spaced according to the standard distance between IC pins. To facilitate building circuits, certain rows or columns are internally connected as common *buses.* Circuit connections are made using 22- or 24 -gauge single-conductor wire, with stripped wire ends inserted into the appropriate holes. To indicate whether a given point is HI or LO, LEDs *(light-emitting diodes)* are commonly used.

Figure 4.3 shows schematics of several typical LS-TTL ICs. Most of these have 14 pins, two of which are used for connecting to the supply voltage V_{cc} (+ 5 V dc) and ground. This leaves 12 pins for gate connections. Obviously, the number of gates that can fit on the IC depends on gate *fan-in,* that is, the number of inputs. Since each NOT gate (also called an *inverter*) requires only two connections, the SN74LS04 chip contains six such gates. Each two-input gate requires three connections, leaving room for only four such gates per IC. Similarly, one IC can accommodate 3 three-input gates, or 2 four-input gates. The reader will note that the gate symbols used on these diagrams are of the MIL type; see Fig. 3.26.

The reader should learn how to interpret the alphanumeric designation printed on ICs. A typical designation might read SN74LS04N. The letters SN (sometimes left off) followed by 74 or 54 indicate the TTL family, with 74

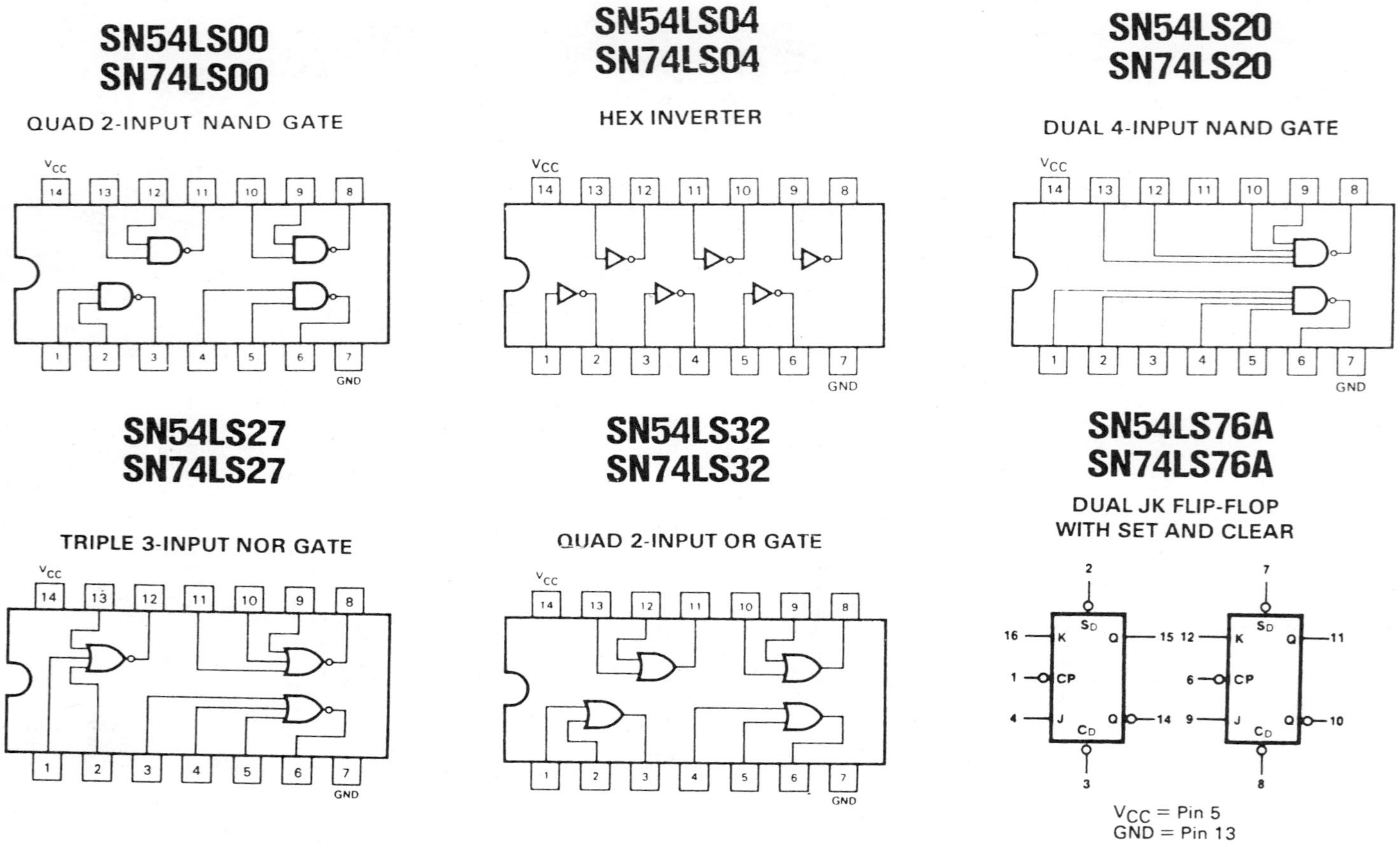

Fig. 4.3. Typical LS-TTL integrated circuits. (Copyright of Motorola, Inc. Used by permission.)

representing normal industrial units, and 54, military specification units. The following LS indicates a low-power Schottky element. The final two or three digits are the important ones, since they define the specific IC. The final letter N represents a plastic case, whereas a C represents a ceramic. There are usually other letters or numbers printed on the unit, but these indicate manufacturer and production series, and are of little interest to the user. If the letters LS are missing (e.g., SN7404N), the unit is of the older TTL type (i.e., not low-power Schottky). The reader should be able to pick out the important two or three digits (04 in this example) that indicate the type of IC (hex inverter, in this case).

54LS-series ICs can function in an extended temperature range from − 55 to + 125°C, as compared to 0 to 75°C for ordinary 74LS-series ICs. Since electronic power supplies often emit considerable heat, poorly ventilated instrument cases can have considerable temperature buildup. Therefore, 54LS-series ICs are preferable for heavy industrial use, in spite of their higher cost.

The supply voltage V_{cc} for all TTL ICs is + 5.0 V dc, with a 0.25 V tolerance for 74LS-series units (0.5 V for 54LS). (Connecting more than + 7 V to the V_{cc} pin, or interchanging V_{cc} and ground connections, is a sure way of instantly ruining the IC.) Gate outputs typically range from 0.25 to 0.35 V for LO and 2.5 to 3.5 V for HI outputs. A gate input is considered LO if it is below 0.8 V, and HI if above 2.0 V.

The output-current capacity of TTL gates is highly asymmetrical. Although exact values vary (see the manufacturer's spec sheet), a typical LS gate can sink an output current of about 8 mA in the LO state, whereas the source output current at HI is only 0.4 mA.

Two improved LS series have been introduced in recent years. One is the "advanced low-power Schottky" series, designated by the acronym ALS instead of LS. They are slightly faster than LS units and use only half the power. The second series is termed FAST TTL, designated by the letter F instead of LS (e.g., 74F04). These are faster yet, but at a cost of increased power consumption. These characteristics are:

	Regular TTL	LS	ALS	FAST
Average propagation delay (nsec)	14	9	7	3.7
Power/gate (quiescent) (mW)	10	2	1	5.5

The increased speed of the ALS and FAST series is important in computing devices, but of no significance in most industrial control systems, whose response time is measured in milliseconds or in seconds rather than nanoseconds. There is, therefore, little point in buying more expensive ALS or F units for most industrial applications.

Finally, a completely different IC family should be mentioned, called CMOS (*complementary metal-oxide semiconductor*). These are based on FETs (*field-effect transistors*), rather than bipolar transistors. CMOS elements enjoy several important advantages. First, their power consumption is of the order of

0.001 mW per gate (i.e., three orders of magnitude less than for TTL gates). This feature makes them especially suitable for battery-operated circuits. Second, supply voltage is not critical, and can vary from 3 to 15 V dc. Third, CMOS gates are much less sensitive to electrical noise than TTL gates, with noise immunity as high as 45% of supply voltage. Their drawbacks: CMOS devices are generally much slower, and they are easily damaged by static electricity. They must, therefore, be handled with great care, especially in low-humidity environments.

4.1.2 Programmable Logic Devices (PLDs)

Fairly complex circuits can, of course, be manufactured as medium- or large-scale integrated circuits. However, custom-made ICs have high development costs and are thus not justified unless large quantities are required. A good way to obtain semicustomized ICs inexpensively is with so-called PLDs (*programmable logic devices*), which are fuse-programmable chips. These chips, mostly belonging to the LS-TTL family, contain a large array of programmable gates connected by microscopic fused links. These fuses can be selectively blown using a special programming unit, thus implementing any complex logic function.

PLDs include PAL (*programmable array logic*), FPLAs (*field-programmable logic arrays*), and PROM (*programmable read-only-memory*). The PAL system, described in detail in Ref. (4.4), uses a programmable AND-gate array, with the AND gates connected to a fixed OR-gate array. In the FPLA system, both AND-gate and OR-gate arrays are programmable, which provides greater flexibility, but makes the programming procedure more complicated. In both systems, chips are also available with NOR or XOR gates, or with the OR-gate outputs connected to D flip-flops so that complete sequential systems can be included on one chip.

To ease the task of programming PLDs, a number of software packages are available for personal computers; see Refs. (4.5) and (4.6). These convert the Boolean equations to be implemented into the data fed to the programming unit. Some also facilitate testing the programmed chip. For several articles on PAL systems, see Ref. (4.7).

4.1.3 Input/Output (I/O) Modules

As stated in Section 4.1.1, typical logic ICs have a HI output of 2.5 to 3.5 V dc, and output currents of 0.4 to 8 mA. While such outputs can serve as inputs to other ICs or even to microcomputers, they are obviously unable to actuate industrial equipment. Therefore, input/output (I/O) modules are needed to interface the electronic logic circuit with the outside world.

The purpose of input modules is to accept electric signals (either ac or dc) from outside equipment (sensors, switches, relay contacts, etc.), and convert them to binary signals suitable for TTL or CMOS circuits. The modules are usually self-contained encapsulated units, and contain three sections, as shown in Fig. 4.4. In the first, the binary input passes through a transient-protection, or arc suppression, circuit (see Fig. 2.4) to prevent damage due to large voltage spikes produced when inductive loads are switched off. The circuit also filters out electrical noise that could falsely trigger the logic system.

The input and output sections of the module are coupled by a so-called *optoisolator*, or *optical coupler*, which contains a light-emitting diode (LED) and a photodiode or phototransistor. The LED transforms the HI input voltage into a light beam that strikes the photodiode. The latter, coupled to a transistor, produces a voltage signal sent to the third, or output, section. Since the optical coupler is an enclosed unit, it is unaffected by stray light. The coupler gives complete electric isolation between the input and output sections, hence, the name optoisolator. This is important to prevent high voltages that might appear at the input from damaging the logic circuit or microcomputer connected to the module. Typical isolation breakdown voltages of optical couplers are several thousand volts. For further discussion of optical couplers, see Refs. (4.8) and (4.9).

The third, or output, section of the input module usually consists of an additional transistor to convert the signal to the required logic level. Input modules are commercially available for various types of input voltages (ac or dc) and output voltage levels.

The function of output modules is to accept logic HI signals from an electronic circuit or microcomputer and convert them to a voltage and current large enough to drive an outside load. In most output modules, the logic signal is connected to an optical coupler, which, in turn, drives a so-called solid-state relay (see Section 4.2.3).

As with input modules, output modules are available for various output voltages. In ac output modules, the optical coupler usually drives a triac or a dual SCR (*silicon-controlled rectifier*). The dc output modules commonly make use of power transistors. All output modules must be protected by transient-protection devices (either internal or external), especially when switching inductive loads.

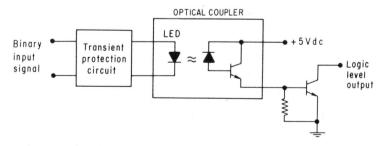

Fig. 4.4. Input module using an optical coupler.

For further discussion of I/O modules, see Section 10.2.3. For a list of manufacturers of I/O modules and of solid-state relays, see pages 112 and 121 of Ref. (4.10).

A fairly recent development is the inclusion of a solid-state switch in a logic IC. This combination is called a PIC (*power integrated circuit*), and it eliminates the need for discrete output modules; see Refs. (4.11) and (4.12). However, the use of PICs is not without problems; see Ref. (4.13).

4.2 RELAYS

There are three basic relay types: Electromechanical relays, reed relays, and solid-state relays. Relays are used for two purposes: as logic switching elements (i.e., control relays), or as current or voltage amplifiers (i.e., power relays). Both applications are discussed here.

4.2.1 Electromechanical Relays

Electromechanical relays (EMRs) consist of an electromagnetic coil and core designed to pull in an armature against a spring (i.e., basically a solenoid), and a number of electrical contacts. The armature is connected to the contacts so that all switch simultaneously when the coil is energized. A typical relay construction is shown in Fig. 4.5.

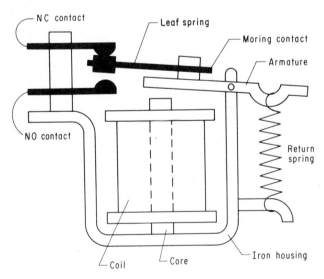

Fig. 4.5. An electromechanical relay.

Solid-state relays (Section 4.2.3) appeared more than two decades ago, and the demise of the EMR has been predicted ever since. Surprisingly, the opposite has occurred. Though, percentagewise, EMRs have lost in relation to solid-state relays, their absolute sales figures have increased steadily. While their use as logic elements is declining, they are being employed in increasing numbers for load handling, that is, as interface elements between electronic logic circuits (whether ICs, microcomputers, or programmable controllers) and the outside devices or loads that the former must control. It is exactly because of the electronics revolution that complex automation systems have become practical and common, and this has widened the base for EMR applications.

Relay contacts are either normally open (NO) or normally closed (NC). The term "normally" refers to the state in which the coil is *not* energized. Relays can have many independent contacts, some NO and others NC, and each contact can be used in a different circuit for a different task. When the coil is energized, all NO contacts belonging to that relay close, whereas all NC contacts open. Relay contacts can be used to implement any logic function, with contacts in series producing the AND function, and parallel contacts, the OR function. The design of relay circuits is discussed in detail in Chapter 5. Relays can also implement RS flip-flops (see Fig. 5.3) for use in sequential systems.

As explained in Section 5.1, relay circuits are usually drawn in the form of so-called *ladder diagrams*. In these, the relay coil and its associated contacts are drawn separately, using the symbols shown in Fig. 4.6. The relay-coil symbol is a circle, containing an identifying number (4, in this example), and the letters CR (standing for "control relay"). All contacts belonging to this relay are labeled 4-CR, no matter how many there are or where they may be connected. (Sometimes, the identification is written CR4 or R4 rather than 4-CR.)

Relays can be purchased with anywhere from a single contact (designated SPST, for *single-pole single-throw*), to as many as 20 contacts. While relay costs, of course, increase with the number of contacts, this relationship is not linear, since most of the costs can be attributed to the coil, armature, linkage, and relay case. Thus, a relay with six contacts typically costs only slightly more than one with four.

In most relays with multiple contacts, these are arranged in the double-throw (also called the "changeover" or "transfer") configuration, as shown in Fig. 4.6(d), where an NO and NC contact have a common pole. Such relays are

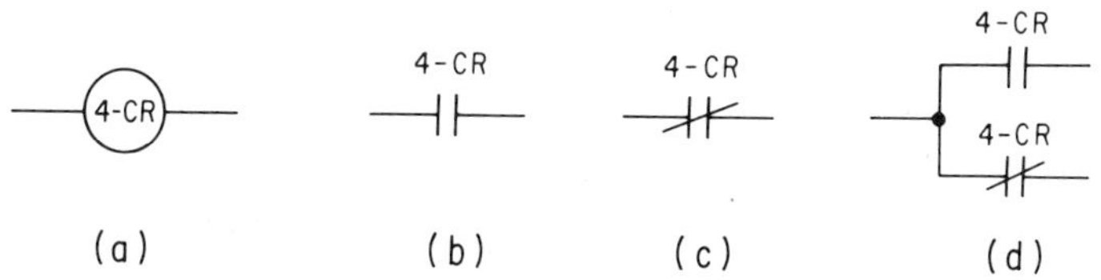

Fig. 4.6. Relay symbols: (a) coil, (b) NO contact, (c) NC contact, and (d) changeover contact.

designated as SPDT, DPDT (i.e., *double-pole double-throw*), 3PDT, 4PDT, etc., depending on the number of poles.

The many available contact configurations are defined by letters. Thus, "Form A" represents a SPST NO contact; "Form B" a SPST NC contact; "Form C," a SPDT contact of type break-before-make; "Form D," a SPDT contact of type make-before-break, and so on. (For an explanation of these terms, see discussion of limit-switch contacts in Section 2.2.1.) For a complete listing going up to "Form Z," see the table on page 200 of Ref. (4.14) or Ref. (4.15).

Relays are available for different coil-actuation voltages, with the common ones being 5, 12, and 24 V dc (for actuation by electronic circuits), and 24, 115, and 230 V ac. There is, of course, no connection between coil voltage and the type of current flowing through the contacts. Therefore, apart from their use as logic elements, relays can be used as "power relays" for several other purposes:

1. Relays provide complete electrical isolation between the control signal (i.e., coil) and output (i.e., contacts).

2. Relays permit a small voltage to control a large one. For instance, an electronic circuit could actuate a 5 V dc coil with the contacts transmitting 115 V ac.

3. Relays act as current amplifiers. For instance, a tiny limit switch with limited current-carrying capacity can actuate a relay coil whose contacts transmit a current driving a large motor.

4. By using a multicontact relay, one input signal can control many different loads (possibly with different voltages for each load).

Relays are available in a tremendous variety of designs and sizes. Reference (4.16) presents a table listing almost 90 relay manufacturers, indicating the types offered by each. In selecting relays, the following points should be considered:

(a) *Size.* This refers to contact-current rating. So-called general-purpose light-duty relays normally have a contact rating of 5 to 15 A and their contact configuration is typically 2 Form C (i.e., DPDT) or 3 Form C (i.e., 3PDT). It should be realized that current capacity is less for dc than for ac. When dc currents are interrupted, arcing occurs, which tends to erode the contacts. This is especially severe with inductive loads, so that arc-quenching circuits (see Fig. 2.4) must be used. In ac circuits, arcing is no problem since the current goes through zero during each ac cycle, which extinguishes the arc. If the relay actuates incandescent lamps, the contacts must also be derated—even though ac is switched—since the inrush current (with cold filament) is about 10 times the steady-state current. General-purpose relays can be expected to last at least 100,000 operations at rated load. While this represents long life if the load is switched once an hour, it is very little for switching frequencies of once per second.

For higher current ratings and longer life, heavy-duty "machine-tool relays" are available. At the other end of the spectrum there are miniature relays suitable for installation on printed-circuit boards, either in combination with electronic circuits, or on their own as replacement for more bulky and costly relay panels; see Refs. (4.17)–(4.19). Some of these are especially designed for use with automatic insertion equipment on automated manufacturing lines. A typical subminiature or "flatback" relay is about 10 mm high, takes up the space of a 16-pin IC on the circuit board, has SPDT or DPDT contacts rated at 1 A, and may cost $2 in large quantities.

(b) *Terminals.* For general-purpose relays, the terminals are either soldered, or of the plug-in type for easy replacement. Heavy-duty relays usually have quick-connect wire lugs. Miniature relays are usually soldered.

(c) *Contact Materials.* There is no universal contact material best for all applications. Contacts made of gold alloys, or gold alloy working against a palladium contact, are usually used for low-current switching or for "dry circuits." (These are circuits in which the contacts open or close while there is no current flow.) While the condition of low-current switching or dry circuits may appear ideal, this is not so: the contact resistance can become quite high, since there is no arcing to penetrate and remove organic condensates or oxides adhering to the contact surfaces. For higher currents (0.5 A or more), gold-alloy contacts are no longer suitable because of erosion caused by arcing, and silver alloys or silver-cadmium oxide are frequently used.

For more information on relay selection, see Refs. (4.15) and (4.20)–(4.23).

After the appropriate relay has been selected, it must be used properly. For example, coil voltage should be between 85 to 110% of rated voltage. Too high a coil voltage produces overheating, and makes the armature slam with excessive force, causing mechanical wear and contact bounce. Too low a coil voltage, surprisingly, also produces overheating, because the armature may not seat completely, so that the coil current does not reach its lower seated value. In addition, there may be arcing caused by poor contact closure or contact chatter. For a relay-troubleshooting table, see Ref. (4.23).

Another point to be considered is transient suppression. Here we must distinguish between coil and contacts. The coil represents an inductive load, and produces a high-voltage spike when switched off. If a dc coil is energized by electronic elements, these can burn out due to such transients unless a transient-suppression method is used. The available methods were listed in Fig. 2.4, but not all are equally suitable for this application, since some can reduce relay speed and life expectancy considerably. The relay contacts themselves may also have to switch dc inductive loads (e.g., motors), and have to be protected from high-voltage transients and the resulting arcing. For further discussion, see Refs. (4.20) and (4.24).

A factor that may or may not be important is switching speed. The time required to switch the relay *on* is called the *operate time*, and equals the *waiting time* (time required for magnetic flux to build up sufficiently to start the armature movement) plus the *transient time* (the time required to complete the armature movement and cause contact closure). The operate time depends on temperature and coil voltage, and typically ranges from 2 msec for subminiature relays to 30 msec for large relays. The *release time* is the time required to switch the relay *off*. It also consists of the waiting time plus the transient time, but is generally less than the operate time, since the flux decays faster than it builds up, and since the spring in the relay mechanism resists switching *on* but aids switching *off*. The operate and release times are of importance in sequential-system design, since they are the reason for the so-called *unstable states* discussed in Section 5.5.2.

Relays have undergone steady improvement during the past two decades. Apart from improved materials, design, and packaging, many new features are available, such as special relay sockets, and relays with status-indicator lamps, press-to-test buttons, and label holders. Because of the increasing use of relays with electronic circuits, the stress is toward relays switching smaller currents and voltages, and coils operating with less power (0.1 W) suitable for direct transistor actuation. For surveys of new relay designs, see Refs. (4.16), (4.19), and (4.25)–(4.28).

4.2.2   Reed Relays

Reed relays are closely related to the reed switches discussed in Section 2.2.3. However, while reed switches are actuated by a moving permanent magnet, reed relays contain several reed capsules actuated by one stationary electromagnet. Thus, the armature and mechanical linkage in regular EMRs are eliminated, and the contacts are replaced by sealed reed tubes or capsules.

Reed relays can be extremely compact, with its magnet and up to 12 contacts encapsulated in a single epoxy unit designed for printed-circuit mounting. Typical life expectancy is up to 10^8 operations, the contact rating up to 1 A, and the operate time up to 0.5 msec. To increase current capacity, mercury-wetted reed contacts are frequently used, which eliminate contact bounce and arcing, but require correct mounting orientation.

For further discussion of reed relays, see Ref. (4.14). Several electronic drive circuits for energizing reed-relay coils, including transient suppression, are described in Ref. (4.29). For a listing of reed-relay manufacturers, see Ref. (4.16).

4.2.3   Solid-State Relays (SSRs)

Solid-state relays (SSRs) are invariably compared with EMRs and reed relays. However, it should be realized that most SSRs can only switch one circuit, that is, they are equivalent to a SPST relay. Thus, SSRs are not suitable as logic devices for implementing switching functions, but only as output elements interfacing logic circuits to outside loads. Hence, SSRs should only be compared to single-contact power relays. (Multicontact SSRs exist, but are expensive.)

With this limitation in mind, SSRs have the following advantages:

1. SSRs switch much faster than EMRs, and do so quietly.
2. If properly applied, the life expectancy of SSRs is indefinite. Switching is clean (no contact bounce and no arcing), and thus there is no contact degradation.
3. For ac switching, SSRs can be designed to always switch at zero current (using "zero-detecting circuits"), so that radio-frequency interference (RFI) is eliminated.
4. SSRs can be switched directly by low-power electronic devices, such as TTL circuits.
5. SSRs are resistant to shock and vibration that might falsely switch EMRs.

However, the drawbacks of SSRs are just as numerous:

1. Their initial cost is greater than that of EMRs (although they may be cheaper in the long run because of longer life expectancy).
2. They can only switch one circuit each (i.e., they are equivalent to a SPST contact). Thus, if several devices must be switched together, multiple SSRs must be used, which multiplies the cost.
3. They are not good as positive shutoff devices, since they have a leakage current of several milliamps in their *off* state. (Open relay contacts, by comparison, have practically infinite resistance.)
4. Whereas EMRs have a contact resistance of only a few milliohms, SSRs inherently have a junction voltage drop of about 1 V. Depending on the current to be transmitted, this generates heat, and may necessitate use of a heat sink.
5. They are not suitable at high ambient temperatures (above 125 °C).
6. SSRs are susceptible to being turned *on* by extraneous transient signals.
7. SSRs usually fail in the *on* state, which may be dangerous.
8. The application of SSRs is not as straightforward as that of EMRs and requires a number of precautions; see Refs. (4.30)–(4.33).

In addition, service personnel often have personal preferences, claiming that they can tell whether a mechanical relay is working by watching or listening, something impossible with SSRs.

For further discussion and comparison between SSRs and EMRs, see Refs. (4.14) and (4.34). For a listing of SSR manufacturers, see Refs. (4.10) and (4.16).

4.3 PNEUMATIC VALVES

A pneumatic control system consists of a compressed-air supply, a control circuit with either pneumatic valves or with *moving-part logic* (MPL) elements, pneumatic sensors, and, finally, pneumatic actuators such as cylinders, rotary actuators, or air motors. Pneumatic actuators are described in Sections 1.4 and 1.5, and pneumatic sensors in Section 2.3. Compressed-air supplies and pneumatic valves are described in this section. The discussion is only intended as a brief introduction to industrial pneumatics. For an in-depth treatment of pneumatics, the reader is referred to Ref. (4.35), or any of the textbooks referenced in Chapter 7.

4.3.1 Compressed-Air Supplies

Compressed-air supplies comprise a compressor switched *on* and *off* by a pressurestat, an air tank, and an air-service, or so-called FRL, unit, whose letters stand for (air) *filter*, (pressure) *regulator* (with pressure gage), and lubricator. In large installations, the compressed air is also dried to minimize moisture condensation in the circuit.

For information on air supplies, see Refs. (4.35)–(4.38). Air compressors and their selection are described in Refs. (4.39) and (4.40). Filtering and drying the compressed air, an important subject often neglected, are discussed in Refs. (4.41)–(4.45).

Since the pressurestat turning the compressor *on* and *off* permits the tank pressure to fluctuate between fairly wide limits, a pressure regulator is needed to supply a more or less constant outlet pressure in the air-supply line. For a description of pressure regulators, see Refs. (4.35), (4.40), and (4.43).

The function of the lubricator is to inject a fine oil mist into the air supply (at a rate of about one oil drop per minute), which serves to prevent corrosion and lubricate sliding surfaces in valves, cylinders, and air motors. Since this oil is eventually exhausted to atmosphere, it tends to contaminate the work environment, which at best is a nuisance and at worst is a health hazard. OSHA regulations strictly limit the amount of oil mist permitted in the work environment. Apart from this, many processes such as manufacture of food products, pharmaceuticals, textiles, paper, and electronics cannot tolerate even small amounts of oil contamination. Hence, the tendency toward oilless pneumatics has been growing, with many manufacturers offering oilless compressors, and valves, air motors, and cylinders designed to operate on dry air; see Ref. (4.46).

4.3.2 Units of Pressure

Because of the large number of units of pressure, it may be useful to discuss them briefly. The classic pressure unit in English-speaking countries has been the *psi* (lb/in.^{2}), with atmospheric pressure at sea level equalling 14.7 psi. This unit, however, is being replaced by metric units. The official SI-system metric pressure unit is the *pascal* (written Pa), defined as $1 \, N/m^2$. The pascal, however, is inconveniently small, since $1 \, psi = 6897 \, Pa$. For this reason, industry is reluctant to adopt the pascal and prefers the *bar*, which equals 100,000 Pa. Since the bar almost equals atmospheric pressure ($1 \, bar = 0.985$ atmospheres $= 14.5 \, psi$), it is easy to visualize and convenient to use.

The typical pressure range for industrial pneumatics is from 4 to 10 bar (60 to 150 psi). Unless higher piston forces are required, the air-supply pressure is usually regulated to 5 bar, since this pressure is obtainable with single-stage air compressors.

Very low pressures are often measured with manometers, using units of "head" or water-column height. Thus, $1 \, bar = 1000 \, cm \, H_2O = 400 \, in. \, H_2O$, and $1 \, psi = 28 \, in. \, H_2O$.

4.3.3 Pneumatic Valve Symbols

The pneumatic valves described in this section are commonly called *directional-control valves*. These are *on–off* valves (i.e., with each flow path either completely open or closed), whose function is to control direction of air flow in the pneumatic circuit. (Similar directional-control valves are used in industrial hydraulics, but the discussion here is limited to pneumatics.)

Most directional-control valves have either two or three discrete positions. Figure 4.7 (a), for example, shows the international (ISO) or United States (ANSI) standard symbol for a three-connection two-position valve, which is called a 3/2 valve from now on. The two rectangles represent the two discrete positions of the valve. Since the connecting tubing is drawn in this case attached to the left rectangle, this means that the valve is presently in the left position.

There are three connections, or valve ports, labeled A, B, and C, respectively. As long as the valve remains in the left position, there is a flow path between ports A and C, while port B is blocked. When this valve is shifted to its right position, port A is blocked, while ports B and C are connected. (The reader should visualize the two rectangles sliding to the left, with the connecting tubing on the drawing remaining stationary.) A valve of this type is commonly called a "three-way valve," but this terminology is illogical and confusing, since there are only two different flow paths or "ways." Hence, this terminology is not used here.

The arrowheads shown on the symbol are optional. They indicate direction of air flow, to help interpret the circuit diagram. Since these arrowheads depend

(a)

(b)

Fig. 4.7. Directional-control valve symbols: (a) a 3/2 valve, and (b) a 5/2 valve.

on how the valve is utilized, they are usually not shown in manufacturers' catalogs.

Figure 4.7(b) shows the symbol for a five-connection two-position (or 5/2) valve. In the left position, ports A and D are connected, and likewise ports B and E, while port C is blocked. In the right position, port A is blocked, while port B is connected to D, and port C to E. Such a valve is commonly called a "four-way valve." (Valves of the 4/2 type also exist, but are used mainly in hydraulic systems. Manufacturers of pneumatic valves normally supply a fifth port, since this provides greater flexibility.)

Certain manufacturers and authors advocate the use of different symbols. Figure 4.8, for example, shows the so-called *hinge-block symbols* for the valves of Fig. 4.7. While hinge-block symbols may appear simpler for many valves, they are awkward for representing, for example, three-position valves. There are also "pneumatic ladder-diagram" symbols that enjoy a certain popularity, and these are described in Section 7.8. Without discussing the relative merits of different symbols, the ISO symbols are used here, since these are accepted as the international standard.

In addition to the rectangles showing the valve positions, the symbol must also indicate how the valve is shifted. Symbols for common actuation methods are shown in Fig. 4.9. Most of these constitute local actuation, but three of them—the solenoid, pilot pressure, and pilot signal amplifier—constitute remote actuation.

Figure 4.9 shows actuation symbols for only one valve position. Actually, the opposite actuation must also exist, because otherwise the valve could never shift back to its original position. Various combinations are possible here. Thus, Fig. 4.10(a) shows a valve with pilot-pressure actuation and a return spring. If the pilot line is under pressure, the spring force is overcome and the valve is in its right position. (Typically, a pilot pressure of over 2 bar is required to overcome the spring force.) If the pilot line is vented to atmosphere, the spring returns the valve to its left position.

In Fig. 4.10(b), a solenoid is substituted for the pilot line, permitting electrical rather than pneumatic remote actuation. In Figs. 4.10(c) and (d), there are no return springs. Instead, the valve is shifted back by activating the opposite pilot line or solenoid, respectively. If neither pilot line nor solenoid is actuated, the valve remains in its previous position because of internal friction, that is, the valve has "mechanical memory." Therefore, such valves are also called "memory valves." If both opposing pilot lines or solenoids are actuated together, we have

(a)

(b)

Fig. 4.8. Hinge-block symbols for (a) a 3/2 valve, and (b) a 5/2 valve.

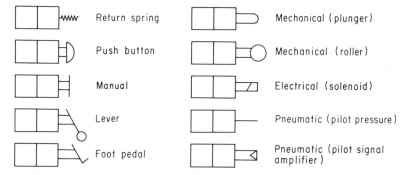

Return spring	Mechanical (plunger)
Push button	Mechanical (roller)
Manual	Electrical (solenoid)
Lever	Pneumatic (pilot pressure)
Foot pedal	Pneumatic (pilot signal amplifier)

Fig. 4.9. Common valve-actuation methods.

trouble: the valve receives contradictory signals with an undefined outcome. In the case of opposing solenoid signals, the solenoids oppose each other, resulting in overheating and likely failure.

As shown in Chapters 5 and 7, it is generally easier to design control circuits using valves without a return spring, since a short pressure or electrical pulse is sufficient to shift the valve. Valves with a return spring, on the other hand, require sustained pilot or solenoid signals to maintain their position, which makes circuit design more difficult.

Figure 4.11 shows some additional pneumatic symbols, and most should be self-explanatory. While there is a specific air-compressor symbol, this is seldom used, since the "air-supply" symbol already includes a compressor, a tank, and an FRL unit, as detailed in Section 4.3.1. This air-supply symbol might appear many times on a circuit diagram, denoting all points connected to the common air supply. The check-valve symbol represents a one-directional valve. Flow from right to left is prevented, since the ball is pushed against the valve seat, thus blocking the passage. Flow from left to right, however, is possible, since the ball is pushed to the right (against a weak spring).

The shuttle valve has a free-floating ball or disk able to seal either of two seats. If either input A or B is pressurized, the ball seals the opposite seat, and output C is HI. If both A and B are HI, the ball position is undefined, but in any case C is HI. If both A and B are LO, the ball position is again undefined, but the air at C is vented through at least one of the two inlets and thus is LO. Hence, the shuttle valve is a pneumatic OR gate with Boolean function $C = A + B$.

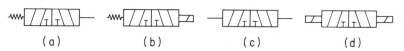

(a)   (b)   (c)   (d)

Fig. 4.10. Four different valve-actuation combinations. (a) Pilot line and return spring, (b) solenoid and return spring, (c) double pilot line, and (d) double solenoid.

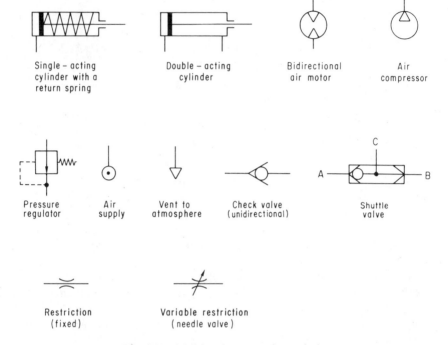

Single – acting cylinder with a return spring	Double – acting cylinder	Bidirectional air motor	Air compressor

Pressure regulator	Air supply	Vent to atmosphere	Check valve (unidirectional)	Shuttle valve

Restriction (fixed)	Variable restriction (needle valve)

Fig. 4.11. Additional pneumatic symbols.

4.3.4 Simple Cylinder-Actuation Circuits

To illustrate use of the pneumatic valve symbols, and to enable the reader to gain some facility in understanding pneumatic diagrams, several simple circuits are shown. In Fig. 4.12, when the push-button valve is pressed, the pilot line of the 3/2 cylinder-actuating valve is pressurized. As a result, air pressure reaches the left cylinder side, and the piston extends. When the push button is released, the valves return to the position shown, and the piston retracts. Note that it is customary to draw all elements in their initial position, that is, before the circuit is actuated.

Figure 4.13 shows a circuit with a double-acting cylinder. Since this cylinder has two inlet lines, an actuating valve with two outlet ports (5/2 or 4/2 valve) is required. This 5/2 valve is labeled VA, and its two pilot lines $A+$ and $A-$, respectively indicating the result produced when each is pressurized.

At the beginning of the sequence, all elements are as shown on the figure. When Start is pressed, pilot line $A+$ is pressurized, shifting valve VA so as to activate its right rectangle. This pressurizes the left piston side, causing the cylinder to extend. When the Start button is released and pilot line $A+$ is vented, valve VA remains in its new position, as explained previously. At the end of the cylinder stroke, the piston rod actuates limit valve a_2, which pressurizes pilot line $A-$ of valve VA, causing the cylinder to retract automatically. Note

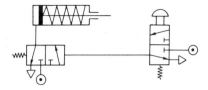

Fig. 4.12. Actuating circuit for a single-acting cylinder.

that if the operator should keep pressing the Start button, both pilot lines $A+$ and $A-$ are pressurized, providing contradictory signals. Hence, valve VA does not shift back, and cylinder A remains extended until the operator decides to release the Start button.

The purpose of the needle valves in the two vent lines of valve VA is to restrict cylinder speed. The left needle valve controls cylinder speed during retraction, and the right one does so during extension. Thus, speed can be adjusted independently for each direction. The needle valve restricts the cylinder exhaust, so that back pressure builds up and restricts the piston speed. While this method does not provide accurate speed control, it is useful where cylinder speed must be restricted to prevent damage to delicate objects.

The circuit of Fig. 4.14 is intended to move the cylinder back and forth automatically, with the option of stopping the cylinder motion at any point. Upon giving the Run signal, the cylinder motion should resume where it was interrupted.

In order to stop the cylinder motion, a 5/3 valve is commonly used. Three-position valves have two pilot lines (or solenoids) and two centering springs. If no pilot line is pressurized, these springs place the valve into its center position, so that both cylinder inlet lines are sealed, stopping the cylinder motion. (*Note*: Due to air compressibility, the piston is not absolutely locked. For absolute locking, hydraulic cylinders must be used.) If either pilot line is pressurized, pilot pressure overcomes the spring forces, shifting the valve so that the cylinder continues moving. Note that the pilot pressures must be sustained signals, since three-position valves have no mechanical memory. The function of valve VB is to provide these sustained pilot signals.

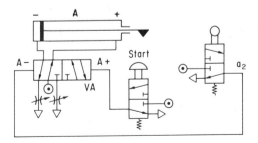

Fig. 4.13. Actuating circuit for a double-acting cylinder for the sequence START, $A+$, $A-$.

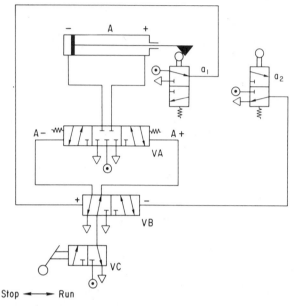

Fig. 4.14. Circuit for continuous cylinder cycling with a Stop possibility during a stroke.

Valve VC is manually operated, but without a return spring. Therefore, it has mechanical memory and always remains in its last position. As long as VC is at Stop, both pilot lines of valve VA are vented, stopping the cylinder motion. When VC is shifted to Run, air passes through valve VB into the appropriate pilot line of valve VA, so that cycling resumes. The reader should have no difficulty tracing the course of events on the figure.

5/3 valves come in several configurations. The most common are "closed-center" which is used in Fig. 4.14, and "open-center," which is shown in Fig. 4.15. In the latter, both cylinder sides are vented to atmosphere when the valve is at the center position, while the air supply is blocked. This does not lock the piston and permits the operator to shift the piston rod manually to any desired position before resuming the sequence.

Two different "two-hand safety circuits" serve as final examples. These are used for actuating dangerous equipment such as punch presses, and they have two push buttons mounted sufficiently apart so that both cannot be reached with one hand. Both push buttons must be pressed simultaneously to actuate the

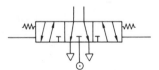

Fig. 4.15. Open-center 5/3 valve.

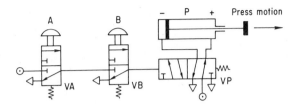

Fig. 4.16. Two-hand safety circuit.

press, and this forces the operator to withdraw both hands from the dangerous area before the press descends.

The problem sounds trivial, and can seemingly be solved by the simple circuit of Fig. 4.16. Two push-button valves VA and VB are connected in series, so that supply pressure can reach the pilot line of VP only if both push buttons are pressed simultaneously. Valve VP, in turn, actuates the cylinder, which represents the punch press. This circuit, however, is useless, because the operator, wanting to make things easier, might disable the safety feature by permanently tying down one of the push buttons with a piece of baling wire or with chewing gum. To prevent this, a number of more sophisticated circuits have been devised, in which the press does not work at all if one button is tied down. One of the best of these, taken from Ref. (4.47), is shown in Fig. 4.17.

If neither A nor B is pressed, the situation is as shown in the figure, with air reaching the shuttle valve and actuating valve VC. However, since pilot line P + is vented, the press is not operated.

If push buttons A and B are now pressed simultaneously, supply air flows through both VA and VB, reaching VC and pilot line P+, thus actuating the press. Note that the line with the restriction is now vented through valve VB. However, the restriction slows down the rate of venting, so that VC remains actuated until the air pressure has a chance to reach the other side of the shuttle valve, from pilot line P+. It should be obvious that there is a timing problem in this circuit. The time during which sufficient pressure remains to keep valve VC actuated until pressure can arrive at the right side of the shuttle valve depends on the size of the restriction and on the volume of air trapped in the tubing

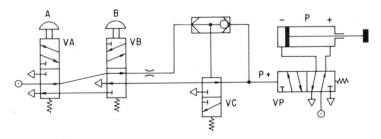

Fig. 4.17. Two-hand "no-tie-down" safety circuit.

between the pilot line of VC and the restriction. The restriction should be chosen to make this time at least 0.2 to 0.3 sec, so that the press operates even if the operator does not manage to press both buttons exactly at the same moment.

If either button is tied down, supply air reaches one of the two blocked input ports of valve VB, and thus cannot proceed. Pressing the second button afterwards does not help, since the pilot line of valve VC has, in the meantime, been vented through the restriction, so that VC blocks the supply air from reaching pilot line $P+$. To operate the press, both push buttons must first be released to reset the system, and then pressed together.

4.3.5   Obtaining Logic Functions from Pneumatic Valves

Figure 4.18 illustrates how basic logic gates can be implemented with pneumatic valves. The *INHIBITION* gate (mentioned in Chapter 3) is so called because a $B = 1$ signal "inhibits" output T from becoming 1. While an OR gate can be implemented by a 3/2 valve as shown, shuttle valves are generally preferred, since they cost about one-third as much. Note that all of the logic gates in Fig. 4.18 have a fan-in of only 2. If a larger fan-in is required, valves must be connected in series, as shown in Fig. 4.19.

To obtain an RS flip-flop, a 5/2 valve without a return spring is used, as shown in Fig. 4.20. The mechanical memory of the valve provides the flip-flop characteristics. Note that the valve is symmetrical. Hence, we can arbitarily define either pilot line as S and the other as R, but this determines which output must be labeled y and which y'.

To obtain more complex logic functions, the basic valve configurations shown here can be combined appropriately. However, a much more efficient method is described in Section 7.4.

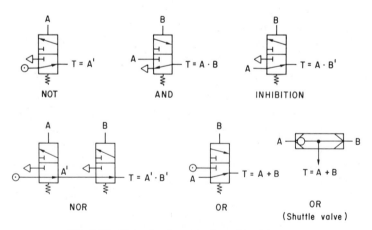

Fig. 4.18. Valve implementation of logic gates.

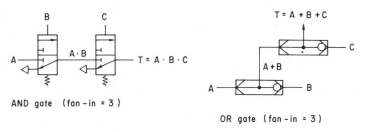

AND gate (fan-in = 3)

OR gate (fan-in = 3)

Fig. 4.19. AND and OR gates with a fan-in of 3.

4.3.6 Valve Construction

Most directional-control valves are of the spool-and-sleeve type. Figure 4.21 shows a 5/2 spool valve schematically. [Compare this to the symbol of Fig. 4.10(c).] Figure 4.21(a) shows the spool position if the last pilot line that has been pressurized was the P_1 line. As a result, there are flow paths between ports A and D, and between B and E, while port C is blocked. If pilot line P_2 is pressurized, the spool shifts to the left, see Fig. 4.21(b), with corresponding changes in flow paths.

To prevent air leakage across spool lands, O rings or other seals (not shown in figure) are generally used. These can either be installed in grooves machined in the spool lands, or in the sleeve. Certain manufacturers eliminate seals by using lapped spools and sleeves with very close clearances to minimize leakage. Such valves cost much more, but have very long life (10^8 cycles, with properly filtered air). Because of their low friction, they need very small actuating forces and have fast response (in the order of 3 msec).

A second type is the poppet valve, shown in Fig. 4.22. This is frequently used for limit valves and other mechanically actuated 3/2 valves. In the position shown, the outlet is vented. When the plunger is depressed, the upper poppet seat seals the passage between the outlet and vent, while the lower one opens the passage between the air supply and outlet. Since poppet valves have no sliding between spool and sleeve, friction is minimized and they are less sensitive to dirt. Also, a large flow passage is produced by small plunger movement, so that flow capacity and speed of response are high. Poppet valves, however, are not very practical for more complex valve configurations. Also, during plunger movement, the air supply is connected to the vent for a short period, which wastes compressed air and can also cause other problems. While poppet-valve designs

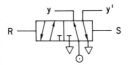

Fig. 4.20. RS flip-flop implemented by a 5/2 valve.

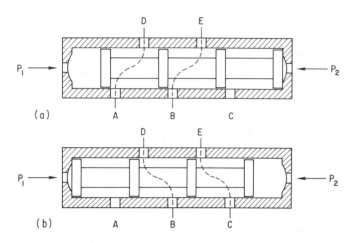

Fig. 4.21. Operation of a 5/2 spool valve.

avoiding this problem exist, these are more complicated and hence more expensive.

Directional-control valves come in a great variety of designs, often with special features. For example, some valves have override buttons so that the valve can be shifted manually, useful for circuit checking and troubleshooting. Some valves have visual indicators, showing valve position by means of small colored balls appearing in a window, as shown in Fig. 4.23. This feature is also a great circuit-checking aid. Some manufacturers, instead of providing built-in indicators, provide an extra threaded port into which an external indicator can be mounted. Some valves operate on oilless air (see the discussion in Section 4.3.1). One manufacturer, see Ref. (4.47), makes valves with plug-in sockets, which facilitates fast exchange, as shown in Figs. 4.23 and 4.24. The sockets interlock to form a solid basic structure, with the tube connections made from below. The circuit tubing is connected underneath the plug-in manifold. If

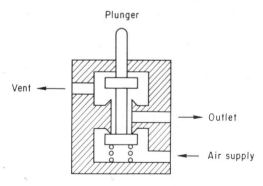

Fig. 4.22. Construction of a 3/2 poppet valve.

Fig. 4.23. A 3/2 directional-control valve, with position indicator and plug-in base. (Courtesy of Clippard Instrument Laboratory, Inc.)

multiples of the same circuit are needed, plastic circuit-manifold subplates can be used. All circuit interconnections are provided within the subplate, which reduces assembly time, avoids tubing errors, and makes for a neat compact circuit. (This technique is analogous to electronic printed circuits.)

For further discussion of valve construction, see Ref. (4.48). A detailed listing of valve manufacturers is found in Ref. (4.49).

4.3.7 Valve Sizing

Directional-control valves come in different sizes, such as 1/16″, 1/8″, 1/4″, and 1/2″, which refers to the flow-passage diameter. Both flow capacity and price increase with valve size.

Valves can be divided into three general classes, depending on the function of

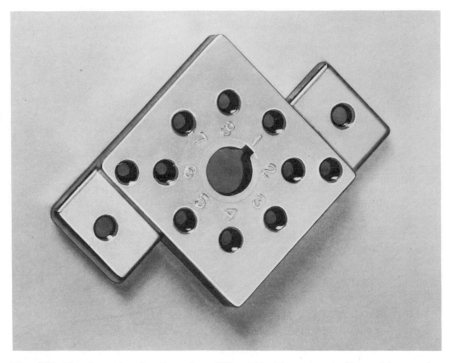

Fig. 4.24. Plug-in socket for the valve of Fig. 4.23. (Courtesy of Clippard Instrument Laboratory, Inc.)

the valve in the pneumatic circuit:

(a) Cylinder-actuating valves, which supply air to and drive the cylinder or air motor.
(b) Limit valves, which sense the piston position. Other sensor valves and manually operated valves can also be grouped together with limit valves.
(c) Control valves, which produce a certain control sequence.

Of these three, only cylinder-actuating valves have to transmit considerable air flow. Limit valves and control valves transmit pressure rather than air flow. Since they actuate pilot lines rather than cylinders, their outlet flow is minimal, depending on the volume of circuit tubing. Therefore, limit and control valves should be as small as possible, to reduce cost and mounting space. Many manufacturers supply special miniature valves for this purpose.

The cylinder-actuating valve must be chosen according to stroke, diameter, and the required speed of the cylinder. If this valve is too small, its low flow rate can limit piston speed seriously. Pneumatic valves are usually sized using the so-called C_V coefficient. A pneumatic valve is said to have $C_V = 1$ if it passes 1 gal/min of water at 1 psi pressure drop. The C_V coefficient of the valve should be stated in the manufacturer's catalog. For example, a typical miniature 1/16″ valve might have a $C_V = 0.03$, and a 1/8″ valve, a $C_V = 0.4$. (It should be stressed that the C_V depends not only on nominal valve size, but also on the design.) The approximate air flow through a valve can be calculated from

$$Q = 22.5 C_V [\Delta P (P_2)/T_1]^{1/2}$$

where

Q = flow [scfm] (i.e., at 14.7 psia and 68°F)

ΔP = pressure drop across the valve [psi]

P_2 = downstream pressure [psia]

For further discussions of valve sizing, see Refs. (4.35) and (4.50)–(4.52). The latter gives a table showing how valve size effects piston speed. For example, a 2″ diameter cylinder, under average conditions, has an estimated piston speed of 28 in./sec when actuated by a 1/4″ valve. For an 1/8″ valve, piston speed is only 9 in./sec.

4.4 MOVING-PART LOGIC (MPL) ELEMENTS

Moving-part logic elements are the result of a process of evolution. Several decades ago, all pneumatic valves were large and cumbersome. As pneumatic control circuits became more complex, it was realized that, except for cylinder-actuating valves, smaller valves can do a better job, being inexpensive and faster. This resulted in a process of valve miniaturization, which was discussed in the previous section. Finally, a number of manufacturers developed special miniature pneumatic elements to implement various logic gates. Since these elements use moving parts, such as diaphragms, springs, disks, balls, and poppets, they are referred to as *moving-part logic* (MPL) elements. They are generally smaller than miniature directional-control valves, and typically cost half as much.

One typical well-known MPL system, described in Refs. (4.35) and (4.53), consists of different units implementing OR, NOT, and AND gates, flip-flops, timers, and other elements. Figure 4.25 shows the NOT element from this system. If input a is *off*, supply air from port b reaches output c and turns it *on*. However, if a is *on*, the pressure on the diaphragm forces the poppet downward, exhausting output c. Thus, the element produces the NOT function, according to $c = a'$. If port b is connected to a second input variable (rather than to the air supply), we get $c = ba'$, so that the element acts as INHIBITION gate.

The elements of this system can operate with a supply pressure between 25 and 150 psi, have a 10 msec response time, and flow coefficients of $C_V = 0.14$ to 0.28. (Thus, they can directly actuate small cylinders, if high piston speeds are not required.) The circuit is connected with plastic tubing, or circuit-manifold subplates containing all circuit connections can be used.

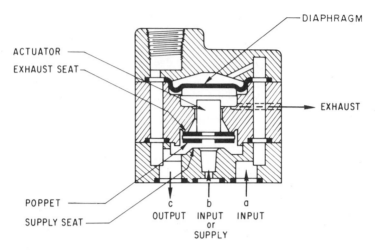

Fig. 4.25. MPL element providing the NOT or INHIBITION function. (Courtesy of The ARO Corporation, Brian, Ohio, USA.)

Another well-known MPL system is described in Ref. (4.54). Its elements operate on 40 to 120 psi supply pressure, with a 3 msec response time. The system includes a YES relay (giving the AND function), a NOT relay (implementing both NOT and INHIBITION functions), a flip-flop or memory relay (using a magnet for latching the element in position until reset), and other

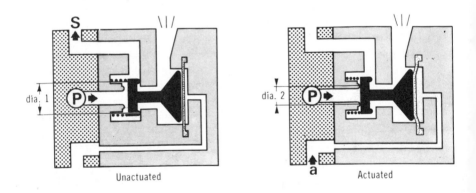

- Output signal S is ON until pilot signal "a" is present. When "a" appears, S is exhausted to atmosphere.
- Relay is snap-acting because area of seat 1 is greater than area of seat 2.

Fig. 4.26. MPL element providing the NOT or INHIBITION function. (Courtesy of Telemecanique.)

Fig. 4.27. Several MPL elements and their mounting arrangement. (Courtesy of Telemecanique.)

elements. The NOT relay is shown in Fig. 4.26. If input pressure $a = 0$, supply pressure P reaches output S. If $a = 1$, P is blocked so that $S = 0$ (i.e., exhausted). If P is replaced by a variable b, this relay implements the INHIBITION function $S = ba'$. Several MPL elements from this system are shown in Fig. 4.27, which also shows their mounting arrangement.

The OR and AND functions can be obtained using so-called "passive" elements, that is, elements without supply air of their own, as shown in Fig. 4.28. The OR gate is a shuttle valve using a poppet disk instead of a ball. The AND gate in the figure uses a double poppet, and produces an output S only if both inputs a and b are pressurized. If, for example, $a = 1$ but $b = 0$, the poppet is pressed to the right by the pressure of a. Thus, this pressure cannot reach S, and output S is vented through b. Passive elements are more compact and less expensive than active ones.

A third MPL system consists of a single universal switching element, described in Ref. (4.55), and shown schematically in Fig. 4.29. The element is extremely small, 20 mm square and 10 mm thick. It contains two pneumatically isolated compartments. The left one has inlet ports x_1 and x_2 acting on a spring-opposed diaphragm. This diaphragm is connected to a pivoted lever, whose right end moves within the right compartment. If $x_1 = x_2 = 0$ (i.e., vented) or if

AND ELEMENT

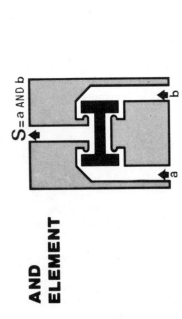

$$S = a \text{ AND } b$$

The AND element delivers an output S any time inputs "a" and "b" are simultaneously present.

— If input "a" appears alone, poppet seats to the right, preventing output.

— If input "b" appears alone, poppet seats to the left, preventing output.

Output S will appear only if "a" and "b" are simultaneously present, because the poppet cannot close-off both inputs.

Note: Output S will appear regardless of poppet position as long as both inputs are present. If one input pressure is higher than the other, the lower pressure will appear at the output.

OR ELEMENT

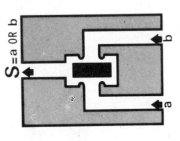

$$S = a \text{ OR } b$$

The OR element delivers an output S whether "a" or "b" or both are present.

— Input "a" alone seats poppet on right hand seat and appears as output S without exhausting at "b".

⌐ Input "b" alone seats poppet on left hand seat and appears as output S without exhausting at "a".

Output S thus appears whether "a" or "b" or both are present.

Note: OR element is sometimes called a shuttle valve.

Fig. 4.28. Passive AND and OR MPL elements. (Courtesy of Telemecanique.)

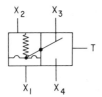

Fig. 4.29. SAMSOMATIC universal MPL logic element.

$x_1 = x_2 = 1$ (i.e., pressurized) or if $x_1 = 0$ and $x_2 = 1$, then the spring pushes the diaphragm down, so that the lever seals inlet x_3 and opens x_4. Outlet port T then assumes the pressure level existing at port x_4. If, however, $x_1 = 1$ and $x_2 = 0$, the diaphragm is pushed against the spring, so that the lever closes inlet port x_4 and opens x_3.

To derive the Boolean function produced by this element, a 16-line truth table should be set up, listing the expected output signal T for each possible combination of the four input signals. The data is then transferred to a Karnaugh map and the output function derived. This task is left as an exercise for the reader (see Problem 4.13 at the end of this chapter), but the final result is

$$T = x_1' x_4 + x_2 x_4 + x_1 x_2' x_3$$

If, by chance, we wish to implement this particular complex function, we have hit the jackpot, since we can do it with one single element. Usually, however, different functions are needed, and these can be obtained by combining several such elements, each of which implements a basic Boolean function according to the following listing (where 0 represents a vented port and 1, the air supply):

For $x_2 = x_4 = 0$: $T = x_1 x_3$ (AND gate)
For $x_2 = x_3 = 0$ and $x_4 = 1$: $T = x_1'$ (NOT gate)
For $x_2 = 0$ and $x_3 = 1$: $T = x_1 + x_4$ (OR GATE)
For $x_2 = x_3 = 0$: $T = x_1' x_4$ (INHIBITION gate, fan-in = 2)
For $x_4 = 0$: $T = x_1 x_2' x_3$ (INHIBITION gate, fan-in = 3)
For $x_3 = 0$ and $x_4 = 1$: $T = x_1' + x_2$ (IMPLICATION gate)
For $x_1 = T$; $x_2 = $ Reset; $x_3 = 1$; $x_4 = $ Set: $T = y$ (flip-flop)

These MPL elements are connected using thin plastic tubing. Alternatively, small "integrated circuits" can be constructed using special connecting plates in which holes are cut and partitions removed to create the necessary air passages. Since this can be done by the user, compact circuits can be built up at low cost.

For an enumeration of the advantages of pneumatic MPL circuits, see Ref. (4.56).

4.5 FLUIDIC ELEMENTS

In 1932, a Rumanian engineer named Henri Coanda noticed an interesting effect while taking a shower: the water stream emerging from the shower head ran along the lower surface of his arm, rather than splashing straight down as would be expected by the law of gravity. The explanation is that the water drags along air particles trapped between it and the surface, producing a partial vacuum. As a result, atmospheric pressure pushes the stream against the surface.

This effect is known as the Coanda effect. However, it was not until 1959 when it was first utilized in a control element. Since then, many other elements have been invented that can implement various logic gates without moving parts, depending solely on interacting air jets, and these are called *fluidic* elements.

At the time, fluidics was viewed as a technical breakthrough, and it was predicted that fluidic elements would eventually replace most other switching elements. These overly optimistic expectations never materialized, mainly for the following reasons.

1. Since fluidic elements have no moving parts, they should theoretically last indefinitely. If made of metal or ceramics, they can withstand high temperatures. The trouble, however, is that fluidic elements are very sensitive to dirt. The slightest trace of oil in the air supply can cause dirt buildup and eventual clogging. Therefore, special "coalescing filters" must be used to completely remove all oil from the compressed air. Since insufficient attention was paid to this initially, many industrial fluidic installations failed to perform reliably, and this gave fluidics a reputation as being unreliable.

2. Since fluidic elements can be mass-produced out of plastics, their price should, in theory, be very low. However, the manufacturers first wanted to recoup their developmental costs, and the price of fluidic elements never really dropped to the level where their use would become economically attractive.

3. Fluidics had the misfortune to appear at a time when the electronic revolution began to take off, and never really succeeded in competing with inexpensive electronic ICs. If fluidics had been invented 20 years earlier, it might have gained a permanent foothold, and, with large production volumes, the cost of the elements could have dropped to the levels originally expected.

For these reasons, fluidics never became popular, and we confine ourselves to briefly describing two types of elements still commercially available. One type, based on the Coanda effect, is called a *wall-attachment* element. A typical wall-attachment flip-flop is shown in Fig. 4.30. The supply air at a pressure of 2 to 15 psi enters supply port S, and exits from an interior nozzle as an air jet. Because of the Coanda effect, this jet attaches itself to one of two interior surfaces and exits at either outlet port O_1 or O_2. At the beginning, the result is random, but assuming that the jet exits at O_1, it continues to do so until a control signal appears at port C_1. Even a weak and short pressure pulse at C_1

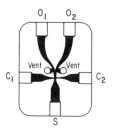

Fig. 4.30. Fluidic wall-attachment flip-flop.

(about 10% of supply pressure is sufficient) causes the jet to flip to the opposite wall and exit at O_2. If the C_1 signal disappears, the jet continues to exit at O_2 until an opposing control signal appears at C_2. Thus, this element acts as an RS flip-flop, with the control ports representing Set and Reset, and the output ports providing state variables y and y'.

The performance of such an element depends on the exact shape of the interior passages, and especially of the vents, which are necessary for successfully coupling successive elements one to another. The output pressure at the outlet port from which the jet emerges is typically 20 to 40% of the supply pressure (called the "pressure recovery").

Figure 4.31 shows an OR/NOR gate wall-attachment element. Although this is not obvious from the figure, the flow passages are modified to prevent the memory effect, and the jet normally exits at outlet O_1. However, a control signal at either control port C_1 or C_2 makes the jet exit at O_2. When the control signal disappears, the jet returns to O_1. Therefore, outlet O_2 implements the OR function $O_2 = C_1 + C_2$, and outlet O_1 implements the NOR function $O_1 = (C_1 + C_2)'$.

A completely different type of fluidic element is the *impact modulator,* described in Ref. (4.57), and shown schematically in Fig. 4.32. The element is a small plastic unit of 20 mm diameter, internally partitioned into two unequal compartments. Supply air enters two opposing input nozzles, producing two impinging jets. The resulting impingement plane is normally formed in the right-hand compartment, so that the outlet line connected to it is pressurized. If, however, control inlet C is pressurized (17% of supply pressure is sufficient), the left jet is deflected, and the impingement plane moves to the left-hand

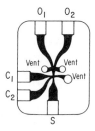

Fig. 4.31. Fluidic wall-attachment OR/NOR gate.

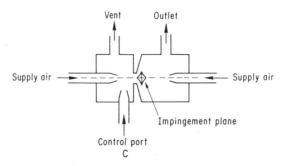

Fig. 4.32. Impact modulator (fluidic NOR gate).

compartment, where the pressure is vented. The outlet line then drops to atmospheric pressure. Actually, there are four such control ports, completely isolated from each other, connected to the left compartment, and pressure at any one of these cuts off the outlet pressure. The impact modulator thus implements a NOR gate, according to Output $= C_1' \cdot C_2' \cdot C_3' \cdot C_4'$. As demonstrated in Sections 3.9 and 3.10, the NOR is a universal gate, and it alone can implement any logic function.

The impact modulator can operate with a wide range of supply pressure (from 0.5 to 20 psi), has a response time of less than 1 msec, a pressure recovery of over 30%, and large fan-out capability of 10 or even greater. It is relatively inexpensive, has small dimensions, and has proven itself reliable.

All fluidic elements suffer from two drawbacks. First, their air consumption is high, since they exhaust air constantly through their vents, even when not switching. (MPL elements, by comparison, use practically no air at steady state, drawing air only during switching.) As a result, large fluidic installations tend to be noisy, and can place a heavy load on the compressed-air supply.

The second drawback pertains to their low output pressures, typically 2 or 3 psi. Since this is insufficient to actuate pilot lines of normal cylinder-actuating valves, special diaphragm amplifiers must be used to boost each output signal of the fluidic circuit to at least 30 to 40 psi. The *on* and *off* states of such an amplifier are shown in Fig. 4.33, which should be self-explanatory. Alternatively, sensitive

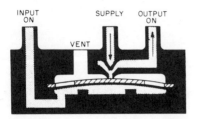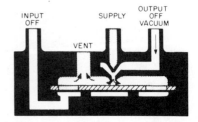

Fig. 4.33. *On* and *Off* states of a diaphragm amplifier. (Courtesy of Air Logic Div., Fred Knapp Eng. Co.)

cylinder-actuating valves with built-in diaphragms in their pilot lines (see Fig. 4.9) can be used. Actually, the fact that fluidic elements work at such low pressures becomes an advantage when using fluidic sensors (discussed in Section 2.3). The low-pressure outputs of these sensors can actuate fluidic elements directly, without the diaphragm amplifiers that are needed where such sensors must actuate conventional valves.

Considering these drawbacks, what is the justification for using fluidics today? This question is discussed in Refs. (4.58) and (4.59), and the conclusion is that fluidics has advantages in certain specialized areas, for instance in explosive environments, where use of electric devices is not permissible. One field of application is in some medical equipment, since fluidics is free of shock hazards, and the elements can be sterilized. In artificial-heart and heart-assist devices, the operating force is usually provided by compressed air, so that it makes sense to also use a fluidic control system. Instead of compressors, air blowers can be used, since they are quieter and produce sufficient pressure to actuate fluidic elements. Fluidics also offers advantages where, for technical reasons, many fluidic sensors (such as air jets) must be used, or where very fast switching is required. Ironically, fluidics has been applied in some assembly equipment for electronic circuits.

In conclusion, it should be mentioned that there exist *analog* fluidic devices, a field quite distinct from the *binary* fluidic elements discussed here. There are many analog fluidic sensors for variables such as temperature, pressure ratio, acceleration, angular rate, and others, and circuits built from proportional fluidic amplifiers use such sensors. These have been used in the control of jet engines and in various military devices (since they are immune to jamming), but the subject is outside the scope of this book.

4.6   ELECTRIC-TO-PNEUMATIC AND OTHER INTERFACING

When combining two different technologies, the problem of interfacing arises. A common problem in industrial automation is interfacing electronics with pneumatics. As described in Section 4.1, electronic ICs are easily combined to create complex electronic logic circuits. Chapters 10 and 11 cover programmable controllers and microcomputers, and both these devices, indispensable in modern automation, produce electric output signals. In order to utilize any of these techniques to drive pneumatic cylinders or other actuators, electric-to-pneumatic interfacing is required.

4.6.1   Solenoid Valves

Solenoid valves are the classical way of converting electric to pneumatic (or hydraulic) signals. A typical solenoid valve is shown in Fig. 4.34. Solenoid valves use a solenoid, discussed in Section 1.2.1, which, when energized, moves a spool

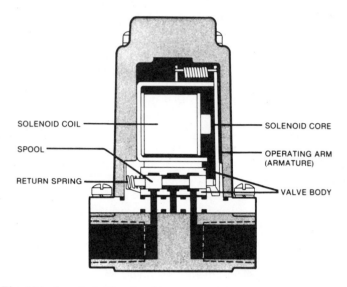

Fig. 4.34. A typical 3/2 solenoid valve. (Courtesy of Alkon Corp.)

(as in the figure) or a poppet, and thus shifts a valve. Solenoid valves generally have two to five ports and are obtainable for various actuating voltages, from 5 V dc to 230 V ac. A general discussion of solenoid valves is found in Ref. (4.60).

Solenoid valves are either direct-acting or pilot-operated. In direct-acting valves, the solenoid plunger makes direct contact with the valve orifice. This makes for simple construction, but requires more power. Therefore, most larger solenoid valves are pilot-operated. The plunger affects flow through a small pilot orifice, and this actuates a diaphragm that closes the main orifice. Thus, high flow rates can be obtained with low solenoid currents. Just as for ordinary valves, the flow capacity of solenoid valves is generally stated using the C_V flow coefficient defined in Section 4.3.7.

The switching time of solenoid valves depends on construction and size, and can range from 3 msec for miniature valves to as high as 50 msec for large sizes. The trend in recent years has been to build miniature and subminiature solenoid valves whose coils can be operated with as little power as 0.5 W. Such valves can be driven directly by electronic circuits using Darlington or other power transistors; see Refs. (4.61) and (4.62). Many miniature valves are designed to be mounted next to each other on air manifolds, permitting a great number of valves to be packed into a small space.

Many manufacturers supply valves with double solenoids, as shown in Fig. 4.35(a).It should be noted, however, that solenoids are relatively expensive, and such valves typically cost twice as much as identical valves with pneumatic actuation. Another problem arises when both solenoids are inadvertently actuated concurrently. The solenoids oppose each other, and are liable to overheat and burn out (see the discussion in Section 1.2.1). The same happens if

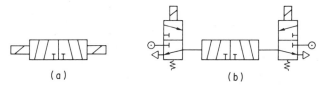

(a)   (b)

Fig. 4.35. Two methods of actuating valves electrically.

the valve spool sticks and fails to shift. To avoid this problem, many manufacturers prefer to use a valve with pneumatic actuation, together with two additional 3/2 valves with solenoids and return springs, as shown in Fig. 4.35(b). While this increases the cost, it does avoid solenoid burnout. If both solenoids are energized, there are contradictory pilot signals on the main valve, but at least the solenoids do not overheat. Similarly, if the main-valve spool sticks the solenoids are not affected.

4.6.2   Miniature Electric-to-Pneumatic Interface Devices

Because of the increasing need to interface electronics with pneumatics, a number of special interface devices have been developed that cannot really be called solenoid valves, even though they perform the same function. One of these devices is the "Minimatic Interface Valve"; see Ref. (4.63). It uses a thin metal spider as the sole moving element, and this moves only 0.007″ to open the valve. The unit is less than 1″ in diameter, uses only 0.65 W power, and can be mounted compactly on air manifolds. It is available for actuating voltages of 6, 12, or 24 V dc.

Another device, named the "Reedex Valve," see Ref. (4.64), is shown in Fig. 4.36. This bears some similarity to reed switches described in Section 2.2.3. The difference is that the moving reed, actuated by an electromagnet, does not make or break an electric contact, but opens a small air passage. Here, too, various dc operating voltages are available, and operating power is as low as 0.5 W.

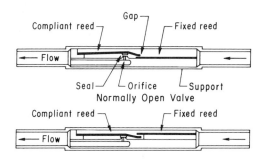

Fig. 4.36. Reedex electropneumatic valve. (Courtesy of C. A. Norgren Co.)

Switching time is only 2 msec. The units can be mounted on air manifolds, or directly soldered to electronic printed-circuit boards.

The idea of mounting electronic-to-pneumatic interface elements directly on electronic circuit boards has been taken up by a number of manufacturers, and the name *electropneumatics* has been coined for this technology; see Ref. (4.65). One manufacturer, see Ref. (4.66), even supplies "pneumatic edge connectors," which make it possible to connect all of the air tubing to such a circuit board in one operation (similar to the use of electric edge connectors). The electro-pneumatic circuit board can be rack-mounted, providing an extremely compact overall system. Another manufacturer, see Ref. (4.67), supplies an electro-pneumatic system with sufficient flow capacity to permit driving cylinders directly.

4.6.3 Interfacing Pneumatics and Hydraulics

As explained in Section 1.4.1, hydraulic actuators are employed where very large actuating forces are required. Although hydraulic solenoid valves are, of course, available, a nonelectric control system is often preferred. Hydraulic control circuits can be built, but these are very expensive, since hydraulic directional-control valves costs up to 10 times as much as equivalent pneumatic valves (see the discussion in Section 1.4.1). Thus, it does not make much sense to use expensive hydraulic valves for purely logic functions.

One way to overcome this problem is to use inexpensive pneumatic valves for the control circuit, employing any of the circuit-design methods presented in Chapter 7. Several manufacturers supply hydraulic cylinder-actuating valves with *pneumatic* pilot lines, and these can be used to interface the pneumatic control system with the hydraulic cylinder or motor.

4.7 COMPARISON BETWEEN DIFFERENT SWITCHING ELEMENTS

Before discussing advantages and drawbacks of various switching elements, it is helpful to study what needs to be connected to what by means of the flow chart of Fig. 4.37. The chart is divided into five vertical areas: The first lists the sensor types available, all of which were discussed in Chapter 2. The middle area lists the switching elements discussed in this chapter and also programmable controllers and microcomputers discussed in Chapters 10 and 11. The fifth area lists equipment to be actuated, as discussed in Chapter 1. The intermediate second and fourth areas are dedicated to the required interface equipment. (Elements enclosed in dashed-line boxes are not always needed.)

The reader who has read Chapters 1, 2, and 4 should be able to follow the chart without further explanation. In doing so, one important point becomes obvious: to minimize the need for expensive interface equipment, it is highly advisable to use the same type of equipment all the way through. For example,

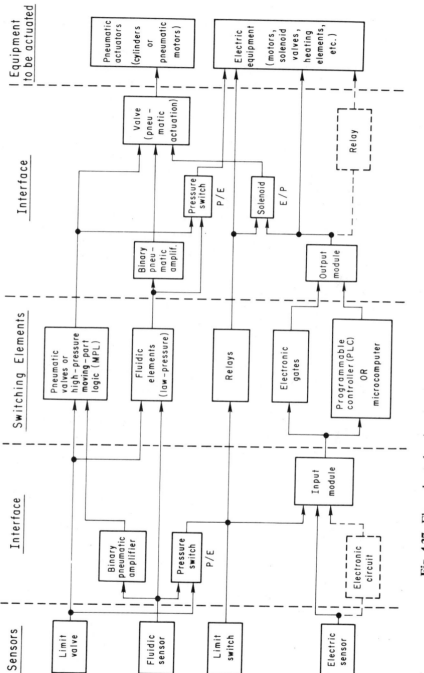

Fig. 4.37. Flow chart showing the equipment used in binary control systems.

159

limit valves can be connected directly to pneumatic valves or to MPL elements, and these can directly drive cylinder-actuating valves having pneumatic pilot lines, with no additional interface elements required. As a second example, limit switches can directly actuate relays which, in turn, can actuate electric equipment, and here, too, no interface elements are needed. On the other hand, using electronic gates to actuate air cylinders tends to be rather expensive, since the electronic system requires input and output modules, and the cylinder-actuating valves require solenoids.

The average cost of different switching elements is listed below:

Electronic gate:	$0.25 per gate (based on use of ICs)
Relays	$3–10 per relay
Valves:	$20–30 per valve (with air actuation)
	$40–60 per valve (with single solenoid)
	$60–90 per valve (with double solenoids)
MPL:	$10–15 per element
Fluidic	$10–15 per element

However, it is meaningless to consider only this list, since overall system cost is what counts. For example, electronic circuits require stabilized power supplies, in addition to the already mentioned I/O modules that cost about $10 to $20 each. Therefore, the very low cost of the electronic gates becomes meaningless if the system requires many I/O modules. Similarly, pneumatic systems require a compressed air supply. If a compressor is already installed in the plant, and if it has sufficient capacity to handle the extra load, then the pneumatic system may turn out to be inexpensive. However, if a new compressor must be purchased, then this has to be taken into account in calculating overall system cost.

These comments should convince the reader that a cost comparison is not as straightforward as it may appear. Reference (4.68) shows how an in-depth cost analysis should be carried out. It is stated there that relative costs vary greatly form one application to another, and a pneumatic control system could cost anywhere from one-half to twice as much as an electrical system.

Table 4.1. provides a comparison between different switching elements, taking various factors into account. Here, too, one should be careful before jumping to conclusions. For example, the extremely fast response of electronic elements is very important in computing devices, but has little significance in industrial automation systems, where the controlled system—be it a cylinder or some machine or process—has relatively slow response. Also if, the electronic circuit actuates a solenoid valve, the delay time of the latter completely cancels the fast response of the former, so that the electronic control system may turn out to be slower than a purely pneumatic system, strange as this may appear.

As to life expectancy, relays are definitely inferior to other devices. However, as already mentioned, this only becomes significant if the relay is to be cycled continuously at a high rate.

TABLE 4.1. Comparison between Different Switching Elements

	Electronic	Relays	Pneumatic Valves	Moving-Part Fluidics	Fluidics
Response time:	5–10 nsec	10–25 msec	10–20 msec	5–10 msec	1–2 msec
Relative size:	Small	Large	Large	Intermediate	Intermediate
Reliability, life expectancy:	Excellent (under suitable conditions)	10^5–10^6 cycles	10^7–10^8 cycles	10^7–10^8 cycles	Unlimited (with clean air)
Sensitivity to high temperatures:	Poor	Intermediate	Good	Good	Excellent
Sensitivity to dirt and corrosion:	Intermediate	Intermediate	Good	Good	Poor
Sensitivity to shock and vibration:	Intermediate	Poor	Excellent	Intermediate	Excellent
Sensitivity to electric noise and radiation:	Poor	Good	Excellent	Excellent	Excellent
Fire danger (with inflammable materials):	Intermediate	Poor	Excellent	Excellent	Excellent
Fan-in:	2–8	> 20	2	2–3	2–4
Fan-out:	5–10	> 20	Unlimited	Unlimited	2–6
Supply air pressure:	—	—	High	Intermediate to high	Low
Air consumption:	—	—	Low	Low	High
Input interface:	Good for electric sensors		Good for pneumatic sensors		
Output interface:	Needs amplification	None for electric equipment	None for pneumatic equipment		Needs amplification

161

A number of factors must be considered before deciding on the type of switching element to be used, for example:

1. *Type of Equipment To Be Actuated.* If mainly electrical equipment must be actuated (e.g., motors, heaters, pumps, conveyors), there is little point in using a pneumatic control system, and the choice is between relays and electronics. On the other hand, for actuating pneumatic cylinders, pneumatic circuits usually provide the least expensive solution.

2. *Type of Sensors Used.* Frequently, the nature of the problem calls for a certain type of sensor. This may affect the choice of switching element, since, as was pointed out, it pays to stay with the same medium, air or electricity.

3. *Plant Conditions.* Are there inflammable or explosive materials? If so, a purely pneumatic system may be preferred. Is there an existing air supply? Does the operating staff have prior experience with a given medium? Is the maintenance staff trained and equipped to handle a certain type of equipment? If not, it may be difficult to convince them to change to something new.

4. *Ratio between I/O Channels and Logic Elements.* A final and important aspect to be considered is the ratio between the number of I/O channels and the number of logic operations that the control system must carry out. This is illustrated in Fig. 4.38, where two extreme cases are shown schematically. In Fig. 4.38(a), the logic system is extremely simple, but there are many input and output channels. This, for example, might be a system with many cylinders, each cylinder extending and retracting only once during the cycle. For each cylinder, there are two limit valves and two pilot lines. Hence, a purely pneumatic system is preferable, since the air circuit is very simple, whereas an electronic circuit requires two input and two output modules per cylinder.

Figure 4.38(b), on the other hand, represents the opposite extreme, a system with a great number of required logic operations, but only one or two input and one or two output channels. This, for instance, might be a single cylinder to be actuated a great number of times, with the logic system containing a counter to

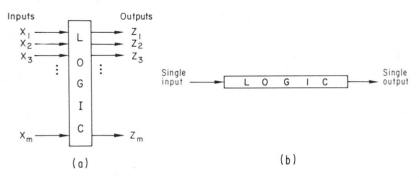

Fig. 4.38. Two extreme cases having different numbers of I/O channels and logic operations.

count the cylinder strokes. Although pneumatic counters exist, counting is best done electronically (see Section 8.4). Since only one or two input and one or two output modules are required for the whole system electronic control is definitely preferable here.

Unfortunately, most practical applications are not as clear-cut, and fall somewhere in between these two extremes. Ultimately, the system designer has to rely on experience and judgment in order to come up with a good decision.

PROBLEMS

4.1. Assume that there are only the ICs shown in Fig. 4.3 at our disposal, and we wish to implement the Boolean function $T = ABC + A'B'C'$. Draw a diagram showing the necessary connections.

4.2. Repeat Problem 4.1 for the function $T = x_1 x_2' + x_1' x_2$.

4.3. Repeat Problem 4.1 for the function $T = ab'c + abd + a'c'd'$.

4.4. The contacts shown in Fig. P4.4 belong to four different relays, W, X, Y, and Z. Write the Boolean equation that defines the excitation of relay coil A.

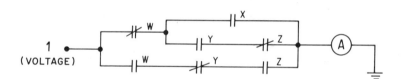

Fig. P4.4. Circuit for Problem 4.4.

4.5. Draw a relay circuit for implementing the function $T = x_1 x_2' + x_1' x_2$.

4.6. Draw a relay circuit for implementing the function $T = AB' + C(B' + D)$.

4.7. Draw a relay circuit for implementing the function $T = ab'c + abd + a'c'd'$. (*Note:* Frequently, it pays to factor out common terms.)

4.8. Draw a relay circuit for implementing the function $T = acd + bcd + abc'$.

4.9. Draw a relay circuit for implementing the function $T = x'y'z + x'yz' + xy'z' + xyz$, assuming that only relays with DPDT contacts are available.

4.10. Draw a pneumatic valve circuit for implementing the function $T = x_1 x_2' + x_1' x_2$.

4.11. Draw a penumatic valve circuit for implementing the function $T = AB' + B'C + CD$.

4.12. Draw a pneumatic valve circuit for implementing the function $T = AB + BC + AC' + B'C'$.

4.13. Derive the output function of the MPL element shown in Fig. 4.29 (and given there).

4.14. Using only MPL elements of the type shown in Fig. 4.29, design a circuit implementing the Exclusive-OR function $T = AB' + A'B$.

4.15. Using only MPL elements of the type shown in Fig. 4.29, design a circuit implementing the function $T = ABC + A'B'C'$.

4.16. Using only MPL elements of the type shown in Fig. 4.29, design a circuit implementing the function $T = a'b + bc$. (*Hint*: One single element is sufficient for the solution.)

4.17. Figure P4.17 shows an MPL element (manufactured by Dreloba of East Germany). The element employs two diaphragms connected by a rod, and this assembly can move sideways depending on the pressure inputs to the element. The two diaphragms and two partitions divide the element into five compartments. The center compartment leads to a port representing the outlet pressure y of the element. The other four compartments have inlet ports A to D. Using a truth table and a Karnaugh map, derive outlet function y as a function of inlet signals A, B, C, and D.

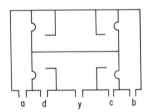

a   d   y   c   b   **Fig. P4.17.** MPL element for Problem 4.17.

4.18. Implement the function $S = A + BC + CD$ using impact modulators.

REFERENCES

4.1. C. Belove (Ed.), *Handbook of Modern Electronics and Electrical Engineering*, Wiley, New York, 1986.

4.2. T. Kohonen, *Digital Circuits and Devices*, Prentice-Hall, Englewood Cliffs, NJ, 1972.

4.3. L. Suckle, "Comparing New Types of Electronic Logic," *Machine Design*, Apr. 7, 1983, pp. 87–91.

4.4. J. Birkner and V. Coli, *PAL Programmable Array Logic Handbook*, Monolithic Memories, Inc., Sunnyvale, CA, 1983.

4.5. L. Teschler, "Programming Logic with PC's," *Machine Design*, Oct. 25, 1984, pp. 67–72.

4.6. J. Birkner, V. Coli, and D. Sackett, "Programming Logic Chips on Personal Computers," *Machine Design*, July 21, 1983, pp. 81–85.

4.7. "Programmable Hardware" (Seven articles on PAL Systems), *BYTE*, Jan. 1987, pp. 194–286.

4.8. R. White, "Using Optical Isolators in Controls," *Control Engineering*, Jan. 1973, pp. 50–53.

4.9. R. Herzog, "Coupling Electrical Signals with Light,"*Machine Design*, June 1973, pp. 80–85.

4.10. "1987 Control Products Specifier," *Control Engineering*, (Special Issue), 2nd ed., Nov. 1986.

4.11. B. Carlisle, "Power Integration Techniques Bring Single-chip Relays," *Machine Design*, Oct. 25, 1984, pp. 22–26.

4.12. S. Robb and J. Sutor, "Comparing Power ICs," *Machine Design*, Feb. 21, 1985, pp. 119–122.

4.13. B. Carlisle, "The Gremlins Lurking in Power ICs," *Machine Design*, Dec. 6, 1984, pp. 107–110.

4.14. Electrical and Electronics Reference Issue, *Machine Design*, May 14, 1981.

4.15. N. Sclater, "Electromechanical Relays," *Design Engineering*, June 1980, pp. 57–62.

4.16. P. Cleaveland, "I & CS Guide to Control Relays," *I & CS*, Nov. 1983, pp. 43–44.

4.17. D. Dattilo, "Replacing Relay Panels with Printed Circuit Boards," *Machine Design*, June 23, 1977, pp. 89–93.

4.18. H. Morris, "Electromechanical Relays Gaining Space on Printed Circuit Boards," *Control Engineering*, Nov. 1982, pp. 78–79.

4.19. B. H. Carlisle, "Electromechanical Relays Find a Niche on the Circuit Board," *Machine Design*, Aug. 6, 1987, pp. 64–68.

4.20. N. Yedevitz, "Back to Relay Basics," *Instruments & Control Systems*, Feb. 1979, pp. 23–27.

4.21. P. N. Budzilovich, "How to Select the Right Relay for Your Application," *Control Engineering*, Nov. 1969, pp. 92–96.

4.22. M. Leonard, "Avoiding Mistakes with Relays," *Machine Design*, July 24, 1975, pp. 54–57.

4.23. R. W. Smeaton (Ed.), *Switchgear and Control Handbook*, 2nd ed., McGraw-Hill, New York, 1987.

4.24. J. Schuessler, "Surpressing Relay-coil Transients," *Machine Design*, Dec. 27, 1973, p. 68.

4.25. K. Pluhar, "Electromechanical Relays—They'll Be With Us for a Long Time," *Control Engineering*, Oct. 1981, pp. 84–96.

4.26. W. R. Flynn, "Switch Inputs, Relay Outputs Remain Mechanical Link in Solid-state Control," *Control Engineering*, Nov. 1983, pp. 68–70.

4.27. W. R. Flynn, "Electromechanical Relays, Switches, Vie with Solid State," *Control Engineering*, Dec. 1984, pp. 49–50.

4.28. S. Bailey, "Relays and Switches Retain Key On-line Role in Today's Digital Micro Control," *Control Engineering*, Nov. 1985, pp. 59–63.

4.29. Gordos Corp., "Drive Circuits for Reed Relays," *Machine Design*, Mar. 20, 1975, pp. 87–88.

4.30. J. R. Pancake, "Solid-state Relays Enhance Computer Control," *Instruments & Control Systems*, June 1980, pp. 33–35.

4.31. (No author listed), "Solid State Relays are Fast, Controllable," *Product Engineering*, Mar. 1979, pp. 47–50.

4.32. S. Schneider, "The Growing Family of Solid-state Relays," *Machine Design*, Aug. 9, 1979, pp. 93–95.

4.33. T. Bishop, "Relays that Fight EMI," *Machine Design*, Jan. 20, 1977, pp. 118–122.

4.34. L. Nelson, "Solid State or Electromechanical Relays?," *I & CS*, June 1986, pp. 63–64.

4.35. F. Yeaple, *Fluid Power Design Handbook*, Dekker, New York, 1984.

4.36. N. R. Stull, "Air Compressors, Conditioning, Costs, and the Crunch," *Hydraulics & Pneumatics*, Part 1: June 1975, pp. 65–70; Part 2: Aug. 1975, pp. 64–67; Part 3: Sept. 1975, pp. 84–86; Part 4: Oct. 1975, pp. 199–201; Part 5: Nov. 1975, pp. 60–62; Part 6: Dec. 1975, pp. 49–57; Part 7: Jan. 1976, pp. 201–205; Part 8: Feb. 1976, pp. 53–55.

4.37. *Compressed Air Systems: A Guidebook on Energy and Cost Savings*, U.S. Dept. of Energy, Washington, DC, 1984, (also abstracted in a series of articles published in *Hydraulics & Pneumatics* from Jan. 1986–Feb. 1988).

4.38. "Air Systems for Profit-Making Designs," *Hydraulics & Pneumatics*, (Report), Apr. 1971, pp. HP1–HP32.

4.39. G. Barnes, "Selecting Small Pneumatic Components," *Mechanical Engineering*, Mar. 1985, pp. 56–63.

4.40. "Fluid Power Reference Issue," *Machine Design*, Sept. 18, 1986.

4.41. W. Petty, "Compressed-air Filters: More Dirt for the Dollar," Machine Design, Jan. 12, 1984, pp. 115–120.

4.42. R. Schneider, "Basics of Compressed-air Filtration," *Hydraulics & Pneumatics*, Nov. 1985, pp. 60–61.

4.43. F. Yeaple, "Air Filters, Regulators and Lubricators," *Design Engineering*, Sept. 1981, pp. 71–75.

4.44. T. Isaacs, "Cleaning and Drying Compressed Air: Why and How," *Hydraulics & Pneumatics*, Nov. 1970, pp. 68–71.

4.45. D. Kirby, "Selecting Compressed-air Dryers," *Machine Design*, Apr. 26, 1979, pp. 164–169.

4.46. R. Beercheck, "Pneumatics Kicks the Oil Habit," *Machine Design*, June 21, 1984, pp. 84–89.

4.47. *Minimatic Modular Components*, Catalog 484-A2, Clippard Instrument Laboratory, Inc., Cincinnati, OH 45239, 1984.

4.48. Report on Directional Control Valves," *Hydraulics & Pneumatics*, Apr. 1985, pp. 50–57.

4.49. Annual Designers Guide," *Hydraulics & Pneumatics*, Jan. 1988, pp. 115–172.

4.50. F. Yeaple, "Pneumatic Directional Valve Performance," *Design Engineering*, Apr. 1981, pp. 83–88.

4.51. T. Goldoftas (Ed.), "C_V Can Help You Save Money," *Hydraulics & Pneumatics,* Apr. 1986, p. 80.

4.52. R. Schneider (Ed.), "Guidelines for Pneumatic Cylinder Sizing," *Hydraulics & Pneumatics,* Sept. 1986, pp. 104–105.

4.53. *ARO Pneumatic Logic Controls,* Catalog 8078-L, ARO Corporation, Bryan, OH 43506, 1987.

4.54. *Technical Handbook,* Telemecanique, Southfield, MI 48076,1982.

4.55. *System 975 Catalog,* Samsomatic, Frankfurt, West Germany, 1986.

4.56. R. A. Moffat and A. J. Hudson, "Air Logic: A Good Choice for Hostile/hazardous Environments," *I & CS,* April 1987, pp. 71–74.

4.57. *Fluidic NOR Logic Elements,* Publication 8200, and *Diaphragm Amplifiers,* Publication 8450, Air Logic Div., Fred Knapp Engraving Co., Racine, W1.

4.58. H. Spuhler, "Where Fluidics Still Makes Sense," *Machine Design,* Aug. 11, 1983, pp. 92–93.

4.59. J. Haertel, "Pneumatic Logic—Present and Future," *Mechanical Engineering,* Mar. 1985, pp. 43–44.

4.60. M. Colaneri, "Solenoid Valve Basics," *Instruments & Control Systems,* Aug. 1979, pp. 27–30.

4.61. K. Crater, "System Approach Reduces Microprocessor to Pneumatics Interfacing Costs," *Control Engineering,* Aug. 1981, pp. 86–87.

4.62. A. Van Gilder, "Digital Control of Fluid Flow," *Machine Design,* Sept. 11, 1986, pp. 83–86.

4.63. *Minimatic Electronic/Pneumatic Interface Valves,* Catalog 984, Clippard Instrument Laboratory, Inc., Cincinnati, OH 45239, 1984.

4.64. *Reedex Valve Catalog,* NCA-81/9-86, C. A. Norgren Co., Littleton, Co.

4.65. R. Beercheck, "Controlling Air with Electronics," *Machine Design,* July 11, 1985, pp. 77–80.

4.66. *Parker Pneutronics,* Catalog 1900, Parker Fluidpower, LDI Pneutronics Corp., Pepperell, MA 01463, 1986.

4.67. F. Yeaple, "Electronic/Pneumatic Circuit Board Operates Air Cylinders Directly," *Design News,* July 22, 1985, pp. 108–111.

4.68. B. McCord, "Simple Checklists Compare Costs of Air vs. Electric Logic," *Machine Design,* Nov. 8, 1979, pp. 108–112.

CHAPTER 5

ELECTRIC LADDER DIAGRAMS

Relays were discussed in Chapter 4. As explained there, each relay consists of one coil and any number of contacts, either normally open (NO) or normally closed (NC). These contacts switch simultaneously whenever the coil is energized. When deenergized, the contacts revert to their normal state.

Three different methods for designing relay control circuits are described in this chapter. These methods are important because—apart from their application to hard-wired relay systems—they provide the basis for programming *programmable controllers*, as described in detail in Chapter 10.

5.1 LADDER DIAGRAMS

Relay control circuits are generally drawn up using so-called *ladder diagrams*. Ladder diagrams differ from conventional wiring diagrams in an important way. Wiring diagrams show the physical arrangement of the various components (i.e., switches, relays, solenoids, motors, etc.) and their interconnections, and are used by electricians to do the actual wiring of a control panel. Ladder diagrams, on the other hand, are more schematic, and show each branch of the control circuit on a separate horizontal row. They are meant to emphasize the *function* of each branch and the resulting sequence of operations.

As shown in Fig. 5.1, the ladder diagram has two vertical lines, the left connected to a voltage source and the right one grounded. Between them, a set of horizontal rows (the rungs of the ladder) represent the different branches of the control circuit. The symbols of various electrical devices are drawn on these lines. Thus, each rung—which may or may not have several parallel branch

168

VOLTAGE   GROUND

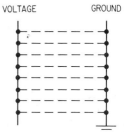

=   **Fig. 5.1.** Framework of a ladder diagram.

lines—represents a separate electrical circuit, providing a current path from the voltage source to ground.

Ladder diagrams use special symbols for the various circuit elements, some of which are shown in Fig. 5.2. (The symbols used to represent switch contacts are shown in Chapter 2 on sensors.) A few comments are in order concerning the relay symbols. According to industrial practice, relay coils and their associated contacts are generally labeled with an identifying number followed by the letters CR (standing for *control relay*). All contacts belonging to a relay are assigned the same number, no matter where they may appear in the ladder diagram. However, in textbooks on switching theory, it is preferred to differentiate between the relay coil and the contacts. Therefore, the coil is generally labeled with capital letter Y followed by a subscript number, whereas the contacts belonging to the same relay are labeled with lowercase y followed by the same subscript. In this chapter, we use this second method of labeling relays, since one of the circuit-design methods to be described requires clear differentiation between relay coil and contacts.

The various ladder-diagram elements can be divided into two groups: electrical contacts and output elements. The contacts include those of push-

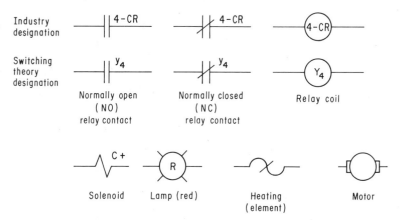

Fig. 5.2. Some ladder-diagram symbols.

button switches (Chapter 3); limit switches, pressure and temperature switches, or other sensors (Chapter 2); and, of course, the relay contacts themselves. The output elements could be any resistive load, such as relay coils, solenoids (usually actuating pneumatic or hydraulic valves), lamps, motors, or any other electrical device to be actuated by the circuit. The difference between contacts and output elements is basic: contacts have negligible *contact resistance* (unless defective), and the circuit made up of these contacts is intended to implement the logic function defining under what conditions the output element is to be actuated. Output elements, on the other hand, always have appreciable electrical resistance.

Each ladder-diagram rung must contain at least one output element, otherwise we get a short circuit. The output elements are commonly drawn at the right edge of the ladder diagram, adjoining the right vertical line.

Figure 5.3 shows a simple ladder diagram, describing how a relay is used to implement an RS flip-flop (see Chapter 3). This circuit operates as follows. When a SET signal is given (by pressing the NO push-button switch in line 1), current reaches relay coil Y_1 (assuming that the NC RESET push button is not pressed). Energizing the relay coil closes the NO relay contact y_1 in line 2. The SET push button can now be released, and current continues to flow to coil Y_1 through this contact y_1, that is, the flip-flop remains SET. Thus, this contact provides the "memory" of the flip-flop, or, using industrial terminology, turns the relay into a self-holding or *latched* relay. The moment the RESET push button is pressed, the memory is broken, and the flip-flop reverts to its former RESET state.

If both SET and RESET signals are given simultaneously (which is "against the rules"), current flow is broken, which makes this flip-flop "reset dominating." Its Boolean equation can be written as

$$Y = (S + y)R'$$

which means that coil Y is energized provided (SET is pressed OR contact y is closed) AND RESET is NOT pressed.

The flip-flop outputs, or *state variables* y and y', are provided by NO and NC relay contacts, respectively, in lines 3 and 4. For the purpose of this example,

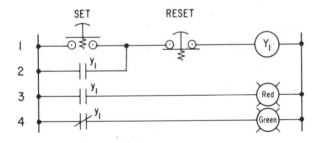

Fig. 5.3. RS flip-flop implemented by a relay.

these connect to a red and green lamp, respectively, giving visual indication of the flip-flop status. In general, these flip-flop outputs are used to actuate other elements, according to need.

Note that the NC contact in line 4 is labeled y_1 and *not* y_1'. This is a matter of convention, and the idea behind it is that the designation written next to any contact is only meant to identify the relay or switch to which this contact belongs, but does *not* represent the binary variable at that location. Since the symbol in line 4 stands for an NC contact, the reader knows that the binary variable appearing to the right of the contact is really y'.

To stress the difference between ladder and wiring diagrams, Fig. 5.4 shows a *wiring diagram* for the same circuit. It shows the actual location of the relay with respect to all other elements. All wires connected to the relay converge at this location, and such a diagram is sometimes called an *attached diagram* (since it shows all input and output lines of a given component *attached* directly to the symbol). To understand this diagram, we need to know that the relay is of the DPDT type (see Chapter 4), and that the various pin numbers signify the following:

Pins 2 and 7: relay coil
Pins 1 and 8: contact poles
Pins 3 and 6: NO contacts
Pins 4 and 5: NC contacts

In the ladder diagram, by comparison, the relay coil and its various contacts are dispersed in different circuits, with each circuit shown on a separate rung. Such a diagram is termed a *detached diagram* (because the relay contacts are shown *detached* from the coil), and its function is to facilitate understanding circuit operation, rather than giving wiring instructions. The difference between these two types of diagrams is even more pronounced for complex circuits.

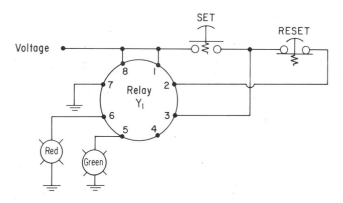

Fig. 5.4. Wiring diagram for the circuit of Fig. 5.3.

More complex ladder diagrams and methods for designing them are presented in the following sections. Ladder diagrams serve as the basis for writing programs for programmable controllers, as discussed in Chapter 10.

5.2 SEQUENCE CHARTS

Sequence charts (also called time-motion diagrams, state diagrams, or bar charts) are useful for visualizing the operation of switching systems. They can be used to describe the step-by-step operation of relay systems, pneumatic systems (see Chapter 7), or any other type of switching system.

To illustrate how sequence charts are constructed, consider the ladder diagram of Fig. 5.5. The relay system shown actuates the two cylinders A and B in Fig. 5.6. Each cylinder is actuated by a 5/2 directional-control valve with solenoid and a return spring. The solenoids are labeled $A+$ and $B+$, respectively, signifying that the cylinder moves in the " $+$ " direction (i.e., extend) whenever the solenoid is energized. Two limit switches, a_2 and b_2, are mounted so as to be actuated when the respective cylinder reaches the extreme " $+$ " position.

The valve symbols used in Fig. 5.6 are explained in Chapter 4. Note that the symbols used for limit switches and solenoids in the pneumatic-circuit diagram (Fig. 5.6) differ from those used for these same elements in the ladder diagram (Fig. 5.5).

The sequence chart corresponding to this system is shown in Fig. 5.7. To construct this chart, we draw horizontal lines for each of the elements taking part in the action, and vertical lines (how many are needed is not known at the beginning) representing the different stages, or steps, in the system's sequence. Note that although the horizontal axis represents time, there is no fixed time scale. Whenever a new event takes place (which might be after 0.1 sec or after 1 h), a new vertical line (labeled with Roman numerals) is allocated. Thus, the time between two adjacent vertical lines depends on when the events occur. Note also that each cylinder is allocated two horizontal lines, to make it possible to

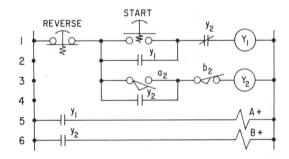

Fig. 5.5. Relay circuit for actuating two cylinders.

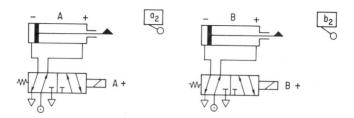

Fig. 5.6. Pneumatic-cylinder circuit controlled by the ladder diagram of Fig. 5.5.

represent cylinder motion between its two extreme positions. All other elements are preferably allocated only a single line (to shorten the diagram). The time period during which a given element is actuated is indicated by a thick line atop its horizontal line, with the beginning and end of actuation shown by short vertical lines.

To shorten the sequence chart, no lines are allocated for the individual relay contacts y. It is sufficient to see whether or not coil Y is energized in order to know the status of contact y.

After the required horizontal and vertical lines are drawn, the sequence chart can be filled in. At stage I, the system is assumed to be in its initial position before the START button has been pressed. We assume both cylinders at their "$-$" positions (retracted), and none of the relays or solenoids actuated. This assumption seems reasonable, but must nevertheless be verified, which can only be done after the diagram has been completed.

At stage II, the START button is assumed to be pressed briefly. This energizes relay coil Y_1, which, in turn, closes NO contact y_1 in line 2. Even though the START button is released right away, relay coil Y_1 remains energized because of this memory contact y_1, as was explained in connection with Fig. 5.3, and this is shown on the sequence chart by means of a thick line on the Y_1 line. Since

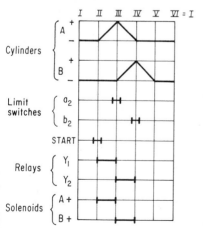

Fig. 5.7. Sequence chart for Figs. 5.5 and 5.6.

contact y_1 in line 5 actuates solenoid $A+$, cylinder A begins to extend, which is shown on the diagram by means of a diagonal line between stages II and III.

At stage III, cylinder A is fully extended, and actuates limit switch a_2. This permits current flow to relay coil Y_2 (line 3). Actuation of relay Y_2 does three actions:

(a) Closes contact y_2 in line 6 and thus actuates solenoid $B+$, so that cylinder B begins to extend.

(b) Opens the NC contact y_2 in line 1. This breaks the memory of relay Y_1 (i.e., resets the flip-flop). As a result, contact y_1 in line 5 opens again and releases solenoid $A+$, so that cylinder A begins to retract.

(c) Closes contact y_2 in line 4. This provides memory to relay Y_2, so that Y_2 remains actuated even after rectraction of cylinder A has opened the contact of limit switch a_2 in line 3.

Cylinder B, when fully extended, actuates limit switch b_2. This breaks the memory of relay Y_2 in line 3, so that solenoid $B+$ (line 6) is released, causing cylinder B to retract.

With that, the sequence is completed, and the system remains at rest until the next START signal. Since the status of all the elements is identical at stages VI and I, the assumptions made at the beginning are verified.

As a safety feature, a REVERSE push-button switch (with an NC contact) is added in line 1. If anything should go wrong during the sequence (e.g., a part jams), the operator can push this button, which breaks the memory of any relay actuated at the time, causing all cylinders to retract.

It should be pointed out that lines 5 and 6 in Fig. 5.5 could be eliminated by placing solenoids $A+$ and $B+$ into lines 2 and 4, in parallel with the relay coils. This is shown in Fig. 5.8. The resulting sequence chart is identical to the previous one, that is, this new circuit produces the identical sequence, even though two relay contacts have been eliminated. In both Figs. 5.5 and 5.8, solenoids $A+$ or $B+$ are actuated if, and only if, relay Y_1 or Y_2, respectively, is actuated. However, the circuit of Fig. 5.8 has one drawback: solenoids usually draw fairly large currents (much larger than those drawn by relay coils), and these currents must pass through the various switch contacts in lines 1 and 3. Frequently, these

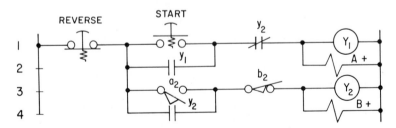

Fig. 5.8. Relay circuit replacing Fig. 5.5 and saving two relay contacts.

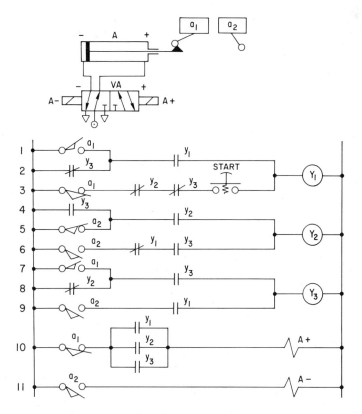

Fig. 5.9. Pneumatic circuit and ladder diagram for the sequence
START, $A+$, $A-$, $A+$, $A-$, $A+$, $A-$.

switch contacts have small current ratings (especially if very small limit switches
are used because of lack of mounting space), and the currents drawn by the
solenoids can severely reduce the switch service life. In Fig. 5.5, this problem is
avoided by supplying the solenoid currents through relay contacts, which
generally have much higher current ratings.

This is not meant to imply that circuits such as that of Fig. 5.8 are never used.
Some solenoids draw very small currents; some limit switches have fairly high
current ratings; and some relay circuits are operated infrequently, so that service
life plays no great role. The circuit designer must consider all these factors.

We now present a second example. The pneumatic circuit and ladder
diagram are shown in Fig. 5.9, and the resulting sequence chart is to be
constructed. Before doing so, three points should be mentioned:

(a) While this problem involves only a single cylinder, there are two limit
switches (instead of only one per cylinder, as in Fig. 5.6). Limit switch a_1 is
actuated when the cylinder is retracted, and a_2 when extended. (Some authors

use the designations a_0 and a_1, or $a-$ and $a+$, for these two limit switches, but a_1 and a_2; b_1 and b_2; etc. are used here.)

(b) It is customary to draw every switch contact as it appears at the beginning of the sequence, that is, nonactuated or actuated—as the case may be—no matter whether it is an NO or NC contact. Thus, contact a_1 in ladder-diagram line 1, which is NC, is shown open, since limit switch a_1 is actuated at the beginning of the sequence, as can be seen from the pneumatic diagram. For the same reason, the NO contact of a_1 in line 10 is shown closed. On the other hand, limit switch a_2 is not actuated at the beginning, hence, all contacts of a_2 are shown in this ladder diagram in their normal positions. (The reader is referred back to Fig. 2.2, where the limit-switch symbols were summarized.) By using the same convention, cylinder-actuating valve VA in Fig. 5.9 is shown in its left position, since that is its state at the beginning of the sequence.

(c) The reader may have noted that Fig. 5.9 calls for many limit-switch contacts: four contacts of a_1 and four of a_2. The chances of finding limit switches with four contacts are slight, since standard limit switches usually come with a single contact or, at best, with a double contact (of the type denoted by SPDT; see Chapter 2). To solve this problem, we use a method that we call *cloning*: an NO contact of the limit switch is connected to an auxiliary relay coil, and the various contacts of this relay provide "clones" of the original limit switch, as shown in Fig. 5.10. Since relays with many contacts are available, any number of clones can be obtained. This technique can also be used if a relay does not have sufficient contacts. We simply connect the last remaining NO contact to the coil of a second relay. The fact that clone contacts are being used is frequently not indicated on the ladder diagram (since it has no bearing on the logic functions being implemented), and the reader is expected to realize what is going on.

The sequence chart for this problem is shown in Fig. 5.11. Note that the cylinder-actuating valve VA in Fig. 5.9 has two solenoids and no return spring. Thus, brief solenoid actuation is sufficient for shifting the valve (as against a valve with a return spring, where sustained solenoid actuation is required). Therefore, valve VA must be included in the sequence chart and is allocated two lines for positions " $+$ " and " $-$," respectively, so that the current valve position can be shown if neither solenoid is actuated. (In the previous time-motion

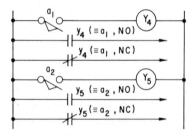

Fig. 5.10. Clone contacts for limit switches a_1 and a_2 in Fig. 5.9.

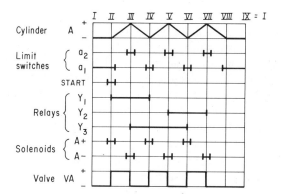

Fig. 5.11. Sequence chart for the circuit of Fig. 5.9.

diagram of Fig. 5.7, the valves were not included, since their states coincided what that of the corresponding solenoid.)

If a three-position valve is used (see Chapter 4), we allocate three horizontal lines for each such valve, with the middle line representing the valve's neutral, or center, position.

To fill in the sequence chart of Fig. 5.11, we again assume that the cylinder is retracted ($-$) and all relays are nonactuated at the beginning of sequence. At stage II, START is pressed. This actuates relay coil Y_1, and, in turn, solenoid $A+$ in line 10. Valve VA thus shifts into its "$+$" position, and cylinder A extends. As a result, limit switch a_1 is released, and its NO contact in line 3 opens. However, actuation of relay Y_1 is maintained by current flow through line 2 and memory contact y_1.

It is left as an exercise for the reader to continue tracing this sequence chart. Whenever a change is detected in the status of any element, this change is entered on the diagram, and all ladder-diagram lines must then be checked to see what effect this change may have on any other element. As seen from Fig. 5.11, the control circuit of Fig. 5.9 causes the cylinder to make three back-and-forth strokes and then halt each time START is pressed. It is also seen that the system comes to rest with all relays nonactuated, which verifies the initial assumption.

We conclude this section by summarizing three different uses of sequence charts:

1. Sequence charts are extremely useful in attempting to understand the operation of ladder diagrams, or of any other switching system. While simple ladder diagrams can be interpreted without them, a diagram such as Fig. 5.9 is difficult to interpret without a sequence chart.

2. Sequence charts provide an efficient method of checking new circuits, since they enable us to trace all events on paper. The sequence chart can point out malfunctions produced by faulty design. For example, if the chart shows that

conditions at the end of the sequence do not match those assumed for the beginning, a design fault is indicated. The sequence chart also permits us to check what might happen if the START button is not released, or if it is released but pressed again later during the sequence. Checking this on Fig. 5.9, we see from line 3 that the START signal only passes provided limit switch a_1 is actuated, *and* relays Y_2 and Y_3 are both not actuated. Checking the sequence chart, we see immediately that these conditions are fulfilled only at stage II, or after stage VIII, which means that pressing the START button during the sequence has no effect whatsoever, in accordance with good circuit design.

3. Sequence charts can also be used for designing new relay control circuits, which is the subject of the next section.

5.3   LADDER-DIAGRAM DESIGN USING SEQUENCE CHARTS

This method is illustrated by means of a relatively simple example, namely, actuating two cylinders according to the sequence START, $A+$, $A-$, $B+$, 10 sec delay, $B-$. The pneumatic diagram for this problem is not shown, since it is identical to that of Fig. 5.9, except that two cylinders are used instead of one. In other words, each cylinder is driven by its 5/2 valve with double solenoids, and actuates two limit switches.

The first step is to draw the required lines for the sequence chart, as shown in Fig. 5.12. At this stage, we do not know yet how many relays will be needed. We assume that one relay Y_1 is sufficient, and, if this assumption should prove false, we can always add more lines later.

The next step is to fill in that part of the sequence chart defined by the specified sequence. Thus, we enter the sequence on the four cylinder lines, and the corresponding limit-switch actuation on the next four lines. Likewise, we show a brief actuation of the START button at stage II, and mark the required changes of valves VA and VB on the four bottom lines.

We now begin to build the ladder diagram stage by stage. We add whatever elements are needed to produce the next step, but must always check that any element added does not interfere with previous steps. All of the resulting activity is entered on the sequence chart, which helps keep track of what is going on. To illustrate:

Step $A+$: Step $A+$ should only take place provided the START button is pressed at the beginning of the sequence. Since the previous sequence ended with step $B-$, which actuated limit switch b_1, we draw the first ladder-diagram line, intended to actuate solenoid $A+$, as shown in Fig. 5.13.

Step $A-$: At stage III, limit switch a_2 is actuated, and this must trigger off the next step $A-$. This can be achieved by line 2 in Fig. 5.14, which shows that a_2 energizes solenoid $A-$. There is, however, a problem: suppose the operator has not yet released the START button. In that case, solenoid $A+$ would still

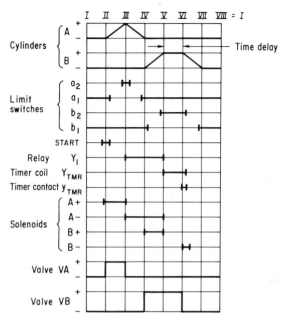

Fig. 5.12. Sequence chart for the sequence START, $A+$, $A-$, $B+$, 10 sec delay, $B-$.

be actuated, and valve VA would have two opposing control signals. As explained in Chapter 4, this is strictly forbidden, since it might cause the solenoids to overheat and burn out. To avoid opposing control signals, we add relay coil Y_1 in line 3 with a NC contact y_1 in line 1. This contact opens and breaks the current flow to solenoid $A+$.

An additional problem now arises: when cylinder A begins to retract, limit switch a_2 is released, so that its NO contact in line 2 opens. This cuts off current to relay coil Y_1, which, in turn, releases solenoid $A-$ and reactuates solenoid $A+$ if the START button should still be pressed. To prevent this undesired turn of events, we add memory contact y_1 in line 3, so that relay Y_1 remains actuated even after contact a_2 has opened.

Step $B+$: Since step $B+$ is to commence only after cylinder A has fully retracted, we connect limit switch a_1 to solenoid $B+$. This however, energizes this solenoid at the very beginning of the sequence, when limit switch a_1 is still actuated. To prevent this, we connect a second NO contact y_1 in series with a_1, as shown in line 4 of Fig. 5.15. As seen from the sequence chart, relay

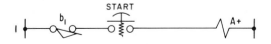

Fig. 5.13. Ladder-diagram line for the steps START, $A+$ (stages I to III).

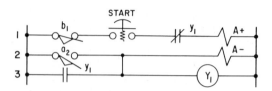

Fig. 5.14. Ladder-diagram lines for the steps START, $A+$, $A-$ (stages I to IV).

Y_1 is not actuated at the beginning of the sequence, so that actuation of a_1 does not energize $B+$ until stage IV.

Steps 10 sec delay, $B-$: When cylinder B has fully extended, it actuates limit switch b_2. We now wish to initiate a 10 s time delay, after which cylinder B should retract. For this relay, we use a timing relay (see Chapter 8 for discussion of timers), which is similar to an ordinary relay, except that its contacts y_{TMR} (NO or NC) switch only when a certain time has elapsed after the timer coil Y_{TMR} was energized.

Figure 5.16 shows the final circuit. The NO contact of limit switch b_2 in line 5 actuates timer coil Y_{TMR} and initiates the delay period. After 10 sec have passed (stage VI), contact y_{TMR} in line 6 closes, energizing solenoid $B-$. However, to avoid opposing control signals, solenoid $B+$ must first be deenergized. This is done by placing the NC contact of limit switch b_2 into line 3. When cylinder B has extended, this contact opens, which breaks the memory of relay Y_1, and thus deactuates both solenoids $A-$ and $B+$. Cylinder B thus retracts the moment solenoid $B-$ is energized at stage VI. As a result, contact b_2 in line 5 opens, deenergizing the timer, and thus also solenoid $B-$ in line 6. When cylinder B has retracted, the sequence is completed.

The reader should realize that this circuit is not the only possible solution. For example, an NC timer contact y_{TMR} could be used in line 3 instead of the NC contact b_2. In that case, relay Y_1 and solenoids $A-$ and $B+$ would remain actuated until stage VI, but the final result would be the same.

In connection with Fig. 5.8, it was explained that sometimes we prefer a circuit in which the large solenoid currents do not flow through the switch contacts. In that case, Fig. 5.16 would have to be modified, as shown in Fig. 5.17.

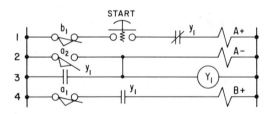

Fig. 5.15. Ladder-diagram lines for the steps START, $A+$, $A-$, $B+$ (stages I to V).

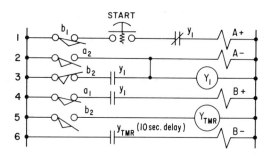

Fig. 5.16. Ladder diagram for the sequence START, $A+$, $A-$, $B+$, 10 sec delay, $B-$.

However, as seen there, this requires two additional relays, which serve no logic function but are used strictly as power relays.

It might be instructive to repeat the above problem, but using cylinder actuating valves with return springs (see Fig. 5.6). These are often preferred, because they cost considerably less than identical valves with double solenoids, since only half the number of solenoids are required. However, their solenoids require sustained actuating signals, instead of the brief signals sufficient when no return springs are used. As a result, additional relays are usually needed in the relay circuit, which somewhat offsets the lower valve cost. The ladder diagram for this case is shown in Fig. 5.18, and the corresponding sequence chart in Fig. 5.19. (Valves VA and VB are not included, since they switch together with their respective solenoids.) It is left as an exercise for the reader to go over these two figures and trace the operation of the circuit. By comparing Fig. 5.18 with Fig. 5.16, it is seen that one additional relay is required.

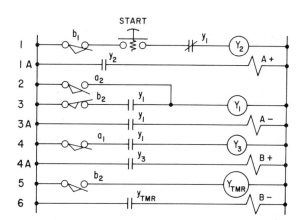

Fig. 5.17. Ladder diagram of Fig. 5.16 modified so that solenoid-actuation currents do not flow through the switch contacts.

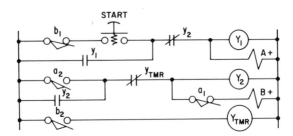

Fig. 5.18. Ladder diagram for the sequence START, $A+$, $A-$, $B+$, 10 sec delay, $B-$ using cylinder-actuating valves with a return spring.

Apart from the cost difference, there is a basic difference between circuits using cylinder-actuating valves with and without return springs. When return springs are used, all cylinders automatically retract during power failure (since the solenoids lose their actuation, but there is still sufficient air pressure in the compressor tank to shift the cylinders). On the other hand, actuating valves without return springs have "mechanical memory," so that all cylinders remain at their last position during power failure. Which method is preferable depends on system requirements, but it is obvious that important safety considerations are involved.

To summarize, the design method based on the sequence chart is probably the one most commonly used in industry, and possibly the most efficient method for relatively simple problems. However, for more complex problems, the results depend to a great extent on the skill and experience of the circuit designer. We, therefore, present two additional methods in this chapter, which are more systematic than the one described in this section.

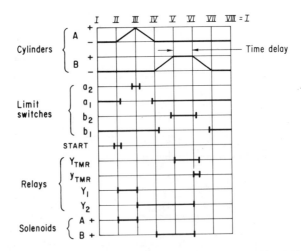

Fig. 5.19. Sequence chart for the ladder diagram of Fig. 5.18.

Readers interested in additional examples of relay ladder diagrams are referred to Refs. (5.1)–(5.4). Reference (5.1) provides a systematic listing of 13 basic circuits for driving single cylinders in different modes, with and without timed delays.

5.4 LADDER-DIAGRAM DESIGN: CASCADE METHOD

The method to be presented here (see Ref. 5.5) does not pretend to minimize the number of required relays. It does, however, provide a convenient way of obtaining a solution for even the most complex problem, without investing a great deal of time and effort. Furthermore, the resulting circuit is so easy to understand that there is no need to draw a sequence chart for this purpose. Also, the method is systematic and completely routine, and thus not dependent on the designer's skill or experience. It is the recommended method when using programmable controllers (see Chapter 10).

5.4.1 Single-Path Sequencing Systems without Sustained Outputs

In this new method, the various steps of the sequence are divided into groups according to the following rule: *a new group must be started the moment it becomes necessary to shut off any output signal actuated during the presently active group.* In other words, any output signal is permitted to remain actuated as long as the group it belongs to remains active.

This rule is best illustrated by a simple example. Suppose we wish to actuate four cylinders, A, B, C, and D, according to the following sequence:

$$\text{START}\left/\underset{\text{I}}{A+, B+, C+}\right/\underset{\text{II}}{C-, A-, D+}\left/\underset{\text{III}}{A+, D-, B-}\right/\underset{\text{IV}}{A-}$$

Assume each cylinder X is actuated, as in Fig. 5.9, by a pneumatic 5/2 valve with two solenoids labeled $X+$ and $X-$, respectively. It is clear that solenoid $X+$ must be shut off the moment $X-$ is actuated, because otherwise we have opposing control signals. Using the previous rule, we divide the sequence into four groups, as indicated before, *so that no letter is repeated within any group.*

The resulting ladder diagram is shown in Fig. 5.20. Each group in the sequence is allocated one relay, connected as an RS flip-flop, as was shown in Fig. 5.3. At any given moment, only the flip-flop corresponding to the currently active group is set, while all others are reset. Therefore, a circuit of this type operates according to the *one-hot* code. As we pass from one group to the next, the next flip-flop is set, and its first task is to reset the previous flip-flop, which automatically shuts off all output signals that were *on* during the previous group. The method is called the *cascade method* because each flip-flop actuates the next one.

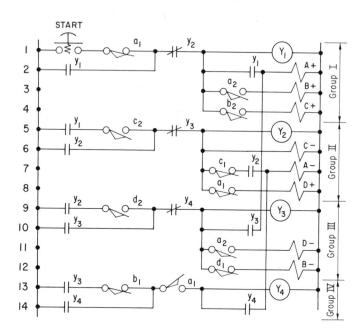

Fig. 5.20. Ladder diagram for the sequence START, $A+$, $B+$, $C+$, $C-$, $A-$, $D+$, $A+$, $D-$, $B-$, $A-$.

We now trace the operation of this circuit. Pressing the START button (line 1) at the beginning of the sequence provides the SET signal for relay Y_1. The y_1 contact connected in line 2 parallel to START provides the memory that converts relay Y_1 into a flip-flop. Once Y_1 is set, solenoid $A+$ (line 2) is actuated, and the sequence begins. Upon completion of the $A+$ stroke, limit switch a_2 (line 3) is closed, actuating solenoid $B+$. Upon completion of the $B+$ stroke, limit switch b_2 (line 4) is closed, actuating solenoid $C+$.

Upon completion of the $C+$ stroke, we must deactivate Group I and activate Group II. The moment limit switch c_2 (line 5) is closed, relay coil Y_2 is set, activating Group II and initiating the first step of Group II, namely stroke $C-$. At the same time, NC contact y_2 in line 1 is now open, breaking the memory of relay Y_1 (i.e., giving the RESET signal for the flip-flop).

Since circuit operation continues in a similar manner, further detailed elaboration is dispensed with. However, it is useful to point out certain features. Note that each relay is reset by means of an NC contact of the next relay (see lines 1, 5 and 9). The only exception is the last relay (Y_4 in this case). This is reset by the NC contact of limit switch a_1 (line 13), which opens the moment the last program step $A-$ is completed. With that, all relays are reset, and the system is ready for the next cycle.

It is also noted that SET signal c_2 for relay Y_2 (line 5) has a y_1 contact connected ahead of it. Likewise, SET signal d_2 for relay Y_3 (line 9) has a y_2

contact connected ahead of it; etc. The purpose of these contacts is to assure that the SET signal for a given relay only takes effect provided the previous relay is active at that moment. Thus, each SET signal is series-connected with a contact of the previous relay. This is necessary to prevent false SET signals in cases where a given limit switch is actuated more than once during the program sequence or where a given limit switch is falsely actuated out of turn.

The third noteworthy feature of the circuit concerns those solenoids that must be actuated more than once during the program cycle, in our example, solenoids $A+$ and $A-$. Since solenoid $A+$ is actuated in both Group I and Group III, we connect an NO contact y_1 ahead of solenoid $A+$ in line 2, and a y_3 contact in line 10. These contacts prevent the voltage from penetrating into the other group while $A+$ is being actuated (this is called a *sneak path*). Similarly, solenoid $A-$ is actuated in Groups II and IV, and we therefore connect a y_2 contact ahead of $A-$ in line 7, and a y_4 contact in line 14.

5.4.2 Single-Path Sequencing Systems with Sustained Outputs

In many industrial automation systems, sustained actuating signals are required. This is best visualized from Fig. 5.6, where the cylinder-actuating valve has only one solenoid and a return spring. To shift such a valve into its "+" position requires a sustained solenoid voltage.

For systems of this type requiring sustained output signals, the previously described method must be modified somewhat. We shall demonstrate this using the same sequence as before:

$$\text{START} \Big/ A+, B+, C+ \Big/ C-, A-, D+ \Big/ A+, D-, B- \Big/ A-$$

The sequence is now divided into groups *so that no letter is repeated within any group*. As is seen, the resulting division is identical to that of the previous example.

Since there are no $A-$, $B-$, $C-$, or $D-$ solenoids, these motions are obtained simply by cutting off the respective "+" solenoid. Contrary to the previous case, this can happen in the middle of a group. As before, the moment a new group is activated, all outputs of the previous group are automatically cut off. If it is required to maintain a certain output into the next group, that output has to be reactivated in that group. To show this and help design the ladder diagram, we draw horizontal arrows underneath the listed sequence, showing up to what point a given output must be maintained. For example, solenoid signal $B+$ must be maintained through part of Group I, all of Group II, and also through Group III up to completion of stroke $D-$. At that point, $B+$ must be cut off, which automatically produces stroke $B-$.

The resulting ladder diagram is shown in Fig. 5.21, which has been drawn

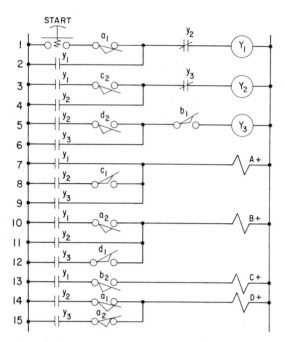

Fig. 5.21. Ladder diagram for the sequence START, $A+, B+, C+, C-, A-, D+, A+,$ $D-, B-, A-$ using cylinder-actuating valves with a return spring.

using the pattern of Fig. 5.5, with the flip-flop lines at the top and the output lines concentrated at the bottom of the ladder. (By comparison, Fig. 5.20 has been drawn according to the pattern of Fig. 5.8, with the output lines drawn directly below the respective relay coils, as discussed in Section 5.2. However, this pattern should not be used for systems with sustained output signals that are maintained from one group to the next, since sneak paths are liable to prevent proper resetting of the previous group.)

The first six lines of Fig. 5.21, representing the three flop-flops, are almost identical to the corresponding lines in Fig. 5.20. The main difference is in the output lines. Since signal $A+$ must be maintained all through Group I, and also through Group II until completion of the $C-$ stroke (see the horizontal arrow below the listed sequence), we connect solenoid $A+$ to an NO relay contact y_1 in line 7, and to y_2 in series with an NC contact of limit switch c_1 in line 8. When stroke $C-$ is completed, this contact opens and cuts off solenoid $A+$, thus producing stroke $A-$. Since solenoid $A+$ must again be actuated all through Group III, $A+$ is also connected to relay contact y_3 in line 9.

Similarly, lines 10, 11, and 12 assure actuation of $B+$, starting with closure of the NO contact a_2 in Group I, through all of Group II, and through Group III until completion of stroke $D-$. At that moment, the NC contact of d_1 opens, cutting off $B+$, which produces stroke $B-$.

Line 13 causes actuation of solenoid $C+$ only during the last part of Group I, starting with completion of stroke $B+$. Finally, lines 14 and 15 actuate $D+$ during the last part of Group II and during the beginning of Group III, until completion of stroke $A+$.

After completion of the $B-$ stroke and of Group III, solenoid $A+$ must be cut off. Since there are no required output signals in Group IV, this group can be dispensed with in this particular example, saving one relay. (Flip-flops are necessary to actuate solenoids, but not to cut them off.) We therefore use the NC contact of limit switch b_1 in line 5 to reset flip-flop Y_3. With that, all groups are inactive, all solenoids are cut off, and, once stroke $A-$ is completed, the sequence has ended.

We conclude this section with a third example, dealing with an automatic mixing system. A START signal must open solenoid valve F (having a return spring) and thereby fill a tank with liquid. When liquid reaches level H, a level switch H is actuated. As a result, valve F must close, and mixer motor M is to operate for a specified time, as measured by timing relay Y_{TMR}. After this time has elapsed, mixer motor M is to stop, and solenoid valve D (also with a return spring) located at the bottom of the tank must open and drain the tank. When the liquid level has declined below a level L, a second level switch L mounted near the tank bottom is *released*, which must close valve D.

The required sequence can be written as follows, where the signals in parentheses indicate the requirements for producing the output signal pointed to by the arrow:

$$\left(\begin{array}{c} \text{START} \\ L \end{array}\right) \Rightarrow F \left/ (H) \Rightarrow F' \right/ (y_{TMR}) \Rightarrow M' \left/ (L) \Rightarrow D' \right.$$

$$
\begin{array}{cccc}
 & M & & D \\
 & Y_{TMR} & & \\
\text{I} & \text{II} & \text{III} & \text{IV}
\end{array}
$$

A good method of systematically defining sequences such as this is the GRAFCET method described in Appendix A.

The resulting solution is shown in Fig. 5.22. The ladder diagram is simple to understand, and the reader should have no difficulty tracing the various steps. Here, too, as in Fig. 5.21, Group IV can be eliminated, since shutting off Group III after level switch L has opened automatically cuts off signal D and thus closes the drain valve. (As is shown in Section 5.5.11, a much simpler solution to this problem is possible.)

5.4.3 Multipath Sequencing Systems

We now illustrate how the cascade method can easily be applied to multipath sequences. Figure 5.23(a) schematically shows a program sequence with two *simultaneous parallel paths*. The program proceeds as a regular sequence up to the completion of step i. At that point, two parallel paths A and B are carried out simultaneously. Path A has j steps, and path B contains k steps; j and k are not

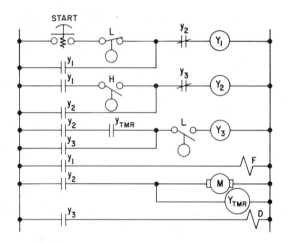

Fig. 5.22. Ladder diagram for an automatic mixing system.

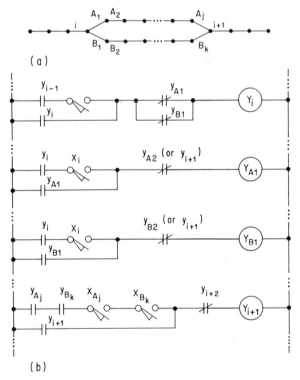

Fig. 5.23. (a) Program sequence with simultaneous parallel paths, and (b) the corresponding ladder diagram.

necessarily equal. Only after both paths have been completed (AND function) does the program continue with the next single-path step $i + 1$.

The corresponding ladder diagram is shown in Fig. 5.23(b). Only the key ladder lines are indicated, with all output lines omitted for clarity. On completion of step i, x_i is actuated, setting flip-flops (i.e., relays) Y_{A1} and Y_{B1}. These flip-flops cover one or more steps each, depending on the way paths A and B must be divided into groups. When both parallel paths are completed, sensor signals x_{A_j} and x_{B_k} are both actuated, setting the next flip-flop Y_{i+1}.

It should be noted that some of the designations are unavoidably ambiguous. Thus, normally closed contacts y_{A2} and y_{B2} (which provide RESET signals for flip-flops Y_{A1} and Y_{B1}, respectively) refer to the *next flip-flop* along the path. For instance, if all of path A should belong to the same group, then y_{A2} would become y_{i+1}. Similarly, contacts y_{A_j} and y_{B_k} refer to the last flip-flops of the two parallel paths. If all of path A should belong to the same group, y_{A_j} would be identical with y_{A1}.

Figure 5.24(a) shows a program sequence with two *alternative parallel paths*. After completion of step i, the next step is either step A_1 or B_1, depending on whether input signal x_P has been set to 1 or 0, respectively. (This x_P signal can be set manually so as to select the desired path, or automatically, depending on outside conditions.) The system continues along the path selected. Once either path A or B is completed (OR function), the system continues with step $i + 1$.

The ladder diagram is shown in Fig. 5.24(b). Again, only key ladder lines are drawn. After step i is completed ($x_i = 1$), either flip-flop Y_{A1} or Y_{B1} is set, depending on whether $x_P = 1$ or 0, respectively. Completion of either step A_j or B_k sets flip-flop Y_{i+1}. The same remarks made in connection with contacts y_{A2}, y_{B2}, y_{A_j}, and y_{B_k} in Fig. 5.23(b) apply here also.

A program with alternative parallel paths is useful for operating multipurpose machines. Obviously, programs with more than two alternative parallel paths can be obtained in a similar manner, with n different x_P variables needed to accommodate 2^n alternative paths. For instance, using x_{P1} and x_{P2}, we could select any one of four alternative paths, depending on whether $x_{P1}x_{P2}$ is set to 00, 01, 10, or 11.

Figure 5.25(a) shows a program sequence with the *option of bypassing certain steps*. At the completion of step i, if input signal $x_P = 1$, then the system goes through program steps A_1 to A_j, and then continues with step $i + 1$. If, on the other hand, $x_P = 0$, then the system jumps directly from step i to $i + 1$.

The corresponding ladder diagram is shown in Fig. 5.25(b). From the first line, it is seen that flip-flop Y_i can be reset by either y_{A1} or y_{i+1}. Flip-flop Y_{A1} is set by the Boolean AND function $x_P x_i y_i$ and reset by y_{A2} (or by y_{i+1} if the bypassed section is all included in one group). Flip-flop Y_{i+1} is set by either the AND function $x_P' x_i y_i$ or by $x_{A_j} y_{A_j}$.

Figure 5.26(a) shows a fourth example of a multipath program: a sequence with the *option of repeating certain steps*. At the completion of step A_j, the system continues with step $i + 1$, provided $x_P = 1$. If, however, $x_P = 0$, then steps A_1 to A_j are repeated indefinitely until x_P becomes 1. Such a circuit is

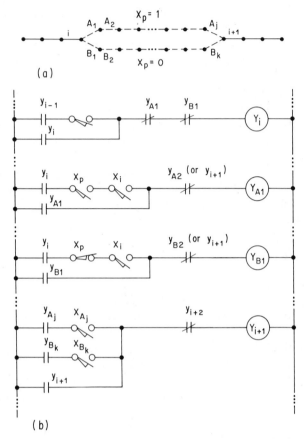

Fig. 5.24. (a) Program sequence with alternative parallel paths, and (b) the corresponding ladder diagram.

useful for systems in which certain operations must be repeated until a desired effect is obtained.

The corresponding ladder diagram is shown in Fig. 5.26(b). It is seen that flip-flop Y_{A1} can be set by either the Boolean AND function $x_i y_i$ or by $x'_p x_{A_j} y_{A_j}$, while it is reset by y_{A2}. The flip-flop y_{A_j} is reset by either y_{A1} or y_{i+1}, depending on whether the steps are repeated or not. Note that at least three flip-flops must be allocated for the repeated steps. If only one or two flip-flops were used for this section of the sequence, they would be set and reset simultaneously, and a malfunction would occur. Thus, even if the rule for dividing the sequence into groups calls for only two groups to cover the repeated steps, a third "dummy" flip-flop must be added. Completion of the last repeated step sets this dummy flip-flop, and the sequence carries on from there, depending on whether $x_P = 0$ or 1.

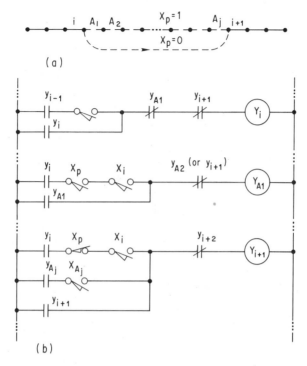

Fig. 5.25. (a) Program sequence with the option of bypassing steps, and (b) the corresponding ladder diagram.

These four examples illustrate the general approach for designing ladder diagrams for multipath sequences. The method presented here is thus extremely flexible, and can easily be adapted to more complicated multipath problems.

5.4.4 Conclusions Concerning the Cascade Method

The cascade method of designing ladder diagrams is simple, and the resulting diagrams are easy to understand. This is a great advantage, which somewhat offsets the fact that more relays are generally required with this method. The method is, therefore, especially suitable for one-of-a-kind circuits, where the time and effort saved in the design process is more important than the cost of an extra relay or two. On the other hand, if the circuit were to be manufactured in quantity (e.g., as part of a machine with large production runs), minimizing relays would become important, and we might prefer to design the circuit using sequence charts (Section 5.3) or the Huffman method (Section 5.5), even though the design effort is much greater. Finally, if the circuit is to be implemented with programmable controllers (see Chaper 10), minimizing relays is of no importance, so that the cascade method would be the method of choice.

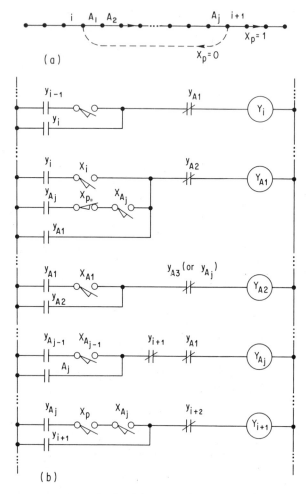

Fig. 5.26. (a) Program sequence with the option of repeating steps, and (b) the corresponding ladder diagram.

A concluding comment concerning the reliability of the cascade method. Many relay circuits suffer from so-called *races*. Thus, even though two relay coils are energized simultaneously, their contacts may not switch at exactly the same moment. Similarly, two contacts of a given relay do not always switch together. If the wrong contact switches first, a malfunction might result in certain circuits, and this possiblity must be taken into account in circuit design. A good circuit is not sensitive to such races; this subject is treated in most textbooks on switching theory (see the references in Chapter 3).

Circuits designed by the cascade method are inherently reliable, since a given flip-flop only resets after the succeeding flip-flop is completely set. Even so, a malfunction caused by a race is theoretically possibly if a relay is defective, and such a case can be demonstrated. Referring to Fig. 5.20, suppose relay Y_3 in line 9 is set. This opens the NC contact y_3 in line 5, resetting Y_2, and finally opening the NO contact y_2 in line 9. If relay contact y_3 is line 10 is defective and does not close completely before y_2 in line 9 has opened, memory is not completely established, and the relay Y_3 may return to its reset condition. Such a situation is extremely unlikely, and the matter is only discussed here to point out the problem of races.

5.5 LADDER-DIAGRAM DESIGN: HUFFMAN METHOD

The method to be described is *the* classic method for designing sequential systems, as described in almost every textbook on switching theory; see Refs. (3.1)–(3.10). Although the method is not easy to master, it produces a circuit with a minimum number of relays. Also, the method can be used for systems with random input signals (Chapter 6), for which the other two methods described in this chapter are not suitable.

5.5.1 Sequential Systems

Switching systems are divided into *combinational* and *sequential* systems. In combinational systems, each binary output is a function of only the present inputs. In sequential systems, on the other hand, some or all outputs also depend on *previous* inputs, that is, on the past history of the system. Thus, sequential systems require memory elements, which usually means flip-flops.

Sequential systems, in turn, are subdivided into *asynchronous* and *synchronous* systems. Asynchronous systems are event-based, which means that a step occurs only after the previous step is successfully completed. Synchronous systems, on the other hand, are time-based, that is, the system is driven by a clock producing pulses at fixed intervals, and each pulse triggers a new step. Computers driven by internal clocks are synchronous systems. In this book, we are mainly concerned with the design of asynchronous systems *with sustained input signals* (rather than pulse inputs), and that is what the reader should look for when consulting textbooks.

Figure 5.27 shows a schematic representation of a sequential system, with a number of inputs x_i and outputs z_j. Depending on memory requirements (discussed later), a number of flip-flops are needed, and each requires a SET and a RESET signal. The functions defining these are called *excitation functions*. Each flip-flop provides a *state variable* y and its logic complement y'. The *combinational system*, which is part of the overall system, receives the various x and y variables as inputs, and then outputs the *output functions* z_j and the excitation functions S_k and R_k. Thus, the design of a sequential system involves, first of all, determining how many flip-flops are required, and then deriving the various excitation and output functions.

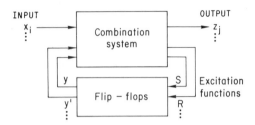

INPUT

OUTPUT

Fig. 5.27. Schematic representation of a sequential system.

5.5.2 Stable and Unstable States

Before discussing the design procedure, it is important to understand the difference between *stable* and *unstable* states.

Suppose that at a certain moment t_0, we send a SET signal to a flip-flop implemented by a relay, as shown in Fig. 5.3. The resulting response is plotted in Fig. 5.28. Because of the relay-coil inductance, a certain time must pass until the coil current builds up to a value sufficient to pull in the coil armature, so that the coil is fully actuated only at moment t_1. Since the armature, mechanical linkage, and contacts all have inertia, we cannot expect instantaneous motion, so that contact y becomes fully closed only at moment t_2. We thus have a total time lag of $t_2 - t_0$ (called the *operate time*), consisting of an electrical and a mechanical lag, which, in a typical relay, might be of the order of 10–20 msec.

A similar lag occurs if a RESET signal is given at moment t_3. The coil current is fully interrupted only at t_4, and the contact fully open only at t_5, giving a total time lag of $t_5 - t_3$. These time intervals, t_0 to t_2 and t_3 to t_5, represent *unstable states*, during which flip-flop output is not consistent with the input signal. (If $S = 1$ and $R = 0$, then y is supposed to be 1, and not 0 as during the t_0-to-t_2 period.) This unstable state lasts only for a short period of time, and automatically turns into a *stable state*, in which input and output signals are consistent with each other.

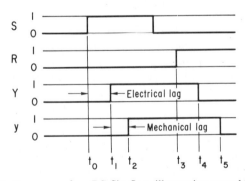

Fig. 5.28. Response of an RS flip-flop, illustrating unstable states.

It should be stressed that unstable states occur with any type of switching element. They occur in electronic flip-flops, except that the unstable state only lasts some nanoseconds, depending on the flip-flop speed of response. The phenonenon is not limited to flip-flops, but exists with any element or any entire circuit. Suppose we have an AND gate giving $T = AB$, and its inputs change from $AB = 10$ to 11. There is a certain time interval (again depending on the gate's speed of response) during which AB is already 11, but the output has not yet switched from 0 to 1. Again, this represents an unstable state, since inputs and output are inconsistent.

The phenomenon of unstable states has an important bearing on the discussion to follow.

5.5.3 Primitive Flow Table

In the following, we use a simple example in order to illustrate the method. Assume a single cylinder A actuated by a 5/2 valve with solenoid $A+$ and a return spring, as shown in Fig. 5.29. The required cycle is very simple: START, $A+, A-, A+, A-$. The figure also includes a partial sequence chart, showing these four cylinder motions as triggered by a short START signal.

We now number each state in the sequence. The input combinations a_1a_2 existing at each state are listed below the diagram. Each time an input signal changes, we assign a new state number. Thus, the above sequence involves eight different states, with the last state at the end of the sequence labeled 1, since it is equivalent to the first state. (Actually, there is a difference: state 1 at the beginning includes the START signal, whereas the final state does not, but we shall disregard the START signal for the time being.)

The next step is to fill in a so-called *primitive flow table*, as shown in Fig. 5.30. This table has a row for each of the eight states, and a column for each possible input combination. Since there are two inputs, a_1 and a_2, there are $2^2 = 4$ possible combinations, and thus four columns. In addition, at the right side of the table, we add an output column for each output signal. Since our example involves only a single output $A+$, there is only one output column.

The table is now filled in as follows. Each of the eight states is entered in its row (according to its number) and its proper column (according to its input

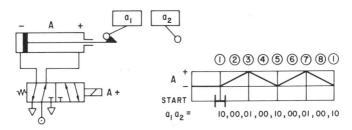

Fig. 5.29. Sequence $A+, A-, A+, A-$.

	a_1a_2				A +
	10	00	01	11	
1	①	2	—	—	1
2	—	②	3	—	1
3	—	4	③	—	0
4	5	④	—	—	0
5	⑤	6	—	—	1
6	—	⑥	7	—	1
7	—	8	⑦	—	0
8	1	⑧	—	—	0

Fig. 5.30. Primitive flow table for the example of Fig. 5.29.

combination), and is encircled, which signifies a stable state. For each stable state, we enter the required output signal in the $A +$ column. For example, in the first row, we want $A +$ to be 1 in order to have the cylinder extend. In the second row, we also enter a 1 in the $A +$ column, since the solenoid requires a continuous signal because of the return spring. In the third row, we enter a 0 in the $A +$ column, since we want the cylinder to retract. The remainder of the $A +$ column is filled in similarly.

We now enter the *unstable states*, using numbers that are not encircled. For example, at stable state ①, the cylinder begins to extend. As a result, limit switch a_1 is released, so that the input combination changes from $a_1a_2 = 10$ to 00. At that moment, we get a brief unstable state 2, which means that an input to the logic system has changed, but the system has not yet responded to this change, so that there is an inconsistency between the system's input and output signals. This unstable state 2, of course, does not last long. After a very brief period (depending on the speed of response of the switching elements used), the system reaches the next stable state, state ② in this case.

The remaining unstable states are filled in similarly. Thus, each time an input change occurs, we go from a stable state ⓚ to the succeeding unstable state $k + 1$ in the same row, and from there to the succeeding stable state ⓚ+1 in the same column but in the new row.

The reader may be mystified as to why we bother with these unstable states to begin with, especially since they only last for such a brief period of time. The answer to this becomes evident in the next section, which deals with *row merging*.

The remaining squares in the flow table are never reached, and they, therefore, get the "Don't Care" symbol ϕ or "—" (see Chapter 3). The reasoning behind this is as follows. The $a_1a_2 = 11$ combination is physically impossible, since the cylinder cannot retract and extend at the same time. Therefore, the entire fourth column has no physical significance. The other empty squares are theoretically possible, but are not utilized in the particular program sequence under discussion. (For example, we cannot go from state ① directly to the $a_1 a_2 = 01$ square in the same row, since the system must first pass through $a_1 a_2 = 00$, state 2, which immediately brings it into the second row.) Since none of these empty squares are ever reached, we "don't care" what might happen there, and therefore enter "—."

5.5.4 Row Merging and Merged Flow Table

We could, in theory, use the primitive flow table to design our control circuit. However, the circuit must keep track or "remember" where it is at any moment, and this requires memory, that is, flip-flops. Each flip-flop has two possible states, $y = 0$ or $y = 1$. Therefore, n flip-flops can differentiate between 2^n different states. Since the previous primitive flow table has eight states, three flip-flops would be required to differentiate between them. (More about that in the next section.)

In order to reduce the number of rows in the flow table, and thus hopefully also the number of required flip-flops or relays, we use a technique called *row merging*. The idea behind row merging is as follows: instead of relying solely on flip-flops to differentiate between the different states, we can also utilize the information supplied by the input signals. We therefore combine, or *merge*, two (or more) rows, provided there is no contradiction between them; which means that there are no differing numbers in the same column. To illustrate, we could merge rows 1 and 2 in the previous primitive flow table, and the result of this merger is shown in Fig. 5.31. The merging is carried out according to the following rules:

1. If there is an unstable state and a stable state in the same column, the merged row gets a stable state.
2. If there is a number and a "—" entry in the same column, the merged row gets the number (with or without circle, as the case may be).
3. If there are only "—" entries in a column, the merged row gets a "—."

The principle behind this merging process is that if the control circuit "decides" that the system is, at this moment, in the merged row 1, 2, it can then identify the exact state it is at by referring to the input signals.

Considering, for example, rows 4 and 5, we see immediately that these cannot be merged, because there are differing numbers, ④ and 6, in the $a_1 a_2 = 00$ column. If we try to merge these rows, we get a contradiction: in row 4, the

1	①	2	—	—
2	—	②	3	—
1,2	①	②	3	—

Fig. 5.31. Merging rows 1 and 2 of Fig. 5.30.

	a_1a_2				y_1	y_2
	10	00	01	11		
1,2	①	②	3	—	1	0
3,4	5	④	③	—	1	1
5,6	⑤	⑥	7	—	0	1
7,8	1	⑧	⑦	—	0	0

Fig. 5.32. Merged flow table with state assignment.

$a_1a_2 = 00$ combination means that we are at stable state ④, so that the system is expected to remain there for the time being, and provide output signal $A+ = 0$. In row 5, however, the same $a_1a_2 = 00$ combination means that the system is at unstable state 6, and is thus expected to move on immediately to stable state ⑥ in the next row, where $A+ = 1$ is called for. It is obvious, therefore, that rows 4 and 5 cannot be merged.

It should now be clear to the reader why we entered the unstable states in the primitive flow table: they provide information necessary to decide which rows may be merged.

Checking the remaining rows in Fig. 5.30, we conclude that the following rows can be merged: 1 and 2, 3 and 4, 5 and 6, and 7 and 8. The result of these mergers is the *merged flow table* of Fig. 5.32. (The reader is asked to disregard the two right-hand columns labeled y_1 and y_2 for now. These are discussed in the next section.) Note, however, that *output columns* ($A+$ in this case) are *not* included in the merged flow table. In fact, rows can be merged even though they have different output signals. It so happens that this statement cannot be illustrated in the present example. However, in a later example (Section 5.5.13), we merge rows having different outputs, and the problem of row merging is discussed in greater detail.

5.5.5 State Assignment

Using the technique of row merging, we succeeded in reducing the eight rows of the primitive flow table to four rows in the merged flow table. Therefore, only two flip-flops, instead of three, are needed to differentiate between the rows. This is done using a process called *state assignment.*

If the merged flow table has only two rows, the problem of state assignment becomes trivial: a single flip-flop is sufficient, and we assign state $y = 0$ to one row and $y = 1$ to the other. By checking the state of y, the system always knows which row it is at. (Note that if the primitive flow table can be merged into a single row, then no state variables are required, and the system is combinational rather than sequential.)

If there are four rows, we need two flip-flops, and these provide four different state-variable combinations: $y_1y_2 = 00$, 01, 10, and 11. The process of deciding which of these to assign to each row is termed the state assignment. We can place any one of these four combinations into the first row, which leaves any of the remaining three combinations for the second row, any of the remaining two for the third, and the last remaining combination for the fourth row. Thus, there are 4! = 24 different possibilities.

It can be shown, however, that most of these 24 possibilities are equivalent. For example, the state assignments

$$y_1 y_2 = 00, 01, 11, 10 \quad \text{and} \quad y_1 y_2 = 00, 10, 11, 01$$

are equivalent, since we can get one from the other simply by exchanging the indices, that is, exchanging y_1 and y_2.

Similarly, the state assignments

$$y_1 y_2 = 00, 01, 11, 10 \quad \text{and} \quad y_1 y_2 = 11, 10, 00, 01$$

are equivalent, since we can get one from the other by exchanging SET and RESET, that is, exchanging y and y' for both flip-flops. Likewise, if we only exchange S_2 and R_2, we find the following state assignments to be equivalent:

$$y_1 y_2 = 00, 01, 11, 10 \quad \text{and} \quad y_1 y_2 = 01, 00, 10, 11$$

In this manner, the 24 state assignments possible with two flip-flops can be reduced to only three distinctly different ones:

(a) $y_1 y_2 = 00, 01, 11, 10$
(b) $y_1 y_2 = 00, 11, 01, 10$
(c) $y_1 y_2 = 00, 01, 10, 11$

Each of these represents a group of eight other equivalent state assignments, which can be derived from the original one by means of the manipulations previously described. Depending on which of these three state assignments is used, we obtain three completely different final solutions. On the other hand, the eight solutions resulting from the eight state assignments belonging to the same group are basically identical, and differ only in how the variables and hardware components are labeled.

If we use three flip-flops instead of two, we can cover $2^3 = 8$ different rows of a merged flow table, and this results in 8! = 40,320 possible state assignments. Here, too, most of these are actually equivalent, and the above number can be reduced to "only" 840 distinctly different state assignments, each of which produces a different solution. (See Chapter 6 for an example involving three flip-flops.) The question of selecting the state assignment—out of the 840 possible ones—in order to get the best (i.e., simplest) solution is complex, with scores of articles and whole chapters written on the subject. The problem is beyond the scope of this book, and is only discussed very briefly here, in Section 5.5.13, and in Chapter 6.

One important role in selecting a state assignment is that *only one state variable should switch as we go from one row to the next.* This automatically excludes groups (b) and (c) from the specified list, leaving only group (a). In group (b), the transition from the first to the second row calls for a change of $y_1 y_2$ from 00 to 11, which is against this rule. Similarly, during transition from the third to the fourth row, the state variables change from 01 to 10. In group (c), we also have two transitions with double changes: from row 2 to 3, and from row 4 back to row 1.

The reason behind this rule is that double changes in state variables can cause so-called *races.* For example, suppose we used a state assignment according to group (b). In order to go from the first row (where $y_1 y_2 = 00$) to the second row (where $y_1 y_2 = 11$), we must give the S_1 and S_2 signals simultaneously, so that both flip-flops become set. However, two flip-flops are never completely identical (no matter whether implemented with relays, electronically or pneumatically), so that one of the two is certain to have a slightly faster response and become set first. Of course, we have no way of knowing which flip-flop is faster. The transition from row 1 to row 2 can, therefore, take place along any one of the following two paths:

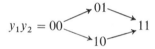

$$y_1 y_2 = 00 \begin{array}{c} \nearrow 01 \searrow \\ \searrow 10 \nearrow \end{array} 11$$

If flip-flop 2 is faster, then the upper path is followed, and the system suddenly finds itself in row 3 (where $y_1 y_2 = 01$). If, on the other hand, the lower path is followed, then the system finds itself in row 4. Depending on other circumstances, the system might find itself "trapped" in row 3 or row 4, which could result in a serious malfunction.

Not all races lead to a malfunction. Those that do are called *critical races*, because the end result depends on which flip-flop "wins" the race. But there are also *noncritical races*, in which the winner has no effect on the end result. The difference is explained in greater detail in Chapter 6. However, to avoid the whole problem, it is best to select a state assignment that avoids races to begin with by following the previous rule.

The merged flow table in Fig. 5.32 shows the state assignment that was selected, listed in the two right-hand columns. It is one of the eight belonging to group (a), and, as is noted, there are no races.

5.5.6 Derivation of Excitation Functions

For each flip-flop, we must derive the SET and the RESET functions. These are often called the *excitation functions* of the flip-flop. Since two flip-flops are used in our example, we must derive four excitation functions, and this is best done using Karnaugh maps (see Chapter 3). To fill these maps, we refer to the merged flow table of Fig. 5.32, and the flip-flop actuation table described in Chapter 3,

Initial	Final	Required	
y	y	S	R
0	0	0	—
0	1	1	0
1	0	0	1
1	1	—	0

Fig. 5.33. Flip-flop actuation table.

Fig. 3.35. Since it is useful to have this table in front of us, it is shown in Fig. 5.33. The Karnaugh maps for the four excitation functions are shown in Fig. 5.34. Note that their row and column designations match those of the merged flow table. This facilitates the process of filling in the maps, since a given square in any map corresponds to the square at the identical location in the merged flow table. Unfortunately, for more complicated problems, this usually becomes impossible, in which case a special "path map" can be used, as shown in the examples of Sections 5.5.11 and 5.5.13.

The Karnaugh maps are now filled in according to the following three rules:

1. *In squares representing stable states, each flip-flop must maintain its present state.*

Example. The left square in the first row represents stable state ①, both in the merged flow table and in the Karnaugh maps. To maintain this state, we must keep $y_1 = 1$ and $y_2 = 0$ (this being the state assignment for the first row). We now refer to the flip-flop actuation table in Fig. 5.33, and see from the last row that for initial $y_1 = 1$ and final $y_1 = 1$ (i.e., y_1 maintained 1), we don't care about S_1, but must keep $R_1 = 0$. We, therefore, enter the "Don't Care" symbol "—" in this particular square of the S_1 map, and a 0 in the R_1 map. The state variable y_2, on the other hand, must be kept 0. This is accomplished by following instructions in the first row of the flip-flop actuation table (initial $y_2 = 0$ and final $y_2 = 0$), and we enter a 0 in the S_2 map, and a "—" in the R_2 map. The reader should check the remaining seven stable states in Fig. 5.32, and trace the corresponding entries in the four maps.

2. *In squares representing unstable states, the flip-flop must go to the succeeding stable state.*

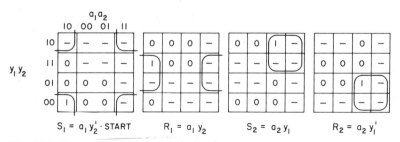

Fig. 5.34. Karnaugh maps for excitation functions corresponding to Fig. 5.32.

Example. The third square in the first row represents unstable state 3. To get from there to stable state ③ in the new row, y_1 must be maintained 1, but y_2 must switch from 0 to 1, since the state assignment for the second row is $y_1 y_2 = 11$. Again, we refer to the flip-flop actuation table for instructions. The last row indicates that we need $S_1 = $ "—" and $R_1 = 0$, and the second row indicates that we need $S_2 = 1$ and $R_2 = 0$, and these are the entries in the third square of the first row in the excitation maps. Again, the reader should check the entries for the remaining unstable states.

3. *Squares having "don't care" entries in the merged flow table get "don't care" entries in the excitation maps.* This is logical, since these squares can never be reached anyway, so that we don't care what is entered there in the maps.

After the four maps have been filled in, the functions are derived using the Karnaugh-map technique described in Chapter 3. The resulting excitation functions are written in Fig. 5.34 under each map. (The START term included in the S_1 function is explained in Section 5.5.8.)†

5.5.7   Derivation of Output Functions

For each output signal, the corresponding *output function* must be derived, and here, too, this is best done using Karnaugh maps. In our example, there is only one output signal $A+$, and the corresponding Karnaugh map is shown in Fig. 5.35. The output maps are filled in by referring to both primitive and merged flow tables, and using the following four rules:

1. *A square representing a stable state gets the output value shown for that state in the primitive flow table.*

Example. The primitive flow table, Fig. 5.30, shows that, for stable states ① and ②, $A+ = 1$, whereas, for stable states ③ and ④, $A+ = 0$. We therefore place 1 entries in the first two squares of the first row, and 0 entries in the two middle squares of the second row (which, according to Fig. 5.32, represent stable states ③ and ④).

2. *If the output remains at the same value (0 or 1) for stable states ⓚ and ⓚ+1, we enter this value in the square representing the unstable state $k + 1$.*

Unfortunately, there is no example of this situation in the present problem. However, it makes sense that if we wish a certain output to remain 0 (or 1) for

---

†In most textbooks on switching theory, relays are utilized as memory elements in a different manner, that is, not in the form of RS flip-flops. While this has the advantage that only one excitation function per relay need be derived, there are two drawbacks. (1) So-called "static hazards" can occur if the design is not carried out properly. (2) Pseudo-Karnaugh maps, to be discussed in Section 5.5.12, cannot be used. Because of these two problems, we are here using relays exclusively in the flip-flop mode, even though this means that two excitation functions per relay must be derived. It can be shown that there is little difference between these two methods as far as the final resulting circuit is concerned.

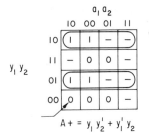

$A + = y_1 y_2' + y_1' y_2$ **Fig. 5.35.** Karnaugh map for output function $A+$.

stable states ⑯ and ⑰, then that same output should also be retained for the intermediate unstable state 17.

3. *If the output changes between stable states* ⓚ *and* ⓚ+ⅈ, *we place a "don't care" entry in the square representing unstable state k + 1.*

Example. As seen from the primitive flow table, $A+ = 1$ at stable state ②, but 0 at stable state ③. We therefore enter "—" at unstable state 3 (third square of first row). Similarly, $A+ = 0$ at ④, but 1 at ⑤. We therefore enter "—" at unstable state 5. The reasoning behind this rule is that it does not really matter whether the output switches to its new value a few milliseconds earlier or later, since the delays in the switching circuit are negligible compared to the mechanical delays of the controlled system.†

4. *Squares having "don't care" entries in the merged flow table get "don't care" entries in the output map.* Again, since these squares are never reached anyway, we don't care what is entered there.

After the output maps have been filled in, the output functions are derived. The result for $A+$ is listed in Fig. 5.35. Note that an arrow is pointing at the 0 entered in the square corresponding to unstable state 1. According to previous Rule 3, we should have entered "—" in that square, since $A+ = 1$ at stable state ⑧ and 0 at stable state ①. The reason for this 0 entry is explained in the next section.

5.5.8 How to Add the START Signal

The solution is now almost complete, except that we have not yet taken care of the START signal. As things stand, the sequence repeats indefinitely, which can be seen by referring to the excitation and output maps. At completion of the sequence, the system reaches unstable state 1 (left square in bottom row), where $S_1 = 1$ and $S_2 = 0$. Thus, flip-flop 1 becomes set, producing $y_1 y_2 = 10$, that is,

---

†Most textbooks on switching theory, which are usually oriented toward the design of computer systems, recommend entering the new output value rather than "—," in order to get a slight increase in the system's speed of response. However, the use of "—" entries can lead to simpler output functions, which means less hardware, and this is of greater importance in industrial automation systems.

the system automatically goes to stable state ① (left square in the top row). Since $A+ = 1$ at that square, the sequence begins anew without waiting for the START command.

The straightforward way of incorporating START in the solution is to consider it as a third input signal, in addition to a_1 and a_2. But this means additional columns in the flow tables, and the various Karnaugh maps would have to accommodate five variables instead of four, thus doubling their size and making the solution much more time-consuming.

To avoid having five variables, we use the trick of completely disregarding START at the beginning, as has been done here. START is now incorporated in the solution obtained so far, using the following reasoning:

In order to get only one cycle at a time, the system must be stopped at the end of the sequence, that is, either at unstable state 1 or at stable state ①. This provides two options, each involving different considerations.

To stop the system at unstable state 1, we refer to the excitation maps, and check which signal produces the transition from unstable state 1 to stable state ①. As already mentioned, this transition is caused by the $S_1 = a_1 y'_2$ signal. We must, therefore, inhibit this signal by multiplying it with START, as indicated in Fig. 5.34. As a result, when unstable state 1 is reached, S_1 remains 0 as long as START $= 0$. Only when START $= 1$ do we get $S_1 = 1$, causing the system to pass to stable state ①.

However, all this is useless unless we made $A+ = 0$ at unstable state 1. If $A+ = 1$ at that state, it is pointless to inhibit the S_1 signal, since the cylinder would begin to move at unstable state 1 before START is given. This explains why 0 instead of "—" was entered in the respective square of the $A+$ map. (A "don't care" entry in that square might be utilized as 1.)

The second option involves stopping the system at stable state ①. Since ① and ② have the identical state assignment, this cannot be done by inhibiting excitation functions. Instead, we must now inhibit the $A+$ output function with START, so that the system cannot pass from ① to ② unless START $= 1$.

This, however, brings up another problem. If we followed the above option, we would write the output function as

$$A+ = y_1 y'_2 \cdot \text{START} + y'_1 y_2$$

which means that the entire upper 4-square cell $y_1 y'_2$ is dependent on the START signal. Thus, unless the operator keeps pressing the START button all during the forward stroke (until unstable state 3 is reached), we would get $A+ = 0$ at stable state ②, so that the cylinder rectracts. To prevent this malfunction, we must split the two 1 entries in the upper 4-square cell into two separate cells, and attach the START signal only to stable state ① (but including other states with "—" entries, if possible). The resulting output map is shown in Fig. 5.36.

The resulting $A+$ function is much longer than that obtained in Fig. 5.35. The conclusion is that, for this particular example, the first option is preferable,

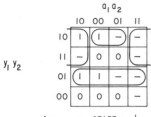

$$A+ = a_1 y_1 \cdot \text{START} + y_1' y_2 + a_1' y_1 y_2'$$

Fig. 5.36. Modified Karnaugh map for the output function $A+$.

that is, START should be attached to the S_1 function. In many cases, however, there is no choice. For example, unstable state 1 sometimes does not appear in the merged flow table, having been eliminated in the merging process. In such cases, we have no choice but to use the second option, that is, attach START to the appropriate output function.

In connection with START, a feature of the state assignment in Fig. 5.32 is discussed briefly. The reader may have wondered why $y_1 y_2 = 00$ was assigned to the last, rather than the first row. This has to do with power breaks (e.g., power failure or the end of the work day). When power returns, we want the system to be at unstable state 1, where it waits for the START signal. Flip-flops implemented by relays are always reset during a power break, so that the system is automatically at unstable state 1, provided state assignment 00 is used there.

It must be stressed that this consideration applies *only to relays*. If electronic flip-flops are used, the initial flip-flop state is normally completely random, so that special provision must be made to initialize the system properly when power returns. When pneumatic valves are used as flip-flops (see Chapter 7), this problem does not exist. Valves have mechanical memory, and therefore automatically retain their last position when air pressure is interrupted.

5.5.9   The Ladder-Diagram Solution

We have now derived the solution functions, and are ready to draw the resulting ladder diagram. In Fig. 5.3, the flip-flop SET signal was provided by a NO switch contact. In the case of a circuit operated automatically rather than by a manual push button, this SET contact must be replaced by a contact circuit implementing the S function derived in Section 5.5.6.

Since the RESET button in Fig. 5.3 actuates an NC contact, it must be replaced by a circuit giving the *complemented* or *inverted* reset function R'. (In other words, this circuit must conduct current as long as the RESET button is *not* pressed.) This means that the derived RESET, or R functions, must first be inverted using the DeMorgan theorems; see Equations (28)–(30) in Chapter 3. We thus get

$$R_1' = (a_1 y_2)' = a_1' + y_2'$$
$$R_2' = (a_2 y_1')' = a_2' + y_1$$

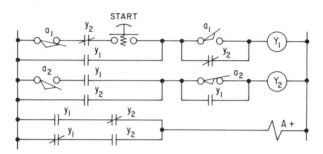

Fig. 5.37. Ladder-diagram solution for the sequence START, $A+$, $A-$, $A+$, $A-$.

The resulting ladder-diagram solution is shown in Fig. 5.37. If the reader is not convinced, the sequence chart should be drawn for this ladder diagram to verify circuit operation.

In Chapter 10, it is shown how relay circuits can be implemented on a programmable controller. The solution can, of course, also be implemented with any type of logic gate, instead of with relays. For instance, if electronic gates are used, we need two RS flip-flops, four AND gates (for the four excitation functions) and two AND gates and one OR gate for the output function. (This assumes that limit switches with both NO and NC contacts are available; otherwise, additional NOT gates are needed.) If Exclusive-OR gates are available, a single such gate produces the output function. In Chapter 7, it is shown how the solution can be implemented using pneumatic valves.

5.5.10   Solution for Cylinder-Actuating Valve without a Return Spring

We now modify the solution, assuming a cylinder-actuating valve with double solenoids $A+$ and $A-$, but with no return spring, as in Fig. 5.9. The resulting primitive flow table is identical to that in Fig. 5.30, except that the single output column $A+$ must be replaced by the two output columns shown in Fig. 5.38.

State	A +	A –
1	1	0
2	–	0
3	0	1
4	0	–
5	1	0
6	–	0
7	0	1
8	0	–

Fig. 5.38. Output columns for the primitive flow table of Fig. 5.30, using valves without return springs.

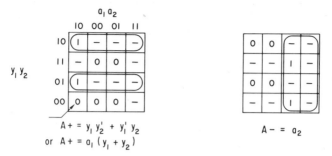

Fig. 5.39. Output maps corresponding to Fig. 5.38.

Since the remainder of the primitive flow table is not changed, it is not repeated here. Note that both output columns contain "don't care" entries. This is because these valves have mechanical memory, and retain their previous position even without an explicit solenoid signal.

Since output signals have no effect on row merging or on state assignment, the merged flow table is identical to that of Fig. 3.32. Similarly, the excitation maps are identical to those shown in Fig. 5.34. The only difference is that the two output maps of Fig. 5.39 replace the one of Fig. 5.35. Note that in the new $A+$ map, the second square in the top row now has a "—" entry rather than 1. As a result, a simplified solution $A+ = a_1(y_1 + y_2)$ becomes possible. If we decide to attach the START signal to $A+$ (rather than to S_1), we get $A+ = a_1(y_1 \cdot \text{START} + y_2)$. Thus, using the second option is practical in this case.

5.5.11 Use of a "Path Map"

A Second Example: Automatic Mixing System. We now apply the Huffman method to the automatic mixing system, which was solved in Section 5.4.2 using the cascade method. Since the program sequence was defined there, it is not repeated here.

The primitive flow table is shown in Fig. 5.40(a), and has four output columns. Since there are three input variables (L, H, and y_{TMR}), there could be eight different input combinations. However, only those of relevance to the problem are listed in the table, in the order in which they appear in the sequence. For instance, combinations 010 and 011 are impossible, since the level cannot possibly be below L and above H at the same time; hence, these columns are not listed.

The merged flow table is shown in Fig. 5.40(b). Since there are only two rows, a single flip-flop is sufficient.

In Section 5.5.6, it was explained that the excitation and output maps should, if possible, have the same configuration as the merged flow table to make it easier to fill in the maps. Looking at Fig. 5.40(b), we see immediately that this is

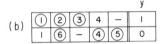

(a)

	LHy_TMR					F	D	M	Y_TMR
	000	100	110	111	101				
	①	2				1	0	0	0
		②	3			1	0	0	0
			③	4		0	0	1	1
				④	5	0	1	–	1
		6			⑤	0	1	0	0
	1	⑥				0	1	0	0

(b)

						y
①	②	③	4	–	1	
1	⑥	–	④	⑤	0	

Fig. 5.40. (a) Primitive flow table, and (b) a merged flow table for an automatic mixing system.

impossible here. To facilitate filling in the maps, it is highly recommended to invest a couple of minutes in first constructing a *path map*, as shown in Fig. 5.41. This has the row and column designations of a standard Karnaugh map, but instead of 1 and 0 entries, we enter the various states appearing in the merged flow table. For example, since the merged flow table shows stable state ① to be at $LHy_{TMR} = 000$ and in the row $y = 1$, we enter ① in that square of the path map corresponding to the same combination of variables. The remainder of the path map is filled in similarly.

We are now ready to fill in the two excitation and the four output maps, which are shown in Fig. 5.42, using the rules listed in Sections 5.5.6 and 5.5.7. Since these maps have identical row and column designations as the path map, we can tell immediately which square corresponds to which state. In other words, instead of figuring out the location of each state separately for each of the six maps, we perform this chore only once, when filling in the path map.

As in the previous example, we incorporate the START signal at the end, adding it to the S signal, and, for this reason, place a 0 into the square corresponding to unstable state 1 of the F output map. The same square in the D map also has a 0, but for a different reason. If it should get a "—" entry, the D function would become $D = y'$, which means that solenoid D would be energized unnecessarily for long periods of time while the system is at unstable state 1 waiting for the next START signal.

The final solution is shown in Fig. 5.43. Only one relay is required, as

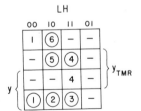

Fig. 5.41. Path map for Fig. 5.40.

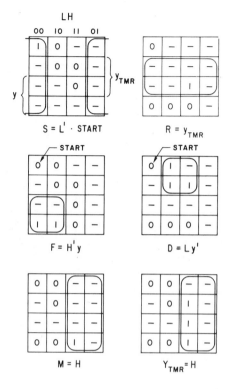

Fig. 5.42. Excitation and output maps for an automatic mixing system.

compared to three in the cascade-method solution of Fig. 5.22. This illustrates the statement made in Section 5.4.2: the cascade method is much easier than the Huffman method, but does not result in a minimum number of relays.

5.5.12 Pseudo-Karnaugh Maps

While the description of the Huffman method is basically complete, some enhancements can be added. The single-cylinder problem treated previously involved two input and two state variables. Every additional cylinder adds two

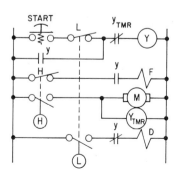

Fig. 5.43. Ladder diagram for an automatic mixing system.

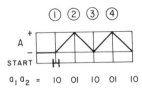

Fig. 5.44. Sequence chart for the sequence START, $A+$, $A-$, $A+$, $A-$.

more input variables (assuming two limit switches per cylinder), and possibly also more state variables, depending on the length and nature of the sequence. It is obvious that, very soon, we will exceed the eight variables that can be handled by Karnaugh maps (see Chapter 3).

To overcome this difficulty, we can utilize *pseudo-Karnaugh maps*, so called because they do not include all theoretically possible combinations of input variables. As an example, we again consider the single-cylinder problem of Fig. 5.29. If we now replace the valve return spring by a second solenoid $A-$ (as in Fig. 5.9), then we can disregard intermediate states 2, 4, 6, and 8 in Fig. 5.29 (at which $a_1 a_2 = 00$), since no solenoid actuation is required at these four states, so that nothing happens there. The resulting modified sequence chart is shown in Fig. 5.44. Instead of eight, there are now only four states.

The resulting flow table is shown in Fig. 5.45. Note that there are only two input-signal columns, a_1 and a_2. The $a_1 a_2 = 00$ states have been eliminated, and the $a_1 a_2 = 11$ states are impossible, so that we are left only with $a_1 a_2 = 10$ and 01. These designations can be shortened to $a_1 = 1$ and $a_2 = 1$. (The dropped 0 need not be explicitly stated, but it is implied). This considerably shrinks the flow tables, and also the resulting Karnaugh maps. Since row merging is not possible in this particular case, Fig. 5.45 represents both primitive and merged flow tables. We therefore add the two columns for the state assignment. (We purposely use the same state assignment as in Fig. 5.32 to obtain a valid comparison between the respective results.)

The excitation and output maps, see Fig. 5.46, have the same configuration as the merged flow table, that is, they contain only two columns rather than four. The resulting excitation and output functions are identical to those obtained previously, as shown in 5.34 and 5.39. The conclusion of this exercise is that by using pseudo-Karnaugh maps, only half the work is required to arrive at the same final solution.

We now illustrate how a pseudo-Karnaugh map for six variables is constructed (four input variables, a_1, a_2, b_1, and b_2, and two state variables, y_1

a_1	a_2	$A+$	$A-$	$y_1 y_2$
①	2	1	0	10
3	②	0	1	11
③	4	1	0	01
1	④	0	1	00

Fig. 5.45. Primitive and merged flow table for Fig. 5.44.

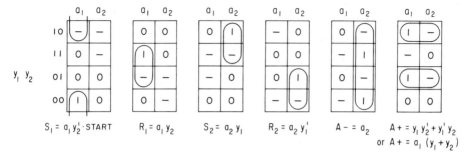

Fig. 5.46. Pseudo-Karnaugh excitation and output maps for Fig. 5.45.

and y_2). The left part of Fig. 5.47 shows a regular Karnaugh map for these six variables, as described in Chapter 3. We first eliminate all squares representing the combinations $a_1a_2 = 00$ or $b_1b_2 = 00$ by cross-hatching the respective areas on the Karnaugh map. Since the combinations $a_1a_2 = 11$ and $b_1b_2 = 11$ are impossible (assuming we are dealing with limit switches for cylinders), we eliminate these areas also, using cross-hatching in the opposite direction. By now, only four columns are left, representing a_2b_2, a_1b_2, a_2b_1, and a_1b_1. These columns are now arranged as shown in the right section of Fig. 5.47, and the result is a six-variable pseudo-Karnaugh map.

An eight-variable pseudo-Karnaugh map is shown later in Fig. 5.53. Figure 5.48 extends this idea to a 12-variable pseudo-Karnaugh map, covering eight input and four state variables. This map consists of 16 submaps, each of which covers the four input variables, a_1, a_2, b_1, and b_2, and the two state variables, y_1 and y_2, as in Fig. 5.47. These submaps themselves are arranged in a similar configuration, but covering the four input variables, c_1, c_2, d_1, and d_2, and the two state variables, y_3 and y_4. Note that all possible combinations of the state variables appear on this pseudo-Karnaugh map, including y_1y_2 or $y_3y_4 = 00$ or $=11$, whereas these combinations have been eliminated for pairs of input variables.

The use of pseudo-Karnaugh maps is discussed in detail in Ref. (3.11). We summarize *all* the conditions that must be fulfilled before pseudo-Karnaugh maps can be used:

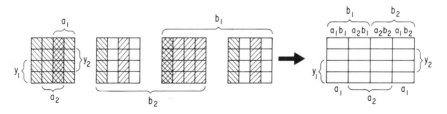

Fig. 5.47. Pseudo-Karnaugh map for six variables.

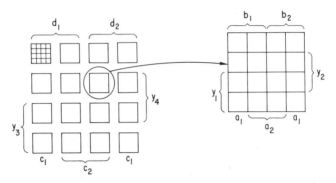

Fig. 5.48. Pseudo-Karnaugh map for 12 variables.

1. The input variables come in pairs, x_1 and x_2, such that the combination $x_1x_2 = 11$ is impossible. (This condition is fulfilled, for example, when the pair of input variables represents two limit switches that cannot be actuated simultaneously.)

2. Combination $x_1x_2 = 00$ is possible, but can be disregarded, since no output signal is required while $x_1x_2 = 00$. (This condition is fulfilled if no sustained output signals are required, for example, with cylinder-actuating valves without a return spring.)

3. The memory elements are RS flip-flops (and not relays requiring sustained excitation functions).

4. Pseudo-Karnaugh maps must be used with special caution when there are parallel output signals (e.g., two different cylinder motions occurring simultaneously). This is illustrated in the following example.

5.5.13 Example Involving Three Cylinders

We now present a third example, which serves to describe several more features of the Huffman method.

The required program sequence for a three-cylinder system is shown in the sequence chart of Fig. 5.49. Note that there are two cases of simultaneous or parallel cylinder motions: between states ② and ③, both cylinders B and C extend; and between states ③ and ④, A extends and C retracts.

The primitive flow table is shown in Fig. 5.50. The sequence begins with state ① at the initial input combination $a_2b_1c_1$. For each succeeding state, additional input columns are added, as required. Altogether, this sequence goes through five input combinations (out of the eight theoretically possible combinations).

Attempting to merge the rows, we find that a very large number of different row mergers are possible. We therefore utilize a so-called *merger diagram* to disclose possible merger combinations. This diagram consists of a circle, shown

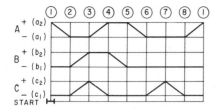

Fig. 5.49. Sequence for three cylinders.

	$a_2b_1c_1$	$a_1b_1c_1$	$a_1b_2c_2$	$a_2b_2c_1$	$a_1b_1c_2$	A −	A +	B −	B +	C −	C +
1	①	2				I	0	−	0	−	0
2		②	3			−	0	0	I	0	I
3			③	4		0	I	0	−	I	0
4	5			④		0	−	I	0	−	0
5	⑤	6				I	0	−	0	−	0
6		⑥			7	−	0	−	0	0	I
7		8			⑦	−	0	−	0	I	0
8	I	⑧				0	I	−	0	−	0

Fig. 5.50. Primitive flow table for problem of Fig. 5.49.

in Fig. 5.51, on which we mark eight points, each representing one of the eight rows of the primitive flow table. We now check every possible combination of rows to see whether a merger is possible. This is best done systematically by checking row 1 against row 2, 1 against 3, 1 against 4, etc., up to 1 against 8; then 2 against 3, 2 against 4, etc., up to 2 against 8; then 3 against 4, 3 against 5, etc., etc.; and, finally, concluding with 7 against 8. Every allowable merger is registered on the merger diagram by drawing a line between the respective points.

Studying the completed diagram, we see, for example, that rows 2, 3, and 4 can be merged into a single row, because there are lines between 2 and 3, 3 and 4, and also between 2 and 4. Similarly, rows 3, 4, 5, and 6 can be merged into a single row. On the other hand, rows 3, 4, 7, and 8 *cannot* be merged, because there is no diagonal line between 4 and 8. We could merge either 3, 4, and 7, or 3, 7, and 8, but not all four rows.

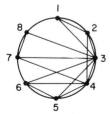

Fig. 5.51. Merger diagram.

By studying all possible merger combinations systematically, two ways are found of merging down to three rows: (1,2)(3,4,5,6)(7,8) or (1,2,3)(4,5,6)(7,8). We can also find 30 additional ways of merging down to four rows, beginning with (1)(2)(3,4,5,6)(7,8) and ending with (1,2,3)(4,5,6)(7)(8). There are countless ways of merging down to five rows, but these are of no interest, since they require three flip-flops, the same as the unmerged primitive flow table.

Each merger combination results in a completely different final solution (or rather, in a different *family* of solutions, since, for each merger combination, we can choose different state assignments, each of which gives a different solution). It would, of course, be completely impractical to try each of the existing 32 options. However, we can make an educated guess by employing the following two rules of thumb:

Rule A. In order to simplify the output functions as much as possible, it is advisable to merge rows with identical or similar outputs.

Rule B. In order to simplify the excitation functions, it is advisable to select a merger combination that eliminates as many unstable states as possible, and creates as many squares as possible with "—" entries.

Rule A can, unfortunately, not be applied in the present example. Although rows 1 and 5, for instance, have identical output signals, their merger is not legal to begin with.

The reasoning behind rule B is that each unstable state appearing in the merged flow table calls for an additional S or R term. Rule B means that we prefer one of the two merger combinations resulting in three rows over any of the 30 remaining combinations resulting in four rows, even though they all require two flip-flops.

It should be stressed that these rules cannot provide an absolute answer, and occasionally a merger combination can be found that does not follow either of these rules, and yet results in a simpler final circuit. Also, rules A and B frequently call for different merger combinations, and we must then decide which rule to satisfy and which to ignore.

Figure 5.52 shows the merged flow table resulting from one of the two merger combinations merging down to three rows. Since two flip-flops are required, we

	$a_2 b_1 c_1$	$a_1 b_1 c_1$	$a_1 b_2 c_2$	$a_2 b_2 c_1$	$a_1 b_1 c_2$	$y_1 y_2$
1,2	①	②	3	—	—	0 0
3,4,5,6	⑤	⑥	③	④	7	1 0
7,8	1	⑧	—	—	⑦	1 1
	1A	—	—	—	—	0 1

Fig. 5.52. Merged flow table.

obtain four combinations of state variables, which means that one combination ($y_1 y_2 = 01$) seems superfluous, since the row it is assigned to is empty. This fourth row is called a *dummy row*, and can be filled with "—" entries, since the sequence does not pass through this row.

We are now faced with a critical-race problem (see Section 5.5.5), even though we chose a state assignment that should avoid races. Whenever the merged flow table contains an odd number of rows, a race must occur when returning from the last to the first row. In this example, when the system reaches unstable state 1 in the third row (where $y_1 y_2 = 11$), we want to return to stable state ① (where $y_1 y_2 = 00$). This calls for giving both R_1 and R_2 signals at unstable state 1. However, if flip-flop 1 should, for some reason, be slower than flip-flop 2, the system would pass from $y_1 y_2 = 11$ to 10 and find itself in stable state ⑤. Since there is no R_1 signal at this state, the system is trapped there, resulting in a malfunction.

To eliminate this critical race, we utilize the dummy row. Instead of giving both R_1 and R_2 at unstable state 1, we give only R_1. This produces $y_1 y_2 = 01$, forcing the system into the square marked $1A$ in the dummy row. We then provide for a R_2 signal in this $1A$ square, enabling the system to continue to stable state ① . We thus prevent the system from going to stable state ⑤ by forcing the transition through the dummy row, as indicated by the arrows. This method of preventing critical races is elaborated further in Chapter 6.

The next stage in the solution procedure is to draw the path map. Since there are six input variables and two state variables, we use an eight-variable pseudo-Karnaugh map, with row and column designations as shown in Fig. 5.53. Note that the arrows in Fig. 5.52 are also entered in the appropriate place on the path map.

The final stage of the procedure is to fill the four excitation maps and six output maps, as shown in Fig. 5.54. We now come to the problem discussed at the end of the previous section concerning the conditions for using pseudo-Karnaugh maps when there are parallel output signals. We must check what might happen at the completion of two (or more) simultaneous cylinder strokes.

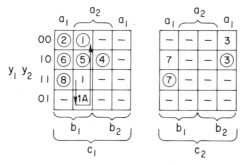

Fig. 5.53. Path map for Fig. 5.52.

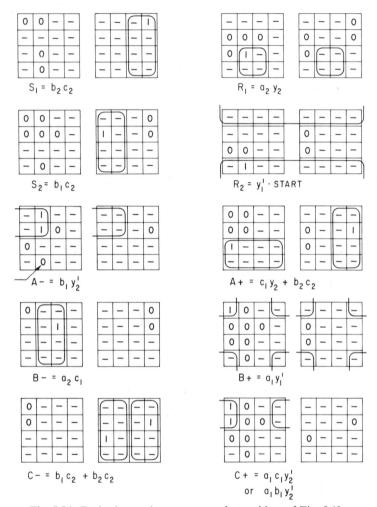

Fig. 5.54. Excitation and output maps for problem of Fig. 5.49.

In the present problem, this means that states ③ and ④ must be checked, these being the "critical states."

To illustrate, consider output map $C-$: since the right submap contains no 0 entries, we are tempted to include all of it in one cell, resulting in $C- = c_2$. However, note that this cell includes critical state ③, at which both $B+$ and $C+$ strokes are completed. Suppose stroke $B+$ takes longer than stroke $C+$. (Cylinder speed, as discussed in Chapter 1, depends on many factors, including cylinder diameter and length, and the nature of the opposing load, and there is no justification for assuming that all cylinder strokes take exactly the same time.) We then get a c_2 signal, and thus a $C-$ command before cylinder B has fully extended, which could have serious consequences. The solution to this problem is to split the c_2 cell into two smaller cells, as shown in Fig. 5.54, giving the output function $C- = b_1c_2 + b_2c_2$. This means that the $C-$ stroke is only initiated at state ③ after *both* limit switches b_2 and c_2 are actuated.

For similar reasons, the solution shown in Fig. 5.54 uses $S_1 = b_2c_2$ (rather than $S_1 = c_2$); $A+ = c_1y_2 + b_2c_2$ (rather than $A+ = c_1y_2 + b_2$); and $B- = a_2c_1$ (rather than $B- = a_2$), which relates to critical state ④. (Drawing the ladder diagram for the above solution is left as an exercise for the reader.)

These difficulties arise because pseudo-Karnaugh maps do not cover those combinations at which both limit-switch signals are 0, so that some information is lost. Because of their great advantage, pseudo-Karnaugh maps should be used whenever possible, even though this precaution must be taken: each cell covering a critical state (i.e., one at which parallel cylinder strokes are completed) must be checked individually, as shown here, and, if necessary, split into two smaller cells, in order to avoid malfunctions if one cylinder should complete its stroke ahead of the other.

5.5.14   Problems Involving More than 12 Variables

The reader may be puzzled about what should be done if even the capacity of pseudo-Karnaugh maps is exceeded, that is, if the problem involves more than 12 variables. The answer is simple: the Huffman method can still be used, provided we do not insist on minimizing the various excitation and output functions. Each of these functions can be written directly from the merged flow table, although not in minimized form.

To illustrate, consider the merged flow table of Fig. 5.32. We can write an S or R expression for each unstable state in this table, depending on the state assignment at the row of the succeeding state, using the address of the unstable state. Thus,

at unstable state 3, we need $S_2 = a_1'a_2y_1y_2'$

at unstable state 5, we need $R_1 = a_1a_2'y_1y_2$

at unstable state 7, we need $R_2 = a_1'a_2y_1'y_2$

at unstable state 1, we need $S_1 = a_1a_2'y_1'y_2'$

If a given S or R signal is required more than once, the respective terms are combined by Boolean addition (OR gate).

From the primitive flow table, Fig. 5.30, we see that an $A+$ signal is required at stable states ①, ②, ⑤, and ⑥. The addresses of these states are found from the merged flow table, giving

$$A+ = (a_1a_2' + a_1'a_2')y_1y_2' + (a_1a_2' + a_1'a_2')y_1'y_2$$
$$= a_2'(y_1y_2' + y_1'y_2)$$

While these functions are more complicated than those in Figs. 5.34 and 5.35, they do not contradict them. In other words, this method is simple and always works, but the resulting solution is not optimal.

5.6 CONCLUSIONS

Three methods for designing ladder diagrams have been presented:

1. *Sequence Chart.* This method is not systematic, and is only recommended for relatively simple problems. The results achieved depend, to a great extent, on the skill and experience of the designer.

2. *Cascade Method.* This method is very simple and systematic, but does not minimize the number of relays. It is useful for both simple and large-scale problems, and the resulting ladder diagram is easy to understand.

3. *Huffman Method.* This method always minimizes the number of relays, but is rather difficult, and requires considerable practice to master fully. It is suitable for small- and medium-size problems. It can also be applied to large-scale problems, but at the cost of obtaining a nonoptimal solution.

The reader should realize that there exist many other methods, most of which are variations of the sequence-chart method or of the Huffman method. A critical comparison of these methods can be found in Ref. (5.6).

PROBLEMS

5.1. Draw the ladder diagram corresponding to the solution of Fig. 5.54.

5.2. Draw the sequence chart corresponding to the ladder diagram of Fig. 5.37.

5.3. Draw the sequence chart corresponding to the ladder diagram of Fig. 5.43.

5.4. Two cylinders A and B are actuated by 5/2 valves with double solenoids, and controlled by the ladder diagram shown in Fig. P5.4. Draw a detailed sequence chart showing the action of each element (i.e., each cylinder, switch, valve, solenoid, relay) following a brief actuation of the START button. Using this sequence chart, determine what happens if the START button is pressed continuously.

5.5. Repeat Problem 5.4., but for the ladder diagram shown in Fig. P5.5.

5.6. Repeat Problem 5.4, but for the system having three cylinders A, B, and C, and for the ladder diagram shown in Fig. P5.6.

5.7. Repeat Problem 5.4, but for the system shown in Fig. P5.7. *Hint:* Allocate three horizontal lines on the sequence chart for the three-position valve VA.

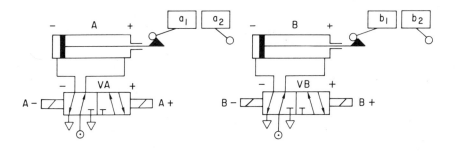

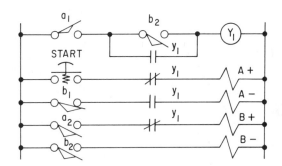

Fig. P5.4. Cylinders and ladder diagram for Problem 5.4.

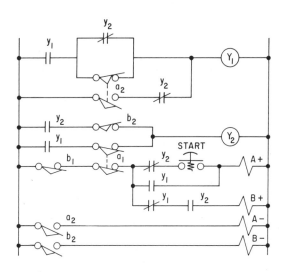

Fig. P5.5. Ladder diagram for Problem 5.5.

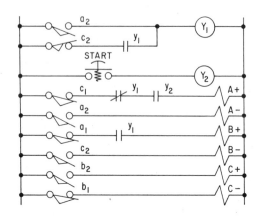

Fig. P5.6. Ladder diagram for Problem 5.6.

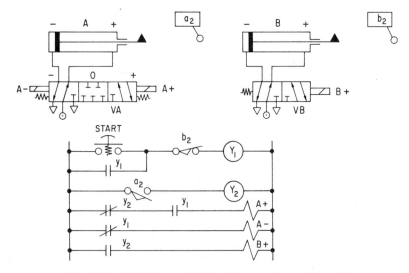

Fig. P5.7. Cylinders and ladder diagram for Problem 5.7.

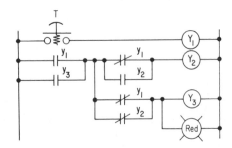

Fig. P5.8. Ladder diagram for Problem 5.8.

5.8. Draw a detailed sequence chart showing the action of each element in the ladder diagram shown in Fig. P5.8, assuming that push-button switch T is pressed and released four times in a row (i.e., $T = 0, 1, 0, 1, 0, 1, 0, 1, 0$).

5.9. **(a)** A single cylinder A is actuated by a 5/2 valve with solenoid $A+$ and a return spring (as in Fig. 5.6). Design a ladder diagram to produce the sequence START, $A+$, $A-$. Check your result by means of a sequence chart.
(b) Repeat part (a), but with a cylinder actuated by a 5/2 valve with double solenoids.

5.10. By means of a sequence chart, design a ladder diagram for the sequence START, $A+$, $B+$, $B-$, $A-$, assuming the use of 5/2 cylinder-actuating valves with double solenoids. *Note:* This sequence represents a common application, with cylinder A clamping a workpiece, while cylinder B lowers and raises a drill spindle to drill a hole.

5.11. Repeat Problem 5.10, but with cylinder A actuated by a 5/2 valve with a single solenoid and a return spring.

5.12. Repeat Problem 5.10, but with cylinder B actuated by a 5/2 valve with a single solenoid and a return spring.

5.13. Repeat Problem 5.10, but with both cylinders actuated by 5/2 valves with a single solenoid and a return spring.

5.14. Repeat Problem 5.10, but including a time delay, giving the sequence START, $A+$, $B+$, time delay, $B-$, $A-$. (See Chapter 8 for a discussion of time-delay relays.)

5.15. Repeat Problem 5.10, but for the sequence

$$\text{START, } A+, B+, \begin{pmatrix} A- \\ B- \end{pmatrix}$$

(*Note:* The last stroke in the sequence signifies the simultaneous retraction of cylinders A and B.)

5.16. Use the cascade method to solve Problem 5.10.

5.17. Use the cascade method to solve Problem 5.11.

5.18. Use the cascade method to solve Problem 5.12.

5.19. Use the cascade method to solve Problem 5.13.

5.20. Use the cascade method to solve Problem 5.14.

5.21. Use the cascade method to solve Problem 5.15.

5.22. Use the cascade method to design a ladder diagram for the sequence START, $A+$, $B+$, $B-$, $B+$, $B-$, $A-$, assuming cylinder-actuating valves with double solenoids.

5.23. Repeat Problem 5.22, but with cylinder-actuating valves with a single solenoid and a return spring.

5.24. Use the cascade method to design a ladder diagram for sequence

$$\text{START, } A+, B+, B-, C+, B+, \text{time delay, } \left(\begin{matrix} A- \\ B- \end{matrix}\right), C-$$

assuming cylinder-actuating valves with double solenoids.

5.25. Repeat Problem 5.24, but with cylinder-actuating valves with a single solenoid and a return spring.

In the following problems, the student may be required—at the instructor's discretion—to supply a complete solution, including ladder diagram, or, alternatively, to develop only the required excitation and output functions.

5.26. Use the Huffman method to solve Problem 5.10.

5.27. Use the Huffman method to solve Problem 5.11.

5.28. Use the Huffman method to solve Problem 5.12.

5.29. Use the Huffman method to solve Problem 5.13.

5.30. Use the Huffman method to solve Problem 5.14.

5.31. Use the Huffman method to solve Problem 5.15.

5.32. Use the Huffman method to solve Problem 5.22.

5.33. Use the Huffman method to solve Problem 5.23.

5.34. Use the Huffman method to solve Problem 5.24.

5.35. Use the Huffman method to design a ladder diagram for the sequence START, $A+$, $A-$, $B+$, $C+$, $B-$, $C-$, assuming cylinder-actuating valves with double solenoids.

5.36. Repeat Problem 5.35, but for the sequence START, $A+$, $A-$, $B+$, $A+$, $A-$, $B-$.

5.37. Repeat Problem 5.35, but for the sequence START, $A+$, $B+$, $B-$, $C+$, $B+$, $A-$, $A+$, $A-$, $B-$, $C-$.

5.38. Repeat Problem 5.35, but for the sequence START, $A+$, $A-$, $A+$, $A-$, $B+$, $B-$. (For the final solution, see the figure for Problem 5.5.)

5.39. Two equally deep holes are to be drilled in blocks of wood. Cylinder A clamps the block, cylinder B lowers the drill, and Cylinder C shifts the block to the location of the second hole. Hence, the required sequence is START, $A+$, $B+$, $B-$, $C+$, $B+$, $B-$, $C-$, $A-$. Design a ladder diagram for this sequence using the Huffman method.

5.40. Using the Huffman method, design a ladder diagram for a "push-to-start/push-to-stop" circuit, that is, the first press on push-button switch T actuates output z, which must remain *on* even after T is released, whereas the second press turns z *off*. (This is identical to the trigger flip-flop discussed in Section 3.9.)

5.41. Repeat Problem 5.35, but for the sequence

$$\text{START}, A+, A-, \begin{pmatrix} A+ \\ B+ \end{pmatrix}, B-, A-$$

5.42. Repeat Problem 5.35, but for the sequence:

$$\text{START}, A+, B+, B-, B+, A-, \begin{pmatrix} A+ \\ B- \end{pmatrix}, A-$$

5.43. Repeat Problem 5.35, but for the sequence

$$\text{START}, A+, B+, A-, A+, B-, A-, \begin{pmatrix} A+ \\ B+ \end{pmatrix}, \begin{pmatrix} A- \\ B- \end{pmatrix}$$

REFERENCES

5.1. M. G. Saake, "Electrical Circuits for Solenoid Valves," *Hydraulics & Pneumatics*, Part 1: Feb. 1970, pp. 67–72; Part 2: Mar. 1970, pp. 101–105.

5.2. M. G. Saake, "Solenoid Valve Circuit Sequences Unloader," *Hydraulics & Pneumatics*, Sept. 1973, pp. 200–201.

5.3. M. G. Saake, "Feedback Signals Automate Pharmaceutical Packaging," *Hydraulics & Pneumatics*, Nov. 1972, pp. 93–96.

5.4. K. Rexford, "Electrical Control for Fluid Power Systems," *Hydraulics & Pneumatics*, Mar. 1964, pp. 69–71.

5.5. D. Pessen, "Ladder Diagram Design for Programmable Controllers," *Proceedings of IFAC Symposium on Components, Instruments and Techniques for Low Cost Automation*, Valencia, Spain, Nov. 1986, pp. 311–315. (Also *Automatica*, May 1989.)

5.6. D. Pessen, *A Critical Comparison of Asynchronous-System Design Methods*, Festo Didactic, Esslingen, West Germany, 1983.

CHAPTER 6

SEQUENTIAL SYSTEMS WITH RANDOM INPUTS

The previous chapter dealt with sequencing systems in which the various steps of the sequence occur in a definite predefined order. Hence, the input signals, (whether originating from limit switches or any other type of sensor,) also appear in a known fixed order.

In many industrial systems, on the other hand, the input signals are completely random, that is, unpredictable. A good example is an elevator control circuit, already mentioned in Chapter 3. At each floor, there are an UP and a DOWN button, and within the elevator, one button for every floor of the building. In addition, there are limit switches at each floor actuated when the elevator passes, so that the control system "knows" the location of the elevator. Thus, if the building has n floors, the control system receives at least $4n$ input signals. Since we cannot predict at which floor the next passenger is liable to appear or where he/she wishes to go to, the order of these input signals is completely random and unpredictable. Depending on these inputs, the control system must decide at which floor the elevator should stop next, in accordance with an operating policy chosen by the circuit designer.

This chapter shows how to design control circuits for random-input systems. Section 5.4.3 of the previous chapter deals with systems having a single random (x_p), and these can be considered as simple examples of random-input systems. Here, however, we deal with systems all (or most) of whose inputs are random. Such problems are best handled by the Huffman method. This method, described in detail in Section 5.5, is now extended for random-input signals.

6.1 EXAMPLE 1: ALARM (ANNUNCIATOR) SYSTEM

The method is explained using a simple example: the design of an alarm (annunciator) system, shown in Fig. 6.1. The system has two binary inputs, x_1 and x_2, and two binary outputs, z_1 and z_2. The state $x_1 = 1$ represents a danger signal, indicating that some condition (e.g., a certain temperature or pressure in an industrial process) is exceeding an allowable limit.

If $x_1 = 1$, the alarm system must produce $z_1 = 1$, which actuates an alarm siren. The operator can shut off this siren by pressing push button x_2, thus acknowledging having received the warning. A momentary x_2 signal can shut off the siren ($z_1 = 0$), replacing it by a flashing red light ($z_2 = 1$), which must continue to flash as long as $x_1 = 1$. In the meantime, the operator (we hope) sees to it that the emergency condition is corrected, and, as soon as $x_1 = 0$ again, we get $z_2 = 0$, and the system returns to its former normal state.

Regardless of which design method is to be used, the first step in solving the problem is to draw a *flow diagram*, as shown in Fig. 6.2. Each state the system passes through is represented by a circle (with an attached state number), and the various input/output signals associated with the state are entered within the circle (as indicated in the key in Fig. 6.2). Arrows show the transition path from one state to the next. The normal course of events described in the previous paragraph is represented here by states 1, 2, 3, 4, 1, respectively, in that order.

Note that some transitions are bidirectional, whereas others are unidirectional. For example, if at state 2, the dangerous situation ($x_1 = 1$) disappears by itself ($x_1 = 0$) before the push button is pressed, we may not want to return to state 1. Instead, we go to a new state, numbered 6, where $x_1 x_2 = 00$ just as in state 1, but where the siren continues to sound. This is done to force the operator to acknowledge the warning by pressing and then releasing push button x_2, which sends the system first to state 5, and then back to state 1. The transition from state 1 to 2 is thus unidirectional, whereas that from state 2 to state 6 is bidirectional.

Note that simultaneous changes of both input signals are not found in Fig. 6.2. The probability of two inputs changing at the identical moment is extremely small. In the design of asynchronous systems with sustained inputs (as taught in most textbooks on switching theory) it is commonly assumed that simultaneous changes do not occur. (The idea behind this assumption is that if such a change should occur, the switching elements themselves "decide" which signal switched first, and react accordingly.)

Subject to this restriction, every possible input change must be accommo-

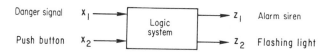

Fig. 6.1. An alarm (annunciator) system.

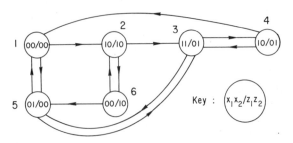

Fig. 6.2. Flow diagram for Fig. 6.1.

dated, even if it seems highly improbable. For example, if someone should press the push button $x_2 = 1$ even though $x_1 = 0$, the system goes from state 1 to state 5, where $z_1 z_2$ remains 00. Releasing x_2 returns the system to state 1 (another example of a bidirectional transition).

In order not to miss any possible transitions when drawing the flow diagram, it is useful to apply this rule: *for a system with n inputs, there must be n arrows leaving each state in the flow diagram* (corresponding to each of the n different input signals that might switch). However, this rule is valid only if all inputs are completely random and if simultaneous changes of two or more inputs are excluded. Since the above system has two inputs, each state in Fig. 6.2 must have two output arrows.

Drawing the flow diagram is often the most difficult part of the design process. It requires an exact definition of system requirements, logical thinking, and good judgment, unlike the remaining design stages, which are almost routine. As mentioned before, having a proper flow diagram is vital, no matter what design method is to be used afterwards. It should be stressed that this flow diagram is not the only one possible for this alarm system. Certain changes could be made (see Problem 6.3 at end of chapter), depending on how we want the system to react under given circumstances, but this is part of the design specifications, and not relevant to the present discussion.

$x_1 x_2$

Row	00	10	11	01	z_1	z_2
1	(1)	2	—	5	0	0
2	6	(2)	3	—	1	0
3	—	4	(3)	5	0	1
4	1	(4)	3	—	0	1
5	1	—	3	(5)	0	0
6	(6)	2	—	5	1	0

Fig. 6.3. Primitive flow table.

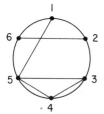

Fig. 6.4. Merger diagram.

In the Huffman method, the next step is to transfer the information in the flow diagram to the primitive flow table, as shown in Fig. 6.3. This table is filled in according to the rules described in Section 5.5.3. Since the flow diagram and primitive flow table contain identical information, albeit in different form, beginners sometimes feel that they can begin directly with the primitive flow table and skip the task of drawing the flow diagram first. The reader is strongly urged not to take this shortcut. The flow diagram provides a graphic representation of what the system is to accomplish, and is very helpful in visualizing the problem and disclosing possible mistakes.

The next step in the Huffman method is that of row merging (Section 5.5.4). The merger diagram is shown in Fig. 6.4. Two ways can be found of merging down to three rows, resulting in merger combinations (1)(2,6)(3,4,5) and (1,5)(2,6)(3,4). (There are also six other ways of merging to four rows, but these are not considered here.) Applying Rule A from Section 5.5.13, we find that the second merger combination (1,5)(2,6)(3,4) complies completely with this rule, since rows 1 and 5 have identical outputs $z_1z_2 = 00$, rows 2 and 6 both have $z_1z_2 = 10$, and rows 3 and 4 have $z_1z_2 = 01$. We therefore choose this merger combination, resulting in the merged flow table of Fig. 6.5.

6.2   CRITICAL AND NONCRITICAL RACES

In Section 5.5.5, it was stated that the state assignment $y_1y_2 = 00, 01, 11, 10$ avoids races, since only one state variable changes state when passing from one row to the next. This statement, however, is only true for sequencing systems,

$x_1 x_2$

	00	10	11	01	$y_1 y_2$
1,5	①	2	3	⑤	00
2,6	⑥	②	3	5	01
3,4	1	④	③	5	11
–	1A	–	–	–	10

Fig. 6.5. Merged flow table.

which proceed through the states in numerical order (and even then, as was shown in Section 5.5.13, only for an even number of rows).

Random-input systems, however, do not proceed through the states in numerical order, but may "jump," as seen from Figs. 6.3 and 6.5. For instance, the system can proceed from state ① in row 1,5 to state ② in the next row. But it may also jump from state ⑤ in row 1,5 to state ③ in row 3,4, and this produces a race, since $y_1 y_2$ is expected to go from 00 to 11. To avoid this race, we first send the system from unstable state 3 in row 1,5 to unstable state 3 in row 2,6, as indicated by the arrow, and only then permit the transition to stable state ③ in row 3,4.

Examining Fig. 6.5 discloses two additional races: proceeding from state ③ to state ⑤, and from state ④ to state ①. In the latter case, the dummy row must be utilized to avoid the race (as in the example of Fig. 5.52).

Use of a different state assignment can, in some cases, eliminate the races. However, this is not so for the present problem, as can be proved. Nevertheless, the problem can be alleviated by using a different state assignment, as shown in Fig. 6.6. The Dummy row is now assigned $y_1 y_2 = 11$ rather than 10, and, as a result, there is only one race, namely, for the transition from state ② in row 2,6 to state ③ in row 3,4. Again, the race is avoided by using the arrow indicated in the table.

The question of whether a given race is critical or noncritical can only be answered after the excitation maps have been completed. The excitation maps for Fig. 6.6 are shown in Fig. 6.7. In order to abide by the arrow entered in Fig. 6.6, we must place a 0 in the third square ($x_1 x_2 = 11$) of the second row ($y_1 y_2 = 01$) of the S_1 map. The R_2 signal at that square then forces the system to go from unstable state 3 in row 2,6 to unstable state 3 in row 1,5 (where $y_1 y_2 = 00$), rather than going to the dummy row (where $y_1 y_2 = 11$). From there, the system proceeds to stable state ③ in row 3,4. As a result of the 0 entry now specified, we can only loop a 2-square cell in the S_1 map, and obtain $S_1 = x_1 x_2 y_2'$ rather than $S_1 = x_1 x_2$, which is the price we pay to avoid the race.

To decide whether this race is really critical, we pose the following question: What would happen if no steps are taken to avoid this race? The answer is that the system might pass to the third square of the dummy row. This would only worry us if the system might get trapped there. However, examining the R_2 map

$x_1 x_2$

	00	10	11	01	$y_1 y_2$
1,5	①	2	3	⑤	00
2,6	⑥	②	3	5	01
–	–	–	–	–	11
3,4	1	④	③	5	10

Fig. 6.6. Improved merged flow table.

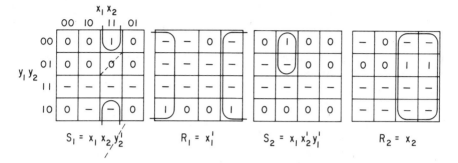

Fig. 6.7. Excitation maps for Fig. 6.6.

and the resulting function $R_2 = x_2$ discloses that an R_2 signal exists at this square in the dummy row, and this assures the system's transition to stable state ③ in row 3,4. Therefore, this race is noncritical, since, no matter which flip-flop wins the race, the system ends up at stable state ③. Therefore, the arrow in Fig. 6.6 is superfluous. Canceling it, we can replace the 0 entry in the S_1 map specified before by an "—" entry (as indicated by the dashed line), which simplifies the S_1 function back to $S_1 = x_1 x_2$.

If, for instance, the R_2 function in this example had been $R_2 = x_2 y_1'$ rather than $R_2 = x_2$, then the race would be critical after all.

6.3 OUTPUT MAPS FOR RANDOM-INPUT SYSTEMS

The two output maps are shown in Fig. 6.8. Note that both output functions are extremely simple. This should come as no surprise, and is the direct outcome of having chosen a merger combination in accordance with Rule A from Section 5.5.13.

When filling in the output maps for random-input systems, we are sometimes confronted by conflicting instructions when attempting to apply the rules of

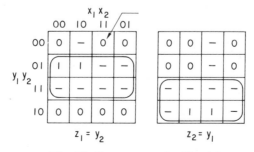

Fig. 6.8. Output maps for Fig. 6.6.

Section 5.5.7. Consider, for example, the third square ($x_1 x_2 = 11$) of the first row ($y_1 y_2 = 00$) of the z_1 output map. It has a 0 entry, with an arrow pointing to it. We can see from the merged flow table of Fig. 6.6 that this square represents unstable state 3. From the primitive flow table, we note that the system can pass through this state on the way from stable state ② (where $z_1 = 1$) to stable state ③ (where $z_1 = 0$). Hence, according to Rule 3 in Section 5.5.7, we should place a "—" entry in the z_1 map. However, the system can also pass through this state on the way from stable state ⑤ (where $z_1 = 0$) to stable state ③ (where $z_1 = 0$). Hence, according to Rule 2, we should place a 0 entry in the z_1 map. Obviously, the demand for a 0 entry dominates over the willingness to accept a "—" entry, since the former represents a legitimate requirement, whereas the latter means that we "don't care."

Unlike in Chapter 5, we shall not show the solution in ladder-diagram form, but limit ourselves to deriving the excitation and output functions. As mentioned in Chapter 5, these functions can be implemented using relays, electronic gates, pneumatic valves, or any other type of switching element.

6.4   PHENOMENON OF CONTACT BOUNCE

The previous example provides a good opportunity to demonstrate the phenomenon of contact bounce. If the solution of Figs. 6.7 and 6.8 is implemented with electronic gates, and if the input signals x_1 and x_2 are produced by ordinary switches, the following malfunction might be observed.

If, at state ④, x_1 goes from 1 to 0 (i.e., the switch opens), the system might end up at state ⑥ (where $z_1 = 1$) instead of at state ① (where $z_1 = 0$). The reason is contact bounce.

If we connect the x_1 signal to a fast oscilloscope, we discover that opening the switch contact does not produce a clean break of the x_1 signal. Because of arcing, the signal is liable to jump back and forth several times between 0 and 1, before finally settling down at 0. Referring to the merged flow table of Fig. 6.6, we see that the first transition of x_1 from 1 to 0 brings the system from stable state ④ to unstable state 1 and then to stable state ①. However, if x_1 now reverts to 1, the system reaches stable state ②, and, after a final reversion to 0, reaches state ⑥.

It is interesting to note that this malfunction does not occur if the solution is implemented by relays or pneumatic elements, since these are much too slow to respond to the very brief input changes produced by contact bounce. However, the speed of response of electronic gates is fast enough to be affected by such brief changes.

The cure to the problem of contact bounce is to attach an RS flip-flop to each switch, as shown in Fig. 6.9. As the upper contact of the SPDT switch opens, the contact leaf moves from S to R of the flip-flop. Arcing has no effect, because the flip-flop remains set as long as $R = 0$. Only when R is contacted does the flip-

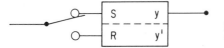

Fig. 6.9. Use of a flip-flop as a switch "debouncer."

flop become reset, and $y = 0$. Special integrated-circuit chips are available for this purpose (e.g., chip SN 74279, "Quad Debouncer," which contains four flip-flops and sells for less than a dollar).

6.5 EXAMPLE 2: BEAM-THICKNESS DETECTION SYSTEM

In the following example, the inputs are *not* completely random. The system is depicted in Fig. 6.10. Wooden beams are transported on a conveyor belt, and all beams whose thickness falls below a certain value must be rejected. For this purpose, we use two sensors, x_1 and x_2 (which could be photoelectric, fluidic, or limit-switch sensors). Sensor x_1 is mounted at the critical height corresponding to the minimum required beam thickness, whereas x_2 is mounted so that every beam passing by reaches its height. The x_1 and x_2 signals are assumed to be 0 when no beam is present and 1 when a beam reaches the sensor height. Whenever a beam below the required thickness passes, a $T = 1$ output signal must be given, and this signal can later be utilized to push the beam off the conveyor (for instance, using a pneumatic cylinder).

It is obvious that a single sensor x_1 is insufficient, since a $x_1 = 0$ signal alone cannot differentiate between a thin beam or the absence of a beam. Mounting both sensors one above the other at same horizontal location and then checking whether $x_1 x_2 = 11$ (beam is okay) or $= 01$ (beam is too thin) does not solve the problem either, because a false 01 signal might occur due to a slight sensor misalignment, or if beam edge is uneven or not exactly vertical.

By utilizing both sensors x_1 and x_2 as shown in the figure, we obtain the flow diagram of Fig. 6.11. Transition from state 1 through states 2,3,4, and back to 1 represents passage of a normal beam. On the other hand, a beam that is too thin gives an x_2 signal alone without first giving $x_1 x_2 = 11$, thus producing a transition to state 5 and then back to 1.

Note that the system has two input variables, and yet states 2, 3, 4, and 5 all have only one output arrow, which seems to contradict the rule cited in Section 6.1. The explanation is that the input signals in this example are not completely

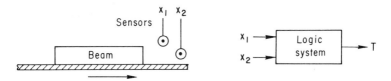

Fig. 6.10. Beam-thickness detection system.

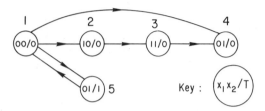

Fig. 6.11. Flow diagram for Fig. 6.10.

random. Once a beam has entered the sensor region, a certain order of events must follow, if we exclude the possibility of the conveyor belt stopping and reversing direction.

The resulting primitive and merged flow tables are shown in Fig. 6.12. Only one flip-flop is required, and the resulting excitation and output maps are shown in Fig. 6.13.

6.6 EXAMPLE 3: BINARY COMBINATION LOCK

This example (just as Example 2) comprises a logic system with two input signals, x_1 and x_2, and one output, T. However, here the inputs are completely random. The following sequence of input combinations is required to switch T from 0 to 1, and then back again to 0:

$$x_1 x_2 = 00, 10, 11, 10, 11, (01 \text{ or } 10), 00$$

produces

$$T = 0, \quad 0, \quad 0, \quad 0, \quad 1, \qquad 1, \qquad 0$$

$x_1 x_2$

	00	10	11	01	T
1	①	2	—	5	0
2	—	②	3	—	0
3	—	—	③	4	0
4	1	—	—	④	0
5	1	—	—	⑤	1

1,5	①	2	—	⑤	y'
2,3,4	1	②	③	④	y

Fig. 6.12. Primitive and merged flow tables for Fig. 6.11.

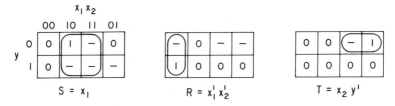

Fig. 6.13. Excitation and output maps for Fig. 6.12.

This sequence might represent some industrial process, in which a certain sequence of input combinations signifies a dangerous situation, which must trigger off an alarm signal $T = 1$.

A second interpretation might be a process in which a certain sequence of operations is required for successful system start-up. Only if this sequence is followed do we get a $T = 1$ signal, which means that it is okay to go ahead.

A third interpretation (less realistic, but perhaps easier to visualize) is a binary combination lock, where x_1 and x_2 represent toggle switches having *on* (1) and *off* (0) positions. The lock opens ($T = 1$) only if the switches go through the specified sequence. To make it difficult for unauthorized persons to open the lock, a wrong step cannot be corrected simply by reversing this step and then trying again. Rather, the system must be returned to $x_1 x_2 = 00$ and the sequence begun anew.

As in the previous example, we exclude simultaneous changes of x_1 and x_2. Also, after having opened the lock ($T = 1$), both x_1 and x_2 must be switched back to 0 (in any order) before the lock closes again ($T = 0$).

The flow diagram for this system is shown in Fig. 6.14. Note that it is divided into two regions. The right region represents the proper sequence that finally opens the lock. The left region, on the other hand, represents the improper sequence, and the only way to leave this region is to return to state 1 and start again.

Note that each state has two output arrows (since there are two inputs, both

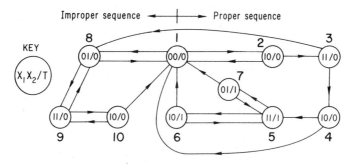

Fig. 6.14. Flow diagram for a binary combination lock.

completely random). In drawing the flow diagram, we use the following reasoning: Each time we reach a new $x_1 x_2/T$ combination, we check whether a state with such a combination already exists on the diagram. If it does not, we must define a new state, If it does, we check whether this state suits our purpose (as far as the following events are concerned). If so, then we use this state; if not, we must define a new state. (Sometimes two states can be proved to be equivalent, using a special technique shown in many textbooks; see also Ref. 6.1.)

For example, if at state 8, we switch x_1 from 0 to 1, we get $x_1 x_2/T = 11/0$. This combination already exists at state 3. However, that state is not suitable for our purpose, since it represents a step toward opening the lock at state 5, whereas state 8 is part of the improper sequence, in which the lock must *not* open. We must, therefore, define a new state 9, in which $x_1 x_2/T = 11/0$ as in state 3, but which does *not* lead to $T = 1$. The switching system is later "taught" to differentiate between states 3 and 9 by means of differing state assignments. For similar reasons, states 2, 4, and 10 all differ from each other, even though in all of them, $x_1 x_2/T = 10/0$.

Having completed the flow diagram, we transfer the information to the primitive flow table of Fig. 6.15. The merger diagram is shown in Fig. 6.16. Unfortunately, it is impossible to merge down to four rows. The best we can do is merge to five rows, which means that three flip-flops are required. The resulting merged flow table is shown in Fig. 6.17. Since three flip-flops provide eight rows of state variables, there are three remaining dummy rows.

The state assignment for Fig. 6.17 was obtained by trial and error, so as to reduce the number of races as much as possible. Two races remain. The first, going from state ③ to state ⑧, is handled by an arrow from unstable state 8 in the second row to the first row. The second race occurs in going from state ④ back to state ①. It is handled by the arrow from unstable state 1 in the third row to the square in the second row having a "—" entry. (Alternatively, we could

$x_1 x_2$

Row	00	01	11	10	T
1	①	8	—	2	0
2	1	—	3	②	0
3	—	8	③	4	0
4	1	—	5	④	0
5	—	7	⑤	6	1
6	1	—	5	⑥	1
7	1	⑦	5	—	1
8	1	⑧	9	—	0
9	—	8	⑨	10	0
10	1	—	9	⑩	0

Fig. 6.15. Primitive flow table for Fig. 6.14.

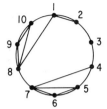

Fig. 6.16. Merger diagram.

draw this arrow from the third to the fourth row, which would result in a slightly different solution.)

The excitation and output maps are now drawn, and these cover five variables, x_1, x_2, y_1, y_2, and y_3. Unfortunately, pseudo-Karnaugh maps cannot be utilized with most random-input systems, since the conditions listed in Section 5.5.12 are not fulfilled. (The input combinations $x_1x_2 = 00$ and 11 not only are possible, but play an important part in the solution, and, therefore, cannot be disregarded.)

In the present example, the use of a path map (see Section 5.5.11) can be dispensed with, since the merged flow table in Fig. 6.17 has the same configuration as a standard five-variable Karnaugh map, with the upper four rows corresponding to the submap for $y_3 = 0$, while the lower four rows represent the second submap for $y_3 = 1$. To stress this correspondence, these submaps are shown in Figs. 6.18 and 6.19 one below the other, rather than side by side.

After the excitation functions are derived, it is discovered that the race in the $x_1x_2 = 01$ column is noncritical. If we go directly from state ③ to state ⑧ by giving $R_1 = 1$ and $S_3 = 1$ concurrently, there is no danger of being trapped in the $y_1y_2y_3 = 101$ dummy row, since the $x_1x_2 = 01$ square of that row is included

$$X_1 X_2$$

Row	00	01	11	10	$y_1y_2y_3$
1,2	①	8	3	②	000
3	—	8	③	4	100
4	1	—	5	④	110
5,6,7	1	⑦	⑤	⑥	010
8,9,10	1	⑧	⑨	⑩	001
—	—	—	—	—	101
—	—	—	—	—	111
—	—	—	—	—	011

Fig. 6.17. Merged flow table for Fig. 6.14.

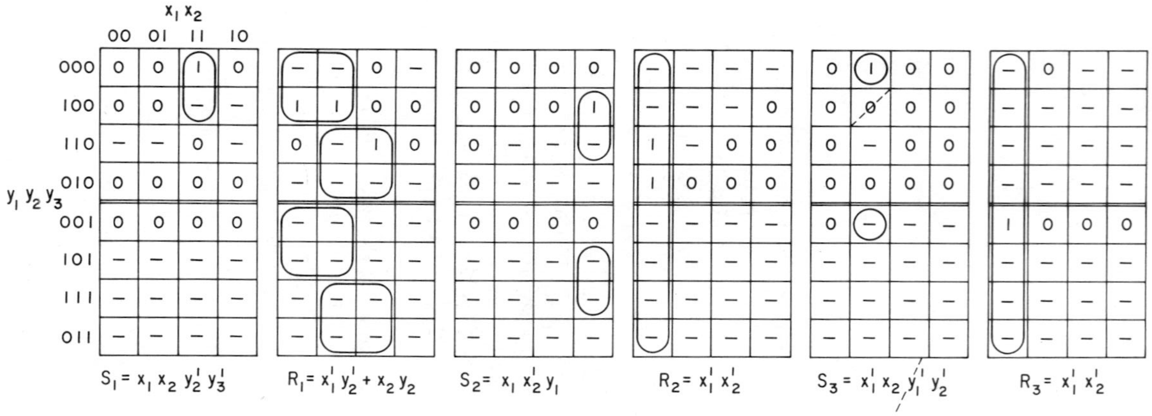

Fig. 6.18. Excitation maps for Fig. 6.17.

o	o	o	o
o	o	o	o
o	–	–	o
–	I	I	I
o	o	o	o
–	o	–	–
–	–	–	–
–	–	–	–

$T = y_1' \, y_2$ **Fig. 6.19.** Output map for Fig. 6.17.

in the R_1 function, which assures that $y_1 y_2 y_3 = 101$ turns into 001, thus sending the system to state ⑧. Therefore, the y_1' term in the S_3 function can be canceled. Similarly, the race in the $x_1 x_2 = 00$ column is also noncritical (since this entire column is included in the R_2 function). However, if we canceled the arrow and thereby the 0 entry and the y_2' term in the R_1 function, the system might pass through the $y_1 y_2 y_3 = 010$ row on the way from state ④ to ①, and we would therefore have to place a 0 in the $x_1 x_2 = 00$ column of that row in the T map. This would spoil our simple T function, so that the loss exceeds the gain. We therefore prefer to retain the arrow, giving the solution shown in Figs. 6.18 and 6.19.

6.7 CONCLUSIONS

The design technique described in this chapter can be applied to many types of manufacturing applications, such as automatic assembly, materials handling, packaging, injection molding, start-up of batch processes, etc. The method can be used not only where alarm signals may be required whenever a malfunction occurs, but also where self-correcting steps must be taken in order to correct the fault discovered.

The method is especially useful where real-time discrete control of very fast processes is required. As explained in Chapter 10, programmable controllers, because of their scanning action, have a fairly slow speed of response (in the order of tens of milliseconds), which may be too slow for fast processes, where extremely fast action must be taken in the case of a malfunction. By implementing the excitation and output functions derived as shown in this chapter using hard-wired electronic elements, a system response in the order of nanoseconds is obtained (i.e., 10^6 as fast as that of a programmable controller). The solution could, of course, also be implemented with relays or pneumatic valves, but then this speed advantage is lost.

This does not imply that the complete control system must be implemented with hard-wired electronics. Most steps of the control cycle could be controlled by the programmable controller, and only those portions where extremely fast response is required could be handled by a hard-wired circuit.

It should be mentioned that there exist other methods for handling random-input systems. For example, Ref. (6.2) describes a method using input-signal transitions rather than signal levels. The reader is referred to Part II of Ref. (5.6) for a detailed comparison of existing methods for random-input systems, and also to Ref. (6.1).

A final comment concludes this chapter, which began with a description of an elevator control system, as a good example of a system with random inputs. The reader is advised not to attempt to design such an elevator system using the method of this chapter. Even for a small building, the number of input variables is so large that solving the problem with the Huffman method is impractical. Since all floors are basically identical, problems such as this are best handled by so-called iterative circuits, which consist of identical modules, each taking care of one floor. Such systems are discussed in Chapter 8.

PROBLEMS

Note: The following problems should be solved using the Huffman method. It is sufficient to derive the required excitation and output functions, without necessarily drawing circuits for implementing these functions. In all problems, exclude simultaneous switching of two or more input signals.

6.1. Repeat the solution for the alarm system of Fig. 6.2, but using merger combination (1)(2,6)(3,4,5). Compare the new with the previous solution, and draw the necessary conclusions.

6.2. Repeat problem 6.1, but using merger combination (1,5)(2,6)(3)(4).

6.3. Redesign the alarm system of Fig. 6.1 such that danger signal $x_1 = 1$ appearing while system is at state 5 actuates alarm siren z_1 instead of flashing light z_2. (A problem arises: How should the siren be shut off? Suggest a reasonable solution to this problem.)

6.4. A sequential system has two input signals, x_1 and x_2, and one output signal, T. At the beginning, $T = 0$. T becomes 1 if and only if $x_1 x_2 = 01$ is directly followed by $x_1 x_2 = 11$. T returns to 0 only if $x_1 x_2 = 00$. Derive the excitation and output functions.

6.5. Repeat problem (6.4), but T becomes 1 if and only if $x_1 x_2$ follows the sequence $x_1 x_2 = 00,01,11$. T returns to 0 if $x_1 x_2 \neq 11$.

6.6. Design a "two-hand safety circuit" for actuating a punch press. In order to have the press descend (by means of signal $T = 1$), the operator must simultaneously press two push buttons, x_1 and x_2. These are mounted with sufficient distance between them so that they cannot both be pressed with one hand. This forces the operator to withdraw both hands from the dangerous region before the press descends. If the operator should attempt to tie either push button down permanently, the press must not operate at all, even if the other push button is pressed. After the press has descended ($T = 1$), release of either push button should return the press ($T = 0$). Design the circuit using the Huffman method.

6.7. JK flip-flops are described in Section 3.9, and they differ from RS flip-flops in that the input combination $JK = 11$ is legal, and causes output y to switch. (In RS flip-flops, $SR = 11$ is not allowed.) We are in urgent need of a JK flip-flop, but have only RS flip-flops and various logic gates in stock. Using the Huffman method, design a circuit that acts as a JK flip-flop, using the available elements.

6.8. T flip-flops are described in Section 3.9, and they differ from RS flip-flops in that they have only one input, T. Each time T goes from 0 to 1, the flip-flop outputs switch state, We are in urgent need of a T flip-flop, but have only RS flip-flops and various logic gates in stock. Using the Huffman method, design a circuit that acts as a T flip-flop, using the available elements.

6.9. A die-protection circuit is to be designed. Disks are to be coined by a pair of dies, as shown in Fig. P6.9. If the START button (not shown) is *held* pressed, we get a $z = 1$ signal, which causes the upper die to descend and coin the disk. However, if the disk is absent or jammed at an angle, z must never become 1, since this might damage the expensive dies. A fluidic back-pressure sensor (i.e., a small hole drilled into the lower die and supplied with air pressure) is used to detect the absence or misalignment of the disk ($x_1 = 0$). Release of the START button produces $z = 0$ and piston retraction, because of the cylinder return spring. Design a logic circuit for

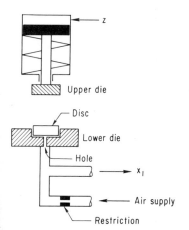

Fig. P6.9. System for Problem 6.9.

operating the cylinder that prevents die damage *even when the small hole is clogged. Hint*: If the hole is clogged, x_1 never returns to 0, even when the disk is absent.

6.10. Parts moving along a production line must have a length L defined by $d_2 > L \geqslant d_1$. To check L, three sensors, x_1, x_2, and x_3, are located under the passing parts, as shown in Fig. P6.10, and each gives a 1 signal while covered by the part. If $L \geqslant d_2$, we want to obtain a $G = 1$ alarm signal. If $L < d_1$, we want a $S = 1$ alarm signal. Either G or S signals (short pulses are sufficient) are later utilized to remove the defective part from the line, but this is not part of the present problem. Design a logic circuit to supply the G and S signals. To simplify the problem, the following assumptions can be made:

1. All parts appear on the line with a minimum distance greater than d_2 between adjacent parts.

2. There are no parts shorter than $L < (d_2 - d_1)$.

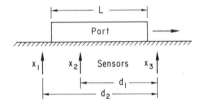

Fig. P6.10. System for Problem 6.10.

6.11. Figures 8.35–8.37 picture an incremental encoder, and the reader is asked to study the accompanying explanation in Chapter 8. As the encoder rotates, two sensors *A* and *B* produce two series of pulses, with a 90-degree phase shift between them, and the direction of this phase shift can be utilized to detect the direction of the encoder rotation. Draw the flow diagram that describes operation of this system, and design the necessary logic circuit to determine the direction, using the Huffman method.

6.12. Two different types of parts, type *A* and type *B*, must be fed alternately into an automatic assembly device. When a type *A* part enters, sensor x_1 produces a short pulse. Similarly, a type *B* part triggers a pulse from sensor x_2. If a part is followed by another part of the same type, an alarm signal $T = 1$ must be set off, see Fig. P6.12. Since this $T = 1$ signal might itself be a pulse, it connects to the SET input of a flip-flop, which then converts the

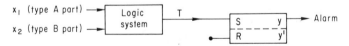

Fig. P6.12. System for Problem 6.12.

short T signal into a sustained y signal. Thus, $y = 1$ represents a malfunction. The operator can cancel $y = 1$ by resetting the flip-flop, provided $T = 0$. (Assume that $x_1 x_2 = 11$ does not occur.) Design the logic system.

6.13. The system in Fig. P6.13 has two inputs, x_1 and x_2, and two outputs, z_1 and z_2. These outputs are dependent on each other, with one always being the logic inverse of the other, that is, $z_2 = z_1'$. If either input x_i switches from 0 to 1, the respective output z_i goes to 1 (if it was 0), or remains 1 (if it was 1). The second output then automatically is 0. On the other hand, when an input x_i switches from 1 to 0, the outputs do not change. Design a logic circuit to fulfill these requirements.

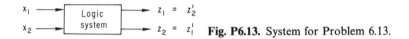

Fig. P6.13. System for Problem 6.13.

6.14. Parts with a rectangular cross section move on a conveyor belt. As shown in Fig. P6.14, three photoelectric sensors, x_1, x_2, and x_3, mounted above the conveyor detect whether the part is "standing up" or "lying down." The sensors work on the reflection principle, that is, a given sensor produces an output voltage while a part is in front of it and reflects the light beam. Design an alarm system that produces alarm signal $T = 1$ whenever two parts that are lying down follow each other, without being separated by a standing part. After T has switched to 1, it must return to 0 only when a standing part passes. *Hint:* It might pay to utilize a new variable defined by $x_4 = x_2 + x_3$.

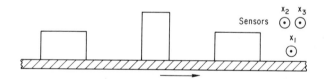

Fig. P6.14. System for Problem 6.14.

6.15. A machine runs as long as it receives a $T = 1$ signal. When a fault occurs, a sensor sends an $F = 1$ signal, which shuts off T. After the fault has been removed ($F = 0$), the machine can be restarted only by pressing a reset push button (giving signal $x = 1$) *twice* in a row. This provision is intended to prevent false restarting of the machine (which might cause great damage) due to accidental touching of the push button. Design a logic system to fulfill the above requirements.

6.16 A logic system, as shown in Fig. P6.16, receives electric power P from the main line, and transmits voltage to a machine through a relay, by means of output $V = 1$, which energizes the relay coil. In case of a power break ($P = 0$), we get $V = 0$. If power should return ($P = 1$), we must prevent automatic supply of voltage $V = 1$ to the machine, since this might produce dangerous machine motions. The operator must first check the machine, and only then renew voltage $V = 1$ by momentarily pressing push-button switch START. Voltage V must only return to 1 provided S changes from 0 to 1 *after* P has returned to 1 (to prevent a disaster in case push-button S should be stuck permanently in the closed position). Design the required logic circuit.

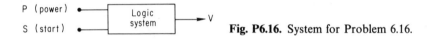

Fig. P6.16. System for Problem 6.16.

REFERENCES

6.1.   E. Fitch and J. Surjaatmadja, *Introduction to Fluid Logic*, McGraw-Hill, New York, 1978.

6.2.   P. Dersin, P. Gallet, and J. Florine, "Committed to Memory: Firmware Transitional Logic in Manufacturing," *Mechanical Engineering*, May 1986, pp. 49–56.

CHAPTER 7

PNEUMATIC CONTROL CIRCUITS

Pneumatic actuators and motion sensors are discussed in Chapters 1 and 2, respectively. In Chapter 4, pneumatic valves and other pneumatic switching elements are described in detail. The present chapter deals with pneumatic control circuits utilizing these previously described elements.

As shown in Chapter 5, pneumatic actuators can be controlled by means of electromechanical relays or by programmable controllers. However, as discussed in Chapters 2 and 4, it is often preferable to use the same power medium throughout the system, avoiding the need for additional interface elements. Also, relays require cylinder-actuating valves with solenoids, which are considerably more expensive. Therefore, pneumatic control circuits are often preferred for small- or medium-size systems.

A number of good books on industrial pneumatics have been published, see Refs. (7.1)–(7.10), and this chapter does not pretend to compete with these. Rather, its purpose is to provide an introduction to the subject, with stress placed on useful techniques that have *not* been described in other books.

Numerous pneumatic-circuit design methods have been described in the past, most purporting to give *the* answer to all problems. In reality, there is no best method, since most methods are advantageous only for certain classes of problems. A critical comparison of many published methods is presented in Ref. (7.11). This chapter describes four different methods, three of which are very useful, yet hardly known among industrial practitioners. A fifth method is the *programmable counter* method described in Chapter 9. Between them, these five methods should provide at least one good solution for every problem the reader is liable to encounter.

To help the reader select the optimum method for a given application, a flow chart is presented in Appendix B.

7.1 CASCADE METHOD OF CIRCUIT DESIGN

The cascade method, first described in Ref. (7.12), is simple to apply, and results in reliable and easily understood circuits. In using the method, it is assumed that each pneumatic cylinder or motor is actuated by a 5/2-valve with double pilot lines (i.e., without a return spring), and that the completion of a stroke is indicated by a limit valve.

The first part of the design procedure is to divide the program-sequence steps into groups, *so that no letter is repeated within any group.* This procedure is illustrated in Section 5.4.1, where a certain four-cylinder sequence is divided as follows:

$$\text{START, } A+, B+, C+ \Big/ C-, A-, D+ \Big/ A+, D-, B- \Big/ A-$$

Group: I   II   III   IV

7.1.1   Example 1

For an economical solution, the number of groups should be kept to a minimum. Sometimes one group can be eliminated by including the last step in the first group. For example, the sequence

$$\text{START, } A+, B+ \Big/ B-, A-, C+ \Big/ C-$$

Group: I   II   III

might be divided into three groups, since steps $C+$ and $C-$ must not be in the same group. However, by assigning $C-$ to Group I, one group is eliminated, as shown:

$$\text{START, } A+, B+ \Big/ B-, A-, C+ \Big/ C-$$

Group: I   II   I

This sequence might represent a system in which cylinder A is used to clamp a workpiece; cylinder B produces some operation, such as cutting, drilling, or punching; and cylinder C removes the workpiece from the station.

When using cylinder-actuating valves with double pilot lines, it is important to avoid contradictory (i.e., concurrent) control signals in the two pilot lines of any valve, since this is almost certain to result in circuit malfunction. In the cascade method, this is avoided by the following procedure. Each group is assigned a pressure manifold line, which must be pressurized only while the particular group is active. Each manifold line supplies air pressure to those limit valves associated with its particular group. Thus, in the last example, limit valves

a_2, b_2, and c_1 get their air supply from manifold line I, whereas b_1, a_1, and c_2 are connected to manifold line II, as shown in Fig. 7.1. (In most other design methods, the limit valves are directly connected to supply air.) Since two opposing pilot lines, such as $C+$ and $C-$, cannot belong to the same group, and since only one group can be pressurized at any moment, contradictory pilot signals are positively avoided.

In order to pressurize the various manifold lines in the proper order, one or more so-called *group valves* or *cascade valves* are employed. The number of such group valves always equals the number of groups minus one. The method is best explained by some examples.

Since, in the present example, there are only two groups, one group valve is sufficient. The group valve is 5/2, with each of its two output ports connected to one of the two manifold lines, which supply pressure to the limit valves. As shown in Fig. 7.1, it is customary to draw the pressure manifold lines as heavy horizontal lines.

It is assumed that at the beginning of the sequence, each valve is in the position shown in the figure. Since the group valve (shown below the manifold lines) is in its left-hand position, Group I is pressurized. When the START button is pressed, pressure passes from manifold line I through limit valve c_1 and the START valve to the pilot line $(+)$ of cylinder-actuating valve VA. As a result, cylinder A extends and actuates limit valve a_2. Pressure then passes from manifold line I through a_2 to the pilot line $(+)$ of cylinder-actuating valve VB, thus causing cylinder B to extend and actuate limit valve b_2.

Note that step $B+$ is the last step in Group I. In order to switch over to Group II, the pressure from limit valve b_2 is connected to pilot line II of the group valve, causing this valve to shift to its right-hand position, which pressurizes manifold line II and vents line I. Line II is connected directly to the pilot line $(-)$ of cylinder-actuating valve VB, so that the first step in Group II, namely $B-$, commences automatically the moment Group II is pressurized.

The reader should now be able to follow the sequence to its conclusion. The method of connecting the valves can be summarized as follows. The output of each limit valve is connected to the pilot input corresponding to the next sequence step, with one exception. The limit valve corresponding to the last step of a given group is *not* connected to the next cylinder-actuating valve, but rather to the pilot line of a group valve, so as to pressurize the manifold line of the next group. This manifold line is then connected directly to the pilot line corresponding to the first step of the next group.

7.1.2   Example 2

As a second example, consider the following single-cylinder cycle, which is solved in Chapter 5 using the Huffman method:

$$\text{START, } A+ \left| A- \right| A+ \left| A- \right.$$
$$\text{Group: } \quad \text{I} \qquad \text{II} \quad \text{III} \quad \text{IV}$$

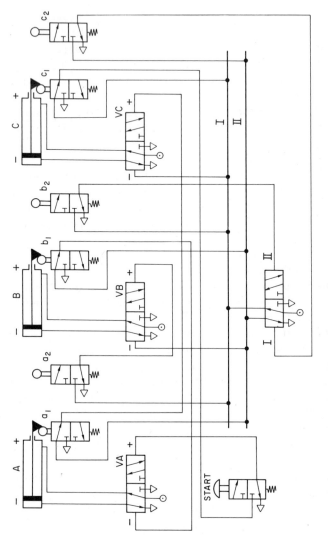

Fig. 7.1. Cascade circuit for Example 1: START, $A+$, $B+$, $B-$, $A-$, $C+$, $C-$.

The sequence must be divided into four groups, requiring three group valves. Figure 7.2 illustrates how the group valves are stacked one above the other in a "tree" array, with each valve supplying air to the one above; hence the name "cascade circuit." When the START button is pressed, pressure reaches pilot line 1, shifting the lowest group valve so that supply air flows through the array into manifold line I. When the time comes to switch over to Group II, pilot line 2 must be pressurized. This shifts the uppermost group valve so that its right-hand square becomes active, which sends air to manifold line II, while line I is vented.

This process repeats itself with the two lower group valves. Note that when the middle valve is shifted, it not only pressurizes manifold line III, but also returns the upper valve to its original position. Similarly, the lowest group valve, when shifted, returns the middle valve to its original position. This is done so that at the end of the sequence, the circuit is ready to begin the next cycle. For more complicated sequences, as many group valves as needed are stacked one above the other, with n valves accommodating $n + 1$ groups.

While cascade circuits are reliable and generally easy to design, they have one great drawback: complications set in whenever the program sequence contains repeated steps, as is shown in this example. The existence of repeated steps not

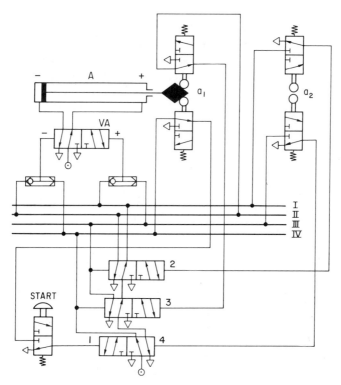

Fig. 7.2. Cascade circuit for Example 2: START, $A+$, $A-$, $A+$, $A-$.

only increases the number of groups, as seen from this example, but leads to two additional complications. First, pilot line VA+, for example, must be actuated twice during the sequence, once in Group I, and then again in Group III. It therefore becomes necessary to isolate the two lines leading from the respective manifold lines to VA+ by means of a shuttle valve (i.e., OR gate). Without such a valve, pressure would penetrate into the manifold line not active at the moment, producing a malfunction. The same applies, of course, to pilot line VA−, which also requires a shuttle valve to isolate between manifold lines II and IV.

A more serious complication occurs with the limit valves. Since limit valve a_2 must be pressurized by manifold lines I and III at different stages of the sequence, and since its output must pressurize two different group-valve pilot lines at different times, a single limit valve is obviously unable to fulfill these conflicting requirements. The solution shown in Fig. 7.2 is to use two separate limit valves for a_2 and likewise for a_1.

Frequently, however, it is difficult to find room within the machine to mount double sets of limit valves; indeed, it is often difficult to find room for a single limit valve. Furthermore, in sequences containing steps repeated more than once, three or even more sets of limit valves would have to be mounted near the cylinder, which becomes completely impractical.

One solution to this problem is shown in Fig. 7.3. Only one limit valve is mounted near the cylinder, and it receives its air pressure from the central air supply. The output of this valve is then led to the pilot lines of as many 3/2 valves (with a return spring) as required, which can be mounted wherever convenient, at any distance from the cylinder. Whenever the limit valve is actuated, these additional valves are also shifted pneumatically. The method is identical to the "cloning" technique described in Section 5.2 in connection with relay contacts.

To summarize, each repeated step in the program sequence requires two additional shuttle valves and two additional 3/2 valves acting as clones of the limit valves. Apart from this, repeated steps increase the number of groups, and thus the number of required group valves. Thus, the circuit becomes cumbersome, and the basic simplicity and economy of the cascade method is lost. The necessary conclusion is that the cascade method is not recommended for

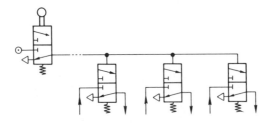

Fig. 7.3. Multiple limit valves using cloning.

sequences having more than one repeated step. For sequences without repeated steps, the cascade method generally provides the simplest and most economical circuit.

7.2 FLOW-TABLE METHOD OF CIRCUIT DESIGN

The flow-table method, first published in its present form in Ref. (7.13), is derived from a method originally published by Cole and Fitch in Ref. (7.14), but includes several important simplifications and improvements. As with the cascade method, it is assumed that each pneumatic cylinder or motor is actuated by a 5/2 valve with double pilot lines, and that the completion of each piston stroke is indicated by a limit valve. [Some material in this section is based on Ref. (7.13), and is used here with the kind permission of *Hydraulics & Pneumatics*, Copyright 1984, Penton Publishing, Cleveland, Ohio.]

7.2.1 Steering Valves

The method is based on the concept of so-called *steering valves*, illustrated in Fig. 7.4. Figure 7.4(a) shows a conventional 5/2 valve with double pilot lines, which acts as an RS flip-flop, as explained in Section 4.3.5. Its two output lines supply the state variable y and its logic complement y'. The active output is determined by which pilot line, SET or RESET, last received a pressure signal.

The valve in Fig. 7.4(b) is identical, except that supply pressure has been replaced by a signal coming from some limit valve, say c_2. As a result, the valve now acts not only as a flip-flop, but also as a passive AND gate, combining c_2 and y (or y') by the logic AND function to produce c_2y and c_2y'. Such a valve is called a steering valve since it sends input signal c_2 to either of two different *addresses*, c_2y or c_2y'.

Suppose we want to send input signal c_2 to any one of three different addresses. This requires a second steering valve, connected in series with the first one, as shown in Fig. 7.5, and providing the three addresses $c_2y'_1$, $c_2y_1y'_2$, and $c_2y_1y_2$. Note that the output c_2y_1 is not used as an independent address, since it is not a self-exclusive term, being included in the two addresses $c_2y_1y_2$ and $c_2y_1y'_2$.

Extending this idea further, Fig. 7.6 shows three steering valves connected in

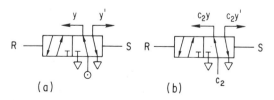

Fig. 7.4. (a) A valve flip-flop, and (b) a steering valve.

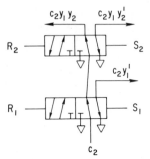

Fig. 7.5. Two steering valves providing three addresses.

series to provide four addresses c_2y_1', $c_2y_1y_2'$, $c_2y_1y_2y_3'$, and $c_2y_1y_2y_3$. Obviously, any number n of steering valves can be connected in this way providing $n + 1$ self-exclusive addresses. At any moment, the input signal reaches one and only one of these addresses, depending on the momentary state of the various steering valves.

The reader may have noted the strong resemblance between the steering-valve array and the way the group valves are connected in the cascade method (e.g., compare Figs. 7.2 and 7.6). However, except for this similarity, the two methods have nothing in common.

7.2.2   Example 3

The flow-table method is now illustrated by four examples. The first is the single-cylinder sequence

$$\text{START}, A+, A-, A+, A-, A+, A-$$

The sequence is entered into a flow table, Fig. 7.7, similar to the primitive flow table described in Section 5.5.3 (Huffman method). There are, however, two

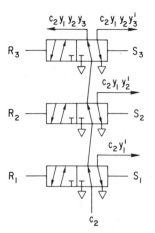

Fig. 7.6. Three steering valves providing four addresses.

Input signals		Output signals	
a_1	a_2	A+	A−
①		I	
	②		I
③		I	
	④		I
⑤		I	
	⑥		I

Fig. 7.7. Flow table for Example 3.

simplifications. First, the various unstable states and the "don't care" conditions that must be entered in the Huffman method (see Fig. 5.30) are left out. Second, the output columns get only 1 entries, with all 0 and "—" entries omitted.

In the Huffman method, all excitation and output functions are derived using Karnaugh maps. In the flow-table method, by comparison, no Karnaugh maps are used. All functions are found directly from the primitive flow table, with no row merging carried out. This is done as follows; see Fig. 7.8:

Each input-signal column is considered in turn. The control system must be able to distinguish between the various states appearing in the same column, and this is achieved by a *state assignment*, that is, each such state is assigned a different steering-valve address. Since there are three states in the a_1 column, two steering valves are required for this column, giving the three addresses a_1y_1', $a_1y_1y_2'$, and $a_1y_1y_2$. Similarly, two more steering valves are needed for the a_2 column, giving the three addresses a_2y_3', $a_2y_3y_4'$, and $a_2y_3y_4$. The chosen state assignments are entered in the table to the left of the state numbers.

Note that there are actually six ways of assigning three addresses to three states (i.e., six different possible state assignments), and each produces a slightly different solution. However, these differences are usually insignificant, so that

Input signals		Output signals	
a_1	a_2	A+	A−
y_1' ① R_3		I	
	y_3' ② $\begin{smallmatrix}S_1\\R_2\end{smallmatrix}$		I
y_1y_2' ③ $\begin{smallmatrix}S_3\\R_4\end{smallmatrix}$		I	
	y_3y_4' ④ S_2		I
y_1y_2 ⑤ S_4		I	
	y_3y_4 ⑥ R_1		I

Fig. 7.8. Completed flow table for Example 3.

the state assignment chosen is generally not critical (unlike the Huffman method).

The next step is to check each state and prepare the steering valves so that each is properly set for the next state. For example, state 2 requires state assignment y_3'. This must be prepared ahead of time by calling for reset signal R_3 at state 1. This resets valve 3, so that its input signal goes to address y_3'. Thus, the moment the a_2 signal arrives, the system automatically goes to state 2. If this y_3' address had not been prepared before, the system might falsely end up at states 4 or 6, resulting in a malfunction.

This procedure is followed for all states. Thus, at state 2, we specify S_1 and R_2 signals in order to set up the $y_1 y_2'$ address to which the a_1 signal of state 3 must be sent. Note that at state 4, we do *not* call for an S_1 signal, even though the address of state 5 is $y_1 y_2$. The reason is that steering valve 1 was already set by S_1 at state 2. Since there has been no R_1 signal in the intervening period, the valve is still in its set position, so that no additional S_1 signal is required. Similarly, there is no S_3 at state 5, even though the address of state 6 is $y_3 y_4$.

The final step is to read the various set, reset, and output signals directly from the table by ANDing the input signal listed at the head of each column with the respective state assignment. We thus get

$$S_1 = a_2 y_3' \qquad S_2 = a_2 y_3 y_4' \qquad S_3 = a_1 y_1 y_2' \qquad S_4 = a_1 y_1 y_2$$

$$R_1 = a_2 y_3 y_4 \qquad R_2 = a_2 y_3' \qquad R_3 = a_1 y_1' \qquad R_4 = a_1 y_1 y_2'$$

The output signals are written down similarly. However, we must differentiate between the three required $A+$ signals at states 1, 3, and 5. Whereas those at states 3 and 5 are unconditional, the one at state 1 should only go into effect if the START button is pressed. This is assured by ANDing the $a_1 y_1'$ address with START, giving the output functions

$$A+ = a_1 y_1' \cdot \text{START} + a_1 y_1 y_2' + a_1 y_1 y_2 = a_1 y_1' \cdot \text{START} + a_1 y_1$$

$$A- = a_2 y_3' + a_2 y_3 y_4' + a_2 y_3 y_4 = a_2 y_3' + a_2 y_3 = a_2$$

(Note that the simplification in the $A+$ function is made possible by the state assignment that was chosen.)

The final circuit based on these equations is shown in Fig. 7.9, where a shuttle valve implements the OR function in the $A+$ expression. For the sake of clarity, most circuit connections are only indicated but not drawn, as this would only make the drawing cluttered and difficult to follow. Also, the figure shows only the control circuit, without the cylinder-actuating valve and limit valves. Altogether, the control circuit requires only five valves (four steering valves and one shuttle valve), apart from the START valve. The author knows of no other method able to provide such a simple solution for this particular example. (If we use the Huffman method, the control circuit would require at least 13 valves instead of 5.)

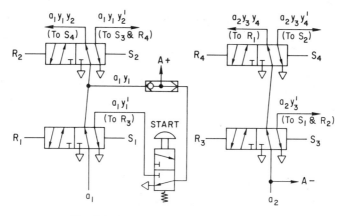

Fig. 7.9. Control circuit for Example 3.

7.2.3 Example 4

As second example, consider the two-cylinder sequence

$$\text{START, } A+, B+, A-, B-, \begin{pmatrix} A+ \\ B+ \end{pmatrix}, A-, B-$$

where the $A+$ and $B+$ strokes in parentheses indicate parallel (simultaneous) cylinder strokes. The flow table for this problem is shown in Fig. 7.10, and has four input columns, since there are four combinations of limit-valve signals.

If in this system, cylinder A should be so slow that during the parallel stroke, it has not even begun to move by the time cylinder B has already reached limit valve b_2, we would have to insert an additional state in the $a_1 b_2$ column between states 5 and 6. However, in the solution presented here, this extreme condition is

Input–signal combinations				Output signals			
$a_1 b_1$	$a_2 b_1$	$a_2 b_2$	$a_1 b_2$	A +	A −	B +	B −
y_1' ①				I			
	② R_2					I	
		y_2' ③ R_3			I		
			y_3' ④ S_1				I
y_1 ⑤ S_2					I	I	
		y_2 ⑥ S_3			I		
			y_3 ⑦ R_1				I

Fig. 7.10. Flow table for Example 4.

excluded. Note that three steering valves are required. No steering valve is assigned to the a_2b_1 column, since this contains only a single state. The excitation and output functions, as read from the table, are

$$S_1 = a_1b_2y_3' \qquad S_2 = a_1b_1y_1 \qquad S_3 = a_2b_2y_2$$

$$R_1 = a_1b_2y_3 \qquad R_2 = a_2b_1 \qquad R_3 = a_2b_2y_2'$$

$$A+ = a_1b_1y_1' \cdot \text{START} + a_1b_1y_1$$

$$A- = a_2b_2y_2' + a_2b_2y_2 = a_2b_2$$

$$B+ = a_2b_1 + a_1b_1y_1$$

$$B- = a_1b_2y_3' + a_1b_2y_3 = a_1b_2$$

The resulting control circuit is shown in Fig. 7.11. Apart from three steering valves and two shuttle valves, three additional valves are required to implement the four input combinations a_1b_1, a_2b_1, a_2b_2, and a_1b_2.

It is of interest to point out the reason for this low number of valves required. Examining the excitation and output functions, we note that a given state variable is *always* coupled with the same input-signal combination. For example, y_1 or y_1' always appears together with a_1b_1, whereas y_2 or y_2' is always linked with a_2b_2. This is no accident, but an inherent feature of the flow-table method, in which every steering valve is assigned to only one flow-table column. As a result, each steering valve can be used to combine an input combination

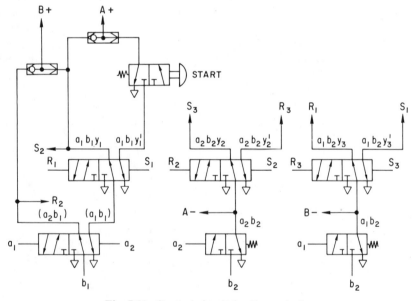

Fig. 7.11. Control circuit for Example 4.

with a state variable, and no additional AND valves are needed for this purpose. In the Huffman method (and others derived from it), many additional valves are needed to give the various AND-function terms contained in the excitation and output relations. In the flow-table method, by comparison, all these terms are automatically produced by the steering valves, and the only AND valves needed are those for the input combinations.

This explains the striking valve economy often achieved with the flow-table method, but also hints at the method's weak point. If several cylinders are involved, the resulting input-signal combinations can become fairly long, so that an excessive number of AND valves may be needed to produce them. In other words, the flow-table method is only advantageous for problems involving relatively few cylinders, although the number of sequence steps can be very large.

In order to reduce the number of AND valves, one 5/2 valve with two pilot inputs can often take the place of two 3/2 valves with return springs. This idea has been applied in Fig. 7.11, where one 5/2 valve *ostensibly* produces both $a_1 b_1$ and $a_2 b_1$ terms. Actually, the valve does not always provide the "true" $a_1 b_1$ and $a_2 b_1$ terms, since it remains in its previous position after cylinder A has begun to move. Thus, we still get the $a_1 b_1$ signal even after cylinder A has left the a_1 position. When the cylinder reaches the end of its stroke, it actuates the a_2 limit valve, at which moment the $a_1 b_1$ output is replaced by $a_2 b_1$. For this reason, these two terms are shown on the diagram in parentheses to indicate that they do not always reflect the true present situation. However, since nothing is to be switched *on* or *off* until the stroke is completed, there is no harm in maintaining the previous term during the cylinder motion.

The only case where it is *not* permissible to use this idea is when there are two parallel cylinder strokes. This explains why the two 3/2 valves giving the $a_1 b_2$ and $a_2 b_2$ terms have not been replaced by a single 5/2 valve. If this had been done, and if, after state 5, cylinder B should reach b_2 before cylinder A has reached a_2, then the $B-$ output signal would be produced falsely after state 5.

To summarize, a single 5/2 valve with double pilot inputs can always be used to provide two input-signal combinations, unless parallel cylinder motions are involved. Use of this idea reduces the number of AND valves by up to one-half.

An alternative method is to use inexpensive passive AND-gate elements, see Fig. 4.28(b), instead of 3/2 valves.

7.2.4 Example 5

The third example concerns the three-cylinder sequence

$$\text{START}, \ A+, \ B+, \ B-, \ C+, \ B+, \ B-, \ C-, \ A-$$

which might, for example, represent a work station in which two holes are to be drilled in a workpiece. Cylinder A clamps the workpiece, B lowers the drill spindle, and C moves the workpiece to the position corresponding to the two holes.

Input – signal combinations					Output signals					
$a_1 b_1 c_1$ ($= a_1$)	$a_2 b_1 c_1$	$a_2 b_2 c_1$ ($= b_2 c_1$)	$a_2 b_1 c_2$ ($= b_1 c_2$)	$a_2 b_2 c_2$ ($= b_2 c_2$)	A+	A-	B+	B-	C+	C-
① R_1					l					
	y_1' ②						l			
		③ S_1 R_2							l	
	$y_1 y_2'$ ④ R_3							l		
			y_3' ⑤			l				
				⑥ S_3			l			
			y_3 ⑦ S_2							l
	$y_1 y_2$ ⑧					l				

Fig. 7.12. Flow table for Example 5.

The flow table for this problem is shown in Fig. 7.12. Although there are eight possible combinations of limit-valve signals, three ($a_1 b_2 c_1$, $a_1 b_1 c_2$, and $a_1 b_2 c_2$) do not occur in this sequence, so that the flow table requires only five input-signal columns.

The reader will realize that the problem of implementing the input-signal combinations becomes more and more troublesome as the number of cylinders is increased. Not only are there more such combinations, but each combination is longer and requires more AND valves. This is so because each valve has a fan-in of only 2. Thus, a single valve can provide an AND term such as ab. To get abc, a second AND valve is needed, with inputs ab and c. Thus, to combine n variables, $n - 1$ AND-valves are required.

As shown in Example 2, the use of one 5/2 valve to replace two 3/2 AND valves improves the situation. However, it pays to look for additional ways of reducing the number of AND valves even further. By inspecting the five headings of the flow table of Fig. 7.12, it is noted that the variables $b_1 c_1$ in the $a_1 b_1 c_1$ term are superfluous, since there is no other column having a heading that includes a_1. Therefore, the $a_1 b_1 c_1$ term can be shortened to a_1. Similarly, the $a_2 b_2 c_1$ term can be replaced by $b_2 c_1$ (since the $a_1 b_2 c_1$ term does not come up), and the $a_2 b_1 c_2$ and $a_2 b_2 c_2$ terms can be replaced by $b_1 c_2$ and $b_2 c_2$, respectively. A systematic way of carrying out these simplifications is shown in the next section. These simplifications result in the solution

$$S_1 = b_2 c_1 \qquad S_2 = b_1 c_2 y_3 \qquad S_3 = b_2 c_2$$

$$R_1 = a_1 \qquad R_2 = b_2 c_1 \qquad R_3 = a_2 b_1 c_1 y_1 y_2'$$

$$A+ = a_1 \cdot \text{START} \qquad A- = a_2 b_1 c_1 y_1 y_2$$

$$B+ = a_2 b_1 c_1 y_1' + b_1 c_2 y_3' \qquad B- = b_2 c_1 + b_2 c_2$$

$$C+ = a_2 b_1 c_1 y_1 y_2' \qquad C- = b_1 c_2 y_3$$

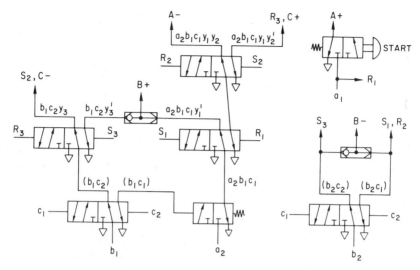

Fig. 7.13. Control circuit for Example 5.

Figure 7.13 shows the resulting control circuit. Note that the 3/2 valve used to give the $a_2b_1c_1$ term could be eliminated by connecting b_1c_1 to the supply-pressure port of limit valve a_2. This limit valve, when actuated, then outputs a pressure representing the $a_2b_1c_1$ term. This technique of using a limit valve as passive AND gate is possible here because the a_2 signal is not required anywhere else. (This idea is also illustrated in Fig. 7.22.)

7.2.5 Map Method of Simplifying Input Combinations

In Example 5, four of the five input-signal combinations are simplified in order to reduce the number of required AND valves. A systematic method of doing this is now shown.

First, draw a pseudo-Karnaugh map covering the input variables involved. (See Section 5.5.12 for a description of these maps.) Since Example 5 involves six limit valves, we draw a six-variable pseudo-Karnaugh map, as shown in Fig. 7.14. Although this looks just like a Karnaugh map used for simplifying logic functions, the use made of it here is quite different.

For each input-signal combination that actually comes up in the given sequence, we place an x in the corresponding square of the map. Each x must then be included in one and only one *loop*, using the following looping rules:

1. Each loop must contain *one and only one* x, but should contain as many adjacent empty squares as possible.
2. Adjacent squares are here defined as in conventional Karnaugh maps. Loops can only contain 1, 2, 4, 8, etc. squares, just as the cells in Karnaugh maps.

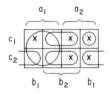

Fig. 7.14. Map for simplifying the input-signal combinations of Example 5.

3. Empty squares may be included in more than one loop.
4. Each loop should be made as large as possible, subject to the above rules.

The designations of the various loops then give the simplified input-signal terms. For example, in the map of Fig. 7.14, we enter an x in five of the eight squares, according to the five input-signal columns of Fig. 7.12. Since the $a_1b_1c_1$ term (the upper left-hand corner of the map) is part of the 4-square loop with designation a_1, then $a_1b_1c_1$ can be replaced by a_1. Similarly, the $a_2b_1c_2$ term can be replaced by b_1c_2, since its square is part of the 2-square loop having that designation. On the other hand, the x in the $a_2b_1c_1$ square cannot be included in any larger loop, which means that this term cannot be simplified.

For four-cylinder sequences, eight input variables are involved, and the map assumes a 4 × 4 configuration. For five-cylinder sequences, the map size is again doubled, and contains two 4 × 4 submaps. For example, assuming the sequence $E+$, $A+$, $B+$, $B-$, $C+$, $C-$, $B+$, $B-$, $D+$, $D-$, $A-$, $E-$, the input combinations appear in the following order: $a_1b_1c_1d_1e_1$, $a_1b_1c_1d_1e_2$, $a_2b_1c_1d_1e_2$, $a_2b_2c_1d_1e_2$, $a_2b_1c_1d_1e_2$, $a_2b_1c_2d_1e_2$, $a_2b_1c_1d_1e_2$, $a_2b_2c_1d_1e_2$, $a_2b_1c_1d_1e_2$, $a_2b_1c_1d_2e_2$, $a_2b_1c_1d_1e_2$, $a_1b_1c_1d_1e_2$, and $a_1b_1c_1d_1e_1$.

At first sight, the task of implementing all these input combinations seems formidable. However, entering each combination in the map of Fig. 7.15 and looping shows that

$a_1b_1c_1d_1e_1$ is simplified to e_1,
$a_1b_1c_1d_1e_2$ is simplified to a_1e_2,
$a_2b_1c_1d_1e_2$ is simplified to $a_2b_1c_1d_1$,
$a_2b_2c_1d_1e_2$ is simplified to b_2,
$a_2b_1c_2d_1e_2$ is simplified to c_2,
$a_2b_1c_1d_2e_2$ is simplified to d_2.

Therefore, only three AND valves are required to produce the terms a_1e_1, a_2b_1, and c_1d_1, and a fourth valve to combine these last two terms into $a_2b_1c_1d_1$.

7.2.6 Example 6

As a final example, we use a modification of Example 3. Here, too, a single cylinder A carries out the sequence

$$\text{START, } A+, A-, A+, A-, A+, A-$$

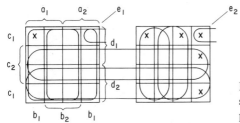

Fig. 7.15. Map for simplifying the input-signal combinations for a five-cylinder problem.

but, for each outward stroke, the total extension becomes less; see Fig. 7.16. At the first $A+$ stroke, the piston reaches limit valve a_4 before retracting. At the second $A+$ stroke, the piston retracts after reaching limit valve a_3, and at the last $A+$ stroke, only a_2 is reached. Sequences of this type frequently appear in packing machines, for instance, where several cartons must be pushed off a belt and lined up in a row. Note that during the first $A+$ and $A-$ strokes, the piston twice actuates a_2 and a_3, but these actuations must have no effect on the sequence. Similarly, during the second $A+$ and $A-$ strokes, a_2 is actuated.

Because of these multiple limit-valve actuations, the flow table of Fig. 7.17 is much larger than that for Example 3, which is shown in Fig. 7.7, and contains 12 instead of only 6 states. If we were to handle this problem as before, we would need eight steering valves (two each in columns a_1 and a_3, and four in column a_2). However, we can simplify the problem considerably by distinguishing between *active* and *passive states*. We define passive states as those at which nothing happens, that is, no action is taken when the system passes through a passive state. Obviously, states 2 and 3 are passive states, since the piston just keeps going when passing through them, and there are no output signals at these states. State 4, however, is an active state, since output signal $A-$ changes to 1. Similarly, states 5, 6, 8, and 10 are all passive states, and this fact is indicated in the flow table by the letter P entered next to the state numbers.

Since nothing occurs at these passive states, there is no need to distinguish between them by means of differing state assignments. However, *we must differentiate between the various passive states and the active states in the same column*. We therefore assign y'_3 to passive states 2, 6, 8, and 10 in column a_2, and y_3 to active state 12 in the same column. This is necessary to avoid having the $A-$ signal, which is produced at state 12, also appear at the passive states. Similarly, we differentiate between passive states 3 and 5 and active state 9 in the a_3 column by assigning y'_4 to the two former and y_4 to the latter. Thus, the number of required steering valves has been reduced from eight to four.

Fig. 7.16. Limit valves for Example 6.

a_1	a_2	a_3	a_4	A +	A −
y_1' ① R_3R_4				I	
	y_3' ② P				
		y_4' ③ P			
			④ S_1R_2	I	
		y_4' ⑤ P			
	y_3' ⑥ P				
$y_1 y_2'$ ⑦ S_4				I	
	y_3' ⑧ P				
		y_4 ⑨ S_2			I
	y_3' ⑩ P				
$y_1 y_2$ ⑪ S_3				I	
	y_3 ⑫ R_1				I

Fig. 7.17. Flow table for Example 6.

Since nothing is to occur at the passive states, we must not specify any set or reset signals at them. Instead, we shift these back to the previous active state. For instance, y_4' is first listed at state 3. Ordinarily, we would enter R_4 at state 2. However, since this is a passive state (with P indicating that no S or R must be placed there), we enter R_4 at state 1 (together with R_3). Similarly, S_1R_2 is entered at state 4, rather than at state 6, etc.

The excitation and output functions resulting from the flow table are as follows:

$$S_1 = a_4 \qquad S_2 = a_3 y_4 \qquad S_3 = a_1 y_1 y_2 \qquad S_4 = a_1 y_1 y_2'$$

$$R_1 = a_2 y_3 \qquad R_2 = a_4 \qquad R_3 = a_1 y_1' \qquad R_4 = a_1 y_1'$$

$$A+ = a_1 y_1' \cdot \text{START} + a_1 y_1 \qquad A- = a_4 + a_3 y_4 + a_2 y_3$$

Drawing of the control circuit is left as an exercise for the reader. As in Fig. 7.9, four steering valves are required, but the circuit also calls for three shuttle valves (instead of only one in Fig. 7.9), because of the two additional OR terms in the $A-$ expression.

7.3 OPERATIONS-TABLE OR CHANGE-SIGNAL METHOD (COLE)

To summarize the previous two sections: the cascade method is ideal for sequences without repeated steps, regardless of the number of cylinders involved; the flow-table method, on the other hand, can easily handle sequences with many repeated steps, provided the number of cylinders is not too large.

There are, however, more complex sequences that involve both many repeated steps and many cylinders, so that neither of the two previous methods is suitable. An economic solution for such problems is provided by the *operations-table method*, developed by J. H. Cole and published in Refs. (7.15)–(7.17). (The method has also been called the *synthesis-table method*, or the *change-signal method*.) While this method can also provide good solutions for simpler sequences, it is not easy to master and apply, so that its use is best limited to more complex sequences for which the previous two methods are unsuitable. A somewhat simplified version of the method is now described using two examples.

As with the previous two methods, the operations-table method assumes cylinder-actuating valves with double pilot inputs.

7.3.1   Example 7

The sequence to be implemented is defined by

$$\text{START, } A+, A-, A+, B+, B-, A-, B+, A+, A-, B-$$

The operations, or synthesis, table for this sequence is shown in Fig. 7.18. In column I, the rows are numbered to help with the explanation. In column IV, the required sequence events are listed. In column II, we then list the input-signal combination prevailing *before* the event listed in column IV has taken place. However, as the name *change-signal method* implies, the method does not utilize the input-signal combinations, but rather the *changes* that take place. Therefore, in column III, we list the change in the input combination that is produced by the previous event.

We now check each input change and, in column V, list the so-called *associated events*. These are the different events that are triggered by the same input change. For example, input change b_1 occurs in row 1 (where it must trigger event $A+$), but also in row 6 (where it must trigger event $A-$). This information is entered in column V. Similarly, input change a_2 must trigger event $A-$ in rows 2 and 9, but event $B+$ in row 4.

The next design step is to differentiate between associated events by means of state assignment. The required state variables are obtained with steering valves connected exactly as in the flow-table method. For example, to distinguish between the two associated events $A+$ and $A-$ listed in row 1, we assign address y_1 to row 1 and y_1' to row 6, and this information is entered in column VI. Since input change a_2 must produce $A-$ in rows 2 and 9, but $B+$ in row 4, we enter y_2 in rows 2 and 9, but y_2' in row 4. Since input change a_1 is associated with three different events, we need two steering valves, and assign $y_3 y_4$ to row 3, $y_3 y_4'$ to row 7, and y_3' to row 10. Finally, we assign y_5 and y_5' to rows 5 and 8, respectively.

The address of each row is obtained by ANDing its state assignment with the input-change signal. Thus, the address of row 1 is $b_1 y_1$, etc. These addresses are

I	II	III	IV	V	VI	VII	VIII	IX	X	XI
Row	Inputs	Input Change	Event	Associated Events	State Assignment	SET	RESET	Shutoff Valves	SET	RESET
1	a_1b_1	b_1	$A+$	$A+, A-$ (1) (6)	y_1		R_6	w_1		
2	a_2b_1	a_2	$A-$	$A-, B+$ (2)(9) (4)	y_2y_6'	S_3S_4		w_1'		R_{w1}
3	a_1b_1	a_1	$A+$	$A+, B+, B-$ (3) (7) (10)	y_3y_4		R_2		S_{w2}	
4	a_2b_1	a_2	$B+$		y_2'	S_5		w_2		
5	a_2b_2	b_2	$B-$	$B-, A+$ (5) (8)	y_5		R_1	w_2'		R_{w2}
6	a_2b_1	b_1	$A-$		y_1'		R_4			
7	a_1b_1	a_1	$B+$		y_3y_4'		R_5		S_{w3}	
8	a_1b_2	b_2	$A+$		y_5'	S_2S_6		w_3		
9	a_2b_2	a_2	$A-$		y_2y_6		R_3	w_3'		R_{w3}
10	a_1b_2	a_1	$B-$		y_3'	S_1			S_{w1}	

Figure 7.18. Operations table for Example 7

used to distinguish between the associated events for the same input change. Thus, output signal $A+$ in row 1 is produced by $A+ = b_1 y_1$, and $A-$ in row 6 is produced by $A- = b_1 y_1'$.

The next step is to check for contradicting output signals. For example, the $A+ = b_1 y_1$ signal occurs in row 1, and $A- = a_2 y_2$ is produced in row 2. However, the $b_1 y_1$ term is still active in row 2, so that there are opposing pilot signals $A+$ and $A-$ simultaneously. To prevent this, we must add additional steering valves called *shutoff valves*, whose state variables are labeled w rather than y. (These shutoff valves can be 3/2 rather than 5/2 valves, since the negated state variables w' are not utilized.) Thus, we must differentiate between rows 1 and 2 by entering w_1 and w_1', respectively, in column IX. This changes the previous $A+$ term from $b_1 y_1$ to $b_1 y_1 w_1$. Since $w_1 = 0$ in row 2, the $A+$ signal is shut off there, thus avoiding getting $A+$ and $A-$ signals at the same time.

Checking succeeding rows for contradictory output signals, we find no contradiction in row 3, since the $A- = a_2 y_2$ signal is not active anymore in that row. Similarly, there is no contradiction in row 4, since the previous $B- = a_1 y_3'$ signal is not active anymore. (a_1 has changed to a_2, and y_3' to y_3.) However, the $B+ = a_2 y_2'$ signal from row 4 is still active in row 5. To prevent a contradiction with $B-$, we enter w_2 and w_2', respectively, in these two rows in column IX. The final contradiction occurs between rows 8 and 9, forcing us to assign w_3 and w_3', respectively, to these rows.

The final, and most difficult, part of the method consists of entering the set and reset signals for the various steering valves in their proper locations. As in the flow-table method, the steering valves must be set or reset ahead of time in preparation for the next state. This means that we ordinarily enter each set or reset signal one row before the row in which the new state variable is required.

Sometimes, however, this leads to problems, because of simultaneous set and reset signals for the same steering valve. For example, we would normally enter R_3 in row 9, giving $R_3 = a_2 y_2$. But this term is still active in row 2, where the R_3 signal cannot be tolerated since we need S_3 in that row. Sometimes, such a problem can be solved by moving up the offending signal by one or more rows. Attempting to move up R_3 to row 8, we find that this causes the $B- = a_1 y_3'$ signal from row 10 to be activated prematurely in row 8. Moving up R_3 further to row 7 is also impossible, since that row has the state assignment $y_3 y_4'$. The only way to solve the predicament in this case is to leave R_3 in row 9, but to differentiate between rows 9 and 2 by means of state assignments y_6 and y_6', respectively, which, of course, requires an additional steering valve.

A similar predicament occurs with the set and reset signals for the shutoff valves. Normally, we would enter S_{w2} in row 3, and R_{w2} in row 4. This, however, would cause the w_2 signal in row 4 to disappear almost immediately, possibly before the $B+$ signal has had a chance to take effect. To avoid such a *hazard*, we move down the R_{w2} signal to row 5, giving $R_{w2} = b_2 y_5$. The moment the b_2 signal appears, R_{w2} becomes effective, switching w_2 to w_2'. (Although there is a very brief overlap between the $B+$ and $B-$ signals, this does no harm, since $B+$ disappears the moment $w_2 = 0$.) Likewise, we move R_{w1} from row 1 to row 2, and R_{w3} from row 8 to row 9.

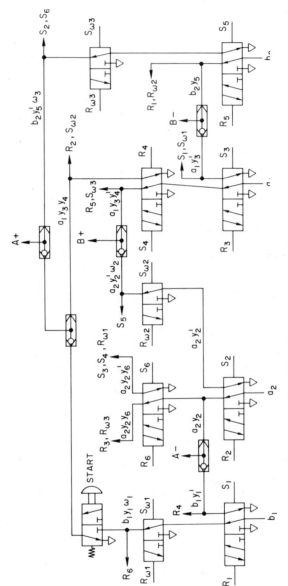

Fig. 7.19. Control circuit for Example 7.

The resulting excitation and output functions are

$$S_1 = a_1 y_3' \qquad R_1 = b_2 y_5$$

$$S_2 = b_2 y_5' w_3 \qquad R_2 = a_1 y_3 y_4$$

$$S_3 = a_2 y_2 y_6' \qquad R_3 = a_2 y_2 y_6$$

$$S_4 = a_2 y_2 y_6' \qquad R_4 = b_1 y_1'$$

$$S_5 = a_2 y_2' w_2 \qquad R_5 = a_1 y_3 y_4'$$

$$S_6 = b_2 y_5' w_3 \qquad R_6 = b_1 y_1 w_1$$

$$S_{w1} = a_1 y_3' \qquad R_{w1} = a_2 y_2 y_6'$$

$$S_{w2} = a_1 y_3 y_4 \qquad R_{w2} = b_2 y_5$$

$$S_{w3} = a_1 y_3 y_4' \qquad R_{w3} = a_2 y_2 y_6$$

$$A+ = b_1 y_1 w_1 \cdot \text{START} + a_1 y_3 y_4 + b_2 y_5' w_3 \qquad A- = a_2 y_2 + b_1 y_1'$$

$$B+ = a_2 y_2' w_2 + a_1 y_3 y_4' \qquad\qquad\qquad\qquad B- = b_2 y_5 + a_1 y_3'$$

The reader will see that a given state variable is *always* combined with the same input signal, a characteristic already noted with the flow-table method. For this reason, here, too, the various steering valves can be utilized as passive AND gates. In the flow-table method, a number of AND valves are needed for implementing the various input-signal combinations. In the operations-table method, by comparison, no such AND-valves are required, since the input-change signal is utilized instead of the complete input-signal combination. Therefore, this method requires no AND valves whatsoever, but only steering valves, and some shuttle valves to implement the OR functions in the output expressions. The method is, thus, especially advantageous for sequences involving many cylinders in which the input-signal combinations could only be implemented with a great number of AND valves.

The final control circuit, shown in Fig. 7.19, is drawn in a similar manner as that with the flow-table method.

7.3.2 Sequence Charts for Pneumatic Circuits

In Section 5.2, sequence charts are described in connection with relay control systems. Such charts are especially useful for verifying the correct functioning of a new control-circuit design. Since the operations-table method just described is not very straightforward and errors are easily made, it is highly recommended to check each design obtained with this method by means of a sequence chart.

The sequence chart for the solution of Example 7 is shown in Fig. 7.20. The chart is best drawn as follows:

The first horizontal lines represent cylinders A and B and their corresponding limit valves. Then follow the lines for the START signal and the various steering

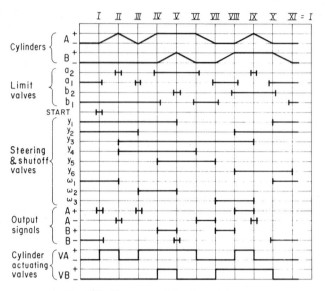

Fig. 7.20. Sequence chart for Example 7.

valves. Finally, we draw lines for the output signals (i.e., pilot signals for the cylinder-actuating valves), and two lines for each cylinder-actuating valve to show the valve position.

The expected cylinder sequence and the resulting limit valve signals are then entered in the first few lines, under the assumption that the control circuit functions properly. Whether it really does so is verified at the end, according to the entries in the lines for the two cylinder-actuating valves, VA and VB.

From the operations table, we note that steering valves y_1, y_2, and w_1 should be in their set position at the beginning of the sequence. We, therefore, draw heavy lines for these valves at the left end of the chart. Again, this assumption must be verified after the chart has been completed by checking that these valves are left set at the sequence end.

The states of the nine state variables y_1 to y_6 and w_1 to w_3 are now plotted on the chart for the course of the complete sequence, in accordance with the set and reset signals listed in the operations table. However, each of these entries must be verified by checking the set and reset functions listed as part of the final solution. It is especially important to check that there are no opposing set and reset signals for any valve, and that no set or reset signal appears unexpectedly a second time during the sequence. These checks can be carried out by following the listed set and reset signals and seeing for how long each remains active, utilizing the input- and state-variable signals already shown on the chart. (If the reader should find it difficult to check this, it is suggested to add a set and a reset line on the chart for each steering valve, and then plot those periods during which these signals are active. This has not been done in Fig. 7.20, since it would require 18 additional lines, but is left as an exercise for the reader.)

After the state-variable lines have all been verified, the lines for output signals $A+$, $A-$, $B+$, and $B-$ should be filled in, according to the output functions listed as part of the solution. Here, too, a check should be made for contradictory signals. These lines should then be utilized to draw the resulting positions of cylinder-actuating valves VA and VB. Finally, the resulting cylinder motions are checked.

The sequence chart, when filled in properly, does not only disclose circuit malfunctions due to improper design, but may also indicate possible simplifications. For example, the chart discloses that shutoff valve w_1 can be dispensed with since, even without it there is no overlap at stage 2 between $A+$ and $A-$, provided the START button has been released. If this w_1 valve is eliminated, the $A+$ signal is maintained as long as the operator presses START, so that the cylinder only retracts when the button is released. If this is acceptable, then the w_1 valve can be eliminated.

7.3.3 Example 8

The second example illustrating this method involves a rather difficult problem. A hole is to be drilled near each of the four corners of a rectangular plate. Cylinder A clamps the plate to a slide table. Cylinder B lowers and raises the drill spindle, drilling a hole with each $B+$ stroke. Cylinders C and D move the table in the x and y directions. Thus, the four state combinations of cylinders C and D move the plate to the four required hole locations. The necessary cylinder sequence can thus be defined as follows:

START, $A+$, $B+$, $B-$, $C+$, $B+$, $B-$, $D+$, $B+$, $B-$, $C-$, $B+$, $B-$, $D-$, $A-$

The operations table for this problem is shown in Fig. 7.21. Since there are only four associated events (for input change b_1), three steering valves are required to provide four different state assignments, y'_1, $y_1y'_2$, $y_1y_2y'_3$, and $y_1y_2y_3$, all of which are combined with input variable b_1.

In entering the set and reset signals, it soon becomes apparent that additional steering valves are required to provide proper addresses for these signals. Consider, for example, S_1 and R_2 in row 6, where the input change is b_2 and the prevailing state assignment is y'_1. However, address $b_2y'_1$ cannot be used, since steering valve 1 is already coupled with input variable b_1. (It should be remembered that a given state variable must always be combined with the same input signal.) To provide proper addresses for the various set and reset signals, three aditional steering valves are required, providing state assignments y'_4, $y_4y'_5$, $y_4y_5y'_6$, and $y_4y_5y_6$, all of which are combined with b_2.

To avoid conflicts between output signals $A+$ and $A-$, or between $B+$ and $B-$, five shutoff valves, w_1 to w_5, are required. By checking the resulting operations table, it is found that there is still a conflict between $A+$ and $A-$ in row 1, caused by the fact that the $S_{w1} = b_1y_1y_2y_3$ signal is still active in row 1 and thus contradicts the R_{w1} signal assigned to that row. As a result, the

Row	Inputs	Input Change	Event	Associated Events	State Assignment	SET	RESET	Shutoff Valves	SET	RESET
1	$a_1b_1c_1d_1$	a_1	$A+$					w'_1	S_{w2}	R_{w1}
2	$a_2b_1c_1d_1$	a_2	$B+$				R_4	w_2		
3	$a_2b_2c_1d_1$	b_2	$B-$		y'_4		R_1	w'_2		R_{w2}
4	$a_2b_1c_1d_1$	b_1	$C+$	$C+, D+, C-, D-$ ④ ⑦ ⑩ ⑬	y'_1				S_{w3}	
5	$a_2b_1c_2d_1$	c_2	$B+$			S_4	R_5	w_3		
6	$a_2b_2c_2d_1$	b_2	$B-$		$y_4y'_5$	S_1	R_2	w'_3		R_{w3}

Column headers (top of table): I Row, II Inputs, III Input Change, IV Event, V Associated Events, VI State Assignment, VII SET, VIII RESET, IX Shutoff Valves, X SET, XI RESET.

7	$a_2b_1c_2d_1$	b_1	$D+$	y_1y_2'				S_{w4}
8	$a_2b_2c_2d_2$	d_2	$B+$		S_5	R_6	w_4	
9	$a_2b_2c_2d_2$	b_2	$B-$	$y_4y_5y_6'$	S_2	R_3	w_4'	R_{w4}
10	$a_2b_1c_2d_2$	b_1	$C-$	$y_1y_2y_3'$				S_{w5}
11	$a_2b_1c_1d_2$	c_1	$B+$		S_6		w_5	
12	$a_2b_2c_1d_2$	b_2	$B-$	$y_4y_5y_6$	S_3		w_5'	R_{w5}
13	$a_2b_1c_1d_2$	b_1	$D-$	$y_1y_2y_3$				S_{w1}
14	$a_2b_1c_1d_1$	d_1	$A-$				w_1	

Fig. 7.21. Operations table for Example 8.

$A- = d_1w_1$ signal is also still active in that row. This problem is solved by moving up S_{w1} from row 13 to row 12, giving $S_{w1} = b_2y_4y_5y_6$. This signal is not active anymore in row 1, since b_2 becomes 0 after row 12.

The various excitation and output functions, as read from the operations table, are

$$S_1 = b_2y_4y_5' \qquad S_2 = b_2y_4y_5y_6' \qquad S_3 = b_2y_4y_5y_6$$

$$R_1 = b_2y_4' \qquad R_2 = b_2y_4y_5' \qquad R_3 = b_2y_4y_5y_6'$$

$$S_4 = c_2w_3 \qquad S_5 = d_2w_4 \qquad S_6 = c_1w_5$$

$$R_4 = a_2w_2 \qquad R_5 = c_2w_3 \qquad R_6 = d_2w_4$$

$$S_{w1} = b_2y_4y_5y_6 \qquad S_{w2} = a_1 \qquad S_{w3} = b_1y_1'$$

$$R_{w1} = a_1 \qquad R_{w2} = b_2y_4' \qquad R_{w3} = b_2y_4y_5'$$

$$S_{w4} = b_1y_1y_2' \qquad S_{w5} = b_1y_1y_2y_3'$$

$$R_{w4} = b_2y_4y_5y_6' \qquad R_{w5} = b_2y_4y_5y_6$$

$$A+ = a_1 \cdot \text{START} \qquad\qquad A- = d_1w_1$$

$$B+ = a_2w_2 + c_2w_3 + d_2w_4 + c_1w_5 \qquad B- = b_2$$

$$C+ = b_1y_1' \qquad\qquad C- = b_1y_1y_2y_3'$$

$$D+ = b_1y_1y_2' \qquad\qquad D- = b_1y_1y_2y_3$$

For a problem as complicated as this, it is vital to check the solution by means of a sequence chart. Drawing this chart and also drawing the final control circuit is left as an exercise for the reader. The control circuit requires 11 steering valves and 3 shuttle valves.

7.4 EFFICIENT VALVE IMPLEMENTATION OF LOGIC FUNCTIONS

This section lays the groundwork for Section 7.5, in which the Huffman method is applied to pneumatic control circuits.

As shown in Section 4.3.5, pneumatic valves can produce the NOT, AND, and OR functions, and can also implement RS flip-flops. However, using each valve to produce only one single function is very wasteful, and results in large, unwieldy circuits. It is shown here that one valve can be made to produce simultaneously two independent and sometimes fairly complex logic functions, to be called a *function pair*. The method is based on the use of logic-function tables first published in Ref. (7.18), in which the available function pairs are systematically listed. (The tables in this section and Fig. 7.22 have been reproduced by courtesy of the ASME from *Transactions of ASME, Journal of Dynamic Systems, Measurement, and Control*, Dec. 1983.)

7.4.1 Description of Logic-Function Tables

Table 7.1 shows the logic functions obtainable from a 3/2 valve with a return spring. Since such a valve has only one output port, it cannot produce a function pair but only a single function. The possibilities here are rather limited, since the valve has only two input ports, labeled 2 and 3, apart from the valve-actuating pilot port labeled P. (The latter could be replaced by mechanical or solenoid actuation.) As seen from the table, this valve can produce seven different logic functions by connecting the input signals as shown. (A 0 in the table signifies a port vented to atmosphere, and 1 stands for supply pressure.) Lines 1 to 6 of the table give the four common logic functions already shown in Chapter 4. Note that the AND and OR functions obtained only have a fan-in of 2. If greater fan-in is required, several valves have to be connected in series. Note also that the OR function can be obtained more economically using a shuttle valve, which costs less than half the price of typical directional-control valves.

Lines 7 to 9 of the table show three other logic functions that can also be obtained from this valve: the INHIBITION function $T = AB'$, the IMPLICATION function $T = A + B'$, and the three-variable function $T = AC + BC'$ for which no name seems to exist in the literature. It is here called the SELECTOR function, since the valve selects either the A or B input, depending on the state of input C. To obtain this function, input variable C must be connected to pilot port P, and variables A and B to ports 2 and 3, respectively.

The 5/2, 6/2, and 5/3 valves shown in Tables 7.2 to 7.4 have two output ports each, and can, therefore, produce function pairs defined by functions T_1 and T_2. All significant function pairs obtainable with these valves are listed in one of these three tables, depending on the number of input variables involved.

TABLE 7.1. 3/2 Valve Connections Yielding a Single Output Function

Line No.	Function Name	Function Boolean Equation	P	2	3
1	YES	$T = A$	A	1	0
2	NOT	$T = A'$	A	0	1
3	AND	$T = AB$	B	A	0
4	AND	$T = AB$	B	A	B
5	OR *	$T = A + B$	B	1	A
6	OR *	$T = A + B$	B	B	A
7	INHIBITION	$T = AB'$	B	0	A
8	IMPLICATION	$T = A + B'$	B	A	1
9	SELECTOR	$T = AC + BC'$	C	A	B

* Use of a shuttle valve is usually less expensive

TABLE 7.2 Valve Connections Yielding Two Separate Output Functions Involving One or Two Input Variables

Line No.	Function Names	Function Boolean Equations	5/2 Valve P	2	3	4	6/2 Valve P	2	3	4	5	5/3 Valve P₁	P₂	2	3	4
10	YES/NOT	$T_1 = A'$ $T_2 = A$	A	0	1	0										
12	YES/AND	$T_2 = B$ $T_1 = AB$					B	A	0	1	0					
13	YES/OR	$T_2 = B$ $T_1 = A + B$					B	1	A	1	0					
14	YES/INHIBITION	$T_1 = B$ $T_2 = AB'$	B	1	0	A										
16	YES/IMPLICATION	$T_1 = B$ $T_2 = A + B'$	B	A	1	0										
18	NOT/AND	$T_1 = B$ $T_2 = AB$	B	A	0	1										
21	NOT/OR	$T_1 = B'$ $T_2 = A + B$	B	0	1	A										
24	NOT/INHIBITION	$T_1 = B'$ $T_2 = A + B'$	B	1	A	0	B	0	1	0	A					
25	NOT/IMPLICATION	$T_2 = AB$ $T_1 = A + B$					B	0	1	A	1					
26	AND/OR	$T_2 = AB$ $T_1 = A + B$	B	B	A	0										
27	AND/OR	$T_2 = AB$ $T_1 = AB'$	B	0	A	0										
36	AND/INHIBITION	$T_2 = AB$ $T_1 = A + B'$										B	A	A	0	1
42	AND/IMPLICATION	$T_1 = AB$ $T_2 = A + B'$					B	A	0	A	1	A	B	A	1	0
43	AND/IMPLICATION	$T_1 = AB$ $T_2 = A + B'$														
45	OR/INHIBITION	$T_1 = A + B$ $T_2 = AB'$					B	1	A	0	A					
46	OR/INHIBITION	$T_1 = A + B$ $T_2 = AB'$					B	B	A	0	A					
47	OR/INHIBITION	$T_1 = A + B$ $T_2 = AB'$										A	B	1	0	1
48	OR/IMPLICATION	$T_2 = A + B$ $T_1 = A + B'$	B	A	1	A										
54	INHIBIT./INHIBIT.	$T_1 = A'B$ $T_2 = AB'$	B	0	A	1										
55	INHIBIT./IMPLICAT.	$T_1 = AB'$ $T_2 = A + B'$										A	B	1	0	0
58	IMPLIC./IMPLICAT.	$T_1 = A + B'$ $T_2 = A' + B$										A	B	1	0	1

Frequently, a given function pair can be obtained in several ways, all of which are listed in the original tables of Ref. (7.18). To save space, the tables presented here usually show only the most economical option for each function pair. (However, the numbering of the original tables has been kept, which explains the missing line numbers.)

As the tables show, many function pairs can only be obtained with a 6/2 or a 5/3 valve. Unfortunately, not many manufacturers supply 6/2 valves (which are equivalent to two individual 3/2 valves with a common pilot port built into one housing, and can thus always be replaced by two 3/2 valves). By comparison, 5/3 valves are readily available, since about half of all manufacturers of pneumatic spool valves offer such a design. The 5/3 valve provides many function pairs unobtainable with any other valve, and especially functions with a fan-in of 3.

The various function pairs have been derived by listing the conditions under which a given output port is pressurized, translating these conditions into a Boolean expression, and then simplifying the expression algebraically or using a Karnaugh map. For a detailed explanation, see Ref. (7.18).

Several comments concerning the tables will help the reader find his way. Table 7.2 shows all valve connections giving function pairs involving only one input variable (line 10), or two input variables (lines 12 to 58). Table 7.3 shows valve connections for three input variables. Since many three-variable functions have no accepted names, they have been named here using word and symbol combinations, for ease of identification. For example, the function $T_1 = A + BC'$ is designated here as "INHIBITION+," signifying that the INHIBITION term BC' is ORed with a third variable.

Table 7.4 shows function pairs involving four or five variables. Some of these functions are too complex to be named, and can only be identified by Boolean expressions.

The reader will note that the YES function appears several times. At first sight, this function seems useless. However, many valves are actuated mechanically rather than by pilot pressure. In all of the tables, pilot pressure P can be replaced by mechanical or solenoid actuation. Assume, for instance, that the 5/2 valve of line 14 represents a limit valve. The state $B = 1$ would then signify that the valve is actuated mechanically. Connecting this valve as in line 14 produces not only the YES function in the form of pressure signal $T_1 = B$ (as with any normal limit valve), but also the INHIBITION function $T_2 = AB'$, which may be needed somewhere else in the circuit, so that one valve has been saved.

A comment about interchanging valve variables might be useful. In any 6/2 valve, we can interchange T_1 and T_2 simply by interchanging input ports 2 and 3 with ports 4 and 5. In the 5/3 valve, T_1 and T_2 can be interchanged by interchanging P_1 with P_2, and port 2 with port 4. For 5/2 valves, T_1 and T_2 cannot be interchanged, since this valve is nonsymmetrical. However, for any type of valve, one can always interchange two or more input variables, and so get a function pair that may appear quite different, but is equivalent to the original one. To illustrate, interchanging A and B in line 24 gives $T_1 = A'$ and $T_2 = A'B$ (instead of $T_1 = B'$ and $T_2 = AB'$). But these function pairs are

TABLE 7.3. Valve Connections Yielding Two Separate Output Functions with Three Involved Variables

Line No.	Function Names	Function Boolean Equations		5/2 Valve P	2	3	4	6/2 Valve P	2	3	4	5	5/3 valve P_1	P_2	2	3	4
59	YES/SELECTOR	$T_2 = C$	$T_1 = AC+BC'$					C	A	B	1	0					
60	NOT/SELECTOR	$T_2 = C'$	$T_1 = AC+BC'$					C	A	B	0	1					
61	AND/OR	$T_1 = AB$	$T_2 = B+C$	B	A	B	C										
66	AND/AND	$T_1 = AC$	$T_2 = BC$					C	A	0	B	0					
70	AND/INHIBITION	$T_1 = AC$	$T_2 = BC'$	C	A	0	B										
73	AND/IMPLICATION	$T_1 = AC$	$T_2 = B+C'$					C	A	0	B	1					
75	AND/SELECTOR	$T_2 = BC$	$T_1 = AC+BC'$	C	A	B	0										
79	AND/SELECTOR	$T_2 = AC$	$T_1 = AC+BC'$					C	A	B	A	0					
81	OR/OR	$T_1 = B+C$	$T_2 = A+C$					C	1	B	1	A					
84	OR/OR	$T_1 = B+C$	$T_2 = A+C$					C	C	B	C	A					
85	OR/INHIBITION	$T_1 = B+C$	$T_2 = AC'$					C	1	B	0	A					
86	OR/INHIBITION	$T_1 = B+C$	$T_2 = AC'$					C	C	B	0	A					
87	OR/IMPLICATION	$T_2 = A+C$	$T_1 = B+C'$	C	B	1	A										
90	OR/SELECTOR	$T_1 = A+C$	$T_2 = AC+BC'$	C	1	A	B										
91	OR/SELECTOR	$T_1 = A+C$	$T_2 = AC+BC'$	C	C	A	B										
94	OR/SELECTOR	$T_1 = B+C$	$T_2 = AC+BC'$					C	1	B	A	B					
95	OR/SELECTOR	$T_1 = B+C$	$T_2 = AC+BC'$					C	C	B	A	B					
96	INHIBITION/INHIBITION	$T_1 = AC'$	$T_2 = BC'$					C	0	A	0	B					
97	INHIBITION/INHIBITION	$T_1 = AB'C$	$T_2 = ABC'$										B	C	0	A	0
99	INHIBITION/IMPLICATION	$T_1 = AC'$	$T_2 = B+C'$					C	0	A	B	1					
100	INHIBITION/IMPLICATION	$T_1 = AB'C$	$T_2 = A+B'+C$										B	C	0	A	1
101	INHIBITION/SELECTOR	$T_1 = AC'$	$T_2 = AC+BC'$	C	0	A	B										
103	INHIBITION/SELECTOR	$T_1 = BC'$	$T_2 = AC+BC'$					C	0	B	A	B					
104	IMPLICATION/IMPLICATION	$T_1 = A+C'$	$T_2 = B+C'$					C	A	1	B	1					
105	IMPLICATION/IMPLICATION	$T_1 = A+B+C'$	$T_2 = A+B'+C$										B	C	1	A	1
107	IMPLICATION/SELECTOR	$T_2 = B+C'$	$T_1 = AC+BC'$	C	A	B	1										
109	IMPLICATION/SELECTOR	$T_2 = A+C'$	$T_1 = AC+BC'$					C	A	B	A	1					
110	SELECTOR/SELECTOR	$T_1 = AC+BC'$	$T_2 = AC'+BC$	C	A	B	A										
112	AND + AND/AND + AND	$T_1 = AB + AC$	$T_2 = AC + BC$										C	A	A	B	C
113	AND + AND/AND +	$T_1 = AB + AC$	$T_2 = A + BC$										C	A	A	B	A
114	AND + AND/INHIBITION	$T_1 = AB + AC$	$T_2 = A'BC$										C	A	A	B	0
115	AND + AND/IMPLICATION	$T_1 = AB + AC$	$T_2 = A + B + C'$										C	A	A	B	1
117	AND + INHIBITION/AND + INHIBITION	$T_1 = AB + AC'$	$T_2 = AB'+AC$										B	C	A	0	A
118	AND + INHIBITION/INHIBITION +	$T_1 = AB + AC'$	$T_2 = A + BC'$										B	C	A	B	A
119	AND + INHIBITION/OR	$T_1 = AB + AC'$	$T_2 = B + C$										B	C	A	B	C
120	AND + INHIBITION/AND	$T_1 = AB + AC'$	$T_2 = BC$										B	C	A	0	B
121	AND + INHIBITION/INHIBITION	$T_1 = AB + AC'$	$T_2 = BC'$										B	C	A	B	0
122	AND + INHIBITION/IMPLICATION	$T_1 = AB + AC'$	$T_2 = B' + C$										B	C	A	0	1
127	AND +/AND +	$T_1 = A + BC$	$T_2 = C + AB$										A	C	A	B	C
128	AND +/INHIBITION	$T_1 = A + BC$	$T_2 = ABC'$										A	C	A	B	0
129	AND +/IMPLICATION	$T_1 = A + BC$	$T_2 = A' + B + C$										A	C	A	B	1
131	INHIBITION +/INHIBITION +	$T_1 = A + BC'$	$T_2 = A + B'C$										C	B	A	1	A
132	INHIBITION +/OR	$T_1 = A + BC'$	$T_2 = B + C$										C	B	A	1	B
133	INHIBITION +/AND	$T_1 = A + BC'$	$T_2 = BC$										C	B	A	B	C
134	INHIBITION +/INHIBITION	$T_1 = A + BC'$	$T_2 = B'C$										C	B	A	1	0
135	INHIBITION +/IMPLICATION	$T_1 = A + BC'$	$T_2 = B + C'$										C	B	A	B	1

Line No.	Function names	Function Boolean Equations	5/2 valve				6/2 valve					5/3 valve			
			P	2	3	4	P	2	3	4	5	P_1	P_2	3	4
		5 variables:													
140		$T_1 = AE + BE'$ $\quad T_2 = CE + DE'$					E	A	B	C	D	B	C	A	E
141		$T_1 = AB + AC' + B'CD$ $\quad T_2 = CE + B'E + BC'D$													
		4 variables:													
142	AND/SELECTOR	$T_2 = CD \quad T_1 = AD + BD'$					D	A	B	C	C				
143	"	$T_2 = CD \quad T_1 = AD + BD'$					D	A	B	C	D				
144	OR/SELECTOR	$T_2 = C + D \quad T_1 = AD + BD'$					D	A	B	1	C				
145	"	$T_2 = C + D \quad T_1 = AD + BD'$					D	A	B	D	C				
146	INHIBITION/SELECTOR	$T_2 = CD' \quad T_1 = AD + BD'$					D	A	B	0	C				
147	IMPLICATION/SELECTOR	$T_2 = C + D' \quad T_1 = AD + BD'$					D	A	B	C	1				
148	SELECTOR/SELECTOR	$T_1 = AD + BD' \quad T_2 = BD + CD'$	D	A	B	C									
149	"	$T_1 = AD + BD' \quad T_2 = CD + BD'$					D	A	B	C	B				
150	"	$T_1 = AD + BD' \quad T_2 = CD + AD'$					D	A	B	C	A				
151	"	$T_1 = AD + BD' \quad T_2 = AD + CD'$					D	A	B	A	C				
152	AND + INHIBITION/AND + INHIBITION	$T_1 = AB + AC' \quad T_2 = CD + B'D$										B	C	A	D
153	AND + INHIBITION/INHIBITION +	$T_1 = A + B'C \quad T_2 = CD + B'D$										B	C	C	D
154	INHIBITION + /INHIBITION +	$T_1 = A + B'C \quad T_2 = D + BC'$										B	C	A	D
155		$T_1 = AB + AC' + B'CD \quad T_2 = C + BD$										B	C	1	D
156		$T_1 = AB + AC' + B'CD \quad T_2 = BC + BD$										B	C	A	C
157		$T_1 = AB + AC' + B'CD \quad T_2 = BC'D$										B	C	D	B
158		$T_1 = AB + AC' + B'CD \quad T_2 = B' + C + D$										B	C	D	0
159		$T_1 = AB + AC' + B'CD \quad T_2 = AB' + AC + B'CD$										B	C	D	A
160		$T_1 = AB + AC' + B'CD \quad T_2 = D$										B	C	A	D

TABLE 7.4. Valve Connections Yielding Two Separate Output Functions with Four or Five Involved Variables

275

TABLE 7.5. Valve Connections Yielding Flip-Flop Output Functions

Line No.		3/2 Valve		5/2 Valve		
		2	3	2	3	4
	No input variables:					
161	$T = y$	1	0			
162	$T_1 = y'$ $\quad$ $T_2 = y$			0	1	0
163	$T_1 = y$ $\quad$ $T_2 = y'$			1	0	1
	One input variable:					
164	$T = Ay$	A	0			
165	$T = Ay'$	0	A			
166	$T_1 = Ay'$ $\quad$ $T_2 = Ay$			0	A	0
167	$T_1 = Ay$ $\quad$ $T_2 = Ay'$			A	0	A
168	$T_1 = Ay$ $\quad$ $T_2 = y'$			A	0	1
169	$T_1 = y$ $\quad$ $T_2 = Ay'$			1	0	A
170	$T = A + y'$	A	1			
171	$T = A + y$	1	A			
172	$T_1 = A + y$ $\quad$ $T_2 = A + y'$			1	A	1
173	$T_1 = A + y'$ $\quad$ $T_2 = A + y$			A	1	A
174	$T_1 = A + y'$ $\quad$ $T_2 = y$			A	1	0
175	$T_1 = y'$ $\quad$ $T_2 = A + y$			0	1	A
176	$T_1 = Ay'$ $\quad$ $T_2 = A + y'$			0	A	1
177	$T_1 = A + y$ $\quad$ $T_2 = Ay$			1	A	0
	Two input variables:					
178	$T_1 = Ay$ $\quad$ $T_2 = By'$			A	0	B
179	$T_1 = A + y'$ $\quad$ $T_2 = B + y$			A	1	B
180	$T = Ay + By'$	A	B			
181	$T_1 = Ay + By'$ $\quad$ $T_2 = By$			A	B	0
182	$T_1 = Ay + By'$ $\quad$ $T_2 = B + y'$			A	B	1
183	$T_1 = Ay'$ $\quad$ $T_2 = Ay + By'$			0	A	B
184	$T_1 = A + y$ $\quad$ $T_2 = Ay + By'$			1	A	B
185	$T_1 = Ay + By'$ $\quad$ $T_2 = By + Ay'$			A	B	A
	Three input variables:					
186	$T_1 = Ay + By'$ $\quad$ $T_2 = By + Cy'$			A	B	C

obviously equivalent, and, therefore, only one of them is listed. In other words, all equivalent function pairs that can be derived from the original one by interchanging input variables are omitted from the tables since they contribute nothing new.

Table 7.5 deals with 3/2 and 5/2 valves with two pilot ports (i.e., without return springs). As mentioned earlier, these act as RS flip-flops, and are sometimes called "memory valves" or "double-impulse valves." As shown on line 162, a 5/2 valve of this type with pilot inputs SET and RESET provides the state variables $T_1 = y'$ and $T_2 = y$.

The utilization of such flip-flop valves as passive AND gates, as in line 166, is not new, and such valves are used as steering valves in the flow-table and the operations-table methods. However, systematic investigation of all possible input combinations has shown that various other completely unexpected function pairs involving the state variable y can also be obtained, and these are listed in Table 7.5.

7.4.2 Search Procedure

The search procedure is quite simple: we first turn to the appropriate table, depending on the number of input variables involved in the desired function pair. If the function pair involves a state variable (i.e., a flip-flop output), then Table 7.5 is used. To facilitate finding the required function pair quickly within each table, the functions are always listed in this order: YES, NOT, AND, OR, INHIBITION, IMPLICATION, and SELECTOR.

The search procedure is illustrated by an example. Suppose we need $F_1 = x_1 x_2'$ and $F_2 = x_1 x_2 + x_2' x_3$. F_1 represents the INHIBITION and F_2 the SELECTOR function. Since three input variables, x_1, x_2, and x_3, are involved, Table 7.3 is searched. Since, in the listing order used, INHIBITION appears ahead of SELECTOR, the table is followed up to lines 96–103, where all the first functions are INHIBITION. Among these, lines 101 and 103 have SELECTOR as the second function, but only line 101 provides the exact function pair needed. The solution thus uses a 5/2 valve connected as in line 101, with x_1, x_2, and x_3 represented by A, C, and B, respectively.

7.4.3 Example Illustrating Use of the Tables

A circuit for operating a silk-screen printing machine is analyzed on page 169 of Ref. (7.19). The solution derived there requires the following logic expressions:

$$A_1 = f y' \qquad C_1 = f \qquad V_1 = m(ay' + by) \qquad SET = bce$$

$$A_0 = f y \qquad C_0 = e \qquad V_0 = d(ay + by') \qquad RESET = ace$$

where variables a, b, c, d, e, and f represent limit-valve signals, m is a manual START signal, and y and y' are flip-flop outputs.

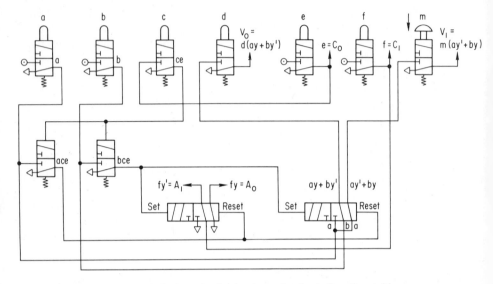

Fig. 7.22. Solution obtained using valve logic-function tables.

It is obvious that A_1 and A_0 can both be obtained from one flip-flop valve, line 166. V_1 and V_0, however, are more complicated. Since two input variables (a and b) are involved together with state variable y, we search lines 178–185 in Table 7.5, and find that line 185 gives exactly the terms within the parentheses. Thus, a single 5/2 valve, together with limit valve d and START valve m, can provide both V_1 and V_0 functions. Figure 7.22 shows the final circuit.

Note that limit valves c and d and manual valve m are used as AND gates, according to line 3 of Table 7.1. The control circuit requires only four valves, apart from the START push-button valve and the various limit valves required regardless of the method used. With conventional circuit design (where each valve provides just one function), 11 extra valves would be needed: 8 for AND functions fy and fy', ay and ay', by and by', ce, bce, ace, $m(ay' + by)$, and $d(ay + by')$; 2 for the OR functions in V_1 and V_0; and 1 flip-flop valve. Thus, seven valves are saved using the technique described here.

Additional examples illustrating use of these valve logic-function tables are found in Sections 7.5 and 7.7.8, and in Ref. (7.18).

7.5   HUFFMAN METHOD APPLIED TO VALVE CIRCUITS

The Huffman method for ladder-diagram design (i.e., for use with relays) is described in Section 5.5. The method involves deriving excitation functions (Section 5.5.6) and output functions (Section 5.5.7). These functions can be implemented with valves instead of relays. To reduce the number of valves needed, the logic-function tables just described can be used to good advantage.

7.5.1 Example 9

The procedure is illustrated using the single-cylinder sequence START, $A+$, $A-$, $A+$, $A-$ as an example. This problem is solved by the Huffman method in Section 5.5, and the results obtained there (see Figs. 5.34 and 5.39) are repeated here:

$$S_1 = a_1 y_2' \cdot \text{START} \qquad S_2 = a_2 y_1$$

$$R_1 = a_1 y_2 \qquad\qquad R_2 = a_2 y_1'$$

$$A+ = y_1 y_2' + y_1' y_2 \qquad A- = a_2$$

Obviously, S_2 and R_2 can be obtained with a single flip-flop valve connected as in line 166. S_1 and R_1 are obtained with a second similar flip-flop valve, but with the $a_1 y_2'$ output connected to the supply port of the START push-button valve. Finally, the $A+$ expression is obtained from two additional flip-flop valves (connected as in lines 162 and 180).

The final circuit is shown in Fig. 7.23, where the table line numbers utilized are shown circled. Three 5/2 valves and one 3/2 valve are required. (As the reader can verify, the flow-table method is more advantageous for this particular example, resulting in a control circuit requiring only three valves.)

7.5.2 Example 10

As a second example, consider the sequence START, $A+$, $B+$, $B-$, $A-$, $B+$, $B-$. The primitive and merged flow tables are shown in Fig. 7.24, and the two excitation and four output Karnaugh maps in Fig. 7.25. (Pseudo-Karnaugh maps, see Section 5.5.12, are used here.)

The resulting valve control circuit is shown in Fig. 7.26. Normally, we should use two separate 3/2 valves to provide AND terms $a_2 b_2$ and $a_1 b_2$. However, we can use the "trick" described in Section 7.2.3, using a single 5/2 valve without a

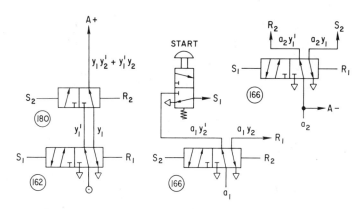

Fig. 7.23. Huffman-method valve solution for Example 9.

a_1b_1	a_2b_1	a_2b_2	a_1b_2	A+	A−	B+	B−
①	2	−	−	1	0	0	−
−	②	3	−	−	0	1	0
−	4	③	−	−	0	0	1
5	④	−	−	0	1	0	−
⑤	−	−	6	0	−	1	0
1	−	−	⑥	0	−	0	1

				y
①	②	3	⑥	0
⑤	④	③	6	1

Fig. 7.24. Primitive and merged flow tables for Example 10.

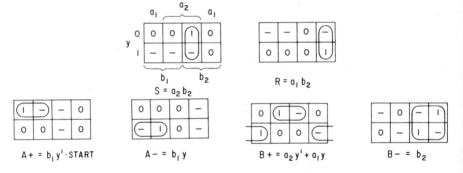

Fig. 7.25. Excitation and output maps for Example 10.

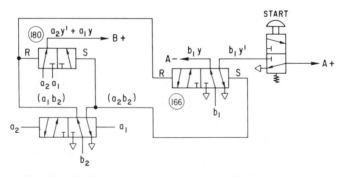

Fig. 7.26. Huffman-method valve solution for Example 10.

280

return spring to produce both a_2b_2 and a_1b_2. (Again, these are shown on the drawing in parentheses to indicate that they do not always represent the true present situation.) As explained there, this technique cannot always be used with parallel cylinder strokes, but these do not exist in the present problem. Thus, the solution requires only two 5/2 and one 3/2 valve, which is more economical than with any other method. (As the reader can verify, both the flow-table and the operations-table methods result in solutions requiring four 5/2 valves and one shuttle valve.)

An alternative technique is to use inexpensive passive AND-gate elements, see Fig. 4.28(b), instead of 3/2 valves.

In conclusion, it should be mentioned that the Huffman method can also be applied to cylinder-actuating valves *with* return springs, in contrast to the other three methods discussed so far, all of which assume actuating valves with double pilot ports. However, use of actuating valves with return springs precludes the use of pseudo-Karnaugh maps (see the discussion in Section 5.5.12), which limits the number of variables that can be handled.

7.6 VARIOUS CIRCUIT DESIGN METHODS

Many pneumatic-circuit design methods have been developed over the years. A critical comparison covering most of these appears in Ref. (7.11). Three of these methods are briefly discussed.

One method was developed by D. Bouteille and described in detail in Ref. (7.19). It is basically a variation of the Huffman method, except that the step of constructing primitive and merged flow tables is completely bypassed. Instead, all information is entered directly on a single pseudo-Karnaugh map. The various set, reset, and output signals are entered in those map squares where they are first needed. Finally, the excitation and output functions are read directly off the map. The method is illustrated using Example 9, namely, the sequence START, $A+$, $A-$, $A+$, $A-$. The pseudo-Karnaugh map for this problem is shown in Fig. 7.27.

The map can be considered equivalent to the squares of the merged flow table in the Huffman method. Whenever passing to a square with a differing state assignment, an appropriate S or R signal must be entered. Thus, we enter S_1 in the first square of the cycle (lower left-hand corner), so that the system can pass from $y_1 = 0$ to $y_1 = 1$. In the next square, we enter $A+$ in order to get the $A+$ stroke, etc. The excitation and output functions are then read directly from the map:

$$S_1 = a_1 y_1' y_2' \cdot \text{START} \qquad S_2 = a_2 y_1 y_2'$$

$$R_1 = a_1 y_1 y_2 \qquad\qquad R_2 = a_2 y_1' y_2$$

$$A+ = y_1 y_2' + y_1' y_2 \qquad A- = a_2$$

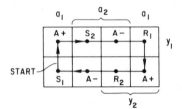

Fig. 7.27. Pseudo-Karnaugh map for Example 9 (the Bouteille method).

By employing certain rules explained in Ref. (7.19), it is found that some of the variables in these excitation functions are redundant, so that they can be simplified to become identical to those of Section 7.5.1.

In this method, there is no systematic search for optimum row merger and state assignment, and the results are largely a matter of luck, although the designer's experience and intuitive ability also play an important role. Similarly, the output and excitation functions are not derived systematically as in the Huffman method, where separate maps are used for each function, and where the "don't care" conditions are entered and utilized systematically. Thus, the design procedure in the Bouteille method is formulated largely in the designer's mind rather than on paper, and optimum results are not assured. In the author's experience, it is easy to make mistakes and include unnecessary variables in some of the expressions. For problems more complicated than this example, the Huffman method often results in a more favorable row merger and state assignment, and thus in a simpler solution.

A variation of the Bouteille method is presented in Ref. (7.20), but with a number of elaborate rules added in an attempt to make the design process more systematic. Here, too, it is the author's feeling that the Huffman method, as developed in Sections 5.5 and 7.5, can achieve the same if not better final results, with less effort.

A completely different method, the Cybergram method developed by E. L. Holbrook, is advocated in Ref. (7.10). The problem of contradictory pilot inputs is solved using so-called impulse valves. These valves convert a continuous signal into a short pulse, which is maintained just long enough to shift a cylinder-actuating valve. (Such impulse-valves are discussed in Chapter 8 under the name of *pulse shapers* or *one-shots*.)

The method is illustrated in detail with many examples in the reference, and often leads to very economical circuits. However, some experts claim that circuits operating with pulses are inherently less reliable than those using sustained signals. One possible source of problems is the needle-valve, or restriction, which is part of the impulse valve and determines the pulse width. This must be properly adjusted, and there is always the danger of a restriction becoming clogged. Also, the Cybergram method is not as systematic as the four methods described in this chapter, so that here, too, the results depend to a considerable extent on the designer's experience and intuition.

To summarize the various recommended methods, the following guidelines are suggested:

1. For sequences involving any number of cylinders but no repeated steps, the *cascade method* almost always leads to the simplest control circuit. The design process is simple and easily understood.

2. For sequences having any number of repeated steps but a limited number of cylinders (two or three), the *flow-table method* is usually preferable. In some cases, the method can still give good results for four or even five cylinders, but this depends on the number of input-signal combinations covered by the sequence. Sometimes, sequences of this type are solved more economically with the *Huffman method* (as in Example 10). However, there is no way of predicting this beforehand, and it is necessary to try both methods and compare the results. The Huffman method is limited to about four or five cylinders, since it uses Karnaugh maps, which can only handle a limited number of variables.

3. For sequences involving *both* repeated steps *and* many cylinders, the *operations-table method* gives the best results. However, this method is not easy to master, and it may be preferable to use *programmable counters* based on the "two-hot" code, as described in Chapter 9. The simplicity and ease of applying programmable counters makes up for the fact that they require more valves than other methods. Another option for complex sequences is to use *programmable controllers*; see Chapter 10.

A flow chart helpful in selecting the optimum control method for a given application is presented in Appendix B.

7.7 EMERGENCY-STOP MODES

It is sometimes necessary to interrupt a sequence because of an emergency condition, such as a jammed machine, a missing or misaligned part, or other malfunction. The operator does this by pressing a so-called "panic button" or STOP button—preferably large, red, and easily accessible.

There are various stop modes that can be chosen, depending on safety considerations for the specific application. Seven of the most useful are described here. Generally, all cylinders in a given system react according to the same stop mode. However, it is often possible to have different cylinders react according to different modes, depending on the specific application of each cylinder.

It should be stressed that all the solutions presented can be used as add-ons to existing control circuits, that is, they can be added without having to redesign or in any way modify the original control system. This is important, since emergency-stop modes are frequently added to an existing system as an afterthought. Furthermore, it does not matter which design method was used to obtain the control circuit; the emergency-stop modes presented here are compatible with all of them.

The following is based on material first published in Ref. (7.21), and is presented here with the kind permission of *Hydraulics & Pneumatics*, Copyright 1978, Penton Publishing, Cleveland, Ohio.

7.7.1   Stop–Restart Circuits

Before describing the different emergency-stop modes, a brief discussion of STOP–RESTART devices is helpful. After any emergency stop, the cause of the malfunction must be removed, after which a RESTART or RESET button is pressed to resume the sequence, usually at the point where it was interrupted. This RESTART button must not be confused with the regular START button used to initiate a new sequence. In other words, the START signal should affect operation only after completion of the previous sequence, whereas the RESTART signal must function at any time after the sequence has been interrupted by a STOP signal.

The simplest STOP–RESTART device consists of a push-button operated 3/2 valve *without* a return spring; see Fig. 7.28(a). Pressing the push button interrupts the *C* ("continue cycle") signal. To make this signal active again, the button must be pulled out in the RESTART direction, since there is no return spring. Sometimes, we want to prevent the operator from restarting the sequence on his own. For this, the valve of Fig. 7.28(b) with two buttons can be used. Both buttons only affect the valve position when they are pushed in; pulling out has no effect. The valve is mounted inside a locked cabinet, with the STOP button outside, but the RESTART button inside. This enables the supervisor—who presumably has the key—to check the cause of the malfunction before deciding to resume operation.

Frequently, in large installations, it is necessary to actuate STOP and RESTART from a remote location, or there may even be several STOP buttons located at strategic locations. As an example, the system of Fig. 7.29 has two STOP buttons. (For each additional STOP button, one more shuttle valve is

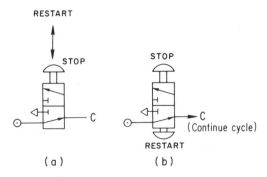

Fig. 7.28. STOP–RESTART valve with (a) a single button, and (b) separate STOP and RESTART buttons.

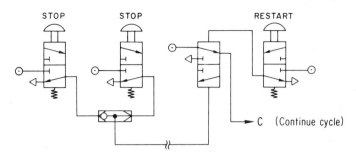

Fig. 7.29. STOP–RESTART system with multiple remote-control STOP buttons.

needed.) Pressing any STOP button momentarily shifts the 3/2 valve with two pilot lines so as to interrupt the C signal.

An equivalent electric STOP–RESTART system is shown in ladder-diagram form in Fig. 7.30. The RESTART contact is connected in parallel with the STOP contacts, rather than in series, so that STOP dominates if both STOP and RESTART buttons are pressed simultaneously.

7.7.2 "No Change" Stop Mode

In this emergency-stop mode, any cylinder at rest when the STOP button is pressed must remain at rest. Any cylinder in motion must complete its stroke and then come to rest.

This stop mode is very easy to achieve, requiring only a single 3/2 valve connected in the line supplying air to the various limit valves, as shown in Fig. 7.31(a). (For cascade control circuits, see Section 7.1, this would be the line supplying air to the lowest group valve.) The moment the C signal is interrupted, the 3/2 valve shifts to its normal position, venting all limit valves to atmosphere.

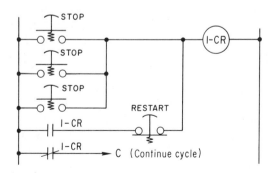

Fig. 7.30. Electric STOP–RESTART system with multiple remote-control STOP buttons.

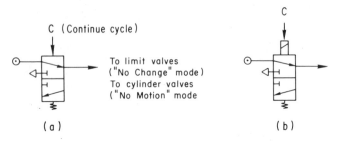

Fig. 7.31. "No Change" and "No Motion" STOP modes with (a) pneumatic, and (b) electric actuation.

Once the limit valves are neutralized, no new sequence step can be initiated. When the C signal is reactivated by the RESTART button, the 3/2 valve again passes air to the limit valves, and the sequence resumes where interrupted. Figure 7.31(b) shows the same valve, but with solenoid actuation. The C signal is produced by a circuit such as that of Fig. 7.30.

7.7.3 "No Motion" Stop Mode

In this mode, actuation of the STOP button must vent pressure on both piston sides. The piston thus comes to a halt, due to internal friction, unless some external force acts on the piston rod. This stop mode is useful if the operator must be able to shift the piston manually to any position.

To obtain this mode, the same 3/2 valve shown in Fig. 7.31 is used, but it must be connected in the line supplying air to the various cylinder-actuating valves, rather than to the limit valves. When C is reactivated, the 3/2 valve again pressurizes the actuating valves, and the sequence resumes where it left off.

7.7.4 "Lock Piston" Stop Mode

The moment the STOP button is pressed, the piston must be locked in position, that is, it should not be free-floating as in the "No Motion" mode. This requires two additional 3/2 or 2/2 valves per cylinder, as shown in Fig. 7.32. One manufacturer, see Ref. (7.22), supplies compact 2/2 valves built into the cylinder fittings for this purpose.

When the C signal is interrupted, the two 3/2 valves shift to their normal positions, in which both cylinder lines lead to a valve port plugged on the outside. As a result, the cylinder lines are sealed, and the air trapped on each side acts as an air cushion, locking the piston. Of course, air compressibility prevents absolute locking. To minimize this effect, the two 3/2 valves should be mounted as close to the cylinder as possible to reduce the volume of trapped air. If absolute locking is required, a hydro-pneumatic circuit must be used. (Such circuits are described in most books on pneumatics.)

The two additional 3/2 valves in Fig. 7.32 could be eliminated by replacing the 5/2 cylinder-actuating valve with a 5/3 valve, that is, a three-position valve

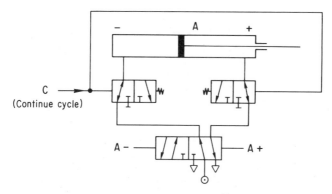

Fig. 7.32. "Lock Piston" STOP mode.

with a closed-center position (see Fig. 4.15). However, this requires a complete redesign of the control circuit, since such a valve requires sustained pilot signals. As already stated, the advantage of the emergency-stop circuits presented here is that they do not require any control-circuit modification.

7.7.5 "Safety Position" Stop Mode

For each cylinder, one of the two end positions, either " $+$ " or " $-$ ", is defined as its safety position, and the piston is to go and/or remain there when the STOP button is actuated, even if this means reversing the direction of motion.

Figure 7.33 shows this stop mode applied to one individual cylinder A. For the purpose of illustration, " $-$ " is defined here as the safety position for this cylinder. As long as $C = 1$, both 3/2 valves pass the $A-$ or $A+$ output signals from the control circuit to the respective $VA-$ and $VA+$ pilot lines, so that the sequence proceeds normally. When $C = 0$, both 3/2 valves switch to their normal positions, so that $VA+ = 0$ (since the line is vented), while $VA- = 1$ (this line is connected to the supply pressure).

If this stop mode is to be applied to all cylinders in the system, the solution becomes considerably simplified. As shown in Fig. 7.34, the right-hand 3/2 valve in Fig. 7.33 is eliminated, with $X+$ connected directly to, and thus identical

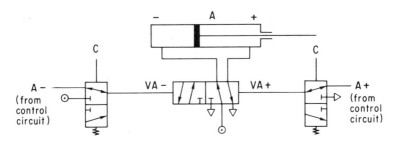

Fig. 7.33. "Safety Position" STOP mode (applied to an individual cylinder).

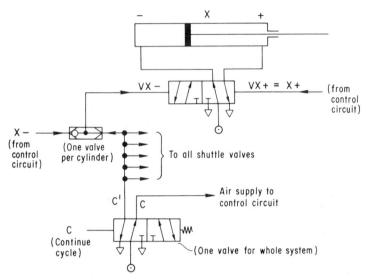

Fig. 7.34. "Safety Position" STOP mode (applied to an entire system).

with, VX +. Instead, one 5/2 valve is needed for the entire circuit to cut off the air supply to the control circuit (i.e., to all except cylinder-actuating valves) when C is interrupted. (For example, if the control circuit is a cascade circuit, this 5/2 valve is connected in the air-supply line leading to the lowest group valve.) The left-hand 3/2 valve in Fig. 7.33 is replaced by a shuttle valve. When $C = 0$, the air supply to all limit valves is cut off, so that the control circuit is unable to send an $X +$ signal. At the same time, C' becomes 1, so that the shuttle valve produces a VX − signal, sending piston X to its safety position (−).

It should be noted that if C is renewed after an emergency stop, the sequence does not necessarily continue as normally scheduled. This is because a cylinder going to its safety position may upset the regular sequence order. This might trigger a limit-valve signal and affect the control circuit in an unexpected manner. It may thus be necessary to reset the whole system and repeat the sequence from the beginning. This problem should be considered before choosing the "Safety Position" stop mode.

7.7.6 "No Change/No Motion" Stop Mode

This combines the "No Change" and "No Motion" stop modes. As before, any cylinder at rest when the STOP button is pressed must be locked by pressure on the piston, but any cylinder in motion should have both sides vented. The supply-pressure line to each cylinder-actuating valve is replaced by two shuttle valves in series, giving the function $C + a_1 + a_2$, as shown in Fig. 7.35.

As long as $C = 1$, the sequence proceeds as planned. When $C = 0$ but either a_1 or $a_2 = 1$ (i.e., the cylinder is at rest), air continues to reach the cylinder, so

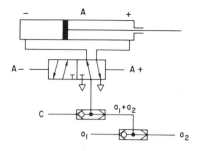

Fig. 7.35. "No Change/No Motion" STOP mode.

that the piston is locked at its rest position. However, if C, a_1, and a_2 are all 0 (i.e., the cylinder is in motion), both piston sides are vented.

7.7.7 "No Change/Lock Piston" Stop Mode

This combines the "No Change" and "Lock Piston" modes. As before, any cylinder at rest when the STOP button is pressed must be kept at rest by pressure acting on the piston; but any cylinder in motion should have both inlet lines sealed off. This is achieved by using the circuit of Fig. 7.32, but with signal C replaced by $C + a_1 + a_2$.

7.7.8 "No Change/Safety Position" Stop Mode

This combines the "No Change" and "Safety Position" stop modes. Any cylinder at rest when the STOP button is pressed must be kept locked at rest position, whereas any cylinder in motion must go to its previously defined safety position.

Two Karnaugh maps, Fig. 7.36, are used to derive pilot-line functions VA+ and VA− for the cylinder-actuating valve. Each map involves four input variables: C, a_1, a_2, and either of the control-circuit outputs $A+$ or $A-$. The maps are filled in as follows.

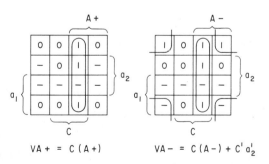

$$VA+ = C\,(A+)$$

$$VA- = C\,(A-) + C'\,a_2'$$

Fig. 7.36. Karnaugh maps for VA+ and VA− functions.

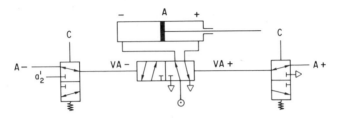

Fig. 7.37. "No Change/Safety Position" STOP mode.

Since $a_1a_2 = 1$ is physically impossible, the "don't care" condition is entered in the third row of both maps.

As long as $C = 1$, the sequence should continue as planned, which means that VA+ and VA− should assume the values of $A+$ and $A−$, respectively, as sent by the control circuit. We, therefore, enter 0s in the empty squares of the $C(A+)'$ and $C(A−)'$ columns, and 1s in the empty squares of the $C(A+)$ and $C(A−)$ columns.

When STOP is pressed, $C = 0$. If the cylinder is at rest at its a_1 position, it must remain there, which means that VA+ must be 0, while VA− can be either 0 or 1. We, therefore, enter 0s in the two $C'a_1a_2'$ squares of the VA+ map, and "don't care" entries in the same squares of the VA− map. Similar arguments apply if the cylinder is at its a_2 position when $C = 0$. We, therefore, place "don't care" entries in the $C'a_1'a_2$ squares of the VA+ map, and 0s in the same squares of the VA− map.

Finally, the two remaining $C'a_1'a_2$ squares represent the situation where the cylinder is in motion when C becomes 0. Assuming again that "−" has been defined as the safety position for cylinder A, we must keep VA+ = 0 and VA− = 1 at these squares to force the piston to go to "−."

The resulting pilot-line functions are derived from the Karnaugh maps in Fig. 7.36, with the final circuit shown in Fig. 7.37. Note that VA− is a SELECTOR function, and uses a 3/2 valve connected as in line 9 of Table 7.1. Note also that Fig. 7.37 is identical to Fig. 7.33, except that the air supply to the left-hand 3/2 valve has been replaced by a_2'. (This a_2' term can be obtained by using a 5/2 rather than 3/2 limit valve, giving both a_2 and a_2'.)

7.8 PNEUMATIC LADDER DIAGRAMS

In Section 5.1, ladder diagrams, commonly used to describe relay circuits, are described. It is also explained that ladder diagrams are *detached diagrams*, as opposed to regular wiring diagrams, which are *attached diagrams*. All the pneumatic diagrams used in this chapter up to the present are of the attached-diagram type.

Because of the advantages of detached diagrams, it should not be surprising that attempts have been made to adapt the ladder-diagram principle to pneumatic circuits. Although pneumatic ladder diagrams are not in general use, they are being employed by several important manufacturers of pneumatic equipment. It is, therefore, appropriate to discuss these diagrams briefly, so that the reader basically understands them. For a more detailed discussion, see Refs. (7.23)–(7.25).

There are several basic differences between electric and pneumatic ladder diagrams. First of all, since air reaching any pneumatic device is eventually vented to atmosphere, there is no return tubing (unlike with hydraulic circuits). Therefore, the vertical line at the right edge of electric ladder diagrams (representing ground) is not needed.

Since those manufacturers using pneumatic ladder diagrams want to attract users already familiar with electric ladder diagrams, they attempt to use the same terminology and symbols, as far as possible. Thus, pneumatic valves are represented as relays and called "relay valves," with valve passages represented by relay-contact symbols. However, confusion can easily result, since the terms "open" and "closed" have opposite meanings in pneumatic and electric circuits. (An "open" electric contact does not transmit current, but an "open" valve transmits air.) To avoid confusion, it is suggested to use the terms "passing" and "blocking," which have identical meanings in both systems.

Figure 7.38 displays common valves, and their equivalent relay-contact symbols. Figure 7.38(a) shows a 3/2 valve with a single pilot line and return spring, equivalent to a relay with a switchover contact. The contact between ports 1 and 2 is normally blocking, and that between ports 3 and 2 normally passing. Figure 7.38(b) shows a 5/2 valve, which is equivalent to four contacts, two normally blocking and two normally passing. Note that these contacts are not independent, but have three common junctions. Such a valve is often used with two or one vented input port, which results in either a switch-over contact, Fig. 7.38(c), or two independent contacts, Fig. 7.38(d).

One obvious limitation of valves, as compared to electric relays, is that the number of valve passages, and, therefore, the number of equivalent contacts, is strictly limited. (This explains why a single electric relay with sufficient number of contacts can often do the work of several valves.) To increase the number of valve passages, 6/2 valves are sometimes used. As shown in Fig. 7.38(e), this is equivalent to two independent sets of switchover contacts.

As in electric ladder diagrams, we differentiate completely between valve passages and valve actuation. The more common types of valve actuation and their equivalent ladder-diagram symbols are shown in Fig. 7.39. For valves with single pilot lines and return springs, the ladder-diagram symbol of the pilot line is identical to the symbol used for relay coils, Fig. 7.39(a). Inside the symbol circle, the letters RV (standing for "relay valve") are followed by an identification number and the letter A. If the valve is a cylinder-actuating (or "power") valve, the letter P is used instead of RV. Valves with double pilot lines without return springs have no relay equivalent. Therefore, the single round coil symbol is replaced by two squares, labeled A and B, respectively, as in Fig. 7.39(b). These are defined such that actuation of B pilot line places all valve passages into their

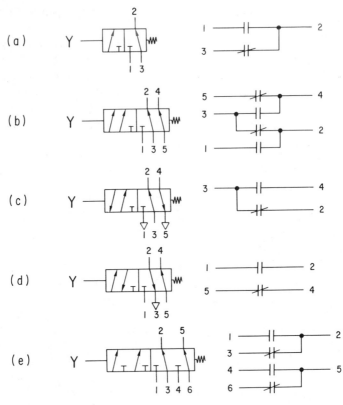

Fig. 7.38. Relay valves with equivalent relay-contact symbols.

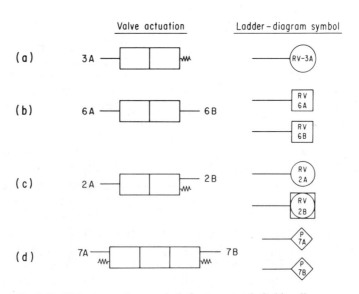

Fig. 7.39. Valve-actuation symbols for pneumatic ladder diagrams.

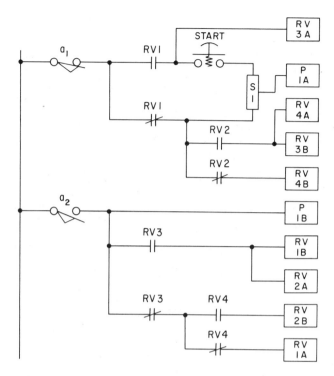

Fig. 7.40. Pneumatic ladder diagram equivalent to the valve circuit of Fig. 7.9.

normal positions, as indicated by the relay-contact symbols used. Figure 7.39(c) shows a valve with double pilot lines and one offset spring, and Fig. 7.39(d) shows a three-position valve (usually a power valve). Pilot lines pressurized at the start of the sequence are often indicated by cross-hatching their symbol to facilitate reading the diagram.

To maintain the similarity between electric and pneumatic ladder diagrams as much as possible, the symbols used for limit valves are identical to those for limit switches (see Chapters 2 and 5). Similarly, symbols for push-button valves are identical to those for push-button switches.

To illustrate the use of these symbols, Fig. 7.40 shows a pneumatic ladder diagram representing the pneumatic circuit of Fig. 7.9. The vertical rectangle designated S1 in the figure is the symbol for a shuttle valve (the 1 is an identification number). Since we are dealing here with a relatively simple circuit, the advantage of pneumatic ladder diagrams may not be obvious from this example. However, as circuits become more complex, the relative simplicity of the ladder-diagram representation becomes more striking.

PROBLEMS

Design pneumatic control circuits for the sequences listed, using any given one (or all) of the following four methods:

(a) Cascade method (including the complete circuit diagram).

(b) Flow-table method. (The solution should include a diagram of the control circuit only, i.e., without the various cylinders, cylinder-actuating valves, and limit valves. Alternatively, the reader need only derive the excitation and output functions.)

(c) Operations-table method. (Requirements are as for the flow-table method.)

(d) Huffman method. (The solution should include a diagram of control circuit, indicating the line numbers from the logic-function tables that are utilized in the solution, as in Figs. 7.23 and 7.26.)

7.1. START, $A+$, $B+$, $B-$, $A-$ (where cylinder A clamps a workpiece, and cylinder B lowers a drill spindle).

7.2. START, $A+$, $B+$, $B-$, $A-$, $C+$, $C-$.

7.3. START, $A+$, $A-$, $B+$, $C+$, $B-$, $C-$.

7.4. START, $A+$, $A-$, $B+$, $A+$, $A-$, $B-$.

7.5. START, $A+$, $A-$, $A+$, $A-$, $B+$, $B-$.

7.6. START, $A+$, $B+$, $A-$, $A+$, $B-$, $A-$.

7.7. START, $A+$, $B+$, $B-$, $B+$, $B-$, $A-$.

7.8. START, $A+$, $B+$, $B-$, $B+$, $A-$, $A+$, $B-$, $A-$.

7.9. START, $A+$, $B+$, $A-$, $B-$, $A+$, $B+$, $B-$, $A-$.

7.10. START, $A+$, $B+$, $B-$, $C+$, $B+$, $A-$, $A+$, $A-$, $B-$, $C-$.

7.11. START, $A+$ (up to a_2), $A-$, $A+$ (up to a_3), $A-$ (see Fig. 7.16).

7.12. START, $A+$ (to a_2), $A-$, $A+$ (to a_3), $A-$, $A+$ (to a_4), $A-$ (see Fig. 7.16).

7.13. START, $A+$, $A-$, $\left(\dfrac{A+}{B+}\right)$, $B-$, $A-$.

7.14. START, $A+$, $B+$, $B-$, $\left(\dfrac{A-}{B+}\right)$, $B-$.

7.15. START, $A+$, $B+$, $B-$, $B+$, $A-$, $\left(\dfrac{A+}{B-}\right)$, $A-$.

7.16. START, $A+$, $B+$, $B-$, $\left(\dfrac{A-}{B+}\right)$, $B-$, $B+$, $B-$.

7.17. START, $A+$, $B+$, $B-$, $\left(\dfrac{A-}{B+}\right)$, $A+$, $B-$, $A-$.

7.18. START, $A+, B+, B-, C+, B+, \begin{pmatrix} A- \\ B- \end{pmatrix}, C-.$

7.19. START, $A+, B+, C+, C-, D+, D-, \begin{pmatrix} A- \\ B- \end{pmatrix}.$

7.20. START, $A+, B+, A-, C+, D+, \begin{pmatrix} C- \\ D- \end{pmatrix}, B-.$

7.21. START, $A+, B+, A-, B-, \begin{pmatrix} A+ \\ B+ \end{pmatrix}, A-, B-.$

7.22. START, $A+, B+, A-, A+, B-, A-, \begin{pmatrix} A+ \\ B+ \end{pmatrix}, \begin{pmatrix} A- \\ B- \end{pmatrix}.$

7.23. START, $A+, \begin{pmatrix} B+ \\ C+ \end{pmatrix}, D+, D-, D+, D-, \begin{pmatrix} A- \\ B- \end{pmatrix}, C-.$

7.24. (Multiple problem) For any one of the four solutions for the sequence of Problem 7.1, add any one of the seven emergency-stop modes described in Section 7.7. As additional challenge, apply two different stop modes to cylinders A and B, respectively.

7.25. Check the solution given in Section 7.2.6 for Example 6 by means of a sequence chart.

7.26. Draw the pneumatic control circuit for the solution given in Section 7.2.6 for Example 6.

7.27. Check the solution given in Section 7.3.3 for Example 8 by means of a sequence chart.

7.28. Draw the pneumatic control circuit for the solution given in Section 7.3.3 for Example 8.

REFERENCES

7.1. E. B. Paterson, *Pneumatics in Industry*, McGraw-Hill, New York, 1984.

7.2. Z. J. Lansky and L. F. Schrader, *Industrial Pneumatic Control*, Dekker, New York, 1986.

7.3. W. Deppert and K. Stoll, *Pneumatic Control*, Vogel-Verlag, Wuerzburg, West Germany, 1975.

7.4. W. Deppert and K. Stoll, *Pneumatic Application*, Vogel-Verlag, Wuerzburg, West Germany, 1976.

7.5. *Pneumatic Handbook*, 5th ed., Trade & Technical Press Ltd., Morden, Surrey, England.

7.6. *Industrial Pneumatic Technology*, Bull. 0275-81, Parker Hannifin Corp., Cleveland, OH 44112. 1980.

7.7. F. Yeaple, *Fluid Power Design Handbook*, Dekker, New York, 1984.

7.8.   H. L. Stewart and J. M. Storer, *ABC's of Pneumatic Circuits*, Howard W. Sams, Indianapolis, IN, 1973.

7.9.   F. S. Van Dijen, *Pneumatic Mechanization*, Kemperman Technical Publ., Culemborg, The Netherlands, 1977.

7.10.   E. L. Holbrook and P. I. Chen, *Design of Pneumatic and Fluidic Control Systems*, PECH Publishers, Milwaukie, OR, 1984.

7.11.   D. W. Pessen, *A Critical Comparison of Asynchronous-System Design Methods*, Festo Didactic, Esslingen, West Germany, 1984.

7.12.   A. M. Salek, "Simplify Your Air Circuits," *Hydraulics & Pneumatics*, July 1961, pp. 65–67.

7.13.   D. W. Pessen, "Fast Design of Pneumatic Sequencing Circuits," *Hydraulics & Pneumatics*, Aug. 1983, pp. 63–65; Oct, 1983, pp. 57–58; Dec. 1983, pp. 26–27; Aug. 1984, pp. 56–57; Oct. 1984, pp. 122, 124, 152.

7.14.   J. H. Cole and E. C. Fitch, "Synthesis of Fluid Logic Networks with Optional Input Signals," *Fluidics Quarterly*, Vol. 2, No. 5, 1970, pp. 22–29.

7.15.   J. H. Cole, *Synthesis of Optimum Complex Fluid Logic Sequential Circuits*, Publ. R68-4, Fluid Power Research Center, Oklahoma State University, Stillwater, 1968.

7.16.   J. H. Cole and E. C. Fitch, "Synthesis of Fluid Logic Control Circuits," *Proceedings of Joint Automatic Control Conference*, Boulder, CO, 1969, pp. 425–432.

7.17.   E. C. Fitch and J. B. Surjaatmadja, *Introduction to Fluid Logic*, McGraw-Hill Hemisphere Publ. Co., New York, 1978, pp. 235–245.

7.18.   D. W. Pessen, "Efficient Use of Directional-control Valves in Fluid-logic Circuits," *Journal of Dynamic Systems, Measurement, and Control*, Vol. 105, Dec. 1983, pp. 272–278.

7.19.   D. Bouteille, *Fluid Logic Controls and Industrial Automation*, Wiley, New York, 1973.

7.20.   P. Rohner, *Fluid Power Logic Circuit Design*, Macmillan, London, 1979.

7.21.   D. W. Pessen, "Emergency Stop Modes for Cylinder Circuits," *Hydraulics & Pneumatics*, Oct. 1977, pp. 162–168; Nov. 1978, p. 98.

7.22.   R. C. Beercheck, "On-board Controls for Pneumatic Cylinders," *Machine Design*, Dec. 6, 1984, pp. 142–144.

7.23.   D. W. Pessen, *Ladder Diagrams and their Application to Pneumatic Circuits*, Festo Didactic, Esslingen, West Germany, 1979.

7.24.   W. G. Holzbock, "Designing with Moving Parts Logic," *Hydraulics & Pneumatics*, Part 1: July, 1979, pp. 59–62, 116; Part 2: Aug. 1979, pp. 64–66; Part 3: Sept. 1979, pp. 100–106.

7.25.   G. Doig, "Pneumatic Logic Circuit Diagrams," *Product Engineering*, Dec. 1979, pp. 49–51.

CHAPTER 8

MISCELLANEOUS SWITCHING
ELEMENTS AND SYSTEMS

In this chapter, a number of additional switching elements and circuits are described. Many of these can be implemented either electrically or pneumatically, hence, this chapter follows the discussion of pneumatic circuits in Chapter 7.

8.1 TIMERS

Timing elements play an important part in many automation systems. Frequently, use of a timer can bypass an awkward sensing problem. To give just one example, liquid-dispensing machines are required to fill containers to a certain level. Rather than attempting to sense this level, many food-industry applications use a timer instead. By keeping the dispensing tube open for a timed period, the amount of liquid dispensed can be controlled fairly accurately. Timers can be electronic, electromechanical, or pneumatic, and there are also hybrid types. These three groups are discussed in turn. For a general survey of timers, see Refs. (8.1)–(8.3).

8.1.1   Timer Modes

In selecting a timer, it is important to decide first what exactly the timer is to do. The most common timer modes are illustrated by the sequence charts shown in Fig. 8.1. Although the timer terms used may vary, the operations should be clear from the chart.

In the *On-Delay* mode shown in Fig. 8.1(a), the timer output goes HI a certain length of time after the control signal has gone HI. The resulting delay period is

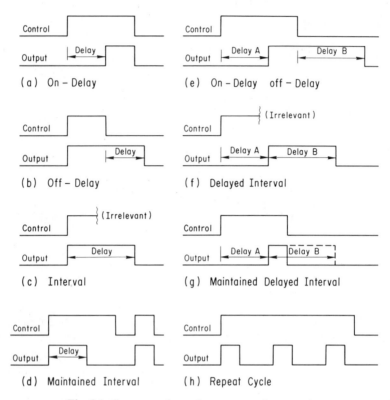

Fig. 8.1. Sequence charts for common timer modes.

usually adjustable. When the control signal goes LO—no matter whether during or after the delay period—the output also goes LO, that is, the timer is reset. A typical use for such a timer is in a plant where a series of machines must be started together. Since most motors draw a very high inrush current on starting, this could overload power lines and blow fuses. By using timers, the starting of the individual motors can be staggered. For many additional examples of industrial applications, see Ref. (8.1).

In the *Off-Delay* mode shown in Fig. 8.1(b), the delay takes effect after the control signal goes LO. A typical application is for a copying machine with a cooling blower. After the machine is shut *off*, the timer keeps the blower working for a certain time to allow the machine to cool down.

Figure 8.1(c) illustrates the *Interval* mode. The timer output remains HI for a set time regardless of what happens to the control input during the interval. A typical application is for a drink dispensing machine, in which a given quantity of liquid must be poured into the cup.

The *Maintained Interval* mode of Fig. 8.1(d) is similar to the Interval mode, except that the control input *does* affect output during the delay period. It provides a safety feature in a timed machine, enabling the operator to stop the machine any time in case of emergency.

Figure 8.1 (e) shows the *On-Delay Off-Delay* mode, which is really a combination of the two modes shown in Figs. 8.1(a) and (b). If the control input goes LO during the first delay period, the timer is reset.

The *Delayed Interval* mode of Fig. 8.1(f) has an On-Delay *A* after the control signal has gone HI, followed by an Off-Delay *B*. Once the cycle has begun, the control signal has no effect on events.

The *Maintained Delayed Interval* mode of Fig. 8.1(g) is similar to the Delayed Interval mode, except that the control signal must remain HI for the cycle to be completed. It can be seen that the three modes in Figs. 8.1(e)–(g) have the same relationship to each other as those of Figs. 8.1(a), (c), and (d).

In the *Repeat Cycle* mode of Fig. 8.1(h), a certain cycle, consisting of a specific HI–LO sequence, is repeated indefinitely, as long as the control signal remains HI. The width of both HI and LO intervals can be adjusted independently.

8.1.2 Electronic Timers

An inexpensive way to build a do-it-yourself timer is to use the NE555 or 556 IC. (The 556 chip contains two separate 555 units.) These chips can be used in two separate modes. In the *monostable* mode, a brief trigger input pulse causes output to go HI for a certain period, which corresponds to the Interval mode of Fig. 8.1(c). By cascading two such units (using a 556 for this purpose), the Delayed Interval mode of Fig. 8.1(f) is obtained. The timing intervals are determined by an exterior resistor and capacitor. Typical intervals obtainable range from microseconds to minutes. In the *astable* mode, the units function as oscillators, according to the Repeat Cycle mode of Fig. 8.1(h). Here, too, the *on* and *off* intervals are determined by two external resistors and one capacitor. Circuits for these and many other NE555 applications are described in Refs. (8.4)–(8.6).

If the NE555 is intended to drive other electronic elements, no special output device is needed. However, if exterior loads must be actuated, then the NE555 output must be connected either to a solid-state relay (SSR) or an electromechanical relay (EMR). These devices and their relative merits are discussed at length in Section 4.2.

If a more substantial self-contained industrial timer is required, there is a wide choice of solid-state devices. For a list of manufacturers, see Ref. (8.7). These contain both the electronic timing circuit, and the output stage which, again, is either an SSR or an EMR. The timing circuit can be analog or digital. Analog timing circuits are similar to the NE555 just discussed. Their accuracy is limited to 1–5% (because of temperature and line-voltage effects), and their maximum timing range to about 10 minutes (because longer times require very large capacitors).

Digital timing circuits are based on counting a source of constant-frequency pulses or oscillations. The time-reference base can be an internal oscillator, and

Fig. 8.2. Timing relay. (Courtesy of Amerace Corp.)

the delay controlled either by varying the oscillator frequency or by setting the counter. By increasing the final count, delays up to days are obtainable. In more modern digital timers, the time-reference base is provided by the 60 Hz (or 50 Hz in Europe) line frequency. Since this is regulated by the power company, very good accuracy and repeatability can be obtained.

Solid-state timers with an electromechanical relay as output stage—a hybrid element—are usually referred to as "timing relays"; see Fig. 8.2. These normally come as a self-contained unit with a plug-in relay, and with an external knob or dial adjustment of the time delay. In the particular timer shown in the figure, one of four different timer modes can be selected by a screwdriver adjustment. For further discussion of solid-state timers, see Refs. (8.8) and (8.9).

8.1.3   Electromechanical Timers

Electromechanical timers are of two types: thermal timers, and synchronous-motor timers. Thermal timers often use bimetal strips (shown in Fig. 2.25), which deflect with temperature change. By sending the control current through a heating element wound around the bimetal strip, the strip heats and deflects, and eventually makes or breaks a contact. This produces a time-delay switch, but if the switch current actuates a relay coil, we have a time-delay relay. Instead of bimetal strips, self-heating thermistors can be used. Their resistance changes sharply with temperature, and this effect is utilized to actuate a relay coil after a certain delay.

Thermal timers are very inexpensive, but also the least accurate of all electric timers, with typical errors of 10% or more. Unlike most other timers in which the delay is easily adjustable by the user, most thermal timers have a fixed factory-set time delay. A typical application of thermal bimetal timers is for automobile flashers, where the strip is heated and then opens a contact, whereupon it cools down and closes the contact. The result is a flashing action at a frequency of about once per second, which is only stopped by switching off the external current supply.

Synchronous-motor timers, by contrast, are much more accurate but also expensive. Since motor speed depends on line frequency, repeat accuracies of better than 0.5% are obtainable. A cam, or set of cams, is mounted on the motor shaft. As the motor turns, each cam mechanically actuates a limit switch, with the actuation periods depending on the cam shape. By using reduction gears to reduct camshaft speed, extremely long timing intervals (days or even weeks) can be obtained. By changing cams, we get, in effect, a programmable timer with a number of output channels. Each limit switch can be connected to some other outside equipment, which is actuated in synchronization according to the cam shapes. This type of programmable cam timer is very similar to the drum programmers discussed in Section 9.1.

8.1.4 Pneumatic Timers

Most pneumatic timers are based on RC circuits (that is, resistance–capacitance), with the resistance produced by an adjustable needle valve, and the capacitance by a small volume tank.

A simple pneumatic On-Delay timer, easily assembled from standard pneumatic components, is shown in Fig. 8.3. Normally, the 5/2 valve is in the position shown, so that the OUTPUT signal is vented. When the CONTROL signal becomes HI (i.e., pressurized), air leaks through the needle valve, causing pressure in the volume tank to build up according to an exponential curve. When this pressure reaches a level sufficient to overcome the valve return spring (typically 2 to 3 bar), the valve shifts, so that the OUTPUT becomes HI and

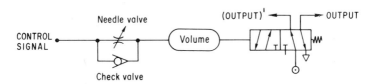

Fig. 8.3. Pneumatic "On-Delay" timer.

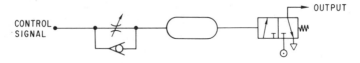

Fig. 8.4. Pneumatic "Off-Delay" timer.

(OUTPUT)' is LO (i.e., vented). The action is identical to that of Fig. 8.1(a), except that both OUTPUT and its logic inverse (OUTPUT)' are available. If the (OUTPUT)' signal is not required, the 5/2 valve can be replaced by a simpler 3/2 valve (as is done in the following figures).

To change the delay period, the needle valve is adjusted. For very long delays, a larger volume tank must be used. The check valve bypassing the needle valve enables the tank to exhaust almost instantly the moment the CONTROL signal goes LO. This makes the OUTPUT also go LO, and prepares the timer for the next actuation cycle.

An Off-Delay timer is obtained by inverting the check valve direction, as shown in Fig. 8.4. When the CONTROL goes HI, the valve switches almost instantly, causing the OUTPUT to go HI also. However, when the CONTROL goes LO, tank pressure has to exhaust through the needle valve, producing a delay before the OUTPUT goes LO, as shown in Fig. 8.1(b).

To obtain an On-Delay Off-Delay timer according to Fig. 8.1(e). the circuit of Fig. 8.5 can be used. This has two needle valves and two opposing check valves. The left needle valve determines Delay A, and the right one Delay B. (Note that the intervals are not accurate, unless sufficient time has elapsed between the *on* and *off* actions to enable the volume to fill up or exhaust completely.)

One drawback of the circuits of Figs. 8.3 to 8.5 is that the valves shift slowly as the pressure in the tank gradually increases or decreases. This effect can cause timing errors as high as 25%. To overcome this problem, the valve (be it 5/2 or 3/2) can be replaced by one with two pilot lines, as shown in Fig. 8.6. The right pilot line has a bias pressure imposed on it by an accurate pressure regulator. When the tank pressure is sufficient to overcome this opposing pilot-line pressure and the internal valve friction, the valve shifts the full distance in one try, giving a snap-action response. This permits a repeat accuracy of about 5%, and also gives more flexibility in adjusting the time interval, since the bias pressure also affects it.

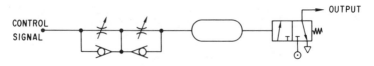

Fig. 8.5. Pneumatic "On-Delay Off-Delay" timer.

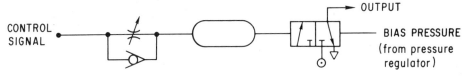

Fig. 8.6. Pneumatic "On-Delay" timer using bias pressure.

One of the factors contributing to the relatively poor accuracy of pneumatic timers is dirt or oil in the air supply, which accumulates in the needle valve and can seriously affect its pneumatic resistance. A second factor is valve friction, which is liable to change with time. To overcome these problems, many manufacturers supply more sophisticated pneumatic timers. One of these uses an enclosed dashpot damper for the timing function, so that the same clean air is recirculated, and no dirt is introduced from the air supply. Another method uses an electronic timing relay that actuates a solenoid valve. Such a hybrid system combines the good accuracy of solid-state timers with the possibility of getting a pneumatic output.

Figure 8.7 shows a hybrid timing relay of the opposite type. Both input and output signals are electric, just as in any relay. The actual timing, however, is

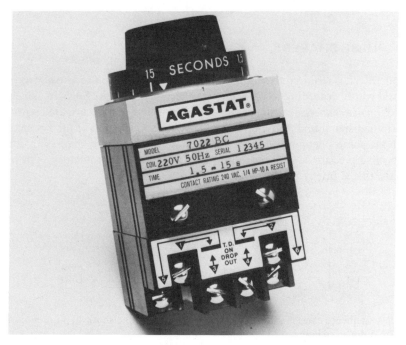

Fig. 8.7. Electropneumatic timing relay (Courtesy of Amerace Corp.)

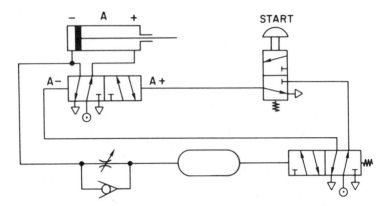

Fig. 8.8. "On-Delay" timer for automatic cylinder retraction.

done by an enclosed pneumatic dashpot device. Repeat accuracy is between 5 and 15%, depending on model.

To conclude this section, Fig. 8.8. shows how a pneumatic On-Delay timer can be used in the Interval timing mode of Fig. 8.1(c) to make a cylinder retract automatically after a certain time. Actuation of the START button causes the cylinder to extend and supplies the control signal to the timing circuit. Note that the cylinder eventually retracts even if the START button is held down during the cycle.

8.2 PULSE SHAPERS

Frequently, it is required to change a step signal or a wide pulse into a brief pulse of fixed width, according to the sequence chart of Fig. 8.9(a). Such an element is called a *pulse shaper*, *monostable*, or a *one-shot*. Pulse shapers are used wherever a sustained signal might interfere with the proper operation of the system. For example, some pneumatic-circuit design methods use pulse shapers to cut off limit-valve pressure signals, and thus prevent getting contradictory pilot-input signals; this is briefly discussed in Section 7.6.

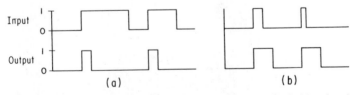

Fig. 8.9. Sequence charts for a pulse shaper (monostable, one-shot): (a) pulse shortening, and (b) pulse stretching.

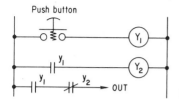

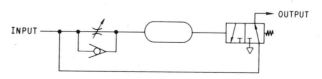

Fig. 8.10. Relay pulse shaper.

Figure 8.9(a) shows a pulse shaper performing "pulse-shortening." The opposite operation is called "pulse-stretching," and is illustrated in Fig. 8.9(b). A very brief input pulse produces a wider output pulse of fixed width.

A number of ICs provide electronic pulse-shaping capabilities, for example, 74LS122. The pulse width, which is controlled by an external timing resistor and capacitor, is in the microsecond range. If wider pulses are required, the NE555 chip mentioned in Section 8.1.2 should be used.

Figure 8.10 shows a pulse shaper using relays. Here, however, the output pulse width cannot be adjusted, but remains constant (in the millisecond range), depending on the operate time of relay Y_2.

Figure 10.20 shows how a pulse shaper can be implemented on a programmable controller.

A pneumatic pulse shaper is shown in Fig. 8.11. As the reader will note, this uses an On-Delay timing circuit, but with the INPUT signal also providing the air supply for the 3/2 valve. The moment the INPUT goes HI, the OUTPUT goes HI also. After a certain time period, the increasing tank pressure shifts the valve, causing the OUTPUT to go LO. If very brief output pulses are required, the tank can be dispensed with, and the effective volume is then that of the connecting tubing.

While the previous circuit acts as pulse shortener, the Off-Delay timer of Fig. 8.4 is also a pulse shaper but acts as a pulse stretcher, as can be seen from Fig. 8.1(b).

Some manufacturers supply self-contained valve units acting as pulse shapers, based on the circuit of Fig. 8.11 or on slightly different schemes. These are sometimes called "impulse valves," but this term should be used with care, because normal valves without return springs and with two pilot lines are sometimes called by that name, since short pulses are sufficient to shift them.

Fig. 8.11. Pneumatic pulse shaper.

8.3 TRIGGER FLIP-FLOPS

Trigger flip-flops (or T flip-flops) are defined in Section 3.9. Unlike other flip-flops, they have only one input, labeled T, and two outputs Q and Q'. Their operation is shown on the sequence chart of Fig. 8.12. Whenever T goes HI, Q changes state, but nothing happens when T goes LO. (However, some T flip-flops work in the opposite mode, changing state when T goes LO).

The T flip-flop is one of the most important switching elements in use. Referring to the sequence chart of Fig. 8.12, we note that a train of pulses introduced at T produces a pulse train at output Q. However, there is only one Q pulse for every two T pulses. In other words, the Q pulses appear at half the frequency of the T pulses. Thus, the T flip-flop acts as *frequency divider*, which makes it extremely useful as a timing device. Electronic quartz watches, for example, use a crystal oscillator producing pulses in the megaherz range. By using a string of T flip-flops connected in cascade fashion, each Q output serving as the T input for the next flip-flop, the original frequency is successively divided by 2, 4, 8, 16, 32, etc. By using counters—discussed in the next section—these pulse trains can be used to accurately measure long intervals such as seconds, minutes, hours, and days.

The same principle is used in computers. The microprocessor found in every computer uses a crystal oscillator and frequency divider to produce pulse trains (typically at 1–10 mHz), and these pulses are used to synchronize the operations carried out by the various computer elements.

A number of ICs implement T flip-flops electronically. One of the most popular is chip 74LS76 (see Fig. 4.3), which is really a dual JK flip-flop. However, by appropriate connections, it can also serve as an RS or as a T flip-flop. To obtain a T flip-flop, the inputs labeled J, K, $\bar{S}$, and $\bar{C}$ are made HI (connected to supply voltage V_{CC}), and the T pulses are connected to the input labeled CP. To reset or *clear* flip-flop output Q to 0, a HI signal is applied to pins 2 or 7, and LO (i.e., Ground) to pins 3 or 8. (The overbar, as in $\bar{S}$, signifies logic inversion, or S'.)

Figure 8.13 shows a T flip-flop implemented by three relays. The sequence chart demonstrates the operation of this circuit. T flip-flop implementation on a programmable controller is shown in Fig. 10.21.

To build a pneumatic T flip-flop, the logic scheme of Fig. 8.14 could be used. It uses an RS flip-flop plus two AND gates. If $Q = 1$, the lower AND gate is enabled, so that the next T pulse resets the RS flip-flop and makes $Q' = 1$. But

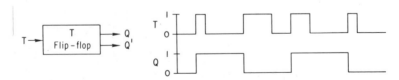

Fig. 8.12. T flip-flop and its sequence chart.

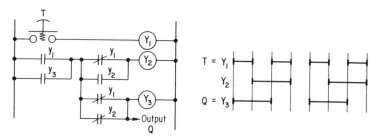

Fig. 8.13. Trigger flip-flop relay circuit and its sequence chart.

now the upper AND gate is enabled, so that the next T pulse sets the flip-flop, and so on. This circuit, however, is sensitive to pulse width. The incoming T pulse must be wide enough to contain the energy required to switch the flip-flop. If, however, the pulse is too wide, it will still be HI when the feedback signal arrives, and will therefore switch the flip-flop a second, third, or fourth time. To avoid this, a pulse shaper is inserted in the T input line, with its pulse width adjusted so that each T pulse, no matter how wide, switches the flip-flop exactly once.

A T flip-flop completely insensitive to pulse width can be designed using the Huffman method for sequential systems; see Problem 6.8. The solution, which requires two RS flip-flops, one NOT gate, and four AND gates is shown in Fig. 8.15. The two flip-flops are called a *master flip-flop* and a *slave flip-flop*, respectively. When input T becomes 1, only the slave flip-flop becomes set, so that $Q = y_2 = 1$. The master flip-flop is set only when $T = 0$, after which the next $T = 1$ signal resets the slave flip-flop, and so on.

By using 5/2 valves as passive AND gates according to the technique described in Section 7.4, this scheme can be implemented using only three valves (apart from the valve providing the T and T' signals), as shown in Fig. 8.16. To reset this T flip-flop, a pressure signal must be applied to R_2 while $T = 0$. This reset line should be connected to R_2 through a shuttle valve to prevent the air from escaping through the vented Ty_1 line.

Several manufacturers supply compact valve units containing pneumatic T flip-flops.

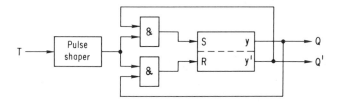

Fig. 8.14. Trigger flip-flop circuit (sensitive to pulse width).

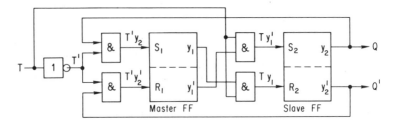

Fig. 8.15. Trigger flip-flop circuit (insensitive to pulse width).

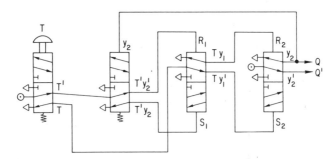

Fig. 8.16. Trigger flip-flop valve circuit (insensitive to pulse width).

8.4 BINARY COUNTERS

Trigger flip-flops serve as basic building blocks for binary counters. A binary UP counter is shown in Fig. 8.17. It counts the pulses appearing at the left T input. A counter with n stages (i.e., T flip-flops) can count up to $2^n - 1$; thus, the counter shown can count to 15. Note that the Q' output of each flip-flop is connected to the T input of the next stage. The Q outputs are used here only for indication; for example, they might actuate lamps for a visual indication of the binary count.

The operation of this counter is shown on the sequence chart of Fig. 8.18, where, at the beginning, the count is assumed zero, so that all Q outputs are 0 and all Q' outputs 1. Since a T flip-flop changes state the moment its T input goes from 0 to 1, this happens when the previous Q output goes from 1 to 0, so that Q' goes from 0 to 1. It is suggested that the reader trace the course of events

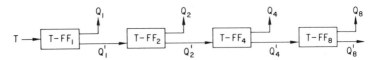

Fig. 8.17. UP counter.

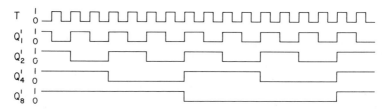

Fig. 8.18. Sequence chart for the UP counter of Fig. 8.17.

on this sequence chart. The corresponding truth table is given in Fig. 8.19. To reset the counter, a reset, or *clear*, line (not shown in the figure) is generally provided, which resets all T flip-flops simultaneously.

Note that when the count reaches 16, all Q outputs return to 0. For higher counts, more stages have to be added. To illustrate, Fig. 8.20 shows an UP counter with six stages, which can count to 63. If the outputs are as shown, the present count is 100110, which is the binary-number equivalent of 38.

It is frequently desired to obtain a signal when the count has reached a certain value. This requires a *decoding* AND gate, as shown in Fig. 8.21, where the gate is connected to pick up a count of 6. Since the binary equivalent of 6 is 0110, the four gate inputs are connected to Q'_8, Q_4, Q_2, and Q'_1. Note that is is not sufficient to connect only Q_4 and Q_2, because then the AND gate output would be 1 also for counts of 7, 14, and 15, and not exclusively for 6.

To display decimal numbers, so-called seven-segment displays are used, which display any digit from 0 to 9 using seven line segments, as illustrated in Fig. 8.22. Such displays are either liquid-crystal displays (LCDs) used in digital

Q_8	Q_4	Q_2	Q_1	Count
0	0	0	0	0, 16
0	0	0	1	1
0	0	1	0	2
0	0	1	1	3
0	1	0	0	4
0	1	0	1	5
0	1	1	0	6
0	1	1	1	7
1	0	0	0	8
1	0	0	1	9
1	0	1	0	10
1	0	1	1	11
1	1	0	0	12
1	1	0	1	13
1	1	1	0	14
1	1	1	1	15

Fig. 8.19. Truth table for the UP counter of Fig. 8.17.

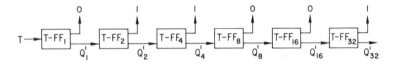

Fig. 8.20. UP counter indicating a count of 100110 = 38.

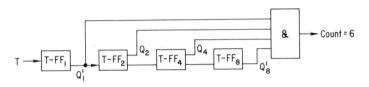

Fig. 8.21. UP counter decoded for a count 0110 = 6.

Fig. 8.22. Seven-segment display of digits 0 to 9.

watches, pocket calculators, digital voltmeters, and so on, or light-emitting diodes (LEDs) preferred in instrumentation because of their better visibility. In either case, a separate decoding circuit is required for each of the seven segments. For example, the decoding circuit designed to actuate the top horizontal segment would consist of eight AND gates connected to decode the numbers 0, 2, 3, 5, 6, 7, 8, and 9, respectively (since these are the digits in which this segment is actuated). The outputs of these eight AND gates are then connected to an OR gate, whose output actuates the segment under discussion. Seven such decoding circuits (one for each line segment) are needed for each decimal digit to be displayed. This seems a formidable task, but, fortunately, IC chips are available for this purpose, such as 74LS47, 48, 247, 248, or 249 (all BCD to seven-segment decoder drivers), which contain all necessary decoding circuits for one decimal digit on a single chip.

To obtain a DOWN counter, the Q output of each stage is connected to the T input of the next stage, as shown in Fig. 8.23. (The Q' outputs are not utilized.) The truth table of Fig. 8.19 applies here also, except that the counting proceeds in the opposite direction. At the beginning, all Q outputs are presumed 0, which represents not only count 0 but also 16. The first incoming T pulse cascades through the whole counter, making all Q outputs go 1, which indicates a count of 15. Each succeeding T pulse reduces the count by one. It is suggested that the reader draw a sequence chart (similar to Fig. 8.18) to trace the operation of this counter.

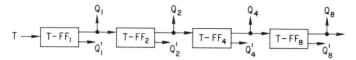

Fig. 8.23. DOWN counter.

Frequently, UP/DOWN counters are required, which can count in either direction. (Such counters, for example, are used with incremental encoders discussed in Section 8.8.2, and must count either UP or DOWN depending on the direction of shaft rotation.) Three stages of an UP/DOWN counter are shown in Fig. 8.24. Each stage requires one OR and two AND gates, in addition to the T flip-flop. If the UP line is HI, the lower AND gates are enabled, so that the Q' outputs actuate the next flip-flop, and the counter counts UP. Conversely, if the DOWN line is HI, the upper AND gates are enabled, and the counter counts DOWN. In either case, the Q outputs are used for count indication (not shown in the figure).

To implement counters electronically, a number of ICs are available, such as 74LS90 and 74LS160, which are UP counters, or 74LS168, 74LS169, and 74LS190 to 193, which are UP/DOWN counters. Some of these present the count as a binary number, whereas others use the binary-coded decimal (BCD) format, which is described in Section 8.7.

Since relays can implement T flip-flops (see Fig. 8.13), they could also be used for counters, although this is seldom done. Pneumatic counters find application where use of electrical devices must be avoided for safety reasons, or where pneumatic outputs are required. Such pneumatic counters are of two types: all-pneumatic counters and hybrid pneumatic–mechanical counters.

All-pneumatic counters use the switching circuits described in Fig. 8.17 or 8.24, with the T flip-flop implemented pneumatically according to Fig. 8.15 or 8.16. Such counters are bulky and costly if more than a few stages are required. Hence, they are only practical for low-count applications, where the counter is reset frequently.

Pneumatic-mechanical counters use an air actuator (diaphragm or small piston) to drive a mechanical ratchet mechanism. For each pneumatic input

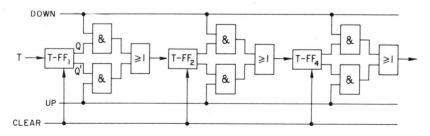

Fig. 8.24. UP/DOWN counter (three stages).

pulse, this ratchet advances one angular step and shifts a numerical display (such as in automobile mileage indicators). Because of the ratchet, these counters can only count in one direction. Usually, the counter can be preset to a certain count, and when this has been reached, it produces a pneumatic output signal that can be utilized as desired.

For a discussion of pneumatic counters, see Ref. (8.10). For a listing of counter manufacturers, both electronic and pneumatic, see Ref. (8.7).

8.5 SHIFT REGISTERS

Shift registers receive binary information, and store and transfer it in the order it was received. As shown in Fig. 8.25, the shift register has a number of modular stages, equal to the number of bits to be stored. Whenever a "Shift" pulse arrives, each stage shifts the bit stored within it on to the next stage. The first stage accepts the present state of input x, whereas the bit in the final stage is discarded. Thus, after the arrival of the next Shift pulse, the bits stored in the shift register of Fig. 8.25 are $x100110110$.

Shift registers find many applications in automation systems, wherever information relating to some object moving along a production line must accompany the object. Consider, for example, a manufacturing line having a number of work stations, at each of which a different operation is carried out. One of these is an automatic inspection station. If a given workpiece is found defective, the inspection station enters a 1 into the shift register. Each time the workpieces move on to the next station, a Shift pulse is sent, so that the 1 bit travels through the shift register in synchronization with the workpiece. Each work station is programmed to examine the bit related to the present workpiece. If this is a 0 (i.e., the workpiece is okay), the operation is carried out, but if it is a 1 (i.e., the workpiece is defective), the operation is skipped, so as to avoid wasting more money on a rejected part. At the last station, the 1 bit can be utilized to remove the defective part from the line.

If more than one bit of information must be transmitted, a "wider" shift register having several parallel tracks can be used, as shown in Fig. 8.26. This might be used, for example, in an automatic sorting or storage line. With four tracks, the workpieces can be classified into 16 different categories. At each work station, different programmed operations may take place, depending on the type of part that has arrived. At the end of the line, the part is stored in one of 16

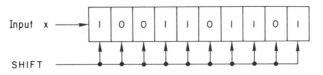

Fig. 8.25. Shift register (10 stages).

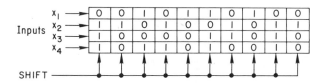

Fig. 8.26. Shift register with four parallel tracks.

different storage bins, depending on the category it belongs to. As with counters, decoding AND gates are needed to distinguish between the various bit combinations in the register.

Figure 8.27 shows how a shift register can be built of standard switching elements. Similar to the T flip-flop of Fig. 8.15, each module contains a master and a slave RS flip-flop, and four AND gates. When the Shift pulse goes HI, the AND gates of each master flip-flop are enabled, and pass any 1 bit on to the S input (and any 0 bit to the R input) of the master flip-flop. As the Shift pulse goes LO, the other two AND gates are enabled, so that the master flip-flop passes its information on to the next slave flip-flop.

Although half the elements could be saved by using only one flip-flop per stage, this would cause the same problem described in connection with Fig. 8.14: if the Shift pulse lasts too long, the various bits would race through several stages all at once, that is, we would get several shift operations in one go. By comparison, the register of Fig. 8.27 is insensitive to the width of the Shift pulses.

A number of ICs implementing shift registers are available, for example, 74LS91 (8-bit shift register), or 74LS164, 165, 166, 194, or 195. Shift registers can also be implemented on programmable controllers, see Chapter 10, or on microcomputers using software.

8.6 SCHMITT TRIGGERS

The Schmitt trigger represents an electronic interface between the analog and binary worlds. As illustrated in the input/output plot of Fig. 8.28, the Schmitt trigger output jumps to HI when the input exceeds a certain value, typically 1.8 V dc. Further increase in input has no effect on the output. The output returns to LO only when the input reaches a much lower value than the previous actuation point, say 0.95 V dc. Hence, this Schmitt trigger has a hysteresis band of 0.85 V.

A typical Schmitt trigger IC is 74LS14, containing six triggers on one chip, each with an inverter (NOT gate) at its output. Hence, the input/output response is as shown in Fig. 8.28, but flipped upside down.

The main use of Schmitt triggers is to convert fuzzy, not well-defined wave forms—for example, as transmitted by an optical sensor—into sharp square waves suitable for actuating a binary counter, as shown in Fig. 8.29. The

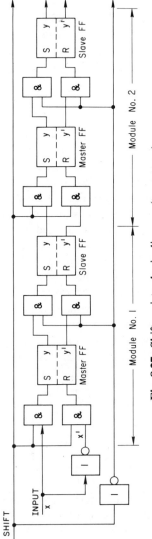

Fig. 8.27. Shift register logic diagram (two stages).

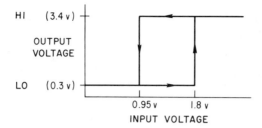

Fig. 8.28. Schmitt-trigger response.

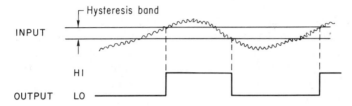

Fig. 8.29. Schmitt-trigger response to a fuzzy wave form.

hysteresis prevents the output from jumping back and forth between LO and HI if the input should oscillate about the actuation point, for example, due to vibration.

8.7 CODES

All of us use codes in our daily lives, whether we realize it or not. When we read or write any decimal number, such as 2908, we are employing the decimal code, in which each digit is assigned a value or "weight" equal to 10 to the power of an integer. Thus, 2908 really means

$$8 \times 10^0 = 8 \times 1 = 8$$
$$+0 \times 10^1 = 0 \times 10 = 0$$
$$+9 \times 10^2 = 9 \times 100 = 900$$
$$+2 \times 10^3 = 2 \times 1000 = 2000$$

which comes out to a total written, in *encoded* form, as 2908.

Decimal numbers are frequently attached to items such as consumer goods by labels containing the familiar bar code. This is used not only in supermarkets and in libraries, but also in industry, where it has become a popular method of reading numerical data attached to an object. For a good discussion of bar codes and their application, see Refs. (8.11) and (8.12).

The codes discussed in this section can be divided into three categories: (1) weighted codes, (2) BCD codes, and (3) cyclic codes. The discussion serves as background for the following section on encoders. Further discussion of codes can be found in any textbook on switching theory (see references in Chapter 3), or in Ref. (8.13).

8.7.1 Weighted Codes

As just illustrated, the decimal code is a weighted code, since the digits, from right to left, have weights of 1, 10, 100, 1000, and so on. However, there are many other weighted codes. The ancient Mayas, for instance, had a numbering system based on 20 (they evidently used both fingers and toes for counting).

Computers use the binary code based on 2, since most switching elements are, by nature, binary, or two-state, elements. In the binary code, the digits, from right to left, have respective weights of

$$1, 2, 4, 8, 16, 32, 64, 128, 256, 512, 1024, 2048, 4096, \text{etc.}$$

Thus, a binary "word" containing n binary digits can express decimal numbers from 0 up to $2^n - 1$.

To translate a decimal number into its binary form, it is handy to refer to the list of the powers of 2 just shown. To illustrate the procedure on decimal number 2908, the list shows that $2048 = 2^{11}$ is the largest power of 2 that is less than 2908. Therefore, the binary digit with weight 2048 becomes 1, leaving a remainder $2908 - 2048 = 860$.

Since 860 is less than $1024 = 2^{10}$, the second binary digit from the left becomes 0.

Since 860 is greater than $512 = 2^9$, the third binary digit becomes 1, leaving a remainder $860 - 512 = 348$.

Since 348 is greater than $256 = 2^8$, the fourth binary digit becomes 1, leaving a remainder $348 - 256 = 92$.

Since 92 is less than $128 = 2^7$, the fifth binary digit becomes 0.

Since 92 is greater than $64 = 2^6$, the sixth binary digit becomes 1, leaving a remainder $92 - 64 = 28$.

Continuing this procedure to the end results in

$$2908 = 1011\ 0101\ 1100$$

A pocket calculator comes in useful for this task. Better yet, the following simple BASIC program does the job. (It should run on any personal computer, though minor modifications may be required depending on the BASIC dialect used.)

```
5 REM*** Converting decimal to binary number
10 INPUT "DECIMAL NUMBER? ";D
15 REM*** Find number of required digits
20 N=0
30 IF D<2^N GOTO 50
40 N=N+1:GOTO 30
50 DIM B(N)
60 X=2^(N − 1)
65 REM***Start conversion
70 FOR J=1 TO N
80 IF D<X THEN B(J)=0:GOTO 110
90 B(J)=1
100 D=D−X
110 X=X/2
120 NEXT J
125 REM***Start print-out
130 FOR J=1 TO N
140 PRINT B(J)
150 NEXT J
160 PRINT:END
```

The opposite task, that of translating a binary number back into its decimal equivalent, is much simpler. We simply add the weights of all binary digits that are 1. Thus, using the previous number, we get

Weight:	2048	1024	512	256	128	64	32	16	8	4	2	1
Digit:	1	0	1	1	0	1	0	1	1	1	0	0

$$= 2048 + 512 + 256 + 64 + 16 + 8 + 4 = 2908$$

Another weighted code, the *hexadecimal* code, which is based on 16, is commonly used in computer machine-language or assembly-language programming. Each digit can have 16 different values, from 0 to 15 (instead of 0 to 9, as in the decimal system). Since everybody is already familiar with decimal numerals, these are also used in the hexadecimal system for values up to 9. For values from 10 to 15, new symbols must be defined, and the letters A to F are used, with A = 10, B = 11, C = 12, D = 13, E = 14, and F = 15.

Although hexadecimal numbers may appear strange, they are not difficult. The digit weights, again from right to left, are $16^0 = 1$, $16^1 = 16$, $16^2 = 256$, $16^3 = 4096$, $16^4 = 65536$, and so on. Thus, the decimal value of a number such as \$B5C is calculated as follows. (The \$ sign indicates a hexadecimal number.)

Weight:	256	16	1
Digit:	B (=11)	5	C (=12)

$$= 11 \times 256 + 5 \times 16 + 12 \times 1 = 2908$$

To convert 2908 back into hexadecimal form, the following procedure is used.

$2908/256 = 11.3$. Therefore, the first digit from the left is $11 = B$, leaving a remainder of $2908 - 11 \times 256 = 92$.

$92/16 = 5.75$. Therefore, the second digit from the left is 5, leaving a remainder of $92 - 5 \times 16 = 12$.

Hence, the third digit is $12 = C$, and the hexadecimal number is $B5C.

It is interesting to note the close relationship between binary and hexadecimal representations of a number. If we divide the above binary representation into groups of four digits (starting from the right), we obtain 1011 0101 1100. If we now consider each group as a separate four-digit binary number (with a decimal value between 0 and 15), and translate each into its hexadecimal equivalent, we obtain the hexadecimal form of the number, namely, $B5C. Or, proceeding in the opposite direction, we could translate each hexadecimal digit into its equivalent four-bit binary form, getting

$$B = 1011 \qquad 5 = 0101 \qquad C = 1100$$

Combining all these binary bits brings us back to the original binary number 1011 0101 1100.

For further discussions of binary and hexadecimal numbers, the reader is referred to books on computers, and especially on assembly-language programming.

8.7.2   Binary-Coded Decimal (BCD) Codes

Since most humans think in terms of decimal numbers, they find both binary and hexadecimal numbers somewhat unnatural and awkward. The BCD code represents a compromise. Although BCD numbers consist solely of binary digits, and are thus suitable for binary switching elements, they maintain the basic structure of decimal numbers, and are thus easily interpreted and visualized.

In the common BCD code (also called the 8–4–2–1 code), each decimal digit maintains its identity, but is expressed in binary form. Again, using the decimal number 2908 as example, this is written in BCD as

$$\begin{array}{cccc}
0010 & 1001 & 0000 & 1000 \\
(=2) & (=9) & (=0) & (=8)
\end{array}$$

It is sufficient to memorize the binary representation of numbers 0 to 9 to interpret BCD numbers easily and without effort. The price that must be paid for this convenience is that more bits are needed to represent a given decimal number in BCD than in "natural" binary code. Thus, a 16-bit binary number can express decimal numbers from 0 up to $2^{16} - 1 = 65,535$, whereas a 16-bit BCD number can express decimal numbers only up to $10^{16/4} - 1 = 9999$.

Many of the ICs used to count or handle numbers use BCD code. For example, since seven-segment displays, discussed in connection with Fig. 8.22, display decimal numerals, it is only natural to drive them with ICs containing the required decoding circuits but based on BCD code, as, for example, chip 74LS47 or 48 (BCD to seven-segment decoder driver).

In many applications, numbers are transmitted in the BCD format from one device to another, sometimes over considerable distances. There is always the possibility of an error in the transmission or receiving process, and, to discover these, so-called *error-checking codes* are used. The simplest error-checking code is the BCD code with a fifth bit added—the so-called *parity*, or *P* bit. This bit is made either 0 or 1, so that the total number of 1 bits in the five-bit word is even. (An odd number of 1 bits could also be used, in which case we speak of an "odd-parity" system.) The resulting error-checking BCD code is shown in the truth table of Fig. 8.30. At the receiving end of the signal, a logic circuit (called a "parity checker") counts the number of 1 bits in each five-bit word, and, if this should turn out odd, gives an error message, and possibly asks for the transmission to be repeated. Parity checkers are available in IC form, for example, 74LS280 (9-bit odd/even parity generator checker), and these make use of iterative circuits, as described in Section 8.9.1.

Unfortunately, error-checking codes are not infallible. For example, if a double error should occur, $7 = 01111$ might come out as 00011, or 01100, or possibly 01001, all of which would be interpreted by the parity checker as a perfectly valid number.

A different BCD code is the so-called "2-out-of-5" code, which is slightly more powerful at error-checking. As shown in the truth table of Fig. 8.31, every five-bit word must have exactly two 1 bits, otherwise the word is invalidated. To make this possible, the weight of the first bit from the left must be reduced from 8 to 7, since the former representation of 7 as 0111 is now unacceptable because of its three 1 bits. A second problem relates to the representation of 0. Representing 0 as 0000 is unacceptable, since this word cannot have two 1 bits even if the *P* bit is made 1. It therefore becomes necessary to represent 0 as 11000. While this

Weight / Number	8	4	2	1	P
0	0	0	0	0	0
1	0	0	0	1	1
2	0	0	1	0	1
3	0	0	1	1	0
4	0	1	0	0	1
5	0	1	0	1	0
6	0	1	1	0	0
7	0	1	1	1	1
8	1	0	0	0	1
9	1	0	0	1	0

Fig. 8.30. Truth table for an error-checking BCD code (with even parity).

Weight Number	7	4	2	1	P
0	I	I	O	O	O
1	O	O	O	I	I
2	O	O	I	O	I
3	O	O	I	I	O
4	O	I	O	O	I
5	O	I	O	I	O
6	O	I	I	O	O
7	I	O	O	O	I
8	I	O	O	I	O
9	I	O	I	O	O

Fig. 8.31. Truth table for the 2-out-of-5 code.

does not agree with the assigned weights of the bits, it does not really matter. (No other option is available, because all the remaining unused 4-bit combinations have three or four 1 bits, and are thus unacceptable.)

To check numbers transmitted according to the 2-out-of-5 code, a logic circuit at the receiving end must count the number of 1 bits, and give an error message if this should be other than 2. This error-checking code is able to catch many double errors not detected by the even-parity error-checking code, such as a change from $2 = 00101$ to 01111. However, this code is also not infallible. Thus, if adjacent 1 and 0 bits should exchange positions the number of 1 bits remains 2 and the error is undetected.

Apart from error-detecting, there also exist error-correcting codes. One method (although expensive) is to transmit each number three times, and compare the results. If they agree, there is probably no error, since the probability of identical errors three times in a row is minute. If there is a discrepancy, a highly democratic method is employed: a "vote" is taken, and a majority of two out of three determines the result.

8.7.3 Cyclic Codes

In cyclic codes, also called "unit-distance codes," only one bit changes between adjacent numbers. By comparison, the natural binary code represents numbers 0 to 3 as 00, 01, 10, 11 respectively. In going from $1 = 01$ to $2 = 10$, or from $3 = 11$ back to $0 = 00$, both bits change, and this can cause problems in certain applications. As was shown in Section 5.5.5, if such a code were used for the state assignment in the Huffman method, critical races can result.

A cyclic code for the same four numbers would be 00, 01, 11, and 10. Since only one bit changes at a time, races are avoided. Note that the cyclic code is not a weighted code, that is, there are no weights attached to the various bits. Instead, the representation used for each number is arbitrarily defined.

How are cyclic codes constructed? One method is to utilize a basic property of Karnaugh maps: adjacent squares differ in only one variable. Suppose we need a cyclic code for eight numbers, 0 to 7. We draw a three-variable Karnaugh map, Fig. 8.32(a), and then mark any closed path going through adjacent squares. The code is then obtained from the addresses of the respective squares, but substituting 1 and 0 for x and x', respectively. The code resulting from Fig. 8.32(a), assuming we start from the upper left-hand square, is 000, 001, 011, 010, 110, 111, 101, and 100. Note that the last and first terms also differ by only one bit, hence the name "cyclic code."

Actually, a great number of such codes exist. For example, we could start at any of the eight squares, or go in the counterclockwise direction, and each of these options gives another cyclic code. We could also choose a different path, such as in Fig. 8.32(b), which gives 000, 001, 101, 111, 011, 010, 110, and 100. If a six-line code is required, the path shown in Fig. 8.32(c) results in 000, 001, 011, 111, 101, and 100. If we need a 10-line code, a four-variable Karnaugh map is needed, but only 10 out of its 16 squares are utilized. Using the path in Fig. 8.32(d) results in the code 0000, 0001, 0011, 0010, 0110, 0111, 0101, 1101, 1100, and 0100. It should be obvious that cyclic codes can only be constructed with an even number of terms.

Instead of Karnaugh maps, the "reflection" method can be used to obtain a symmetrical cyclic code. The method works as follows: a cyclic code for only two lines is obviously 0, 1. We now write these numbers below each other, draw a line of symmetry, and write the mirror image below this line, resulting in

$$\begin{array}{c} 0 \\ 1 \\ \hline 1 \\ 0 \end{array}$$

To differentiate between the two top and the two bottom lines, we must add a second bit, and enter 0s in the two top lines and 1s in the two bottom lines. This results in

$$\begin{array}{c} 00 \\ 01 \\ \hline 11 \\ 10 \end{array}$$

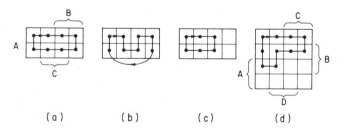

Fig. 8.32. Use of Karnaugh maps to obtain cyclic codes.

Number	C_1	C_2	C_3
0	0	0	1
1	0	1	1
2	0	1	0
3	1	1	0
4	1	1	1
5	1	0	1

Fig. 8.33. Reflected cyclic code for six numbers.

and we have a cyclic code for four numbers. To extend this to eight numbers, we repeat the process. We draw a new line of symmetry, write the mirror image, and then add four 0s and four 1s in the third bit from the right, resulting in

$$
\begin{array}{c}
000 \\
001 \\
011 \\
\underline{010} \\
110 \\
111 \\
101 \\
100
\end{array}
$$

This procedure can be repeated indefinitely to produce reflected codes of any length (also called "Gray codes"). The number of lines thus obtained is 2^n, with n an integer. If less lines are needed, any number of line pairs at the top and bottom can be canceled. For example, to obtain six lines, lines 000 and 100 are canceled, resulting in a reflected cyclic code defined by the truth table of Fig. 8.33.

8.8 ENCODERS

The task of encoders is to convert angular or linear position to an equivalent binary signal from which the position can be deduced. Thus, encoders are a type of analog-to-digital (A/D) converter, with position being the analog input. Encoders find wide use as feedback elements in numerically controlled (NC) machines and in robots, which are discussed in Chapter 13.

Encoders can be linear or angular, depending on the type of motion they measure. The principle of operation is similar, but there is a basic difference: the length of a linear encoder must equal the amount of linear motion it is to accommodate, Hence, linear encoders are generally long and expensive. Angular encoders, by comparison, are small disks. Such an encoder might, for instance, measure rotation of a motor shaft driving a machine-tool table through a ball screw. The exact table position can then be inferred from a knowledge of shaft angle, provided we know the ball-screw lead. Angular encoders are much less expensive than linear ones, but they only provide indirect measurement of the linear motion. Any elastic deformation or inaccuracy in the ball screw affects accuracy of the measured position.

Encoders can be classified into two basically different types: *absolute-position* (or *coded-pattern*) encoders, and *incremental* encoders. Most encoders utilize either optical or magnetic measuring means. The following is limited to angular optical encoders, both absolute-position and incremental. For detailed discussions of encoders, see Chapter 7 of Ref. (1.33), and Refs. (8.14–(8.17).

8.8.1 Absolute-Position (Coded-Pattern) Encoders

Optical angular absolute-position encoders (also called coded-pattern encoders) consist of a rotating disk made of a transparent material. The disk is divided into a number of equal angular sectors, depending on the resolution required, and a number of concentric circular bands. Each band is transparent in certain sectors but opaque in others, producing a characteristic pattern such as shown in Fig. 8.34. To keep the explanation simple, only three bands are used here, providing for $2^3 = 8$ sectors, or a resolution of $360/8 = 45$ degrees. (Normally, 8 to 12 bands are used for high resolution, but the principle of operation is the same.)

Each band has a light source sending a beam through the disk and, on the opposite side, a photosensor receiving this beam. Depending on the angular sector momentarily facing these sensors, they transmit a bit pattern representing the angular disk position. For example, if the bit pattern is 010, then the sector between 4:30 and 6:00 o'clock is facing the sensors.

Note that a cyclic-code pattern is used on the encoder. If a natural binary-code pattern were used, a transition from, say, 001 to 010 would produce a race between the two right-hand bits. Depending on which photosensor responded faster, the output would go briefly through 011 or through 000. In either case, a momentary false bit pattern would be sent. Cyclic codes avoid such races.

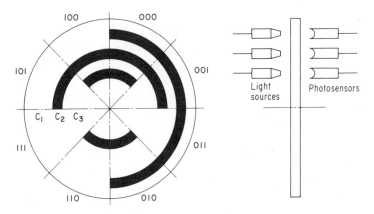

Fig. 8.34. Coded-pattern encoder.

However, many absolute-position encoders do use a natural binary-code pattern, and avoid races by utilizing two sets of sensors arranged in V formation.

A so-called decoding circuit is required to interpret the encoder signals. In its most primitive form, this could consist of eight AND or INHIBITION gates, each set up to detect a given bit pattern. Problems 8.13 and 8.14 deal with the design of decoding circuits for an eight-section encoder. A more elegant solution is provided by an iterative circuit; see Section 8.9.2.

The resolution obtainable with coded-pattern encoders is limited by the number of bands on the encoder disk, and, hence, on the disk diameter. For instance, for eight bands, the resolution is $2^8 = 256$ sectors, or $360/256 = 1.4$ degrees. Twelve-band encoders also exist, but are more expensive. For higher resolution, a second encoder could be used, coupled to the first encoder by step-up gearing. Similarly, we may wish to know how many complete revolutions the encoder has made, and this can be measured by a second encoder coupled to the first by step-down gearing (for example, designed to advance one sector for each revolution of the first encoder). Hence, by using several encoders connected by appropriate gearing, any desired range can be covered with any desired resolution.

8.8.2 Incremental Encoders

Incremental encoders, as shown in Fig. 8.35, have only a single band consisting of alternate transparent and opaque sectors. As the encoder turns, the photosensor sends a quasi-sine wave to a Schmitt trigger, which transforms this into a sharp square wave, that is, a series of pulses. These go to an UP/DOWN counter, whose count represents the encoder position. Commercially available incremental encoders typically give from 200 to as high as 5000 pulses per turn.

Compared to coded-pattern encoders, incremental encoders have four main advantages:

1. They are simpler and less expensive.
2. They need no decoding circuits, only a counter.
3. Their range is only limited by the counter capacity. Thus, it is unnecessary to use additional encoders with step-down gearing in order to increase the range that can be covered.
4. They have a floating zero, that is, the measurement origin can be chosen at any point by resetting the counter.

As against these, there are three drawbacks:

1. Incremental encoders do not measure absolute position, but only incremental changes. Therefore, any mistake in the count is carried along to all subsequent counts.

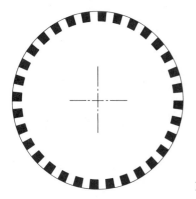

Fig. 8.35. Incremental encoder.

2. Interruption of power means the loss of measuring-system reference. By comparison, a code-pattern encoder indicates absolute position at all times, hence the name "absolute-position encoder."

3. Incremental-encoder systems are more noise-sensitive. Transient voltage spikes penetrating into the counting circuit might falsely affect the count.

One important question has not yet been answered: How does the UP/DOWN counter know in which direction to count? To detect the direction of disk rotation, a second light source and sensor are used, displaced with respect to the first one so that the two sine waves sent by the light sensors are 90 degrees out of phase. This is referred to as *quadrature*, and is illustrated in Fig. 8.36, where the two sensors are labeled A and B. The resulting two square waves are shown in Fig. 8.37. For the UP direction, the A wave is seen to lead B by 90 degrees. At a certain point on the sequence chart, a change of direction is assumed to take place, causing the A wave to lag rather than lead B. By using an appropriate logic circuit able to distinguish between these two conditions, the UP/DOWN counter is instructed in which direction to count. (Problem 6.11 deals with the design of such a circuit using the Huffman method.)

Apart from the A and B pulses, many commercial encoders also provide a so-called index pulse, which appears once every revolution. This can be used as a check, or where it is only required to count the total number of disk revolutions.

A simple *but inaccurate* direction-detecting circuit is shown in Fig. 8.38. (It is presented here only to illustrate the problems involved.) It uses a D flip-flop

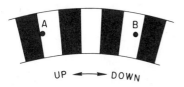

Fig. 8.36. Use of two sensors A and B with a 90-degree phase shift for detecting encoder direction.

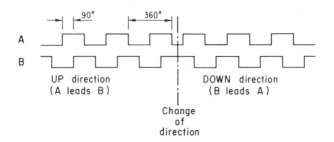

Fig. 8.37. Incremental-encoder output for UP and DOWN directions.

(such as IC chip 74LS74) and two AND or NAND gates. As described in Section 3.9, the D flip-flop transfers the bit present at the D (or "Data") input to the Q output at every LO-to-HI transition of the CK ("Clock") input. Operation of this circuit can be studied by means of a sequence chart, but this is left as an exercise for the reader; see Problem 8.15. This sequence chart discloses under what conditions the circuit gives inaccurate results. Specifically, if the encoder changes direction at certain positions, false DOWN pulses are generated and these accumulate and gradually increase the error. Even worse, the circuit is sensitive to "dither": encoder-disk vibration about one of the sensor switching points will generate a train of UP or DOWN pulses, even though the encoder is not really rotating, an effect called "encoder runaway." The hysteresis band in the Schmitt trigger should prevent this effect, unless the amplitude of vibration is very large.

An accurate direction-detecting circuit, published in Ref. (8.18), is shown in Fig. 8.39. This uses four D flip-flops instead of one, but is completely insensitive to dither, and does not accumulate errors upon change of direction. The reader can be convinced by drawing a sequence chart. A different approach to the problem is shown in Ref. (8.16).

A simple do-it-yourself encoder can be constructed by drilling 100 or possibly 200 small holes evenly spaced along a metal disk circumference, with the hole diameters equal to half the hole center distances. The H21A1 "Opto Slotted Coupler" described in Ref. (8.19) provides both an infrared emitting diode and a phototransistor in one self-contained unit, with a slot wide enough to accommodate the edge of a thin encoder disk. Two such optocouplers are needed

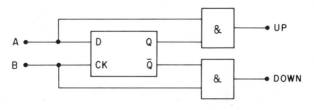

Fig. 8.38. Simple (but inaccurate!) direction-detecting circuit for an incremental encoder.

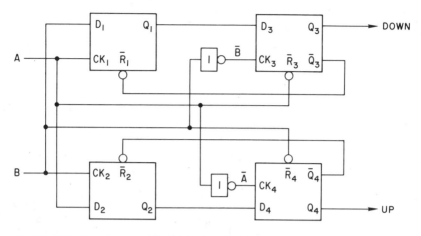

Fig. 8.39. Accurate direction-detecting circuit for an incremental encoder.

to provide quadrature signals. Provision for adjusting the relative position of these couplers with respect to the encoder disk is required to obtain reasonably accurate results. The two output signals should be sent through Schmitt triggers (e.g., 74LS14) and then to the circuit described in Fig. 8.39. The UP and DOWN pulses from this circuit go to a BCD UP/DOWN counter (consisting of one 74LS192 chip for each decimal digit), and then through a 74LS47 or 74LS48 (seven segment decoder/driver) to the seven-segment LED display. An alternative solution is to use integrated circuit SN74LS2000 (Texas Instruments), which includes the direction-detecting circuit and UP/DOWN counter all on one chip.

If a more accurate high-resolution encoder is required, a commercial unit has to be purchased. High-resolution encoders use a stationary stator or mask containing the same number of holes or slits as the rotating disk, and a collimating lens to reduce edge or fringe effects. This is necessary to obtain clear *on–off* pulses where the holes or slits and the gaps between them are extremely small. For a discussion of error sources in optical encoders, see Refs. (8.20) and (8.21). Interfacing optical encoders to computers is discussed in Ref. (8.22).

In conclusion, another application for incremental encoders should be mentioned. By connecting encoder output to a frequency-to-voltage converter (such as the ICs LM2907N or LM2917N), the encoder can be used to measure shaft speed.

8.9 ITERATIVE CIRCUITS

Iterative circuits (also called cascade circuits, although they have nothing in common with the cascade method of Chapter 7) consist of a chain of identical modules connected in series, with the modules receiving information in parallel.

Their use can lead to dramatic simplification of the switching circuit, compared to conventional design methods, as is illustrated through three examples.

8.9.1 Parity Detector

To demonstrate the advantages of iterative circuits, we first design a parity detector for the error-checking BCD 8–4–2–1 code using conventional methods, and then repeat the design with an iterative circuit. Each number from 0 to 9 is expressed in the error-checking BCD code by five bits, as shown in the truth table of Fig. 8.30. The parity detector must accept these five bits, and send a $T = 0$ output if the number is valid (i.e., has an even number of 1 bits). An invalid number must result in $T = 1$.

The information in the truth table is transferred to the five-variable Karnaugh map of Fig. 8.40. All ten combinations appearing in the truth table are valid numbers, and therefore get 0 entries on the map; all others get 1 entries, either because they have an odd number of 1 bits or because they are not part of the BCD code (such as the combination 11110, for example, which would represent 15 were it a valid number). The resulting output T is

$$T = x_8(x_4 + x_2 + x_1'P' + x_1P) + x_4(x_1'x_2'P' + x_1x_2P' + x_1x_2'P + x_1'x_2P)$$

$$+ x_4'x_8'(x_1x_2'P' + x_1'x_2P' + x_1'x_2'P + x_1x_2P)$$

which would require a great number of logic gates to implement.

The iterative-circuit solution for this problem is shown in Fig. 8.41, and consists of only four Exclusive-OR (or XOR) gates (see Section 3.9 for a description of the XOR function). The five code bits, x_8, x_4, x_2, x_1, and P, enter the circuit simultaneously, in parallel. An XOR gate output of 1 signifies that an odd number of 1 bits has been received up to that module. Thus, if $x_8 = x_4 = 0$ or $x_8 = x_4 = 1$, the first XOR gate gets a 0 output. If, however, either x_8 or x_4 (but not both) is 1, the output of this first gate is 1, indicating an odd number of 1 bits. This is repeated at each gate, with output T indicating the final result.

Not only is the iterative circuit much simpler than the solution based on Fig. 8.40, but it has two additional advantages. It is easier to understand, and it can,

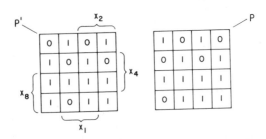

Fig. 8.40. Karnaugh map for parity-detector output.

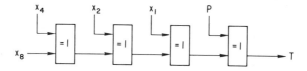

Fig. 8.41. Iterative parity detector consisting of four XOR gates.

if necessary, be extended to any number of digits, simply by adding additional XOR gates. By comparison, if a parity detector for a six-bit number had to be designed by conventional methods, a completely new solution would have to be derived using a six-variable Karnaugh map, and the resulting solution would be even more complicated.

8.9.2 Translating Binary to Reflected Cyclic Code

As a second example, an iterative circuit for translating from natural binary to reflected cyclic code is designed. As a starting point, Fig. 8.42 compares the numbers 0 to 15 expressed in these two codes. Notice that the first digits from the left are identical in both codes. Comparing the second digits, note that these are identical in all rows in which the previous digit of the binary code was 0, but are different if this bit was 1. The same principle holds for all other digits in the table. These results are summarized in the truth table of Fig. 8.43, where N_i represents a certain bit of the natural-binary code, and N_{i-1} and C_{i-1} are the bits in the two codes one column further to the right. The truth table is identical to that of the XOR function, and the results can be summarized as

$$C_{i-1} = N_i \oplus N_{i-1}$$

where the $\oplus$ symbol stands for the XOR function.

Decimal value	Natural binary code	Reflected cyclic code
0	0 0 0 0	0 0 0 0
1	0 0 0 1	0 0 0 1
2	0 0 1 0	0 0 1 1
3	0 0 1 1	0 0 1 0
4	0 1 0 0	0 1 1 0
5	0 1 0 1	0 1 1 1
6	0 1 1 0	0 1 0 1
7	0 1 1 1	0 1 0 0
8	1 0 0 0	1 1 0 0
9	1 0 0 1	1 1 0 1
10	1 0 1 0	1 1 1 1
11	1 0 1 1	1 1 1 0
12	1 1 0 0	1 0 1 0
13	1 1 0 1	1 0 1 1
14	1 1 1 0	1 0 0 1
15	1 1 1 1	1 0 0 0

Fig. 8.42. Comparison between natural-binary and reflected cyclic codes.

N_i	N_{i-1}	C_{i-1}
0	0	0
0	1	1
1	0	1
1	1	0

Fig. 8.43. Truth table for translating natural-binary into reflected cyclic code.

Hence, the required iterative circuit consists of a chain of XOR gates connected according to Fig. 8.44, where N_m and C_m represent the first bits from the left. The natural-binary code bits serve as inputs to the XOR gates, and the cyclic-code bits are their outputs. The circuit is not limited to four-bit numbers, but can be extended indefinitely for any number of bits by adding more XOR gates.

To translate in the opposite direction, from the reflected cyclic code back to the natural-binary code, the same truth table of Fig. 8.43 can be used, but with the two right-hand columns interchanged, that is, the N_i and C_{i-1} columns are now the input columns, and N_{i-1} is the output column. The resulting function becomes

$$N_{i-1} = N_i \oplus C_{i-1}$$

and the resulting iterative circuit shown in Fig. 8.45. Such a circuit can serve as decoding circuit for an absolute-position encoder based on the cyclic code.

8.9.3 Binary Comparator

As final example, an iterative binary comparator is designed. The function of such a comparator is shown schematically in Fig. 8.46. The comparator receives two binary numbers A and B (with any number of bits), and has three possible output signals. One of these must be 1 and the other two 0, depending on whether $A < B$, $A > B$, or $A = B$. Such comparators are, for instance, used in

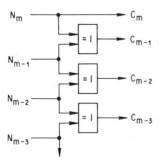

Fig. 8.44. Iterative circuit for translating natural-binary into reflected cyclic code.

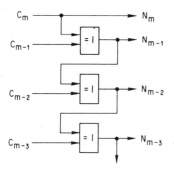

Fig. 8.45. Iterative circuit for translating reflected cyclic into natural-binary code.

numerical control systems, or any digital control system selecting one of three possible outputs (such as Forward, Backward, or Stop), depending on the relationship between the desired value A and the actual value B of the controlled variable.

A single module of the comparator is shown in Fig. 8.47. The two inputs are bits A_i and B_i of two n-bit numbers A and B. The module contains two INHIBITION gates with respective outputs $A_i'B_i$ and A_iB_i'. If $A_iB_i' = 1$, then $A_i > B_i$ (since $A_i = 1$ while $B_i = 0$). If $A_i'B_i = 1$, then $A_i < B_i$. If neither of these two conditions prevail, then $A_i = B_i$.

To compare two n-bit numbers, n such modules are required, connected as shown in Fig. 8.48. The comparison procedure is as follows: first, the two most significant digits A_n and B_n are compared. If $A_n > B_n$, then $A > B$; or, if $A_n < B_n$, then $A < B$. In either case, what happens with the other less-significant digits is irrelevant. Only if $A_n = B_n$ is there any point in comparing the next two digits, A_{n-1} and B_{n-1}, and the same procedure is repeated.

The $A_i < B_i$ outputs of the n modules are all led to an OR gate, so that if one of these outputs is 1, the conclusion is that $A < B$. Similarly, all $A_i > B_i$ outputs are connected to a second OR gate, which indicates whether $A > B$. The modules are connected so that each $A_i \neq B_i$ signal completely inhibits operation of all lower modules by keeping the output of all succeeding INHIBITION gates at 0, regardless of module inputs, If, however, $A_i = B_i$, then the next module is enabled to carry out its comparison. The final module produces an $A = B$ signal only if every $A_i = B_i$.

It is obvious that the method works only because the binary numbers A and B are expressed in the natural-binary code, with the weight of any digit being twice that of the succeeding digit (so that, for example, 1000 is greater than

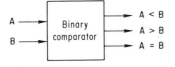

Fig. 8.46. Binary comparator.

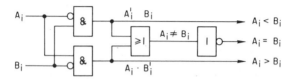

Fig. 8.47. Single module of an iterative binary comparator.

0111). Numbers in the cyclic code, for example, could not be compared in this fashion, but must first be translated into the natural-binary code.

This example, too, illustrates the advantage of iterative circuits. The circuit works with any number of digits, with each digit requiring an additional identical module. Integrated circuits implementing this principle are available, for example, 74LS85, which includes four comparator modules on a single chip.

In conclusion, it might be pointed out that all three examples presented here are combinational systems, since none of them contain flip-flops. However, many iterative circuits use flip-flops and are thus sequential systems. A typical example is an elevator control system. For n floors, there are $2n - 2$ UP or DOWN buttons, and n destination buttons inside the elevator. In addition, there are at least two limit switches per floor to signal elevator passage. A control system with that many input variables would be too complex to be designed by the Huffman method. Using iterative circuits, a standard module can be designed, depending on the exact control strategy required, with one module assigned to each floor. Since the control system must remember

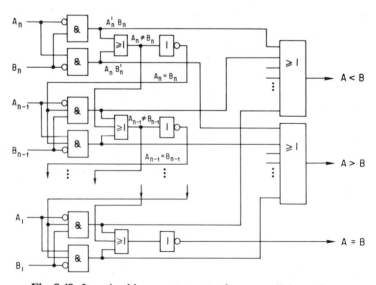

Fig. 8.48. Iterative binary comparator for two n-digit numbers.

previous button actuations that have not yet been serviced, flip-flops are required, so that this iterative circuit would be a sequential system.

For further discussion of iterative circuits, see most textbooks on switching theory, as listed in Chapter 3.

PROBLEMS

8.1. Integrate a pneumatic timer into the cascade-method solution for Problem 7.1 so that there is a 10-sec delay between the end of $B +$ and the beginning of $B -$ stroke.

8.2. Integrate a pneumatic timer into the cascade-method solution for Problem 7.1 so that the sequence only begins 10 sec after the START button has been pressed.

8.3. Design a pneumatic control circuit *not* based on the cascade method for the sequence START, $A +$, $B +$, $B -$, $A -$ by simply connecting each limit-valve output to the succeeding pilot-line input. This circuit does not function properly because of contradictory pilot signals. Modify this circuit by adding one or more pulse shapers so as to cure the defect.

8.4. Design a logic circuit that receives a steady train of pulses from an external oscillator, and a command signal x. Each time an $x = 1$ signal arrives, the circuit should output exactly nine successive pulses.

8.5. Modify the UP counter of Fig. 8.20 so that it can function as an electronic stop watch. The counter should receive a steady train of pulses from an external oscillator, whose frequency can be adjusted. The stop watch should be able to measure time periods up to 10 sec, with a resolution of 0.1 sec. The readout of the watch is to be binary.

8.6. An electronic logic circuit sends a decimal digit expressed in BCD (8-4-2-1) code by means of four binary digits, x_8, x_4, x_2, and x_1. This decimal digit is to be displayed on a seven-segment display illustrated in Fig. 8.22. Design a decoding circuit, shown schematically in Fig. P8.6, that actuates the middle horizontal segment of the display. Hint: First, fill in a truth table for output signal T; then transfer its contents to a Karnaugh map and derive the T function.

Fig. P8.6. Decoding circuit for Problem 8.6.

8.7. As described in Section 1.3.2, step motors are frequently "ramped" during starting and stopping to avoid exceeding the maximum pulse rate permitted under inertial loading. Design a simple, somewhat primitive, ramping circuit that whenever a START pulse is given outputs two low-frequency pulses (for start-up), followed by seven high-frequency pulses (for running), and, again two low-frequency pulses (for stopping). Use an external oscillator providing constant-frequency pulses, and any additional logic elements you want. To keep things simple, assume that the high-frequency output pulses have twice the frequency of the low-frequency ones. Check your solution by means of a sequence chart.

8.8. The figure shows a mechanism that takes a single line of beer cans arriving on a conveyor belt, and places them in six-pack configuration. Each arriving can triggers a limit switch. The first three cans are deflected to the left side; see Fig. P8.8(a). When the fourth can triggers the switch, a pneumatic cylinder is retracted, which changes the mechanism position, Fig. P8.8(b), so that the fourth, fifth, and sixth cans line up on the right side. When the seventh can triggers the switch, the cylinder extends and returns the mechanism to its original position, releasing the six-pack and starting a new cycle. Design a logic circuit, using a binary counter, that switches cylinder position every three cans. (The mechanism is taken from Ref. 8.23.)

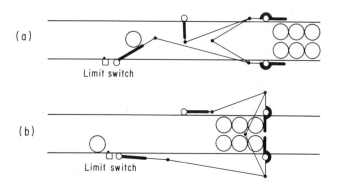

Fig. P8.8. Mechanism for Problem 8.8.

8.9. Translate each of the following decimal numbers into **(a)** a binary number, **(b)** a hexadecimal number, and **(c)** a BCD number:

(1) 333

(2) 4026

(3) 7113

(4) 10,254

(5) 15,010

(6) 217,666

8.10. Translate each of the following binary numbers into **(a)** a decimal number, **(b)** a hexadecimal number, and **(c)** a BCD number:

(1) 111000

(2) 1010000

(3) 10110001

(4) 1100111001

(5) 100110110001

(6) 101010101010

8.11. Translate each of the following hexadecimal numbers into **(a)** a decimal number, **(b)** a binary number, and **(c)** a BCD number:

(1) $24

(2) $2B

(3) $CBA

(4) $1F7D

(5) $FFFF

(6) $A771

8.12. Translate each of the following BCD numbers into **(a)** a decimal number, **(b)** a binary number, and **(c)** a hexadecimal number:

(1) 1000   0000   0110

(2) 1000   1001   0100

(3) 0001   1001   0111   0101

(4) 0100   0110   0110   1001

(5) 0101   0111   0110   0001   1001

(6) 1001   0011   0101   0000   0111

8.13. Design a decoding circuit for the eight-sector absolute-position encoder shown in Fig. 8.34. The circuit has three inputs, C_1, C_2, and C_3 (these are the photosensor signals), and eight outputs A to H (one for each sector), as shown in Fig. P8.13. The circuit should contain eight output gates, one for each output, A to H.

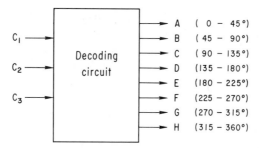

Fig. P8.13. Decoding circuit for Problem 8.13.

8.14. Repeat Problem 8.13, but instead of eight outputs, there are only three outputs, B_1, B_2, and B_3, that actuate three lamps, thus displaying the encoder position in natural-binary code. (For the first sector, 0–45°, the count is to be $0 = 000$, and for the final sector, 315–360°, it should be $7 = 111$.) *Hint:* The problem is best handled by setting up a truth table with three input and three output columns, and then transferring the information to three Karnaugh maps, in which the B output functions can be derived.

8.15. Draw a detailed sequence chart for the direction-detecting circuit of Fig. 8.38 that discloses possible malfunctions. Hint: Draw pairs of lines (0 and 1) for the signals A, B, Q, $\bar{Q}$, UP and DOWN. Enter A and B square waves for either direction of motion, with changes of direction at various encoder positions, and also including "dither." Then fill in the other lines, and check whether the UP and DOWN pulses agree with the actual encoder motion. Under what conditions is there encoder "runaway"? Under what conditions are extraneous DOWN pulses generated?

8.16. A street is lighted by a row of street lamps. Occasionally, a lamp may burn out, but because of budgetary restrictions, the city fathers have decided to send a repair crew only after three adjoining lamps have failed (since this creates a dangerous dark zone). Design an iterative circuit that gives a warning signal if three adjoining lamps are out. (Assume that the operation of each lamp is signaled by a photosensor.)

8.17. Solve Problem 6.12 using binary counters instead of the Huffman method.

8.18. Solve Problem 6.14 using a binary counter instead of the Huffman method.

REFERENCES

8.1. R. W. Smeaton (Ed.), *Switchgear and Control Handbook*, 2nd ed., McGraw-Hill, New York, 1987, Chapter 3.

8.2. N. Andreiev, "Timing Techniques—A Wide Range of Choices," *Control Engineering*, Apr. 1974, pp. 38–41.

8.3. J. C. Schwartz, "Understanding Timers for Better Control," *Instruments & Control Systems*, Dec. 1975, pp. 21–25.

8.4. F. M. Mims, *555 Timer IC Circuits*, Engineer's Mini-Notebook, Catalog No. 276-5010, Radio Shack, Tandy Corp., Fort Worth, TX 76102, 1984.

8.5. R. C. Frostholm, "Miniaturizing with Timers on a Chip," *Machine Design*, July 10, 1975, pp. 78–81.

8.6. J. Mattis and D. McCranie, "Time it with Integrated Circuits," *Instruments & Control Systems*, March 1974, pp. 55–58.

8.7. "1987 Control Products Specifier," *Control Engineering*, (Special Issue), (2nd Ed.) Nov. 1986.

8.8. R. Mayer, "The meaning Behind Time-delay Relay Specs," *Machine Design*, Apr. 20, 1978, pp. 50–54.

8.9. C. N. Benoit, "What to Know Before Specifying Electronic Timers," *Instruments & Control Systems*, Jan. 1974, pp. 61–64.

8.10. R. Culbertson, "Counters," *Hydraulics & Pneumatics*, Oct. 1985, pp. 67–72.

8.11. C. R. Asfahl, *Robots and Manufacturing Automation*, Wiley, New York, 1985, Chapter 2.

8.12. D. Bahniuk, "Speeding Data Entry with Bar Codes," *Machine Design*, Feb. 12, 1987, pp. 140–144.

8.13. M. Kutz (Ed.), *Mechanical Engineers' Handbook*, Wiley, New York, 1986, Chapter 3.

8.14. H. N. Norton, *Handbook of Transducers for Electronic Measuring Systems*, Prentice-Hall, Englewood Cliffs, N J, 1969 pp. 192–211.

8.15. W. Simon, *The Numerical Control of Machine Tools*, Edward Arnold, London, 1973, Chapter 3.

8.16. W. E. Snyder, *Industrial Robots: Computer Interfacing and Control*, Prentice-Hall, Englewood Cliffs, NJ, 1985, pp. 24–33.

8.17. J. D. Montgomery, "Optical Shaft Encoders," *Machine Design*, Sept. 12, 1985, pp. 89–90.

8.18. J. Borenstein, *The Nursing Robot System* (D. Sc. Thesis), Technion, Israel Institute of Technology, 1987, Fig. A.8.

8.19. Opto Slotted Coupler H21A1 and H22A1 data sheets, *Opto Electronic Device Data*, p. 3–34, Motorola Inc., Phoenix, AZ, 1983.

8.20. N. Walker, "Guarding Against Errors in Optical Encoders," *Machine Design*, Oct. 21, 1982, pp. 105–109.

8.21. S. A. Wingate, "Tracking Down Errors in Linear Encoders," *Machine Design*, Feb. 20, 1986, pp. 93–98.

8.22. E. Rapp and L. C. Smith, "Connecting Optical Encoders to Computers," *Machine Design*, July 8, 1982, pp. 93–97.

8.23. J. G. Tokarski and K. M. Marshek, "Novel Mechanisms II," *Mechanical Engineering*, July 1975, p.38.

CHAPTER 9

SEMIFLEXIBLE AUTOMATION: HARDWARE PROGRAMMERS

The control circuits, whose designs are described in previous chapters, are each intended for one specific application. If the requirements change (which often happens in industrial practice), the circuit must be redesigned, and, even worse, if the control circuit has already been built, it has to be rewired or reconnected. Hence, this kind of automation is termed *fixed automation*, each circuit being intended for a fixed application.

In contrast, Chapters 10 and 11 deal with *flexible automation*, in which microcomputer-like devices perform the required control functions, which are executed according to the program stored in the device's memory, that is, by means of software. Changing the requirements generally does not call for modifying the hardware, but only for modifying the program.

This chapter discusses an intermediate solution: use of hardware-type devices that bear no resemblance to computers, but can easily be programmed for any application. We call this kind of automation *semiflexible automation*.

9.1 DRUM PROGRAMMERS (STEPPING SWITCHES)

Drum programmers have to a great extent been displaced by programmable controllers (see Chapter 10). Nevertheless, they are discussed briefly, especially since many programmable controllers can be programmed to simulate a drum programmer. Hence, it is useful to know how these devices operate.

A typical drum programmer, as shown in Fig. 9.1, consists of a cylindrical drum having an array of holes into which plastic knob-like inserts can be pressed. These holes are arranged in a number of rows (equal to the number of

Fig. 9.1. Drum programmer. (Courtesy of Amerace Corp.)

steps in the sequence cycle) and a number of columns (equal to the number of output signals). A typical drum programmer might have 24 rows and 20 columns, although drums with up to 100 rows and columns exist. The drum is mounted on bearings and connected to a stepping motor whose function is to rotate the drum through angular increments corresponding to one row at a time.

At the base beneath the drum are a number of limit switches aligned with the columns, that is, one switch per column. The *active row* is defined as that row presently contacting the limit switches. Any column having a plastic insert in this active row actuates the switch assigned to it through physical contact between the insert and the switch actuating lever. Each switch is connected to an outside device.

Drum programmers can be operated in two different modes:

1. The motor driving the drum can be a timing motor, so that the drum is stepped at a fixed rate (i.e., synchronous operation).
2. The operation can be event-based, with the drum stepping to the next row upon arrival of a feedback signal signifying that the previous sequence step has been completed (i.e., asynchronous operation).

Synchronous operation is much simpler, since it does away with the need for sensors to check completion of each step and with the wiring connecting each sensor to the programmer. However, it is usually much slower than event-based operation, since the speed of the timing motor must be sufficiently slow to accommodate the slowest step in the sequence. Thus, time is wasted during all faster steps. By contrast, with event-based operation, the drum steps the moment an event is completed. Event-based operation is also more reliable. If the controlled system should stick due to some mechanical malfunction, the drum programmer waits until the trouble is fixed, rather than blindly go on stepping, as with synchronous operation.

We now show how the drum programmer is programmed. For the sake of illustration, assume that six cylinders, A to F, are to be actuated according to the sequence

$$\text{START, } A+, B+, B-, C+, C-, D+, A-, \begin{pmatrix} E+ \\ F+ \end{pmatrix}, F-, F+, F-, F+, \begin{pmatrix} D- \\ E- \\ F- \end{pmatrix}$$

We also assume that cylinders A, B, and C have actuating valves with a single solenoid and a return spring, whereas D, E, and F are actuated by valves with double solenoids, as illustrated in Fig. 9.2.

Assume that the drum has 24 rows and 20 columns. If we "unwind" the drum surface, we get the table shown in Fig. 9.3, where the horizontal rows represent steps 1 to 14, and the vertical columns the 10 limits switches being used. (Unused rows and columns are omitted.)

We now list the various sequence steps in the column labeled "Desired Event." In the next column, labeled "Signal for ADVANCE," we enter the limit-switch signal required to verify completion of the desired event. Note that parallel events (such as in steps 9 and 14) require the AND function to assure that *all* the events belonging to the step are completed. (These AND functions can be implemented with electronic AND gates, or by connecting the corresponding limit-switch contacts in series.) The drum programmer has a separate connecting post for each of the 24 rows, and the drum advances to the next row

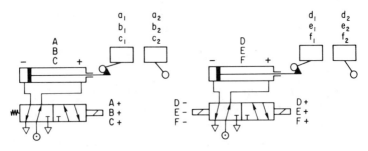

Fig. 9.2. Six-cylinder system for 14-step sequence.

Step	Desired event	Signal for advance	Switches I A+	II B+	III C+	IV D+	V D-	VI E+	VII E-	VIII F+	IX F-	X Motor
1	⟋	START										
2	A +	a_2	X									
3	B +	b_2	X	X								
4	B −	b_1	X									
5	C +	c_2	X		X							
6	C −	c_1	X									
7	D +	d_2	X			X						
8	A −	a_1										
9	E + F +	e_2 f_2						X		X		
10	F −	f_1									X	
11	F +	f_2								X		
12	F −	f_1									X	
13	F +	f_2								X		
14	D − E − F −	d_1 e_1 f_1					X		X		X	
15-24	GO HOME	⟋										X

Fig. 9.3. Solution for the example of Fig. 9.2 using a drum programmer.

only if a voltage appears at the proper connecting post. For example, if the system is currently at step 7, then row 7 is the active row, and the drum remains there until the d_2 limit switch is actuated, sending a voltage signal to the connecting post of row 7.

Each of the nine valve solenoids is connected to one of the available limit switches I to IX, as indicated at the top of the table. The drum is then programmed by placing inserts in each hole marked by an X. Note the difference in handling valves with and without return springs. For valves with return springs, the single solenoid must be provided with a continuous signal for as long as the cylinder is to remain extended. Thus, for example, inserts are placed into the $A +$ column for all rows from steps 2 to 7. At step 8, cylinder A is to retract, and this is achieved by simply not placing an insert. On the other hand, for valves with double solenoids, a single insert suffices for cylinder extension, but a second one is needed for retraction; see, for example, the $E +$ and $E -$ columns for steps 9 and 14.

Since the drum has 24 rows and only 14 of these are needed, rows 15 to 24 are not utilized, and the drum is programmed to step through these rows without delay ("Go Home"). This is done by placing inserts into rows 15 to 24 of column X, whose limit switch is connected to the drum motor. Thus, the drum returns automatically to row 1 and stops there until the next START signal, whereupon it steps to row 2 and the cycle begins anew.

The sequence can easily be modified by changing the positions of the inserts. Alternatively, if spare drums are available, different programs can be stored and the drum exchanged.

Instead of using drums with holes and inserts, it is possible to use cams mounted along a shaft, with each cam actuating a limit switch (or, if pneumatic circuits are to be actuated, a limit valve). Depending on the cam shape, the switch is either actuated or not. Such devices are, of course, less flexible when it comes to changing the sequence, since cams must be cut to the proper shape as compared to merely shifting plastic inserts. However, mass-produced cam drum programmers (usually with plastic cams) find wide use in appliances such as washing machines, where the water pump, solenoid valves, heating element, centrifuge, etc. are operated according to one or more fixed programs.

Rotating-cam limit switches are basically the same as the cam drum programmers just discussed. The difference is that the shape of each cam is adjustable, sometimes even while the cam is in motion. This provides much greater flexibility, since no special cams have to be cut, and the program can easily be changed at any time. Naturally, such devices are much more expensive than mass-produced fixed-cam drum programmers, and are, therefore, not used in consumer goods such as washing machines, but only for the control of industrial processes. A typical rotating-cam limit switch is shown in Fig. 9.4.

This leads us to a group of devices that includes programmable timers and programmable limit switches, which exist in a no-man's land located between such elements as limit switches (Chapter 2), timers (Chapter 8), and programmable controllers (Chapter 10).

Fig. 9.4. Rotating-cam limit switch. (Courtesy of Gemco Corp.)

9.2 PROGRAMMABLE TIMERS AND LIMIT SWITCHES

The shaft of a rotating-cam limit switch can be linked mechanically to a machine, so that the cams turn at a speed proportional to machine speed. In this way, various elements of a production system can be synchronized. A second method is to drive the shaft by a synchronous timing motor, in which case the device becomes a *programmable timer*. In both methods, the device works on a time base without closed loop or feedback signals, unlike the event-based operation discussed in connection with drum programmers.

The next stage of sophistication is to replace some or all elements of this programmable timer by solid-state components. Thus, the limit switches actuated by the cams can be replaced by solid-state relays. Next, the timing motor can be replaced by a solid-state timer, and the cams by optically read programmed cards, or even by electronic PROM memory modules. For further discussion of *solid-state programmable timers*, see Ref. (9.1).

This bring us to *programmable limit switches*. These act like programmable timers, except that they do not have an absolute time base. Instead, the time base is provided by a rotary transducer linked mechanically so as to rotate once for each complete machine cycle. This transducer could be an absolute-position encoder outputting a BCD signal (see Chapter 8), or an analog resolver producing an output voltage that is then converted electronically into a BCD signal. The transducer can, if necessary, be at a distance from the programmable limit switch.

Programmable limit switches usually have a digital display of the shaft position, as shown in Fig. 9.5. The output signals are produced electronically

Fig. 9.5. Solid-state programmable limit switch. (Courtesy of Gemco Corp.)

instead of with the use of cams. The device is programmed either using thumbwheels (straightforward and easy to understand) or using a small keyboard, in which case the program is stored in solid-state memory, and the device becomes very similar to the programmable controllers discussed in Chapter 10. Programmable limit switches are further discussed in Ref. (9.2).

9.3   CARD AND TAPE READERS

For these devices, the program information is stored on punched tapes (paper or plastic) or cards. The information is read using photocells or electric brushes. The brush must be wide enough to provide signal continuity for consecutive holes (i.e., make-before-break action). As with drum programmers, each column in the tape or card provides an output signal, provided a hole is present in the active row.

Punched tapes have the advantage in that there is practically no limit as to sequence length. If desired, the two tape ends can be connected to produce a continuous loop, so that the sequence repeats automatically.

As with drum programmers, card and tape readers can be stepped either in a time-based or event-based manner. Punched tapes are, of course, much less expensive and more compact than drums, which is an advantage where many programs must be stored. On the other hand, any change requires preparation of a new tape.

Card and tape readers have been largely replaced by programmable controllers or microcomputers, in which the programs are stored either on magnetic media (tape or disk), or in solid-state memory.

9.4   MATRIX BOARDS

Figure 9.6 shows part of a matrix board. Underneath the board are a number of horizontal wires (A to E) and vertical wires (1 to 5), located in different planes so that there is normally no electric contact between them. To connect any row

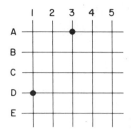

Fig. 9.6. Part of a matrix board.

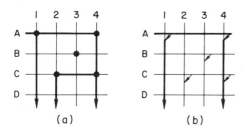

Fig. 9.7. Matrix board (a) with a sneak path, and (b) without sneak path.

with a given column, a plug is inserted at the appropriate junction. In the figure, two such plugs are shown, connecting wires A and 3, and also D and 1.

Figure 9.7(a) shows a matrix board with five plugs. Obviously, any voltage applied to row A reaches columns 1 and 4, because of the plugs at junctions A–1 and A–4. However, as indicated by the thick lines, the voltage from column 4 penetrates row C (because of the plug at C–4), and thus also column 2 (because of the plug at C–2). This is termed a "sneak path," because lines A and 2 were not intended to be connected.

To avoid sneak paths, plugs with built-in diodes are used, as shown in Fig. 9.7(b). Assuming that direct current is used, the current can only flow in the direction of the arrow. Thus, voltage applied to row A can reach columns 1 and 4, but the voltage from column 4 cannot penetrate row C, because the current would have to flow against the arrow.

It should be stressed that matrix boards are not programmers in their own right. Rather, they are commonly used in conjunction with other devices to facilitate changing connections between points. Thus, a matrix board might be used to connect a drum programmer or a programmable controller to a controlled system, so that connections can be changed easily by shifting the plugs on the board, rather than rewiring the system.

Obviously, two points can also be connected using a wire with banana plugs. However, if many such wires are needed, it results in a so-called "rat's nest," that is, a tangle of wires difficult to trace or to untangle. A matrix board, by comparison, is much neater: a glance is sufficient to tell which lines are connected, and the plugs are easily removed or shifted, since they do not interfere with each other. Also, some manufacturers supply plugs with built-in LEDs that glow when voltage is present. This makes it possible to tell at a glance which lines are live.

9.5 PROGRAMMABLE COUNTERS (SEQUENCERS)

Programmable counters (also known by various other names, such as step counters, programmable sequence controllers, ring-counter programmers, modular sequencers, etc.) consist of a number of identical modules, with each module assigned to carry out one step or event of the sequence.

9.5.1   Advantages of Programmable Counters

Figure 9.8 shows a schematic representation of a programmable counter. For now, we disregard the actual content of the modules. Instead, the counter can be visualized as a black box having n input lines (x_1 to x_n) and n output lines (z_1 to z_n). Only one module is active at any given time. If module i is active, then its output z_i is "hot" (i.e., logic 1), and thus actuates any equipment connected to it. This initiates step i, and when this is completed, input signal x_i becomes 1 (due to an appropriate sensor connected to line x_i). The moment $x_i = 1$, module $i + 1$ becomes active and module i is turned *off*, thus initiating the next sequence step. After the last step is completed, sensor signal x_n automatically reactivates module No. 1, and the system is ready for the next cycle (hence the name "ring-counter programmer").

Programmable counters possess several important advantages:

1. Programming is extremely easy. All that is required is to connect the various sensors to the input lines x, and the equipment to be actuated to the output lines z, according to the desired sequence. No special design method has to be mastered, and the circuit design time is almost zero.
2. For the same reason, sequence changes are very easy to carry out, simply by changing input and output connections. The system thus represents the ultimate in flexibility.
3. The method is suitable for sequences of any length, by connecting additional modules, depending on sequence length. Similarly, if the sequence is shortened, any unused modules can be removed and utilized elsewhere.
4. All modules are identical, and can therefore be easily built by the user.
5. The method is suitable for any type of logic elements: pneumatic valves, moving-part logic elements, electronic logic gates, etc.
6. Because of its extreme simplicity, the programmable counter is easy to explain to maintenance and operating personnel.
7. Trouble shooting is very simple: thus, if a certain sequence step i should fail to take place, we first check whether $z_i = 1$. If so, then the fault lies in the equipment to be actuated. If $z_i = 0$, we check whether $x_{i-1} = 1$. If it is

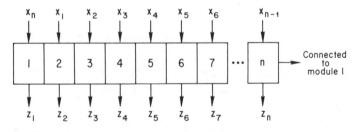

Fig. 9.8. Schematic representation of programmable counter.

not, then the fault lies in the sensor indicating completion of the previous step. If $x_{i-1} = 1$ and $z_i = 0$, then the fault lies in module i, which can readily be replaced by an identical spare module.

8. The method is useable with various START and STOP modes, and with multipath sequences—more about that later.

After having read this impressive list of advantages, the reader may wonder why any other method should ever be employed. The answer is simple: programmable counters are wasteful as to the number of required elements. Thus, they are not suitable where element economy is the primary objective, for example, where a control circuit for a specific sequence must be duplicated many times. On the other hand, for one-of-a-kind circuits, the engineering time saved in circuit design and the other advantages just listed may more than make up for the cost of the additional switching elements required.

9.5.2 Sequences with Parallel and/or Repeated Events

For simple program sequences (i.e., without parallel or repeated events), the programmable counter is connected as just described. However, for parallel events, additional AND gates are required, and repeated events require additional OR gates. This is illustrated by means of the following hypothetical sequence for actuating cylinders (assuming cylinder-actuating valves without return springs):

$$\text{START}, A+, B+, C+, A-, \begin{pmatrix} B- \\ C- \end{pmatrix}, A+, A-$$

For this sequence, the programmable counter is connected as shown in Fig. 9.9. Module 6 produces parallel events $B-$ and $C-$. Therefore, the resulting sensor signals b_1 and c_1 must be connected to module 7 through an AND gate to assure that the next step $A+$ only commences after both $B-$ and $C-$ are completed.

The sequence also has repeated events $A+$ and $A-$, each of which occurs twice. Therefore, the two output signals from modules 2 and 7 must be connected to $A+$ through an OR gate, in order to prevent short-circuiting the outputs of these modules. The same applies to modules 5 and 8. If these outputs were connected, the "high" output signal coming from the presently active module would penetrate into the other inactive module and cause a malfunction. The OR gate prevents this by isolating the outputs.

Note that these auxiliary AND and OR gates are *not* part of the standard modules of the programmable counter, but must be added by the user where required, as just illustrated.

Also note that modules 1 and 2 can be combined by ANDing the a_1 and START signals, thus saving one module. Usually, no additional AND gate is needed for this, since the a_1 signal can simply be connected as input to the device producing the START signal (which is usually a push-button switch, or a 3/2

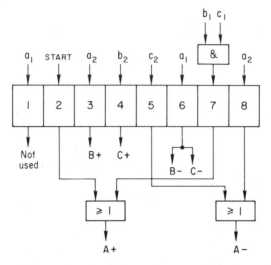

Fig. 9.9. Programmable-counter circuit for a sequence with both parallel and repeated events. (Assumes cylinder-actuating valves without return springs.)

valve with push-button actuation and a return spring). This produces a so-called "passive AND gate" (see Chapter 7).

If cylinder-actuating valves with return springs are to be used, sustained output signals are required, and the programmable counter has to be connected as shown in Fig. 9.10. Note that the output lines of modules 6 and 8 are not utilized. This is because of the absence of $X-$ pilot lines. The $X-$ stroke is obtained by cutting off the $X+$ pilot signal.

Because of the need for sustained outputs, OR gates are required here even if there are no repeated actions. Also, these OR gates may require a large number

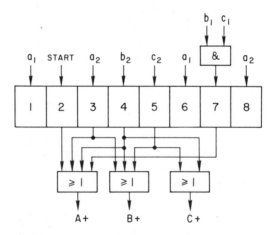

Fig. 9.10. Programmable-counter circuit for the sequence of Fig. 9.9, but using cylinder-actuating valves with return springs.

of inputs, which can cause problems if the available OR gates only have a fan-in of 2 (e.g., shuttle valves). One way to solve this problem is to replace these OR gates by one auxiliary flip-flop, which provides a sustained output until it is reset. When doing this, we are, in effect, replacing the cylinder-actuating valve with a return spring by one without a return spring. It would, of course, be much simpler to use valves without return springs to begin with, and this is the recommended course of action when using programmable counters.

9.5.3 Construction of Programmable Counters

A number of manufacturers offer pneumatic programmable counters, which use either miniature pneumatic valves, or moving-part logic (MPL) elements (described in Chapter 4). One of these is shown in Fig. 9.11. The modules, based on MPL elements, are mounted on a rail, with each module engaging the two adjoining ones, which takes care of the required internal connections. The tubing for input and output signals is connected at the back. Each module also has a red indicator button, which pops out when the module is active—a help in troubleshooting. For a description of another commercial programmable counter, see Ref. (9.3).

While ready made programmable counters provide neatly packaged units convenient to use, the user can save money by assembling the modules. For this, the do-it-yourself user has to know the content of the module. The purpose of this section is to supply this information.

The construction of the individual module depends mainly on the operating code used. Although there are a number of possible codes that could be utilized, see Refs. (9.4) and (9.5) for a detailed discussion, the most practical ones are:

1. the one-hot code,
2. the two-hot code,
3. the accumulating code.

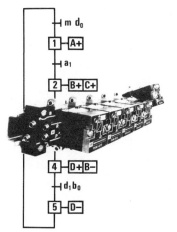

Fig. 9.11. Programmable counter based on MPL elements. (Courtesy of Telemecanique.)

The logic diagram of a programmable counter using the one-hot code is shown in Fig. 9.12. Each module consists of one RS flip-flop and one AND gate, with the AND gate providing the flip-flop SET signal. Assume that flip-flop 1 is presently set. As a result, output signal $y_1 = 1$, and this serves as output z_1, which actuates any equipment required for sequence step 1. Flip-flop output y_1 is also connected to the AND gate of module 2, thus enabling this AND gate to accept sensor signal x_1, which appears when step 1 is completed. This, in turn, sets flip-flop 2, causing $y_2 = 1$.

When any flip-flop output y_i becomes 1, it does three things:

(a) Turns on output z_i, thus initiating the next step.
(b) Resets the previous flip-flop $i-1$.
(c) Enables the AND gate of the next module $i + 1$.

It is obvious from this description that only one flip-flop is set at any given time, hence the name "one-hot code." The purpose of the AND gates is to prevent setting a false flip-flop in case of repeated events. For example, referring to the sequence of Fig. 9.9, note that the a_2 signal enters both modules 3 and 8. If these AND gates were not present, this a_2 signal would set both flip-flops 3 and 8, which contradicts the principle of the one-hot code. The AND gate in module 3 is only enabled when $y_2 = 1$, so that flip-flop 3 is not set by the a_2 signal associated with step 7. Thus, the various modules are only activated in their proper order.

From Chapter 8, we realize that programmable counters can be considered as a special type of shift register, in which a single 1 bit is shifted through the various stages.

It should be stressed that all flip-flops, AND gates, and connections between the modules shown in Fig. 9.12 are inside the black box comprising the

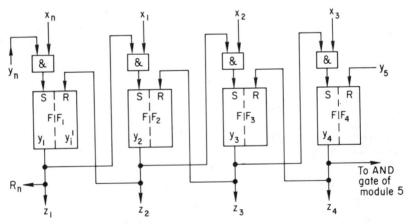

Fig. 9.12. Programmable counter based on the one-hot code.

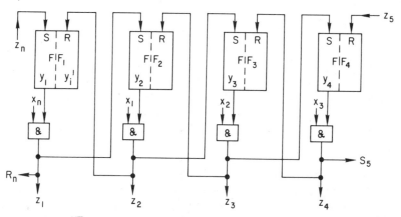

Fig. 9.13. Programmable counter based on the two-hot code.

programmable counter, and therefore not visible to the user. All the user sees are input connecting points x_1 to x_n, and outputs z_1 to z_n. The only exceptions are the auxilary AND and OR gates that may have to be added, as described in connection with Fig. 9.9.

Figure 9.13 shows a programmable counter using the two-hot code. Here, too, each module consists of one flip-flop and one AND gate, but the AND gate is connected at the flip-flop output. The operation is similar to that of the one-hot code counter, with one difference. Input signal x_i produces not only the output signal z_{i+1}, but also the RESET signal for flip-flop i and the SET signal for flip-flop $i + 2$, so that two flip-flops $i + 1$ and $i + 2$ are in their set conditions simultaneously, hence the name "two-hot code."

As was first pointed out in Refs. (9.4) and (9.5), pneumatic programmable counters based on the two-hot code have an important advantage: only a single 3/2 valve is required per module, as illustrated in Fig. 9.14. This is accomplished by utilizing the 3/2 valve as both flip-flop and passive AND gate, using the

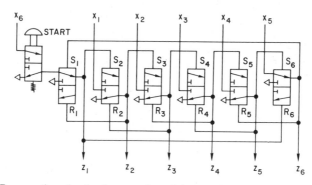

Fig. 9.14. Pneumatic-valve implementation of the two-hot code programmable counter (six stages).

principle explained in Section 7.4; see line 164 of Table 7.3. (Since the inverted flip-flop outputs y' are not utilized, a single-output 3/2 valve can be used, rather than a more expensive 5/2 valve.) Thus, the hardware required is only one 3/2 valve per module, rather than two 3/2 valves needed in counters based on the one-hot code. (Of course, the additional auxiliary AND and OR gates shown in Fig. 9.9 may also be required, as explained there.)

(Note that the idea of using passive AND gates cannot be used with the one-hot code, since the counter of Fig. 9.12 requires the y_i signal separately, and this is not available if the 3/2 valve is used as both a flip-flop *and* passive AND gate, as in Fig. 9.14.)

As against this important advantage, the two-hot code counter unfortunately also has a drawback: any output signal z_i is only 1 as long as input signal x_{i-1} remains 1. This does not matter if z_i actuates equipment not requiring sustained actuating signals (such as cylinder-actuating valves without return springs). However, it can cause problems if sustained actuating signals are required (such as for valves with return springs). To illustrate, assume that the program sequence includes stroke $A+$, followed by two parallel strokes $A-$ and $B+$ carried out simultaneously. Completion of $A+$ produces sensor signal a_2, which in turn must produce actuating signal, $B+$. However, since stroke $A+$ is immediately followed by $A-$, the a_2 signal disappears. If the circuit of Fig. 9.13 is used, the resulting $B+$ signal also disappears, so that the return spring in the actuating valve of cylinder B prevents completion of stroke $B+$.

This drawback can be overcome by making it a point to use only cylinder-actuating valves without return springs. If other equipment requiring sustained signals must be activated, the problem can be solved by adding an auxiliary flip-flop at the module output, as explained in Section 9.5.2. In other words, the momentary output signal of the module sets this flip-flop, which then provides the required sustained signal. When this signal needs to be cut off later in the sequence, the corresponding module must reset the auxiliary flip-flop.

Because of the 50% reduction in the number of required valves or MPL elements, it is recommended that the two-hot code be used for all pneumatic programmable counters. (The idea is not applicable to electronic gates.)

With the third possible operating code listed, the accumulating code, a new flip-flop is set at each step without resetting any previous ones. Thus, during step 1, only flip-flop 1 is set. During step 2, flip-flops 1 and 2 are set, and so on. By the end of the sequence, all flip-flops are in their set condition. They must then all be reset together before the sequence can restart. A programmable counter based on this code is described in Refs. (9.6) and (9.7). This kind of counter is advantageous where cylinder-actuating valves with return springs must be used, since the accumulating code automatically provides sustained output signals. To cut off any output, auxiliary INHIBITION gates must be added. The accumulating counter has two drawbacks:

1. The modules are not identical anymore, since some consist of a flip-flop, and others of an AND gate, depending on the character of the sequence. The user must decide which element to use for each module, and also when to add an

auxiliary INHIBITION gate. Thus, the advantage of having standard identical modules and almost zero circuit design time has been sacrificed.

2. The method only works properly if each flip-flop remains at its previous condition when both SET and RESET signals are given simultaneously (i.e., so-called "memory dominating" flip-flops). Ordinarily, most directional-control valves without return springs fulfill this condition. However, in some applications, the limit valves may be connected to a separate air-supply line having its own pressure regulator, so that we cannot be sure that all "Logic 1" signals have identical pressure levels. Thus, if the SET signal reaching the flip-flop should have a higher pressure level than the RESET signal, the flip-flop becomes "set dominating," and the circuit might malfunction.

9.5.4   Programmable-Counter Operation

When a newly assembled programmable counter is operated for the first time, it is necessary to initialize it, in order to place all the flip-flops into their proper initial condition. For the one-hot code, this is done by setting the first flip-flop, and resetting all others. For the two-hot code, the first and last flip-flops must be set, and all others reset. For safety reasons, it is advisable to first disconnect the air supply or electric power to all position sensors (i.e., limit valves or switches) to prevent arbitrary cylinder motions while the counter is being initialized.

If the programmable counter is made of pneumatic valves, it remains in its last position when the air supply is shut off, because of the valve's mechanical memory. Thus, when the air supply is renewed, the counter continues at that sequence step at which it left off. If it is desired to skip the remaining steps and start the sequence again from the beginning, it is necessary to reinitialize the counter, as just described, and also any cylinder-actuating valves that may not be in their proper initial position.

In applications where initializing has to be done frequently, it may be worthwhile to permanently connect a line carrying the initializing signal to the proper flip-flop SET and RESET inputs and cylinder-actuating valves, using OR gates (i.e., shuttle valves, for pneumatic systems) so that the various inputs remain isolated. With such an arrangement, the counter can be initialized by pressing a single button.

With programmable counters made of electronic gates, reinitializing has to be done after each power interruption, since electronic flip-flops generally assume a random state when power is resumed.

A second aspect of programmable-counter operation relates to START operating modes. In most applications, a simple START button, as in Fig. 9.14, is sufficient to start the sequence. Sometimes, however, there are more sophisticated requirements, and these can easily be satisfied with programmable counters. Three such special START operating modes are discussed here:

Maintained START Signal. Safety considerations may require that the operator keep pressing the START button until a certain step in the sequence is reached. This is easily accomplished by ANDing the START

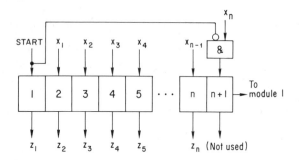

Fig. 9.15. Programmable counter with a single-cycle START mode.

signal with each of the x inputs up to the last counter module at which the
START signal is to be maintained. Once that module is reached, the
sequence continues normally even though the START button is released.

Single-Cycle START Signal. Each START signal must produce one and only
one cycle. For safety reasons, the cycle can only be repeated if START is
actuated *after* the previous cycle is completed. This assures the operator's
presence at the beginning of the cycle, and can easily be obtained by using
the modification shown in Fig. 9.15.

As seen from the figure, one additional counter module $n + 1$ is required,
and also one auxiliary INHIBITION gate giving the output $x_n(\text{START})'$,
which serves as input to module $n + 1$. When the START signal is first
given, module 1 is activated, and the sequence begins. When the last
sequence step n is completed, sensor signal x_n becomes 1, but this signal
cannot pass the INHIBITION gate unless START has reverted to 0. If the
operator attempts to tie down the START button permanently, the
counter stalls at module $n + 1$ and blocks the next cycle. START must first
be brought back to 0, and then reset to 1 to initiate the next cycle.

Single-Step Operation This mode is useful for testing a new sequence, for
diagnosing faults, and for adjusting the controlled machine or system. It is
easily obtained by cutting off the air supply to the position-sensing limit
valves (or voltage to the limit switches), and then introducing short air-
supply pulses through a special push-button valve each time an additional
sequence step is desired. Without the air supply, the limit valve cannot
send an x signal to the next counter module, so that the sequence halts.

9.5.5   Programmable Counters for Multipath Sequences

Relay circuits for multipath sequences are described in Section 5.4.3 of Chapter
5. The same principles can be used with programmable counters. (Figures 9.16
to 9.19 have been reproduced from Ref. 9.5 with kind permission of Longman,
London.)

Figure 9.16 shows the adaptation of a one-hot code programmable counter
to a sequence with *two simultaneous parallel paths*. As seen from the figure, two

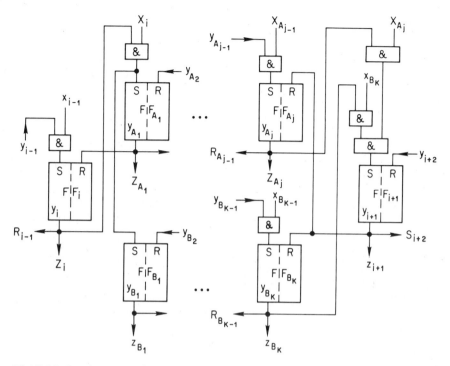

Fig. 9.16. One-hot code programmable counter for two simultaneous parallel paths.

parallel counter sections must be installed for the parallel paths A and B. Completion of step i is signalled by $y_i x_i = 1$. This sets both flip-flops A_1 and B_1, thus actuating paths A and B simultaneously. Completion of path A is indicated by $y_{A_j} x_{A_j} = 1$, and that of path B by $y_{B_k} x_{B_k} = 1$. Two auxiliary AND gates are needed to produce these terms. (Since the paths are not necessarily of equal length, j and k do not have to be equal.) These two signals are then connected through the AND gate of module $i + 1$, supplying the SET signal to flip-flop $i + 1$ only after *both* paths are completed. The sequence then continues along the single path, starting with output z_{i+1}.

Figure 9.17 shows a one-hot code programmable counter for handling *two alternative paths, A or B*. Such an arrangement is useful for controlling multipurpose machines or systems. The path to be implemented is chosen by an outside signal p, which could be introduced manually, or automatically using the output of some sensor or logic circuit. If $p = 1$, path A is followed, whereas $p = 0$ selects path B. Here, too, completion of step i is signalled by $y_i x_i = 1$. At that point, $p = 1$ sets flip-flop A_1, whereas $p = 0$ sets flip-flop B_1. The $y_{A_j} x_{A_j}$ and $y_{B_k} x_{B_k}$ terms are connected through an OR gate, so that completion of *either* path sets flip-flop $i + 1$. Note that several auxiliary gates are required, apart from the regular AND gates belonging to each module.

If there are more than two alternative paths, more than one p signal is required. Thus, the combination of two inputs p_1 and p_2 could be used to select

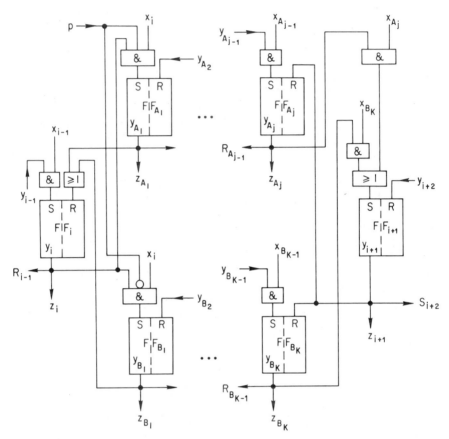

Fig. 9.17. One-hot code programmable counter for two alternative parallel paths (path A for $p = 1$ and path B for $p = 0$).

between four alternative paths, depending on whether $p_1 p_2 = 00, 01, 10,$ or 11. Similarly, n p signals can handle 2^n alternative paths.

Figure 9.18 shows a circuit giving the *option of skipping certain sequence steps*. Upon completion of the last obligatory step i, $y_i x_i = 1$. If at that moment $p = 1$, then flip-flop A_1 is set, and the sequence continues through the optional steps of the A branch up to A_j, and then on to the next obligatory step $i + 1$. If, however, $p = 0$, then steps A_1 to A_j are skipped, and the counter jumps directly to step $i + 1$.

As a final example of multipath programs, Fig. 9.19 shows a circuit giving the *option of repeating certain steps*. Up to step A_j, the counter implements a single-path sequence. Upon completion of step A_j (indicated by $y_{A_j} x_{A_j} = 1$), if $p = 1$, then flip-flop $i + 1$ is set, and the sequence continues without repeating any steps. If however, $p = 0$, then flip-flop A_1 is set, and steps A_1 to A_j are repeated.

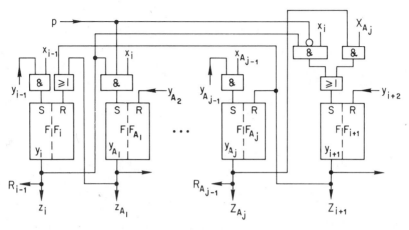

Fig. 9.18. One-hot code programmable counter with the option of skipping steps (steps A_1 to A_j are skipped if $p = 0$).

As long as p remains 0, these steps are repeated again and again. (For this circuit to function properly, j must be > 2. If there are only two repeated steps, a third "dummy" module must be inserted into the counter.)

In the four examples just given, programmable counters using the one-hot code are used. As explained previously, the two-hot code is preferable with pneumatic programmable counters. Circuits for these four examples using the two-hot code are presented in Ref. (9.5).

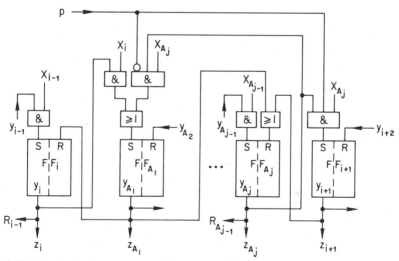

Fig. 9.19. One-hot code programmable counter with the option of repeating steps (steps A_1 to A_j are repeated if $p = 0$).

9.5.6   Conclusions

Programmable counters have been used for many years in Europe. For some reason, they have never achieved the popularity they deserve in the United States. Because of their simplicity, ease of application, and flexibility, they should be considered seriously for small, and medium-size applications, for which the purchase of a programmable controller (see Chapter 10) cannot be economically justified. In fact, we could define the programmable counter as a "poor man's programmable controller."

The main application of programmable counters is in controlling pneumatic actuators. Since the counter modules can be connected directly to the actuating valves, the considerable cost of the I/O modules required with programmable controllers or microcomputers is eliminated. As shown in Section 9.5.3, pneumatic counters are best implemented using the two-hot code.

Programmable counters can easily be assembled using electronic flip-flops and AND gates. Printed-circuit boards containing a number of such electronic counter modules have been marketed in the past. Alternatively, integrated-circuit chips implementing shift registers (see Chapter 8) could be utilized. However, because of the low voltage and current outputs of such electronic modules, I/O modules must be added to interface with the controlled equipment, just as with programmable controllers or microcomputers.

PROBLEMS

For the following sequences, draw diagrams similar to Fig. 9.9 that show the input and output connections, and any auxiliary gates or flip-flops that may be required with a programmable counter.

9.1.   START, $A+$, $A-$, $B+$, $C+$, $B-$, $C-$ using cylinder-actuating values without return springs.

9.2.   Repeat Problem 9.1, but with cylinder-actuating valves with return springs, and a programmable counter based on the one-hot code.

9.3.   Repeat Problem 9.2, but with the two-hot code.

9.4.   START, $A+$, $A-$, $B+$, $A+$, $A-$, $B-$ using cylinder-actuating valves without return springs.

9.5.   Repeat Problem 9.4, but with cylinder-actuating valves with return springs, and a programmable counter based on the one-hot code.

9.6.   Repeat Problem 9.5, but with the two-hot code.

9.7.   START, $A+$, $A-$, $\left(\begin{matrix} A+ \\ B+ \end{matrix} \right)$, $B-$, $A-$ using cylinder-actuating valves without return springs.

9.8. Repeat Problem 9.7, but with cylinder-actuating valves with return springs, and a programmable counter based on the one-hot code.

9.9. Repeat Problem 9.8, but with the two-hot code.

9.10. START, $A+$, $\left(\dfrac{B+,\ B-}{C+,\ C-}\right)$, $A-$ with simultaneous parallel paths, using cylinder-actuating valves without return springs, and a programmable counter based on the one-hot code.

9.11. START, $A+$, $\overset{\nearrow(B+,\ B-)\searrow}{\searrow(C+,\ C-)\nearrow}A-$ with alternative parallel paths, using cylinder-actuating valves without return springs, and a programmable counter based on the one-hot code.

9.12. Solve Problem 8.8 using a programmable counter.

REFERENCES

9.1. P. G. Mesniaeff, "Understanding Solid-state Timers," *Machine Design*, June 11, 1981, pp. 139–141.

9.2. S. Kumar, "Limit Switches You Can Program," *Machine Design*, July 9, 1981, pp. 135–140.

9.3. D. D. Payne, "Pneumatic Sequencers," *Machine Design*, June 9, 1983, pp. 89–93.

9.4. D. W. Pessen and G. Golan, "Do-it-Yourself Programmable Controllers," *Hydraulics & Pneumatics*, Oct. 1975, pp. 182–187.

9.5. D. Pessen and W. Huebl, *Programmable Sequence Controllers for Automation Systems*, Longman, London, 1979.

9.6. B. E. McCord, "New Technique Avoids Common Pitfalls in Designing Pneumatic Controls," *Machine Design*, Oct. 11, 1979, pp. 92–97.

9.7. B. E. McCord, *Designing Pneumatic Control Circuits*, Dekker, New York, 1983.

CHAPTER 10

FLEXIBLE AUTOMATION: PROGRAMMABLE CONTROLLERS

10.1 INTRODUCTION

Programmable [logic] controllers (or PLCs) are microcomputer-like instruments designed to control industrial equipment. Producing *on–off* voltage outputs (but also analog signals), they can actuate elements such as electric motors (and thus pumps, conveyor belts, or any other motor-driven equipment), solenoids (and thus pneumatic or hydraulic solenoid valves), fans, heaters, alarms (such as warning lights or horns), and other electric equipment. PLCs are vital components of modern automation systems. They were first applied in automobile assembly plants about 20 years ago but, by now, they have penetrated almost every industry. Their importance is mirrored by the fact that a conference and exhibit devoted solely to programmable controllers is held each year in the United States. At the 1987 conference, more than 100 manufacturers exhibited their programmable controllers and associated equipment.

In its most basic and original form, the PLC is a software-based general-purpose equivalent of a relay panel; however, the typical PLC can do many things that electromechanical relays cannot do, such as timing and counting. Since PLCs are programmed like microcomputers, using an easy-to-learn programming language (more about that later), a given PLC can be programmed to control a variety of machines or systems. Most important, the program can easily be changed for new jobs or changes in production routines. PLCs are thus much more flexible than hard-wired relay panels.

PLCs generally take up much less space and cost less than medium- or large-size relay panels, since a single PLC can often replace several hundred relays.

Using a PLC also eliminates the often appreciable cost of wiring the relay panel it replaces. On the other hand, there might be little economic justification in purchasing a PLC to solve a small control problem that can be handled by five or six relays—although some PLC manufacturers claim otherwise. Apart from the cost factor, PLCs are usually more reliable, since relays have a limited life (typically in the order of 10^5 to 10^6 duty cycles). Also, many PLCs include various diagnostic features that not only allow self-checking, but also the checking of the interface equipment to which they are connected.

Early PLCs were called "programmable logic controllers," and were designed only for logic-based sequencing jobs (*on–off* signals). Many of today's modern PLCs also accept proportional signals (either in analog or digital form), and can perform simple arithmetic calculations or comparisons. The more sophisticated ones can also generate analog outputs, and even act as PID (proportional, integral, and derivative action) process controllers. For these reasons, the word "logic" and the letter "L" were dropped from the name long ago. This frequently causes confusion, since the letters "PC" mean different things to different people, for example, "Pocket Calculator," "Printed Circuit," "Program Counter" (as part of a microprocessor's internal architecture), and, of course, "Personal Computer." To avoid this confusion, there has been a tendency lately to restore the letter "L" and revive the designation "PLC," and this practice is followed here.

It might be useful at this point to outline the differences between PLCs and microcomputers:

1. In theory, microcomputers can be programmed to perform most of the functions of PLCs. However, general-purpose microcomputers are not built to operate reliably under industrial conditions, where they can be exposed to heat, humidity, corrosive atmosphere, mechanical shock and vibration, electromagnetic noise, unreliable ac power with dropping voltages, voltage spikes, etc. PLCs, by comparison, are especially designed for industrial environments.

2. While microcomputers can be interfaced with external equipment, this requires special circuit cards. PLCs, by comparison, come with input or output (I/O) modules available for different voltage levels, and especially designed to connect to industrial equipment. PLCs are easily interfaced with hundreds of input and output lines, something difficult to do with most microcomputers.

3. PLCs usually contain various diagnostic features, which facilitate troubleshooting. They are built for easy maintenance: defective modules are simply exchanged, rather than replacing components.

4. PLCs are usually programmed using relay-type ladder diagrams (at least, in the United States), although programming languages similar to BASIC are becoming more common. This is so because many potential users are familiar with relay-circuit ladder diagrams (see Chapter 5).

5. Although many PLCs are able to accept analog data and to perform simple arithmetical operations, they really cannot compete with microcomputers when it comes to complicated mathematical routines.

6. PLCs are usually much slower than microcomputers. This is because the PLC scans the program line by line (a feature discussed in Section 10.4), and only comes back to a given line after one complete scanning cycle. This might typically take anywhere from 5 to 50 msec, depending on PLC design and memory size. While this scanning speed is generally sufficient for most industrial systems, it might be a limitation with fast feedback loops under PID control.

For further discussion on the relationship between PLCs and microcomputers, see Ref. (10.1).

10.2 PLC CONSTRUCTION

There are hundreds of PLC models marketed by scores of different companies, but all have at least three elements in common; see Fig. 10.1. The heart of the PLC consists of the central processing unit (CPU) with associated memory. The CPU receives input signals from the various input modules and, based on these and on the program stored in memory, decides on the appropriate output signals, which it then transmits to the respective output modules. The input and output modules provide the necessary interface between the PLC and the machine or system to be controlled.

In addition to these elements, Fig. 10.1 also shows a programming unit. This is required to load the program into the PLC's memory. In general, this unit is not required for PLC operation, that is, it can be removed after the program has been loaded, and utilized somewhere else. Thus, a plant using several PLCs has only to purchase a single programming unit.

PLCs are classified into four general types, according to size: micro-, small, medium, and large PLCs, and these designations generally refer to memory capacity and/or the number of I/O (input/output) modules that can be accommodated. While there is no universal agreement on the exact definition of these different PLC sizes, a typical classification is as follows:

	Memory Size (words)	I/O Capacity (modules)
Micro-PLC:	256	Up to 64
Small PLC:	256–2K	Up to 128
Medium PLC:	2K–12K	Up to 512
Large PLC:	>12K	>512

It should be realized that the difference between micro-, small, medium, and large PLCs lies not only in their memory and I/O capacity, but also in the features they offer. The micro-PLCs are intended to be little more than relay replacers, with added timer and counter capabilities. Small PLCs may or may not have arithmetic capabilities, but these are generally restricted to so-called "integer math." The larger PLCs, on the other hand, often approach the

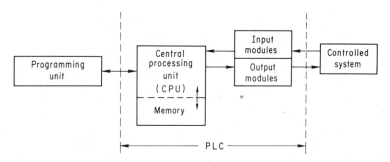

Fig. 10.1. Block diagram of a programmable controller.

capabilities of microcomputers, in that they can handle floating-point arithmetic. They also offer many other sophisticated features, including analog output signals (such as PID control action).

For survey articles listing presently available PLCs and their respective features, see Refs. (10.2)–(10.5). For general information on PLCs, the reader is referred to Ref. (10.6), which is a 10-part PLC course. Considering the vital importance of PLCs in industrial automation, it is surprising that few books have been published on the subject. Two notable exceptions, and highly recommended, are Refs. (10.7) and (10.8).

We now discuss the various PLC elements—programming unit, memory, and I/O modules—in greater detail.

10.2.1 PLC Programming Units

These units range from small, hand-held portable units, sometimes called "manual programmers," to cathode-ray tube (CRT) terminals consisting of a computer-style keyboard with a video screen.

Manual programmers are similar in appearance to large pocket calculators, having a number of keys and a display, either light-emitting diodes (LEDs) or a liquid-crystal display (LCD). Each logic element of the ladder diagram is entered separately, one at a time, with series or parallel connections achieved by using the AND or OR keys, respectively. The NOT key is used for specifying a normally closed contact. (The programming method is explained in detail in Section 10.3.) A typical manual programmer is shown in Fig. 10.2.

Apart from entering the ladder-diagram program into the PLC, the programming unit can also be used to check the program, that is, read back the information stored in a given memory location. Two methods are used to display this information. In simpler units, the information contained in each "program word" (which represents a given ladder-diagram element) is displayed in alphanumeric form. In more sophisticated programming units, a small portion of the ladder diagram entered into memory is actually shown in graphic form by means of the LCD.

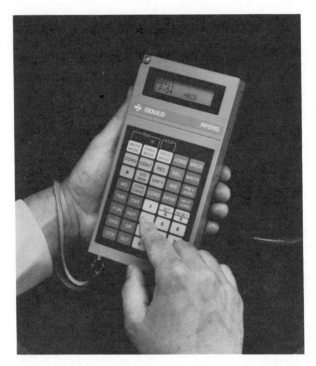

Fig. 10.2. Hand-held manual PLC programmer. (Courtesy of Gould Industrial Automation Systems, North Andover, MA, USA.)

Many programming units have double-function keys, with the upper function selected by first pressing a SHIFT key (just as in a typewriter or computer keyboard). By this means, the total number of keys is reduced. In principle, there is nothing wrong with this, provided the upper functions are not needed frequently. With some units, however, the SHIFT key must be used for practically every word, which makes the task of entering the program awkward and more error-prone.

The programming unit is generally connected to the PLC by a cable, which is easily disconnected for portability. With some PLCs, the programming unit can be optionally attached firmly to the PLC, remaining there during operation. In such cases, the unit should be provided with a keylock. Removal of the key prevents unauthorised persons from tampering with the program stored in memory.

Many programming units have a facility for transferring the stored program to tape, and conversely, for reading a program stored on tape and sending it back into the PLC's memory. This important feature makes it possible to save a collection of programs for different applications, and to load any program without having to retype it. Although some manufacturers supply special tape recorders for this purpose, many PLCs are compatible with standard household cassette recorders.

Some programming units permit on-line programming, that is, the program can be modified while the PLC is running. Thus, the system does not have to be shut down during a program modification. However, according to some experts, on-line programming can create serious safety hazards, since certain output signals might undergo unexpected changes during program modification.

Apart from the previously mentioned features, all programming units have diagnostic capabilities of one sort or another. These may comprise any of the following:

(a) Indicating the "power flow" within each ladder-diagram rung, which makes it possible to check whether voltage is reaching any given point on the ladder diagram during actual operation.

(b) Forcing any input or output signal either *on* or *off*. This makes it possible to determine whether a fault is located in the PLC or in the program, or whether the equipment connected to a given input or output module is to blame.

(c) Showing error code numbers on the programmer display. These indicate the nature of the fault, be it an illegal entry into memory, an electrical fault within the PLC itself, or within one of the I/O modules.

The more sophisticated programming units consist of video, or CRT, terminals. These display several ladder-diagram lines at a time, and can also directly show power flow within each line during operation, which greatly facilitates troubleshooting. With such units, the program is usually entered by moving a cursor along the screen (using four cursor-moving keys for this purpose), and when the cursor reaches the location where the next element is to be added, pressing additional keys. Most such units also have facilities for connecting a printer, so that the ladder diagram or the resulting program can be printed and stored in hard-copy form (sometimes even with additional documentation and remarks). Figure 10.3 shows a programming unit of the CRT type, and Fig. 10.4 shows a typical ladder-diagram section appearing on the CRT screen.

The trouble with most programming units is that they are only usable with one specific PLC model, or, at best, with one family of PLC models from the same manufacturer. There are some programming units marketed that are claimed to be compatible with "most major PLCs." However, the logical solution to this problem is to use microcomputers as programming units. There are already a number of PLC manufacturers using IBM-compatible microcomputers together with an appropriate software package as programmers, and the trend in this direction is gathering momentum. The reasons for this are clear.

The cost of a special-purpose CRT programming unit designed for one specific PLC is inherently high, because of the low sales volume involved. (A customer purchasing dozens of PLCs might buy only one single programmer.) Thus, no PLC manufacturer is able to build a CRT programmer that can compete with standard mass-produced personal microcomputers. The use of a microcomputer as programmer also has additional advantages. The computer

Fig. 10.3. CRT-type PLC programmer. (Courtesy of Allen-Bradley Co., Industrial Computer and Communication Group.)

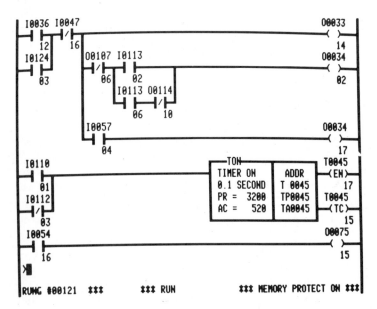

Fig. 10.4. Ladder-diagram section appearing on the CRT screen of Fig. 10.3. (Courtesy of Allen-Bradley Co., Industrial Computer and Communication Group.)

can print documentation, and even (using appropriate software) help in the task of writing the PLC program. Furthermore, many customers may already have a suitable microcomputer available. And if not, they can utilize the one they are purchasing for other applications.

Indeed, some experts predict that eventually most PLCs will be programmed by microcomputers, and that small manual programmers will only be used for micro- or small PLCs, or as portable programming units that operating personnel can easily carry about the plant.

10.2.2 PLC Memory

Memory capacity is usually specified in terms of bytes or of words, with each byte generally containing 8 bits (sometimes 16), and each word containing one or two bytes. In choosing a PLC, the available memory capacity plays an important role. Smaller (micro-) PLCs usually have fixed memory capacity. In the larger PLCs, memory is expandable. With some units, this expansion can be carried out by the user, using plug-in memory units, whereas with others, the PLC must be returned to the manufacturer for this purpose.

It should be realized that the way memory is utilized in a specific PLC is just as important as absolute memory size. For example, are one or two instructions required to enter a given ladder-diagram element? Furthermore, are one, two, or even more bytes required to store a given instruction? The answers to these questions have a vital bearing on the memory size required. Furthermore, some of the memory may be reserved for internal PLC use (executive programs, scratch pad work area, input/output data, etc.) and is thus not available for storing the user's program. A prospective purchaser would thus do well to inquire as to how much memory is actually allocated for the program, and how many bytes are required per element.

The only way to know for sure how much memory will be needed for a given automation problem is to write the program, and then make a calculation based on the just described information. However, a rough idea can be obtained using a rule of thumb. For example, Ref. (10.6) suggests that an average of about 20 relay contacts are required in a typical ladder diagram for each output signal. Since the number of outputs is easily determined from a description of the problem, a rough idea concerning the total number of contacts can be obtained. A different rule of thumb suggests multiplying the total number of input and output points by 10 to get the total expected number of contacts. In general, one program instruction is required for each contact. It is recommended to purchase an additional 25–50% memory capacity to allow for program modifications and future expansion.

After having estimated the required memory capacity, the user must decide on the type of memory required. Electronic memory is divided into volatile and nonvolatile types. Volatile memory loses its contents during power breaks. To avoid the resulting program destruction, volatile memory needs a battery backup to take over during a power break. The batteries are either of the rechargeable nickel-cadmium type, or lithium batteries, with a shelf life of several years. Note that the battery backup only preserves the program. It is not intended to keep the PLC operating during power breaks, since its voltage and current capacity is insufficient to actuate the I/O modules.

We now briefly describe the memory types available, both volatile and nonvolatile. The different types are designated by various initials, which may seem mysterious to the uninitiated, such as:

RAM (Random-Access Memory). RAM is volatile. It has the advantage of being compact, inexpensive, and easily programmable. RAM is either of the TTL (transistor-transistor logic) type, or CMOS (complementary metal oxide semiconductor) type. Today, the majority of PLC manufacturers use CMOS RAM memory because of its lower power consumption (important in connection with the just discussed battery backup), and much higher noise immunity.

R/W (Read/Write) Memory. This term is often used synonymously with RAM. Frequently, however, R/W is used to designate memory based on magnetic cores (rather than semiconductors). Magnetic-core memory has the advantage of being nonvolatile, yet it can be freely programmed. However, it is more expensive and takes up more space than semiconductor-type RAM. It is often used in larger-sized PLCs, where there are less size constraints, and where memory cost represents only a small part of the overall system cost.

ROM (Read-Only Memory). This is used to permanently store a fixed program that is never to be changed. ROM, being nonvolatile, is often used to store the PLC's executive program, but rarely for storing the user's application program.

PROM Programmable Read-Only Memory). This is nonvolatile and can be programmed, but only using special equipment. Once programmed, the PROM chip cannot be erased or altered; hence, it is rarely used for storing application programs.

EPROM (Erasable Programmable Read-Only Memory). This is similar to PROM, but the chip can be completely erased by exposing it to ultraviolet light. After erasure, the chip can be reprogrammed using a special EPROM loading device. Being nonvolatile, EPROM is commonly used in PLCs whenever more-or-less permanent programs are to be stored.

EEPROM (Electrically Erasable Programmable Read-Only Memory). This is a relatively new memory type that is non-volatile, yet easily programmable just as RAM. No special loading device is required, and individual bytes can be erased and reprogrammed. In spite of its higher cost, the use of EEPROM is becoming increasingly popular.

To summarize, RAM is usually preferred for program development and debugging, because of the ease of making program changes. Once the program has been finalized, it is frequently transferred to EPROM, which is more reliable under industrial conditions, being nonvolatile and insensitive to electrical noise. Similarly, many PLCs installed by OEMs (original-equipment manufacturers) as part of some machine or system use EPROM, because the program is not supposed to be changed by the user.

Some manufacturers market PLCs with interchangeable EPROM modules. This lets the user store different programs, or even "recipes" for batch processes, with the program easily exchanged by plugging in different modules.

10.2.3 I/O (Input/Output) Modules

The need for I/O modules is discussed in Chapter 4, in connection with electronic switching elements. The function of these I/O modules is to provide the necessary interface between the PLC and the controlled system. The input modules translate the incoming signals (for example, from limit switches, manual switches, pressure switches, thermostats, or other types of sensors as discussed in Chapter 2) to 5 v dc, which the PLC can work with. The output modules, on the other hand, translate the low-current 5 V dc signals coming from the PLC to the high-voltage high-current signals required to actuate industrial equipment. I/O modules are available for different voltages, such as 115 V ac, 230 V ac, 24 V ac, 24 V dc, and 5 V dc (for connecting to computers, LED displays or electronic elements), etc. There are also output modules with a relay output through which the user can send any desired voltage.

Figure 10.5 shows a typical PLC with attached I/O modules and their

Fig. 10.5. PLC with I/O modules. (Courtesy of Uticor Technology, Inc.)

connecting terminals. The I/O modules are usually packaged in units of 4, 8, or even more. Although the voltage levels of the various I/O modules installed in a PLC can be mixed as required, the modules built into a given unit are generally of the same type. Thus, if only units with eight modules are available, we would have to purchase eight modules of one type, even though we might only need a single module of that particular kind. On the other hand, units containing a large number of modules are generally more compact with respect to panel space per module, which becomes of importance in large installations having hundreds of I/O modules.

I/O modules, classified in chart form in Ref. (10.9), can be divided into three general types, depending on the kind of signals handled:

1. Binary (*on–off*), single-bit,
2. binary, multibit,
3. analog.

The single-bit binary modules come for various voltage levels, as already mentioned. There are also many special-purpose I/O modules available. For example, most PLC manufacturers offer high-speed counter input modules, adapted to count high-frequency pulses coming, for example, from an incremental encoder (see Chapter 8). Such modules can typically count pulses at a frequency of several kilohertz. (The regular counters available in every PLC repertoire are severely limited in counting speed because of the PLC's slow scanning rate, which is discussed later.) An example of a special-purpose output module is one designed to output a pulse train for driving stepper motors; see Ref. (10.10). For a detailed listing of other special-purpose I/O modules, see Ref. (10.11).

I/O modules generally require an external power supply, that is, the voltages required to drive the various limit switches or other sensors on one hand, and those sent by the output modules to the controlled system on the other, are usually *not* supplied by the PLC. There are some exceptions, however. So-called "dry-contact" input modules are designed to sense contact closure without the need for an external power supply connected to the field device.

I/O modules generally have an LED status indicator, which shows whether the given module is *on* or *off*. This is of great help in tracking down malfunctions, since it shows immediately whether the fault is in the PLC or in the field device. Many output modules are protected by a built-in fuse, but some manufacturers require the user to supply the fuse. Another handy feature is a blown-fuse indicator.

The multibit binary I/O modules are used for several special-purpose devices. There are multibit input modules for accepting numerical data entered by means of thumbwheel switches, for accepting signals from bar-code readers, or from absolute-position encoders (Chapter 8). There are also modules for accepting BCD (binary-coded decimal) signals. Multibit output modules exist for sending alphanumeric data to seven-segment LED displays or to other peripheral equipment.

The analog-type I/O modules are becoming of ever-increasing importance as PLCs are being applied to more sophisticated applications. Apart from I/O modules for various analog dc voltage levels, there are modules with a 4–20 mA or 10–50 mA current range that are connected to process-control instrumentation, which commonly uses these ranges.

There are many analog input modules for special applications, for example, for low-level input voltages (in the 40 mV range) that are connected to standard thermocouples. These not only convert the thermocouple voltage to a signal representing temperature (taking the thermocouple calibration curve into account), but even have built-in cold-junction compensation. Other input modules are designed for pressure, flow, or strain-gauge load-cell transducers. A typical PLC application for such a load cell might be in a weighing device that weighs parts packed into a container. The signal from the transducer is compared to a constant stored in PLC memory. The PLC allows more parts to be added until the preset weight is reached.

Analog output modules exist for driving analog valves and actuators, using the PID (proportional, integral plus derivative) control algorithm. PLCs with analog input modules and PID output modules are useful for controlling batch processes; see Ref. (10.12). There are also output modules for driving servo motors, analog meters, or chart recorders.

It is obvious that few PLC manufacturers can offer every existing I/O module. However, some PLCs come with a very limited I/O module selection. Most micro-PLCs, for example, work only with single-bit binary I/O signals. The prospective user should, therefore, make sure that the required I/O modules are available, before deciding on a particular PLC model.

Since I/O modules are fairly expensive ($15–20/module), they often represent the major part of total PLC cost, especially for systems with many I/O channels. The high cost can be explained by the fact that I/O modules do more than merely convert voltages. An input module designed to accept ac signals requires, first of all, a bridge rectifier for converting the ac to dc. Next, there is a filter to cut down electrical noise and switch contact bounce. (The phenomenon of contact bounce is discussed in Chapter 6.) Then follows a so-called Schmitt trigger, which determines whether the input signal has reached the required threshold level. If so, the signal is recognized as *on*. The *on* signal (i.e., logic 1) is then passed through an optical coupler (light-emitting diode coupled to a phototransistor) whose function it is to electrically isolate the input signal from the PLC, preventing excessive voltages from entering and destroying the PLC circuits. The output of this coupler is then transmitted to a logic circuit, which supplies a 0 or 1 to the PLC data bus. In addition, there is the already mentioned LED for status indication, and, of course, the required packaging, which must be designed to withstand industrial conditions, and provide facilities for panel mounting and for conveniently connecting and labeling the input lines.

I/O modules are discussed in Part 5 of Ref. (10.6), where it is stated that for reliable operation, input modules should draw at least 2–3 W of power through the sensor switch contacts (this power being externally supplied, as already mentioned). Some input modules have higher input impedances, and thus draw less power. This may seem an advantage, but modules with high input impedances have lower noise immunity and, other factors being equal, are more liable to pick up false signals from adjacent field wiring.

Output modules also contain several stages, with the isolation stage being either an optical coupler or a reed relay. The final output voltage is usually supplied by a power transistor (for dc outputs), or by a triac or SCR (for ac outputs). A very important part of the output module is a filter and/or other protective device that guards against destructive voltage peaks. These can be especially dangerous where the output module must shut off inductive loads, which can cause huge reverse voltages. Some of these protective schemes are discussed in Part 7 of Ref. (10.6), and in Chapters 5 and 10 of Ref. (10.7).

There have been several important developments in recent years concerning I/O modules. The most striking of these is undoubtedly the increasing use of "remote I/O" modules, available with most larger PLCs. Instead of locating the I/O modules next to the PLC, as shown in Fig. 10.6(a), they are mounted near the field devices, which may be located as much as two miles from the PLC, as shown in Fig. 10.6(b). The resulting reduction in wiring cost is obvious: instead of requiring two long wiring runs per I/O module, only two (or sometimes four) wires or fiber-optic links are required for each cluster of I/O modules. Each such cluster can contain anywhere from 32 to 256 I/O points, and the PLC can connect to several clusters. The cluster has its own power supply and logic circuit, which permits it to communicate with the PLC (multiplexing), and connect the appropriate I/O module. Thus, hundreds of wire runs are eliminated. (The system can be compared to a telephone switchboard, which can connect any of a large number of telephones to the single outside line.) When using remote I/O, it is important that diagnostic data (such as the *on–off* status

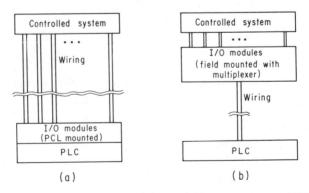

Fig. 10.6. (a) PLC-mounted I/O modules, and (b) remote-mounted I/O modules.

of each I/O module, fuse condition, etc.) can be monitored from the PLC location.

Another recent development is the increasing use of "intelligent I/O." This denotes I/O units with an on-board microprocessor that can solve dedicated control problems independently of the PLC, thus greatly reducing the system response time (otherwise limited by the PLC's scanning rate). Such systems can perform preprocessing of input data, and carry out closed-loop control functions (such as PID control, servo positioning, stepper motor control, etc.). For further discussion of intelligent I/O, see Ref. (10.13).

We conclude this section with a brief discussion of I/O simulators. These are mostly small units containing anywhere from 16 to 32 toggle switches, and a similar number of output lamps. The simulator can be connected to the PLC as a temporary substitute for the I/O modules, and is very useful as a troubleshooting aid, and for testing and debugging new programs. The operator tries the program by observing the lamps (which represent output modules) and manually actuating the proper switches (input modules) in simulation of the controlled system. Testing a new program with a simulator can avoid catastrophic damage to the controlled system caused by program bugs.

10.3   PROGRAMMING THE PLC

PLC programming languages are often classified according to four types:

1. ladder-diagram based,
2. Boolean expressions,
3. functional blocks,
4. English statements (similar to the computer language BASIC).

The first two are the most common PLC languages, used with most small or medium-sized PLCs. They are convenient for programming sequence-type circuits with *on–off* outputs, using contacts of various kinds, timers, and counters.

Once we get into analog control, with the need for comparisons, data manipulation, calculations, etc., the use of functional blocks or an English-statements type language often becomes more practical. Ladder-diagram languages are popular because engineers and technicians with years of relay experience are familiar and feel comfortable with them. However, an increasing number of PLCs are programmed in English-statements type languages, because of the increasing use of PLCs for analog control, and because people are familiar with BASIC as used in personal computers. Some experts predict that ladder-diagram languages (which have never been popular in Europe) will eventually disappear; see also Ref. (10.14).

Actually, the division between the first three languages listed is not very distinct. In the author's opinion, ladder-diagram and Boolean-expression

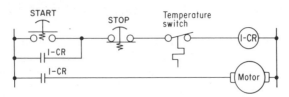

Fig. 10.7. Relay ladder diagram for motor control.

programming amounts to practically the same thing, as is demonstrated later. Furthermore, many ladder-diagram languages use certain functional blocks as part of the ladder diagram, so that the differences become blurred.

To facilitate PLC programming, increasing use is being made of personal computers. For example, Ref. (10.15) describes how a computer can help with drawing the ladder diagram, and with taking care of the necessary documentation.

We begin the discussion by showing how ladder diagrams are loaded into the memory of a typical PLC. (The actual design of ladder diagrams for PLCs is discussed in detail in Section 10.4. For now, we assume that the ladder diagram already exists.) The ladder-diagram programming languages of various manufacturers differ, sometimes considerably and sometimes only in minor details. It is impossible to cover all these variations. In the following examples, we therefore use a hypothetical but typical language for the sake of illustration, and mention common variants where appropriate.

Suppose we want to load the short ladder diagram of Fig. 10.7, which is designed to actuate a motor. From Chapter 5, we recognize this as representing a flip-flop, with the START and STOP push buttons providing SET and RESET, respectively. An additional RESET signal is provided by a normally closed contact of a temperature switch installed in the motor housing. (This is a safety device, intended to shut off the motor in case of overheating.)

The first step in preparing this ladder diagram for PLC use is to draw an I/O assignment table, as shown in Fig. 10.8. This table shows which I/O module is to be connected to each input or output element. The number chosed for each module is arbitrary, depending on the number of I/O modules available in the particular PLC, and on which modules are still free.

Input module	Output module	Connected to
X 7		START
X 8		STOP
X 9		Temperature switch
	Y 3	Motor

Fig. 10.8. I/O assignment table for Fig. 10.7.

The ladder diagram of Fig. 10.7 is now adapted for PLC use, as shown in Fig. 10.9. Several important points should be noted:

1. The various I/O modules act just like relays, although these are software-implemented within the PLC. In other words, actuating a given module is equivalent to actuating a relay coil, so that contacts of that relay (whether NO or NC) can be used elsewhere to represent the input or output signal. Furthermore, the number of contacts available in the PLC for any given relay is unlimited (unlike hardware relays, which usually have only four, six, or eight contacts each). Thus, a contact with a given designation can be used on the PLC ladder diagram repeatedly as often as needed.

2. Since the input modules act like relays, we can substitute relay contacts (with the prefix X followed by a number) for the original switch contacts. Thus, the NO contact of the START push button is replaced by relay contact $X7$ (this number arbitrarily chosen), and the NC contacts of the STOP push button and of the temperature switch are replaced by NC relay contacts $X8$ and $X9$ respectively. Therefore, PLC ladder diagrams consist mainly of relay-contact symbols, which may appear strange at first. We can tell what each contact stands for by referring to the I/O assignment table. In our example, X stands for input signals, and Y for outputs.

3. As with input modules, the output modules also act as relay coils, with unlimited numbers of associated contacts having Y designations. Thus, the hardware relay 1-CR in Fig. 10.7 is not required anymore, its function taken over by output module $Y3$, which not only actuates the motor, but also functions as a relay. The memory contact 1-CR in the second line of Fig. 10.7 is thus replaced by contact $Y3$. The third line in Fig. 10.7 can be completely eliminated, being replaced by the connection of output module $Y3$ to the motor, as indicated in the I/O assignment table. (Note that in the hard-wired ladder diagram, this line was needed to prevent the motor from drawing large currents through the relatively small switch contacts. In the PLC implementation, such caution is unnecessary, since there is no current flow between the three input modules $X7$, $X8$, and $X9$, and output module $Y3$. The current implied by Fig. 10.9 does not flow physically, since the PLC ladder diagram is only symbolic, representing the flow of information within the PLC, as determined by the software. Therefore, it is not even necessary for the various input modules and the output module in a given rung to operate at identical voltage levels.)

The ladder diagram of Fig. 10.9 is now entered into our hypothetical PLC by keying in the following commands or "words" with the PLC programming unit:

```
0  LOAD      X7  ENTER
1  OR        Y3  ENTER
2  AND NOT   X8  ENTER
3  AND NOT   X9  ENTER
4  OUT       Y3  ENTER
```

As each line is entered by pressing the appropriate keys, the word number (first number in each row) and the nature of the command is indicated on the

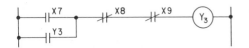

Fig. 10.9. Ladder diagram of Fig. 10.7 in PLC format.

programming unit, either by means of an LED display, or by displaying the actual ladder-diagram line on an LCD. When satisfied that the command has been typed properly, the programmer presses the "ENTER" key, which enters the word into memory, and brings up the next word number. Note that the command "LOAD" usually indicates the beginning of a new ladder rung, and "OUT" signals the end of the rung.

When using CRT programmers, the program is entered in a somewhat different manner. The ladder diagram is actually drawn on the screen by moving a cursor to the desired screen location and then pressing the appropriate keys, which draws the required contact at that location, as shown in Fig. 10.4.

This brings us to the supposed difference between the first two PLC programming languages mentioned previously: ladder-diagram based and Boolean-expression languages. Some authors define the method of drawing the diagram directly on a screen as being a "ladder-diagram language," whereas the method described first is called a "Boolean-expression language," since we used the Boolean AND, OR, and NOT functions. However, the difference is really only a technicality, since, for either method, the ladder diagram must first be drawn. Once this is done, entering it into memory is easy, no matter which method is used. We shall, therefore, not differentiate between these two methods here, but consider both as ladder-diagram based.

As a second example, consider the ladder-diagram rungs in Fig. 10.10 (part of a larger ladder diagram). Note that solenoid $C+$ is actuated twice during the cycle: first, when relay 2-CR is actuated AND limit switch $b+$ is closed; and second, when relay 6-CR is actuated. The I/O assignment table is shown in Fig. 10.11, and the resulting ladder diagram in PLC format in Fig. 10.12.

Several remarks are in order. Relay coil 2-CR cannot be replaced by an output module (as done in the previous example), because this relay is needed for two different output signals, $B+$ and $C+$. We, therefore, use what is called an "internal relay" of the PLC, designated by the letters CR followed by a number. These internal relays operate just like the relays imagined to be part of every output module; that is, they are considered to have an unlimited number of NO

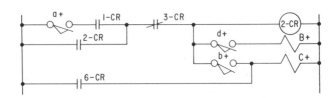

Fig. 10.10. Ladder-diagram segment illustrating the repeated actuation of solenoid $C+$.

Input module	Output module	Connected to
X 3		a +
X 4		b +
X 5		d +
	Y 12	B +
	Y 13	C +

Fig. 10.11. I/O assignment table for Fig. 10.10.

and NC contacts, which can be used anywhere in the ladder diagram as needed. The only difference is that they are *not* connected to any output module. (The number of I/O modules in a PLC is limited by their relatively high cost. Internal relays, by comparison, are software-implemented and require no external hardware. Therefore, the number of internal relays available in any PLC is usually sufficiently large so that no great effort has to be made to economize, as is necessary with hardware relays.)

A second remark concerns the repeated actuation of solenoid $C+$. This is accomplished by ORing (i.e., connecting in parallel) the various conditions under which $C+$ is actuated. (With most PLCs, a given relay coil may not be specified more than once in the program.) It might appear at first sight that the NC relay contact CR3 should be included between contacts CR2 and $X4$ in Fig. 10.12. While this is not a mistake, it is unnecessary, since contact 3-CR in Fig. 10.10 provides the RESET signal for relay coil 2-CR, so that closure of contact 2-CR automatically implies that contact 3-CR conducts.

The commands for keying Fig. 10.12 read as follows:

```
0  LOAD      X3    ENTER
1  AND       CR1   ENTER
2  OR        CR2   ENTER
3  AND NOT   CR3   ENTER
4  OUT       CR2   ENTER
5  AND       X5    ENTER
6  OUT       Y12   ENTER
7  LOAD      CR2   ENTER
8  AND       X4    ENTER
9  OR        CR6   ENTER
10 OUT       Y13   ENTER
```

Two variants are now discussed. Many PLCs do not permit more than one OUT command in a single rung. (See the instruction manual for information on this point.) In that case, output $Y12$ must be placed in a separate rung preceded by contact CR2 (since we want to actuate $Y12$ only if CR2 is SET), and by $X5$. Thus, the command LOAD CR2 ENTER is inserted between the words 4 and 5.

Another important variant exists because many PLCs do not differentiate between the different types of contacts by prefix letters, such as X, Y, or CR used

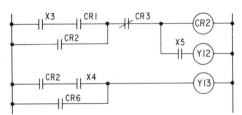

Fig. 10.12. Ladder diagram of Fig. 10.10 in PLC format.

in the previous examples. Instead, they do so by assigning address blocks for the different types of contacts or elements. A typical hypothetical list of such address blocks or "reference numbers" might look as follows:

Input modules:	Reference numbers 000 to 037
Output modules:	Reference numbers 040 to 067
Internal relays:	Reference numbers 100 to 477
Internal relays (latching):	Reference numbers 500 to 577
Timers/counters:	Reference numbers 600 to 677
Shift registers:	Reference numbers 700 to 777

Latching relays, listed here, differ from ordinary relays in that their *on–off* status is retained if the PLC is shut off (e.g., during a power failure), and that they have separate SET and RESET inputs (just like flip-flops).

With many PLCs, the reference numbers are written in the octal number system, which has 8 as base rather than 10. In this system, there is no digit for 8 or 9, 8 being written as 10, and 9 as 11. For example, the number 477 in octal code is equivalent to the decimal number

$$4 \times 8^2 + 7 \times 8^1 + 7 \times 8^0 = 4 \times 64 + 7 \times 8 + 7 \times 1 = 319$$

Using this alternative method of specifying contacts, the reference numbers $X3$, $X4$, $Y12$, and $Y13$ in Figs. 10.11 and 10.12 might be replaced by reference numbers such as 005, 006, 043, and 044, respectively, and the relay designations CR2 and CR6 might become 102 and 106. While this method reduces the number of required keys on the programming unit, in the author's view, it makes programming less convenient. When studying a ladder diagram having such reference numbers, it is impossible to recognize the type of contacts or coils unless the list of reference numbers was memorized or is kept next to the ladder diagram. This makes it very awkward for the uninitiated to interpret a given diagram. In the examples to follow, we therefore employ the first method, and continue using the X, Y, CR, and other letter designations.

In order to enter ladder rungs more complex than those of Figs. 10.9 and 10.12, the use of a LIFO ("last in, first out") memory stack is required. This can be compared to a push-down stack of plates in a restaurant: additional plates coming from the dishwasher are piled on stop of the stack. Whenever a plate is required, it is taken off the top; that is, the last plate in is the first one out.

To illustrate how the LIFO stack is used, assume we want to program the ladder rung in Fig. 10.13. If we program this as follows:

```
0  LOAD  X2     ENTER
1  AND   CR10   ENTER
2  OR    X4     ENTER
3  AND   CR11   ENTER
4  OUT   Y5     ENTER
```

we are implementing the Boolean equation

$$Y5 = (X2 \cdot CR10 + X4) \cdot CR11$$

rather than the desired equation

$$Y5 = (X2 \cdot CR10) + (X4 \cdot CR11)$$

This is so because the PLC does not recognize the conventional order of operations of Boolean algebra. Instead, any contact added by means of the AND (or OR) command is added in series (or in parallel, respectively) to everything that was entered previously in that rung. By using the LIFO stack, the rung of Fig. 10.13 is properly programmed as follows:

```
0  LOAD  X2     ENTER
1  AND   CR10   ENTER
2  LOAD  X4     ENTER
3  AND   CR11   ENTER
4  OR    LOAD   ENTER
5  OUT   Y5     ENTER
```

Note that word 2 begins with LOAD, even though the rung has not yet been completed by an OUT command. The PLC interprets this by beginning a new line, and, in the meantime, storing all of the previously entered contacts $(X2 \cdot CR10)$ in the LIFO stack (which is resident within the PLC memory). The $X4$ and CR11 contacts are next connected in series (words 2 and 3). The OR LOAD command in word 4 causes the PLC to recall $(X2 \cdot CR10)$ from the LIFO stack, and connect this in parallel with the line keyed in afterwards $(X4 \cdot CR11)$.

The AND LOAD command is used in a similar manner. Also, several rung

Fig. 10.13. Example of the use of a LIFO memory stack.

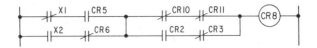

Fig. 10.14. Example of the multiple use of a LIFO stack.

portions can be stored consecutively in the LIFO stack by using consecutive LOAD commands, with the portion stored last always the one withdrawn first. As an example of these points, see the rung of Fig. 10.14, which is programmed as follows:

```
 0  LOAD  NOT   X1     ENTER
 1  AND         CR5    ENTER
 2  LOAD        X2     ENTER
 3  AND   NOT   CR6    ENTER
 4  OR    LOAD         ENTER
 5  LOAD  NOT   CR10   ENTER
 6  AND   NOT   CR11   ENTER
 7  LOAD        CR2    ENTER
 8  AND   NOT   CR3    ENTER
 9  OR    LOAD         ENTER
10  AND   LOAD         ENTER
11  OUT         CR8    ENTER
```

The LOAD command in word 5 sends the previous four contacts $(X1' \cdot CR5 + X2 \cdot CR6')$ to the LIFO stack. The next LOAD in word 7 sends $(CR10' \cdot CR11')$ to the top layer of the stack, which automatically pushes the previous contents of the top layer down by one layer. The OR LOAD (word 9) recalls $(CR10' \cdot CR11')$ from the stack, and connects it in parallel with $(CR2 \cdot CR3')$, and the following AND LOAD (word 10) recalls the first four contacts from the stack (these having by now returned to the top layer), and connects them in series with everything that follows.

Sometimes, judicious rearrangement of the contacts can reduce the number of times the LIFO stack must be used, and thus simplify the program. For example, the rung in Fig. 10.15(a) would have to be programmed as

```
0  LOAD   X1     ENTER
1  LOAD   X2     ENTER
2  LOAD   X3     ENTER
3  AND    X4     ENTER
4  OR     LOAD   ENTER
5  AND    LOAD   ENTER
6  OUT    Y1     ENTER
```

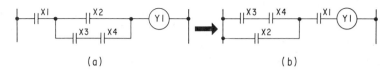

Fig. 10.15. Rearrangement of ladder-diagram rung.

By first interchanging the order of $X1$ and $X2 + X3 \cdot X4$, and then exchanging the two lines $X2$ and $X3 \cdot X4$, we obtain Fig. 10.15(b), which can be programmed without using the LIFO stack as follows:

```
0   LOAD   X3   ENTER
1   AND    X4   ENTER
2   OR     X2   ENTER
3   AND    X1   ENTER
4   OUT    Y1   ENTER
```

While timers are programmed differently in different PLCs, they are usually treated as a special type of relay coil, again with an unlimited number of NO and NC contacts. To illustrate the use of timers as programmed on a typical PLC, we use the ladder diagram of Fig. 10.16, which is meant to flash a warning light ($Y1$). The circuit consists of two timer relay coils, TMR1 and TMR2, both programmed to turn *on* 0.5 sec after current reaches the coil. (These are, of course, not hardware timers, but implemented solely by PLC software.) Even micro-PLCs usually provide a fair number of timers, each of which can be programmed for a different time interval (usually in increments of 0.1 or 1 sec).

The first two rungs in Fig. 10.16 act as an oscillator. Assuming TMR2 turns *off* at the beginning, the NC contact TMR2 in the upper rung closes so that, 0.5 sec later, the coil of TMR1 goes *on*. As a result, its NO contact TMR1 in the second rung closes so that, 0.5 sec later, the coil of TMR2 goes *on*. During the next PLC scan, this opens NC contact TMR2 in the first rung, which resets TMR1, whereupon TMR1 immediately resets TMR2. Now TMR2 is *off* again, and, at the next scan, the cycle begins anew. The system therefore oscillates at 1 cycle/sec, with TMR1 being *on* half this time. In the third rung, contact $X1$ (representing an alarm condition) connects through contact TMR1 to output module $Y1$, which actuates a red light. Provided $X1$ is *on*, the light flashes at

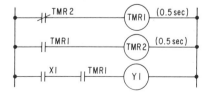

Fig. 10.16. Circuit for flashing warning light.

0.5 sec intervals. The diagram can be programmed as follows:

```
O   LOAD   NOT   TMR2   ENTER
1   OUT          TMR1   ENTER
2   5              ENTER
3   LOAD          TMR1   ENTER
4   OUT           TMR2   ENTER
5   5              ENTER
6   LOAD          X1     ENTER
7   AND           TMR1   ENTER
8   OUT           Y1     ENTER
```

The command "5" in words 2 and 5 specifies the timing interval to be five 0.1 sec periods, or 0.5 sec.

There are considerable differences in how timers are handled with different PLCs. In some, the timer coil is not preceded by an OUT command. In other PLCs, the timer coil cannot be at the end of the line, but must be connected to an internal relay coil ending the line. In some PLCs, timers have two parallel input lines, one being an "ENABLE" signal and the second "RESET." As long as RESET is *off*, the timer continues timing, provided ENABLE is *on*. If ENABLE goes *off*, the timing is interrupted, but resumes the moment ENABLE goes *on* again. This results in an accumulating timer, analogous to a stop watch that can be turned *off* and *on* again repeatedly without resetting. Only a RESET signal sets the elapsed time back to zero.

Counters are programmed in ways similar to timers, except that they always have at least two input lines: one to input the pulses or events to be counted, and the second to zero the counter. Some PLCs provide UP/DOWN counters, which require a third input line to indicate whether the counter is to count UP or DOWN. Since this is difficult to show with regular ladder-diagram symbols, counters are usually indicated using "functional blocks" (i.e., the third of the four programming methods mentioned previously). While it is possible to program using solely functional blocks, these blocks are frequently used within the ladder-diagram format, as shown in Fig. 10.17.

In this figure, CTR3 counts up to 120, and then actuates a lamp or other device, Y2. (Most PLCs provide a fair number of independent counters.) The event to be counted is the closure of contact X2 (which represents any event

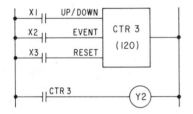

Fig. 10.17. UP/DOWN counter (set to count to 120), shown by a functional block.

connected to input module $X2$). The status of contact $X1$ determines whether the counter is to count UP or DOWN. Finally, closure of contact $X3$ zeros the counter. When $X3$ is opened, the counter resumes counting. In the lowest rung, NO contact CTR3 closes when the count 120 is reached, and then actuates output module $Y2$. The diagram is programmed as follows:

```
0  LOAD  X1      ENTER
1  LOAD  X2      ENTER
2  LOAD  X3      ENTER
3  OUT   CTR3    ENTER
4  120           ENTER (specifies the count)
5  LOAD  CTR3    ENTER
6  OUT   Y2      ENTER
```

Another facility offered by practically all PLCs is the use of a "master control relay" (MCR), sometimes also called an "interlock." This provides the possibility of disabling a number of consecutive ladder-diagram rungs if a certain condition is fulfilled. The coil of the MCR is programmed in the same way as any other relay coil, except that the designation MCR is followed by a number, which signifies the number of consecutive outputs to be under control of the MCR. If the MCR coil is *off*, these outputs become inactive. Other PLCs achieve the same by means of an interlock (or IL) command, with an IL-END command signifying the end of the ladder diagram portion to be under control of the interlock.

A similar command available with most PLCs is the JUMP command, which transfers the PLC scan to any succeeding program rung, skipping everything in between, provided the JUMP condition is fulfilled. With most PLCs, jumps are only possible in the forward direction, so that JUMP is not quite equivalent to the "IF ... THEN GO TO" command in computer BASIC. The difference between the MCR and JUMP commands is that the former shuts off all outputs within its field of control, whereas the latter leaves them unchanged.

In many PLCs, the permissible number of contacts per line, or of lines per rung, is unlimited. In others (especially those using CRT programmers), there may be a maximum number of allowable contacts per line, such as eight. If this is insufficient, the line can be effectively extended by ending it with an internal relay coil, and then using an NO contact of that relay to start a new "branch" of the original line.

Most PLCs offer many other programming commands, but since many of these are specific to particular PLC models (especially in the way they are used and programmed), they are not discussed here, and the reader is referred to the instruction manual for the particular PLC.

The use of functional blocks and of English-statement languages for programming PLCs are not discussed here, again because the details are specific to a particular PLC. We only mention briefly some of the functions that can be programmed easier using these two programming languages than with ladder diagrams. These include, first of all, the four basic arithmetic operations, with input data and results stored in registers (i.e., memory areas set aside for that purpose). Then there are data-manipulation operations, such as comparing two numbers, and logic matrix operations (which means performing logic operations such as AND, OR, Exclusive OR, etc., on the contents of two registers on a bit-by-bit basis). Furthermore, there are data-transfer operations that shift data blocks from one PLC location to another. Finally, there are operations that convert data from one form to another, for example, from binary to BCD or the reverse. Most of these operations are similar to ones carried out in computer programming.

Another important function adapted from computer programming is the use of subroutines. Many of the more advanced larger PLCs offer this feature, which consists of storing frequently repeated program portions, and then using them whenever required within the main program. This technique makes it possible to prepare libraries of common subroutines, possibly prepared at different times by different programmers. This is sometimes called "structured programming"; see Ref. (10.16).

In conclusion, the GRAFCET method of programming PLCs should be mentioned briefly. GRAFCETs, described in Appendix A, are basically flow diagrams used to specify or define a required control sequence. By utilizing an appropriate computer program, it is possible to convert a GRAFCET directly into a PLC program for certain PLCs. This interesting development is mentioned in Ref. (10.17).

10.4   CONSTRUCTION OF LADDER DIAGRAMS FOR PLCs

While all PLC manufacturers supply manuals showing how the ladder diagram is to be entered into memory, they usually provide little help in designing the diagram itself. In Chapter 5, three methods for designing ladder diagrams are described. However, these are intended for hard-wired relays, and are not necessarily the best choice for PLC use. We therefore outline the differences between relay and PLC circuits, and afterwards describe two new methods for designing PLC ladder diagrams.

10.4.1   Differences between Relay and PLC Circuits

1. The current flow in relay circuits can take place in any direction. In PLC circuits, however, the "current flow" (software-implemented, and therefore imaginary) takes place *only* from left to right. Consider, for example, the ladder diagram of Fig. 10.18. If this were a relay circuit, the Boolean expression for actuating coil CR2 would be $CR2 = X3 \cdot X5 + X1 \cdot X4 \cdot X5$, where the $X1 \cdot X4 \cdot X5$ term represents a so-called sneak path. If this circuit is used as part of a PLC program, this sneak path does not exist (since the PLC "current" cannot flow from right to left through contact $X4$), so that we would only get

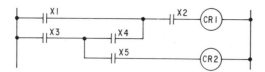

Fig. 10.18. Relay circuit with a "sneak path."

$CR2 = X3 \cdot X5$. Whether or not this difference is an advantage depends on circumstances (e.g., whether or not we are interested in the $X1 \cdot X4 \cdot X5$ term), but it must certainly be taken into account by the programmer.

2. Relays have a limited number of contacts. Even worse, the limit switches and other switches used in hard-wired circuits generally have only a single contact, or, at best, an SPDT (changeover) contact. All this affects the way relay ladder diagrams are designed.

In PLCs, by comparison, an unlimited number of contacts (both NO and NC) are available for every relay and every I/O module. Furthermore, the number of available internal relay coils is usually very large. There is, therefore, no great need to economize and to spend a lot of time to save a few contacts or relays, as would be the case with relay circuits. This fact, by necessity, affects the programming style when using PLCs. In general, it is preferable to make the program as clear and as easy to understand as possible, even if this requires some additional contacts or relay coils. (More about this question in Section 10.4.4.)

3. PLC ladder diagrams are strictly two-dimensional, so that there can be no crossover lines. Furthermore, contacts cannot be placed in vertical lines, so that a hard-wired rung such as shown in Fig. 10.19(a) must be converted as shown in Fig. 10.19(b) to make it suitable for PLC programming.

4. Perhaps the most fundamental difference between relay and PLC circuits lies in the fact that the PLC scans each rung successively. In hard-wired relay circuits, all ladder-diagram rungs are active simultaneously, that is, we have parallel operation, and the order in which the rungs are drawn is completely immaterial. This parallel operation sometimes causes problems. Suppose a relay coil having several contacts is energized. The various contacts should then open

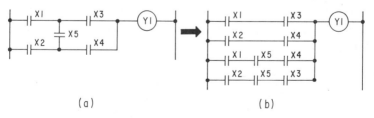

(a)   (b)

Fig. 10.19. (a) Rung with contact in a vertical line; (b) equivalent rung suitable for a PLC.

or close together, but frequently they do not, which can cause races and malfunctions.

In PLC circuits, on the other hand, each rung is scanned in turn, in the order in which they were entered into memory. When the last program word is reached, the PLC returns to the top word, and a new scan begins. We thus get serial rather than parallel operation. When a certain relay coil is energized, nothing happens to a particular contact of that relay until the scan reaches that contact. Thus, if a relay has several contacts, we can predict exactly in what order these will open or close, namely, according to their order within the program. Thus, races as such do not exist, but there is another problem instead. The order of the rungs within the ladder diagram can become critical, as is shown in what follows.

10.4.2 Effect of Scanning Time

The effect of scanning is important, yet hardly discussed in the literature. It is therefore covered here in detail.

The time required for the PLC to carry out one scan is of the order of 5–50 msec, with 10–20 msec being typical. The time depends on the particular PLC and, more important, on the length of program memory. Other things being equal, scanning time is roughly proportional to memory length. Some PLCs have an "END" command, which should be placed at the end of the program. When "END" is reached, the PLC begins a new scan, rather than continuing to scan the remaining unused memory built into the PLC. Thus, the scanning time can be reduced considerably for short programs.

In general, the scanning time should be as short as possible, as otherwise the PLC is unable to sense very brief events. For example, suppose we want to count parts passing by on a conveyor belt. The parts are detected by a photoelectric cell connected to an input module. Each part passing in front of the cell produces a brief pulse, the pulse width depending on the part length and conveyor speed. If this pulse width is shorter than the scanning time, it might fall between two successive scans of the input module, so that the PLC would miss the pulse altogether. (As mentioned in Section 10.2.3, this problem can be solved using special high-speed counter input modules, available with many PLCs.)

For systems where a very fast response to some very brief event is required, it might pay to design a special hard-wired electronic switching circuit (using the method described in Chapter 6) for handling this particular task, and let the PLC take care of the remainder of the control problem.

With most PLCs, the status of all I/O modules is updated at the beginning of each scan cycle. However, some PLCs provide for a scan interrupt, during which a given I/O module can be updated without waiting for the scan cycle to be completed. This feature helps in "catching" fast-changing inputs.

While short scanning times are, in principle, desirable, very short times may not provide any actual benefit, because of the relatively slow speed of response of most input modules. As explained in Section 10.2.3, most input modules contain

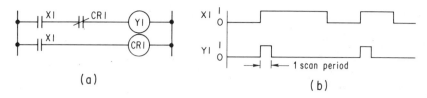

(a)   (b)

Fig. 10.20. (a) One-shot circuit for PLC implementation, and (b) the resulting sequence chart.

a filter to cut down electrical noise, and this produces an inherent time delay of the order of 5–10 msec. Scanning times shorter than this, therefore, provide little benefit.

We now give two examples showing how the PLC scanning action affects circuit operation, and can even be put to good use.

Figure 10.20 shows a one-shot or pulse-shaper circuit, which converts every up-going step of input $X1$ to a brief pulse at output $Y1$ lasting exactly one scanning period. Before the step input appears, relay CR1 is *off*, so that NC contact CR1 in the upper rung is closed. Therefore, step input $X1$ turns output $Y1$ *on*, following which the scan reaches the second rung, turning CR1 *on* also. Only after the scan is completed is the upper rung reached again, whereupon NC contact CR1 is opened, and $Y1$ turned *off*. Note that the time that $X1$ remains *on* has no effect on $Y1$, which always goes "HIGH" for the duration of one scan period.

It is important to realize that the order of the two rungs in Fig. 10.20 is critical for successful operation of the circuit. If the order were reversed, $X1 = 1$ would turn CR1 *on* at the very beginning, whereupon the NC contact CR1 opens, so that $Y1$ would never get a chance to go *on*.

If this circuit is implemented using a hard-wired relay, the order of the two rungs is immaterial, since both operate simultaneously. The pulse width, in that case, equals the switching time of the relay.

A second example is shown in Fig. 10.21, which represents a trigger flip-flop (see Chapter 3), or "push-to-start/push-to-stop" circuit. The input push button (not shown) is connected to input module $X1$, and $Y1$ is the circuit output. To understand the operation of this circuit, it is useful to draw a sequence chart.

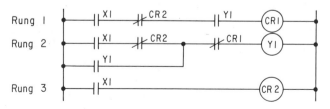

Fig. 10.21. Trigger flip-flop circuit for PLC implementation.

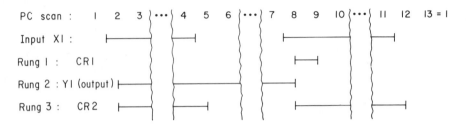

Fig. 10.22. Sequence chart for the circuit of Fig. 10.21.

However, the type of sequence charts used for hard-wired relay circuits and described in Chapter 5 is not really suitable for PLC ladder diagrams. We, therefore, suggest some modifications to make the chart useful for checking PLC programs, and illustrate this method in Fig. 10.22.

In relay sequence charts, the order of the various horizontal lines is immaterial, since all circuits operate simultaneously. In PLC sequence charts, it is important *first* to draw the lines corresponding to the various input signals (there is only one in this example), since the inputs are usually sampled and updated at the beginning of each scanning period. Next, we draw a line for each rung, taking care to draw these lines *in the same order* in which the rungs appear in the ladder diagram, since this is the order in which they are scanned. Each line represents the coil of the internal relay or output module that terminates the respective rung in the ladder diagram.

The second modification relates to the horizontal time divisions, indicated by numbers at the top of the chart. In relay sequence charts, these time divisions represent events, triggered by a change in some input signal (i.e., we are dealing with *asynchronous* systems), and there is no fixed time scale, and therefore no constant time difference between adjacent time divisions. In this new type of PLC sequence chart, on the other hand, each time division represents one PLC scan. Since these scans occur at a constant frequency, we have a *synchronous* system, and there is a fixed time scale, depending on the scan period.

We now go through the operation of the circuit of Fig. 10.21, and study how this sequence chart is filled in. (Figure 10.21 is assumed to be part of a much longer ladder diagram, but only the first three rungs, labeled 1, 2, and 3, are of interest here.) It is suggested that the reader follow this description in detail, since it is helpful in knowing the way the PLC scanning action affects program operation.

Scan 1: Since input $X1 = 0$, all three outputs CR1, Y1, and CR2 remain 0.

Scan 2: Assuming that $X1$ went 1 during the previous scan, this new state is sensed at the beginning of scan 2. We now study each rung *in the correct order*.

    Rung 1: Since Y1 is still 0, CR1 remains 0.

    Rung 2: Since $X1 = 1$ but coils $CR1 = CR2 = 0$, we get $Y1 = 1$.

    Rung 3: Since $X1 = 1$, we get $CR2 = 1$.

Scans 3 and 4:

> Rung 1: Though $X1 = Y1 = 1$, the NC contact of CR2 maintains $CR1 = 0$.
>
> Rung 2: Though coil $CR2 = 1$, the memory contact of $Y1$ maintains $Y1 = 1$.
>
> Rung 3: Since $X1 = 1$, CR2 remains 1.

As long as $X1$ remains 1, there are no further changes. We therefore draw two vertical break lines, and continue with scan 4. The break lines indicate that an indefinite number of scans occur between scans 3 and 4.

Scan 5: Assuming that $X1$ went 0 during scan 4, this new state is sensed at the beginning of scan 5.

> Rung 1: Since $X1 = 0$, CR1 remains 0.
>
> Rung 2: $Y1$ remains 1 because of memory contact $Y1$.
>
> Rung 3: CR2 goes 0.

Scans 6 and 7: No further changes take place. Draw break lines between scans 6 and 7.

Scan 8: Assuming $X1$ goes 1 during scan 7, we have:

> Rung 1: Since we still have coil $CR2 = 0$ and $Y1 = 1$, CR1 goes 1.
>
> Rung 2: Since coil $CR1 = 1$, the memory of $Y1$ is broken. Hence, $Y1 = 0$.
>
> Rung 3: Since $X1 = 1$, $CR2 = 1$.

Scan 9:

> Rung 1: Since $Y1$ is now 0, CR1 goes 0.
>
> Rung 2: Since coil $CR2 = 1$, $Y1$ remains 0.
>
> Rung 3: CR2 remains 1.

Scans 10 and 11: No further changes take place.

Scan 12: Assuming $X1$ goes 0 during scan 11, no changes take place in rungs 1 and 2, but CR2 in rung 3 goes 0. The cycle is complete, and we have now returned to the same state as at scan 1.

From following this listing of events, we realize that the order of the rungs in Fig. 10.21 is vital for proper circuit operation. For example, if rung 3 were to be placed at the beginning, ahead of rungs 1 and 2, then $Y1$ could never become 1 (since $X1 = 1$ produces $CR2 = 1$, and the NC contact of CR2 is connected in series with $X1$ in rung 2). The reader should be able to discover other malfunctions that would be caused by changing the rung order. Thus, the circuit functions properly only due to the PLC's scanning action.

For this reason, the circuit of Fig. 10.21 would not function with hard-wired relays. For example, when $X1$ becomes 1, there would be a race between the NC contact CR2 and memory contact $Y1$ in rung 2. If contact CR2 opens before contact $Y1$ has closed, current flow to coil $Y1$ is interrupted, so that relay $Y1$ never becomes energized. Here, too, the reader should be able to discover other races that would take place. (To design this relay circuit properly without races, the Huffman method described in Chapters 5 and 6 can be used.)

10.4.3 PLC Ladder Diagrams for Sequencing Problems

Many PLCs have special provisions for programming sequencers. These generally simulate the action of drum programmers, described in Chapter 9. The basic action is quite simple: by means of a STEP command, the sequencer advances from step to step, and, for each such step, the PLC program contains instructions concerning which output modules should be turned *on* or *off*.

Some of these so-called sequencers work on a time basis, that is, the sequencer advances to the next step at fixed time intervals. This method has the advantage in that no sensors are required to announce the completion of each step. However, the method is very inefficient timewise, since the time interval must be large enough to accommodate the shortest action occurring in the whole cycle, which means that time is wasted during all other steps. Also, such a system is less reliable, since the PLC does not sense any stoppage or delay in the sequence.

A real asynchronous sequencer is event-based: the sequencer must only advance to the next step if an input signal has been received announcing the completion of the previous step. A typical PLC sequencer, software-implemented, acts as shown in Fig. 10.23(a). At each step, a given sequencer contact is closed, and this can actuate one or more output modules. Every time a STEP signal arrives, the next sequencer contact closes, and the previous one opens. To get a true asynchronous stepper, the circuit of Fig. 10.23(a) has to be complemented by Fig. 10.23(b). Each sequencer contact is ANDed with the input signal denoting completion of the particular step, and the resulting lines are all connected in parallel (ORed) to actuate the internal relay coil CR(STEP), which stands for the STEP signal.

By the time all this is done, the PLC program can become quite long. Also, many PLCs do not provide such a sequencing facility. We therefore suggest a different method, which can be used with any type of PLC, is easy to understand, and is easy to apply. It is basically the same as the relay cascade method described in Chapter 5, first published in Ref. (10.18).

Since this method is described in detail in Chapter 5, it is only outlined here. Briefly, it consists of dividing the required cycle into groups, such that no

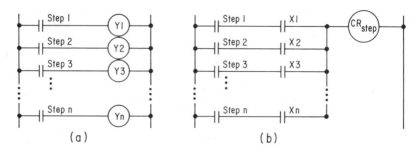

Fig. 10.23. Asynchronous PLC sequencer.

opposing output commands appear in the same group. Opposing commands are defined as those that may not be *on* at the same time. Or, in other words, *a new group must be started the moment it becomes necessary to shut off any output actuated during the present group.*

To illustrate, we use the same example from Chapter 5. Suppose we want to actuate four cylinders A, B, C, and D according to the sequence

$$\text{START, } A+, B+, C+ \left| C-, A-, D+ \right| A+, D-, B- \left| A- \right.$$

$$\quad\quad\quad \text{I} \quad\quad\quad\quad \text{II} \quad\quad\quad\quad\quad \text{III} \quad\quad \text{IV}$$

Assume that each cylinder X is actuated by a pneumatic 5/2 valve with two solenoids, $X+$ and $X-$, respectively. It is clear that $X+$ must be shut off the moment $X-$ is to be energized. Therefore, the sequence must be divided into four groups, as indicated, so that no letter is repeated in any group.

Each group is now allocated one control relay, connected as an RS flip-flop, as shown in Fig. 5.3 in Chapter 5. The resulting ladder diagram is shown in Fig. 5.20. For the first group, the START signal provides the SET signal for the flip-flop. For all succeeding groups, the SET signal consists of an NO contact of the previous flip-flop, connected in series with the sensor signal indicating completion of the last step of the previous group. The RESET signal of each flip-flop consists of an NC contact of the next flip-flop. (The last flip-flop, however, is reset by the sensor for the last program step.) In this way, only one flip-flop is set at any given time (one-hot code).

To implement this circuit on a PLC, slight modifications should be made, first of all, because the PLC ladder diagram must be two-dimensional (no crossing of lines is allowed); and second, because many PLCs do not allow ladder rungs with multiple outputs. The resulting modified ladder diagram is shown in Fig. 10.24. (To simplify matters, the various input and output signals are shown directly on this figure, rather than presenting an I/O assignment table and then using the corresponding X or Y designations.)

Note that repeating output signals (such as $A+$ and $A-$ in the above example) are actuated by two ladder lines connected in parallel. Any output signal that is to appear at the beginning of a new group is produced by an NO contact of the relay assigned to that group. All other outputs are produced by two contacts in series: an NO contact of the relay assigned to its group, and the sensor signal indicating the completion of the previous step.

In Chapter 5, the unlikely but possible occurrence of a race in one-hot relay circuits is discussed. In the PLC implementation of such circuits, the possibility of races is completely eliminated, provided the various groups are programmed in chronological order, as shown in Fig. 10.24. Because of the scanning action of the PLC, the fact that flip-flop CR_n is SET produces a RESET of flip-flop CR_{n-1} only during the following scan, so that there is absolutely no possibility of a race between the NO contacts of CR_{n-1} and CR_n.

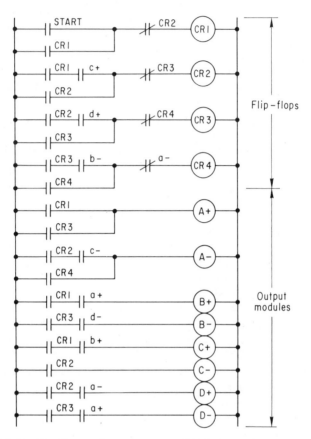

Fig. 10.24. PLC ladder diagram for the sequence START, $A+$, $B+$, $C+$, $C-$, $A-$, $D+$, $A+$, $D-$, $B-$, $A-$.

As shown in Chapter 5, this cascade method can also be adapted for systems requiring sustained outputs, and for multipath sequences (i.e., with simultaneous parallel paths, alternative parallel paths, options of bypassing certain steps or of repeating certain steps). The solutions described there can be applied directly to PLC ladder diagrams. These cases are simple examples of systems with a single random input signal. More complicated systems with random inputs are discussed in the next section.

10.4.4 PLC Ladder Diagrams for Systems with Random Inputs

This section deals with asynchronous systems with random inputs, that is, in which the various steps do not occur in a fixed predefined order. While most PLCs have JUMP commands, these usually permit jumps only in the forward direction, and thus are not suitable for handling such problems. Generally, only large high-cost PLCs have bidirectional conditional jumps of the "IF . . . THEN

GO TO" variety. We therefore present a general method for random-input systems, suitable even for the simplest PLC.

The method to be described is partially based on the Huffman method covered in Chapters 5 and 6. The Huffman method leads to an absolute minimum in the number of relays required. However, the method is relatively difficult to master thoroughly, and time-consuming to apply. Its use is, therefore, justified only when using hard-wired relay panels, where each relay saved represents a reduction in system cost and complexity.

As already discussed, there is no urgent need to save relays when working with PLCs. Even so, we want to keep the ladder diagram reasonably simple, for several reasons:

1. A long program takes longer to enter into the PLC's memory.
2. A long program is generally more difficult to understand or check.
3. If the program is too long, the memory capacity may be insufficient where small inexpensive PLCs are used.
4. As already discussed, with PLC's having an END command, the scanning rate depends on the amount of memory actually used. Thus, the shorter the program, the faster the PLC's speed of response.

The method to be presented here is much simpler than the Huffman method. Although it does not minimize the number of relays, it represents a good compromise between program length and the time required to come up with a reasonable solution. Also, it is applicable to large problems involving a great number of input variables, whereas the Huffman method is limited to a number of variables that can be handled with Karnaugh maps. [The method is reprinted from Ref. (10.19) by permission of the Council of the Institution of Mechanical Engineers.]

The method is explained using an example used in Chapter 6, namely, the design of an alarm or annunciator system. The basic particulars of this system are not repeated here, and the reader is referred to the explanation found there.

The first step in *any* method for handling random-input systems is to draw a flow diagram, as shown in Fig. 10.25. This diagram differs from Fig. 6.2 in Chapter 6 in one particular detail: it provides for simultaneous changes of both input signals x_1 and x_2, and these are shown in Fig. 10.25 by means of dashed arrows. The probability of two inputs changing at exactly the same moment is extremely small. In fact, in the design of random-input systems with sustained inputs—as taught in most textbooks on switching theory—it is commonly assumed that such simultaneous changes do not occur. (The idea behind this assumption is that if such a change should occur, the switching elements will "decide" which signal switched first, and will react accordingly.)

Such an assumption, however, is not valid where the solution is to be implemented on a PLC, because of the way the PLC scans the program line by line. The typically scanning period of 10–20 msec is sufficiently long so that

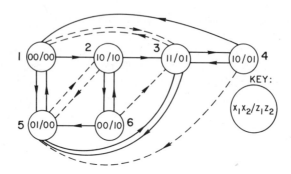

Fig. 10.25. Flow diagram for an alarm system.

during the scan, two or more inputs could possibly change state. Thus, this possibility must be accounted for, and hence the dashed arrows in Fig. 10.25.

There are, however, applications (not the present example) where the order of the input signals is not completely random. In such applications, discussed in Section 6.5, most simultaneous input changes, and even some single changes, are physically impossible, so that the corresponding arrows in the flow diagram are missing.

The next step consists of drawing the primitive flow table and of merging the rows, which results in the merged flow table. This is described in detail in Chapter 5, and is not repeated here. These two flow tables, based on the flow diagram of Fig. 10.25, are shown in Figs. 10.26 and 10.27, where the circled numbers represent stable states, and the uncircled numbers unstable (transition) states.

As shown in Chapter 5, the next step in the Huffman method is to differentiate between the various rows in the merged flow table by a so-called state assignment, using combinations of state variables (i.e., flip-flop outputs or relay outputs). Karnaugh maps are then filled in for each state variable and each output variable, and the so-called excitation functions and output functions are derived from these maps. However, these steps are time-consuming, and require good knowledge of switching theory. We therefore present a different method,

X_1X_2

00	10	11	01	z_1z_2
①	2	3	5	00
6	②	3	5	10
1	4	③	5	01
1	④	3	5	01
1	2	3	⑤	00
⑥	2	3	5	10

Fig. 10.26. Primitive flow table corresponding to Fig. 10.25.

X_1X_2

Row	00	10	11	01	State Assignment
1,5	①	2	3	⑤	y_1
2,6	⑥	②	3	5	y_2
3,4	1	④	③	5	y_3

Fig. 10.27. Merged flow table.

which is much simpler and faster. Although the resulting solution requires somewhat more relays than the Huffman method, this should be of little concern when using PLCs.

The state assignment in the suggested method is as simple as could be: we simply assign one flip-flop output y_i to each row in the merged flow table. In this example, we therefore require three flip-flops, with outputs y_1, y_2, and y_3, respectively, as indicated in Fig. 10.27. For each row i, the assigned state variable y_i is 1, while all others are 0. (This is identical to the one-hot code used in Section 10.4.3.)

We can now write the output functions directly from the merged flow table. Since $z_1 = 1$ in states 2 and 6 (see Fig. 10.26), and $z_2 = 1$ in states 3 and 4, we can write

$$z_1 = y_2 \tag{10.1}$$

$$z_2 = y_3 \tag{10.2}$$

The set and reset functions for the three RS flip-flops are somewhat more difficult to write. Each unstable state listed in the merged flow table means that the system should move to the succeeding stable state. To achieve this, a set signal is required for the flip-flop assigned to that stable state. For example, the only way to reach the second row is from unstable state 2 in the first row. The "address" of this state consists of the Boolean product of the state variable (y_1) and the input combination (x_1x_2'), namely, $y_1x_1x_2'$. We thus get the set function for flip-flop 2:

$$S_2 = y_1x_1x_2' \tag{10.3}$$

Similarly, the third row can only be reached from either of the two unstable states 3 in rows 1 and 2. This results in

$$S_3 = (y_1 + y_2)x_1x_2$$

However, to simplify the solution, we can use the following rule:

Rule. If a given column contains only *one* repeated number, we can use the input combination of that column alone for the set and reset functions.

Applying this rule to the $x_1 x_2$ column (which contains only 3s) simplifies the S_3 function to

$$S_3 = x_1 x_2 \tag{10.4}$$

This means that we also get an S_3 signal at stable state ③, where it is not really needed (since the flip-flop is already set), but also does no harm.

For flip-flop 1, the first row can be reached from unstable state 1 in the third row (address $y_3 x_1' x_2'$), or from either of the two unstable states 5 in rows 2 and 3. This results in

$$S_1 = y_3 x_1' x_2' + (y_2 + y_3) x_1' x_2$$

Applying the previous rule simplifies this to

$$S_1 = y_3 x_1' x_2' + x_1' x_2$$

At this point, it is appropriate to briefly discuss the problem of system start-up, which is relevant for any system, no matter what design method is used. Suppose system power is shut off (e.g., power failure, or the end of the work day). When power is turned *on* again, we want the system to start out at state ① before any inputs have appeared. One way to achieve this is to have a special start-up button, which initializes the system properly by supplying S_1, R_2, and R_3 signals, thus placing the system into state ①. However, with little effort, automatic initialization can be obtained. To achieve this, an S_1 signal is required in the $x_1' x_2'$ column, not only in the third row ($y_3 = 1$), but also if $y_1 = y_2 = y_3 = 0$, which represents the situation after a power interruption. Both requirements can be combined by using the $S_1 = y_2' x_1' x_2'$ term. This includes not only the third row, but also the first row where S_1 is not needed but does no harm. The final modified expression for S_1 thus becomes

$$S_1 = y_2' x_1' x_2' + x_1' x_2 \tag{10.5}$$

The various reset signals are derived using the following consideration. Whenever a new stable state ⓚ is reached from the previous unstable state k, the flip-flop corresponding to that unstable state must be reset. For example, when the system reaches state ②, it must reset flip-flop 1 assigned to state 2. This means that we need a reset signal R_1 at $y_2 x_1 x_2'$ (the address of state ②). In addition, unstable state 3 in row 1 leads to stable state ③ in row 3. This requires an additional reset signal R_1 at $y_3 x_1 x_2$ (the address of state ③). Combining these two gives the total reset function

$$R_1 = y_2 x_1 x_2' + y_3 x_1 x_2$$

However, noting that the $x_1 x_2$ column contains only the number 3, we apply the previous rule and simplify R_1 to

$$R_1 = y_2 x_1 x_2' + x_1 x_2 \tag{10.6}$$

Similarly, we need R_2 signals at states ③ and ⑤, giving

$$R_2 = y_1 x_1' x_2 + y_3 x_1 x_2$$

Applying the previous rule twice simplifies R_2:

$$R_2 = x_1' x_2 + x_1 x_2 = (x_1' + x_1) x_2 = x_2 \tag{10.7}$$

Finally, we need R_3 signals at states ① and ⑤, giving

$$R_3 = y_1 x_1' x_2' + y_1 x_1' x_2 = y_1 x_1' (x_2' + x_2) = y_1 x_1' \tag{10.8}$$

We are now ready to construct the PLC ladder diagram. As explained in Chapter 5, an RS flip-flop can be constructed using a relay as shown in Fig. 10.28(a), where the manual SET push button actuates an NO switch contact, and the RESET push button actuates an NC contact. In the case of an automatically operated circuit, Fig. 10.28(b), the $(SET)_1$ contact must be replaced by a contact circuit producing the Boolean function S_1 previously derived. Since the $(RESET)_1$ button actuates an NC contact, it must be replaced by a circuit giving the *inverted*, or *complemented*, reset function R_1'. (In other words, this circuit must conduct current as long as the RESET function is 0. This means that the various R functions [Equations (10-6)–(10-8)] previously derived must first be inverted using the DeMorgan theorems, see Equations (3-28)–(3-30) in Chapter 3. This results in

$$R_1' = (y_2 x_1 x_2' + x_1 x_2)' = (y_2' + x_1' + x_2)(x_1' + x_2') \tag{10-6A}$$

$$R_2' = x_2' \tag{10-7A}$$

$$R_3' = (y_1 x_1')' = y_1' + x_1 \tag{10-8A}$$

[Note that Equation (10-6A) can be further simplified to $R_1' = x_1' + y_2' x_2'$ by using Boolean algebra.]

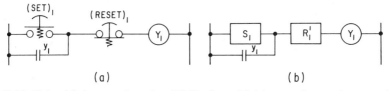

Fig. 10.28. Relay implementation of an RS flip-flop with (a) manual set and reset, and (b) automatic set and reset.

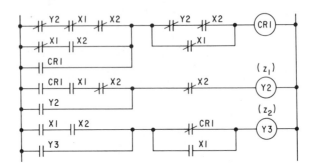

Fig. 10.29. Ladder diagram for the problem of Fig. 10.25.

Utilizing Equations (10-1)–(10-5) and (10-6A)–(10-8A) and the pattern of Fig. 10.28(b) results in the ladder diagram of Fig. 10.29. In this discussion, we have purposely used the relay designation Y_i (for coils) and y_i (for relay contacts), as in Chapters 5 and 6, to facilitate comparison with the Huffman method shown there. However, to make Fig. 10.29 compatible with the PLC ladder diagrams used in this chapter, we replace relay coil Y_1 and its contacts y_1 by the designation CR1. Relay coil Y_2 becomes output module $Y2$ (actuating output z_1), while relay contacts y_2 become output-module contacts $Y2$. Similarly, relay Y_3 becomes output module $Y3$ (actuating output z_2).

A second example is now presented. Some simple problems result in a merged flow table having only two rows. In such cases, a slight modification of the method results in a much shorter ladder diagram.

Consider the flow diagram for the example of Fig. 6.10 in Chapter 6. The primitive and merged flow tables are shown in Chapter 6, but are repeated in Fig. 10.30. Using the one-hot state assignment, we would assign y_1 and y_2, respectively, to the two rows of the merged flow table. However, the solution can be simplified considerably if we assign to these rows y' and y instead, so that only

(a)

X_1X_2

	00	10	11	01	T
	①	2	–	5	0
	–	②	3	–	0
	–	–	③	4	0
	1	–	–	④	0
	1	–	–	⑤	1

(b)

①	2	–	⑤	y'
1	②	③	④	y

Fig. 10.30. (a) Primitive flow table, and (b) merged flow table.

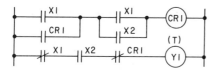

Fig. 10.31. Ladder diagram for the problem of Fig. 10.30.

one flip-flop is required. The resulting equations are

$$S = x_1 x_2' \qquad R = x_1' x_2' \qquad R' = x_1 + x_2 \qquad T = x_1' x_2 y'$$

The blank square in the merged flow table (address $x_1 x_2 y'$) contains a dash, since there is no direct transition from state 1 ($x_1 x_2 = 00$) to state 3 ($x_1 x_2 = 11$). However, if we assume that such a transition could take place, we would insert a 3 in this blank square. This act does no harm in this case, since the transition cannot occur, so that the system never reaches this particular square anyway. The result, however, is a further simplification, since the SET signal now becomes

$$S = x_1 x_2' + x_1 x_2 = x_1$$

The resulting ladder diagram is shown in Fig. 10.31, where Y and y have been replaced by CR1, and output T by output module $Y1$.

We conclude this section with a third example, which is much more complex. Assume that the primitive and merged flow tables are as shown in Fig. 10.32.

$X_1 X_2$

	00	01	11	10	T_1	T_2
	(1)	2	—	3	0	1
	1	(2)	4	—	0	0
	6	—	5	(3)	0	0
	—	7	(4)	8	0	1
	—	7	(5)	8	1	0
	(6)	2	—	3	1	0
(a)	1	(7)	4	—	1	1
	6	—	5	(8)	1	1

	(1)	(2)	4	3	y_1
	(6)	2	5	(3)	y_2
	1	(7)	(4)	8	y_3
(b)	6	7	(5)	(8)	y_4

Fig. 10.32. (a) Primitive flow table, and (b) merged flow table.

Since output T_1 must be 1 at stable states 5, 6, 7, and 8, this output function can be written directly as

$$T_1 = x_1 x_2 y_4 + x_1' x_2' y_2 + x_1' x_2 y_3 + x_1 x_2' y_4$$

which can be simplified to

$$T_1 = x_1 y_4 + x_1' x_2' y_2 + x_1' x_2 y_3$$

Similarly, output T_2 must be 1 at stable states 1, 4, 7, and 8, giving

$$T_2 = x_1' x_2' y_1 + x_1 x_2 y_3 + x_1' x_2 y_3 + x_1 x_2' y_4$$
$$= x_1' x_2' y_1 + x_2 y_3 + x_1 x_2' y_4$$

The excitation functions are

$$S_1 = x_1' x_2' y_3 + x_1' x_2 y_2$$

(which, for automatic initialization, should be changed to $S_1 = x_1' x_2' y_2' y_4' + x_1' x_2 y_2$) and

$$S_2 = x_1' x_2' y_4 + x_1 x_2' y_1$$
$$S_3 = x_1' x_2 y_4 + x_1 x_2 y_1$$
$$S_4 = x_1 x_2 y_2 + x_1 x_2' y_3$$
$$R_1 = x_1 x_2 y_3 + x_1 x_2' y_2$$
$$R_2 = x_1' x_2 y_1 + x_1 x_2 y_4$$
$$R_3 = x_1' x_2' y_1 + x_1 x_2' y_4$$
$$R_4 = x_1' x_2' y_2 + x_1' x_2 y_3$$

The drawing of the resulting ladder diagram is left as an exercise for the reader.

10.5 PLCs vs. RELAY PANELS: COST CONSIDERATIONS

A basic decision to be made is whether or not to purchase a PLC for a given automation application. It is hoped that the reader is by now convinced that an application requiring hundreds of control relays is best handled by a PLC. The question becomes more controversial with small control systems, which can be handled by, say, 5 or 10 relays. Is there justification for purchasing a PLC for such an application? We attempt to present both sides of the argument.

Most manufacturers offer so-called micro-PLCs, especially designed to replace small relay panels; see Refs. (10.20) and (10.21). These PLCs might typically have 12 or 16 I/O modules, and be advertised to sell for something like $200–400. (Occasionally, this price only applies to OEM quantities.) Usually, this price does not include the programming unit, which might cost another $200–300. The fact that one programming unit can be used for many PLCs is small comfort to the prospective purchaser who believes that, for the time being, only a single PLC is required. Furthermore, additional I/O modules, if needed, cost $15–20 per module. Also, if large output currents are required, the output modules may be unable to supply these, and exterior output relays are needed as current boosters.

Comparing all this to a relay panel for the same job may, at first sight, lead to the conclusion that the PLC is much more expensive. Standard off-the-shelf relays with three SPDT contacts having a 10 A capacity can be purchased for about $5 each, and these can be connected directly to all field devices without the need for I/O modules. However, this $5/relay cost does not reflect the total installed cost of the system. We need a panel for mounting the relays, into which the necessary mounting holes must be drilled. We require relay sockets, so that the relays can be plugged in and out should replacement become necessary. Furthermore, the man-hours required to hard-wire the relay circuit adds appreciably to total cost.

If the relay circuit requires timers or counters, these must be purchased, and are quite expensive if they are of industrial quality. A PLC, by comparison, comes with timing and counting capabilities at no additional cost.

Apart from these advantages, there are a number of less tangible advantages associated with the PLC that are difficult to cost. The most important of these is flexibility. In a PLC installation, the program can easily be modified or even completely changed. With relays, this requires costly circuit rewiring. Furthermore, the PLC usually provides an ample number of relays, and an unlimited number of contacts per relay, so that the programmer can afford to be flexible, and need not spend extra time trying to economize when designing the circuit.

And, finally, there is the question of reliability. PLCs are supposed to be more reliable than relays, which, in general, is probably true. However, when a PLC does fail (the PLC power supply and the output modules are reported to be the main cause), an electronic technician is needed to handle the repair, whereas a defective relay can easily be pulled out and replaced. Furthermore, the whole question of reliability can be somewhat misleading. Studies have shown that about 90% of failures in relay-controlled systems take place in the various sensors, 5% in the actuators, and only about 5% in relays. Thus, if the relays are replaced by a PLC, the 95% of failures attributed to sensors and actuators still occur. Only the remaining 5% due to relays are reduced, but not completely eliminated. On the other hand, when failures do occur, the diagnostic features available in most PLCs make it much easier to locate the failure, so that system downtime is greatly reduced. Methods to program PLCs to help detect faults are described in Refs. (10.22)–(10.24).

Considering all these points, the proper conclusion is that hard-wired relay panels are probably cost effective only for very small systems, provided no counters or timers are required, and that the program is fixed so that no future rewiring is likely. Whether a "very small" system should, for the purpose of this discussion, be defined as one having 5 to 10 relays, or possibly 10 to 20, is a matter of debate. The answer probably depends on various other factors, specific to the given application.

10.6   SELECTING A PLC

Unfortunately, most advertising brochures do not supply sufficient information to help the prospective purchaser make an intelligent decision. It is, therefore, highly recommended to ask the sales representative to supply a copy of the user's manual for the PLC being considered. The buyer is then able to judge whether:

1. the manual is clearly written,
2. the PLC is convenient to use, and its programming language sufficiently simple so that the operating personnel can master the programming procedure by self-study, without having to attend a special course.

References (10.7) and (10.8) each devote a whole chapter to the question of selecting the most suitable PLC; see also Parts 4 and 5 of Ref. (10.6). Some of the factors that should be considered are mentioned in connection with the various features available in programming units (Section 10.2.1), memory units (Section 10.2.2), and I/O modules (Section 10.2.3).

One important feature of many PLCs is the ability to communicate with other PLCs or with a computer, using so-called "data highways." This capability, also called "multiple slaving," is of great importance in large-scale automation, for example, where different production steps in a complex manufacturing process must be synchronized and coordinated. There is a very strong trend toward this kind of system, which is analogous to what is called "distributed process control." Rather than having one very large PLC attempt to control the whole system, the system is divided into smaller units, with each unit or machine controlled by a small or even micro-PLC. These PLCs are then linked to a larger PLC or to a computer, that coordinates the whole system. Whereas a large centrally controlled system can become extremely complicated to program, a distributed system makes the job of programming and writing the documentation much easier.

To accommodate the increasing demand for such systems, many PLC manufacturers offer a family of PLCs of different sizes, employing common hardware (e.g., I/O modules, memory units, etc.), and a common programming language that is upward compatible. (This means that a program written for the micro-PLC also works with the largest PLC, but the reverse is not necessarily true.) In addition, interface cards are available (of the RS-232C or RS-422 type) to permit linking each PLC to others, to a computer, or to a printer. Prospective purchasers who have reason to believe that they may wish to expand their system in the future should, therefore, look for a PLC that is part of such a family. For further discussion of this subject, see Refs. (10.7), (10.8), (10.25), and (10.26).

A large chart intended to help in selecting a suitable PLC is presented in Ref. (10.27).

10.7 INSTALLING AND USING THE PLC

After the PLC is purchased, it must be properly installed, the installation tested, the operating program written, and the system started up. These aspects are discussed in detail in Refs. (10.7), (10.8), (10.28), and (10.29). The latter reference, especially, provides useful tips concerning safety considerations. As stated there, because PLCs are so easy to reprogram, there is a tendency to do sloppy programming and to overlook safety problems, which would be carefully planned for in a hard-wired system. Some of these safety problems include:

1. Emergency-stop switches and other emergency circuits should be hard-wired and not programmed through the PLC, so that they remain operative in spite of PLC failure.

2. Unauthorized personnel should be prevented from making program changes that may lack safety considerations (or, even worse, canceling existing, possibly inconvenient, safety features). This can be done by using a PROM or an EPROM; or, if RAM is used, by having a keylock to prevent program changes without the key.

3. Outputs actuated by latched relays can be especially dangerous, since these relays retain their state during power failure. When power returns, dangerous machine motions are liable to occur.

4. NO or NC switch contacts should be chosen as needed for greatest safety. For example, if a certain cylinder position is less safe, an NC limit switch should be used to detect that position. Then, if the switch fails to make contact, or if connecting wires break, the PLC shows an unsafe position. In very critical applications, a switch with both NO and NC contacts can be used, with these contacts connected to two separate input modules. The PLC can then be programmed to verify that *both* contacts are giving the proper signal, before proceeding with the machine cycle.

5. As with limit switches, photocells and proximity sensors should be chosen to be fail-safe. For example, a dangerous condition should *break* (rather than make) the photocell beam, so that bulb failure indicates an unsafe condition.

Similarly, proximity sensors should output an *off* signal when the unsafe condition exists.

6. Many PLCs have self-checking features, and shut off when a fault is detected. What happens with the various output signals in such a case? Are they automatically turned *off*, or are they frozen at their last state? (Some PLCs provide both options.) Not all outputs are necessarily safe when turned *off*.

7. Critical motions should not be controlled by a timer, since mechanical systems might stall or slow down. Completion of a critical step should always be verified by a limit switch or other suitable sensor, and not be taken for granted just because the expected time has passed.

8. On-line program changes (with PLCs that allow on-line programming) can produce unexpected dangerous output signals. The same applies when forcing outputs (i.e., turning outputs *on* or *off* manually during troubleshooting), since this may unexpectedly turn *on* other outputs, too.

9. Requiring a RESET button to be pushed twice in the event of a serious fault can prevent an accidental machine restart that might cause a disaster. (The double activation of the RESET button could be verified by the PLC either using a counter or using the methods described in Sections 10.4.3 or 10.4.4. See also Problem 6.15 in Chapter 6, which deals with this problem.)

While the basic techniques of PLC programming are discussed in Sections 10.3 and 10.4, there are certain formal procedures that should be followed for efficient development of large programs. Flow charts should be drawn at the beginning to define exactly what the program is to accomplish. Good documentation should be written during the software design process, and any later changes clearly documented. All safety features included in the program should be explained. Without proper documentation, it is difficult if not impossible to understand a program written years ago by someone else. If an I/O simulator is available (see Section 10.2.3), it should be used to test each portion of the program as it is written. For further discussion of program development, see Ref. (10.30).

10.8   EXAMPLES OF PLC APPLICATIONS

This chapter concludes with a brief description of several typical PLC applications.

Reference (10.31) describes an energy-saving system for a metal foundry. The PLC prevents large spikes in electricity consumption by shutting off auxiliary equipment, and scheduling operations to reduce power peaks. Before the system was installed, peak demand during any month ranged from 4000–7000 kW. The PLC system succeeded in reducing this peak demand by 1000–2500 kW. The resulting savings in maximum-demand charges and in overall charges amounted to $150,000 per year.

Reference (10.32) describes a plant preparing turkey feed according to 30 different formulas, using 41 different ingredients. The control system uses three PLCs with a total of 60 inputs, 215 outputs, and 41 D/A (digital-to-analog) modules controlling variable-speed dc drives. The PLC system resulted in a 200% increase in production, in addition to more consistent mixtures, and safer and more comfortable working conditions.

Other applications are described in Ref. (10.33), including a system for batch control of coffee roasting. A PLC ramps the roasting temperature (done by increasing the temperature set point every 2 sec), and then holds the maximum temperature for a certain period.

Reference (10.7) describes a great number of PLC applications, including control of a grain elevator, in which the PLC controls conveyors, slides, elevators, opening and closing of chutes, and grain-weighing. The PLC also blends various grain mixtures as required, and provides alarm signals in case of emergency situations. By using the PLC, the plant can be handled by two or three operators per shift, as compared to five or six that were previously required.

Further PLC applications can be found in Ref. (10.34), and in Parts 8 and 9 of Ref. (10.6), including a description of a very large system controlling a cement plant. Four PLCs are used, having a total of 740 digital I/O modules, 300 analog input modules, and 200 PID-loop output modules. In another cement plant, described in Ref. (10.7), the PLC installation is reported to have cost $15,000, but the resultant fuel savings repaid this cost within four months.

PROBLEMS

Draw a ladder diagram and write the required PLC program for implementing each of the following sequences, assuming use of cylinder-actuating valves with (a) double solenoids, and (b) a single solenoid and a return spring.

10.1. START, $A+$, $A-$, $A+$, $A-$, $B+$, $B-$.

10.2. START, $A+$, $B+$, $B-$, $B+$, $B-$, $A-$.

10.3. START, $A+$, $B+$, $B-$, 10 sec delay, $B+$, $B-$, $A-$.

10.4. START, $A+$, $A-$, $B+$, $C+$, $B-$, $C-$.

10.5. START, $A+$, $A-$, $B+$, $C+$, $B-$, 5 sec delay, $C-$.

10.6. START, $A+$, $B+$, 10 sec delay, $\left(\begin{matrix} A- \\ B- \end{matrix}\right)$.

10.7. START, $A+$, $B+$, $B-$, $C+$, $B+$, 5 sec delay, $\left(\begin{matrix} A- \\ B- \end{matrix}\right)$, $C-$.

10.8. START, $A+$, $B+$, $B-$, $C+$, $B+$, $B-$, $C-$, $A-$.

10.9. START, $A+$, $B+$, $B-$, $B+$, $A-$, $\begin{pmatrix} A+ \\ B- \end{pmatrix}$, $A-$.

10.10. START, $A+$, $B+$, $A-$, $A+$, $B-$, $A-$, $\begin{pmatrix} A+ \\ B+ \end{pmatrix}$, $\begin{pmatrix} A- \\ B- \end{pmatrix}$.

10.11. START, followed by $A+$, $A-$ repeated 20 times.

10.12. START, followed by the following sequence repeated automatically 10 times: $A+$, $B+$, 5 sec delay, $B-$, $A-$.

10.13. Solve the sequence of Problem 10.1 as a synchronous system (i.e., without using sensors), with one step taking place every 5 sec.

10.14. Solve the sequence of Problem 10.2 as a synchronous system (i.e., without using sensors), with one step taking place every 10 seconds.

10.15. Solve the sequence of Problem 10.4 as a synchronous system (i.e., without using sensors), with one step taking place every 10 seconds.

Using the method described in Section 10.4.4 for systems with random inputs, draw a ladder diagram and write the required PLC program for solving each of the following problems at the end of Chapter 6:

10.16. Problem 6.3.

10.17. Problem 6.4.

10.18. Problem 6.5.

10.19. Problem 6.6.

10.20. Problem 6.8.

10.21. Problem 6.9.

10.22. Problem 6.10.

10.23. Problem 6.12.

10.24. Problem 6.14.

10.25. Problem 6.15.

REFERENCES

10.1. L. Teschler, "Differences Shrink between Computers and PCs," *Machine Design*, June 11, 1981, pp. 113–119.

10.2. P. Cleaveland, "Guide to Programmable Controllers," *I & CS*, March 1988, pp. 32–37.

10.3. W. Flynn, "1987 Programmable Controller Update," *Control Engineering*, Jan. 1987, pp. 70–79.

10.4. J. Donovan, "Programmable Controller Update: A Guide to Specifications," *Plant Engineering*, Mar. 28, 1985, pp. 44–67.

10.5. "1987 Buyer's Guide of PLCs," *Programmable Controls*, Jan./Feb. 1987, pp. 29–83.

10.6. 10-Part PC Course, *Instruments & Control Systems*, Feb. 1980, pp. 21–25; Mar. 1980, pp. 25–31; Apr. 1980, pp. 57–61; May 1980, pp. 43–47; June 1980, pp. 37–40; July 1980, pp. 37–40; Aug. 1980, pp. 45–47; Sept. 1980, pp. 67–70; Oct. 1980, pp. 55–59; Nov. 1980, pp. 51–54.

10.7. C. Jones and L. Bryan, *Programmable Controllers—Concepts and Applications*, IPC/ASTEC, Atlanta, GA, 1983.

10.8. R. E. Wilhelm, *Programmable Controller Handbook*, Hayden Book Co., Hasbrouck Heights, NJ, 1985.

10.9. "Programmable Controller I/O Selection Guide" (pull-out chart), *I&CS*, Sept. 1986, pp. 87–94.

10.10. R. Rufener, "Controlling Motion with PCs," *Machine Design*, June 25, 1981, pp. 95–99.

10.11. K. E. Ball, "Special Purpose I/O," *Programmable Controls*, July/Aug. 1987, pp. 37–43.

10.12. G. Blickley, "Batch Process Controls Using Programmable Controller," *Control Engineering*, July 1984, pp. 81–84.

10.13. M. Wylie, "Intelligent I/O: New Smarts for PCs," *I&CS*, Jan. 1985, pp. 59–61.

10.14. Product Marketing Manager, Siemens Energy and Automation, Inc., "PLC Programming Languages: A Comparison," *I&CS*, Mar. 1986, pp. 57–58, 60, 69–70.

10.15. M. Babb, "Using a Personal Computer for Ladder Logic and Documentation," *Control Engineering*, July 1986, pp. 47–49.

10.16. O. Ibsen, "Programmable Controller Functions are Enhanced by Structured Programming," *Control Engineering*, Feb. 1984, pp. 100–102.

10.17. J. H. Richardson, "Programming Languages Vie for Control," *I&CS*, Dec. 1986, p. 41.

10.18. D. Pessen, "Ladder-diagram Design for Programmable Controllers," *Proceedings of IFAC Symposium on Low-Cost Automation*, Valencia, Spain, Nov. 1986, pp. 311–315. (Also *Automatica*, May 1989.)

10.19. D. Pessen, "Using Programmable Controllers for Sequential Systems with Random Inputs," *Proceedings—Institution of Mechanical Engineers*, Vol. 201, No. C4, 1987, pp. 245–249.

10.20. Y. Tabata, "Using Micro PLCs," *I&CS*, Mar. 1986, pp. 45, 48–50, 55.

10.21. N. Rouse, "Mini PCs Take Over Small Control Jobs," *Machine Design*, Feb. 9, 1984, pp. 54–56.

10.22. J. Benedetto, "Preventing Errors in Programmable Control," *Machine Design*, Oct. 9, 1980, pp. 172–176.

10.23. D. Cherba, "Programming PCs to Detect Faults in Machines or Processes," *Control Engineering*, Feb. 1981, pp. 57–60.

10.24. W. A. Neal, "Keeping Tabs Via Programmable Control," *Mechanical Engineering*, July 1986, pp. 78–80.

10.25. T. Miller, "New PCs Exemplify Trends to Smaller Size and Distributed Network Compatibility," *Control Engineering*, Jan. 1983, pp. 49–51.

10.26. E. Kompass, "Low Cost Programmable Controller is Distributable in Large Systems," *Control Engineering*, Oct. 1984, p. 123.

10.27. Gould Electronics, "Programmable Controller Selection Guide" (Pull-out Chart), *I&CS*, Mar. 1987, pp. 71–78.

10.28. P. Bartlett, "Installing a PC," *Instruments & Control Systems*, Aug. 1980, pp. 45–47.

10.29. W. Rice, "Safety Tips for PC Users," *I&CS*, July 1984, pp. 33–37.

10.30. D. Penz, "Organizing PC Software Development," *I&CS*, Part 1: Feb. 1982, pp. 53–57; Part 2: Mar. 1982, pp. 73–76.

10.31. (No author listed), "Programmable Controller Supervises Foundry Operations," *I&CS*, May 1983, pp. 75–76.

10.32. (No author listed), "Programmable Controller Automates Feed Company," *I&CS*, May 1983, p. 78.

10.33. R. Merritt, "Some PC Application Ideas," *I&CS*, Jan. 1982, pp. 63–65.

10.34. P. Cleaveland, "Programmable Controller Application Ideas," *I&CS*, Mar. 1984, pp. 41–44.

CHAPTER 11

FLEXIBLE AUTOMATION: MICROCOMPUTERS

Microcomputers have scores of applications. If we disregard those of a nontechnical nature, such as computer games or word processing, and also technical applications consisting purely of calculating data, we come to the subject of this chapter: use of the microcomputer for controlling industrial systems.

Computer-control applications are also referred to as *on-line* or *real-time* applications. These, in turn, can be divided into *continuous-state* or *analog* control versus *discrete-state* or *binary* (*on–off*) control. In the former, the input and output variables of the computer can change continuously (within a certain range), whereas in the latter, these variables are of a binary nature. Since this book is concerned mainly with binary elements, the discussion in this chapter also deals mainly with binary or discrete computer control, with stress on the process of interfacing the computer to the controlled system. Readers interested in continuous-state computer control can find a great number of books on the subject, such as Ref. (11.1), which also contains a chapter on discrete-state control.

It is assumed that the reader has an elementary knowledge of the BASIC programming language. This is not meant to imply that BASIC is preferable to other languages, but BASIC is used here since it is simple, and most users of personal computers are already familiar with it.

11.1 MICROCOMPUTERS FOR CONTROL APPLICATIONS

Microcomputers are only suitable for control applications if they have a so-called "open-ended architecture." This means that they possess input and output lines through which the computer can be connected to the controlled system.

One manifestation of open-ended architecture is that the computer contains one or more "expansion slots" into which peripheral interface boards or cards can be inserted. Each such board is connected by an "edge connector" to a flat cable, which emerges from the back of the computer and leads to the controlled system.

Among the most popular microcomputers with open-ended architecture are the Apple II Plus or IIe, and the IBM PC. The Apple II Plus/IIe (which has by now been superseded by the much more sophisticated Apple IIGS) has several limitations. Its memory is basically limited to 64K bytes (1K equals 1024 bytes), it uses a relatively slow 8-bit microprocessor, and it has very poor screen resolution. For these reasons, this computer is considered obsolete for general-purpose computing. However, these drawbacks are not significant for binary-control purposes, where the Apple has several pronounced advantages: (1) Its architecture is very simple and straightforward, which makes the job of interfacing easier. (Using only 8-bit data lines is an advantage here.) (2) It uses simple, easily mastered machine language. (3) Many books and articles on interfacing the Apple have been published. Likewise, a great deal of software and hardware for interfacing this computer is available.

For these reasons, the Apple II Plus/IIe is used for illustrating the principles discussed in this chapter. Once the reader understands these, they can easily be applied to any other computer. Whenever there is significant difference between the Apple and the IBM PC, information concerning the latter is printed within square brackets, [ ], to make it easier for the reader to find.

11.2 MICROPROCESSORS VS. MICROCOMPUTERS

The terms microprocessor and microcomputer are often confused or used interchangeably. Strictly speaking, a microprocessor consists only of a *central processing unit* (CPU). This is the unit in which the various mathematical, logical, and other operations are carried out, and that controls execution of a program. A microprocessor alone has little value. It must be connected to memory, either of the ROM (read-only memory) and/or RAM (*random-access memory*) type. (See Section 10.2.2 for a description of the different kinds of memory.) The memory stores the program that the microprocessor must execute, and also any intermediate and final results.

To turn a microprocessor and memory into a microcomputer requires input and output devices (also called peripheral devices). The input device is usually a keyboard, although a mouse or a light pen can also be used. The output device is generally a video or CRT (*cathode-ray tube*) monitor and/or a printer. In addition, we use disk drives or cassette tapes for both input and output. Whereas the microprocessor itself costs very little, the peripheral equipment can account for as much as 99% of the total system cost.

Microprocessors alone are mainly used for *dedicated* OEM (*original-equipment manufacturer*) applications. For example, when we read that many modern automobiles use microprocessors to control the ignition and fuel system for increased fuel economy, microprocessors rather than microcomputers are meant. Obviously, there is no keyboard, no printer, and no monitor involved, and the driver has little possibility of interacting with the system. The car manufacturer employs an inexpensive microprocessor, with its fixed operating program and other necessary data stored on a ROM chip. Such microprocessor systems are being used in ever-increasing numbers in various consumer applicances.

Since the program stored in ROM memory can only be changed by replacing the ROM chip, a microprocessor system does not really constitute flexible automation. For this, a microcomputer is required, in which the program (in RAM) can be modified by means of a keyboard, or loaded into RAM from a disk drive. Hence, the following discussion pertains more to microcomputers than to microprocessors.

Programmable controllers (PLCs), discussed in Chapter 10, also use microprocessors in conjunction with ROM or RAM. Whereas PLCs are less suitable for numerical calculations, they are more robust than microcomputers, being especially designed to operate under difficult environmental conditions. For a comparison between these two types of devices, see Section 10.1.

11.3 MICROCOMPUTER ARCHITECTURE

Since this book is not primarily about computers, the discussion on microcomputer architecture is limited to those basic essentials necessary to understand later sections. For a more detailed description, the reader is referred to Refs. (11.2)–(11.6).

The basic architecture of the Apple II is shown schematically in Fig. 11.1. A clock generator (upper left-hand corner) oscillates at a frequency of about 1 MHz, so that one cycle (consisting of one upgoing and one downgoing step) occurs each μsec (microsecond). These clock signals are utilized to synchronize the various computer operations, as described later. The microprocessor, or CPU, of the Apple is the 6502 integrated circuit manufactured by several companies. [Most IBM PC models use the 8088 microprocessor manufactured by the Intel Corp.] The CPU is connected to the memory blocks by means of three different *buses*. The term bus refers to a number of parallel wires, each carrying one bit of binary information.

(a) *Address Bus.* This bus consists of 16 output lines. Since each line can be either HI ($=1$) or LO ($=0$), there are $2^{16} = 65,536$ different memory locations that can be addressed. This explains why the Apple is limited to 64K $= 65,536$ memory locations. The memory location addressed is the decimal-number equivalent of the binary pattern placed by the CPU on the address bus, as is illustrated later. Note that the address bus is one-directional, with data always flowing out of the CPU. [The IBM PC has a 20-bit address capability, and can

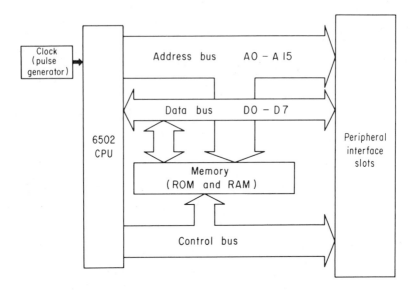

Fig. 11.1. Microcomputer block diagram.

thus cover 1000K of memory. However, at any given time, only 64K of this is within reach.]

(b) *Data Bus.* This bus consists of only eight lines, that is, the bus can transmit one 8-bit byte of information, representing decimal numbers from 0 to 255. Thus, if analog data is to be transmitted along the data bus, the available resolution is limited to $1/255 = 0.4\%$. (However, for internal calculations, greater precision is obtainable by combining two or more bytes, using so-called double-precision routines.) The data in the data bus can flow in both directions: it can emanate from the CPU and be sent to RAM locations or to outside devices; or it can flow from these outside devices, or from RAM or ROM, back into the CPU. This data coming from memory can represent numerical information, or it can represent operation codes instructing the CPU what action to take next (see Section 11.14). [While the IBM PC uses a 16-bit microprocessor, its data bus can only transfer 8 bits at a time to and from memory. To transfer 16 bits, two memory cycles are required. Surprisingly, the 8088 microprocessor has no explicit data bus. Instead, the lowest 8 bits of the address bus serve as data bus during part of the cycle, using a technique known as *multiplexing.*]

(c) *Control Bus.* This consists of 21 additional lines [18 for the IBM PC] sending various command signals to the ROM and RAM, and to the expansion slots. Only a few of these are generally used for interfacing the computer to outside equipment, as described later. The control bus is one-directional, with all control signals emanating from the CPU. For a detailed description of the control lines, see Ref. (11.3) [or Ref. (11.4), for the IBM PC].

The 64K bytes of memory in the Apple are organized as follows, with each section dedicated to specific purposes:

Decimal Memory Locations	Purpose
0–1023	System RAM (some of this is free)
1024–3071	Text and low-resolution graphics
3072–8191	Free (programs are usually stored here)
8192–24575	High-resolution graphics (or for programs)
24576–49151	Free (programs can be stored here)
49152–49279	Built-in I/O locations (for keyboard, etc.)
49280–49407	I/O lines for eight expansion slots (0 to 7)
49408–53247	Available for additional RAM or ROM (in slots 1 to 7)
53248–65535	ROM (the BASIC interpreter and computer operating system are stored here)

[In the IBM PC, the memory utilization is more complicated, and the available memory space depends on the exact configuration of the computer. In the most basic configuration, free memory space available for BASIC programs consists of a 36K work space extending from 28K to 64K, or 28672 to 65535. For a more detailed description of memory organization, see Ref. (11.7).]

As shown in the next section, binary data can be stored in any RAM location by the CPU, or can be sent to the outside through one of the expansion slots (also called *peripheral interface slots*). This operation is called *memory write*. Likewise, the CPU can read binary data stored in memory or coming in through the expansion slot, and this operation is called *memory read*. Since data in ROM cannot be changed, we can read ROM but not write into it, hence the name "read-only memory." Both memory reads and writes are explained in the following section.

11.4 MEMORY READS AND WRITES

In BASIC, the contents of a memory location is read using the PEEK command. The format of this command is illustrated by the following program line:

$$A = PEEK \text{ (address)}$$

where "address" can be any number between 0 and 65535. After the above command is executed, the variable A (any other variable can, of course, be used) accepts the value stored in the specified memory location. Since an 8-bit CPU is used, A can have a value between 0 and 255, depending on the 8 bits stored in the location defined by "address." [Even though the IBM PC uses a 16-bit microprocessor, the PEEK command also returns a value between 0 and 255.] If a negative address is entered, the Apple adds 65536 to it. Thus, the statement $X = \text{PEEK}(-16384)$ is equivalent to $X = \text{PEEK}(49152)$.

Note that PEEK commands do not obliterate the value stored in memory. Thus, any location can be PEEKed repeatedly without affecting the data stored there. Also, note that if nothing has been specifically stored in a given memory location, the PEEK command is liable to come up with any random result, with 255 as likely as anything else (since bit voltages not deliberately kept LO have a tendency to float to HI).

It is instructive to study what happens within the computer while a PEEK command is executed. Figure 11.2 shows a memory-read cycle, lasting 1 μsec. $A0–A15$ represents the 16-bit address bus, and $D0–D7$ the 8-bit data bus. The other three lines, $\phi0$, $\overline{DS}$, and $R/\overline{W}$, are three of the previously mentioned 21 control-bus lines. Line $\phi0$ is the 1 μsec timing signal emanating from the clock generator. Line $\overline{DS}$ (*device select*) is described in Section 11.7. Line $R/\overline{W}$ (*read/write*) remains HI whenever a PEEK command is given. When this $R/\overline{W}$ line is HI, the CPU establishes contact with the memory address cited in the PEEK command. About one-half cycle later, shortly after the $\phi0$ clock signal has gone HI, the data stored in the memory address is placed on the data bus $D0–D7$.

[The memory-read cycle in the IBM PC is similar, but not identical. Instead of the $\phi0$ clock signal, the cycle is initiated by an upgoing ALE (*address latch enable*) pulse. Instead of $R/\overline{W}$, there is a downgoing $\overline{MEMR}$ (*memory-read*) pulse. The whole cycle takes somewhat less time: 0.84 instead of 1 μsec.]

To change the contents of a memory location (i.e., memory write), the POKE command is used. Unlike the PEEK command, the address in the POKE command is *not* enclosed in parentheses. The format is as follows:

POKE address,value

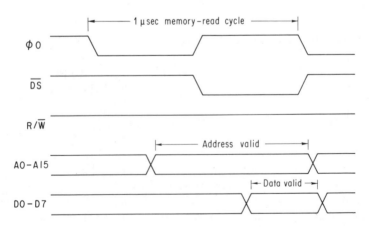

Fig. 11.2. Memory-read cycle.

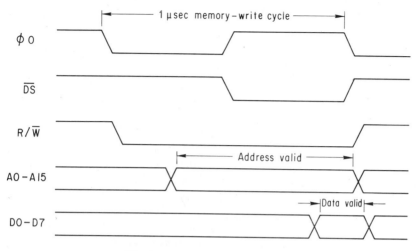

Fig. 11.3. Memory-write cycle.

For example, the command POKE 20000,91 means that 91 is to be stored in memory location 20000. Any byte previously stored in this location is discarded. Note that both the address and the value used in the command could be a variable or even an algebraic expression.

Obviously, a POKE command is ineffective if the address cited represents a ROM location, since ROM contents cannot be changed. POKE commands should only refer to free, unused RAM locations not being utilized for other vital computer-system functions, since otherwise a serious malfunction could result.

Figure 11.3 illustrates events during a 1 μsec memory-write cycle. When a POKE signal is given, $R/\overline{W}$ goes LO (since $W = 1$ so that $\overline{W} = 0$). [In the IBM PC, the $R/\overline{W}$ line is replaced by a $\overline{MEMW}$ (*memory-write*) line for write cycles.] As a result, the CPU establishes contact with the memory address cited in the POKE command. About one-half cycle later, $\phi 0$ goes HI, after which the data specified by the POKE command is transferred to the cited memory location.

[In the IBM PC, both PEEK and POKE commands must be preceded by a *DEF SEG* (*define segment*) command. This is because any memory location is defined by two bytes. The first one, specified in the *DEF SEG* command, defines the base address of a 64K block of locations, whereas the second one, specified by the PEEK or POKE command, defines the location within this block, that is, the offset value of the location as referred to the base address of the block.]

11.5   I/O COMMANDS

In the previous section, we described the memory-read and -write operations, and showed how, by means of POKE and PEEK commands, information can be transferred into or out of memory. This is all we have to known if we only want to move information *within* the computer. However, our purpose here is to discuss computer interfacing, which requires moving information from the controlled system (e.g., from sensors) into the computer, and then having the computer send command signals out to the controlled system.

There are two distinct methods for handling such I/O (input/output) operations, depending on the type of microcomputer involved. These methods are *isolated I/O, or I/O-mapped I/O,* versus *memory-mapped I/O.*

Microcomputers using I/O-mapped I/O [such as the IBM PC] have a special I/O bus through which the data is transmitted. Each I/O port has a unique I/O address, and special INP and OUT commands must be used to gain access to these I/O ports. Thus, to receive input data, the command might be

A = INP(62)

which causes variable A to accept the value transmitted through the port having address 62. Similarly, the command

OUT 62,91

transmits 91 to the output port having address 62. If 8 bits are used to define the I/O port address, then 256 ports can be accommodated.

In microcomputers using memory-mapped I/O (such as the Apple), there is no special I/O bus. Instead, a block of memory is assigned to act as an I/O bus, with each I/O port having a specific address within this block. In other words, the I/O devices are treated as memory. To receive input data, a PEEK command is used, as shown in the previous section, except that the address cited must be that of the I/O port at which the data is expected to enter. Similarly, to send data out, the POKE command is used, and here, too, the address used must be that of the desired output port.

[The IBM PC supports *both* I/O-mapped and memory-mapped I/O. Each option has pros and cons, as described in Ref. (11.7). When I/O port read or write cycles occur, special signal lines on the control bus labeled $\overline{IOR}$ and $\overline{IOW}$ take the place of the $\overline{MEMR}$ and $\overline{MEMW}$ lines, respectively, that were used with memory-mapped I/O. Generally speaking, 512 input port and 1024 output port addresses are available.

In addition to the previous two options, the IBM PC provides a third one, called DMA (*direct-memory access*). This means that I/O data is transferred directly between memory and I/O ports, bypassing the CPU completely. A special DMA controller chip installed in the computer is used for this. Since DMA I/O is more complicated, it is only employed where the extra speed it provides is essential.]

In the Apple II Plus/IIe, memory addresses 49152 to 53247 are reserved for I/O lines. For general-purpose interfacing, only the block 49296 to 49407 is available, and this is distributed among seven peripheral interface slots as follows:

> Slot 1: Locations 49296 to 49311
> Slot 2: Locations 49312 to 49327
> Slot 3: Locations 49328 to 49343
> Slot 4: Locations 49344 to 49359
> Slot 5: Locations 49360 to 49375
> Slot 6: Locations 49376 to 49391
> Slot 7: Locations 49392 to 49407.

Thus, each slot can accommodate 16 different I/O ports. Section 11.10 shows how all of these can be utilized. Practically speaking, however, one of these seven interface slots is generally used for connecting the disk drive, a second for the printer, and a third may be connected to a color monitor. This means that only four slots may be available for interfacing other outside devices. [The IBM PC only has five interface slots, which means that only two or three may be available for connecting to other outside devices.]

It should be stressed that the block of addresses from 49296 to 49407 cannot be utilized as regular memory. Thus, POKEing a byte into any one of these locations may produce some outside effect, but the POKEd byte is not retained in memory.

This section has led us to the subject of computer interfacing, which is continued in the following sections. For a general discussion of computer interfacing, see Refs. (11.1), (11.2), (11.5), (11.6), and (11.8)–(11.15). For books dealing specifically with interfacing the Apple computer, see Refs. (11.16)–(11.18) [whereas Ref. (11.7) discusses interfacing of the IBM PC].

11.6 ANALOG VS BINARY I/O

Whenever we input information from outside equipment by means of the PEEK [or INP] command, we get a complete 8-bit byte, whether we want to or not. This byte can represent analog or digital data, and both cases are now illustrated.

Suppose we want to measure temperature by means of a thermocouple. A typical thermocouple might produce an output voltage from 0–8 mV for a 0–200°C temperature range. (Although the voltage vs. temperature plot is not absolutely linear, it is assumed linear for this discussion.) Using an electronic data-conditioning circuit (which might consist of a couple of operational amplifiers and potentiometers), this 0–8 mV range is transformed into a 0–5 V range. As indicated in Fig. 11.4, this voltage is connected to an A/D (*analog-to-digital*) converter. Such converters, available as relatively inexpensive ICs, are discussed in all books on computer interfacing.

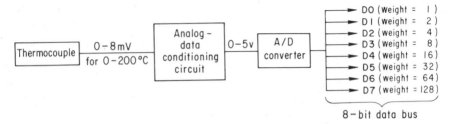

Fig. 11.4. Example of analog-data input to a computer.

Since we are dealing here with a microprocessor having an 8-bit data bus, we use an 8-bit A/D converter, which places one complete byte on the data bus. (The hardware needed to connect the A/D converter to the data bus is described in Section 11.9.) Depending on the individual bits $D0$ to $D7$, this byte can range from 0 to 255, which represents:

Byte	A/D Input (V)	Thermocouple Voltage (mV)	Temperature (°C)
00000000 = 0	0	0	0
11111111 = 255	5.00	8	200
01100101 = 101	1.98	3.17	79.2

where the last line illustrates how intermediate values are interpreted by interpolation.

To illustrate an input byte representing binary data, assume that the computer must obtain information from eight different binary sensors, such as limit switches, or any other type of binary sensor described in Chapter 2. As shown in Fig. 11.5, each of these eight sensors is connected to one of the eight lines of the data bus (again, using special hardware to be described in Section 11.9). Note that not all of these eight input lines have to be utilized. However, any unconnected line usually floats to HI, unless deliberately grounded.

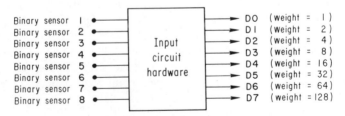

Fig. 11.5. Example of binary-data input to a computer.

When the computer receives the 8 bits on its data bus, it does not know whether these represent analog or binary data. A PEEK command always converts the binary-bit pattern received into an equivalent decimal number (using the bit weights shown in the figure), and this is the number indicated. For example, if binary sensors 1 and 8 have HI outputs but all others are LO, the number $1 + 128 = 129$ is returned by the PEEK command. This number, as such, is of little significance. Rather, we are interested in the outputs of the individual sensors. This information can be obtained by converting the decimal number returned by the PEEK into its binary equivalent, for example, by using the BASIC program presented in Section 8.7.1 for this purpose. (This problem is referred to as *bit testing*, and is solved very simply in assembly language using a process called *masking*.)

A similar situation prevails for output signals. Whenever the computer is asked to send a command to outside equipment by means of the POKE [or OUT] command, the decimal value POKEd is first converted by the computer into its 8-bit binary equivalent, and these 8 individual bits are sent out, no matter whether all of them are utilized or not. Again, this output data can represent analog or binary information.

If the output byte represents analog information, the 8 bits are fed through the data bus to a D/A (*digital-to-analog*) converter, which changes the binary-bit pattern into an analog voltage (usually in the 0–5 V range). This, in turn, could then be used to actuate a final control element, such as a motor or control valve, by means of appropriate interface elements.

If the output byte represents binary information, the 8 bits on the data bus (again first going through appropriate hardware that is described in Section 11.8) are connected each through a separate line to a different binary device, such as a solenoid valve or a relay. If less than 8 devices are connected, then some of these lines remain unused, even though a 1 or 0 signal appears on each. For example, if only one device is to be actuated (connected, say, to line $D0$), and is to be turned *on*, then line $D0$ must be HI, while all remaining lines are irrelevant. Thus, the value POKEd could be any odd number from 1 up to 255, since the $D0$ line is HI for all odd numbers.

11.7 SIGNIFICANCE OF THE $\overline{DS}$ (DEVICE SELECT) LINE

It is important to understand the purpose of the $\overline{DS}$ signal (shown in Figs. 11.2 and 11.3), since it plays a vital role in the next three sections. As seen in those figures, this $\overline{DS}$ signal goes LO (signifying that $DS = 1$ or HI) during each memory-read or -write cycle. However, this $\overline{DS}$ signal does not appear automatically at each peripheral interface slot. [The $\overline{DS}$ signal, which represents a great convenience in interfacing, is not available in the IBM PC. As a result, complete decoding must be employed in this computer, as explained in Section 11.10.]

As explained in Section 11.5, each slot is assigned 16 addresses, so that it can accommodate a maximum of 16 different I/O devices. To make the following discussion more specific, from now on, we always refer to one of these slots, say slot 7, whose 16 addresses are from 49392 to 49407. The $\overline{DS}$ line goes LO (i.e., device select goes HI) *at slot 7* each time there is a PEEK or POKE command referring to one of these 16 addresses. All other slots receive no $\overline{DS}$ LO signal at this time.

For technical reasons that we do not discuss, these $\overline{DS}$ LO pulses are synchronized with the $R/\overline{W}$ pulses in such a manner that they can only be detected if tested together, using a circuit such as in Fig. 11.6.

Suppose we send a PEEK command referring to one of the 16 addresses of slot 7. As shown in Fig. 11.2, the $R/\overline{W}$ line goes HI, since PEEK calls for a memory-read cycle. The NOT-gate output (representing $\overline{R/W}$) in Fig. 11.6 therefore goes LO. The moment the $\overline{DS}$ line also goes LO (halfway through the cycle, as shown in Fig. 11.2), both inputs to the lower NOR gate are LO, so that the gate output, designated here as IN 7, goes HI. This signifies that slot 7 is ready to accept input data from some outside device, as called for by the PEEK command. Exactly how this data is inputted is shown in Section 11.9.

Suppose now that we send a POKE command referring to one of the addresses of slot 7. As shown in Fig. 11.3, the $R/\overline{W}$ line goes LO (meaning that W is HI), since POKE calls for a memory-write cycle. The moment the $\overline{DS}$ line also goes LO, both inputs to the upper NOR gate are LO, so that its output, designated as OUT 7, goes HI. This means that slot 7 is ready to output data to some outside device, as called for by the POKE command. Exactly how this is done is shown in Section 11.8.

Since, in this section, we are for the first time connecting actual hardware (in the form of a logic circuit containing three gates) to a peripheral interface slot, we should briefly discuss how this is done in practice. The most convenient way is to install an empty board (card) especially designed for the peripheral interface slot. Specific interface circuits can then be soldered on this board. For experimental or classroom use, it is best to keep this board empty, and to install jumper wires from the slot pins to the back of the board, where an edge connector leading to a 40-conductor flat cable is connected. This cable is then led out of the computer to any outside circuit board or device, as described in

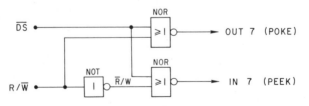

Fig. 11.6. OUT or IN signals following POKE or PEEK commands.

Ref. (11.16). In this fashion, it is possible to access any of the points at the peripheral interface slot from outside the computer. Experimental circuits can easily be built on a so-called prototype board (described in Section 4.1.1) connected to the flat cable.

> *Warning.* Never insert or remove a board or card from the computer while power is *on*. This is a sure prescription for disaster, and usually destroys a number of ICs in the computer and/or on the card instantly.

11.8 OUTPUT PORTS

As shown in Fig. 11.6, the computer emits an output signal only when both $\overline{DS}$ and $R/\overline{W}$ lines go LO. As seen from Fig. 11.3, this situation prevails only for one-half cycle, that is, for about 0.5 μsec. It is only during this short period that the data specified by the POKE command appears on the data bus $D0$ to $D7$ leading to slot 7.

Since 0.5 μsec is too short a time to actuate any equipment or produce any useful result, we must use so-called *output latches* to convert these short pulses to sustained signals. The data then remains stored in these latches unchanged, as long as no subsequent POKE signal referring to the same slot is sent. [The problem is identical in the IBM PC, in which valid data remains on the data bus for only about half of the 0.84 μsec memory-write cycle, which is the period during which the $\overline{MEMW}$ signal remains LO.]

The output latches consist basically of D flip-flops, that is, we need one D flip-flop for each output bit, or eight for each 8-bit byte. As described in Section 3.9, the D flip-flop transfers the D (data) bit to Q on the LO to HI transition of the CK (clock) signal. Thus, a simple 1-bit output port might appear as shown in Fig. 11.7, where the D flip-flop could consist of the IC 74LS74 (containing two independent D flip-flops on one chip). Since $\overline{SET}$ and $\overline{RESET}$ inputs have built-in inverters (NOT gates) in this particular IC, they must be connected to $V_{CC} = +5$ V dc, so that both SET and RESET are effectively LO.

In practical output latches, we have no need for the $\overline{SET}$, $\overline{RESET}$, and $\overline{Q}$

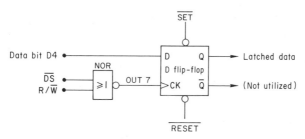

Fig. 11.7. Single 1-bit output port.

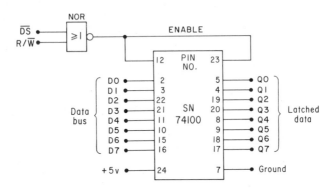

Fig. 11.8. An 8-bit output port.

connections. On the other hand, we generally want to send out more than one bit at a time. Hence, IC manufacturers offer a number of special output-latch ICs especially designed for this purpose, such as the 4-bit SN74LS75, or the 8-bit SN74100. In these, the $\overline{\text{SET}}$ and $\overline{\text{RESET}}$ connections have been eliminated. The output Q follows the value of input D as long as the ENABLE (clock) signal is HI. The moment ENABLE goes LO, the present Q bit is latched.

A complete 8-bit output port using the SN74100 is shown in Fig. 11.8. (Since the SN74100 costs about four times as much as the SN74LS75, it is more economical to use two of the latter for an 8-bit output port.) When both $\overline{DS}$ and $R/\overline{W}$ lines go LO, the NOR-gate output goes HI, thus enabling the port, so that each latch output Q assumes the value of its corresponding data-bus line D. At the end of the memory-write cycle, both $\overline{DS}$ and $R/\overline{W}$ go HI, so that ENABLE goes LO, and the various Q bits become latched.

11.9 INPUT PORTS

As explained in Section 11.7, any PEEK command referring to one of the 16 addresses from 49392 to 49407 causes the Apple to read the 8 bits which, at that moment, are placed on data bus $D0$ to $D7$ by any outside device.

It is important to realize that these eight input signals *cannot* be connected directly to the data bus. This is because dozens of different devices may be connected to the computer. While all of these are attempting to feed the computer with data simultaneously, the computer can only read one at a time, by means of an appropriate PEEK command. If all these devices were connected directly to the data bus, the bus would simply produce a short circuit between them. To illustrate this, Fig. 11.9 shows what would happen to a specific data line, say $D3$, of the data bus. (There are, of course, eight such lines.) To make things easy to visualize, the input devices are assumed to be simple toggle switches connected to $+5$ V and Ground. The figure shows only three such

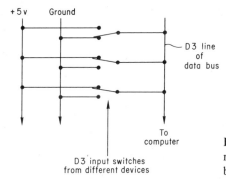

Fig. 11.9. Short circuit produced by connecting outside devices directly to a data bus.

switches connected to the *D*3 data line, although there might be many more. Assume that the uppermost switch happens to be *off* (i.e., connected to Ground), while the other two are *on* (connected to +5 V). It is obvious from the figure that there is a short circuit between +5 V and Ground, so that data line *D*3 can never become HI. In other words, if one single switch is set to Ground, *all* inputs are shortened to LO.

To avoid such a situation, we must connect each input bit to the data bus through a so-called *tri-state buffer*. Unlike binary elements, which have only two possible output states, 0 or 1, the tri-state buffer has three: 0, 1, and "high impedance." The tri-state buffer can be thought of as an electronic equivalent of a simple switch. This is illustrated in Fig. 11.10, where the upper row shows the tri-state buffer symbol with the various possible signals for the three states, and the lower row shows the equivalent switch positions. In the first two states, the $\bar{E}$ (ENABLE) SIGNAL is 0 (so that *ENABLE* = 1, because of the built-in NOT gate). As a result, the buffer output equals its input, no matter whether 0 or 1. This is equivalent to a closed switch that transfers any voltage connected to it. In the third state, $\overline{\text{ENABLE}}$ = 1 (the buffer is *not* enabled), so that the output is disconnected and appears as an open circuit (i.e., a high impedance). This is equivalent to an open switch, in which the input signal is irrelevant.

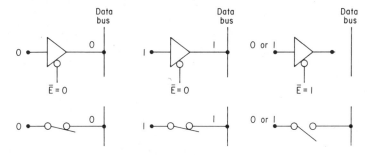

Fig. 11.10. Three possible states of a tri-state buffer and their switch equivalents.

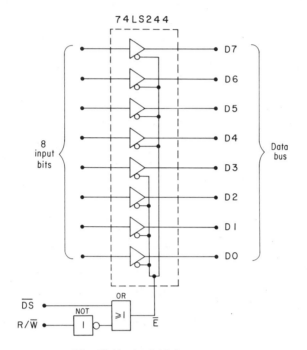

Fig. 11.11. An 8-bit input port.

If each of the switches in Fig. 11.9 is connected to the data bus through a tri-state buffer, short circuits can be avoided. Since each input device is assigned a different address, we must use an address decoding circuit (discussed in the next section) so as to enable only one tri-state buffer at a time. In this way, only one of the many devices connected to the $D3$ data line can actually pass its signal at any given moment, with all others disconnected, so that short circuits are avoided. (This can be visualized as analogous to a telephone network. A particular telephone can potentially connect to any one of millions of others, provided the right number is dialled, but, at any moment, only one of these can actually be connected.)

It should be kept in mind that each address refers to an eight-bit byte. Hence, we need eight separate tri-state buffers for a given input-device address (unless we are not interested in utilizing all of these 8 bits). Therefore, manufacturers supply single ICs containing eight independent tri-state buffers, so that a complete byte can be placed on the data bus in one go. For example, the IC 74LS244 (which has 20 pin connections) uses two separate $\overline{\text{ENABLE}}$ lines, each controlling four buffers. A number of other ICs are available, but most of these have only 16 pins and can thus only accommodate six buffers, so that two such ICs are required to accommodate 1 byte.

To complete this section, Fig. 11.11 shows how an IC, such as the 74LS244, is used to connect eight different binary input devices (or, alternatively, the output of an 8-bit A/D converter) to the data bus. (It is important to note that each input bit must be explicitly HI or LO. Disconnected inputs should not be used, since most TTL elements interpret these as HI. If a LO input is intended, the input line should be grounded.) Whenever $\overline{DS}$ is LO and R/W is HI, the OR-gate output connected to $\overline{E}$ becomes LO, so that all eight tri-state buffers are enabled and transmit their input data to the data bus. When the memory-read cycle is completed, $\overline{DS}$ goes HI, so that $\overline{E}$ is HI, and the input device is effectively disconnected from the data bus. (Note that the 74LS244 requires a LO signal to be enabled, unlike the output latch IC of Fig. 11.8. Hence, the present enable circuit uses an OR gate, instead of the NOR gate used in Figs. 11.6–11.8.)

11.10   ADDRESS DECODING

As already explained in Sections 11.5 and 11.7, each slot is assigned 16 different addresses, so that it can, *if utilized properly*, be connected to 16 separate 8-bit input/output devices. Still using slot 7 for purposes of illustration, these 16 addresses are 49392 to 49407. Any PEEK or POKE command referring to any of these addresses causes the $\overline{DS}$ line of slot 7 to go LO.

In constructing the output or input ports of Figs. 11.8 and 11.11, the $\overline{DS}$ signal was used by itself, without further "decoding." Working in this fashion, it is impossible to connect more than a single input or output device to slot 7. (If, for example, we attempted to connect two 8-bit input devices, each through its own 74LS244 chip as shown in Fig. 11.11, we are again in danger of getting short circuits, since both 74LS244 chips are enabled simultaneously whenever $\overline{DS}$ of slot 7 goes LO and $R/\overline{W}$ goes HI.) In other words, we are using the whole slot for one single device, and are thus wasting the potential for connecting 15 other devices.

In order to utilize all 16 addresses assigned to the slot, we must use a technique called *address decoding*. To illustrate the idea of decoding, suppose we have four input signals, x_1 to x_4, and we want to obtain an output only for the combination $x_1x_1x_3x_4 = 1011$. We could use the decoding circuit shown in Fig. 11.12 for this purpose, in which the AND gate acts as "decoding gate."

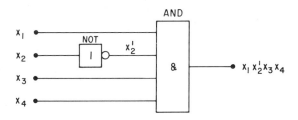

Fig. 11.12. Decoding circuit for $x_1x_2x_3x_4 = 1011$.

Consider now the binary equivalents of the slot 7 addresses 49392 to 49407:

$$49392 = 1100\ 0000\ 1111\ 0000$$

$$49407 = 1100\ 0000\ 1111\ 1111$$

Thus, the address range is given by 1100 0000 1111 $\phi\phi\phi\phi$, where the ϕ symbol represents either 0 or 1. Hence, if a $\overline{DS}$ pulse appears at slot 7, this means that the $A15$ to $A4$ bits on the address bus must be 1100 0000 1111, whereas the four least significant bits $A3$ to $A0$ could be either 0 or 1.

The Apple computer itself carries out the decoding of the $A15$ to $A4$ bits in order to decide whether to send the $\overline{DS}$ pulse to slot 7 or to some other slot, and this is called *partial decoding*. [There is *no* partial decoding in the IBM PC.] However, we must decode the remaining $A3$ to $A0$ bits in order to reach any *specific* one of the 16 addresses assigned to the slot. For example, to reach address 49398, bits $A3$ to $A0$ must represent $49398 - 49392 = 6$, that is, $A3$, $A2$, $A1$, $A0 = 0110$. The resulting decoding circuit for this address is shown in Fig. 11.13. (This circuit is analogous to the circuit of Fig. 11.6, except that now only the address 49398 is being used, whereas, in Fig. 11.6, all of slot 7 can accommodate only one output and one input port.) Thus, any POKE 49398,X command produces a HI pulse at the OUT 49398 line, and this can be used as an ENABLE signal for the SN74100 chip shown in Fig. 11.8, so as to output the byte X to whatever devices are connected to this output port. Similarly, any $Y = $ PEEK(49398) command produces a LO pulse at the $\overline{\text{IN}\ 49398}$ line, and this can be used as an $\overline{\text{ENABLE}}$ signal for the tri-state buffers of Fig. 11.11, so that the variable Y assumes the decimal equivalent of the byte coming in at the input port.

Since either input or output port can be enabled—never both simultaneously!—depending on whether the $R/\overline{W}$ line is HI or LO the moment $\overline{DS}$ goes LO, we can assign both an input *and* an output port to the same address, and they do not interfere with each other. This means that each of the

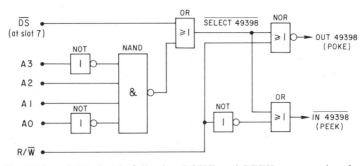

Fig. 11.13. OUT and IN signals following POKE and PEEK commands referring to address 49398.

seven slots in the Apple can accommodate 16 input and 16 output ports, provided address decoding is employed. This makes for a total of 112 input and 112 output ports for the computer. (If necessary, 256 additional addresses per slot become available by using the address block 49408–51199, as explained in Ref. (11.17), but this rarely becomes necessary.)

Suppose we want to utilize all 16 addresses of a given slot. This requires constructing 16 decoding circuits, together having 16 NAND gates (one for each of the 16 addresses represented by $A3, A2, A1, A0 = 0000$ up to 1111), and also four NOT gates, to produce $\overline{A3}, \overline{A2}, \overline{A1}$ and $\overline{A0}$, respectively. Fortunately, this tiresome task can be bypassed by using a single IC chip, such as the 74LS154 "4-line to 16-line decoder." As the name implies, this IC has 4 input lines, connected to $A3, A2, A1,$ and $A0$, respectively, and 16 output lines. One and only one of these 16 outputs is LO at any given time, depending on the momentary state of the four inputs.

Many other decoding ICs are available for different purposes, for example, the 74LS138, which is a "3-line to 8-line decoder." Actually, the Apple II uses such a decoder for its partial decoding to select one of the peripheral interface slots, depending on the values of address lines $A4, A5,$ and $A6$. This partial decoding represents a considerable advantage when interfacing the computer.

[In the IBM PC, there is no partial decoding. Thus, even if we only wish to connect a single exterior device to one of the five expansion slots, we must use full decoding to specify the address to be used, no matter whether this is an I/O port address or whether memory-mapped I/O is being used. This naturally makes interfacing somewhat more complicated. Various possible decoding circuits are described in Ref. (11.7). A good general discussion of address decoding is found in Ref. (11.9).]

11.11   SUMMARY OF COMPUTER INTERFACING

This brief section summarizes all that has been discussed so far concerning computer interfacing by means of the block diagram of Fig. 11.14. The figure applies to a single 8-bit input and a single 8-bit output port. The reader should note the directions of signal flows. Whereas the address and control busses are one-directional, the data bus is bidirectional, depending on whether there is a read or write operation.

Apart from the logic interface, outlined on the drawing by dashed lines, a power interface is also required, consisting of eight input and eight output modules, as described in Sections 4.1.3 and 10.2.3. Although these can be dispensed with for laboratory applications, they are essential for most industrial applications to protect the computer and associated electronic circuits from high-voltage surges, and for other reasons already described. These I/O power modules tend to be expensive and, if many are required, are liable to account for a major percentage of the total system cost.

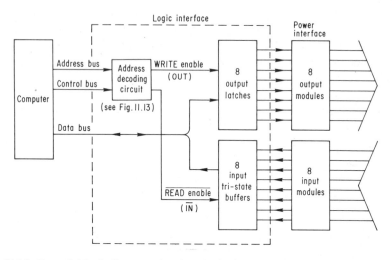

Fig. 11.14. Overall block diagram showing the interface between a computer and the outside world.

11.12   PROGRAMMABLE INTERFACE ADAPTORS

To facilitate the task of interfacing computers, various so-called *programmable interface adaptors* (also known by other names) are available. These are fairly large ICs (usually having 40 or more pins) containing sufficient output latches, tri-state input buffers, and partial decoding circuits to accommodate two or three I/O ports. The characteristic feature of these adaptors is that they permit the user to define each port (and sometimes even individual lines) as input or output ports by means of program commands, that is, using simple POKEs. Some of these adaptors are quite sophisticated and can also perform counting and timing functions. Considering that all this is available for the modest cost of $3-5 per adaptor, they are certainly worth their price.

One of the easiest adaptors to use is the 8255 PPI (*programmable peripheral interface*), manufactured by the Intel Corp. While it is intended primarily for use with Intel microprocessors [such as used in the IBM PC], it can also be used with other computers, with minor adaptations. The 8255 PPI has three I/O ports labeled *A*, *B*, and *C* (for a total of 24 I/O lines), and each port can be programmed by an appropriate POKE command to function either as an input or an output port. Port *C* can be split, with four lines functioning as inputs and the other four as outputs. There are also more sophisticated modes of operating involving "handshaking." (This means that data is only sent if a BUSY/READY line indicates that the outside device is ready to accept or send data; this subject, however, is beyond the scope of this chapter.)

Apart from the *A*, *B*, and *C* ports, there is a fourth port acting as control port. By POKEing an appropriate *control word* to this control port, the 8255 is instructed as to the desired mode of operation, and as to the direction of each of the other three ports or half ports. Since there are a total of four ports, each having its own address, the 8255 uses four of the 16 available slot addresses. Thus, up to four 8255 chips can be assigned to each slot, for a total of 12 I/O ports. This, of course, is less efficient memorywise than using individual input and output ports, as described in the preceding sections (which permitted using up to 32 rather than only 12 ports per slot), but this is the price that must be paid for convenience.

To select a specific one of the four 8255 chips that might be installed in a given slot, address lines $A2$ and $A3$ are used, together with an appropriate external decoding gate. To select any one of the four ports in the chip, address lines $A0$ and $A1$ are used, connected directly to the chip without the need for external decoding. For exact instructions on connecting and programming the 8255 PPI, see Ref. (11.16) or the appropriate Intel data sheet.

Although this is not mentioned in Ref. (11.16), the 8255 PPI will not operate properly with the Apple computer, unless the pulse reaching the $\overline{WR}$ line (pin 36 of the PPI) is stretched to about 400 nsec. This can be done using the IC 74LS122 or 123 (retriggerable monostable multivibrator), described in Section 8.2, or using any pulse-stretching circuit described in the literature.

Another example of an interface adaptor is the 6820 or 6821 PIA (*programmable interface adaptor*) manufactured by Motorola, Inc., or the equivalent 6520 manufactured by MOS Technology. This device is more complicated to program than the 8255 PPI, but offers greater flexibility. Although there are only two I/O ports (instead of three), each individual data line can be independently programmed to function as either input or output. This feature is useful in applications, such as alarm systems, that require a great number of input signals from various sensors, but only have one output. Even though the 6820 PIA has only two I/O ports, it still requires four address locations. This is because the "data direction registers," which specify the direction of each individual data line, require two addresses each. Again, the reader is referred to Ref. (11.16) or to the manufacturer's data sheet for detailed instructions.

A third interface adaptor, the 6522 VIA (*versatile interface adaptor*) manufactured by MOS Technology, is an enhanced version of the 6520 or 6820, offering such features as counting and timing, but with increased programming complexity. Although the 6522 was specifically designed for use with the 6502 microprocessor used in the Apple, it does not ordinarily function with the Apple because of a synchronization problem. To make it operate properly, a 80 nsec delay must be introduced into the $\phi1$ clock-signal line. An easy (though expensive) way to solve this problem is to purchase a John Bell Engineering, Inc., "6522 Parallel Interface" card, which can be placed into any peripheral interface slot, and contains two 6522 VIA chips, together with the required 80 nsec time delay. Thus, this card provides a total of four I/O ports.

Although exact operating instructions are out of place here, it may be instructive to give a simple example. Each of the four ports comes with a data direction register (which defines the direction of each of the eight data lines), and a data register (which determines the actual data bits sent in or out), and each of these two registers has its own address location. Taking one of the four ports, labeled PA, as an example, the address of its data direction register is 50179, and that of its data register is 50177 (all this under the assumption that the card is installed in slot 4).

A POKE 50179,0 command defines all eight lines of this port as input lines, whereas a POKE 50179,255 defines all as output lines. To split the port, we can POKE any intermediate value. To illustrate, a POKE 50179,1 defines data line $D0$ as output (since its binary weight is $2^0 = 1$), and all others as input. A POKE 50179,97 makes data lines $D0$, $D5$, and $D6$ output lines (since their respective weights add up to $1 + 32 + 64 = 97$), while lines $D1$, $D2$, $D3$, $D4$, and $D7$ remain input lines.

Once the direction of each line is defined, the data is sent in or out using PEEK or POKE commands referring to address 50177 (for this particular port). The decimal numbers PEEKed or POKEd have the same significance as far as the individual bits are concerned, as explained in Section 11.6.

There exist other interface adaptors, such as the 6530, 6532, and the 8155 PIA described in Ref. (11.9); the last apart from its I/O ports, also provides a programmable counter and timer. However, caution should be used, since not every adaptor is compatible with every computer.

11.13   APPLICATION EXAMPLE: RAMPING A STEP MOTOR

The technique of ramping step motors is described in Section 1.3.2. Briefly, it consists of gradually increasing the frequency of the input pulses during start-up in order to avoid exceeding the maximum acceleration permissible under inertia loading. Once the motor is brought up to speed ("slewing"), the permissible pulse rate is limited by load, motor, and motor-controller characteristics. During deceleration, the pulse rate must be decreased gradually to avoid overshoot. If the permissible pulse rate is exceeded at any time, the motor is liable to skip some pulses, so that its shaft position, from then on, is in permanent error.

This ramping problem is first solved using a BASIC program. The purpose of this exercise is to demonstrate the limitations of BASIC, and afterwards to show how a brief machine-language subroutine can easily be inserted into the BASIC program to speed up the critical portion.

The example is based on a student-lab experiment developed at the author's institute. To understand the BASIC program, certain information is necessary. The step motor used produces a 1.8 degree shaft rotation per pulse (i.e., 200 pulses per revolution). Shaft position is measured by a homemade incremental encoder providing 100 pulses per revolution, and connected to an UP/DOWN counter with a six-digit LED display, as described in Section 8.8.2.

Rather than build a logic circuit to activate the four motor phases in their proper order, a special UCN-4204B "stepper-motor translator driver" (manufactured by Sprague Electric Co.) is used to drive the motor. This IC not only provides the proper driving logic, but also includes four output driving transistors with transient-protection diodes. The IC has two input connections. One is labeled "Direction Control," and determines the direction of motor stepping, according to whether this input is HI or LO. The second is labeled "Pulse Input," and accepts 5 V driving pulses from the computer, each pulse causing the motor to advance one step. The IC is able to supply a maximum output current of 1.5 A at 20 V, and is thus not intended for very large step motors. Automatic thermal shutdown is provided internally to prevent damage to the IC by overheating.

In order to control the pulse rate, a delay is introduced after each pulse. This delay consists of the BASIC program line

FOR I = 1 to D:NEXT I

which does nothing but use up time, with D being a measure of the delay. Each increase of D by 1 produces an additional 1 msec delay.

To help understand the program, the variables used here to characterize the ramping procedure are defined in Fig. 11.15. At the start of motion, a fairly large delay value $D = DA$ is used, so as to start the motor slowly. After each pulse, D is decremented by an amount DD until reaching DB, which represents the maximum permissible motor speed (the *slewing rate*). To stop the motor, D is incremented by DD after each pulse, until D again reaches DA. This represents the last pulse, after which the motor comes to a stop.

A BASIC program for ramping the step motor is listed in Fig. 11.16. It is assumed that a John Bell Engineering "6522 Parallel Interface Card," described in the previous section, is used. Lines 20 and 30 define the data lines $D0$ of both ports PA and PB as output lines. In line 130, the desired motor-shaft angle (expressed in terms of the counter six-digit LED display) is specified. Line 140 translates this to a number $N2$ in terms of step-motor pulses. If this value of $N2$ equals the present motor position $N1$, then no further motion is necessary, and line 145 ends the run. Otherwise, line 150 calculates the total number of pulses NN that are required. If $NN > 0$, then line 160 POKEs a 1 bit into the $D0$ data line of port PA. Since this line is connected to the "Direction Control" connection of the UCN-4204B "stepper-motor translator/driver," it instructs the motor to step in the UP direction. Conversely, if $NN < 0$, line 170 makes the motor step DOWN. Finally, line 180 defines N as the absolute value of NN, since the sign of NN is already taken into account.

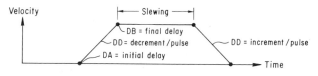

Fig. 11.15. Step-motor ramping parameters.

```
10   HOME : REM     Stepper Ramping
20   POKE 50178,1: REM    Line D0 of port PB outputs pulses
30   POKE 50179,1: REM    Line D0 of port PA determines direction
40   N1 = 0: REM    N1 = total movement
120  PRINT : PRINT "PLEASE ZERO COUNTER!": PRINT
130  INPUT "DESIRED NEW SHAFT ANGLE COUNT? ";A2
140  N2 = A2 * 2: REM    angle in terms of pulses
145  IF N1 = N2 GOTO 490: REM    already on target
150  NN = N2 - N1: REM    required number of pulses
160  IF NN > 0 THEN  POKE 50177,1: REM    UP direction
170  IF NN < 0 THEN  POKE 50177,0: REM    DOWN direction
180  N =  ABS (NN): PRINT
190  PRINT "INPUT RAMPING INFORMATION:"
200  INPUT "INITIAL DELAY COUNT? ";DA
210  INPUT "FINAL (SLEWING) DELAY COUNT? ";DB
215  IF DA = DB THEN DD = 0:NA = 1: GOTO 260
220  INPUT "DELAY-COUNT DECREMENT/PULSE? ( >0, PLEASE!)   ";DD
225  IF DD = 0 GOTO 220
230  NA =  INT ((DA - DB) / DD + 1)
231  REM  no. of required acceleration pulses
232  IF N = > (2 * NA) GOTO 240
234  PRINT : PRINT "SPECIFIED STEP IS TOO SHORT"
235  PRINT "TO REACH SLEWING SPEED!": PRINT
236  NA =  INT (N / 2): GOTO 260
240  DB = DA - (NA - 1) * DD
250  PRINT : PRINT "ACTUAL FINAL DELAY COUNT = ";DB
260  D = DA: REM    present delay count
261  REM    *** begin acceleration ***
280  FOR P = 1 TO NA: REM  no. of acceleration pulses
290  POKE 50176,1: POKE 50176,0: REM  one pulse
300  FOR I = 1 TO D: NEXT : REM  delay
320  D = D - DD: REM  decrease delay
330  NEXT P
331  REM    *** after acceleration, start slewing ***
340  IF N = 2 * NA GOTO 410
350  FOR P = 1 TO N - 2 * NA: REM    no. of slewing pulses
360  POKE 50176,1: POKE 50176,0
380  FOR I = 0 TO D: NEXT
400  NEXT P
401  REM    *** after slewing, start deceleration ***
410  FOR P = 1 TO NA: REM  no. of deceleration pulses
420  POKE 50176,1: POKE 50176,0
440  FOR I = 1 TO D: NEXT
460  D = D + DD: REM  increase delay
470  NEXT P
480  N1 = N1 + NN: REM    update total shaft movement
490  PRINT : PRINT "MOTION COMPLETE": PRINT
500  GOTO 130: REM    start new run
```

Fig. 11.16. BASIC program for ramping a step motor.

The program now prepares the parameters needed for the ramping routine. Lines 200 to 220 ask the user to input the desired values of DA, DB, and DD, as defined in Fig. 11.15. In line 230, the computer calculates how many pulses NA to assign to the acceleration section. Assuming a symmetrical ramping program, NA is also the number of pulses assigned to the deceleration section. This leaves $N - 2NA$ pulses for the slewing (i.e., constant velocity) section; see line 350. If too many pulses are used for accelerating and decelerating, or if the total movement N is too short, the motor never reaches the slewing speed, and this situation is handled by lines 232 to 236.

At this point, the preparatory work is completed, and motor stepping commences. Acceleration is produced by lines 261 to 330, slewing by lines 331 to 400, and deceleration by lines 401 to 470. Since many remarks are included in the program listing, the reader should have no difficulty in following the program. Note that the input pulses for the UCN-4204B driver are produced by first POKEing a 1 and then a 0 into address 50176, which represents data line $D0$ of port PB.

After the motor comes to a standstill, line 480 updates the shaft position $N1$, and line 500 automatically begins a new run by asking for a new shaft-angle count.

When using the program for the first time with a specific motor, the acceleration rate is set by beginning with $DD = 0$ (i.e., constant velocity), and then gradually decreasing DA until the smallest DA is found at which the motor still steps reliably. Then, DD is gradually increased until the largest DD (acceleration) is found that still results in reliable stepping. Finally, the maximum permissible slewing rate is determined by gradually decreasing DB. Reliable stepping is easily confirmed by means of the counter display, which should always agree with the shaft angle specified in line 130 no matter in which direction the motor is being stepped.

The most favorable ramping values of DA, DB, and DD depend not only on motor characteristics and supply voltage, but also on motor load. It is instructive to mount a small flywheel on the motor shaft, and thus study the effect of inertia loading on the ramping values.

If the motor is sufficiently large with respect to its load, it may well turn out that it can step reliably at constant velocity even with DB set to 0. (At $DB = 0$, the delay in line 380 has, in effect, been eliminated.) This is because BASIC programs are very slow. With line 380 eliminated, the pulse rate depends on the time required for the computer to execute the slewing routine of lines 350 to 400, and this results in about 50 pulses/sec. This, then, represents the maximum pulse rate attainable with a BASIC program.

Since good step motors that are not excessively loaded should be able to step at a much higher rate than 50 steps/sec, this means that the motor's full potential cannot be reached with this BASIC program. To increase the attainable stepping rate, an assembly-language (i.e., machine-language) program must be used. Rather than writing the whole program in assembly language, it is sufficient to change critical lines 280 to 470 into an assembly-language subroutine, and insert this into the BASIC program. How this is done is shown in Section 11.15.

11.14 ASSEMBLY-LANGUAGE (MACHINE-LANGUAGE) PROGRAMMING

As previously suggested, assembly-language programs run much faster than BASIC programs. How much faster depends on the specific program, but, in general terms, it can be said that they are faster by a factor of 100 up to 1000. Unfortunately, assembly-language programs are much more tedious to write, understand, and "debug." Therefore, they are only used where their speed is essential, such as for real-time control of fairly fast systems.

To understand how assembly-language programming works, it is necessary to have a basic idea of how the CPU (central processing unit) or microprocessor is organized. Referring to the 6502 microprocessor used in the Apple II Plus/IIe, there are six so-called registers. These are internal memory locations used for storing temporary information, executing program instructions, and keeping track of progress. [By comparison, the 8088 microprocessor used in the IBM PC has 14 registers. Although this provides greater programming flexibility, it also takes longer to master the assembly language if the full potential of the microprocessor is to be utilized.] The six registers of the 6502 are now described briefly.

1. *Accumulator.* This is the most important register, and takes part in almost all arithmetic and logic operations. The accumulator is 8 bits wide, that is, it can store exactly one byte. This byte can be transferred in either direction between the accumulator and any memory location, or between the accumulator and the other registers.

2. *X-Register.* This is also an 8-bit register that can store one byte. It is commonly utilized for counting, but, unlike the accumulator, cannot perform addition or subtraction.

3. *Y-Register.* This is similar to the X-register.

4. *Program Counter.* This is a 16-bit register, and keeps track of progress by storing the address of the program instruction currently being executed. This register requires 16 bits, since it must be able to point to any address between 0 and 65,535.

5. *Stack Pointer.* The use of a LIFO (*last in, first out*) stack is described in Section 10.3 in connection with programmable controllers. The 6502 contains a stack 8 bits wide and 256 bytes deep, using memory locations $100 to $1FF for this purpose. (As explained in Section 8.7.1, the $ sign indicates that the number is expressed in hexadecimal notation.) Thus, the stack can store up to 256 bytes at a time. The stack pointer is 8 bits wide and, in contrast to the stack itself, can

store only one byte. This byte represents the address at the top of the stack, so that the CPU knows which memory location to go to each time a byte is to be added to or taken off the stack. The stack is accessed automatically by the CPU to store temporary data, for instance, when executing subroutines or so-called "interrupts."

6. *Processor Status Register.* Unlike the other five registers, which store true 8-bit numbers, this register stores individual bits that carry information about the current status of the CPU. These bits thus have no significance as numbers, but are used for a variety of housekeeping chores.

With this brief description of the registers, we can illustrate how the computer is programmed. This is done using so-called *instruction codes* or *operational codes* (*opcodes*). For example, suppose we want to load a certain number into the accumulator. The instruction code for this is LDA (*load accumulator*) followed by the number to be loaded. There are, however, several ways of specifying the number to be loaded. In the *immediate mode*, the # sign is used, followed by the number expressed in hexadecimal notation. Note that in assembly-language programming, *all* numbers are expressed in hexadecimal notation. Thus, to load decimal number 255 into the accumulator, we write LDA #$FF. If the # sign is omitted, the CPU loads into the accumulator the number presently stored in *memory location $FF*; this is called *absolute addressing*. This is equivalent to a PEEK command in BASIC. Just as in PEEK commands, an LDA $FF command only reads but does *not* alter the data stored in memory location $FF.

To transfer data from the accumulator to memory, the STA (*store from accumulator*) instruction is used. Thus, the command STA $C400 means that the byte presently in the accumulator is stored in memory location $C400 (or 50176 in decimal location). This is equivalent to the POKE command in BASIC. Here, too, STA commands do not remove or alter the byte presently in the accumulator.

Another example of an instruction code causing data transfer is the LDX #$12 command (*load into x*), which causes the number $12 = 18 to be loaded into the X-register. On the other hand, LDX $12 causes the byte presently stored in memory location $12 to be loaded into the X-register. LDY commands do the same for the Y-register.

There are a number of instructions for transferring data between registers. Thus, TXA transfers a byte from the X-register to the accumulator, whereas TAX does exactly the opposite. Instructions TYA and TAY do the same, but with respect to the Y-register. Note that all of these instructions do not alter the byte stored in the contributing register, but only that in the recipient one.

The instruction INC followed by a memory location increments the number stored in that location by 1, whereas INX and INY do the same with respect to the X- or Y-registers, respectively. To decrement the number, we use DEC, DEX, or DEY, respectively.

At this point, it is appropriate to explain the difference between assembly and machine language, two terms often inaccurately used synonymously. Actually, the microprocessor is unable to understand instructions such as LDX, DEY, and so on. To be exact, each of these instructions really consists of an eight-bit byte stored in memory. Using hexadecimal representation, each such byte is written more compactly as a two-digit number. Thus, the actual opcodes for several of the instructions discussed so far follow:

DEC: $CE
DEX: $CA
DEY: $88
INC: $EE
INX: $C8
LDA: $A9

A true machine-language program is written using these hexadecimal opcodes, and this is the only language the microprocessor understands. Note that programs written in BASIC, FORTRAN, or any other "high-level" language must first be translated, or *compiled*, into machine code before they can be executed by the microprocessor. In the case of BASIC, this is done automatically by a so-called *interpreter* resident in most microcomputers. The user may not even be aware of the process, but this is the reason why BASIC programs are slow.

Obviously, writing a program in machine language is very tedious, unless the programmer has memorized all the hexadecimal opcodes. Similarly, machine-language code is difficult to interpret. That is where assembly language, which uses so-called *mnemonics* (memory aids) comes in. It is easier to remember that LDA means "LoaD Accumulator" than to remember the code A9. However, after a program is written in assembly language, it must be translated into machine code. This is done using a so-called *assembler*, a special computer program written for this purpose. A number of assemblers are commercially available for the Apple as programs stored on disk. Apart from translating each instruction into machine code, most assemblers also perform other housekeeping tasks that greatly facilitate programming. Thus, they organize the machine code in the memory, permit the definition of "labels" (equivalent to line numbers in BASIC), permit the addition of remarks, and so on.

It should be mentioned that the Apple II Plus/IIe comes with a built-in "miniassembler." This *only* translates mnemonic instructions into machine code *without* performing any housekeeping functions. Thus, the miniassembler is not convenient for long assembly-language programs, but is perfectly adequate for short subroutines to be inserted into a longer BASIC program. For instructions on using this miniassembler, see Ref. (11.3).

The 6502 microprocessor has 56 different instructions in its instruction set, one-quarter of which have been described here. [By comparison, the 8088 used in the IBM PC has over 150 instructions, and is thus more difficult to master.] For a detailed description of these instructions and how they are used, see, for example, Refs. (11.19) or (11.20). This chapter does not pretend to teach assembly-language programming, for which a complete book is required. Our aim is to provide a very brief, and therefore superficial, idea of what it is all about. For this purpose, we utilize the BASIC program for step-motor ramping from the previous section, and replace that part of the program that generates the pulses by a much faster assembly-language subroutine.

11.15 ASSEMBLY-LANGUAGE STEP-MOTOR RAMPING SUBROUTINE

Referring to the BASIC program listed in Fig. 11.16, our first step is to cancel program lines 261 to 470, since these are to be replaced by the assembly-language subroutine.

The next step is to transfer essential data from the BASIC to the assembly-language program. This is done by means of POKE statements. A given POKE statement stores an eight-bit byte in a specific memory location, from where it can later be transferred to the accumulator or to the X- or Y-registers by instructions such as LDA, LDX, or LDY. (This is similar to placing a message into a mailbox to be picked up later by the recipient.) The POKE statements required for our example follow, with the accompanying REMarks providing full explanation. (Note that the memory locations used in the following POKE statements have been chosen arbitrarily. However, it is vital to select locations not being used for other purposes, such as for storing the program, since these would otherwise be overwritten.)

261	POKE 32768,D	:	REM	Places initial delay between pulses $D = DA$ (in msec) into memory location $8000 (the hexadecimal equivalent of 32768).
262	POKE 32769,DD	:	REM	Places delay decrement or increment DD per pulse (in msec) into location $8001.
263	POKE 32770,NA	:	REM	Places number of acceleration pulses NA, as calculated in line 230 or 236, into location $8002.
264	SP = N − 2*NA	:	REM	Number of slewing pulses.
265	POKE 32771,SP	:	REM	Places number of slewing pulses into location $8003.
267	POKE 32773,NA	:	REM	Places number of deceleration pulses, which equals number of acceleration pulses NA, into location $8005.
268	POKE 32774,0	:	REM	Places a 0 "flag" into location $8006.

269 IF N = NA*2
    THEN POKE
    32774,1   : REM   If no slewing can occur, the flag in location
                                      $8006 is set to 1.
270 CALL 37632   : REM   Begins assembly-language subroutine.

The CALL statement causes the CPU control to jump to the specified address (37632 = $9300) and begin executing the assembly-language instructions found there and in successive locations. Here, too, address 37632 has been chosen arbitrarily, but first making sure that we are entering "free territory" not occupied by anything else.

We have now reached the assembly-language subroutine, which is listed in Fig. 11.17. Before explaining each statement, note the following general points.

Assembly-language programs—unlike BASIC programs—use no line numbers. The numbers shown in the left-hand column in Fig. 11.17 are added solely to aid in the explanation.

Instead of line numbers, each assembly-language instruction is assigned a memory location. While the first statement LDA # $01 is placed in location $9300 (due to our CALL 37632 statement in line 270), this does not mean that the next statement will be in location $9301. As a matter of fact, it is in location $9302, because the first instruction requires room for *two* bytes (one for the opcode corresponding to LDA, and the second for the data $01). The various assembly-language instructions require anywhere from one to three bytes, depending on their nature. The assignment of memory locations for each instruction is handled automatically by the assembler. (However, the locations can also be calculated manually by the programmer, if desired, by referring to tables showing the number of bytes required for each opcode.) When using the Apple miniassembler, the memory locations assigned to each instruction are automatically printed on each line, but these are not shown in Fig. 11.17.

We now commence with an explanation of the program. Lines 1 to 4 are intended to send one pulse to the stepping motor (and are thus equivalent to line 290 in the BASIC program). In line 1, a 1 is loaded into the accumulator, and in line 2, this 1 is sent to memory location $C400, which is equivalent to 50176. Thus, these two lines are the equivalent of the BASIC statement POKE 50176,1. In lines 3 and 4, the process is repeated, but this time a 0 is loaded and sent in order to complete the pulse.

In line 5, the initial delay between pulses (in milliseconds) that was POKEd into location $8000 by the new BASIC line No. 261 is loaded into the Y-register.

In line 6, the number $C8 = 200 is loaded into the X-register in preparation for producing a 1 msec delay. In line 7, this number is decremented by one, producing 199, 198, 197, and so on, each time this line is executed.

The instruction BNE in line 8 stands for *branch if not equal to zero.* This means that if the result of the previous instruction DEX is not a zero, program execution jumps to the address represented by the label "A." In our example, "A" refers to the previous line 7, so that the instruction DEX is repeated. If,

Line	Address	Assembler Code	Remarks:
1	9300:	LDA #$01	
2		STA $C400	POKE 50176,1
3		LDA #$00	
4		STA $C400	POKE 50176,0 for 1 pulse
5		LDY $8000	Load delay into Y-register
6	"B"	LDX #$C8	Load 200 into X-register
7	"A"	DEX	
8		BNE "A"	1 msec delay
9		DEY	
10		BNE "B"	Full delay
11		DEC $8002	Subtract one pulse
12		BEQ "C"	Finished accelerating
13		SEC	Set Carry before subtraction
14		LDA $8000	
15		SBC $8001	Reduce delay
16		STA $8000	Store new delay
17		JMP $9300	Continue accelerating
18	"C"	LDA $8006	Load 'No slewing' flag
19		BNE "F"	No slewing! Start deceler.
20		LDA #$01	
21		STA $C400	
22		LDA #$00	
23		STA $C400	1 pulse
24		LDY $8000	Load delay into Y-register
25	"E"	LDX #$C8	Load 200 into X-register
26	"D"	DEX	
27		BNE "D"	1 msec delay
28		DEY	
29		BNE "E"	Full delay
30		DEC $8003	Subtract one pulse
31		BNE "C"	Continue slewing
32	"F"	LDA #$01	
33		STA $C400	
34		LDA #$00	
35		STA $C400	1 pulse
36		LDY $8000	Load delay into Y-register
37	"H"	LDX #$C8	Load 200 into X-register
38	"G"	DEX	
39		BNE "G"	1 msec delay
40		DEY	
41		BNE "H"	Full delay
42		DEC $8005	Subtract one pulse
43		BEQ "I"	Finished deceleration
44		CLC	Clear Carry before addition
45		LDA $8000	
46		ADC $8001	Increase delay
47		STA $8000	Store new delay
48		JMP "F"	Continue deceleration
49	"I"	RTS	Return to BASIC program

Fig. 11.17. Assembly-language program for ramping a step motor.

however, the result *is* equal to zero, no branch or jump takes place, and program execution continues at the line 9. It should be obvious to the reader that this BNE instruction is equivalent to the BASIC statement "IF...THEN GOTO." Since the initial value loaded in the X-register is 200, the loop is executed 200 times before continuing on to line 9. Since each DEX–BNE loop uses approximately 5 μsec, 200 such loops produce a 1 msec delay.

In line 9, the delay value loaded into the Y-register in line 5 is decremented by 1. The BNE instruction in line 10 checks whether zero has already been reached. If not, label "B" returns program execution to line 6, so as to produce another 1 msec delay. Only after the full delay that was called for has occurred, does program execution continue at line 11. (Lines 5 to 10 serve the same function as line No. 300 in the BASIC program.)

Since one pulse has now been sent to the motor, the DEC $8002 instruction in line 11 subtracts 1 from the number of acceleration pulses that are still needed, as stored in location $8002. The BEQ (*branch if equal to zero*) instruction in line 12 checks whether all the acceleration pulses called for have been sent. If so (that is, if the number presently stored in $8002 has reached zero), then program execution is sent by label "C" to line 18, which is the beginning of the slewing region, in which the motor steps at maximum constant speed. Otherwise, execution continues at line 13. (Lines 11 and 12 serve the same function as lines 280 and 330 in the BASIC program.)

The delay between pulses must now be reduced by the decrement stored by BASIC line 262 in location $8001. As preparation for any subtraction, the SEC (*set carry*) instruction of line 13 must be executed, but the explanation for this is not discussed here. After that, line 14 loads the previous delay from location $8000 into the accumulator, and the SBC (*subtract with carry*) instruction in line 15 subtracts the decrement stored in location $8001 from the previous delay. The resulting new reduced delay is placed back into location $8000 by the STA instruction of line 16. (Lines 13 to 16 are equivalent to line No. 320 in the BASIC program.) The JMP (*jump*) instruction of line 17 returns program execution to address location $9300 (line 1) for the next pulse.

In the BASIC program, line 340 is inserted to check whether the motor ever reaches slewing speed. If not, the deceleration procedure at line 410 begins. The equivalent check is here carried out by lines 18 and 19. In line 18, the "flag" that had been stored in location $8006 by BASIC lines 268 or 269 is loaded into the accumulator. Line 19 checks the nature of this flag. If it is a 1 (i.e., *not* zero), slewing is skipped by transferring program execution to line 32, which commences the deceleration. If, however, the flag is zero, no branch is performed, and execution continues with Line 20.

Lines 20 to 23 produce one pulse, and are identical to the previously explained lines 1 to 4. Similarly, lines 24 to 29 are identical to previous lines 5 to 10, and produce the required delay. Since this delay remains constant during slewing, the decrementing procedure of lines 13 to 16 is not carried out here. All that is required is to keep track of the number of pulses that have been sent. This is done by lines 30 and 31, which return execution to line 20 as long as pulses are still required. When the number of required slewing pulses have been sent, no branch is taken in line 31, and execution continues in line 32. (Note that lines 30 and 31 perform the same function as lines 11, 12, and 17, though slightly differently.)

The deceleration procedure commences with line 32. It is almost identical to the acceleration procedure, except that the delay must be increased rather than decreased. To do this, the ADC (*add with carry*) instruction in line 46 is used. Just as every subtract instruction has to be preceded by the SEC instruction (line 13), so every add instruction must be preceded by a CLC (*clear carry*), line 44. Again, the explanation for this is not discussed here.

The BEQ (*branch if equal to zero*) instruction in line 43 checks whether the required number of deceleration pulses have been sent. If so, a branch to line 49 is taken, where the RTS (*return from subroutine*) instruction exits the assembly-language subroutine, and returns program execution to the next line (i.e., line 480) of the BASIC program.

A final note: when using the miniassembler of the APPLE, the address locations assigned by the miniassembler to every instruction are shown on the screen, and these are used instead of the labels shown in the listing of Fig. 11.17.

To save this assembly-language program, the necessary command is BSAVE B.RAMPING,A$9300,L$85, where B.RAMPING is the name given to this program (the "B" stands for "binary"), A$9300 represents the starting address, and L$85 the program length (with some factor of safety). In order to merge the two programs, the line

15   PRINT CHR$(4)"BLOAD B.RAMPING"

is inserted at the beginning of the BASIC program. When this program is RUN, its first action is to load the machine-language program from the diskette into the computer's memory, starting at address $9300, in preparation for line 270.

In running this combined program, we find that it works fine, except for one problem. If SP, the number of slewing pulses POKEd into location 32771 in line 265 should exceed 255, an "ILLEGAL QUANTITY" error message results. This is because we are dealing with an 8-bit microprocessor, so that memory locations can only hold numbers from 0 to 255. To solve this problem, we must split SP into a high and a low byte. The high byte equals the integer value of SP/256, and the low byte equals SP minus 256 times the high byte. These two bytes are now POKEd into separate memory locations using the following two lines:

266   POKE 32772,INT(SP/256)   : REM   Places HI byte of SP into location $8004.

265   POKE 32771,SP − 256*INT(SP/256)   : REM   Places LO byte of SP into location $8003. This line replaces previous line 265.

The assembly-language program of Fig. 11.17 must now be modified to make use of these two bytes. This is done by inserting the following seven lines between lines 29 and 30:

Line No.

29A		LDA $8004	(Test HI byte)
29B		BEQ "J"	(If HI byte = 0, continue with line 30)
29C		LDA $8003	(Test LO byte)
29D		BNE "K"	(If both bytes are not 0, decrement LO byte)
29E		DEC $8004	(If LO byte = 0, decrement HI byte)
29F	"K"	DEC $8003	(Decrement LO byte. Decrementing 0 gives FF)
29G		JMP "C"	(Continue slewing)
30	"J"	DEC $8003	(Subtract one pulse)

The program now operates properly, with SP having any value up to $16^4 - 1 = 65535$. If even higher values should be required, the method can be extended using a third, even higher byte.

If we did not use an artificial delay to slow down the pulses sent to the step motor, the assembly-language program would produce one pulse approximately every 40 μsec. This compares to one pulse every 20 msec with the BASIC program. Thus, the assembly-language program is about 500 times faster. Naturally, in the application under discussion, this high speed cannot be utilized, since the stepping motor cannot possibly handle 25,000 pulses per second. Using the equipment described in Section 11.13, the fastest ramping parameters that could be used are $DA = 12, DB = 5$, and $DD = 1$. Since the unit time-delay used in this assembly-language program is 1 msec, $DB = 5$ corresponds to a delay of 5 msec, or 200 pulses/sec, which is four times as fast as with the BASIC program.

11.16 CONCLUDING REMARKS

The example of the previous section was deliberately chosen to be very simple. The reader may have received the impression that assembly-language programming is very easy; this is certainly not so. At the same time, it is important to dispel the mistaken notion that assembly-language programming is a "black art" to be mastered only by a selected group of initiates. The truth lies somewhere in between.

A great number of topics connected with assembly-language programming have not been mentioned. These include, among others, the use of flags and interrupt routines. Since the computer does not provide error messages in response to mistakes in assembly-language programs (as opposed to the error messages conveniently produced in BASIC), error detection and program debugging are much more difficult. It can be said that considerable experience is required to become a really good assembly-language programmer.

For these reasons, it is recommended to write the major part of most programs in BASIC, and only use assembly-language subroutines for those portions where speed is essential (especially for loops that must be repeated many times). There is absolutely no point in using assembly language for the interactive data-inputting routines at the beginning of a program, or for the routines used at the end of the program to display or print out results. The main theme of Ref. (11.20) is to show how various assembly-language subroutines can be inserted into BASIC programs.

Returning to the subject of computer interfacing, here, too, many important topics have not been discussed. These include such topics as handshaking (i.e., continuing program execution only after receiving a signal from an outside device indicating readiness to continue); interrupts (i.e., stopping normal program execution and jumping instead to a different routine, in response to some outside event, especially in applications in which the computer must handle various tasks simultaneously); use of A/D and D/A converters (important in handling analog data); and the use of serial data transmission (used for long-distance data transmission, in which the individual bits of a byte are sent one after the other, rather than in parallel). Serial communication is often performed by the well-known RS-232C serial communication card, used to establish communication between different computers, or between computers and programmable controllers. For discussion of all these important topics, the reader is referred to Refs. (11.5)–(11.18).

The use of microcomputers to help solve automation problems is becoming commonplace. The question is usually whether to use a microcomputer or a programmable controller. As discussed in Chapter 10, programmable controllers are generally more reliable in difficult industrial environments, and are especially built to handle a large number of I/O lines. Microcomputers, on the other hand, are preferable where a great deal of data processing and numerical calculation is required (such as in robot control), and where the number of I/O lines is limited. For further discussion of microcomputer applications, see Refs. (11.1) and (11.21)–(11.23).

PROBLEMS

11.1. (a) Using the Apple II Plus or IIe computer, what is the result if you enter a POKE 30000,77 command, followed by a PRINT PEEK (30000)?

     (b) Repeat part (a), but using the address 40000 instead of 30000?

     (c) Repeat part (a), but using the address 50000 instead of 30000?

     (d) Repeat part (a), but using the address 60000 instead of 30000?

11.2. Which peripheral interface slot in the Apple II Plus/IIe receives a $\overline{DS}$ signal as a result of these commands?

     (a) A = PEEK(49300).

     (b) POKE 49300,200.

     (c) POKE 49300,255.

     (d) B = PEEK(49350).

     (e) POKE 49380,22.

11.3. Calculate the output of an 8-bit A/D converter having a 0–5 V input range if its input voltage is:
   (a) 1.2 V.
   (b) 3.5 V.
   (c) 4.4 V.
   (d) 4.9 V.

11.4. Calculate the input voltage of an 8-bit A/D converter having a 0–5 V range, if its output is:
   (a) 10
   (b) 75
   (c) 154
   (d) 245

11.5. Eight switches are connected (through appropriate hardware) to data bus $D0–D7$. What is the result of the appropriate PEEK command for the following conditions:
   (a) The switches connected to $D0–D3$ have HI outputs, and the switches connected to $D4–D7$ have LO outputs.
   (b) The switches connected to $D0–D3$ have LO outputs, and the switches connected to $D4–D7$ have HI outputs.
   (c) Switches connected to $D0$, $D2$, $D4$, and $D6$ have HI outputs, and those connected to $D1$, $D3$, $D5$, and $D7$ have LO outputs.
   (d) Switches connected to $D0$, $D2$, $D4$, and $D6$ have LO outputs, and those connected to $D1$, $D3$, $D5$, and $D7$ have HI outputs.

11.6. Eight switches are connected (through appropriate hardware) to data bus $D0–D7$. Determine the output of each switch if the appropriate PEEK command produces the following values:
   (a) 19
   (b) 88
   (c) 149
   (d) 233

11.7. Design a decoding circuit (using only NOT and AND gates) for *fully* decoding the following:
   (a) address 49300
   (b) address 49399
   (c) address 45355

11.8. Design a decoding circuit (using only NOT and AND gates) for *partially* decoding the eight least significant bits of each of the addresses specified in Problem 11.7, assuming that the eight most significant bits have already been decoded within the computer.

11.9. Draw the necessary circuit for sending one byte to some outside device by means of the command POKE 49402,xxx. (The circuit should include the necessary decoding gates and output latches.)

11.10. Using the John Bell 6522 "parallel interface card,"
  (a) What BASIC commands are required to send the number 173 to Port *A*?
  (b) Repeat part (a), but using assembly language.

11.11. Write a brief assembly-language subroutine (to be incorporated into some BASIC program) that produces five successive upgoing pulses.

11.12. Repeat Problem 11.11, but with 1 msec delays between successive pulses.

11.13. Repeat Problem 11.11, but sending 10 successive pulses, with the delay between successive pulses increasing with each pulse from 1 to 9 msec.

11.14. Repeat Problem 11.13, but with the delay between successive pulses decreasing with each pulse from 10 to 2 msec.

11.15. Write an assembly-language subroutine that produces 80,000 successive upgoing pulses.

11.16. Sixteen LED lamps are to be actuated by means of two ICs 74100 (output latches) mounted on the same card. This card is inserted in slot 7 of the Apple computer. Draw the required logic circuit, and write several BASIC commands to illustrate how the different LEDs can each be actuated individually.

11.17. A large number of industrial processes are to be controlled by analog signals, using the Apple computer. Each process has a single input supplied by the computer through an 8-bit D/A converter. The process output, as measured by an appropriate sensing element, goes to an A/D converter, that sends an 8-bit signal back to the computer. Calculate the maximum number of processes that can be accommodated by a single computer slot, if we use
  (a) an interface built using the ICs 74100 and 74LS244
  (b) 8255 PPIs
  (c) 6522 VIAs
  (d) a Bell Engineering "6522 Parallel Interface Card."

REFERENCES

11.1.   C. D. Johnson, *Microcomputer-Based Process Control*, Prentice-Hall, Englewood Cliffs, NJ, 1984.

11.2.   D. L. Cannon and G. Luecke, *Understanding Microprocessors*, Texas Instruments Inc. (Radio Shack, Tandy Corp., Fort Worth, TX 76102), 1979.

11.3.   *APPLE II Reference Manual*, Apple Computer Inc., Cupertino, CA, 1980.

11.4.   *IBM Personal Computer Technical Reference*, IBM, 1983.

11.5.   H. S. Stone, *Microcomputer Interfacing*, Addison-Wesley, Reading, MA, 1982.

11.6.   J. F. Craine and G. R. Martin, *Microcomputers in Engineering and Science*, Addison-Wesley, Reading, MA, 1985.

11.7. L. C. Eggebrecht, *Interfacing to the IBM Personal Computer*, Howard W. Sams, Indianapolis, IN, 1983.

11.8. W. G. Houghton, *Mastering Digital Device Control*, Sybex Computer Books, Berkeley, CA, 1987.

11.9. B. B. Brey, *Microprocessor/Hardware Interfacing and Applications*, Charles E. Merrill Publ. Co., Columbus, OH, 1984.

11.10. C. K. Yuen, K. G. Beauchamp, and G. P. Robinson, *Microprocessor Systems and their Applications to Signal Processing*, Academic Press, New York, 1982.

11.11. J. C. Cluley, *Interfacing to Microprocessors*, McGraw-Hill, New York, 1983.

11.12. R. C. Holland, *Microcomputers and their Interfacing*, Pergamon, Oxford, 1984.

11.13. R. C. Holland, *Integrated Circuits and Microprocessors*, Pergamon, Oxford, 1986.

11.14. D. A. Fraser, R. Gregory, B. Hawken, B. Holsworth, G. Jones, and M. Ryal, *Introduction to Microcomputer Engineering*, Halsted Press (Wiley), New York, 1985.

11.15. D. D. Givone and R. P. Roesser, *Microprocessors/Microcomputers: An Introduction*, McGraw-Hill, New York, 1980.

11.16. J. E. Uffenbeck, *Hardware Interfacing with the Apple II Plus*, Prentice-Hall, Englewood Cliffs, NJ, 1983.

11.17. J. A. Titus, D. G. Larsen, and C. A. Titus, *Apple Interfacing*, Howard W. Sams, Indianapolis, IN, 1981.

11.18. J. W. Coffron, *The Apple Connection*, Sybex Computer Books, Berkeley, CA, 1982.

11.19. R. Hyde, *Using 6502 Assembly Language*, Reston Publ. Co., Reston, VA, 1981.

11.20. C. W. Finley and R. E. Myers, *Assembly Language for the Applesoft Programmer*, Addison-Wesley, Reading, MA, 1984.

11.21. C. R. Asfahl, *Robots and Manufacturing Automation*, Wiley, New York, 1985.

11.22. D. M. Auslander and P. Sagues, *Microprocessors for Measurement and Control*, Osborne/McGraw-Hill, New York, 1981.

11.23. T. P. Leung and W. K. Chick, "Micro-computer Control for Low Cost Automation," *Measurement and Control*, Vol. 15, No. 2, Feb. 1982, pp. 67–71.

CHAPTER 12

INTRODUCTION TO ASSEMBLY AUTOMATION

This chapter deals with purely mechanical devices—no electronics, pneumatics, or switching circuits. In the final stage of many manufacturing systems, the various parts must be assembled into a finished product. This can be done using a fixed special-purpose machine, a technique called hard automation, and is only justifiable if huge production volumes are required. For small- or medium-size production runs, it is more economical to employ general-purpose devices, such as pneumatic cylinders, manipulators, or robots, controlled by fixed control circuits, programmable controllers, or microcomputers. If either of the latter two control methods are employed, we have what is called soft or flexible automation.

In either case, whether hard or flexible automation is employed, the parts to be assembled must be fed to the robot or to the assembly device properly oriented and at the required rate. If this is not done efficiently, the efforts of the most sophisticated robot or assembly machine are frustrated, and the money invested in them wasted. Devices that perform this feeding and orienting function are the main subject of this chapter.

The subject of assembly automation has been studied intensively at the University of Massachusetts, with the results described in Refs. (12.1) and (12.2). A good summary of this work is also found in Chapter 3 of Ref. (12.3).

12.1 NONVIBRATORY FEEDING AND ORIENTING DEVICES

There are a great number of devices for feeding parts automatically, and the choice depends on the shape of the parts. Within the framework of this short chapter, it is only possible to describe a few typical examples. Some feeders feed the parts without attempting to orient them, whereas others also perform automatic orienting. Hence, feeding and orienting are best discussed together.

In general, the parts start out dumped randomly in a container or hopper. There are many types of hopper feeders that remove the parts from the hopper and place them into or onto a sloping track, along which they move by gravity to the assembly machine. For example, Fig. 12.1 shows a *bladed-wheel hopper feeder*. As the wheel rotates, the blades agitate the parts so that they tend to drop into the sloping track and thus slide out of the hopper.

Figure 12.2 shows the *centerboard hopper feeder*. The centerboard oscillates up and down through the mass of parts, picking up only those that happen to be in the proper orientation. To do this efficiently, the edge of the centerboard must be properly shaped. For cylindrical parts, the edge must have a circular groove encircling about one quarter of the cylinder periphery, and the width of the centerboard should be equal to or slightly larger than the part diameter. At the top of the stroke; the groove is in line with the track opening, so that any parts that have landed inside the groove slide naturally into the track.

For efficient operation, the centerboard should have a slow upward travel but a quick return stroke. A short dwell at the top of the stroke allows time for the parts in the groove to slide into the track. Cams can be employed to produce this kind of programmed motion, although so-called quick-return linkages—used in many machine tools such as shapers or planers—can also be used.

The shape of the centerboard edge must be designed to accommodate the shape of the parts. For disk-shaped parts, for example, the groove should be a thin deep slot, as shown in Fig. 12.3(a). For screws, bolts, or rivets, a similar deep slot aligns the parts head up, so that the device not only feeds but also orients the parts; see Fig. 12.3(b). An arrangement for feeding and orienting L-shaped parts is shown in Fig. 12.3(c), where a stationary baffle plate guides the parts into the

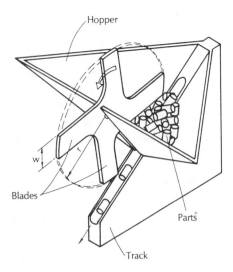

Fig. 12.1. Bladed-wheel hopper feeder. (From Ref. (12.2), by permission of Dept. of Mech. Eng., Univ. of Mass.)

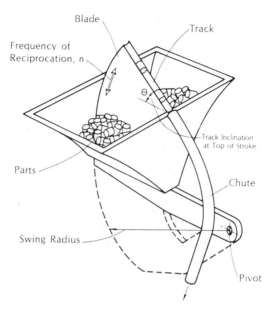

Fig. 12.2. Centerboard hopper feeder. (From Ref. (12.2), by permission of Dept. of Mech. Eng., Univ. of Mass.)

proper position. The angle machined into the centerboard edge causes parts wrongly oriented to slide off and fall back into the hopper.

Whereas the centerboard of Fig. 12.2 oscillates, there is also a *rotary-centerboard hopper feeder* suitable for U-shaped parts, as shown in Fig. 12.4. The rotation of the bladed wheel agitates the part, causing some of them to fall into the shaped groove in the hopper bottom with proper orientation. The wheel then picks up some of these parts and places them onto the slanted delivery track.

A completely different principle is employed in the *reciprocating-tube hopper feeder*, which is shown in Fig. 12.5. The delivery tube reciprocates up and down

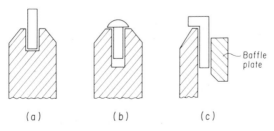

Fig. 12.3. Shape of a centerboard slot for (a) disk-shaped parts, (b) screw-shaped parts, and (c) L-shaped parts.

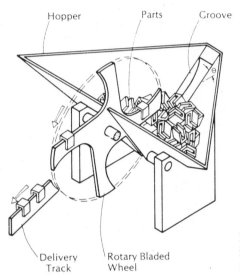

Hopper   Parts   Groove

Delivery Track   Rotary Bladed Wheel

Fig. 12.4. Rotary-centerboard hopper feeder. (From Ref. (12.2), by permission of Dept. of Mech. Eng., Univ. of Mass.)

through a funnel-shaped hopper. (In some designs, the tube is stationary and the hopper reciprocates, but the general principle is the same.) The open end of the tube is cut at an angle, so that incorrectly oriented parts slide off during the tube motion. Only parts with proper orientation are able to enter the delivery tube. Here, too, the relative motion between tube and hopper serves to agitate the parts.

Important pioneering work in the development of part-feeding devices has been carried out at the Department of Mechanical Engineering of the University of Massachusetts. The results were first published in Ref. (12.2), and the majority of figures in this chapter have been reproduced (by permission) from this important book, which can be considered as the "Bible" of small-part feeding devices.

The book not only describes most important part-feeding methods, but also classifies the parts using a systematic coding system that characterizes their shape. A great number of design sheets are presented for various combinations of part shapes and feeder types, and provide valuable design information concerning the constructional parameters of the feeder, and the feeding rates that can be expected for various part dimensions. Figure 12.5 shows such a design sheet for the reciprocating-tube hopper feeder feeding cylindrical parts. The sheet presents equations for calculating the recommended inner diameter of the delivery tube, and shows a graph indicating the expected feed rate. As this graph shows, feed rate increases with a decreasing length/diameter ratio of the part. However, for $L/D < 1.5$, the part cannot be oriented anymore. A brief description of the content of Ref. (12.2) and of how the data for the various design sheets were obtained is given in Refs. (12.4) and (12.5).

Another design sheet from Ref. (12.2) is reproduced in Fig. 12.6, and pertains to the so-called *stationary-hook hopper feeder*. This feeder is especially suitable

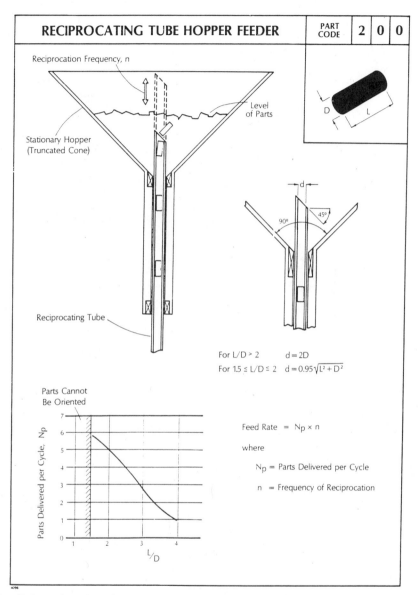

| RECIPROCATING TUBE HOPPER FEEDER | PART CODE | 2 | 0 | 0 |

Reciprocation Frequency, n

Level of Parts

Stationary Hopper
(Truncated Cone)

Reciprocating Tube

For L/D > 2 $d = 2D$

For $1.5 \leq L/D \leq 2$ $d = 0.95\sqrt{L^2 + D^2}$

Parts Cannot Be Oriented

Parts Delivered per Cycle, N_p

L/D

Feed Rate $= N_p \times n$

where

N_p = Parts Delivered per Cycle

n = Frequency of Reciprocation

Fig. 12.5. Design sheet for a reciprocating-tube hopper feeder. (From Ref. (12.2), by permission of Dept. of Mech. Eng., Univ. of Mass.)

for fragile parts that might be damaged by some other hopper feeders. A rotating disk turns within the stationary hopper. When the parts come into contact with the leading edge of the stationary hook, they are guided toward the periphery of the disk, and finally led to the delivery chute on the hopper wall. As stated on the design sheet, the recommended disk diameter is 36 times the part diameter. The graph shows that feed rate increases with decreasing *L/D* ratios of the parts.

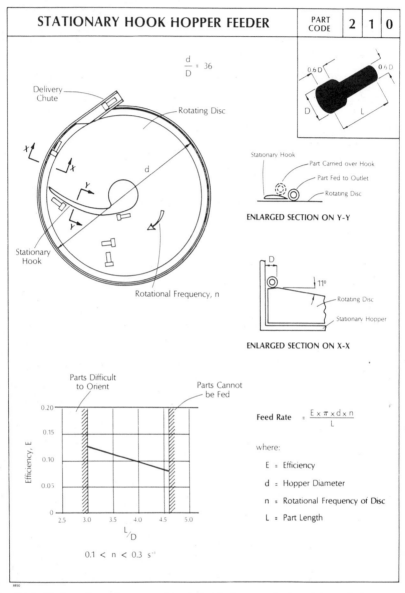

| STATIONARY HOOK HOPPER FEEDER | PART CODE | 2 | 1 | 0 |

$$\frac{d}{D} = 36$$

Delivery Chute

Rotating Disc

Stationary Hook

Part Carried over Hook

Part Fed to Outlet

Rotating Disc

ENLARGED SECTION ON Y-Y

Stationary Hook

Rotational Frequency, n

$11°$

Rotating Disc

Stationary Hopper

ENLARGED SECTION ON X-X

Parts Difficult to Orient

Parts Cannot be Fed

Efficiency, E

$$\text{Feed Rate} = \frac{E \times \pi \times d \times n}{L}$$

where:

E = Efficiency

d = Hopper Diameter

n = Rotational Frequency of Disc

L = Part Length

L/D

$0.1 < n < 0.3 \text{ s}^{-1}$

Fig. 12.6. Design sheet for a stationary-hook hopper feeder. (From Ref. (12.2), by permission of Dept. of Mech. Eng., Univ. of Mass.)

However, for $L/D < 3.0$, the parts are difficult to orient. On the other hand, for $L/D > 4.6$, the parts cannot be fed anymore.

For flat disk-shaped parts with $L/D < 0.2$, the *revolving-hook hopper feeder* shown in Fig. 12.7 is suitable. The hook rotates above the stationary hopper base, so that the parts are guided along the inside curve of the hook to the center hole of the base, where they drop into the delivery chute. A hood prevents parts

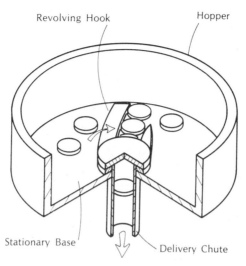

Revolving Hook

Hopper

Stationary Base

Delivery Chute

Fig. 12.7. Revolving-hook hopper feeder. (From Ref. (12.2), by permission of Dept. of Mech. Eng., Univ. of Mass.)

in the hopper from blocking the hole. A drastic reduction in feed rate occurs if hook velocity approaches a critical value specified by a graph in Ref. (12.2).

For feeding parts that tend to tangle, the *tumbling-barrel feeder* shown in Fig. 12.8 is used. This is a rotating barrel having four vanes attached to the inner barrel surface, parallel to the barrel axis. As the barrel rotates, parts are picked up by these vanes and randomly dropped onto a vibratory rail at the center of the barrel. Most of these fall back into the barrel, but those few that land on the rail properly oriented remain there, and then slide down along the rail. An electromagnetic vibrator is attached to the rail to facilitate this sliding motion. Figure 12.8 provides dimensional details pertaining to feeder construction and expected feed rate.

Parts used in tumbling-barrel feeders should be rigid enough to resist bending, since the tumbling action can subject the parts to considerable loads. These feeders tend to be noisy, but lining the inside walls with rubber or cork can help reduce both noise and damage to the parts.

As a final example, Fig. 12.9 shows the *magnetic-disk hopper feeder*. The parts—which must be of ferromagnetic material and have a fairly large flat surface—are picked up by magnets mounted within a rotating disk as this disk turns inside the hopper. Some of the parts become attached to a magnet, and are thus lifted and brought to the delivery chute at the top, where they are detached from the magnet and guided down into the chute. Parts not properly oriented are thrown back into the hopper.

This section has presented only a small selection of the many nonvibratory feeders that are available. Some of the numerous other very ingenious devices for feeding and orienting parts of various shapes that have been invented are described in Refs. (12.6) and (12.7). The important point to remember is that

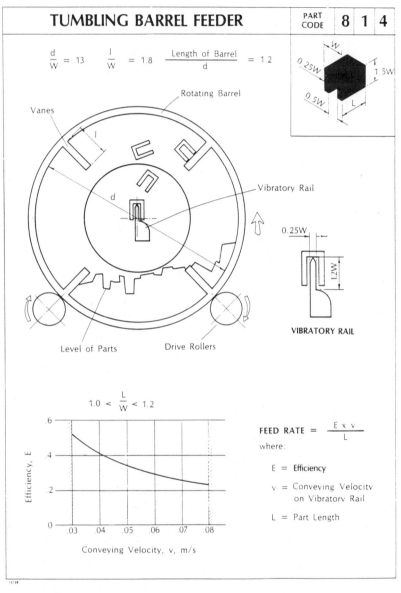

Fig. 12.8. Design sheet for a tumbling-barrel feeder. (From Ref. (12.2), by permission of Dept. of Mech. Eng., Univ. of Mass.)

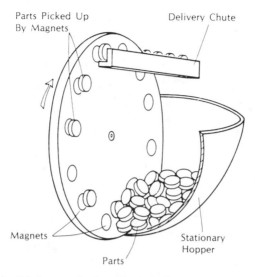

Fig. 12.9. Magnetic-disk hopper feeder. (From Ref. (12.2), by permission of Dept. of Mech. Eng., Univ. of Mass.)

there is no universal feeding device. Each type of part—depending on its size and shape—requires its own specific feeder design.

12.2 VIBRATORY FEEDING AND ORIENTING DEVICES

For feeding very small parts, *vibratory feeders* are very popular. These consist of a hopper or bowl, as shown in Fig. 12.10, mounted to a heavy base by several leaf springs. An electromagnet produces the vibration. Because of the nature of

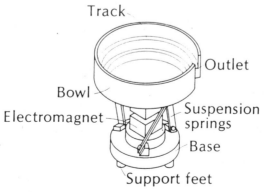

Fig. 12.10. Vibratory-bowl feeder. (From Ref. (12.2), by permission of Dept. of Mech. Eng., Univ. of Mass.)

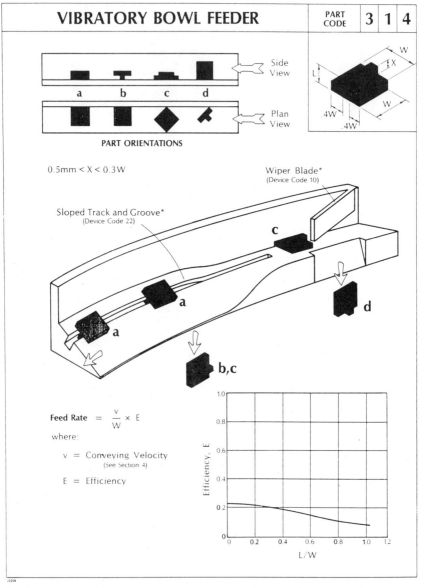

VIBRATORY BOWL FEEDER

Side View

a   b   c   d

Plan View

PART ORIENTATIONS

0.5mm < X < 0.3W

Wiper Blade*
(Device Code 10)

Sloped Track and Groove*
(Device Code 22)

c

a

a

d

b,c

Feed Rate $= \dfrac{v}{W} \times E$

where:

v = Conveying Velocity
(See Section 4)

E = Efficiency

Efficiency, E

L/W

Fig. 12.11. Design sheet for a vibratory-bowl feeder for orienting T-shaped parts. (From Ref. (12.2), by permission of Dept. of Mech. Eng., Univ. of Mass.)

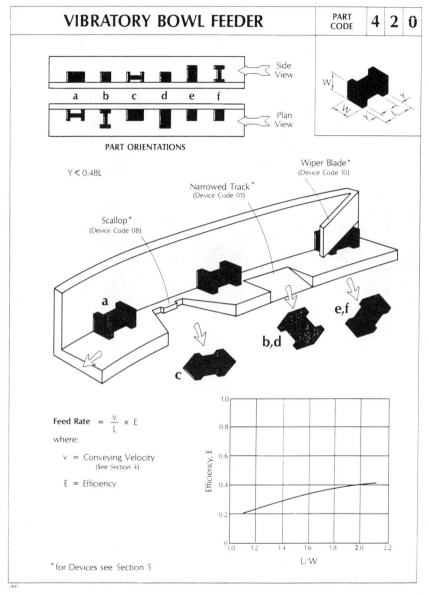

VIBRATORY BOWL FEEDER

PART CODE **4 2 0**

Side View

a b c d e f

Plan View

PART ORIENTATIONS

Y < 0.48L

Wiper Blade*
(Device Code 10)

Narrowed Track*
(Device Code 01)

Scallop*
(Device Code 08)

a

c

b,d

e,f

Feed Rate $= \dfrac{v}{L} \times E$

where:

v = Conveying Velocity
(See Section 4)

E = Efficiency

* for Devices see Section 5

Efficiency, E

L/W

Fig. 12.12. Design sheet for a vibratory-bowl feeder for orienting H-shaped parts. (From Ref. (12.2), by permission of Dept. of Mech. Eng., Univ. of Mass.)

Fig. 12.13. Straight-line vibratory feeder (Photo courtesy of Popper Technologies, Ltd., Haifa, Israel).

the leaf-spring constraint, there are both torsional vibration about the vertical axis of the bowl *and* translational vibration in the vertical direction. As a result, any parts lying on the slanted helical track are pushed forward, and gradually creep upward along the track until reaching the track outlet. For a mathematical analysis of the principles involved, see Ref. (12.1).

By proper design of the feed track, the vibratory-bowl feeder can also be used for orienting parts. As shown in Fig. 12.11, a T-shaped part can land on the track with any of four possible orientations, labeled *a*, *b*, *c*, or *d*. Parts with orientation *d* are pushed off the track by a wiper blade designed for this purpose. Parts with orientations *b* or *c* fall off by themselves. Only parts with orientation *a* can continue along the slot machined into the track.

A track for orienting H-shaped parts is shown in Fig. 12.12. Parts with orientations *e* or *f* are pushed off by the wiper blade, and those with orientations *b* or *d* fall off on their own at the place where the track narrows. In order to eliminate parts with orientation *c*, the track has a narrow ledge with a scalloped profile. In the end, only parts having the desired *a* orientation remain.

Appropriate tracks for numerous other part shapes are described in Ref. (12.2).

Straight-line vibratory feeders can produce higher feeding rates than bowl feeders. Figure 12.13 shows such a feeder, designed to feed cartridge cases in several parallel tracks. Vibration causes properly oriented cases to fall into one of the tracks, so that the case shoulder is on the top. A barrier bar with openings at the bottom allows cases sitting within one of the tracks to pass, while incorrectly oriented cases are held back.

12.3 PARTS TRANSFER

After the parts are oriented in a feeder device, it often becomes necessary to transport them to some other work station. If fairly long distances are involved, this is best done by *gravity-feed tracks*, through which the parts slide by the force of gravity, as shown in Fig. 12.14. By using twisted tracks, it becomes possible to change the orientation of the parts, and even turn them over by 180 degrees. The tracks must be designed properly to prevent jamming. Reference (12.1) devotes almost a whole chapter to the proper design of gravity-feed tracks. For a graphical method of designing gravity-feed tracks, see Ref. (12.8).

Frequently, the parts are accumulated inside some track or discharge tube using one of the feeding devices described in the previous sections, and it is then

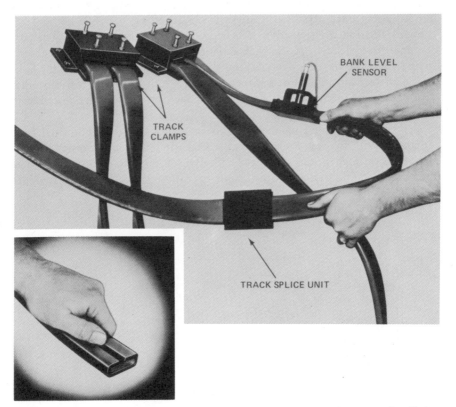

Fig. 12.14. "Maxiflex" gravity-feed track. (Courtesy of Spectrum Automation Co.)

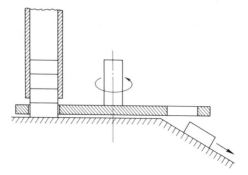

Fig. 12.15. Disk feeder.

required to transfer them to a nearby work location one at a time. Many devices are available for this purpose; see, for example, Fig. 12.15, which shows a so-called *disk feeder*. A disk with one or more holes large enough to accept a part rotates about a vertical axis. When the hole reaches the tube, one part drops into the hole. As the disk continues to rotate, the part is carried along until it drops onto a sloping track and slides to the work location.

Figure 12.16 shows a so-called *slide escapement*, also used to deliver one part at a time. The slide reciprocates back and forth. When the slider hole reaches the feeder tube at the end of the return stroke, one part only can drop into the hole. On the forward stroke, this part is then delivered to the exit tube. Various other types of escapement mechanisms used to feed one part at a time are described in Refs. (12.1) and (12.6).

The subject of indexing mechanisms is mentioned in Section 1.1.2, in connection with the well-known Geneva wheel. Indexing mechanisms transfer each part through a certain angle, followed by a period of dwell or rest (intermittent motion) during which some operation is carried out on the part.

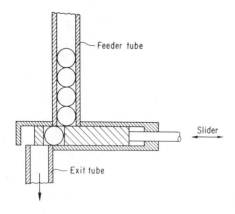

Fig. 12.16. Slide escapement.

Each angular position of the indexing mechanism represents a work station, with two of the positions required for part entry and exit. For example, the Geneva wheel of Fig. 1.2 has four slots, and thus produces four dwell positions. Geneva wheels with up to 12 slots have been constructed, so that more work stations can be accommodated.

Other indexing devices use ratchet or cam mechanisms. Many manufacturers supply special indexing tables with numerous work stations. These are frequently driven by a pneumatic cylinder connected to the table through a ratchet and pawl. Another method uses a rack-and-pinion drive, with the pinion connected to the table through a unidirectional clutch. Thus, in the forward direction, the cylinder turns the table. The clutch disengages during the return stroke, so that the table remains at rest. In many applications, the critical property of the indexing mechanism is its angular positioning accuracy. This is so because the accuracy of the operations carried out on the part frequently depends on the accuracy with which the part is held in position.

A more flexible method of transferring parts from one location to another is by means of so-called *pick-and-place units*, as shown in Fig. 12.17. These are simple robot-like manipulators, usually driven pneumatically. They generally have from two to four degrees of freedom, with the linear motions produced by

Fig. 12.17. Pick-and-place unit. (Courtesy of Norgren-Martonair.)

pneumatic cylinders, and the angular motions by pneumatic rotary actuators (see Section 1.5.1). Unlike robots (discussed in Chapter 13) with continuous position control, pneumatic pick-and-place devices use positive stops or adjustable limit switches or limit valves, so that each motion can only stop at one given point. A typical pick-and-place device might grip the part to be transferred using magnetic, vacuum, or purely mechanical means. The part might then be raised (linear motion) and transported to above the delivery point (combined linear and rotary motion), after which the part is again lowered (linear motion) and finally released. The work sequence of these motions can be controlled by a fixed pneumatic logic circuit (see Chapter 7), a relay circuit (Chapter 5), a programmable counter (Chapter 9), or a programmable controller (Chapter 10).

12.4 PARTS DESIGN FOR AUTOMATED ASSEMBLY

Human workers display considerably more dexterity than machines. Humans are able to take care of differences in part orientation, can visually inspect, classify, and reject parts, compensate for slight differences, and carry out complex manual motions requiring considerable agility. For these reasons, humans can easily perform manual assembly tasks that are beyond the capabilities of most automatic assembly machines.

These facts must be considered when designing parts that are to be assembled automatically. Unless these parts are designed with the limitations of automatic assembly in mind, the project is liable to be a failure. Hence, design for automatic assembly is becoming of increasing importance, and has been the subject of considerable research effort. Results of this research can be found in Refs. (12.9)–(12.11), in addition to the previously cited Ref. (12.1). Some of the conclusions are as follows:

1. Parts should preferably be symmetrical, so that orienting is not necessary. If, however, the part cannot be made symmetrical, the asymmetry should be made as pronounced as possible. Parts with slight asymmetry are the most difficult to orient. It is sometimes advisable to add a nonfunctional lip, shoulder, or other feature to the part just to make it easier to orient.

2. Parts should be designed to avoid tangling or nesting; otherwise, it might be impossible to separate them in the feeder. Sometimes nonfunctional ribs or pins can be added to prevent nesting. Open-ended springs or ring washers tend to tangle. By using square-ended springs and closed ring washers, this tendency is reduced.

3. Integrate components as much as possible. By using modern manufacturing techniques such as precision die-casting, or injection molding for plastic parts, it is frequently possible to combine parts in a single integrated unit, thus eliminating several assembly steps.

4. Avoid bad-quality components. In manual assembly, these are easily detected and rejected by the worker. In automatic assembly, they can cause jamming and costly assembly-line stoppage.

5. The finished assembly should have a pronounced base component that can be positioned accurately in a stable position, and to which most of the other parts are attached directly. Preferably, most assembly steps should involve only simple straight-line motion from the top, in the vertical direction. It is difficult to build assembly machines producing complex curved motion, or motion at an angle.

6. Guide surfaces should be used to help the components slide into position, in spite of a slight misalignment. For example, screws should end with oval or cone points, rather than with flat or slightly chamfered ends.

References (12.1), (12.9), and (12.10) describe a method developed at the University of Massachusetts for classifying parts according to shape, so as to determine their suitability for automatic assembly. A coding system is used to systemize the method, similar to the coding system described in Ref. (12.2) in connection with part-feeding methods. Thus, the two handbooks of Refs. (12.2) and (12.10) complement each other.

12.5 ASSEMBLY ECONOMICS

This chapter concludes with a few words about the economic aspects of assembly automation. It is a fallacy to believe that the change from manual to automatic assembly always results in savings. This is certainly not the case where small production volumes are involved. In many cases, any cost savings that do occur are really due to the fact that the product has been redesigned to make it suitable for automatic assembly, and this redesign alone reduces manufacturing costs even if manual assembly were used.

The problem of assembly economics is not so simple, and is analyzed in detail in Refs. (12.1), (12.9), and (12.12). Some of the variables that must be included in the decision-making process are annual production volume per shift, the number of parts in the assembly, the quality of the parts, possible product-style variations, possible design changes, the number of different products to be assembled by the machine, and capital investment cost. It is shown in these references how these factors must be taken into account in order to decide between manual assembly, special-purpose automatic assembly systems (i.e., fixed automation), and programmable assembly systems (i.e., flexible automation).

Some of the material in Refs. (12.9) and (12.10) can also be found in abbreviated form in the set of articles of Refs. (12.13)–(12.16). The main point of these articles is that the appropriate assembly method should be identified *before* the design stage is completed. The product should then be especially designed to be suitable for the particular assembly method chosen, which can reduce manufacturing costs and increase assembly productivity considerably.

REFERENCES

12.1. G. Boothroyd, C. Poli, and L. Murch, *Automatic Assembly*, Dekker, New York, 1982.

12.2. G. Boothroyd, C. Poli, and L. Murch, *Handbook of Feeding and Orienting Techniques for Small Parts*, Dept. of Mechanical Engineering, University of Massachusetts, Amherst, 1977.

12.3. C. R. Asfahl, *Robots and Manufacturing Automation*, Wiley, New York, 1985.

12.4. L. E. Murch and C. Poli, "Analysis of Feeding and Orienting Systems for Automatic Assembly. Part 1: Non-vibratory Feeding Systems," *Journal of Engineering for Industry*, Vol. 99B, No. 2, May 1977, pp. 302–307.

12.5. L. E. Murch and C. Poli, "Analysis of Feeding and Orienting Systems for Automatic Assembly. Part 2: Vibratory-bowl Feeding Systems," *Journal of Engineering for Industry*, Vol. 99B, No. 2, May 1977, pp. 308–313.

12.6. N. P. Chironis, *Machine Devices and Instrumentation*, McGraw-Hill, New York, 1966.

12.7. (No author), *Hopper Feeders as an Aid to Automation*, Machinery Publ. Co., London.

12.8. L. E. Murch and T. Campbell, "A Quick Graphic Way to Design Gravity Feed Tracks," *Machine Design*, June 26, 1975, pp. 46–49.

12.9. G. Boothroyd, *Design for Assembly*, Dept. of Mechanical Engineering, University of Massachusetts, Amherst, 1983.

12.10. G. Boothroyd, *Design for Assembly Handbook*, Dept. of Mechanical Engineering, University of Massachusetts, Amherst, 1980.

12.11. M. M. Andreasen, S. Kahler, and T. Lund, *Design for Assembly*, IFS (Publications) Ltd., Bedford, England, 1983.

12.12. G. Boothroyd, "Economics of Assembly Systems," *Journal of Manufacturing Systems*, Vol. 1, No. 1, 1982, pp. 111–127.

12.13. G. Boothroyd and P. Dewhurst, "Design for Assembly: Selecting the Right Method," *Machine Design*, Nov. 1983, pp. 94–98.

12.14. G. Boothroyd and P. Dewhurst, "Design for Assembly: Manual Assembly," *Machine Design*, Dec. 8, 1983, pp. 140–145.

12.15. G. Boothroyd and P. Dewhurst, "Design for Assembly: Automatic Assembly," *Machine Design*, Jan. 26, 1984, pp. 87–92.

12.16. G. Boothroyd and P. Dewhurst, "Design for Assembly: Robots," *Machine Design*, Feb. 23, 1984 pp. 72–76.

CHAPTER 13

ROBOTICS AND NUMERICAL CONTROL

Robots are originally an invention of science fiction, the term first coined in 1921 by the Czech playwright Karel Capek. About 20 years later, the term "robotics" was first used by Isaac Asimov, but also in connection with his well-known science-fiction stories. Many–some believe, all—science-fiction ideas eventually turn into reality. In the case of robots, it took another 20 years until the first industrial robot, developed by J. Engelberger and G. Devol, was manufactured in the early 1960s by Unimation Inc., a company especially established for this purpose.

Today, the world "robot population" numbers tens of thousands, with about half of all robots in Japan. The number of robot manufacturers in the world is close to 50, and robots can be found in a great variety of industries performing a great variety of tasks.

Contrary to popular misconception, the purpose of robots is not simply to displace workers and thus cause wide unemployment, although this is undoubtedly an unfortunate temporary by-product of robotics. Robots can help improve the quality of life by taking jobs that are difficult, monotonous, unhealthy, or downright dangerous for humans. Three typical examples are spot-welding of automobile frames (monotonous and tiring), spray painting of automobile bodies (unhealthy), and working in high-radiation zones of nuclear reactors (dangerous).

This chapter only gives a very brief introduction to this fascinating topic. For an in-depth treatment of robotics, the reader is referred to Refs. (13.1)– (13.5).

13.1 BASIC ROBOT DEFINITIONS

The Robotics Industries Association (RIA) defines robots as follows:

A robot is a reprogrammable, multifunctional manipulator designed to move materials, parts, tools, or specialized devices through variable programmed motions for the performance of a variety of tasks.

The word *reprogrammable* in this definition implies the ability of changing the robot motion by means of software, that is, by modifying a computer program. This property is, of course, basic for flexible automation, as opposed to hard automation, where the program can only be changed by means of hardware modifications.

The main part of the robot is the *manipulator*, which is a mechanism performing the required motion. The lower end of the manipulator is generally attached to the floor or some fixed base, although there are also mobile robots able to move freely along one or more axes. At the other end of the manipulator is a *wrist*, which is able to turn about one, two, or three axes, to which a so-called *end effector* is attached. This could be a *gripper* intended to pick up and transfer parts, or some tool such as a welding gun, paint-spraying nozzle, or other device designed for a specific task.

The various manipulator links and the end effector are controlled by a control system. This generally consists of a micro- or minicomputer working through special electronic control circuits, with position or angle being the controlled variable. Thus, the control system is identical to what is referred to as *numerical control* (NC), used for the past three decades in the machine-tool industry. Numerical control is discussed in Section 13.3.

The control system actuates the robot drive. This can be electric (using either dc servo motors or step motors), hydraulic (using hydraulic motors or cylinders actuated by a so-called servo valve, which is a hydraulic valve with electric actuation), or pneumatic. Frequently, a combination of media is used, with the various robot links driven electrically or hydraulically, but the gripper actuated pneumatically.

Many applications require only a simple robot able to execute discrete motions. For this, binary or *on–off* control is sufficient, rather than continuous control. Robots of this type are generally driven by pneumatic cylinders and rotary actuators. They are often referred to as *pick-and-place manipulators* or *nonservo robots*, and are discussed in the previous chapter. The motion limits of pick-and-place manipulators are usually set by mechanically adjustable limit switches or limit valves. The motion sequence can be controlled by a hard-wired relay circuit (or by a fixed pneumatic valve circuit), in which case the device does not meet the previously cited definition of a robot, since the system is not really reprogrammable. If, however, the motion sequence is controlled by a programmable controller (see Chapter 10), then the previous definition is met, but some refuse to recognize even such a system as a true robot (because motion limits can only be changed by hardware modifications).

13.2   BASIC MANIPULATOR CONFIGURATIONS (GEOMETRY)

The basic manipulator configurations are illustrated in the following four figures. Figure 13.1 shows the *rectangular* or *Cartesian* manipulator, and the associated coordinate system used to define the location of the end effector. The motion between the three robot links is linear sliding motion. One advantage of this design is that the manipulator can be made very rigid. For large-size robots, the links moving in the horizontal plane can travel on overhead rails (*gantry-type* robot), which makes for great rigidity and accuracy. Also, it is easy to drive the end effector at constant speed along a straight line, which is difficult to accomplish with other configurations. In spite of this, cartesian robots are not popular, because they are unable to reach hidden points (i.e., points invisible from the robot base). Also, the *work envelope* (which is the volume that can be reached by the end effectors) is smaller than for other configurations with identical robot floor space, as illustrated later.

Figure 13.2 shows the *cylindrical* manipulator configuration, so-called because the work envelope has the shape of a cylinder. It uses linear sliding motion for two of the three possible motions, but rotary motion for movement about the vertical axis (base rotation). As seen in Fig. 13.2(b), the end-effector coordinates are defined by a polar-coordinate system in the horizontal plane. The end effector can easily be moved along a straight line in the vertical or in the radial direction, but any other straight-line motion is difficult to achieve.

The *spherical* manipulator configuration is shown in Fig. 13.3. Its work envelope is a partial sphere. The manipulator has two rotating axes, combined with linear motion in the radial direction. The end-effector location is defined by spherical coordinates. Although a spherical manipulator can produce straight-

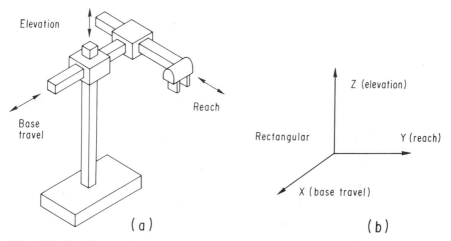

Fig. 13.1. (a) Rectangular or cartesian robot configuration, and (b) the resulting coordinate system. (From Ref. (13.3), courtesy of John Wiley & Sons.)

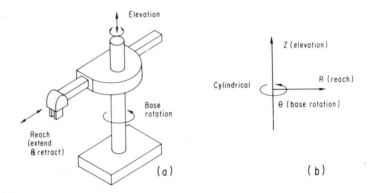

Fig. 13.2. (a) Cylindrical robot configuration, and (b) the resulting coordinate system. (From Ref. (13.3), courtesy of John Wiley & Sons.)

line motion easily only in the radial direction, it has more flexibility to reach hidden spots than the previous two types.

Figure 13.4 shows the fourth basic configuration, referred to as an *articulated* manipulator. There are three rotating axes, but no linear motion. This configuration resembles the action of a human arm, with rotation both at the shoulder and elbow, and it has more flexibility in reaching hidden spots than any other design.

The work envelopes obtained for these four basic manipulator types are shown in Fig. 13.5. Notice that the work envelope of the articulated manipulator is difficult to define, although resembling a sphere. The work envelope of a robot has a double significance. Primarily, it shows the areas that can be reached by the end effector, and thus the types of tasks that can be assigned to the robot. However, there is also a safety aspect. Workers must keep out of the work-envelope region while the robot is active, otherwise serious accidents can result. Japan has the dubious distinction of being the site of the world's first robot-caused fatal accident (which occurred in 1981, when a robot started moving

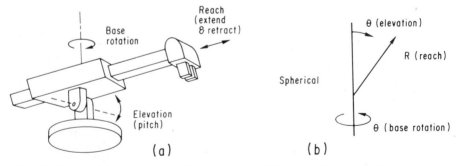

Fig. 13.3. (a) Spherical robot configuration, and (b) the resulting coordinate system. (From Ref. (13.3), courtesy of John Wiley & Sons.)

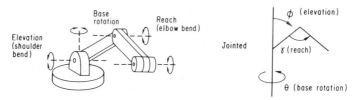

Fig. 13.4. (a) Articulated (jointed) robot configuration, and (b) the resulting coordinate system. (From Ref. (13.3), courtesy of John Wiley & Sons.)

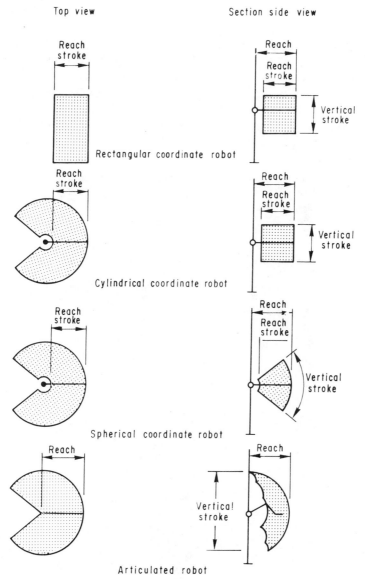

Fig. 13.5. Robot work envelopes for common configurations. (From Ref. (13.3), courtesy of John Wiley & Sons.)

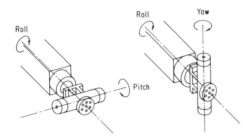

Fig. 13.6. Roll, pitch, and yaw axes for robot wrist. (From Ref. (13.1), courtesy of John Wiley & Sons.)

unexpectedly, and pinned a worker against another machine). For detailed discussions of robot safety measures, see Refs. (13.2) and (13.3). The analysis of the manipulator's work envelope is discussed in Ref. (13.6).

Apart from the three degrees of freedom existing in each of the previously described manipulator configurations, we must also consider possible motion of the wrist, that is, at the point at which the end effector is attached to the robot forearm. Whereas wrist motion has little effect on the work envelope, it does

Fig. 13.7. Articulated-configuration robot (ASEA Robotics Inc.) loading an NC lathe (Technion Robotics Laboratory).

have a bearing on the dexterity with which the robot can perform various tasks. The robot wrist can have anywhere from one to three degrees of freedom, as illustrated in Fig. 13.6. The three resulting motions are called *roll, yaw,* and *pitch,* terms traditionally describing the motion of ships or airplanes.

Figure 13.7 shows a commercial articulated-type robot, whose wrist has two degrees of freedom, giving this robot a total of five degrees of freedom. While some very simple robots have as few as three degrees of freedom and some complex ones have more than six, most industrial robots have five or six degrees of freedom. Since each degree of freedom must have its own independent control system, these degrees of freedom are often referred to as *control axes,* or simply *axes.* Each control axis with its controller and associated components and circuits represents a numerical-control system. Basically, there is no difference between the control axes of a robot and those of a numerically controlled machine tool. The nature of numerical control is discussed in the next section.

13.3 NUMERICAL-CONTROL (NC) SYSTEMS

Numerical control (referred to as NC from now on) has been used with machine tools and other production equipment for several decades. It refers to machines in which the workpiece and/or tool are positioned automatically by a control system, according to previously specified numerical data. A number of important advantages can be listed for NC:

1. Increased machine output.
2. Less labor is required, since one machinist can supervise several machines.
3. Higher accuracy and better repeatability. Once the machine is set up properly, the results do not depend on the machinist.
4. Because of item 3, very limited inspection is required, and there are practically no rejects.
5. By using NC machines with several control axes, a number of motions can be carried out simultaneously. This makes possible the accurate machining of very complex shapes (such as turbine blades).
6. Set-up time is short, since the program is stored on tape or in computer memory. Hence, small production runs become economically feasible, which minimizes the need for maintaining large stocks, thus saving capital investment and storage space.

With all these advantages, it is not surprising that NC has found wide application not only in machine tools but also in many other fields, such as pipe-bending machines (e.g., for automobile exhausts), sheet-metal forming, punch presses (with the sheets to be punched clamped on a work table moving in both x and y directions, according to the coordinates of the required hole), riveting, welding, flame-cutting, automatic-drafting, and automatic-inspection machines. NC has also found wide application in electronic manufacturing, where it is used to drill holes in circuit boards, insert components, and solder. In addition to all these older applications, NC is now used in robots. For a general discussion of NC, see Refs. (13.1) and (13.7)–(13.9).

13.3.1   Control Axes of NC Systems

NC systems are characterized by the number of control axes. For example, positioning a work table (such as that of a drill press or punch press) in the x and y directions requires two control axes. Lowering and raising the drill head requires one additional control axis. Angular positioning of a tool (such as in a milling machine) requires from one to three additional control axes, depending on the number of axes of rotation. Naturally, the complexity and hence the cost of the NC machine depends, to a great extent, on the number of control axes. Milling machines with up to 13 control axes can be found, but these have more than one cutting tool working simultaneously on the workpiece. Apart from the control axes, the control system may also control other variables, such as tool selection, tool rotational speed, coolant flow, and so on.

13.3.2   Closed-Loop NC System

The control system of an NC control axis can operate either in the closed-loop (i.e., using feedback) or in the open-loop mode. A typical closed-loop control system for a single control axis is shown in block-diagram form in Fig. 13.8.

The first block on the left represents the program to be executed by the control axis (for instance, the x coordinates to be traced by a cutting tool). In the past, the program was usually stored on punched paper tape and read by an optical reader. Today, magnetic tape or a computer program is more common.

Punched paper tape uses eight hole columns, with an additional column of smaller sprocket holes placed between the third and fourth column, as shown in Fig. 13.9. These feed the tape through the tape reader, and are deliberately located off-center to prevent inserting the tape upside down.

Two types of codes are employed for encoding the information in the tape. One is the EIA244A code, summarized in the figure. Columns 1 to 5 represent numbers in BCD code with an odd parity bit, as described in Section 8.7.2.

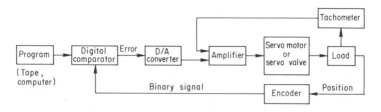

Fig. 13.8. Simplified block diagram of a closed-loop NC system (one control axis).

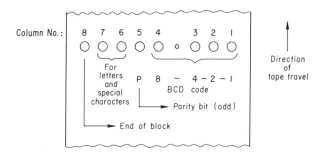

Fig. 13.9. EIA 244 code used in NC punched tapes.

Columns 6 and 7, together with the unused combinations in columns 1 to 5, represent letters and special control characters, and a punched hole in column 8 represents end-of-block of information or a "carriage return." A second, and more modern, code is the ASCII code, commonly used in computer data transmission. In this code column 8 is used for the parity bit, but *even* parity is used. For a more detailed description of these codes, see Refs. (13.1) and (13.10).

The next element in the block diagram of Fig. 13.8 is a digital comparator, whose task it is to compare the actual table or cutting-tool position (as measured by an encoder) to the required position (as determined by the program). This comparator can be built using an iterative circuit, as described in Section 8.9.3. In its simplest form, the comparator has three possible outputs, UP, ZERO, or DOWN, depending on whether the required position is greater than, equal to, or less than the actual position, respectively. In more sophisticated systems, the comparator outputs a digital signal representing the actual magnitude of the error.

The error is sent through a digital-to-analog (D/A) converter, to obtain an analog voltage that can be used to drive a servo amplifier. The amplifier output either drives a servo motor, or, in the case of a hydraulic drive, a hydraulic servo valve, whose flow opening is proportional to the input voltage. While dc servo motors are used for small- or medium-size systems, hydraulic drives are generally preferred where large power output is required. Servo motors are coupled to the load using either gearing or ball screws (depending on whether the load is to rotate or have straight-line motion). In hydraulic drives, the servo valve either drives a hydraulic motor or a cylinder.

As shown in Fig. 13.8, a tachometer is connected to the load to send a velocity-feedback signal to the amplifier. This is utilized to improve the system's dynamic response (see any textbook on feedback control), and thus also the surface finish of the workpiece.

The function of the servo motor, hydraulic motor, or cylinder is, of course, to move the load (i.e., table or cutting tool) in the required direction so as to reduce and eventually eliminate the error. The actual load position is continuously checked by the feedback element, which usually consists of an encoder. As discussed in detail in Chapter 8, encoders can be optical or magnetic, rotary or linear, and absolute-position or incremental. No matter what type, their function is always the same: to convert the load position into an equivalent binary signal, from which the load position can be deduced. Thus, encoders are really a special type of analog-to-digital (A/D) converter, whose input is mechanical position rather than voltage. The encoders used in robots measure the position of the various robot links, rather than of machine-tool tables or cutting tools.

13.3.3 Absolute vs. Incremental Commands

The instructions sent by the program to a given control axis can be expressed in two basically different ways, using either *absolute* or *incremental commands*. With absolute commands, the required load position is specified using absolute coordinates referred to a fixed reference or "home" position. With incremental commands, the new position is specified in terms of the required *change* from the present position. The difference is illustrated by a system with two control axes x and y, and with four successive load positions specified by means of both methods, for sake of comparison:

Step	Absolute Commands		Step	Incremental Commands	
A	x: 0000	y: 0000	A	x: 0000	y: 0000
B	x: 0000	y: −3000	B	x: 0000	y: −3000
C	x: 2000	y: −3000	C	x: 2000	y: 0000
D	x: 2000	y: 0000	D	x: 0000	y: 3000

Absolute commands have the advantage that any error or inaccuracy in a given step has no effect on subsequent steps. With incremental commands, by comparison, errors are accumulative, and are carried along to all subsequent steps. On the other hand, incremental commands may be preferable where a distance between two given points (such as center-to-center distance between two holes) must be held to within a close tolerance, whereas their absolute position may be of less importance. In most modern NC machine tools, the programmer has the option of using either method, depending on which is more convenient for a given application.

13.3.4 Point-to-Point vs. Continuous-Path Control

In many NC applications, the tool or the table to which the workpiece is attached must be moved from one point to the next, but the path that is followed is of no importance. A typical example is a punch press or a drill press, where holes are to be punched or drilled at specific locations. As long as these locations are reached accurately, it does not matter how the machine gets there. For such applications, NC machines with so-called *point-to-point control* are used.

With point-to-point control, the programmer has no control over the path followed. For example, suppose we want the machine to move from points 1 to 2, as shown in Fig. 13.10(a). At the beginning of motion, both servo motors most likely run at the same maximum speed, so that the path is 45 degrees from the x axis. Once the required y coordinate is reached, the y-axis motor stops, and the x-axis motor continues to drive the load in the x direction.

In more sophisticated applications, the exact path followed *is* important, for example, where a specified surface or contour must be machined. Here, *continuous-path control*, also called *contouring*, must be employed; see Fig. 13.10(b). To accomplish this, the two servo motors for the x and y axes are synchronized and kept in step by timing pulses, so that any desired path can be followed by sending more pulses to one axis than to the other. Another method is to vary the voltages supplied to the two dc servo motors, and thus vary their speed. Whatever method is followed, the process of synchronizing the two (or more) servo motors is termed *interpolation*.

The interpolation is carried out by special electronic circuitry or by means of a computer. The simplest type of interpolation is *linear interpolation*, which provides only straight-line motion. Any curve can be built up by using many very short line segments (as short as 0.001 mm). Most interpolators can also do *circular* and *parabolic* interpolation, and these require fewer programming commands to produce a given curve. For example, a given circular arc can be obtained by specifying only the arc center and beginning and end points. With continuous-path control, incremental commands are often preferred, since these usually produce a smoother joint between adjacent path segments.

It should come as no surprise that continuous-path control systems are considerably more expensive than point-to-point ones. This applies not only to machine tools, but also to robots. Robots with point-to-point control cost less, and find wide use in such applications as spot welding, hole drilling, and simple assembly tasks. Sometimes, the path followed by the robot end effector is of some importance, because the arm must be led around existing obstructions to avoid collisions. Even so, point-to-point control can be used, with a collision-free path assured by programming several intermediate transit points.

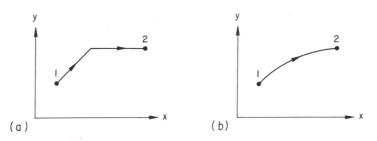

Fig. 13.10. Possible path with (a) point-to-point control, and (b) continuous-path control.

In many robot applications (arc welding, spray painting), the exact path followed *is* important, so that continuous-path control must be used. As already mentioned, any point-to-point system can seemingly be made into a continuous-path system by programming many sufficiently short point-to-point segments. Whereas the path can thus be approximated to any desired accuracy, the resulting motion is slowed down considerably, since each point programmed requires a certain minimum execution time.

13.3.5 Open-Loop NC System

NC systems can be simplified greatly and their cost lowered by working in the open-loop mode, as illustrated in Fig. 13.11. A step motor (described in detail in Chapter 1) is used instead of the servo motor, and this eliminates the need for the digital comparator, D/A converter, servo amplifier, tachometer, and encoder that appeared in Fig. 13.8. For continuous-path control, the frequency of the pulses actuating the step motor of each control axis is controlled so as to obtain the necessary relative motor velocities.

While open-loop NC systems are less expensive, they are also less accurate. Since there is no feedback, the control system cannot compensate for elastic deformation in the drive system, or for other inaccuracies. Also, if the load should unexpectedly exceed the step motor's capacity, the motor might skip steps. Such step-motor errors are accumulative, and are carried along from one step to the next. The only way to eliminate such an accumulated error is to zero the control system frequently with respect to an established reference point. In spite of these drawbacks, open-loop NC is very popular for applications in which the loads are fairly low and fairly *constant*, such as simple drill presses, small lathes, and machines for electronic-circuit assembly. They are not practical where great accuracy is required, or where the part being manufactured is very expensive (so that errors would be costly).

These considerations apply not only to machine tools, but also to robots. Although there are small robots using step motors in the open-loop mode, these are mostly for educational use. In robots, the loads that might be encountered are less predictable than with machine tools, so that there is more danger of having the step motor skip steps. Hence, most industrial robots work with closed-loop control.

Figure 13.12 shows a small robot with articulated configuration, intended for educational use. This robot uses six step motors in the open-loop mode. Three of these drive the manipulator links (base rotation, shoulder rotation, and elbow rotation), and the remaining three actuate the gripper (roll, pitch, and gripper

Fig. 13.11. Block diagram of an open-loop NC system (one control axis).

Fig. 13.12. "Minimover" robot with a step-motor drive (Microbot, Inc.).

closure). Thus, without counting gripper closure, this robot has five degrees of freedom. Programming and control is done on a microcomputer interfaced to the robot by a special interface card, also shown on the picture.

13.3.6 Computer Numerical Control (CNC)

The history of numerical control encompasses four distinct stages. In the first stage, which began after World War II, each NC machine was an independent unit obtaining its program from punched paper (or mylar) tape. While computers were sometimes used to prepare these tapes, this was done "off-line," and the computer did not interfere in the actual running of the machine. The tape was read optically, and the machine controller, consisting of electronic hardware, interpreted the tape program, carried out interpolation, comparison, and so on.

The second stage, beginning in the sixties, included the use of a central "mainframe" computer to control a number of individual NC machines in the plant on a time-sharing basis. This avoided the need for individual punched tapes and controllers. This method was called *direct numerical control* (DNC). Because of the high cost of large mainframe computers, this method was only suitable for large plants that had such a computer to begin with. The method required long cable runs extending from the computer to each individual NC machine, and these cables themselves sometimes caused problems. But the main reason for the abandonment of DNC was that any failure of the central computer would paralyze the whole plant.

With the appearance of inexpensive micro- and minicomputers in the late seventies, the third stage, called *computer numerical control* (CNC) developed. Here, each NC machine has its own microcomputer, eliminating the need for time-sharing and for long cables. At the same time, a great deal of the hardware existing in the original NC machines could be eliminated, as described in Refs. (13.9) and (13.11). Today, most NC machines being manufactured are of the CNC type.

The final stage of development is that of supervisory or hierarchical numerical control. In this method, a number of CNC machines are connected to a central computer that does not interfere in their second-by-second operation. Rather, the central computer performs housekeeping functions, such as keeping production records, storing CNC programs to be supplied to each machine on demand, keeping track of local machine shutdowns, coordinating the work of individual machines, and so on. Supervisory control is being used successfully in many plants, especially larger ones. The same idea is used in robotics, where a central computer often supervises and synchronizes the work of a number of individual robots. Frequently, programmable controllers (Chapter 10) are employed for this purpose. Since programmable controllers can perform counting and timing functions, they are ideal for synchronizing a number of robots or other CNC machines, and can thus replace the supervisory computer, especially in applications not requiring complicated numerical calculations.

13.4 ROBOT KINEMATICS

Robot kinematics involves two main problems: the *direct kinematic problem* and the *inverse kinematic problem*. The direct kinematic problem consists of determining position, velocity, and acceleration of the end effector in cartesian so-called *world coordinates*, from a knowledge of the motion of the various drive elements (motors, cylinders, and so on) expressed in so-called *joint coordinates*. This problem is relatively easy to solve using straightforward spatial trigonometry.

The inverse kinematic problem, on the other hand, poses the opposite question: What must be the motion of each drive element in joint coordinates in order to bring the end effector to a certain position defined in world coordinates, or to have the end effector follow a certain path with a certain velocity and acceleration. This inverse kinematic problem is much more difficult to solve, and generally requires matrix algebra and other mathematical techniques.

To illustrate both problems, a trivial example is used: a three-degree-of-freedom manipulator with a spherical configuration. The coordinates θ, ϕ, and r of the end effector P are shown in Fig. 13.13. The rotational motions through

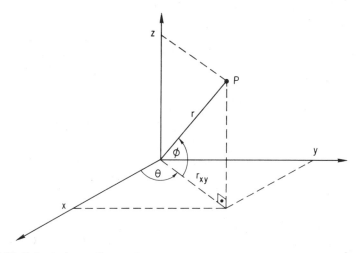

Fig. 13.13. Spherical coordinates θ, ϕ, and r of a manipulator with an end effector P.

angles θ and ϕ are produced by two motors, whereas linear motion along the radius r is produced by a cylinder, ball screw, or other linear-motion device.

Knowing the three joint coordinates θ, ϕ, and r, the Cartesian world coordinates x, y, and z of P are easily found as follows:

$$r_{xy} = r \cdot \cos \phi \qquad (13\text{-}1)$$

$$x = r_{xy} \cos \theta \qquad (13\text{-}2)$$

$$y = r_{xy} \sin \theta \qquad (13\text{-}3)$$

$$z = r \cdot \sin \phi \qquad (13\text{-}4)$$

and with that, the direct kinematic problem is solved.

To solve the inverse kinematic problem, we first calculate the required radius r from

$$r = (x^2 + y^2 + z^2)^{1/2} \qquad (13\text{-}5)$$

Dividing Equation (13-3) by (13-2) gives

$$\theta = \arctan \frac{y}{x} \qquad (13\text{-}6)$$

Dividing Equation (13-4) by (13-1) gives

$$\phi = \arctan \frac{z}{r_{xy}} = \arctan \frac{z}{(x^2 + y^2)^{1/2}} \qquad (13\text{-}7)$$

The inverse kinematic problem becomes much more complex for articulated robots, and especially if wrist motion is also taken into account, producing five or six degrees of freedom. Sometimes, there is no solution, which means that the specified manipulator state cannot be obtained with the given manipulator. Solving the inverse kinematic problem is of great practical importance, since the robot-control computer must do this continuously—on-line and in real time—in order to drive the various control axes in the required manner. This is done using so-called *trajectory interpolator* algorithms. A great deal of research effort has been carried out to develop more efficient techniques for solving the inverse kinematic problem, and thus faster trajectory interpolator algorithms, since the operating speed of the robot depends on these to a great extent. Obviously, the introduction of faster computers also helps to speed up the trajectory interpolation.

For a detailed discussion of the inverse kinematic problem, see Refs. (13.2), (13.3), (13.12), and (13.13).

13.5   ROBOT GRIPPERS

Grippers are the most common type of robot end effector. On one hand, grippers are subject to a great deal of wear and tear. On the other hand, the gripper is itself liable to damage the part being gripped, if it is not properly suited for the task. Hence, the design and selection of the gripper is important.

The majority of grippers are of the two-finger type, as shown in Fig. 13.14, which shows (a) an external gripper, and (b) an internal gripper gripping the part from within an internal bore. Both designs use a cylinder to actuate the gripper, with a linkage transforming linear to rotary motion.

Grippers can be actuated electrically (using motors or solenoids) or pneumatically (using cylinders). Pneumatic gripper actuation is common, even where the robot drive itself is electric or hydraulic, because of several advantages. Pneumatic cylinders are very inexpensive, and weigh much less than electric actuators producing the same force. This is of great practical importance, since any weight attached to the gripper reduces the "payload" that the robot is able to lift. Unlike motors or solenoids, pneumatic cylinders do not overheat and burn out if overloaded. Also, pneumatic systems are compliant (due to air

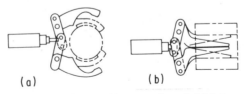

(a)   (b)

Fig. 13.14. Two simple robot grippers: (a) external, and (b) internal (from Ref. (13.3), courtesy of John Wiley & Sons).

compressibility), which is of advantage where delicate parts with irregular surfaces must be gripped.

For very delicate or fragile parts, we can use a pneumatic gripper circuit working at two different air-pressures. At the beginning of gripper closure, very low pressure is applied to the actuating cylinder, so that the gripper jaws close slowly, and the part being gripped is not damaged by shock. When both jaws touch the part, the pneumatic circuit senses this, and automatically increases pressure to the level required for lifting the part. The pneumatic circuit for this system is described in Ref. (13.14).

In applications where parts of differing widths must be gripped, a gripper with parallel jaws, as in Fig. 13.15, is preferred. Two 4-bar linkages provide the parallel motion of the jaws, which have straight gripping surfaces suitable for gripping flat parts. For round parts, jaws with concave gripping surfaces are used.

Sometimes it is advantageous to use twin grippers attached to the same wrist, as shown in Fig. 13.16. Assume, for example, that the robot's task is to remove a finished part from a machine, place it on a finished-part conveyor, and then bring a new raw part from a feed conveyor and load it into the machine. Using twin grippers, the robot arm can approach the machine with the raw part already held in one of the grippers, remove the finished part with the other gripper, and immediately load the raw part. The robot then deposits the finished part and brings a new one while the loaded part is being machined. Thus, the idle time ordinarily wasted by the machine waiting for the next part is minimized and the production rate increased.

One of the problems with industrial robot applications occurs where the robot is expected to handle various parts differing greatly in size, shape, and mechanical properties. Such situations occur, for example, in many assembly operations. One solution is to have a selection of different grippers available,

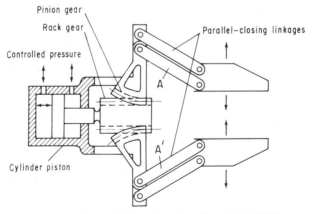

Fig. 13.15. Robot gripper with parallel-motion jaws (from Ref. (13.3), courtesy of John Wiley & Sons).

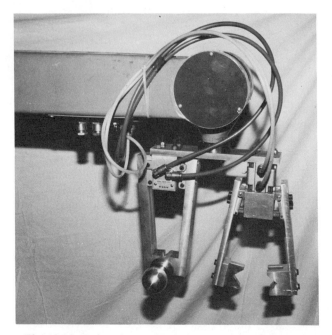

Fig. 13.16. Twin grippers (Technion Robotics Laboratory).

and program the robot to exchange its gripper automatically, according to need. (This basic idea has been used for decades in automatic machine tools, which are able to change the cutting tool being used.) This method, however, slows down robot operation, since several seconds are wasted each time the gripper is being exchanged. To solve this problem, a great deal of effort has been made to design so-called "universal grippers" suitable for parts of any size or shape. Some of the proposed designs, as described in Refs. (13.3) and (13.15), are quite ingenious, and include many-fingered grippers of hand-like design, and various other ideas. None of them, however, can claim to be completely universal.

A common problem in assembly automation occurs where the robot is expected to insert a round part into a bore, also referred to as the "peg-in-hole" problem. There would be no problem if the robot were completely accurate, and if the hole were located exactly where the robot expects it to be. However, any misalignment, lateral or angular, between the peg and hole is liable to cause wedging or jamming. One solution is to use *part-compliant tooling*, which means that a special compliant device is inserted between the robot wrist and gripper. This device must deflect sufficiently so as to permit smooth insertion of the peg in spite of misalignment.

One of the best known of these devices is the *remote center compliance* device, known as RCC, and described in Refs. (13.1), (13.3), and (13.16). The principle of operation of one type of RCC device is illustrated in Fig. 13.17. The device in its neutral position, as shown in Fig. 13.17(a), can be pictured as consisting of two

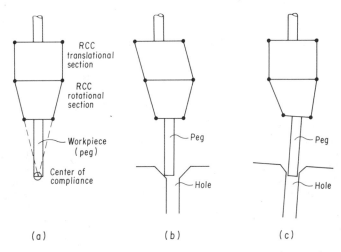

Fig. 13.17. Two-dimensional representation of an RCC device (a) in the neutral position, (b) with translational displacement, and (c) with rotational displacement.

independent 4-bar linkages. The upper one is a parallelogram linkage. If there is lateral misalignment between the peg and hole, this linkage shifts sideways, as shown in Fig. 13.17(b), so that the peg remains vertical but is displaced laterally. (The lateral force necessary to cause this motion is produced by a slight chamfer that must be machined into the outer edge of the hole.) The lower 4-bar linkage is not a parallelogram. Any angular misalignment between peg and hole produces a moment on the peg, causing this lower 4-bar linkage to rotate slightly, until the peg becomes aligned with the hole, as shown in Fig. 13.17(c). The device is designed so that this rotation occurs about a point located at the lower end of the peg, hence the name "remote center" compliance.

Note that Fig. 13.17 is only intended to show the principle of operation. Actually, the devices are three-dimensional, quite differently constructed, and contain elastomer elements to provide some stiffness. Several typical RCC devices commercially available are shown in Fig. 13.18.

13.6 ROBOT SENSORS

Robots can be classified according to three degrees of sophistication. The least sophisticated are the nonservo or pick-and-place robots, which have binary or *on−off* control, so that motion only stops at the end of a stroke, or wherever a limit switch is installed. Then there are robots with continuous control, whose end effector can be placed at any point within the work envelope. In both of these two types, the robot carries out its assigned program regardless of what might be happening in its work environment. For example, if the robot is programmed to place a peg into a hole, it goes through the corresponding

Fig. 13.18. "ROBOWRIST" RCC devices (Photograph courtesy of Lord Industrial Automation, Lord Corporation, 118 MacKenan Drive, Cary, NC 27511-8200, USA.)

motions even if the peg—or the hole—is absent. If some obstacle enters the robot's programmed path, a collision ensues, with possibly serious consequences.

The third degree of robot sophistication consists of "intelligent robots." These use one or more sensors, whose signals affect robot operation. Thus, the robot is able to interact with its environment, and react to changing conditions. We must differentiate between robot systems in which the basic program remains fixed and those in which the program changes according to the information received from the sensors. In the former, the robot may be programmed to execute the next sequence step only after receiving a sensor signal confirming that the previous step has been completed, or other necessary conditions fulfilled. The program itself never changes, only the timing varies according to conditions. Such robot systems are not truly "intelligent" even though they do use sensor signals.

Only the second type of system can really be defined as "intelligent." In such systems, the basic program itself is changed during operation, depending on external conditions. For example, if an obstruction is sensed, the robot modifies its path. Depending on the sensor signals received, a different program branch may be followed, steps may be skipped or repeated, or some emergency routine initiated. The difference between these two types of robot systems with sensors is analogous to that between sequential systems with fixed-order inputs (described in Chapter 5) and those with random inputs (discussed in Chapter 6).

Robot sensors, very much like the sensors discussed in Chapter 2, can be classified as either contacting or noncontacting. Contact sensors, also called *tactile sensors*, respond to contact between the robot end effector and the workpiece. In its most simple form, the tactile sensor could consist of a limit switch installed in the robot gripper (or in the gripper-actuation mechanism), whose contacts close when the gripper jaws touch the workpiece.

Other tactile sensors are considerably more complex. Some, for example, consist of an array of several hundred tiny pressure cells arranged in matrix form within the inner gripper surface. Each cell sends a binary signal if pressure is applied to it. Such sensors not only detect presence of an object, but can supply information as to size, shape, or orientation of the grasped object. The robot-control computer must, of course, be programmed to utilize this information (for instance, using pattern-recognition routines), so that the arm can react accordingly and accept or reject the part, change its orientation, sort parts according to size or shape, and so on.

Many tactile sensors measure the force and/or torque between the end effector and object. Such sensors typically consist of several elastic beams with built-in strain gages, with the unit installed between the robot wrist and end effector. To supply full information, the sensor should measure six components, namely, the applied forces in the x, y, and z directions, and the torques about these three axes. For many applications, however, measurement of the forces is sufficient, so that a simple three-component sensor, such that shown in Fig. 13.19 and described in Ref. (13.17), can be used.

The sesor in the figure consists of a thin-walled cylinder (labeled 1), having eight strain gages mounted on its surface, so as to measure forces in the x, y, and z directions. The thick-walled cylinders 2 and 3 are intended to protect cylinder 1 against excessive forces. If forces in the x or y direction should exceed a permitted limit, the resulting bending moment produces contact between cylinder 3 and the lips on cylinder 2 at sections B and C, thus preventing further

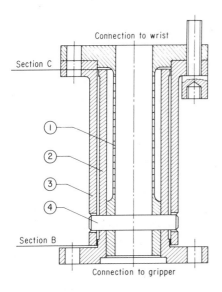

Fig. 13.19. Three-component force sensor for a robot gripper (Technion Robotics Laboratory).

deflection. This design permits making cylinder 1 extremely thin (0.5 mm wall thickness), which results in high sensor sensitivity, and yet protects the sensor from damage. Torsion pin 4 protects the device from excessive axial torsion.

Noncontact robot sensors can consist of any of the photoelectric or proximity sensors described in Chapter 2, which signal presence or absence of an object. Other noncontact sensors, called range detectors, measure distance of an object from some reference point. These use methods such as ultrasound (as in self-focusing cameras), infrared, or lasers.

The most sophisticated type of robot sensing involves artificial vision, which is a subject all by itself; see Ref. (13.18). Vision systems use one or more cameras (usually not mounted on the robot itself), each connected to an image digitizer, which converts the image to a set of digital signals sent to the computer's memory. The computer is programmed to process, interpret, and then utilize the image. [This is discussed in Chapter 15 of Ref. (13.3), and in Ref. (13.5).] One typical application of artificial vision is that of *pattern recognition*, already mentioned in connection with tactile sensors. Using pattern-recognition procedures, the robot can identify parts by their outline, no matter which way the parts may be oriented. Thus, the robot could be programmed to pick up one specific type of part, to classify parts, to distinguish different part orientations, and so on.

The subject of robot sensors is becoming of increasing importance, since robots are expected to carry out increasingly complicated tasks. Technical conferences on this topic are held each year, and many papers and books on the subject have been published; see, for example, Ref. (13.19).

13.7   ROBOT PROGRAMMING

Robots can be programmed in two basically different ways: *on-line* and *off-line*. On-line programming, also referred to as *teach programming*, consists of leading the robot manually through its required motions, and storing these in the control-computer memory. The robot later repeats the motions it has been "taught" whenever called upon to do so. In off-line programming, on the other hand, a computer program is written (using any one of a number of special robot programming languages) and later loaded into the control-computer memory.

Teach programming can itself be divided into two distinct methods. The first makes use of a so-called control box, or *teach pendant*, see Fig. 13.20, a programming device having a number of push buttons, toggle switches, or a joy stick. Using the teach pendant, the operator can control all robot axes, including those of the end effector, and thus make the robot move from one state to the next. When the next state is reached, a button is pressed, and the corresponding joint coordinates of the robot are stored in memory. The robot speed during this teaching phase is usually fairly slow (for safety reasons), but later, during actual operation, the robot repeats the steps taught to it at maximum speed.

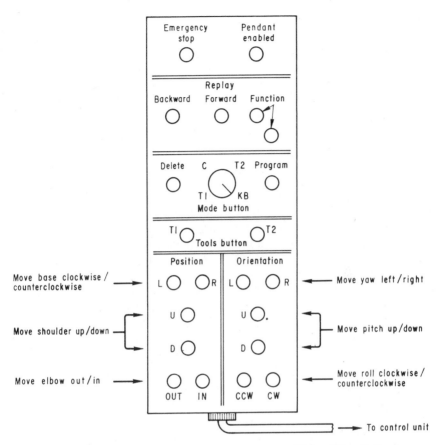

Fig. 13.20. Teach pendant (from Ref. (13.3), courtesy of John Wiley & Sons).

Teach-pendant programming is best suited for point-to-point programming. It can also be used for continuous-path programming by dividing the required path into a large number of short segments and using appropriate interpolation routines. For full programming flexibility, the teach pendant should allow the programmer to work in three types of coordinates: *world coordinates* (i.e., using a Cartesian or *x-y-z* coordinate system fixed to the robot base), *joint coordinates* (i.e., controlling the angle or displacement of each robot link with respect to the adjacent link), and *tool coordinates* (using a coordinate system attached to the base of the robot wrist). Tool coordinates are useful where the tool must maintain a certain orientation, for example, a screwdriver that must turn and move axially, and at the same time remain aligned with the screw axis.

Teach-pendant programming is probably the most popular robot programming method. It is easy to learn and does not require special programming skills. Its main drawback is that the robot is unavailable for productive work during the programming phase. This may not be objectionable where the program, once taught to the robot, remains in use for a long production run. However, if production runs are short, the robot has to be reprogrammed frequently, and may spend most of its time not performing useful work.

The second teach-programming method consists of leading the robot end effector manually along the required path. The robot computer samples the various joint coordinates at regular intervals during this process, and stores them in memory for later "replay." This method is especially suitable for continuous-path applications, such as with arc-welding or paint-spraying robots. Obviously, the robot can only be as skilled in performing its job as the person who taught it. Any small mistakes or path irregularities are later repeated by the robot. Hence, expert welders, painters, or other craftsmen must be employed to do the actual teaching. This teaching method is often referred to as *lead-through teaching*, walk-through teaching, or manual dry-run mode. Unfortunately, great confusion exists concerning these terms, and some authors apply any of these three terms to the teach-pendant method.

Lead-through teaching can only be carried out if all the brakes are released, and the oil pressure is shut off in the case of hydraulic robot drives. Even then, it may still be impossible to move the end effector manually if the drive-system transmission uses self-locking gears or lead screws. Just as with the teach-pendant method, the robot is unavailable during the teaching phase.

To bypass these problems, lightweight robot simulators—also called dummy robots, programming arms, or teaching arms—are often used. These have no drive system of their own, but have handles attached to the end effector, and are often counterbalanced with special weights to make it easier to manipulate the end effector along the required path. The simulator uses encoders or other position sensors to keep track of the various joint motions and send them to the computer memory for storage. The only drawback of this method is the extra cost of the programming simulator.

Off-line programming, using a computer keyboard, is undoubtedly the most powerful, but also the most tedious, of the three programming methods. Unfortunately, there is as yet no standard robot programming language. Each manufacturer uses a different language, and a great number of these exist. Among the better known are VAL (used by Unimation-Westinghouse, Inc.), AML (IBM Robotics), RAIL (Automatix), and T3 (Cincinnati Milacron). Some manufacturers use standard computer languages, such as BASIC or Pascal, which are already widely known, and modify them for robot control by the addition of appropriate commands, For example, the Microbot "Minimover" educational robot shown in Fig. 13.12 uses ARMBASIC, which is regular BASIC with six additional special commands. In ARMBASIC, certain computer keyboard keys can be used instead of a teach pendant to teach the robot the required path, using point-to-point control. This robot also has a simple force sensor sending a signal when the gripper contacts an object, and this feature can be used to measure the width of the object.

Off-line programming eliminates most of the robot downtime, although the robot is still unavailable during the inevitable program debugging. Thus, the method is especially useful where small or medium-size production runs require frequent reprogramming. Also, the use of a programming language makes it easier to carry out on-line calculations, accept various sensor signals, and make decisions as to branching, emergency routines, and so on. Off-line programming can be greatly facilitated by integrating the procedure with existing data bases and CAD/CAM systems.

One drawback of off-line programming is that it does not take into account positional errors due to elastic deflections of the robot structure. These deflections not only depend on the robot load at the end effector, but also change with robot position. One solution to this is to use a combination of off-line and teach-pendant programming. After the initial off-line programming, the robot coordinates for certain critical points can be corrected using the teach pendant.

A technique very helpful in robot programming and in program testing and debugging is that of *robot animation* or *graphic simulation*. Using a graphic computer terminal and appropriate software, robot motion can be examined on the computer screen. Programming mistakes, or mishaps such as possible collisions, can easily be checked beforehand, and the program corrected without tying up the robot or damaging equipment. The user can start experimental programming, or test different robots before making a commitment to purchasing a certain model. Figure 13.21 is a robot-animation picture showing the robot

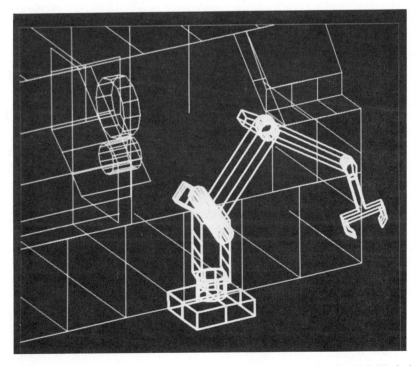

Fig. 13.21. Animation picture of the robot and NC lathe shown in Fig. 13.7 (Technion Robotics Laboratory).

position in relation to its work station. (The picture was obtained using a robot-animation program developed at the Technion; see Ref. 13.20.) For further discussion of robot graphic simulation, see Refs. (13.21) and (13.22).

13.8   GENERAL CONSIDERATIONS FOR ROBOT APPLICATION

Apart from the points discussed in the foregoing sections, there are many other aspects that should be considered before deciding whether to apply robots to a given production process. These include such questions as economic justification, creating a suitable robot workplace environment, safety problems, human factors, and others. Whole books have been written on these aspects of robotics; see, for instance, Ref. (13.23). Obviously, these can only be touched on very briefly in this concluding section.

The question of robot economics is closely linked with that of creating a suitable robot work environment. It is a common fallacy to think that a robot has only to be purchased and placed on the production line, taking the place of one or more workers. If the robot is to load and unload parts into and out of a machining center, these parts must be fed automatically to the robot at the proper rate and with correct orientation, employing the part-handling techniques described in the previous chapter. Similarly, the unloaded finished parts must be removed by a conveyor belt, or by other means. Furthermore, the robot work envelope should be enclosed by a safety barrier to prevent people from entering the area while the robot is in operation. Sensors are required to shut off the robot automatically if someone is present within the work envelope, and additional safety measures may be needed. If the robot performs an assembly operation, the various parts must be fed accurately positioned, so that the robot can find each part at its proper location. If the robot is to do spray painting or spot welding, the part painted or welded must be accurately positioned, otherwise, the paint or the weld are applied at the wrong location.

These are only some examples of what is involved in preparing a proper work environment for the robot. As a rule of thumb, it has been suggested that the total price of the robot installation is about two to three times that of the robot alone. For more detailed examples, see Chapter 30 of Ref. (13.3).

The question of robot economics is usually not straightforward. After having calculated the estimated cost of a projected installation, we must calculate the expected savings. It is another common fallacy to believe that robots can work faster than humans. In general, this is not so. However, the robot maintains a steady pace, does not get tired, take lunch breaks, or go on strike. Hence, in the long run, its output usually exceeds that of the worker it replaces.

What is more difficult to evaluate in financial terms is the increase in work quality. The robot, if properly programmed and set up, does not make mistakes, and consistently maintains the same quality of workmanship. For example, a robot programmed to make 25 spot welds on an automobile frame never "forgets" one of them, and all 25 welds are exactly where they are supposed to be. Hence, inspection can be reduced to a minimum, and rejects can become almost nonexistent. In jobs such as spray painting, the robot, if properly taught, consistently applies just the right amount of paint to each area. This not only reduces paint consumption, but prevents paint "runs" caused by excessive paint. The result is a consistently high-quality finish and increased customer satisfaction.

All of the above factors are difficult to evaluate ahead of time, but experience has shown that considerable savings can be expected, provided the right robot has been selected for the right application. Again, as a rule of thumb, it is generally held that a robot installation, which requires considerable financial investment, only pays for itself if the robot works for at least two 8-hour shifts each day. For a description of a more accurate economic analysis, see Refs. (13.1) and (13.2), or Chapter 33 of Refs. (13.3).

There are, of course, robot applications in which monetary considerations are secondary, and where the robot is employed without regard to possible savings. These include jobs that are unhealthy or downright hazardous for human workers. Any activities involving intense heat, vibration, noise, or exposure to dangerous chemicals are performed advantageously by robots.

Not every task is suitable for robots. A number of criteria are listed in Chapter 29 of Ref. (13.3). It is suggested there that robots are generally not suitable for operations where cycle times of less than 5 sec are required, where loads exceed 500 kg, or where a positioning accuracy better than 0.1 mm is required. Since most robots cannot cope with a disorderly environment (unless equipped with a sophisticated vision system), the application should not involve randomness in workpiece position or orientation. (Part feeders and orienting devices must first be employed to create a predictable environment.) Furthermore, both extremes of complexity should be avoided when choosing a robot application. Very simple jobs can usually be carried out with less expense using hard automation, or possibly by several pneumatic cylinders controlled by a programmable controller (Chapter 10) or by a programmable counter (Chapter 9). Very complex jobs, on the other hand (for example, processes involving more than 10 different workpieces) may be too much for the robot to handle efficiently.

The same precaution against extremes applies to lot size. Very short production runs, involving less than 25 pieces, are not suitable for robots, since the robot will be inactive most of the time, waiting to be reprogrammed for the next run. On the other hand, very large production runs, such as several million pieces per year, are handled better by fixed automation systems, since robots are not sufficiently fast to handle such huge quantities. In other words, robots are most suitable for intermediate-size runs.

The subject of robot safety is obviously an extremely important one. A number of precautions can and should be taken to prevent work accidents. The most dangerous period occurs while the robot is being repaired, programmed, or tested, and this for two reasons. First, the robot is liable to do unexpected things, and second, people are liable to be present within the robot work envelope during this time. Good discussions of robot safety problems and recommended precautions are found in Ref. (13.2) and in Chapter 35 of Ref. (13.3).

Finally, there is the aspect of human factors, which can involve such disciplines as psychology, sociology, and labor relations. Before planning the introduction of robots, it is important to assure the cooperation of everyone involved, from management down to work supervisors and the workers; see Chapter 32 of Ref. (13.3). If this is not done, the whole project is liable to become a failure. This principle, of course, applies equally to the introduction of any type of industrial automation, but a robot seems more likely to arouse strong human emotions than say, a step motor or a pneumatic cylinder. This is possibly because the robot looks and acts more like humans than do any of the other devices discussed in this book.

REFERENCES

13.1.   C. R. Asfahl, *Robots and Manufacturing Automation*, Wiley, New York, 1985.

13.2.   Y. Koren, *Robotics for Engineers*, McGraw-Hill, New York, 1985.

13.3.   S. Nof (Ed.), *Handbook of Industrial Robotics*, Wiley, New York, 1985.

13.4.   D. McCloy and D. M. Harris, *Robotics: An Introduction*, Halsted Press (Wiley), New York, 1986.

13.5.   E. Kafrissen and M. Stephans, *Industrial Robots and Robotics*, Reston Publ. Co., Reston, VA, 1984.

13.6.   Y. C. Tsai and A. H. Soni, "Accessible Region and Synthesis of Robot Arms," *Journal of Mechanical Design*, Vol. 103, No. 4, Oct. 1981, pp. 803–811.

13.7.   R. S. Pressman and J. E. Williams, *Numerical Control and Computer-Aided Manufacturing*, Wiley, New York, 1977.

13.8.   N. O. Olesten, *Numerical Control*, Wiley (Interscience), New York, 1970.

13.9.   J. Pusztai and M. Sava, *Computer Numerical Control*, Reston Publ. Co., Reston, VA, 1983.

13.10.   R. V. Miskell, "Tape Codes and Formats for Numerical Control," *Instruments and Control Systems*, Mar. 1971, pp. 115–118.

13.11.   L. C. Smith, "Servocontrol Through Software," *Machine Design*, May 25, 1978, pp. 70–75.

13.12.   W. E. Snyder, *Industrial Robots: Computer Interfacing and Control*, Prentice-Hall, Englewood Cliffs, NJ, 1985.

13.13.   C. S. Lee, "Robot Arm Kinematics, Dynamics and Control," *Computer* (*IEEE*), Vol. 15, No. 12, Dec. 1982, pp. 62–80.

13.14.   D. W. Pessen, "Tactile Gripper System for Robotic Manipulators," *Proceedings of the Twelfth International Symposium on Industrial Robots*, Paris, July 1982, pp. 411–416.

13.15.   D. T. Pham and W. B. Heginbotham (Eds.), *Robot Grippers*, IFS (Publications) Ltd., Bedford, England, 1986.

13.16.   J. K. Krouse, "Compliant Mechanisms," *Machine Design*, Jan. 24, 1980, pp. 86–90.

13.17.   J. Borenstein, R. Weill, and D. Pessen, "Triaxial Force Sensor for Industrial Robots," *International Journal of Manufacturing Systems*, Vol. 13, No. 3, 1984, pp. 155–163.

13.18. ME Staff, "Vision Systems Make Robots More Versatile," *Mechanical Engineering*, Jan. 1985, pp. 38–43.

13.19. A. Pugh (Ed.), *Robot Sensors, Vols. 1 and 2*, IFS (Publications) Ltd., Bedford, England, 1986.

13.20. S. Zombach, *Integration of Robot and Lathe in Flexible Manufacturing Cell* (M. Sc. Thesis), Technion, Israel Institute of Technology, 1987.

13.21. J. Kacala, "Robot Programming Goes Off-line," *Machine Design*, Nov. 7, 1985, pp. 89–92.

13.22. S. J. Kretch, "Robot Animation," *Mechanical Engineering*, Aug. 1982, pp. 32–35.

13.23. J. F. Engelberger, *Robotics in Practice*, Kogan Page Ltd., London, 1980.

APPENDIX A

GRAFCET METHOD FOR SPECIFYING INDUSTRIAL SEQUENCES

GRAFCET (*graphical function chart*) is a tool for specifying industrial control sequences by means of a diagram. To illustrate the method, Fig. A.1 shows the GRAFCET corresponding to the automatic mixing sequence described in Section 5.4.2.

As seen from the figure, the GRAFCET consists of a column of numbered blocks, each of which represents a sequence *step*. The initial step 1 represents "system ready to begin sequence," and is always shown by double lines. Brief symbolic names or notations can be added under the step number, if desired.

The vertical lines joining adjacent step blocks represent *transitions*. Each transition is associated with a logical condition called *receptivity*, which is defined by a Boolean expression written next to a short horizontal line crossing the transition line. If the receptivity is "logic 1," the transition is enabled, and the system passed on to the next step.

A given step is either *active* or *inactive*. A transition can only originate from an active step. Once a transition has taken place, the next step becomes active, and the previous one inactive.

The actions to be taken at each step are listed within adjacent rectangles drawn to the right of the step block. Here, too, comments can be added, if desired.

From Section 9.5 on programmable counters, it should be evident that their schematic representation bears a close resemblance to GRAFCET. (Compare the step blocks in Fig. A.1 with the module blocks in Fig. 9.9.)

GRAFCET can also be used to depict any of the multipath sequences described in Section 9.5.5. For example, two simultaneous parallel paths (see Fig. 9.16) are depicted in GRAFCET by horizontal double lines, as shown in Fig. A.2.

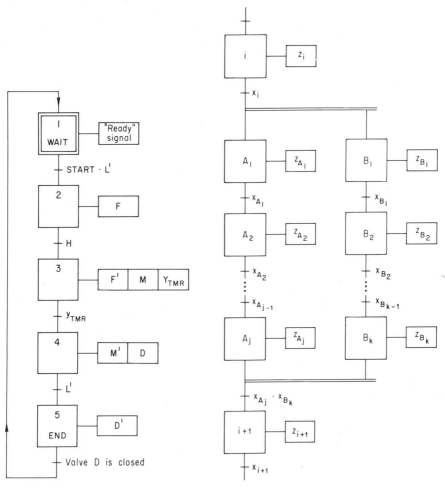

Fig. A.1. GRAFCET for an automatic mixing system.

Fig. A.2. GRAFCET for simultaneous parallel paths.

As a second example, the alternative parallel paths implemented in Fig. 9.17 are depicted in GRAFCET as shown in Fig. A.3.

For the many other features included in the GRAFCET method, see Refs. (A.1) and (A.2).

The GRAFCET method, which originated in France and has been adopted as the French national standard, is becoming increasingly popular in many countries. In Germany, however, a slightly different method is being used, called FUP ("FUnction Plan"). The basic idea behind FUP and GRAFCET is the same, and the differences relate to details in the way the diagram is drawn. To illustrate the difference, Fig. A.4 shows the FUP for the same sequence described by the GRAFCET of Fig. A.1.

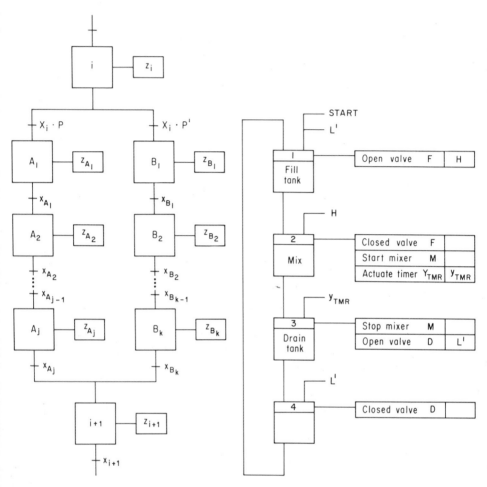

Fig. A.3. GRAFCET for alternative parallel paths.

Fig. A.4. FUP for an automatic mixing system.

The first difference is the way the transition conditions are shown. If more than one condition must be fulfilled, these are listed below each other (see conditions START and L' for step 1), rather than writing the AND-function term as in GRAFCET. If an OR function or a more complex Boolean relation is called for, standard logic symbols are used.

The second difference relates to the output signals. Multiple parallel actions are listed in rectangles drawn one below the other (rather than arranged horizontally, as in GRAFCET). In addition, the square to the right of each rectangle can be utilized to list the sensor signal resulting from the successful completion of the action.

As with the GRAFCET method, FUP can also be used to specify multipath sequences. For more details, see German standard DIN 40719.

REFERENCES

A.1. *"GRAFCET"—A Function Chart for Sequencial Processes*, Publ. by ADEPA, 17 Rue Perier, B.P. No. 54, 92123 Montrouge Cedex, France, 1979.

A.2. *Manual 02.1987 "Book 3—Grafcet Language*, Telemecanique Inc., 901 Baltimore Boulevard, Westminster, MD 21157, 1987.

APPENDIX B

FLOW CHART FOR SELECTING SEQUENCE-CONTROL SYSTEM DESIGN METHOD

The flow chart shown in Fig. B.1 is intended to help the reader select the most appropriate method for designing sequence-control systems from among the various methods described in Chapter 5, 7, and 9.

This chart is *not* intended to serve in the selection of the appropriate switching element. It is assumed that a decision has already been made as to whether to use relays, pneumatic valves, or other elements. Since the chart relates only to fixed-automation circuits, programmable controllers (Chapter 10) are not included.

For the reader who has read Chapters 5, 7, and 9, the flow chart should be self-explanatory.

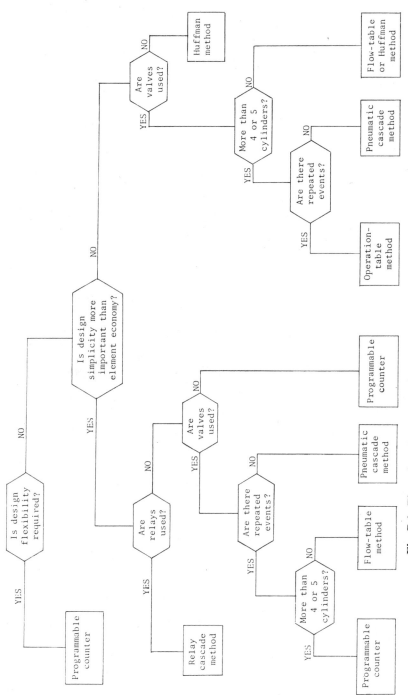

Fig. B.1. Flow chart for selecting a sequence-control system design method.

INDEX